NOAH
WEBSTER
—AND THE—
AMERICAN
DICTIONARY

NOAH WEBSTER
—AND THE—
AMERICAN DICTIONARY

David Micklethwait

McFarland & Company, Inc., Publishers

Jefferson, North Carolina, and London

Library of Congress Cataloguing-in-Publication Data

Micklethwait, David.
Noah Webster and the American dictionary / David Micklethwait
p.   cm.
Includes bibliographical references and index.
ISBN 0-7864-0640-2 (library binding : 50# alkaline paper) ∞
1. Webster, Noah, 1758–1843.   2. Webster, Noah, 1758–1843. American dictionary of the
English Language.   3. Encyclopedias and dictionaries — History and criticism.   4. English
language — United States — Lexicography.   5. English language — 19th century — Lexicography.
6. Lexicographers — United States — Biography.   7. Educators — United States — Biography.   I. Title.
PE65.W5M53   2000
423'.092 — dc21   99-39094
CIP

British Library Cataloguing-in-Publication data are available

Manufactured in the United States of America

*McFarland & Company, Inc., Publishers
Box 611, Jefferson, North Carolina 28640
www.mcfarlandpub.com*

For Tina, who made it all possible

Contents

NOAH WEBSTER LL.D.

Frontispiece to the *American Dictionary*, 1828; from a painting by S. F. B. Morse

Preface

The subjects of this book are the motivations, and the methods, first of Noah Webster himself, and then of later compilers of "Webster's" dictionaries. "No man but a blockhead," said Johnson, "ever wrote, except for money."[1] Boswell did not agree: "Numerous instances to refute this will occur," he commented, "to all who are versed in the history of literature." Certainly there are people who publish for reasons of vanity, but Johnson would have classed them among the blockheads.

Whether one writes for fame or money, or for both, the task is greatly simplified by borrowing what has already been written by somebody else. The author's profits may disappear, however, if others are free to borrow from him. The profession of author can only be profitable when writers have the benefit of copyright. As one English judge said, "Copyright is the sickle by which the author reaps his reward." The first English Copyright Act came into force in 1710, but the word "copyright" was not used until some years later. Boswell used it when writing about Johnson's 1755 Dictionary,[2] but his *Life of Johnson* was published in 1791, and "copyright" was not defined in Johnson's Dictionary until Archdeacon Todd added it, in an edition completed in 1818. Before Johnson there was no legal wrong that would have been described as infringement of copyright, but the corresponding moral wrong, plagiarism, was much older.

Etymologically, plagiarism involves stealing people — *plagae* were nets used for snaring animals and for kidnapping, though the word *kidnapping* originally implied a more narrowly defined commercial purpose than kidnappers have today. The first dictionary to record the practice was Phillips' seventeenth century *New World of Words*: "*Kidnappers,* those that make a Trade of decoying and spiriting away young Children to ship them for Foreign Plantations."[3] Bailey's definition, in 1724, is "KIDNAPPER, a Person who makes it his Business to decoy either Children or young Persons to send them to the *English* Plantations in *America.*"

The use of the word *Plagiarius* for a literary kidnapper dates back to Martial, so that Thomas Cooper's *Thesaurus Linguæ Romanæ & Britannicæ,*[4] in 1584, gives two meanings: "He that stealeth away a mans children," and "He that stealeth bookes." The latter might mean a book-thief, but Adam Littleton's *Latine Dictionary in Four Parts*[5] shows that it was the contents that were stolen, rather than the books themselves: "Plagiarius … *he who steals or filches out of other mens writings, and pretends himself to be the Author.*" Noah Webster would define plagiarism as "introducing passages from another man's writings and putting them off as one's own," by which definition he was himself a lifelong plagiarist. He was also, as it happens, a kidnapper of words. He made it his business to spirit away words from English books and transport them into his own, to be offered for sale in America.

Webster was described by the publisher of a competing dictionary as "a vain, weak, plodding Yankee, who aspired to be a second Johnson." Vain, he certainly was, and he was also a Yankee, being a native of Connecticut. "Plodding," if it means diligent and methodical, is an essential characteristic of a lexicographer. The assertion that Webster aspired to be a second Johnson was true in relation to his great Quarto dictionary, but it was nothing to be ashamed of. Johnson's Dictionary was published

1

three years before Webster was born, and it was a conservative work even then. It was seriously out of date by the time Webster published his *American Dictionary*, in 1828.

What of the plagiarism? Much of Webster's *American Dictionary* was lifted straight from Johnson, and where Webster created space by leaving out bits of Johnson, he filled most of it with excerpts from other reference books. "A chief qualification for authorship," he wrote, "is a dextrous use of an inverted pen and a pair of scissors." The pen was a quill, and inverting it provided a useful brush for applying glue. A modern word-processor still calls the equivalent process "Cut and Paste," and it has always been a common technique in lexicography — the first English dictionaries borrowed from Latin-English dictionaries, and later English dictionaries borrowed from earlier ones. What makes it interesting in Webster's case is that he became very upset when he suspected anyone of borrowing from him.

The result of his borrowing, it must be said, was a better dictionary than Johnson's. Boswell called Johnson "great and good," which he certainly was. He was a great writer, and a good man. Johnson's Dictionary is a good book, but it is not a great dictionary. The *American Dictionary* is not without faults, but for the ordinary purposes of a dictionary, it is better than Johnson's. As for the greatness or goodness of Webster the man, you must form your own conclusions.

Sources and Materials

When Noah Webster travelled round America in the early days of the Republic, he used to count the houses in each town he visited. He would then exchange his figures for those collected by other enthusiasts in other towns. For years, he kept records of the weather. He was an insatiable collector of information. When he came across an interesting word in his reading, he put that in his collection, too, and later he put it in a dictionary. It was the same with documents. In 1782, when the War of Independence was still being fought, Webster asked a friend to give him a letter of recommendation for the spelling book and grammar that he proposed to write. That letter was still in his possession when he died, more than sixty years

later. During those sixty years he had moved house, perhaps ten or a dozen times. His son-in-law, Chauncey Allen Goodrich, wrote of him:

He learnt ... to preserve documents of all kinds with the utmost care. All that he had ever written, all that had been written against him, every thing that he met with in newspapers or periodicals which seemed likely to be of use at any future period, was carefully laid aside in its appropriate place, and was ready at a moment's warning.... He filled the margins of his books with notes and comments containing corrections of errors, a comparison of dates, or references to corresponding passages in other works, until his whole library became a kind of Index Rerum, to which he could refer at once for every thing he had read.[6]

By his will, Webster made arrangements for the safekeeping of his papers. They went first to his son William:

I also commit to the care of my said son my manuscripts, & the volumes of pamphlets, newspapers bound or unbound containing any of my writings, & all other papers respecting my family, & my diplomas and letters; also the national portrait gallery, to be carefully preserved by him during his life; And my will is that these books & papers shall descend to his eldest surviving son, if he shall belong to the religious denomination of his forefathers, called congregational; if not, my will is that all the books and papers then entrusted to my son shall pass into the possession of the eldest of my surviving grandsons, of the congregational religion or denomination.

When his father died in 1843, William Webster had a wife, Rosalie, and two sons, Eugene and Stuart. He lost all three to the American Civil War. Rosalie was a Southerner, which put her and William on opposite sides, and they separated. Eugene followed his mother, Stuart his father, and the two sons joined opposing armies. In 1864, within a period of little more than a month, both of them died — one from wounds, the other from illness caused by exposure in military service. William and Rosalie then divorced. William later remarried, but had no more children. He was the last "Webster" descended from the lexicographer.

Two people wrote to William's widow expressing an interest in acquiring the Webster papers. One was Webster's eldest grandson, Pinckney Ellsworth, who claimed them under Webster's will; the other was the distinguished collector Gordon Lester Ford, who wanted to

buy them. He married Webster's grandchild, Emily Ellsworth Fowler, whose mother, Harriet, was Webster's third daughter.[7] In the end, Ford got the papers, though whether direct from William's widow or via Pinckney Ellsworth I do not know. Ford's collection became part of the New York Public Library, which is where the Webster papers now are, with Ford's own substantial additions, including many of William's own papers. This is by far the largest accumulation of Webster material, and it has been the major resource for all recent research. In the pages that follow, I shall mention the Library often, but to do so every time I refer to something from its collection would be unduly repetitive. All the letters from which I quote are there, unless I say otherwise.

Other major collections of Webster-related manuscript material are in the Connecticut Historical Society in Hartford, in the Sterling Memorial Library at Yale, and in the Pierpont Morgan Library. All of these I have used, and to each I extend my thanks.

Because I worked mainly from original documents, I have not relied much on earlier biographical treatments of Webster. I shall, however, mention some of them from time to time, and those I must introduce to you.

Two of Webster's sons-in-law edited "Webster" dictionaries published in the years immediately following Webster's death, and each of those editors wrote a biographical memoir that was included in the work. The first was in the "University" edition of 1845, edited by William Fowler; the second, in Merriam's first Webster Dictionary, the 1847 Quarto, edited by Chauncey Allen Goodrich. Unseen by users of those dictionaries, a bitter struggle was fought between Fowler and Goodrich for control of Webster's literary legacy. The outcome of that struggle determined the development not only of the dictionary, but also of the American way of spelling. Fowler wrote a rambling account of his brother-in-law Goodrich's devious maneuvering, put it in a pamphlet called *Printed but not Published,* and gave copies to friends and relations.

The first full-length biography of Webster was by a historian, Professor Horace Scudder, in the series "American Men of Letters," published in 1883. It is not a work of profound research — apart from anything else, Scudder did not have access to the Webster papers — but it gives a balanced and reasonably accurate account of Webster's life and work. Scudder's biography, however, did not please Webster's granddaughter, Emily Ellsworth Fowler Ford, because it seemed to her "to discolor his character, to belittle his work as well as his aims, and to make him out an egotist of persistent self-conceit in his career." To set the record straight, Mrs. Ford started to compile her own book, *Notes on the Life of Noah Webster.*[8] She, being the wife of Gordon Lester Ford, did have access to the Webster papers, and she was in touch with Webster's surviving friends and relations. She delayed completing her book, however because her aunt, Webster's fourth daughter, Eliza, for some reason opposed its publication, and Mrs. Ford lost interest in the book when her husband died. It was eventually finished and edited by her daughter, Emily Ellsworth Ford Skeel, by whom it was privately published in 1912. It contains extensive quotations from items in the Webster papers, many of which were there published for the first time. Mrs. Ford, who is always said to have been Webster's favorite grandchild, sought to paint a picture of him as, in private, a pious and devoted family man, and, in public, a noble and disinterested patriot. Even so, she (or her daughter) included material showing unattractive aspects of Webster's character — he expected unquestioning obedience from his children and grandchildren, and he was often accused of excessive vanity.

It is not always easy to tell which parts of the book were written by Mrs. Ford and which by her daughter, but it makes no difference. For convenience I shall refer to the author as "Mrs. Ford," while recognizing that Mrs. Skeel was responsible for many passages. It is a weakness of the book that it sometimes fails to submit Webster family folklore to critical examination. There is a story, for example, that little Emily Fowler was corresponding with Webster *in Latin* at the age of four. The date given for Webster's Latin letter to Emily is 9 February 1830 (when Emily was not quite three and a half), but this is a misreading — the year was actually 1838.[9]

Mrs. Skeel also assembled the materials for the splendid *Bibliography of the Writings of Noah Webster,* which was edited by Edwin H.

Carpenter and published by the New York Public Library.

Noah Webster, Schoolmaster to America, by Harry R. Warfel, was published in 1936, but it is still the best all-round biography of Webster. Professor Warfel also edited a useful selection, *Letters of Noah Webster*,[10] and he and his wife, Ruth, jointly (under the combined and revolting name "Harruth Lefraw") published a collection of what was said to be Webster's poetry. In fact at least two of the poems had been kidnapped by Webster from Cowper.

Warfel said of Scudder's biography that it was "a jaunty critical sketch in which the author achieves admiration for Webster despite an evident prejudice against him." The accusation of prejudice is unjustified; Scudder's book shows no signs of his having formed a view adverse to Webster before he started, though he may have ended up not liking Webster very much. Scudder, in my view, managed to balance his admiration for Webster's good qualities and considerable achievements with a realistic assessment of his weaknesses. If anything, it is Warfel who displays an "evident prejudice" *in favor* of Webster.

Noah Webster by John S. Morgan is a superficial biography almost entirely derived from Warfel's.[11]

Next we must notice *The Long Journey of Noah Webster* by Richard M. Rollins[12]. This is a modern "psychological" biography — "an attempt ... to understand the ways in which an individual internalized the events, ideas, values and beliefs of his age." For Rollins, the changes in Webster's opinions over the years resulted from his suffering a series of traumatic rejections. Webster certainly did change his opinions, but I do not find that Rollins' "internalizations" provide any convincing explanations. Furthermore, Rollins not only imagines Webster's inner thoughts but also fabricates incidents and conversations, often unsupported by any evidence at all, and he does not explain that this is what he is doing. He writes, for example, "[Webster] discussed many topics with Tom Paine."[13] That would be interesting if it were true, but Webster himself says no more than that he met Paine once, when he was introduced to him "for the purpose of seeing his model of an iron bridge in miniature."

I am here criticizing Rollins for making things up, not for making mistakes. Anyone can make mistakes, which one forgives in the hope that one's own mistakes may be forgiven. Sometimes, however, mistakes may have alarming implications. Rollins describes Webster's "blue-backed speller" as a "small book simply bound in blue cloth."[14] In the eighteenth and early nineteenth centuries, American schoolbooks generally (not just Webster's spelling books) had certain common characteristics — they were usually very badly printed on extremely inferior paper, and they were held together by two broad strips of cloth, between thin wooden boards covered in plain blue paper. As time passed, standards of paper, printing, and binding improved, and the wooden boards were replaced by cardboard; but Webster wanted to maintain the get-up of his product, and insisted that later editions of his spelling book should continue to be covered in blue paper, as the earliest editions had been. Thus it became known as the "blue-backed speller"; but it was *not* "bound in blue cloth." Can Rollins have written his book without ever seeing a copy?

Rollins also edited *The Autobiographies of Noah Webster*, which contains autobiographical material of three sorts: first, excerpts from Webster's letters, publications, and manuscripts; second, a *Memoir of Noah Webster, LLD*, which Webster wrote, apparently for publication, though it was never published in his lifetime; and third, Webster's diary. The original *Memoir* (which is in the Sterling Memorial Library at Yale) is in 53 sections on separate sheets, generally numbered at the head of each sheet. It covers the period up to June 1825, by which time Webster had completed the manuscript of the *American Dictionary*. I shall refer to excerpts by number, but they are to be conveniently found in Rollins' *Autobiographies*. The *Memoir* does not read like autobiography because Webster writes of himself in the third person. Most of his diary can be found in Rollins' *Autobiographies* and in *Ford*, both transcribed from the original, which is now in the New York Public Library. Mrs. Ford's transcription is preferable — she suggests corrections in square brackets when an entry does not make sense, or where names she recognizes are misspelled, and when she finds a word she cannot read, she writes "[illegible]." Rollins ignores the illegible words.

An excellent study of the development and sales history of Webster's Spelling Book is *A Common Heritage: Noah Webster's Blue-Back Speller*, by E. Jennifer Monaghan.[15] It does not, however, investigate the sources of Webster's material, as I have made some attempt to do.

With regard to Webster's Dictionary, two books must be mentioned. The first is *Noah's Ark: New England Yankees and The Endless Quest*, by Robert Keith Leavitt.[16] This was published by G. & C. Merriam Company in 1947 to mark the centenary of their first Webster dictionary. The first half of the book describes Webster's life and lexicography; the second half gives an account of "the War of the Dictionaries"—the commercial contest between Webster's Dictionary and Worcester's—and describes the development of the Merriam line of "Webster" dictionaries after Webster's death.

Finally, *Dr. Johnson and Noah Webster: Two Men and Their Dictionaries*, by David Littlejohn, is an entertaining essay, showing how the very different personalities of the two men are reflected in their dictionaries. It was published in a necessarily limited edition, because every copy has bound in at the back two corresponding pages, one from the first edition of Johnson's Dictionary, the 1755 folio, the other from Webster's quarto *American Dictionary* of 1828. This is fun, but it is not quite appropriate to our purposes, because Webster's source was not the first edition of Johnson. Webster used a Quarto Johnson, the 1799 eighth edition. One sentence of Littlejohn I shall quote without comment:

I had intended, at the outset, to try very hard not to reveal how much I had come to dislike Noah Webster, junior, Esquire, in the course of this work: but I fear it may have leaked out.

PLA'GIARISM, n. [from *plagiary*.] The act of purloining another man's literary works, or introducing passages from another man's writings and putting them off as one's own; literary theft.*

The multiplicity of books for instructing us in our vernacular language is an evil of no small magnitude. Every man has some particular notions which he wishes to propagate, and there is scarcely any peculiarity or absurdity for which some authority may not be found. The facility of book-making favors this disposition, and while a chief qualification for authorship is a dextrous use of an inverted pen, and a pair of scissors, we are not to expect relief from the evil.*

*From *An American Dictionary of the English Language*, by Noah Webster, LL.D., 1828.

LESTER'S HISTORY

OF THE

UNITED STATES

ILLUSTRATED IN ITS FIVE GREAT PERIODS:

COLONIZATION,
CONSOLIDATION,
DEVELOPMENT,
ACHIEVEMENT,
ADVANCEMENT.

BY

C. EDWARDS LESTER,

AUTHOR OF

"THE GLORY AND SHAME OF ENGLAND," "THE LIFE AND VOYAGES OF AMERICUS
VESPUCIUS," "MY CONSULSHIP," "THE GALLERY OF
ILLUSTRIOUS AMERICANS,' ETC., ETC., ETC.

VOLUME I.

NEW YORK:
P. F. COLLIER, PUBLISHER,
1883.

Introduction

The "Trinity of Fame"

Let us start with a little game. I would like you to go back in your imagination, something over one hundred years. You are in New York, towards the end of the nineteenth century. From there, you must look yet further back, over the panorama of American history, from Columbus up to your present day. You have in your mind's eye a span of almost four hundred years. If you really want to get into character, you will wish to know that your name is Charles Edwards Lester, the Rev. Lester, and you have just finished writing *Lester's History of the United States.* You have divided your book into "Five Great Periods": Colonization, Consolidation, Development, Achievement, and Advancement. Of all the characters in this historical pageant, you have to choose just three — the three whose reputations are most sure to last — as a "Trinity of Fame." The first two, Christopher Columbus and George Washington, are not difficult; but who gets the third spot? Franklin? Jefferson? Abraham Lincoln, perhaps?

The reader will by now have wondered why I set this puzzle in a book about the life and works of Noah Webster. With that substantial clue (but not, I think, without it) your guess might be correct. This is the passage:

Noah Webster is the all-shaping, all controlling mind of this hemisphere. He grew up with his country, and he molded the intellectual character of her people. Not a man has sprung from her soil on whom he has not laid his all-forming hand. His principles of Language have tinged every sentence that is now, or will ever be uttered by an American tongue. His genius has presided over every scene in the Nation. It is universal, omnipotent, omnipresent. No man can breathe the air of the continent, and escape it.... He has done more for us than Alfred did for England, or Cadmus for Greece. His books have educated four generations. They are forever multiplying his innumerable army of thinkers, who will transmit his name from age to age. Only two men have stood on this soil of the New World, whose fame is so sure to last — Columbus its Discoverer, and Washington its Saviour. Webster is, and will be its great Teacher; and these three make our Trinity of Fame.

That extraordinary encomium was not mere obituary enthusiasm, nor was it a publisher's puff, though G. & C. Merriam, as publishers of *Webster's Dictionary*, did pay Lester $100 for the right to use it in their advertisements. It was the considered judgment of a serious writer of history. Indeed, one can safely say that it was an opinion that Lester consistently held, since he used the same passage in two books published nearly thirty years apart. The history book was published in this form in 1883, which is a useful date to have in mind, as it was exactly 40 years after Webster's death, and 100 years after the publication of his spelling book. Today, Webster's name is known because it is on innumerable dictionaries, but the basis of Webster's fame, for Lester, was not the dictionary at all — it was a humble spelling book, designed to help children learn to read. It was the spelling book, not the dictionary, that had "educated four generations" when Lester was writing his history. The quoted passage first appeared in a ghastly book published in 1854 called *Glances at the Metropolis — A Hundred Illustrated Gems.* Where the preface should have been, it had a "Salutation," saying that the object of the book was "to cluster together, into a string of pearls, the brightest and best American things."

OPPOSITE: **The title page from *Lester's History of the United States.***

Webster was the first pearl on the string. Not one to waste good work, Lester used the same passage again in his later history books, the only significant alteration being to increase the number of Webster-educated generations from three to four.

Webster's "blue-backed speller," as it became known, was a publishing phenomenon. In its several forms, it is said to have sold as many as 100 million copies. A century after its first publication it was still selling more than a million copies a year. Had he not written the spelling book, Webster would never have produced his great dictionary, for it was only with money derived from the spelling book that he survived long lean years of lexicography. The year the spelling book was published, 1783, was also the year in which the War of Independence ended, which was no accident. Webster wanted to supply an American spelling book to replace the English books in use in American schools; it was an educational Declaration of Independence. As things turned out, though this could not have been foreseen, it made Webster the first American who made a living from having written a book.

In a long lifetime he wrote many books, but we shall be looking in detail at only the two I have already mentioned — the spelling book, published when he was just 25, and the *American Dictionary*, published 45 years later, when he was 70. It was not his first dictionary; he published a small one in 1806, which we shall look at also, though more briefly.

Those three books have a curious characteristic in common. Each was based on an earlier work by somebody else. In each case, the earlier work was English, but it was widely used in America. Webster, who was a fervent nationalist, wanted American students to rely on American books (particularly if their patriotism persuaded them to buy *his* books), but he found it easier to make improvements to an existing work than to start afresh. It is often said that Webster, through these particular books, was responsible for the way Americans spell today. There is a germ of truth in that, but it is an oversimplification. As we shall see, Webster's views on spelling were eccentric and inconsistent, and the recommendations that were peculiarly his own were never accepted.

Webster's spelling book claimed to be, and indeed really was, an improvement on Thomas Dilworth's *New Guide to the English Tongue*, first published in England in 1740. The *Compendious Dictionary* of 1806 was "an enlargement and improvement of Entick's spelling dictionary, which public opinion, both in Great Britain and the United States, has pronounced the best compilation of the kind."[1] The *American Dictionary* of 1828 was based on, and intended to replace, Johnson. To each, Webster wrote a long preface or introduction to display both the shortcomings of the earlier work and his own erudition. This was a sort of literary conjuring trick; the flourishes of the silk handkerchief in the right hand distract the audience, who fail to see what the left hand is up to. Webster loudly proclaimed what was wrong with Dilworth or Johnson so that the reader would not notice how much of their work he had quietly appropriated.

The sort of literary borrowing that Webster practiced was in no way unusual. Lexicographers had always made use of earlier dictionaries. Johnson himself built his superstructure on foundations provided by Bailey, and Walker said in the preface to his dictionary that Johnson's was regarded as "lawful plunder" by all later lexicographers. Entick's little dictionary was largely Johnson's, reduced from two large folio volumes to one pocket-sized square duodecimo.

What makes Webster's situation diverting is that he was very cross when his books became market leaders in their turn, and others borrowed from him as he had from Dilworth and Johnson. It is also curious that so dedicated a plagiarist should have been a pioneer of copyright law. In 1782, he was a qualified lawyer. He realized that if he wanted to make money out of his then-unpublished spelling book he would need the protection of copyright; but America had none. Since there was at that time no central government with power to pass a copyright law, Webster set about lobbying to secure copyright protection (for his own book rather than for authors generally) in the separate states. To keep the goose laying its golden eggs, updated versions of the spelling book were produced whenever copyright was about to expire. During Webster's lifetime, it was given two major face-lifts. Forty-five years after his earlier efforts, we find Webster once again lobbying to

improve copyright protection, this time for the benefit of his big dictionary.

Those of Webster's critics who realized how much of his material he had copied from others thought it comical when they saw him drawing attention to his copyright to deter competitors who might be tempted to copy from him. Nevertheless, it was legitimate for him to do so. In recycling bits of Dilworth, Entick, or Johnson, Webster was not himself infringing any copyright. Those works were old and were never protected in America anyway. If by his efforts he created a new copyright work, he was entitled to enforce that right against infringers. Webster, however, went further than that. He regarded it as *morally wrong* for later compilers to make use of ideas that he had incorporated into his spelling book, even when they were ideas that he had himself taken from elsewhere, and even long after his copyright had expired. He objected when others included in their dictionaries words that (he thought) were not to be found in any dictionary but his own. When he adopted an idea, or a word, it became, he thought, his own exclusive property.

It was a characteristic of Webster's mental makeup that he never seemed to notice that many of the criticisms he directed at others might with equal justice have been applied to himself. I quoted at the beginning of this book a footnote from the Introduction to the *American Dictionary*:

The multiplicity of books for instructing us in our vernacular language is an evil of no small magnitude. Every man has some particular notions which he wishes to propagate, and there is scarcely any peculiarity or absurdity for which some authority may not be found. The facility of book-making favors this disposition, and while a chief qualification for authorship is a dextrous use of an inverted pen, and a pair of scissors, we are not to expect relief from the evil.

Webster was responsible for a great many books for instructing Americans in their vernacular language. With some justice, he was often accused of propagating very peculiar notions indeed. Also, quite a large proportion of each of the books we shall be looking at could have been put together by the application of a pair of scissors and a pot of paste to the pages of other men's books. When he wrote this footnote, Webster was not looking inwards.

Another example. In the course of a long life,

Webster often changed his opinions, not only on matters relating to language, but also in politics and in religion. He was not ashamed of this, and he was always willing to acknowledge that his earlier views had been mistaken. What he would not accept was that his *present* view might be mistaken also. No matter how often he had changed his opinion, he was always unshakeably convinced that he was right. He would quote words spoken to him by Benjamin Franklin many years before: "Sir, I have been all my life changing my opinions"; but this was to persuade others that they might be mistaken when they refused to agree with him, and he never applied the same solvent to the glue of his own convictions.

Along with his certainty that his current opinions were right, Webster had an insatiable urge to show the world that those who disagreed with him were wrong. He spread his opinions in letters, newspaper articles, books, and pamphlets. The opening words of a letter he sent to Samuel Adams in March 1784 were typical. Bear in mind that he was then an unknown, out-of-work schoolmaster, and Adams was one of the most important men in America. He wrote:

Sir,
The importance of this communication will, I flatter myself, be sufficient apology for the freedom I take of writing to a gentleman with whom I have not the honor of an acquaintance....

In writing that letter, he was disregarding the advice given him several years earlier by his tutor at Yale, the Rev. Joseph Buckminster. In October 1779, the year after Webster's graduation, Buckminster had written to him:

you must endeavor not to be forward in applying ... to persons with whom you have but a slight acquaintance.... Such is the perverseness of human nature they will be disposed to ridicule you and perhaps set you down among those who have too high an opinion of their own importance....

Webster's weaknesses were always more apparent to those around him than they were to Webster himself. He had the courage given him by the strength of his convictions, and he really believed that the world would be a better place if only it would listen to him, and learn. To some degree, this may be commended as an effort by a seeker of truth to root out error, but

by many of his contemporaries he was seen as a vain, opinionated, self-publicizing busybody. Certainly, reading the prefaces to the spelling book and dictionary, one does get the feeling that the contest is not just between one book and another, but between man and man. If Webster had not believed in himself, however, he would never have achieved what he did; only the certain knowledge that he was right (mistaken as it often was) kept him going through years of discouragement and adversity. In his favor, it cannot be denied that he was painstaking, methodical, and an extraordinarily hard worker.

The next aspect of Webster's character I want to reflect on is his veracity. Sometimes, though not very often, I suspect him of deliberate untruthfulness. There are other times when he tells the exact truth, and I suspect him of attempting a deception. These are not always easy to spot. When Webster speaks in his own words, bear in mind that he chose his words carefully, and they may mean just what they say *and no more*. Take, for example, the matter of his involvement in the War of Independence. When he wanted to give himself greater credibility in a political argument, he said that he had "volunteered his services, shouldered the best musket he could find, marched up the Hudson in sight of the flames and smoking ruins of Kingston, encountering the hardships of a soldier's life to which he had not been inured, to lend his feeble aid in checking the enemy. This he did for the purpose of defending the country...." Every word of that is literally true, but it is misleading because it suggests that he was involved in some sort of battle, which he was not. In the year 1777, Webster, with his father and his two brothers, set off in a contingent of militia to join a battle, which turned out to be over before they got there. Hearing the news "Burgoyne is taken!" they heaved a sigh of relief, turned round, and went home. Webster did, indeed, shoulder his musket, but he put it down again without having had to fire a shot. That was the total of his military experience.

If Webster was consistently guilty of careful truthfulness, this may sometimes be revealing. By looking to see what he wrote, we may be able to draw inferences about what he chose not to write. Let me give you an example. When he was accused of having copied the syllable divi-

sion of his spelling book from Thomas Sheridan, his response was, "I have never seen any schoolbook upon such a plan." The suspect word here is "schoolbook." Webster had indeed taken the idea from Sheridan, but Sheridan's books were not *schoolbooks.*

Towards the end of his life, Webster sometimes displayed the very opposite of careful truthfulness, making statements that were not true at all. Here is an excerpt from a letter to a newspaper, in which he complained of the use made of his books by his competitors, contrasting their behavior with his own:

Every book I write is a fund for others, who copy what they want & publish it with their own materials. Every Spelling Book which I have seen, (& I have thirty or forty) contains the most important parts of my Spelling Book. These plagiarists adopt my plan, & copy most of the book....

It is a consolation to me that as far as my recollection will aid me, I have never copied a sentence from any other man's writings, & in my writings for the youth of my country, no passage is recollected which I shall regret in the last hours of my life.

The assertion that Webster "never copied a sentence from any other man's writings" is quite absurdly inaccurate, but my feeling is that his making such a statement is not evidence of progressive dishonesty so much as of progressive blindness to facts. Webster had for many years portrayed himself as a courageous innovator whose bold ideas were unfairly adopted by others, and in the end he came to believe in his own story.

Family Connections

Webster was born in West Hartford, Connecticut, in 1758 — three years after the publication of Johnson's Dictionary — and he died in New Haven in 1843. Eighty-four years full of incident. Apart from a short visit to Europe to complete his dictionary, he never left America, where politics were all-important. He lived through the war that gave birth to the United States, saw Washington's unanimous election as President in 1789, and lived to see, already apparent by 1843, the cracks in the fabric that threatened the breakup of the Union. In Europe, his contemporaries included Napoleon, Beethoven, and Jane Austen, who were all born between his tenth and twentieth birthdays, and

he outlived them all. Though he wrote on politics both as a pamphleteer and as a newspaperman, this is not an aspect of his life with which we are much concerned, but we must try to see him in his social and historical context.

His biographers like to start with the Colonial governors in his family tree. In the male line, he was a direct descendant of John Webster, governor of Connecticut from 1656 to 1657, and his mother was a great-granddaughter of William Bradford, governor of Plymouth Colony from 1621 to 1651. Webster was proud of them, too. When a Philadelphia newspaper mockingly reported that "Noah Webster jun. Esq." had sunk to the humble office of a teacher of children in that city, Webster (who did not have a high opinion of the average schoolmaster) retorted that "his ancestors governed provinces fifty years before Pennsylvania was settled"[2] That was true, but it gives a misleading impression of Webster's own circumstances. His forebears governed provinces *before* Pennsylvania was settled, but they did not govern anything *after* that time. The last of Webster's gubernatorial ancestors stopped governing more than a hundred years before Webster himself was born.

In Webster's time, there was a ruling elite in Connecticut society. It was an aristocracy not of the idle rich, but of men of solid worth. They were serious, hard-working Congregationalist folk who received their education at Yale and went on to take their places in government, in the church, in the law, and in society. Their sons and their daughters intermarried and passed on their respectable virtues. Webster was *not* born into this class. His father, also called Noah, was a farmer in West Hartford. He was neither particularly intelligent nor very successful, but he did for his fourth child what many men in his situation would not have done — he gave him an education. Finding among his brood an ugly duckling more interested in reading than farming, he sent the boy to a tutor to prepare him for Yale, and he mortgaged his farm to pay the fees.

Webster was the first of his family to receive a college education, and it opened a gap between him and them that would never close. Yale introduced him to members of the Connecticut ruling class. Compared with what he had known, it was a different world, peopled by the educated, sophisticated, and self-assured. And he wanted to belong to it. He became ashamed of his family, both socially and educationally. Also, there was the matter of religion. To be accepted in Connecticut society, one had at least to appear to practice the established Congregationalist religion, but it was not necessary to be fanatical about it. Webster went to church on Sundays, but (until his religious awakening when he was nearly 50) this was conventional polite behavior, far removed from the ingrained piety of his parents. Indeed, embracing the values of his fellow students in preference to those of his family turned Webster, for a while, into something like a free-thinking rationalist. After his religious awakening, he explained what had happened to him at Yale in a letter to his brother-in-law Thomas Dawes:

Being educated in a religious family under pious parents, I had in early life some religious impressions, but being too young to understand fully the doctrines of the Christian religion and falling into vicious company at college, I lost those impressions.

The choosing of names for children is governed by fashion as well as by religious conviction, and fashions were certainly changing between 1750 and 1800, so it may not be safe to rely on the different names chosen by father and son as indicating different levels of piety. Notice, anyway, that Webster's parents gave religious or biblical names to four of their five children: Mercy, Abraham, Jerusha, Noah, and Charles. In eighteenth century America, "first" or "given" names were still "christian names." Webster's children, by contrast, were called Emily, Frances Juliana (known as Julia), Harriet, Mary, William, Eliza, and Louisa. Another son, Henry, died when only a few weeks old. Webster, our Webster that is, disliked the name Noah, and would not allow it to be given to any of his grandchildren. He signed nearly all his private letters, even the most personal and affectionate ones to his wife and children, "N. Webster."

What you have next to read, however, is not a letter written by Webster; it is a letter that was written to him by his elder brother Abraham. It would be unfair to choose this one simply as an example of the Webster family piety set down on paper — it was written after the death of Abraham's only son, an event likely to

provoke reflections on divine providence in anyone — but the piety is certainly there in indigestible chunks.

Lebanon December 3d 1814

Dear Brother

God in his Holy and wise Providence has seen fit to take from me my only and beloved son under Circumstances peculiarly aggrevating. He was called with the melitia to Sacketts Harbor the beginning of September where he enjoyed comfotable health untill about the 20th of Octr, when he was attacked with the Diare. He remained in the barracks 5 or 6 days and thus no doubt suffered greatly being as we learn neglected by the Surgeon — he walked out of Camp about a mile and in the course of a few days by the help of waggons was conveyed 10 miles and lodged with a family where as we have reason to believe he had good attention paid to him a Physion was called but no relief of his Disorder could be obtained he languished there 12 day and then expired but not untill as we humbly hope God of his Sovereign mercy had bowed his wicked heart and brought him to submit to Jesus Christ and to trust in him alone for pardon and forgiveness. The Ground of our hope we build upon verbal information from the family where he lodged and where he Died. they sent us word that they had reason to believe he left the wold a true penitent and that a Clergy man who visited him and his Physician who is said to be a professor of Religion entertained a hope for him — what his state now is we have not business to enquire. God has Disposed of him as his infinite wisdom saw would be most for his own Glory. our duty is Cheerfully to submit to his Holy will in all things and to rejoice that we are in the hand, of just such a God as he is who will do no injustice to any of his Creatures. Gods way are marvelous and his Judgments are a great deep which the short line of understanding cannot fathom who knows but in his Eternal counsel he Determined to take this very method to bring my dear Son to a sense of his corrupt heart, to take him a distance from a Father's house cast him among strangers visit him with sickness and no earthly relative to look to, in his distress he might be led to look to God alone and stay himself on the mighty God of Jacob who knoweth but God ment by taking away the son cutting away the principle Earthly prop, the Parents might be led to rest themselves on the Lord in whome is Ever lasting strength.

Dear Brother, Divine Providence has be exceedingly kind to me and my family since we have lived in this region has bestowed many undeserved favours upon us both special and common but I have been unthankfull my heart was too lifted up with pride and I have not rendered unto him according to benefits received. He the is therefore justly testifying his displeasure against me for my sin and ingratitude.

My Son in Law Amos Blair went to assist Seymour and help him home he arrived 24 before his desease he was rational and conversed freely said he had a desire to se his parents before he left the world if it had been Gods will but hoped he felt resigned he repeatedly Desired his nurs to boulster him up in the bed and read a Chapter in the Bible which she did, and he prayed with aparent engagedness audibly. He was Decntly interred in the common Grave Yard in the Town of Adams a Sermon was Preached on the occasion Amos Blair the only relative present. His case never was represented to me very alarming if it had bee I should have visited him myself. Died November 21st aged 25 years, & 2 days.

My health is much better than it was a year ago and so is my wifes and Sophia they both unite with me in love to you and family.

Pray for your afflicted brother.

That letter was written much later than the period we are now considering, but it shows the patterns of thought of the household in which Webster grew up. Abraham was educated in the same religious family as Noah, under the same pious parents; unlike Noah he never lost the "religious impressions" left on him by that upbringing. Even if we allow for the unhappy circumstances in which the letter was written, we still have an oppressive weight of theology. If that was the style in which the young Webster, fresh from Yale, was habitually addressed by his family, one can imagine how uncomfortable it made him. A further source of embarrassment, of which the letter is a sufficient example, is the fact that the other members of his family were not masters of grammar, and their spelling was extremely erratic.

While you have that letter still in mind, think for a moment what you would do if your elder brother wrote to you in great distress, to tell you that his only son had died just two days after his 25th birthday. What Webster did we can see from Abraham's next letter, written exactly a year later:

Lebanon December 3d 1815

Dear Brother

Two years and more have elapsed since I have heard a word from you. It is an old saying that no news is good news. I therefore rest easy in my mind with regard to you and family concluding that if any thing had taken place which was needfull for me to know you would have written....

Webster had not troubled to answer his brother's earlier letter. As I have said, he aspired

to join a higher class of society than that of his parents and poor Abraham.

Webster never did succeed in joining the ruling class. He dined at their tables, and they at his. Sometimes they used him to publicize their opinions in books, articles, or pamphlets, but they did not admit him to their counsels. When there were Federalists in power, Webster supported and echoed the Federalist line, but they faded with Jefferson in the presidency (though more slowly in Connecticut than elsewhere), and Webster became increasingly isolated. In the end, he was the last fossil Federalist, lamenting that there were political parties in opposition to one another, and distrustful of democracy.

While never himself accepted as a member of the elite, Webster achieved the next best thing by marrying some of his daughters to their sons. The first step up the social ladder was his own marriage. His wife was very definitely from a class above his own, and it is perhaps significant that he found her outside Connecticut. Rebecca Greenleaf was the daughter of a Boston merchant. Webster met her on a visit to Philadelphia, shortly before he was teased in the papers for taking up teaching there.

Rebecca's Boston background was so different from Webster's in West Hartford that he made his parents modify their behavior to avoid offending his new wife. This was recorded by his grand-daughter, Emily Ellsworth Fowler Ford:

Some of the ruder village habits surprised [my] grandmother in her first visits to her husband's family. She was a girl of city training and French descent, out of a family of unusual elegance and breeding, while her husband had been living [away] from home for years. He was also so shocked at one custom that he told his Father "Becky should never visit him again until things were different." These were at once changed, and though the neighbors grumbled at first at the "Boston fashion," it was finally followed by all of them, much to the improvement of their comfort.[3]

One would like to know what the older Websters' disgusting habits were.

The Connecticut society into which Webster's elder daughters married was a complicated network of interconnections. I shall demonstrate this by introducing to you members of three families. To begin with, it is all pretty simple, but it ends up being difficult to grasp without the aid of a diagram. Do not worry about this. The complexity of the structure is what I want to show, and it is not necessary for you to remember the details.

Let us begin with one of Webster's classmates at Yale, Oliver Wolcott. Definitely ruling class. He succeeded Alexander Hamilton as secretary of the Treasury, and after that was Governor of Connecticut from 1817 to 1827. His father, who was one of the signers of the Declaration of Independence, had himself been state governor in 1796-97.

Next, meet the brothers Chauncey and Elizur Goodrich. Their father was the Rev. Dr. Elizur Goodrich, one of the trustees of Yale. Chauncey, the elder brother, was a year younger than Webster. He graduated from Yale in 1776, was tutor there from 1779 to 1781, and in 1781 was called to the bar in Hartford, at the same time as Webster. He went on to become a representative in Congress (1795–1801). In 1807 he became a U.S. senator, taking the seat of another of Webster's classmates, Uriah Tracey, who had died. Chauncey Goodrich's second wife, Mary Ann, was Oliver Wolcott's sister.

Elizur Goodrich followed a similar course to his brother, being a Yale graduate, then a tutor, and then called to the bar. He was a professor of law at Yale from 1801 to 1810, but before that he had joined his brother for a couple of years in Congress. Later, when Chauncey was Mayor of Hartford, Elizur was Mayor of New Haven. Webster's second daughter, Julia, married Elizur's son, Chauncey Allen Goodrich, whose aunt was a Wolcott.

Neither of the Goodrich brothers was governor of Connecticut, but Chauncey did get to be lieutenant governor.

Finally, let me introduce some Ellsworths. Oliver Ellsworth was some years older than Webster. Webster was a lodger in Oliver's house in Hartford in the summer of 1779, when the latter was practicing law there and Webster was teaching school. Ellsworth went on to become chief justice of the United States. He married Abigail Wolcott, and one of their sons, William Wolcott Ellsworth (a classmate at Yale of Chauncey Allen Goodrich), married Webster's eldest daughter, Emily. William was a member of the House of Representatives, and later became governor of Connecticut.

William had a twin brother, Henry Leavitt Ellsworth. Their mother was a Wolcott. When Emily Webster became Emily Ellsworth, the twin became her brother-in-law. He married Chauncey Allen Goodrich's sister Nancy, who was, of course, the daughter of Elizur Goodrich, the niece of Mary Ann Wolcott, and Julia Webster Goodrich's sister-in-law.

In the next generation, that of Webster's grandchildren, William Wolcott Ellsworth's son Oliver married Caroline Cleveland Smith, whose first cousin, Roswell Smith, married Oliver's first cousin, Annie Ellsworth, daughter of Henry. Roswell Smith was one of the founders of what became *Century Magazine* and the Century Publishing Company. Oliver's son, William Webster Ellsworth, went into the Century business, and was involved in the publication of the *Century Dictionary*.

The final and neatest knot between the Webster, Ellsworth, Goodrich and Wolcott threads was tied at the wedding of William Webster Ellsworth's first cousin Julia. Two of her great-grandfathers were Noah Webster and Chief Justice Ellsworth, and she married Henry Goodrich Wolcott, who was the great-grandson of Oliver Wolcott, and descended from the Goodriches as well.

Those of Webster's children who married outside this Connecticut tangle also brought him a feeling of moving closer to the seats of power. His third daughter Harriet's first husband, Edward Cobb, was Rufus King's nephew. Better still, William's marriage to Rosalie Stuart almost made Webster a relation of George Washington. Rosalie's mother, before her marriage to Dr. David Stuart, was the widow of Washington's stepson, John Parke Custis.

Two Particular Poets

Before we go on, I want to introduce two poets from Webster's time at Yale, who have parts to play in our story. The first is Timothy Dwight, who was tutor to the class a year ahead of Webster's. Webster's class petitioned to have him for their tutor in their final year, but without success. He was a man of formidable intellect who, after spending some years at Greenfield Hill as minister, farmer, and schoolmaster, returned to Yale as president. His authority in the Congregationalist church was such that

he was known as "Pope" Dwight. He was the author of a turgid epic, *The Conquest of Canaan*, written between 1771 and 1777, but not published until 1785. Webster read it as a student, and composed a sycophantic poem, "To the Author of *The Conquest of Canaan*," which he sensibly suppressed at the time, but published ten years later when he needed something to fill a page of his *American Magazine*.

Hail, rising genius, whose celestial fire
Warms the glad soul to tune the sacred lyre;
Whose splendid lays in epic song adorn
A theme which infidels and sceptics scorn;
Sing the bold feats of Joshua's valiant hand
Who rears his standard in Canaan's land;
Before whose arm, the numerous squadrons slain
Heap the broad field and drench the embattled plain;
The vanquished nations tremble at his frown
And laurel'd conquests all his labours crown.

There is plenty more in the same vein, and worse. Dwight is compared to Homer, Virgil, and "god-like Milton," and Webster looks forward to the day

[when] o'er the land these glorious arts shall reign
And blest Yalensia lead the splendid train.
In future years unnumber'd Bards shall rise
Catch the bold flame and tower above the skies;
Their brightening splendor gild the epic page
And unborn Dwights adorn th'Augustan age.

By the time the *Conquest* was published, Webster's judgment had matured, and he could see that it was unreadable. With nice discernment, he sent a copy to George Washington, who would not have wished to read it anyway.

The first of the unnumber'd bards to catch Dwight's bold flame and have a shot at gilding the epic page was Webster's best friend, Joel Barlow. Barlow was poor, like Webster, because his father had died, and his inheritance was only just sufficient to see him through college. He was the class poet, and could knock off a few dozen lines on "The Prospect of Peace" which his friends thought were better poetry than they could have written. This modest success and the lack of any serious competition convinced Barlow that he was a real poet, and because he was such a nice chap, nobody liked to tell him that he was wrong. As a result, he spent thirty years on a simply ghastly poem in which Columbus is transported from his prison cell in a dream and shown the whole history of

America from the earliest times to the distant future. In its first form it was called *The Vision of Columbus*, a small book with a list of subscribers at the end that reads like a who's who of American society in 1787. All of Barlow's friends subscribed for copies (Webster took two), and no doubt they told him how much they had enjoyed reading it. Barlow became known as a major literary figure, and with that encouragement, he beavered away on an inflated version of his poem, published twenty years later under the grandiose title of *The Columbiad*. It had illustrations specially painted and engraved in England, and was beautifully printed and bound. It was said to be the finest book ever produced in America, and if you disregard the content, it probably was. Francis Jeffrey was not one of Barlow's friends, and was brutally frank in the *Edinburgh Review*:

Webster's closest friend at Yale, the poet, man of business, and diplomat, Joel Barlow.

In his cumbrous and inflated style, he is constantly mistaking hyperbole for grandeur, and supplying the place of simplicity with huge patches of mere tameness and vulgarity. This curious intermixture, indeed, of extreme homeliness and flatness, with a sort of turbulent and bombastic elevation, is the great characteristic of the work before us....

Thus the whole history, past, present, and future, of America, and inclusively of the whole world, is delivered in the clumsy and revolting form of a miraculous vision; and thus truth is not only blended with falsehood and fancy, but is presented to the mind under the mask of the grossest and most palpable fiction. Mr. Barlow, of course, judges differently of his plan.

Despite the reviewer's dislike of the poem, he could not deny that it came in handsome packaging:

There is one thing, however, which may give the original edition of Mr. Barlow's poem some chance of selling among us, — and that is, the extraordinary beauty of the paper, printing and embellishments. We do not know that we have ever seen a handsomer book issue from the press of England; and if this be really and truly the production of American artists,

we must say, that the infant republic has already attained to the very summit of perfection in the mechanical part of bookmaking.

By chance, the same volume of the *Edinburgh Review* brought Webster, Dwight, and Barlow together again, 25 years after they first met at Yale. It is in a wonderfully acid review of *Travels in America*, by Thomas Ashe:

Though we are certainly of opinion, that the second-rate pamphleteers of that country write incomparably better than Mr. Ashe, it is no doubt true, that America can produce nothing to bring her intellectual efforts into any sort of comparison with that of Europe. Liberty and competition have as yet done nothing to stimulate literary genius in these republican states. They have never passed the limits of humble mediocrity, either in thought or expression. Noah Webster, we are afraid, still occupies the first place in criticism, Timothy Dwight and Joel Barlow in poetry....

Another Trinity of Fame!

1. Schoolteacher and
Student of Law, 1778–1782

When he graduated from Yale in 1778, what was Webster to do? His friend Barlow lingered in New Haven hoping to be appointed to a tutorship. Meanwhile, Barlow courted Ruth Baldwin, the sister of Abraham Baldwin, his friend and a former Yale tutor who would later become a Georgia senator. Barlow won the girl but not the tutorship, so he became an army chaplain. In this, he was following Abraham Baldwin's advice and example. By temperament, Webster would have been better suited to the church than was Barlow, but Yale had too far undermined his religious convictions. He liked the idea of practicing law, but that would involve further study, and his father could not continue to support him. He described his sad situation in No. 5 of the *Memoir*:

The subject of this memoir was now cast upon the world, at the age of twenty, without property, without patrons, and in the midst of a war which had disturbed all occupations; had impoverished the country; and the termination of which could not be foreseen. He remained some time at his father's house; and while there, his father put into his hands an eight dollar bill of continental currency, then worth three or four dollars; saying to him "take this; you must now seek your living; I can do no more for you."

In the state of anxiety which his condition produced, N.W. employed his time in reading; and among other books, he read Johnson's *Rambler*. This book produced no inconsiderable effect on his mind; and he then resolved that whatever was to be his fate in life, he would pursue a most exact course of integrity and virtue. This sentence of the great moralist, "To fear no eye, to suspect no tongue, is the great prerogative of innocence; an exemption granted only to invariable virtue," was indelibly impressed on his memory.

Johnson would be the father figure Webster admired, emulated, and rebelled against for the rest of his life. Fifty years later, the *Rambler* provided a symbolic quotation for the title page of Webster's *American Dictionary*—Webster using Johnson's words to describe what Webster had done to Johnson:

He that wishes to be counted among the benefactors of posterity, must add, by his own toil, to the acquisitions of his ancestors.

The *Memoir* continues:

As N.W. was under the necessity of immediate employment to obtain subsistence, not having means to enable him to prepare for professional business, he took charge of a school in Glastonbury....

By the standards of the day, Webster was overqualified for a schoolmaster, but he could think of nothing better to do. He spent the winter of 1778 teaching school in Glastonbury, Connecticut, a place that he already knew because his Yale class had been evacuated there when the war had made food scarce in New Haven. The following summer, he was teaching in Hartford. He lodged with Oliver Ellsworth, hoping to study law under Ellsworth in his spare time. That winter, he taught in West Hartford and for the last time lived at home with his parents.

He found that it was not easy to study law while teaching, and in the summer of 1780 he tried another strategy. He went to live in the home of the registrar of deeds in Litchfield, Connecticut, Jedidiah Strong, and worked as an assistant in Strong's office. At the same time, he studied law with Strong and with Tapping Reeve, who founded the Litchfield law school and would later provide a recommendation for Webster's spelling book. In the spring of 1781,

Webster was examined with nearly twenty other candidates for admission to the bar in Litchfield. All were rejected, perhaps because the practicing members of the bar were alarmed at the prospect of so large an increase in their number. Undaunted, Webster went immediately to Hartford, where he was examined at the same time as Chauncey Goodrich. Both of them were admitted to the bar.

This qualification entitled Webster to put "Esquire" after his name. He was proud of that. He would later be mocked in the *Freeman's Journal* for his use of the name "Noah Webster Jun. Esquire":

Who in his senses ever used the appellation esq. to a schoolmaster? a *flagellator anorum* to be called esq.! fie! fie! such a contradiction of terms! we might with equal propriety call a Hottentot, a Yankee, or a Savage a refined Frenchman.

In September 1781, Webster took his M.A., another step up from his humble beginnings.

Being entitled to practice at the bar is by no means the same thing as being able to earn a living at it. Webster would make the attempt later, but, in the summer of 1781, it was back to school. The difference this time was that the school, in Sharon, Connecticut, was Webster's own. He placed an advertisement in the *Connecticut Courant*:

The subscriber, desirous of promoting Education, so essential to the interest of a free people, proposes immediately to open a school at Sharon, in which young Gentlemen and Ladies may be instructed in Reading, Writing, Mathematicks, the English Language, and if desired, the Latin and Greek Languages — in Geography, Vocal Music, &c. at moderate price of Six Dollars and two thirds per quarter per Scholar. The strictest attention will be paid to the studies, the manners and the morals of youth, by the public's very humble servant,

Noah Webster, Jun.

P.S. If any persons are desirous of acquainting themselves with the French Language, they may be under the instruction of an accomplished master in Sharon.

Sharon, June 1, 1781.

Webster himself taught everything except French. He had never studied French, but he found "an accomplished master" already living in Sharon. This was a Swiss Huguenot pastor, the Rev. Mr. Tetard, who was prepared to teach French in Webster's school, and to teach French to Webster as well.

Sharon sheltered a number of New York families who had taken refuge from the war, and Webster made contacts that would be useful to him later. Robert Gilbert Livingston's family was there, and Mrs. Theodosia Prevost, a widow who later married Aaron Burr; both sent children to Webster's school. Another pupil was Laura Canfield, whose father, John Canfield, was a lawyer in Sharon and a member of the Connecticut legislature. The school is said to have been conducted in the attic of the house of Cotton M. Smith, whose son Jack (John Cotton Smith) would later serve as governor of Connecticut immediately before Webster's classmate Oliver Wolcott. Jack Smith's sister, Juliana, then aged 19, ran a literary society in Sharon and produced a manuscript magazine, *The Clio, a Literary Miscellany*, made up of contributions from members of the society, including Webster. While Jack was away at Yale, Juliana gave him the news in the form of a diary. It contains a dispassionate view of Webster that expresses very much the conclusion I have come to — that he was a hard-working fellow who adopted other people's ideas. Juliana compared him unfavorably with the Smiths' horse, which was also called Jack:

Mr. Webster has not the excuse of youth, (I think he must be fully twenty-two or three), but his essays — don't be angry, Jack, — are as young as yours or brother Tommy's, while his reflections are as prosy as those of our horse, your namesake, would be if they were written out. Perhaps more so, for I truly believe, judging from the way *Jack Horse* looks 'round at me sometimes, when I am on his back, that his thoughts on the human race and their conduct towards his own might be well worth reading. At least they would be all *his own*, and that is more than can be said of N.W.'s. In conversation he is even duller than in writing, if that is possible, but he is a painstaking man and a hard student. Papa says he will make his mark.

The curious history of Webster's school in Sharon is neatly summed up in three entries from another diary, that of Robert Gilbert Livingston:

July 1st   Noah Webster began school. I sent Cornelia, Catherine, and Helen.

Oct. 1st. Webster began his school, second term.

Oct. 9th. Webster dismissed his school and left town.

It is not known for certain why Webster left Sharon so suddenly. Some say that it was due to disappointment in love, the lady being either Juliana Smith or a Miss Rebecca Pardee, but I have found no confirmation of this in Webster's writings. Whatever the cause, it does not seem to have been such as to offend the people of Sharon, who remained well disposed towards him.

Three years later, he wrote a description of "Juliana—*A real Character*" for his school reader—the third part of the *Grammatical Institute*—which may have been intended as a picture of Juliana Smith:

1. Juliana is one of those rare women whose personal attractions have no rivals, but the sweetness of her temper and the delicacy of her sentiments. An elegant person, regular features, a fine complexion, a lively expressive countenance, an easy address, and those blushes of modesty that soften the soul of the beholder; These are the native beauties, which render her the object of universal admiration.

2. But when we converse with her, and hear the melting expressions of unaffected sensibility and virtue that flow from her tongue, her personal charms receive new lustre, and irresistibly engage the affections of her acquaintances.

3. Sensible that the great source of all happiness is purity of morals and an easy conscience, Juliana pays constant and sincere attention to the duties of religion. She abhors the infamous, but fashionable device of deriding its sacred institutions.

4. She considers a lady without virtue as a monster on earth; and every accomplishment, without morals, as a polite deception. She is neither a hypocrite nor an enthusiast; on the contrary, she mingles such cheerfulness with the religious duties of life, that even her piety carries with it a charm which insensibly allures the profligate from the arms of vice....

27. If it is possible for her to find a man who knows her worth, and has a disposition and virtues to reward it, the union of their hearts must secure that unmingled felicity in life, which is reserved for genuine love, a passion inspired by sensibility, and improved by a perpetual intercourse of kind offices.

The romantic view is that this passage proves Webster to have been in love with Juliana Smith, a fact confirmed by his later giving the name Juliana to his second daughter. Of course it is possible. A young man of twenty, fresh out of an all-male university, often falls in love with the first attractive girl he meets. Perhaps Webster himself was the profligate allured by Juliana's charm from the arms of vice? This sort

of speculation is rather fun, but definite conclusions cannot be formed without evidence, and you have seen all the evidence that there is. Three days before he wrote that description of "Juliana" he noted in his diary, "Finished my remarks on Domestic happiness and the character of Emilia, Institute 3d part." Emily was the name he gave to his first child, but I am not aware of any suggestion that he had been romantically involved with a lady of that name. More probably he gave names that he liked to the ladies described in the reader, and, because he liked the names, he gave them to his children as well.

Whatever the reason for Webster's sudden departure from Sharon, it must have affected him deeply at the time, and he tried to give up teaching. He spent the winter of 1781 wandering from place to place in an unsuccessful search for "mercantile employment." By January 1782, however, he was back in Sharon (and on good terms with the Smiths). He thought of reopening his school there and prepared another prospectus. Though the idea may not have been his own, he was ahead of his time in drawing attention to the need for "the literary improvement of females":

On the first of May will be opened at Sharon in Connecticut, a school, in which children may be instructed, not only in the common arts of reading, writing, and arithmetic, but in any branch of Academical literature. The little regard that is paid to the literary improvement of females, even among people of rank and fortune, and the general inattention to the grammatical purity and elegance of our native language, are faults in the education of youth that more gentlemen have taken pains to censure than to correct. Any young gentlemen and ladies, who wish to acquaint themselves with the English language, geography, vocal music, &c., may be waited upon at particular hours for that purpose. The price of board and lodging will be from six to nine shillings, lawful money per week, according to the age and studies of the Scholar; no pains will be spared to render the school useful.

Sharon, April 16th, 1782   NOAH WEBSTER

N.B. The subscriber has a large convenient store in Sharon for storing articles of any kind, where they may be secured at a moderate expense.

The school, however, did not reopen, so later in May 1782 Webster left Sharon and went wandering once more. This time, he arrived in Goshen, in Orange County, New York. Having

no other way of earning a living, he started teaching again. It was here in Goshen that Webster conceived the idea of compiling his own spelling book and prepared the first draft. One of his later autobiographical recollections puts it in a nutshell:

In the year 1782, while the American army was lying in Newburgh, I crossed the Hudson, established a school in Goshen, & compiled an elementary book which was published in 1783 under the title of The First Part of the Institute.

We shall examine Webster's spelling book, "The First Part of the Institute," but first we must get to know the competition.

2. Two Earlier Spelling Books

Dilworth

DILWORTH, Thomas, a diligent schoolmaster, whose spelling book, book-keeper's assistant, schoolmaster's assistant, miscellaneous arithmetic, &c. are well known as useful and popular books. He was for some time engaged at Stratford-le-bow with Dyche, and then set up a school for himself at Wapping. He died 1781.[1]

When Webster was himself a schoolboy, and when he was teaching, Thomas Dilworth's *A New Guide to the English Tongue* was by far the most widely used spelling book on both sides of the Atlantic. First published in 1740, by 1795 it was in its 97th edition in London, and many editions were published elsewhere. The first recorded printing outside London was by Benjamin Franklin in Philadelphia, in 1747.

Notice that, before Dilworth set up his own establishment a few miles nearer central London, he taught in Thomas Dyche's school. Dyche proposed many of the spelling reforms that America later adopted, and we shall meet him again.

Before we explore Dilworth's spelling book in detail, let us give some thought to the meaning of the word "spelling." If I say "Abraham Webster could not spell," I mean, and you understand me to mean, that he used the wrong letters when writing many words. An educated Englishman writes "diarrhoea"; an American, "diarrhea"; Abraham wrote "Diare." This sort of "spelling," choosing the appropriate letters and putting them in the correct or conventional order, is properly called *orthography*, which means "writing right." The name "spelling book" suggests a book that teaches orthography. There are, however, other and older senses of "spelling" that have to do not with writing, but with reading. We are still familiar with the idea of "spelling out" a word — "c-a-t, spells cat" — this is what the Vicar of Wakefield meant when he said that his wife "could read any English book without much spelling." To Dilworth "spelling" had a yet earlier meaning that is now quite unfamiliar. It meant dividing words up into syllables. This is illustrated by some questions and answers from Part III of the *New Guide*:

OF SYLLABLES

Q. What is a syllable?

A. A syllable is either one letter; as a; or more than one; as, man.

OF SPELLING OR DIVISION OF SYLLABLES

Q. How do you divide your syllables?

A. By taking words asunder into convenient parts, in order to show their true pronunciation, and original formation, which is commonly called spelling.

For Dilworth, a spelling book was a book that taught children to read by dividing words into syllables. Teaching orthography was only a secondary aim.

The fact that Dilworth's speller was so successful shows that, when children are learning to read, almost any simple book will do to practice on. By any sort of academic standard, however, it is a poor performance. Look again at his definition of *syllable*: "A syllable is either one letter or more than one." Certainly, letters are the stuff that syllables are made of, but what *is* a syllable? Dilworth's definition is not just uninformative, it is actually misleading; a single *vowel* can form a syllable, but most single *letters* cannot; and "more than one letter"

covers everything from "an" to "Encyclopædia Britannica."

In the following question and answer, Dilworth gave two reasons for dividing words into separate syllables: "to show their true pronunciation" and "to show their original formation." Having two such aims simultaneously can cause difficulties, because it may not be possible to hit both targets at the same time. Sometimes, the division of a word that shows its original formation suggests a false pronunciation; alternatively, showing the correct pronunciation distorts the structure of the word. This is not a thrilling topic, but it is of some importance to our study, because one of Webster's main criticisms of Dilworth was of his method of dividing words into syllables. What Webster claimed to be his own major contribution was the introduction of his improved system of dividing words.

Webster would avoid Dilworth's difficulty by making the indication of pronunciation the only reason for dividing a word into syllables. He may have been right, as the spelling book was intended to teach children to read words, not to understand them, but my sympathy is with Dilworth.

Dilworth's solution to the problem, *in theory*, was to divide a word in such a way as to show its meaning and formation, and, where this suggested a false pronunciation, to put a particular mark (") by the vowel to indicate that the word would have to be divided in a different way to show the pronunciation correctly. That may not be clear, but it could hardly be more obscure than Dilworth's explanation:

I have consulted the method of spelling or dividing syllables in long words, both according to their sound, and to the rules of grammar; and therefore in the perusal of this essay towards spelling, you will find that whenever a word occurs, that may be divided one way by sound, and another by grammar, the scholar is directed how to understand the doubtful division by this mark (") over the right side of the vowel, which, according to the sound, ought to be joined with the following consonant, which is nevertheless contrary to the rules of grammar; and therefore divided in such a manner as you see them printed.

An example may help. The word *promise* is pronounced with a short *o*; this can be shown by dividing it *prom-ise*, but that conceals the derivation from *pro* and *mitto*. On the other

hand, dividing it *pro-mise* suggests that the *o* is long, as in *pro-scribe*. Dilworth prints it *pro"mise*. The division shows the prefix *pro*, and thus reflects the derivation of the word; the mark in the middle indicates that the pronunciation would be better shown by making the *m* part of the first syllable.

If he had managed consistently to apply this principle, Dilworth would deserve high marks, but usually he did not even try. In practice, he divided words not according to their meaning, or their derivation, or their pronunciation, but according to a set of very silly rules. For example:

RULE I

Q. What is the first general rule for division of syllables?

A. A consonant between two vowels goes to the latter syllable; as, ba-nish

His own example serves to show how silly the system is. Dividing *banish* as he does, *ba-nish*, misleads as to the pronunciation because it suggests that the *a* is long, and it conceals a useful suggestion by hiding the word *ban*. One can sympathize when it is impossible to get two things right simultaneously, but here, when it would be easy to get both right, he contrived to get both wrong.

Dilworth did not devise any of this himself. He copied it, not very cleverly, from his former employer Thomas Dyche. Dilworth's title, *A New Guide to the English Tongue*, was intended to suggest that his work was a replacement for Dyche's *A Guide to the English Tongue*, a spelling book first published in 1707. The point was emphasized by the appearance of Dilworth's title page, which copied both the types and the layout used by Dyche. Dyche was the inventor of the mark ("), which he explained in this way:

As to the dividing of syllables, the learned Philologers themselves are not agreed in their opinions: for some would have us stick close to the Latin rule, laid down in our common grammars, as thinking it most commendable, that our language be reduced to the standard of the learned languages: while others are of opinion with Cominius, "That consonants should be joined with that vowel that gives the softest sound to the ear." And I must confess, that, in teaching children to read, I think the ear is the best guide. But I have found out a method, which probably will oblige both parties: for the words are divided according to

CORRECTED, ENLARGED, AND IMPROVED.

A

GUIDE

TO THE

𝕰nglish Tongue.

IN TWO PARTS.

The FIRST, proper for Beginners, showing a Natural and Easy Method to pronounce and express both Common Words, and Proper Names; in which, particular Care is had to show the Accent, for preventing Vicious Pronunciation.

The SECOND, for such as are advanced to some Ripeness of Judgment, containing Observations on the Sounds of Letters and Diphthongs; Rules for the true Division of Syllables, and the Use of Capitals, Stops, and Marks: with large Tables of Abbreviations, and Distinctions of Words; and several Alphabets of Copies for Young Writers.

TO WHICH IS ADDED,

An APPENDIX, containing many additional Lessons in Prose and Verse: First, in Words of One Syllable only; and then mixed with Words of Two, Three, Four, Five, Six, and Seven Syllables: and further improved with new Fables and Cuts.

By T. DYCHE, School-Master, Stratford-Bow.

GAINSBOROUGH:

PRINTED BY AND FOR H. MOZLEY.

1811.

Price Fifteen-pence bound.

A new Edition, carefully corrected and improved.

A NEW. GUIDE

TO THE

𝕰nglish Tongue.

IN FIVE PARTS.

I. Words both common and proper from one to six syllables; the several sorts of monosyllables in the common words being distinguished by tables, into words of two, three, and four letters, &c. with six short lessons at the end of each table, not exceeding the order of syllables in the foregoing tables. The several sorts of polysyllables, also being ranged in proper tables, have their syllables divided, and directions placed at the head of each table for the accent, to prevent false pronunciation; together with the like number of lessons on the foregoing tables, placed at the end of each table, as far as to words of four syllables, for the easier and more speedy way of teaching children to read.

II. A large and useful table of words that are the same in sound, but different in signification; very necessary to prevent the writing of one word for another of the same sound.
III. A short, but comprehensive Grammar of the English Tongue, delivered in the most familiar and instructive method of Question and Answer, necessary for all such persons as have the advantage only of an English education.
IV. An useful Collection of Sentences in prose and verse, divine, moral, and historical; together with a select number of Fables. And,
V. Forms of Prayer, for Children, on several occasions.

The whole being recommended by several Clergymen and eminent Schoolmasters, as the most useful Performance for the Instruction of Youth.

By THOMAS DILWORTH,

Author of the SCHOOLMASTER'S ASSISTANT, YOUNG BOOK-KEEPER'S ASSISTANT, &c. and Schoolmaster in *Wapping.*

DERBY:

PRINTED BY AND FOR HENRY MOZLEY.

1821.

Price Fifteen-Pence, bound.

The nearly identical title pages of Dyche and Dilworth.

the rules of the Latin grammarians: and where a consonant would sound better to the ear, with the following vowel, than that before it, I have placed this mark (") which was invented purely for that purpose; and I call it the double accent, because the bearing of the accent or stress of the voice, upon that syllable, draws the consonant to the preceding vowel, in the sounding of the words, which, by the rule of spelling, ought to be separated from it. Thus we spell ve-stry, vi-sit, ba-nish; but we pronounce ves-try, vis-it, ban-ish; and they that do not like the Latin rule of spelling, may with ease teach with these tables according to the ear, because the words are everywhere marked, where the rule and the ear disagree.

Notice that Dyche called the mark (") a "double accent"—a description Dilworth did not use.

Dilworth's first six rules for the division of syllables were copied almost verbatim from Dyche. As Dyche explained, but Dilworth did not, the rules do not work in English because they were devised by grammarians for dividing up Latin words. Dilworth's unhelpful definition of "syllable," however, was not copied from Dyche; it was Dilworth's own. In Dyche, the instructive dialogue is between "M," the master, and "S," the scholar. Dilworth copied the words of the first answer, but not the second:

M. WHAT is spelling?

S. To spell is to take words asunder into convenient parts, in order to show their true pronunciation, and original formation.

M. What is a syllable?

S. Every part of a word, so separated, and distinctly sounded, is a syllable or comprehension of the sound of a vowel or diphthong, either by itself, or with one or more consonants.

That is not entirely straightforward, but Dyche did say that he intended the second part of his book (in which it appears) "for such as are advanced to some Ripeness of Judgment."

Dilworth's *New Guide* is not an exciting book, but Webster's later fame and fortune were built on its foundations, and we must try to get to know it better.

The Preface is mainly remarkable for the playful way in which Dilworth put the first word of each paragraph on the first page at the end of the preceding paragraph. I can think of no explanation for this stylistic eccentricity. Thereafter, Dilworth used his Preface for the more normal purpose of explaining what was wrong with earlier works (in his case, Dyche's *Guide*):

In the several praxes, or lessons of monosyllables hitherto published in our mother tongue, instead of rising step by step, children are taught to jump before they can go; and if they prove incapable to take such long strides, as reach sometimes from monosyllables of two, to others of seven or eight letters, before they are informed of those coming between, they must be thumped and lugged forward, without being once instructed in the right knowledge of the most common and useful parts of our tongue. Certainly this is as barbarous in literature, as it would be cruel in behaviour, to bid a child take care how it comes upstairs, and then to beat it because it cannot stride up seven or eight steps at once.

The first of the five parts of the *New Guide* takes up more than half the book. Dilworth's description of it in the title page gives some idea of his mechanical method and his turgid style:

Words both common and proper from one to six syllables; the several sorts of monosyllables in the common words being distinguished by tables, into words of two, three and four letters, &c. with six short lessons at the end of each table, not exceeding the order of syllables in the foregoing tables. The several sorts of polysyllables, also being ranged in proper tables, have their syllables divided, and directions placed at the head of each table for the accent, to prevent false pronunciation; together with the like number of lessons on the foregoing tables, placed at the end of each table, as far as to words of four syllables, for the easier and more speedy way of teaching children to read.

To avoid Dyche's mistake, Dilworth takes one step at a time, with mathematical exactitude. He starts with single letters. We are shown the Alphabet (in alphabetical order, of course) in Roman, Italian, and English type (i.e., roman, italic, and gothic). Also, the names of the letters are written out phonetically, from *a, bee, see* to *double yu, eks, wi*, and *zed*. Then he gives us monosyllables, starting from *ba* and *ab*. The logical structure does not need any explanation:

TABLE I						TABLE II			
ba	be	bi	bo	bu	ab	eb	ib	ob	ub
ca	ce	ci	co	cu	ac	ec	ic	oc	uc
da	de	di	do	du	ad	ed	id	od	ud
fa	fe	fi	fo	fu	af	ef	if	of	uf
ga	ge	gi	go	gu	ag	eg	ig	og	ug

and so on, all the way up to

za	ze	zi	zo	zu	az	ez	iz	oz	uz

The only remotely interesting thing to notice here is that the chanting out loud of a table of this sort was the origin of the mystical incantation "fee fi fo fum." Dilworth cannot claim the credit for inventing it, however, since these tables go all the way back to *An A B C for chyldren*, published in about 1561.

Dilworth's Table III bursts boldly into three letters:

bla	ble	bli	blo	blu
bra	bre	bri	bro	bru ... and so on

By now, we are ready for words, starting with "Words of two letters, viz. one vowel and one consonant," the first example of Dilworth's mania for tortured table titles. The next table is "Words of three letters, viz. one vowel and two consonants." Later, we find "Words of four letters, viz. two consonants and two vowels; the latter vowel serving only to lengthen the sound of the former, except where it is otherwise marked." Still further, "Words consisting of five, six, &c. letters, viz. a diphthong and the rest consonants, except some few which end in e final." For these word lists, we are spared the rows and columns of "ab eb ib ob ub," because the strings of words of similar form vary in length. We have, for example, "Bag cag fag gag hag nag rag tag" extending to eight words, but only two in "Beg leg." I find myself trying to read these meaningless strings into a form of narrative. "Am an as at ax" sounds like a frank admission of inability to chop wood. Some complicated role reversal is implied in "Be he me, we ye." "Dot got hot ... pot, rot, sot" tells

a sad story of dissipation in the tropics. If you would like to try playing this game yourself, have a go at "Lax wax. Rex sex vex. Fix six."

Having reached words of three letters, Dilworth himself starts to string them together in dismal and improving sentences:

No man may put off the law of God
The way of God is no ill way.
My joy is in God all the day.
A bad man is a foe to God.

There is a page of this stuff, 23 sentences, in which the word "God" appears 19 times. Webster would condemn it, saying that the too frequent repetition of "the name of the Deity" led to profanity. "Experience shows," said young Webster, "that a frequent thoughtless repetition of that sacred word, which, in our Spelling Books, often occurs two or three times in a line, renders the name as familiar to children as the name of their book, and they mention it with the same indifference." This is surely nonsense; children, just as well as adults, distinguish between "God" in a biblical or moral sentence, and "God!" as a profane exclamation. If familiarity with the name of God led to profanity, the clergy would swear more than anyone. Dilworth himself apologized for his sentences, but on other grounds. "It must be acknowledged," he said, "that the first six lessons do but just make English: yet, I hope, whoever considers the difficulty of composing sentences to be read in lessons, wherein each word is confined to three letters, will readily overlook the baseness of the language...." That is nonsense too. What is wrong with Dilworth's sentences is that they are stupefyingly dull and therefore do not encourage children to want to learn to read. There is no excuse for this. A story, rich in human interest and instructive in the ways of the world, can be written in words of no more than three letters. Here is one I made up myself. It may not be high art, but it is a lot less boring than old Dilworth. It is deliberately cast in an American idiom.

The Red Hat

Dad got Mom a new hat. It was a red hat.
Mom put the new hat in the car. The car was red too.
Sid sat in the car. Sid was a fat man.
Sid sat on the hat. Was Dad mad at Sid?
Dad set the dog on Sid. The dog bit Sid in the leg.

See Sid hop off to get a cop!
Dad may end up in the pen.
Mom has had a fit.
Mom and Dad can sue the fat man Sid who sat on the hat.
The fat man can sue Dad who set the dog on him.

Back to Dilworth. We left him at words of three letters. He grinds methodically on, through words of four letters to words of five and six letters (still monosyllables, thus far) interspersed with his usual oppressive sentences. The sentences are uniformly biblical in style, and some of them are biblical in origin as well, though he says in the Preface that "in these lessons taken from scripture," he sometimes "substituted an easy word in place of one of more difficult pronunciation."

Next, we have disyllables, beginning with a list of "Some easy words accented on the first syllable, whose spelling and pronunciation are nearly the same;" then "Words accented on the first syllable; the spelling and pronunciation being different"; then dissyllables with the accent on the second syllable. After that we work our way upwards through words of three, four, and five syllables (with the accent now on this syllable, now on that) to the dizzy pinnacle of "Words of six syllables," and the opportunity to get to know *Ab-el-beth-ma-a-cah* and *Be-ro-dach-Ba"la-dan*. Those of you who are still awake will be objecting that "Berodach-Baladan" is not one word of six syllables, but two words of three syllables, joined together by a hyphen. Of course you are right, but that is Dilworth's way. "Proper names of four Syllables" include *Chipping Norton, Chipping Ongar, Philips Norton, Shepton Mallet, Sutton Colefield* and *Wotton Basset.* In five syllables, we have *Cleburg Mortimer* and *Sturminster Newton.* (Foreigners may need to be told that these are all, more or less, the names of towns or villages in England.) This is not the only example of oddity in Dilworth's tables. In the very first word list, "Words of two letters, viz. one vowel and one consonant," he includes *py* and *vy*, which not even the most lax Scrabble rules would allow. And *uncircumcised* is a five syllable word, with the accent on the fourth syllable.

Tables of "Proper names of persons, places, &c. or words usually beginning with a capital" form the final section of Dilworth's Part I. As you would expect, they are arranged in an

alphabetical-orderly manner, starting with "Proper names of one syllable," from *Ann* to *York*, and working up through more and more syllables to *Me-di-ter-ra-ne-an* and *Me-so-po-ta-mi-a*. The one, two, and three syllable words are mostly place names in the British Isles, though there are personal and biblical names, and the names of some places overseas. *Flo"ri-da* is in "Proper names of three syllables," and *Phi-la-del-phi-a* is among the fives.

Part II of the *New Guide* is "A table of words, the same in sound, but different in spelling and signification." It occupies eight pages, going from

> Ail, to be troubled
> Ale, malt liquor

to   Ewe, a sheep
> Yew, a tree
> You, yourself.

Part III is A "Practical English Grammar." Until its last section, Part III is in the form of questions and answers (I have shown you those dealing with syllables and spelling). There is no need for us to examine this part of the book in greater detail. As a grammar, it is really rather bad, though it can be said in its favor that it is not oppressively biblical. In a letter to the *American Mercury* Webster wrote, "I shall make no remarks on his Grammar, as it has been long since exploded and its place supplied with better."[2] We can follow Webster's example. When he came to compile his own grammar, Webster did not start from Dilworth, but from Lowth's *Introduction*.

The last section of Dilworth's Part III is a list of abbreviations. The selection is curiously haphazard. They include the names of some books of the Bible, but not all, some degrees (A.B., B.A., A.M., M.A., L.L.D., B.D., D.D., M.D.), some Roman numerals (I,V,C, and D, but not X or M), and various bits of Latin. Some of the entries are particularly English, including G.R. (*Georgius Rex, George the King*), titles of nobility, abbreviations of the names of English counties, and a disproportionate number of professors of Gresham College (Ast. P.G.C., P.M.G, and Prof.Th.Gr.).

Part IV contains 38 sentences in prose, followed by thirty 32 sentences in verse, each of six lines. Even here, Dilworth's mania for alphabetical order is apparent. Both in prose and in verse, the sentences beginning with *A* come first, then those beginning *B*, and so on. This is completely pointless, since the initial letter bears no relation to the content of the sentence, and one is unlikely to want to find a particular sentence by means of an alphabetical search.

The final section of Part IV is the only jolly thing in the whole book. It contains Select Fables. There are twelve fables, each illustrated with a woodcut. The quality of the woodcuts varies greatly from one edition to another. Rather than attempting to describe them, I shall give you one to look at.

Part V contains a few pages of prayers. There are "Public Prayers for the Use of Schools — In the Morning," and "In the Evening." Then there are "Private Prayers" (morning and evening again), followed by "Grace" (before and after Meat), and prayers for "Before going into Church," "For a Child seating himself in Church," and for "When Divine Service is ended." To the very end, Dilworth is holy, and methodical, and dull.

Fenning

The Introduction to Part I of Webster's *Grammatical Institute* is a sustained attack on Dilworth. It mentions no other spelling book, and from the Introduction alone one might suppose that Webster's only sources were his own fertile imagination and Dilworth. There are, however, two places later in the *Institute* where Webster mentions Fenning.

Daniel Fenning's *Universal Spelling Book* was first published in London in 1756, but it was still in print a hundred years after that. Fenning no doubt hoped to replace Dyche and Dilworth, but none of these books overcame the others, and in England all three continued to be widely used. Fenning's Preface shows that he had his eye on the American market as well; it is addressed "To every impartial Reader, but more particularly to such as have the Care of the Protestant Schools in Great Britain and Ireland, and his Majesty's Plantations Abroad."[3] Among several American editions, there were printings in Boston in 1769 and in 1771.

One of Fenning's improvements was to abandon the Dyche-Dilworth rules for dividing English words as if they were Latin. This is explained in the Preface:

Evil be to them that evil think. *Also*, Throw a Crust to a surly Dog and he will bite you.

FABLE X. *Of the good-natured Man and the Adder.*

A GOOD-NATURED Man being obliged to go out in frosty weather, in his return home he found an Adder almost frozen to death, which he brought with him, and laid before the fire.

As soon as the creature had received fresh life by the warmth, and was come to herself, she began to hiss, and fly about the house, and at length killed one of the children.

Well, says the man, if this is the best return that you can make for my kind offices, you shall even share in the same fate yourself; and so he killed her immediately.

THE MORAL.

Ingratitude is one of the blackest crimes that a man can be guilty of: it is hateful both to God and man, and frequently brings upon such a graceless wretch all that mischief, which he either did, or thought to do to another.

A fable from Part IV of Dilworth.

8. As for not giving more Examples concerning the dividing of Syllables, I assure you, Gentlemen, that I have been commended for saying that I wilfully omitted it; because as the Learned themselves differ so much about it, it is out of the Question to fill a Book with unnecessary Stuff and long Harangues, that are nothing else but Stumbling-Blocks even to adult Persons, and much more to Children.

9. Therefore as the shortest and plainest Way must certainly be the best, I would lay down but one Rule in teaching Children, and that is this, to teach them to divide all Syllables, as full and as near the true Sound as possible, without any Regard to the Latin or any critical Cavils: — Thus I would not divide Master, Sister, Vestry &c. Ma-ster, Si-ster, Ve-stry, because here the first syllable is weak and imperfect, but I should chuse rather to teach them to spell thus, Mas-ter, Sis-ter, Ves-try, &c. because here the first Syllable of all the Words has a full and true Sound, and the second Syllable will naturally follow.

In the book itself, Fenning gave examples:

N.B. Words divided as they
ought to be pronounced
(See the Preface)

As-pect	Flus-ter	Jus-tice	pros-trate
Bas-ket	frus-trate	Mas-ter	pub-lish
bas-tard	Glis-ter	Nos-tril	pun-ish
bush-el	glit-ter	Os-trich	Res-cue
Clus-ter	gob-let	Pas-tor	res-pite
cus-tard	gris-tle	pis-tol	Sis-ter
cus-tom	Hos-tage	pop-lar	sys-tem
Dis-taff	ho-nour	pro-blem	Ves-try
dis-tant	Jas-per	pros-per	ves-ture
dis-tinct	I-mage	pros-pect	Whis-per

I have transcribed the words exactly as they appear in my 1773 Fenning (the 20th edition). Three of the words are not divided according to Fenning's rule (they should be hon-our, prob-lem and Im-age), but this may be the fault of the printer. I have a later (post-Webster) edition in which those mistakes do not appear.

While on the subject of dividing words into syllables, it is convenient to consider another of Webster's criticisms of Dilworth. For Webster, terminations such as *-tion*, *-sion* and *-cious* were always pronounced as one syllable, and he could see no reason why they should not be shown as one syllable when words were divided in a spelling book. Dilworth divided each of those terminations into two syllables. He listed *mo-ti-on* as a word of three syllables; *pen-si-on-er*, *Sal-va-ti-on* and *su"spi-ci-ous* each had four syllables. Unfortunately, he was not sufficiently careful in the way that he thought — or ex-

plained his thoughts — to enable us to be certain how he pronounced these words, since he appears to say that *ti* followed by a vowel may be pronounced either as one syllable or as two:

ti before a vowel, is sounded like *si* or *sh*; as in nation: except when *s* goes immediately before it; as celestial: or at the beginning of a word; as tied: or in derivatives; as, mightier, mightiest, emptied.

That is a summary of a whole page of Dyche. Dilworth's tables contain a great many words ending in *-tion*, and in every case the termination is divided. If Dilworth is right to say that *ti* before a vowel sounds like *sh*, then dividing *-tion* into two syllables must be wrong.

Fenning seems to have been aware of this problem. His rules for pronunciation give evidence of a more discerning ear than Dilworth's, and of a more affected manner of speech than Webster's. This is Fenning's master-scholar dialogue:

M. *Have* ci, sci *and* ti, *always their natural Sound?*

S. No; for they all sound like *shi*, before *o* in particular; but *ci* and *ti* sound also like *shi* before *a*: Thus *vicious, tenacious,* &c. are pronounced *vishious, tenashious; Conscience, conscious,* &c. are pronounced *Conshience, conschious,* &c. and *Motion, Oration,* are sounded like *Moshun, Orashun,* &c.&c. so also *partial, special,* &c. are pronounced *parshial, speshial,* &c.

It will be seen that in most of these words Fenning sounded the *i*, and it was therefore not appropriate for him to reduce Dilworth's number of syllables, as Webster would do. Fenning included *gra-ci-ous-ly* in his list of "Words of four Syllables, accented on the first Syllable," because he pronounced it as a word of four syllables. The termination *-tion*, is different, for there Fenning did *not* pronounce the *i*. Like Webster, he pronounced *motion* and *oration* as words of two and three syllables respectively. If he had been as bold as Webster, Fenning would have put all Dilworth's *-tion* words in tables of words of one syllable fewer than the tables Dilworth had them in. Fenning was not that bold, but he wanted to avoid Dilworth's mistake — so he left such words out altogether. In Fenning's tables of two, three, and four syllable words (he does not go beyond four syllables), accented on this syllable and that, and divided, there is not a single word ending *-tion*. If this was deliberate, as I think it must have been,

Fenning forgot himself toward the end of his book. There, he put a little dictionary, in which the meaning of words is explained, the words being separated into nouns, adjectives, and verbs, and into words of two, three, and four syllables. These lists contain several words ending in *-tion*, and in each case the termination has been counted as two syllables. He included *motion* in the list of "Nouns Substantive of three Syllables," even though he had earlier explained that it was "sounded like Moshun."

At least one of Fenning's contemporaries, Ann Fisher, was bolder than he was; she wrote a spelling book and a grammar (published separately, as Webster would do 20 years later) and she opted clearly and unequivocally for writing *-tion* and similar terminations as one syllable. Thus in her *Practical New Grammar*, she wrote:

The Endings, *cial, tial, cian, sion, tion,* should not (according to the modern Way of pronouncing) be parted in Spelling, being so many distinct Sounds, which cannot be divided without being corrupted; for the *ci, si,* and *ti,* are always sounded like *sh,* in the last Syllable of Words; as *Ar-ti-fi-cial, Sub-stan-tial, Ma-gi-cian, E-gyp-tian, Per-sua-sion, Sal-va-tion.*

We cannot accuse Webster of copying from Fisher, because there is no evidence that he ever saw her works. What this passage does show, however, is that Webster was not the first to teach children to write *per-sua-sion* in three syllables, and he was certainly not entitled to complain if others did so.

It is not necessary for us to examine Fenning in greater detail at this stage. When we look at Part I of the Grammatical Institute, I shall point out where Webster's book has features in common with Fenning's. The fact that Webster mentioned Fenning shows that he had the *Universal Spelling Book* before him when he compiled his own, and therefore had the opportunity to adopt Fenning's ideas if he wanted to. Of course Webster may independently have noticed the same faults in Dilworth that Fenning had earlier seen. In any case, the fact that Fenning had already made certain corrections or improvements to Dilworth would not be a reason for Webster to refrain from doing the same thing, whether he thought of them independently or was taught them by Fenning, indeed it would have been perverse to reproduce features of Dilworth that he had come to believe to be wrong. If it was legitimate for Webster to

learn lessons from Fenning, however, it would be equally legitimate for others later to learn from Webster. That "sauce for the goose" argument was something Webster did not like, but he must have been able to see it, and it led him vehemently to deny that he had found any of "his" ideas in the works of other writers.

Whatever the rights and wrongs of adopting other people's *ideas*, there is no justification for copying their *text*. As we shall see, Webster sometimes did that too.

As usual with Webster, his references to Fenning are in disparagement rather than acknowledgment. The first is at the end of his table headed "Words, the same in sound, but different in spelling and signification." Webster wrote,

N.B. In this Table I have omitted several words which are found in Dilworth and Fenning; either because the *English* differs from the *American* pronunciation, or because they have inserted words together as nearly the same in sound, which may lead into errour. For instance the words *consort* and *concert* are placed together in Dilworth and they are commonly pronounced alike; but it is an offence against propriety; and I chose to admit no words but such as sound exactly alike.

That is not an express admission of borrowing from Dilworth or Fenning, but by claiming to have omitted several of their words, Webster implied that some at least of the words he did not omit were taken from them. Also, Webster's heading, "Words, the same in sound, but different in spelling and signification," was copied from Dilworth verbatim.

Webster's criticism of Dilworth and Fenning was rather subtle, because what he said of them was true, but it implied a greater degree of incompetence than either was guilty of. Dilworth did include in his table a few sets of words whose sounds were similar but not identical. He should not have done so, because his heading said that the table contained "words, *the same* in sound"; it was not a very serious error as there were only two or three sets of words in the table that did not sound the same; Webster cited a single example as if it were one of many. He also suggested that Fenning was guilty of making the same mistake, but Fenning was not. He copied most of Dilworth's table and added some words of his own, but he realized that the sets of words were *not* all identical in sound, so

he changed the heading. He called them "A Collection of Words *nearly alike* in Sound, but different in Spelling and Signification."

In his other reference to Fenning, Webster does admit to having made use of Fenning's material, and his attack on Fenning is correspondingly more direct. Fenning's spelling book contains not only "some useful Fables," but also "some natural and entertaining Stories." The second of these stories, which occupies several pages of the book, is "Life truly painted in the natural History of Tommy and Harry." Harry, Tommy's elder brother, was "a sullen perverse Boy from his Cradle." He fell into bad company and wasted his inheritance, "Drinking, Swearing, Lying, Gaming, and sitting up all Night," and he was finally shipwrecked and eaten by wild Beasts. Tommy was of quite a different character: "EveryBody praised him, because he was a sober, good-natured Child, and very dutiful and obliging." He worked hard, married well, and became rich. "Thus you see, that as *Harry* followed nothing but Vice, he lived a wretched Life, and died a miserable Death; but *Tommy* was always a pattern of Virtue and Goodness, and still lives happy."

Webster's *Institute*, too, contained "The Story of Tommy and Harry," but it was not by any means a direct copy of Fenning's tale. Webster explained in a footnote:

The substance of this fictitious narrative is taken from Mr. Fenning's Spelling Book. In the original, the language is flat, puerile, and ungrammatical; for which reason, I have taken the liberty to make material alterations and throw the whole into a shorter compass. It is necessary that a style fitted to the capacities of youth should be plain and simple, and the words very easy and familiar; but to admit the low, childish vulgar expressions of children into any book is inexcusable. Children will learn vulgarisms and even barbarisms enough, without the assistance and authority of a book from which they imbibe the elements of knowledge. A style may be plain and suited to the understanding of a child; and yet correct, grammatical, and even elegant. And [it] is or *ought* to be the business of one who writes for children, to unite plainness with propriety, and simplicity with purity of style. This would have a tendency to correct some of the barbarous corruptions of language, which are instilled into children by parents and nurses, and which are seldom entirely eradicated afterwards. Parents have another practice of telling to children awful stories of ghosts and witches, which most commonly frighten them to such a degree that they remain cowards to their death. This last practice is highly *criminal*; the former may perhaps bear a softer appellation.

That criticism of Fenning is almost entirely unjustified. His story is no literary masterpiece, and it is a bit long-winded, but it is quite readable. Furthermore, one reads it hopefully, but in vain, looking for those vulgarisms and barbarisms by which children or their language are likely to be corrupted. Quite apart from that, the passage quoted above is a very odd way to introduce a story. It is as if I were to write a book called *The Sad Story of Cathy and Heathcliff*, with a Preface saying: "The substance of this fictitious narrative is taken from Miss Bronte's novel, *Wuthering Heights*. The original is ill-written, badly structured, and much too long; for which reason I have taken the liberty to make material alterations and throw the whole into a shorter compass." The obvious explanation for copying another man's work is laziness, but whatever his other faults may have been, Webster was not lazy. So what was he up to? Why copy Fenning's story at all? Why not write his own? In part, it was no doubt because Webster was never much of a creative writer, but there was more to it than that. The answer, I think, is that by explaining what was wrong with Fenning's story and rewriting it as it should have been written, Webster was able to make a point that would not have been so clear if he had just written a new and better story of his own. At its simplest, he showed that Noah Webster was a cleverer fellow than Daniel Fenning. Webster's spelling book, as a whole, gave Dilworth the same treatment — first the explanation of Dilworth's faults, then the rewriting. Noah Webster was a cleverer fellow than Thomas Dilworth too. Later, he would rewrite Entick's Dictionary and then Johnson's. When he had finished that, he had a go at the Authorized Version of the Bible.

3. The Development of the English Dictionary, 1604–1783

1604–1755: From Cawdrey to Johnson

If one asks a moderately well-informed reader, "Who wrote the first English dictionary?" the most common answer is "Samuel Johnson?"— because Johnson's is the only early English dictionary that most people have heard of — but there were English dictionaries 150 years before Johnson's. Now try this one: "Who wrote the first American dictionary?" If you answered "Noah Webster?" you were wrong too, but only by a few years. Strangely enough, the correct answer is "Samuel Johnson"— not *the* Samuel Johnson, but an American of the same name. It is tempting to construct on this foundation a theory of significant coincidence between names and occupations, but the two events cannot be shown to be independent — the American may have been influenced to produce a dictionary by the fact that he had the same name as a famous lexicographer. Later, Webster's work would be appropriated by two unrelated people, thousands of miles apart; both were called Ogilvie, and both produced an "Imperial" Dictionary. Perhaps there is something in the theory after all. I shall tell their stories in due course. Meanwhile, let us consider what a dictionary is and should contain, and contemplate the art, the business, and the history, of the English dictionary.

Imagine a simplified world in which the only people involved are *lexicographers*, who compile dictionaries; *publishers*, who sell them; and *users*, who buy them. It might be supposed that the aims of all three coincide, that the lexicographer wants to write, and the publisher to sell, just such a dictionary as the user needs

and therefore wants to buy. This is seldom the case. The publisher's purpose is usually to make as much money as possible, which means that he has to induce users to buy his dictionary in preference to those of competing publishers. To make it appear more attractive, he puts more into it than is in the competitors' dictionaries. They react by publishing new dictionaries containing yet more. Dictionaries get bigger and bigger, and the user finds himself compelled to buy a great mass of material that he neither wants nor needs. The greater part of most modern English dictionaries is never used at all.

Consider definitions. The primary purpose of a dictionary is to explain the meaning of words — but *which* words? Is it necessary to define them all? Surely not. To use a dictionary, one must be able to read; and before learning to read, one must be able to speak. Every user comes to his dictionary with a basic vocabulary, which he does not need to have explained. At the other extreme, there are polysyllabic words of such fuliginous obscurity that only a pedant would ever use them.[1] Our average reader avoids everything written by such people, and therefore does not need to have those words explained either. Between these two extremes, then, lies an area containing words that our user will encounter, but does not understand — those are the only words he needs his dictionary to explain. The boundaries of the area are not in the same place for all readers, and for each individual they move as he gets older; at first, he learns the meaning of more and more words, and the area of familiar words within the boundary expands; later, he finds that he cannot remember the

33

meaning of some of the words that once he knew. The basic principle, however, is true for all readers: they do not need definitions either of familiar words or of words they never encounter.

The same principle does not apply to two-language or multilingual dictionaries — a translator may need to look up even the simplest of words. A bilingual dictionary containing a complete vocabulary is therefore a respectable article of commerce, and such dictionaries existed for a very long time before English dictionaries were thought to be necessary at all.

Then, during the sixteenth century, the English language enjoyed a sudden and riotous expansion. There were various reasons for this. In part, it was because men of learning started to use the language more — to be more widely read, they published books in English instead of Latin; in part, it was due to increased contact with foreigners through trade and exploration; and in part it was due to the sheer exuberant vitality of Elizabethan England. The result was that many new words came into use, particularly words borrowed from Latin and Greek, which were not understood by people without a classical education. The English dictionary came into being to explain such words.

The first was Robert Cawdrey's *A Table Alphabeticall*, published in 1604. Its content and purpose were thus described on the title page:

A

Table Alphabeticall, conteyning and teaching the true writing, and vnderstanding of hard vsuall English wordes, borrowed from the Hebrew, Greeke, Latine, or French, &c.
With the interpretation thereof by *plaine English words, gathered for the benefit & helpe of Ladies, Gentlewomen, or any other unskilfull persons.*
Whereby they may the more easilie and better vnderstand many hard English wordes, which they shall heare or read in Scriptures, Sermons, or elsewhere, and also be made able to vse the same aptly themselues.

Two things are to be noticed in that title page. First, observe that Cawdrey's *only* purpose was to interpret "hard English words" by the use of "plaine English words"; it would never have occurred to him to include an interpretation of the "plaine English words" as well, because everybody knew what they meant. Secondly notice that the book was particularly directed to ladies and gentlewomen — as a class, unskillful persons who learned to read and write, but did not learn Latin.

The arrangement of a table in alphabetical order was something of a novelty in 1604, and Cawdrey included instructions on how to use it:

If thou be desirous (gentle Reader) rightly and readily to vnderstand, and to profit by this Table, and such like, then thou must learne the Alphabet, to wit, the order of the Letters as they stand, perfectly without booke, and where euery letter standeth: as (b) neere the beginning, (n) about the middest, and (t) toward the end. Nowe if the word, which thou art desirous to finde, begin with (a) then looke in the beginning of this Table, but if with (v) looke towards the end. Againe, if thy word beginne with (ca) looke in the beginning of the letter (c) but if with (cu) then looke toward the end of that letter. And so of all the rest. &c.

You might think that since this was the first English dictionary, Cawdrey had to write it himself from scratch; in fact, he managed to gather most of his material from other earlier works. Its basis was a vocabulary at the end of an English language manual and grammar, *The English Schoole-Master* by Edmund Coote, published in 1596. Cawdrey took nearly half his three thousand words from Coote, amounting to about 90 percent of Coote's list. Thomas' Latin-English dictionary furnished a further 40 percent or more of Cawdrey's words, and provided definitions for many of the words he had taken from Coote. The nature of the borrowing from Thomas, as well as the way in which Latin words were turned into English with very little alteration, can be seen in the following list:

Thomas, 1596 edition	Cawdrey, 1604
Hectice,... An Hecticke fever, inflaming the heart and soundest or substantiallest part of the bodie.	*Hecticke*, inflaming the heart and soundest part of the bodie.
Hemisphaerium,... Halfe the compasse of the visible heaven....	*Hemisphere*, halfe the compasse of heaven, that we see.
Homonymia, ... When divers things are signi-fied by one word.	*Homonimie*, When divers things are signified by one word.
Horizon,... A circle dividing the halfe sphere of the firmament from the other halfe which we doe not see.	*Horizon*, ... A circle dividing the halfe of the firmament, from the other halfe which we see not.
Incendo,... To inflame: to set fire on a thing: to burne: to incense,... to stirre up ... to make verie angrie, to vexe, moove, or chafe:...	*Incend*, kindle, burne, vex or chafe, to incense, to stirre up, or set on fire, or to anger.
Neotericus,... One of late time.	*Neotericke*, One of late time.
Obnubilo,... To make darke with cloudes.	*Obnubilate*. to make darke.
Palinodia,... A recantation,... an unsaying of that one hath spoken or written.	*Palinodie*, a recanting or unsaying of anything.
Pervivacia,... Obstinacie, headinesse, stiffenecked-nesse.[2]	*Pervivacie*, obstinacie, stifneckednes.

Such borrowing would be a characteristic of most later lexicography. It is the subject of a delightful book from which comes much of the information in this chapter (including the above table). The book is called *The English Dictionary from Cawdrey to Johnson, 1604–1755*, by De Witt Starnes and Gertrude Noyes, and it is an indispensable companion to anyone interested in the subject. The authors traced the borrowings in the family tree of English dictionaries over a period of a hundred and fifty years, as well as the sources of much of the material brought into the family from outside. It is an exemplary work.

A Table Alphabeticall was followed by other "hard words" dictionaries during the seventeenth century. The next was John Bullokar's *An English Expositor* (1616), which claimed to explain "termes of art" in various branches of learning such as "Logicke, Philosophy, Law, Physicke, Astronomie, etc., yea and Divinitie it selfe," as well as "the great store of strange words, our speech doth borrow, not only from the Latine, and Greeke, (and from the ancient Hebrew) but also from forraine vulgar languages round about us."

Cawdrey responded to Dr. Bullokar's book by taking its title. His last edition, published in 1617, was called *A Table Alphabeticall, or The English Expositor*.

The first English dictionary that actually called itself a "dictionary" was that of Henry Cockeram, published in 1623. The title page of the fifth edition (1637) shows it still to be concerned with the explanation of "hard words," to ladies in particular:

The English
DICTIONARIE:
OR,
An Interpreter of
hard Englifh Words.

Enabling as well Ladies and Gentlewomen, young Schollers, Clerkes, Merchants; as alfo ftrangers of any Nation, to the underftanding of the more difficult Authors already printed in our Language, and the more fpeedie attaining of an elegant perfection of the Englifh tongue, both in reading, fpeaking, and writing.

The fifth Edition, revifed and enlarged.

By *H. C.* Gent.

LONDON,
Printed by *I. H.* for *Edmund Weaver*, and are to be fold at the Greyhound in S. *Pauls Church-yard.* 1637.

In the first edition, "H.C. Gent." acknowledged that he owed a debt to Cawdrey and Bullokar. His book was said to be "a Collection of the choicest words contained in the Table

Alphabeticall and English Expositor, and of some thousand of words never published by any heretofore."

Back in 1604, Cawdrey had suggested that his book would enable "unskilled persons" not merely to *read* but also to *use* hard English words, but he did not offer any assistance with using such words, other than the familiarity that would result from repeatedly looking them up; the *Table Alphabeticall* only translated hard words into plain. Cockeram did more — he offered translation both ways. The *English Dictionarie* was in fact divided into three parts, headed "The First Part of the English Dictionary," "The Second Part of the English Translator," and "The Third Part, treating of Gods and Goddeses, Men and Women, Boyes and Maids, Giants and Devils, Birds and Beasts, Monsters and Serpents, Wells and Rivers, Herbs, Stones, Trees, Dogs, Fishes, and the like." The first part was equivalent to Cawdrey, explaining the meaning of hard words. The second part translated plain words or phrases into fancy words. Instead of "a Scholler" and "a Schoolemaster," the reader was offered the words *disciple* and *pedagoge*. For "smallnesse," substitute *tenuity, gracillity, exiguity* or *parvity*. A writer of elegant English does not "Seale" his letters, he *obsigillates*. The three-part arrangement was explained in "A Premonition from the Author to the Reader":

The first Booke hath the choisest words themselves now in use, wherewith our Language is inriched, and become so copious, to which words the common sense is annexed. The second Booke contains the Vulgar words, which whensoever any desirous of a more curious explanation by a more refined and elegant speech shall looke into, he shall there receive the exact and ample word to expresse the same: Wherein, by the way, let mee pray thee to observe, that I have also inserted (as occasion served) even the *mock-words* which are ridiculously used in our Language, that those who desire a generality of knowledge, may not be ignorant of the sense even of the *fustian-termes,* used by too many who study rather to be heard speake, than to understand themselves. The last Booke is a recitall of severall persons, Gods and Goddeses, Giants and Devils ... to the intent that the diligent learner may not pretend the defect of any help which may informe his discourse or practice.... By the way, I would entreat thee, gentle Reader, that thou wouldest have care to search every word according to the true Orthography thereof; as for Physiognomie, in the letter *P.* not in *F.* for Cyn-

icall, in *Cy.* not in *Ci.* and where thou meetest with a word marked thus * know you that it is now out of use, and onely used of some ancient Writers. Thus what I have done is (Reader) for thy benefit: accept it, and make use of it, so shall I finde reward in my labours, and rest thy friend,

> H.C.

The "last Booke" contains an interesting variety of encyclopedic information, including instructions on how to catch a tiger without getting eaten:

Tyger, a truculent beast, and the swiftest of all other beasts; wherefore they are taken very young in the dammes absence, and carried away by them on horsebacke; who hearing the cry of the old Tyger following after them, doe of purpose let fall one of the whelpes, that while she beareth that backe, they in the meane time may escape safe with the other to the ship...

That threefold division of the dictionary was a novelty when Cockeram introduced it, but in 1663 it was copied in a new edition of Bullokar's *Expositor*, which also took a number of words from Cockeram. The last revision of Cockeram, in 1670, responded, as Cawdrey had previously, by taking a word from Bullokar's title. It was called *The English Dictionary; or An Expositor of Hard English Words*. That edition, however, did not contain the "second Booke."

The next significant English dictionary was *Glossographia*, by Thomas Blount (or Blunt), published in 1656. It was another "hard words" dictionary, and was the first to purport to give "*Etymologies*" as well as "*Definitions*." It also included "*Historical Observations*" that were said to be "Very useful for all such as desire to understand what they read." Most of the "Etymologies" consisted of no more than the corresponding Latin word, put in brackets after the English — not an arduous task, since Blount had taken much of his material from Latin-English dictionaries. Blount was also the first to cite authorities, including with the entries abbreviations of the names either of authors who had used the words or of earlier dictionaries in which they had appeared. Blount added these to words, as he explained, "that I might not be thought to be the innovator of them."

Blount made no secret of the fact that he had gathered his material from the works of others. "To compile and compleat a Work of this nature and importance," he told the reader,

"would necessarily require an *Encyclopedie* of knowledge, and the concurrence of many learned Heads;... I profess to have done little with my own Pencil; but have extracted the quintessence *of Scapula, Minsheu, Cotgrave, Rider, Florio, Thomasius, Dasipodius,* and *Hexams Dutch,* Dr. Davies Welsh Dictionary, *Cowels* Interpreter &c .and other able Authors, for so much as tended to my purpose...." The compilation of his dictionary from all these sources took up, so he said, "the vacancy of above Twenty years."

Just because it had taken him so long to compile his own book, Blount was very annoyed when another appeared, less than two years later, which borrowed much of his material. This was Edward Phillips' *New World of English Words.* Phillips was Milton's nephew, and Milton took charge of him, and of his brother, when their mother (his sister) died. Phillips' occupation is always described as "hack writer," and Blount's accusation that he was employed by an unscrupulous bookseller to compile the *New World of Words* therefore seems likely to be true.

It is often said that Phillips' title was suggested by one of Blount's sources, the Italian-English dictionary *A Worlde of Wordes,* by John Florio (1598); but it is possible to find Phillips' inspiration much closer to hand. In *Glossographia,* Blount's address to the reader gave examples of many obscure words that he had come across in books and in business, that were not to be found in earlier dictionaries; he described them as "this new World of Words."

Phillips' *New World of Words* purported to give etymologies, as had Blount, but in general these were no more than the identification of the language from which the English word was immediately derived. The main addition it made to Blount's *Glossographia* in content was the inclusion of proper names, both historical and mythological. Its major advantage, however, was not so much in content as in form — *Glossographia* was a scruffy and somewhat ill-printed little octavo; the *New World of Words* was a handsome small folio, and a pleasure to read. Despite the competition, *Glossographia* went into a second edition in 1659 (reissued in 1661), with further editions in 1670, 1674 and 1681.

A novel and interesting feature of the *New World of Words* was the inclusion of an impressive list of experts. In the first edition, they were introduced by these words in the title page: "For the greater honour of those Learned Gentlemen and Artists that have been assistant in the most Practical Sciences, their Names are affixed in the next Page." Since that was preceded by a list of 41 "Arts and Sciences" whose terms were said to be included in the dictionary, it might be taken to mean that the "Learned Gentlemen and Artists" had been "assistant" to Phillips in the preparation of his dictionary. In later editions, those words disappeared from the title page, but the list of experts remained, headed "The Names of those Learned and Ingenious Persons (most of them now living) Eminent in, or Contributory to any of those Arts, Sciences, or Faculties contained in this following Work." In fact, the "Learned and Ingenious Persons" had nothing to do with the dictionary at all — most of them were not even the authors of works Phillips had used in preparing it — and on a careful reading of Phillips' words it can be seen that he made no greater claim than that these people had made contributions to the arts and sciences that he dealt with. One or two of them, indeed, had been dead too long to have been able to give any direct assistance. However, it is hard to see any reason for such a list other than to suggest, untruthfully, that the experts named had helped in the preparation of the dictionary.

In 1670, Blount, who was a barrister, published a law dictionary, and for some reason he came to believe that its content had been transcribed by Phillips to form the basis of a competing dictionary, *Nomothetes,* published soon afterwards. The following year, the *New World of Words* went into a third edition. This was all too much for Blount to bear, and in 1673 he published a blistering attack on Phillips, which he called *A World of Errors Discovered in the New World of Words, or General English Dictionary, and in Nomothetes, or The Interpreter of Law-Words and Terms.* It contained this address:

To The Reader

Must this then be suffered? A Gentleman for his divertisement writes a Book, and this Book happens to be acceptable to the World, and sell; a Bookseller, not interested in the Copy, instantly employs a Mercenary to jumble up another like Book out of this,

with some Alterations and Additions, and give it a new Title; and the first Author's out-done, and his Publisher half undone.

Thus it fared with my *Glossographia*, the fruit of above Twenty years spare hours, first published in 1656. Twelve moneths had not passed, but there appeared in Print this *New World of Words, or General English Dictionary*, extracted almost wholly out of mine, and taking in its first Edition even a great part of my Preface; onely some words were added and others altered, to make it pass as the Authors legitimate off-spring. In these Additions and Alterations he not seldom erred, yet had not those errors been continued, with new supplies to a Second and third Impression, so little was I concerned at the particular injury, that these Notes (in great part collected from the first Edition) had never reproached the Theft to the World. ...

Soon after we find a *Catalogue* prefixed of the names of divers Learned Persons of this Age, *Eminent in or contributory to any of those Arts, Sciences, or faculties contained in the following Work*. Whereby the Author would at least obscurely insinuate, that those Learned Persons had contributed to or assisted him in it, thereby to advance his reputation; but I believe nothing less, having heard some of the chief of them utterly disown both the Author and his Work.

Blount followed this with details of Phillips' borrowings, and quoted, with scathing comments, some of his mistakes. For example:

Bigamy, The marriage of two Wives at the same time, which according to Common Law hinders a man from taking holy orders.

Here our Author speaks some truth, at peradventure: For he that marries two Wives at the same time commits Felony, and the punishment of Felony is Death; which (suppose it be by hanging) may very well hinder him from taking holy Orders....

Quaver, A measure of time in Musick, being the half of a Crotchet, as a Crotchet the half of a Quaver, a Semiquaver, &c.

What fustian is here? Just so, two is the half of four, and four the half of two; and Semi-quaver is explicated by a dumb '&c.'

Blount's criticisms of *The New World of Words* were well-deserved, but the beliefs about *Nomothetes* that prompted the attack were entirely mistaken. In the first place, the book was not Phillips' work at all; it was compiled by one Thomas Manley. Also, though there was some similarity between Manley's definitions and Blount's, it was for the most part due to the fact that both of them had been copying from Cowel's *Interpreter*.

Phillips was not in the least put out by Blount's attack. In the next edition of *The New*

World of Words, in 1678, he quietly corrected the mistakes that Blount had pointed out, and he inserted a list of words headed: "A Collection of such affected words from the Latin and Greek, as are either to be used warily, and upon occasion only, or totally to be rejected as Barbarous, and illegally compounded or derived." The words were almost entirely taken from the 1670 edition of Blount's *Glossographia*.

The last two noteworthy English dictionaries issued in the seventeenth century were Elisha Coles' *An English Dictionary* (1676) and the anonymous *Gazophylacium Anglicanum* (1689). The former was a "hard words" dictionary based on Phillips', with the addition of cant words taken from Richard Head's *The Canting Academy* (1673). The latter was an etymological dictionary based on Stephen Skinner's *Etymologicon Linguae Anglicanae* (1671). Skinner had taken many of Phillips' definitions, which he translated into Latin. The *Gazophylacium Anglicanum* translated part of Skinner's work back into English.

It may not be meaningful, but it is conveniently memorable that the first "hard words" English dictionary appeared at the beginning of the seventeenth century, and the first "Compleat Collection" of English words at the beginning of the eighteenth, and in the year that Queen Anne came to the throne, 1702. This was the *New English Dictionary* by "J.K." There has been some disagreement about the identity of J.K., but the prevailing view seems to be that it was John Kersey, who later produced a much enlarged edition of Phillips' *New World of Words* (1706), and then, under his own name, the *Dictionarium Anglo-Britannicum* (1708).

In the Preface to J.K.'s *New English Dictionary* can be seen the signs of a conservative backlash. The exuberant enlargement of the English vocabulary by uncontrolled borrowing from abroad had gone too far, and the pendulum was beginning to swing the other way:

However, it must be acknowledged, That the Design of this Ingenious Author [Coles] ... is very different from ours; That apparently being to oblige the Publick, with as large a Collection as possibly could be made, of all sorts of hard and obsolete Words, both domestick and foreign.... Whereas, ours is intended only to explain such English Words as are genuine, and used by Persons of clear Judgment and good Style; leaving out all those foreign Terms, that in Mr. Coles' time were viciously introduced into our

Language, by those who sought to approve them-selves Learned rather by unintelligible Words than by proper Language.

It is easy to understand why J.K. wanted to exclude from his dictionary foreign words that had been "viciously introduced into our Lan-guage." It is at first less clear why he should have wanted to include simple words — surely the reasons for leaving them out were just as valid in 1702 as they had been in 1604? The ex-planation is that he was directing his attention to a function of the dictionary not previously considered. All the earlier dictionaries con-tained definitions of hard words, and some gave information on etymology; this dictionary was concerned with *spelling*. It had, therefore, a twofold aim — to show the recommended spelling of *all* proper English words, and in ad-dition to explain the meaning of those that were "difficult." Both these aims are mentioned in the title page:

A New English Dictionary: or a Compleat COL-LECTION Of the Most Proper and Significant Words, Commonly used in the LANGUAGE; with a Short and Clear Exposition of *Difficult Words and Terms of Art*.
The Whole digested into Alphabetical Order; and chiefly designed for the benefit of Young *Scholars, Tradesmen, Artificers*, and the *Female Sex*, who would learn to spell truely; being so fitted to every Capac-ity, that it may be a continual help to all that want an Instructer.

Starnes and Noyes are very critical of the rudimentary nature of the definitions of com-mon words in the *New English Dictionary*. They say that "derivatives, related words, and some very common words are merely listed without explanations. Many of the definitions seem shockingly haphazard...." They give examples such as

Ake, as, my head akes.
And, and if, and not.
Any, anyone, anywhere, &c.
An *Apron*, for a Woman, &c.
An *Arm* of a man's body, of a tree, or of the sea.
An *Elephant*, a Beast.
A *Goat*, a Beast.
May, the most pleasant Month of the Year.

That criticism shows a misunderstanding of the aims of the book, which comes from com-paring it with later dictionaries rather than ear-lier ones. In a modern dictionary, the entry for every word is supposed to contain a definition, but in 1702 it was well known that familiar words did not need to be defined. It is also ex-tremely difficult to frame satisfactory defini-tions of simple words. As Johnson would ex-press it fifty years later, "To explain, requires the use of terms less abstruse than that which is to be explained." The least abstruse terms cannot be explained at all, because there are no simpler words from which to construct the ex-planation. An encyclopædia can give a *descrip-tion* of a goat, but that is not the same thing as *defining the word*.

What are quoted above are inadequate as definitions because they were not supposed to be definitions at all; they merely served to iden-tify words whose spelling or usage was being demonstrated.

Kersey's later *Dictionarium Anglo-Britan-nicum* (1708), was in the seventeenth century tradition, claiming to be "an Interpreter of Hard Words," and many of the simple words that were in the *New English Dictionary* did not appear in it. It is said to have been the first abridged dictionary, supplying the need for something cheaper and more portable than the enlarged revision of Phillips' dictionary that Kersey had published two years before. It also contains a fine early example of a patriotic Pref-ace:

To Conclude, the Compiler has no other View, than to render himself, at least in some Measure, Ser-viceable to his Native Country, and upon all Occa-sions, to express his Zeal for promoting the Publick Benefit.

Kersey's larger dictionary, the 1706 *New World of Words*, used Phillips' work as no more than a foundation. Much of the original was left out, but Kersey still ended up more than doubling the number of entries, so that less than half the Kersey-Phillips was Phillips. He explained why:

It was judg'd expedient to leave out all Abstracts of the Lives of Eminent Persons, Poetical Fictions, Ge-ographical Descriptions.... In the room of these, are inserted near Twenty Thousand hard Words and Terms in all Arts and Sciences....

Those twenty thousand technical terms, more than the total number of entries in the pre-vious edition of the *New World of Words*, came from the *Lexicon Technicum* of John Harris.

This was the first English encyclopedia, and was published in one volume in 1704. A supplementary A–Z volume appeared in 1710, and in later editions the material was "digested into one Alphabet," and it became a two-volume work.

The next major figure in the world of English lexicography was Nathan Bailey, who dominated the market until Johnson came onto the scene. In 1721, Bailey published a solid octavo under the title *An Universal Etymological English Dictionary*. The word "Universal" shows that the dictionary contained more than just hard words. Indeed Bailey claimed that it included "many Thousand Words more than either Harris, Philips, Kersey, or any English Dictionary before extant." Such boasts would become a regular feature of competition between rival dictionaries, since the one with the most words in it was bound to be the best.

J.K.'s reason for including plain words was to give their spelling, while his definitions were mainly for hard words; Bailey's excuse for being universal was the "Etymological" character of his dictionary, and once again, definitions were not always needed. The title page makes it clear that derivations were to be given for all words, but only "difficult" words were to be explained:

An Universal Etymological ENGLISH DICTIONARY comprehending The Derivations of the Generality of Words in the English Tongue..... and also A brief and clear Explication of all difficult Words ...

In Bailey, therefore, we still find, as in J.K., such entries as

BEAR ... a certain wild Beast.
A DOG ... a Quadrupede well known.
A GOAT ... a Beast.
HORSE ... a Beast well known.

According to Starnes and Noyes, Bailey took "almost every item from Kersey's *Dictionarium Anglo-Britannicum* with identical definitions but with etymologies added.... These Kersey items comprise more than two-thirds of Bailey's list." Bailey, however, borrowed from many other sources as well, and Starnes and Noyes imagine him working in just the way that we shall see Webster working on the *American Dictionary* a hundred years later, "surrounded by sources which he constantly compares and each of which he taps for its speciality."

In keeping with its etymological nature, Bailey's dictionary had an Introduction in which he gave some thoughts on the subject of language in general, and a short history of the English language in particular.

An Universal Etymological English Dictionary was immensely successful. For 50 years, a new edition appeared every two or three years, reaching a thirtieth edition in 1802. In 1727 Bailey published a second octavo volume with a subtly different title. The first volume was *An Universal Etymological English Dictionary*; the second was called *The Universal Etymological English Dictionary ... Vol. II*. It contained what Bailey "would before have inserted in the first volume had there been Room," words he had discovered later, and "others communicated to me by some Persons of generous and communicative Dispositions." In addition, to fill up space, he included in Volume II several words that were in the first volume as well. The first edition of Volume II had a few woodcuts, mainly coats of arms, and many more pictures were added for the second edition (1731), which was said to be "Illustrated with above Five Hundred CUTS." Bailey explained the reason for them: "whereas bare verbal Descriptions and Explications of many Things, especially in Heraldry and the Mathematicks, produce but a faint and imperfect Idea of them in the Mind, I have here given Cuts or engraven Schemes for the more clear apprehending them." There is a particularly pleasing illustration of "Antipodes," showing smartly dressed little men standing on the top and the bottom of a ridiculously small globe.

As a guide to pronunciation, Bailey's Volume II placed an accent to indicate the stress in polysyllables, and this was later introduced into the first volume also. In the first two editions of Volume II, the accent was always placed immediately following a vowel, and its sole purpose was to show which syllable was stressed. In the third edition of Volume II, published in 1737, a more sophisticated system was introduced, in which the placing of the accent indicated not merely the stressed syllable, but also whether the vowel in that syllable was long or short. If the accent was placed immediately after the vowel, it was a long vowel; if after the following consonant or consonants, the vowel was short. Thus in 1731, (under the old system)

ANTI'PODES [in *Geograyby*] ſuch Inhabitants of the Earth, who dwell in oppoſite Pa-
rallels of Latitude, and under the oppoſite
half of the ſame Meridian, and walk with
their Feet directly oppoſite one to another.
The Antipodes have the ſame Length of Day
and Night, but at contrary Times; when it is
Noon with the one, it is Midnight with the
other; and the longeſt Day with one is the
ſhorteſt with the other; they have likewiſe
the ſame Degree of Heat and Cold; they have likewiſe
their Summer and Winter, the Riſing and Setting of the
Stars quite contrary one to another.

Bailey's definition of Antipodes, taken from the Folio *Dictionarium Britannicum* of 1730. The 1731 Octavo has the same definition, but the picture is reversed.

bi'nary and *bi'shop* were both accented after the *i*, even though the vowel is long in the first word and short in the second. In 1737, the difference in pronunciation was shown by moving the accent in the word with the short vowel. That edition accented the words *bi'nary* and *bish'op*.

The relationship between the two volumes of Bailey's octavo dictionary is a puzzle that not even Starnes and Noyes were able to explain. The principal oddity is that, apart from the transfer of some words from the second volume to the first, the two maintained an entirely separate and independent existence. The first volume, complete from A to Z, went through its multitudinous editions as if the second volume did not exist; it was never described as "Volume I," except when a binder was making a matched pair of the two volumes. Most people only had the first volume, and used it as their dictionary without feeling that any part was missing. "Volume II," which was so described on the title page, was also complete from A to Z, and came out much less often. There were only seven editions between 1727 and 1776, and they were not timed to coincide with editions of the first volume. Furthermore, the content of Vol. II varied considerably between one edition and another.

In 1723, after the first publication of Bailey's

octavo, but before the first edition of the second volume, appeared *A Dictionary of all the Words Commonly used in the English Tongue*, by our old friend Thomas Dyche, author of *The Guide to the English Tongue* and sometime employer of Thomas Dilworth. This may be seen as the antithesis of the "hard words" dictionaries of the seventeenth century. They had contained only hard words, because hard words were the only ones that needed to be defined. Dyche's work, usually referred to by its later title, *The Spelling Dictionary*, was intended for children, and therefore it did *not* contain hard words. A strict logician might suggest that, since it had no hard words, it did not need any definitions either. Dyche was a logical man, and his dictionary had no definitions. It was an alphabetical word list, intended to show spelling and pronunciation.

In the Preface to *The Spelling Dictionary*, Dyche set out some proposals for spelling reform:

3. By the leave of my good Friends, the Printers, and Correctors of the Press, I would propose, not to use many Letters in a Word, when fewer may do as well. Hence (ck) *need not be together in the end of such borrow'd Words as* concentric, Lyric, magnetic: *but I retain it in all* English *Words for Antiquity's sake. One* (l) *may commonly serve at the End of a Word, as well*

as two; so I hope the liberty I have taken that way may be pardonable. I think also, that (e) *final may be left out, when it does not lengthen a syllable, as in* doctrine, rapine, humane, handsome, &c. *which may better and more expeditiously be written* doctrin, rapin, human, handsom....

5. *There are some Words sounded so differently from their Letters, that I think the best way would be to spell them by the Ear. For Instance, I approve the words* Count, account, accountant, gage, gager, Lievtenant, skeptic, skeleton, *rather than* Compt, accomptant, gauge, gauger, Lieutenant, sceptic, sceleton, *as they are commonly written.*

6. *Latin substantives in* (-or) *become English ones in* (-our); *tho' I think that* (u) *to be unnecessary, because, when the word increases, it drops, as* humour, humorist, humorsom. *But to propose my single Opinion against the public Vogue, I must confess, is a hazardous Enterprize; for Custom will bear a man down, unless he find a good Number of Candid Friends to support him....*

In the dictionary itself, Dyche used many reformed spellings, but, as often happened with spelling reformers, he did not always remember to give effect to his own proposals. Thus the -*ck* termination was shortened in the "borrow'd" words *beatific, concentric, critic, lyric, magic* and *magnetic;* it was unaltered not only in the "English" words *frolick* and *traffick,* but also in the "borrow'd" word *Almanack.* The final *e* was removed from many words, such as *apocalyps, facil, sanguin, hurrican,* and *headach,* but it remained in *doctrine,* which was one of Dyche's examples, in the Preface, of a word from which it should be removed. The French -*que* was changed in *opake, risk, grotesk* and *checker,* but remained in *pique, oblique, antique* and *Exchequer.* The silent *b* was removed from the end of *benum* but not from *thumb.* The termination -*our* was changed to -*or* in a great many words, but remained unchanged in many others. Another reform that is now familiar in modern American spelling is the change of -*re* to -*er;* Dyche favoured that too, in such words as *theater, luster, scepter* and *specter,* but failed to apply it to *lucre.* The word *groveling* also has an American look to it, but the double *l* remained in *traveller* and *leveller.* It may well have been Dyche's *Spelling Dictionary* showing pronunciation that gave Bailey the idea of including accentuation when he first compiled the second volume of his octavo.

Bailey's final and finest dictionary was the folio *Dictionarium Britannicum,* which ap-

peared in 1730. It claimed to have been "Collected by several Hands, the Mathematical Part by G.GORDON, the Botanical by P.MILLER. The Whole Revis'd and Improv'd by N.BAILEY," but it is not easy to see what the "several Hands" collected before Bailey revised and improved it, since the basis of the folio was Bailey's two octavo volumes. Some of the material in them was left out, but not a great deal was added. Some of the material that was added came from a new encyclopedia, Ephraim Chambers' *Cyclopaedia; Or, An Universal Dictionary of Arts and Sciences,* which had been published two years earlier. Many of the "cuts" were the same as those in the second volume of Bailey's octavo, but, surprisingly, the Introduction to the first volume was left out. In fact, the only things in the 1730 folio were the Dedication (signed by George Gordon as well as Nat Bailey), the main body of the dictionary, and what called itself "An Alphabetical Table of the Names of Persons and Places in GREAT BRITAIN, with their several Etymologies." That heading was misleading, since many of the names had nothing to do with Great Britain at all (those listed under Z were Zabulon, Zachariah, Zedekiah, Zerubbabel and Zimri).

Bailey's folio went into a second edition in 1736. The "several Hands" disappeared from the title page, but were replaced by another named collaborator. Bailey was assisted in the Etymological Part "by T.LEDIARD, Gent. Professor of the Modern Languages in Lower Germany." Lediard did not sign his name to the Dedication, because there wasn't one, but he did provide a Preface by enlarging the Introduction from Bailey's octavo. This considered the history of the English language, and the question of whether the original language spoken by Adam survived the confusion at the building of the Tower of Babel. There was also some discussion of "the constant Resemblance between the Genius of each People and the Language which they speak":

The *French* who are a people of great Vivacity have a Language that runs extreme Lively and Brisk, and the *Italians* who succeeded the Romans have quite lost the Augustness and Nervousness of the Latin and sunk into Softness and Effeminacy, as well in their Language as their Manners....

The *English* who are naturally Blunt, thoughtful and of few Words, use a Language that is very short, concise and sententious.

After the Preface, and immediately before the dictionary itself, Bailey slipped in an advertisement:

N.B. Youth Boarded and Taught the Latin, Greek and Hebrew Languages, Writing Accounts, and other parts of School Learning, in a Method more easy and expeditious than is common; by the Author, at his House in Stepney, near the Church.

The 1736 folio was much larger than the 1730 edition, because it included a motley variety of odds and ends mostly derived from earlier editions of Volume II of the octavo. There were, for example, lengthy explanations of popular proverbs. Starnes and Noyes disapprove of these inclusions, saying that they make the second edition of Bailey's folio inferior to the first "from the point of view of lexicography," though they concede that "the very features which seem regrettable from a modern point of view may well have conduced most to [Bailey's] enormous contemporary popularity." I cannot share their regret. It is one thing to object to the inclusion in a dictionary of a whole lot of material that nobody wants or needs, but it is quite another to attack Bailey for not playing by the rules of twentieth-century lexicography. What he included was material that his eighteenth century purchasers enjoyed reading, and which persuaded them to buy his book.

We now come to *A New General English Dictionary* (1735). This brings us the news that Thomas Dyche has died, for it was "Originally begun by the late Reverend Mr. *THOMAS DYCHE*, School-Master at *Stratford-le-Bow*, Author of the *Guide* to the *English Tongue*; the *Spelling Dictionary*, &c. And now finish'd by *WILLIAM PARDON*, Gent." As you would expect from Dyche, it marks accented syllables, but that was not a novelty as it had earlier been done by Dyche himself in his *Spelling Dictionary* (the one with no definitions) and then by Bailey. The novelty in Dyche and Pardon was the inclusion of "A Compendious English Grammar," though the Grammar itself was not very good. Also becoming apparent in this dictionary is a sense of discomfort with the nondefinition of plain words. Even in his great folio, Bailey saw no reason to say more about a goat than that it was "an Animal well known." William Pardon, Gent. (for I have no doubt that he was to blame) started from Bailey, but added

a variety of information about the goat's smell, appearance, uses, and personal habits:

GOAT (S.) An Animal well known among us, horned, and when any thing aged of a very rank Smell, the Milk of the She's is reckoned peculiarly useful for Consumptive Persons; it was one of the clean Beasts of the *Israelites*, and used in their Sacrifices; when young is excellent eating; this creature is reported to be exceedingly pleased with the Act of Copulation, from whence those Persons who are immoderately addicted to Women are called *Goats, Letchers,* &c.

Because the work was in competition with Bailey's "Universal Etymological" octavo, Pardon stressed the advantage of *not* giving etymologies:

In the following Dictionary, *Derivations and Etymologies are entirely left out: First, because of their Uncertainty, in a very large Number of Instances: And, Secondly, upon Account of their Uselessness to those Persons that these Books are most helpful to, which are commonly such, whose Education, Reading and Leisure are bounded within a narrow Compass; and therefore such Helps and Hints, as were judged more universally beneficial, are substituted in their Room....*

The first helpful hint was to indicate by means of a letter in brackets whether a word was (S) a Substantive, (A) an adjective, (V) a Verb, or (P) anything else. "P" stood for "Particle."

We are now within 20 years of Johnson's folio, and there are only two dictionaries from those years that I want to look at. The first is Benjamin Martin's *Lingua Britannica Reformata* (1749), which Starnes and Noyes describe as "a dictionary with a plan." In a manner of speaking, Martin was not a man with just one plan, but a man with two plans. His own was to produce an octavo dictionary in which he would methodically incorporate, and improve upon, the good points of all the earlier dictionaries; the other, which may have helped him in shaping his ideas, was Johnson's *Plan of a Dictionary of the English Language*, published in 1747.

Martin's title page enumerated under eight headings the points to be covered in his dictionary. The first five are lexicographically the most important:

I. UNIVERSAL; Containing a Definition and Explication of all the Words now used in the English Tongue, in every *Art, Science, Faculty,* or *Trade*.

II. ETYMOLOGICAL; Exhibiting and Explaining the true Etymon or Original of Words from their respective Mother-Tongues, the *Latin, Greek, Hebrew*, and *Saxon*; and their Idioms, the *French, Italian, Spanish, German, Dutch*, &c.

III. ORTHOGRAPHICAL; Teaching the True and Rational Method of Writing Words, according to the usage of the most Approved Modern Authors.

IV. ORTHOEPICAL; Directing the True Pronunciation of Words by Single and Double Accents; and by Indicating the Number of Syllables in Words where they are doubtful, by a Numerical Figure.

V. DIACRITICAL; Enumerating the Various Significations of Words in a Proper Order, viz. *Etymological, Common, Figurative, Poetical, Humorous, Technical*, &c. in a Manner not before attempted.

It will at once be seen that the first two of those headings, Universal and Etymological, echoed the title of Bailey's octavo. Next came Orthography and Orthoepy (that is to say spelling and pronunciation), which were Dyche's specialist subjects. Indeed, Martin followed Dyche more closely than had William Pardon, Gent., for he used Dyche's system of "directing the true pronunciation of words by single and double accents" whereas Pardon had used only the single accent.

If Martin did, as he claimed, show spelling "according to the usage of the most Approved Modern Authors," this was good lexicographical practice — describing not prescribing — showing how it was, not how the lexicographer thought it ought to be. It has the additional advantage that it enables us to see (to the extent that Martin got it right) how "the most Approved Modern Authors" were spelling before Johnson started interfering. In the matter of the *-our* or *-or* termination, things were pretty much where they stand in England today — *armour, colour, favour, honour, humour and labour* spelled with the *u*; *author, error* and *tenor* without. Modern practice was reversed in that Martin had a *u* in *horrour* but not in *dolor*; *superiour/superior* was given both ways. Johnson would spell all those words with *-our* except *author*. The *k* had disappeared from the end of *magic, public, prolific* and *traffic* (to all of which Johnson would restore it) but it was present in *garlick*.

In the change from the French termination *-re* (as in *chambre*) to the English *-er* (*chamber*), Martin recorded a transitional moment slightly in advance of the position where Britain

has since got stuck. The alternative spellings *center* and *centre* are given, with Martin himself using *center* at that point in the dictionary, but elsewhere (for example in the definition of *diameter*) using *centre*. *Theatre* and *theater* are likewise given as alternatives; Martin uses *theatre*. *Sabre* and *lucre* are only given with *-re*, and *caliber* only with *-er*. There is evidence of transition also in the change of the *-que* termination to *-k* in such words as *risk, cask* and *burlesk*; similarly the spelling *lacker* is preferred to *lacquer*. Other phonetic spellings given as alternatives are *ax/axe, plough/plow*, and *straight/strait*.

It is in the matter of definitions that Martin is generally credited with innovation, for his was the first English dictionary in which different senses of the same word were carefully distinguished and separately numbered. That was not as difficult to achieve as it might at first appear; Martin made use of two-language dictionaries, where different senses have to be separated because the translations of the different senses will not be the same. He gave credit to those sources in his Preface:

A Critical and accurate Enumeration and Distinction of the several Significations of each respective Word must be allow'd by all to be indispensably the chiefest Care of every Writer of Dictionaries. And yet nothing is more certain, than that all our English Dictionaries are more notoriously deficient in this important Particular than in any other; indeed it has never been attempted in any of them that I have seen. The Authors have contented themselves with barely transcribing one from another a few (and those not always the principal) Acceptations, in a promiscuous Manner, without any Order or proper Arrangement. This grand Defect it has been my principal Care to supply, and indeed was the greatest Motive to my undertaking this Work. And that I might acquit myself more perfectly herein, I laid before my Amanuensis Ainsworth's Latin Dictionary, and the Royal French Dictionary; where, in the English Part, as the Authors were obliged to consider every different Sense of an English Word, in order to make a proper Translation thereof into each respective Language, this task was by that Means greatly facilitated....

In the department of plain words, Martin does not try to construct meaningful definitions when it is neither possible nor necessary to do so. A dog, a cat, a cow, a bull and a goat are all animals or beasts "well known." An apple is "a fruit well known," and so is a gooseberry.

Bound in with the first edition of *Lingua*

Britannica Reformata is what is described in the dictionary's title-page as "An INTRODUC-TION containing A Physico-Grammatical ESSAY." The Essay is actually a separate work of 111 pages; it has its own title page bearing the date 1748, a year earlier than the dictionary.

It is a remarkable document, which traces the development of the spoken language not only socially and historically, but anatomically. It also follows the development of writing, explaining the interrelation of different alphabets. The careful student is instructed in the ancestry of English, and will master, along the way, the basics of "the Original Mother Tongues, the Hebrew, Greek, Latin and Teutonic; with their respective Idioms [i.e. dialects], the Italian, French, Spanish, Saxon and German." Some of the early passages touch upon subjects that would later be of consuming interest to Webster:

Many of the learned have thought that this ancient German, Celtic, or as it was most commonly call'd, Teutonic language was an original one, or one of those we have derived from the confusion of tongues at Babel; yea, some have gone farther, and insisted on its being the vernacular tongue of Adam, his family, and descendants....

The old Britains, as has been observ'd, were a part of the ancient Celtæ, and their language a dialect of the Celtic tongue, and is still the same in substance as ever. We call it Welsh, and their country Wales; because the Latin *Wallia*, is from Gallia; and Welsh from Wallish, and that from Gallish or Gauls by a change of the letters G or Gu, for W, which is very common. For the Britains were thought by the ancient Saxons to be from Gallia (or France) and so call'd them Gaules.

But a Britain or Welshman in his own tongue is call'd Cymro, or Cumro, which seems to imply an affinity or relation to the ancient Cimbri or Cimmeri, a people of Jutland, and one of the nations of the Celtæ. These Cimbri are supposed by learned antiquarians to be the descendants of, and to derive their name from Gomer, the eldest son of Japhet, and Grandson of Noah. And this seems very probably the high antiquity of our famous ancestors of Britains.

Martin said in his Preface that, "as nothing before has been attempted in this Kind, I have reason to hope it will meet with a favourable Reception." It seems that it didn't, for the Physico-Grammatical Essay did not appear in later editions of his dictionary.

The last pre-Johnson dictionary that I want to look at makes an interesting contrast to all the others. In its conception it is, to my way of thinking, the most sensible of the lot. Its compiler shared my view that a practical everyday pocket dictionary needs to explain only the words that the user will encounter, but does not understand. It need not trouble with words that are familiar to him, or with words that he is unlikely ever to meet, or with "particles" that nobody ever needs to look up. In an address to the reader, the compiler explained why his dictionary was better than those of Bailey, Dyche & Pardon, and Martin:

As incredible as it may appear, I must avow, that this dictionary is not published to get money, but to assist persons of common sense and no learning, to understand the best *English* authors: and that, with as little expence of either time or money, as the nature of the thing would allow.

To this end it contains, not a heap of *Greek* and *Latin* words, just tagged with *English* terminations: (for no good *English* writer, none but vain or senseless pedants, give these any place in their writings:) not a scroll of barbarous *law expressions*, which are neither *Greek, Latin,* nor good *English*: not a croud of technical terms, the meaning whereof is to be sought in books expresly wrote on the subjects to which they belong: not such English words as and, of, but; which stand so gravely in Mr. *Bailey's, Pardon's,* and *Martin's* dictionaries: but 'most of those hard words which are found in the best *English* writers.' I say *most*; for I purposely omit not only all which are not hard, and which are not found in the best writers: not only all law-words and most technical terms, but likewise all, the meaning of which may be easily gathered from those of the same derivation. And this I have done, in order to make this dictionary both as short and as cheap as possible.

I should add no more, but that I have so often observed, the only way, according to the modern taste, for any author to procure commendation to his book is, vehemently to commend it himself. For want of this deference to the publick, several excellent tracts lately printed, but left to commend themselves by their intrinsic worth, are utterly unknown or forgotten. Whereas if a writer of tolerable sense will but bestow a few violent encomiums on his own work, especially if they are skilfully ranged in the title-page, it will pass thro' six editions in a trice; the world being too complaisant to give a gentleman the Lie, and taking it for granted, he understands his own performance best.

In compliance, therefore, with the taste of the age, I add, that this little dictionary is not only the shortest and the cheapest, but likewise, by many degrees, the most correct which is extant at this day. Many are the mistakes in all the other *English* dictionaries

which I have yet seen. Whereas I can truly say, I know of none in this; and I conceive the reader will believe me: for if I had, I should not have left it there. Use this help, then, till you find a better.

The quotation in that passage was from the title page of the dictionary, in which the author had indeed "skilfully ranged" a violent (but short) encomium on his own work:

> THE COMPLETE English Dictionary,
> Explaining most of those HARD WORDS,
> Which are found in the BEST
> *ENGLISH* WRITERS.
> By a Lover of *Good English*
> and *Common Sense.*
> N.B. The AUTHOR assures you,
> he thinks this is the
> best *English* DICTIONARY in the World.

The tone is lighthearted, but the author's aim was absolutely serious. We may even believe his assertion that his purpose in publishing the dictionary was not to get money — because he was John Wesley, and he prepared the dictionary to help his followers to understand the Christian Library that he had published, and his other educational and religious works.

In this survey of the development of the dictionary, from Cawdrey in 1604 to Wesley in 1753, we have seen the different elements appear one by one. To begin with, definition or explanation was the sole purpose, and the dictionary was limited to "hard" words. Blount added etymology and authorities; Phillips, a history of the English language and a list of "experts." "J.K." in 1702 made the first "Compleat Collection Of the Most Proper and Significant Words," to show their spelling. Dyche, followed by Bailey, accented words to indicate pronunciation, and Bailey put illustrations in the pages of text. Dyche & Pardon added a grammar. Martin combined various of these elements, with separately numbering the different senses of words. He did not put pictures in the text, but he did include six plates, illustrating mostly mathematical figures, as a separate section between the Physico-Grammatical Essay and the dictionary itself.

From several points of view, the reign of Queen Anne (1702–1714) seems to mark a significant watershed. There lies the boundary between the dictionaries of "hard words" and the "universal" dictionaries; and there we see a reaction against nonsensical polysyllables, in favor of a style more suited to a Newtonian clarity of thought. Also, Anne was the last Stuart sovereign and was succeeded on the throne of England by an elector of Hanover, who did not speak English. It was natural, later, to look back on the years following the Glorious Revolution of 1688 as a golden age. Finally, the first English Copyright Act, familiarly known as the Statute of Anne, was passed in 1709.

That act came into force on April 10, 1710. The book trade had earlier recognized that a publisher could acquire from an author an exclusive right to print the author's work, but such rights were enforced by the Stationers' Company, on behalf of one member against another, rather than by courts of law. The Stationers' Company kept a register of proprietors of "copies" both before and after the Statute of Anne. When Blount wrote that Phillips had been employed by "a Bookseller, not interested in the Copy," he was referring to that right; he meant, in modern terms, that Phillips was employed by a publisher who had no interest in Blount's copyright, and therefore no right to reproduce Blount's material. The word *copyright* was not used until much later — more than fifty years after the first copyright act came into force. In the statute itself, "Copy" is used. The "copies" that were registered before the statute would later be described as "common law copyrights," but no one attempted to enforce them in the common law courts until after the Statute of Anne had created statutory copyright, nor indeed until after the first statutory copyrights had expired.

1755 Johnson's Dictionary

It was in 1746 that Johnson signed a contract to compile a dictionary. The work appeared, in two large folio volumes costing £4.10.0d. the set, in 1755. If one had to identify its distinctive contribution to the development of the English dictionary, it would be the addition of a wealth of illustrative quotations. In certain other respects, however, Johnson took a step backwards, so that he does not fit quite comfortably into a picture of a regular advance, each compiler adding to the work of those who had gone before. This is because Johnson was not aiming at quite the same target as earlier

English lexicographers. Eighteenth century England looked with envy across the channel, to the *Dictionnaire* of the Académie Française. This contained, or was supposed to contain, the definitive statement of what was correct in the French language. England was thought to need the same sort of authoritative dictionary. Swift, in 1712, published *A Proposal for Correcting, Improving, and Ascertaining the English Tongue*, in which he called for some means to be found "for ascertaining and fixing our language forever."

It was rather remarkable that Johnson should have been offered the job, since he was not a writer of established reputation. The person responsible for the choice was one of the consortium of publishers who financed the work, Robert Dodsley. Johnson, like many other lexicographers before and since (including Webster), had been a schoolmaster. Having given up teaching in Lichfield, he travelled to London with one of his former pupils, the actor David Garrick, each of them hoping to make his fortune. Johnson had with him *London, a Poem*, a satire in imitation of Juvenal, which he tried in vain to sell to numerous London publishers. Finally, when he was near to destitution and despair, he came to Robert Dodsley, who took the poem and eventually paid him ten guineas for it. Without those ten guineas, and perhaps more significantly without the reputation given him by the publication of his work, the Johnson of Boswell's *Life* might never have come into being. Johnson appreciated this, calling his friend Doddy "the only bookseller in London that found out I had any genius." When Dodsley later compiled an all-purpose textbook, *The Preceptor: containing a General Course of Education*, Johnson wrote the Preface.

When he started on the dictionary, Johnson, like Swift, thought that it might be possible to "ascertain and fix our language for ever," but he soon realised that a living language is always going to change. He explained his own change of mind in a beautiful passage in the Preface:

Those who have been persuaded to think well of my design, will require that it should fix our language, and put a stop to those alterations which time and chance have hitherto been suffered to make in it without opposition. With this consequence I will confess that I flattered myself for a while; but now begin to fear that I have indulged expectation that

neither reason nor experience can justify. When we see men grow old and die at a certain time one after another, from century to century, we laugh at the elixir that promises to prolong life to a thousand years; and with equal justice may the lexicographer be derided, who, being able to produce no example of a nation that has preserved their words and phrases from mutability, shall imagine that his dictionary can embalm his language, and secure it from corruption and decay, that it is in his power to change sublunary nature, and clear the world at once from folly, vanity, and affectation.

Even though Johnson accepted that his dictionary could not preserve the language from alteration, he would nevertheless make the attempt. His motive can be seen in the passage quoted above: He did his best to resist inevitable change, because that change was bound to be in the direction of "corruption and decay." Johnson believed, like many of his contemporaries, that the English language had reached something like the pinnacle of perfection, and that any change must therefore be for the worse. Indeed, his was the classic conservative belief, that things had been at their best a generation or two earlier, and that the process of corruption was already well under way.

Johnson therefore set out to include in his dictionary all respectable English words. This led him into the difficulty we have noticed in relation to the earlier eighteenth-century dictionaries, of framing satisfactory definitions of simple words. He was himself well aware of the problem, explaining it in his Preface:

That part of my work on which I expect malignity most frequently to fasten is the *Explanation*; in which I cannot hope to satisfy those, who are perhaps not inclined to be pleased, since I have not always been able to satisfy myself. To interpret a language by itself is very difficult; many words cannot be explained by synonymes, because the idea signified by them has not more than one appellation; nor by paraphrase, because simple ideas cannot be described. When the nature of things is unknown, or the notion unsettled and indefinite, and various in various minds, the words by which such notions are conveyed, or such things denoted, will be ambiguous and perplexed. And such is the fate of hapless lexicography, that not only darkness, but light, impedes and distresses it; things may be not only too little, but too much known, to be happily illustrated. To explain, requires the use of terms less abstruse than that which is to be explained, and such terms cannot always be found; for as nothing can be proved but by supposing something intuitively known, and evident

without proof, so nothing can be defined but by the use of words too plain to admit a definition....

Some explanations are unavoidably reciprocal or circular, as *hind, the female of the stag; stag, the male of the hind:* sometimes, easier words are changed into harder, as *burial* into *sepulture* or *interment, drier* into *dessicative, dryness* into *siccity* or *aridity, fit* into *paroxysm;* for the easiest word, whatever it be, can never be translated into one more easy. But easiness and difficulty are merely relative, and if the present prevalence of our language should invite foreigners to this dictionary, many will be assisted by those words which now seem only to increase or produce obscurity. For this reason, I have endeavoured frequently to join a *Teutonick* and *Roman* interpretation, as to CHEER, to *gladden,* or *exhilarate,* that every learner of *English* may be assisted by his own tongue.

In that last paragraph, there is an unexpected echo of the second part of Cockeram's *English Dictionarie,* where "Vulgar words" were translated into "a more refined and elegant speech." Indeed, Cockeram did actually suggest using *Sepulture* for *Buriall,* and *Aridity* for *drynesse.* Cockeram, however, was teaching hard words to unlearned folk such as "Ladies and Gentlewomen, young Schollers, Clerkes and Merchantes," who were not Johnson's intended readers. Those who could afford a book as expensive as Johnson's Dictionary, whether they were English or foreign, were likely to have had a classical education, and for them the "Roman" word *interment* was not just the equivalent of the "Teutonick" *burial,* it was a definition as well, bringing before the mind's eye a picture of "putting into the earth." Of course, no English reader needed an explanation of *burial* anyway, which was why Johnson mentioned foreigners, who might be using his dictionary to help them learn English.

Johnson's quotations were primarily intended to help towards the understanding of words. What could not readily be *explained* might nevertheless be *illustrated.* In addition, Johnson had the idea that the quotations could usefully be made to serve for the purposes of moral or intellectual instruction:

When I first collected these authorities, I was desirous that every quotation should be useful to some other end than that of the illustration of a word; I therefore extracted from philosophers principles of science; from historians remarkable facts; from chymists complete processes; from divines striking exhortations; and from poets beautiful descriptions. Such is design, while it is yet at a distance from

execution. When the time called upon me to range this accumulation of elegance and wisdom into an alphabetical series, I soon discovered that the bulk of my volumes would fright away the student, and was forced to depart from my scheme of including all that was pleasing or useful in *English* literature, and reduce my transcripts very often to clusters of words, in which scarcely any meaning is retained; thus to the weariness of copying, I was condemned to add the vexation of expunging. Some passages I have yet spared, which may relieve the labour of verbal searches, and intersperse with verdure and flowers the dusty desarts of barren philology....

Some of the examples have been taken from writers who were never mentioned as masters of elegance or models of style; but words must be sought where they are used; and in what pages, eminent for purity, can terms of manufacture or agriculture be found? Many quotations serve no other purpose, than that of proving the bare existence of words, and are therefore selected with less scrupulousness than those which are to teach their structure and relations.

For explaining the meaning, structure, or relations of words, Johnson's Dictionary has many more quotations than are necessary. Some of them may be the truncated remains of moral lessons that Johnson had hoped to include, but then had to cut down to leave only "the word for the sake of which they are inserted, with all its appendant clauses, ... carefully preserved." Others, one feels, were never necessary for any explicative, moral or instructional purpose whatsoever, but were included because Johnson liked them. As a whole, the quotations make the dictionary enjoyable to read — without them it would more nearly resemble "a dusty desart of barren philology" — but they do not much illuminate the meaning of words. For the most part, one would understand the words without either definition or illustration.

Spelling was one of the areas in which Johnson's authoritative dictionary was intended to provide stability and certainty. A century before Johnson, some orthographical freedom was quite acceptable. In Blount's *Glossographia* (1656), for example, the very definition of the word *Centre* contains the sentence "The earth is called the Center of the world." Uncertainty of that sort is an encouragement to change, and in the eighteenth century British spelling fashions were changing. We have seen that the termination *-ick* in such words as *publick, magick* and *fantastick* was being shortened to *-ic,* and

-*our* was giving way to -*or*. In Blount, one finds such spellings as *error, armor* and *ill-favored*. Those changes were well under way, and the new forms were already preferred in some dictionaries, before the publication of Johnson's in 1755.

Johnson, however, was a man with an orderly mind. He did not like what he called an "unsettled and fortuitous" orthography, and he did his best not just to stem the tide of change, but to force it some way back. He restored the *k* to *fantastick*, and the *u* to *errour*. In the grammar attached to his dictionary, he explained why phonetic spelling, though theoretically desirable, was not a practical possibility:

Such would be the orthography of a new language to be formed by a synod of grammarians upon principles of science. But who can hope to prevail on nations to change their practice, and make all their old books useless? or what advantage would a new orthography procure equivalent to the confusion and perplexity of such an alteration?

He gave examples of some of the systems of phonetic spelling that had been proposed in the past, and ended with a dry comment on more recent events:

We have since had no general reformers; but some ingenious men have endeavoured to deserve well of their country, by writing *honor* and *labor* for *honour* and *labour*, *red* for *read* in the preter-tense, *sais* for *says*, *repete* for *repeat*, *explane* for *explain*, or *declame* for *declaim*. Of these it may be said, that as they have done no good, they have done little harm; both because they have innovated little, and because few have followed them.

1755–1783 From Johnson's Dictionary to Webster's Spelling Book

The reputation of Johnson's Dictionary was so great that no effective competitor arose to challenge it for over seventy years. Webster would eventually provide that competition, but not until 1828. In 1755, Bailey's publishers tried to compete, issuing an enlarged version of Bailey's folio, edited by Joseph Nicol Scott, but it was not a success. What purported to be later editions of the Scott-Bailey, issued to coincide with new editions of Johnson, were made up from unsold sheets of the 1755 edition, with new title pages. Johnson's Dictionary was issued initially in two folio volumes and later in quarto; in either form it was a large and expensive work, and the sort of people who were likely to buy it wanted nothing but the best. Johnson was considered to be the best.

Johnson also put out an octavo abridgment, in two volumes but often bound together. Here, he did not succeed in dominating the market. The demand was greater, and Bailey's octavo, which was well established, continued to sell.

Among the octavo dictionaries, indeed, there was a notable new arrival, John Ash's *New and Complete Dictionary of the English Language*, published in 1775. Ash is remembered for two things. First, he was the only lexicographer until very recently who was bold enough to include the words *fuck* and *cunt* in a general English dictionary, and offer definitions more or less in English. Bailey's octavo had both words, but explained them only in Latin—*fœminam subagitare*, and *Pudendum Muliebre*. Ash's entries were models of lexicographical excellence, explaining the meaning of the words in a way that is entirely inoffensive, and at the same time warning against using them:

Cunt (*s. a low and vulgar word, from* cunnus) The female pudendum.
Fuck (*v.t. a low vulgar word*) To perform the act of generation, to have to do with a woman.

Ash's Dictionary is otherwise remembered because it contains a ludicrous mistake in the etymology of the word *Curmudgeon*. This was the entry:

Curmudgeon (*s. from the* French cœur, *unknown, and* mechant, *a correspondent*) A miser, a churl, a griper.

That remarkable piece of nonsense came directly from Johnson's Dictionary:

Curmudgeon. *n.s.* [It is a vitious manner of pronouncing *cœur mechant*, Fr. An unknown correspondent.] An avaricious churlish fellow; a miser; a niggard; a churl; a griper.

Johnson, of course, supposed that his readers did not need to have *cœur méchant* translated, but he was careful to give the source of his information. The way in which Ash contracted Johnson's definition is typical of the manner in which later compilers of lesser dictionaries made use of Johnson's; the carelessness of the supposed etymology shows how little thought went into the process.

Ash's mistake became a surprisingly long-lived literary joke. Seventy-five years later (when nobody was using Ash's Dictionary anyway) the compiler of a French-English Dictionary said that he had never consulted Ash, "who, after his etymology of *curmudgeon*, can inspire no confidence."[3]

A further reduction of Johnson, smaller, that is to say, than Ash's, was Entick's *New Spelling Dictionary*, a little square duodecimo with one-line definitions. It filled an important niche in the market, and was widely used both in England and in America. Entick is significant for our purposes because Webster said that it was the only dictionary he consulted while compiling his spelling book. Later, he would base his own first dictionary, the *Compendious* of 1806, on it, and when we come to look at the *Compendious* we shall examine Entick in greater detail.

One feature of a modern dictionary that Johnson was felt to have neglected was the indication of pronunciation. Because he was addressing a literate readership who already knew how to speak, Johnson generally gave no help with pronunciation other than showing primary stress. Only in a few exceptional cases did he do more, as where he explained that *clothes* is always pronounced *clo's*, a fact one might have deduced from Herrick's rhyme:

> Whenas in silks my Julia goes
> Then, then I think how sweetly flows
> The liquefaction of her clothes.

Johnson's lack of interest in pronunciation suggested an opportunity to later lexicographers looking for a gap in the post-Johnson market. In the period between the publication of Johnson's Dictionary in 1755 and Webster's compiling his spelling book in 1782, pronouncing dictionaries were produced by Buchanan, Sheridan, Johnstone, Kenrick, and Perry.

In 1757, James Buchanan published *Linguæ britannicæ vera pronunciatio: or, a New English dictionary .... designed for the use of schools, and of foreigners, etc.* Its purpose, as he later wrote, was "to obviate a vicious provincial dialect, and to remove the complaints of foreign gentlemen, desirous of learning English.... Accordingly, in the above-mentioned Dictionary, I marked the long and short sounds of the vowels through-

out the alphabetical words, distinguished every quiescent letter, pointed out the number of syllables each word consisted of where doubtful, and ascertained the various sounds of the vowels and diphthongs, and of the single and double consonants, &c." [4]

Next, we have Thomas Sheridan, who as a child spent much time in the company of his godfather, Jonathan Swift. Swift was a close friend of Sheridan's father and wrote *Gulliver's Travels* while staying at the Sheridans' house in County Cavan, in Ireland. Thomas Sheridan, the son, became an actor, theatrical manager, playwright, and teacher of elocution. His son, Richard Brinsley Sheridan, was a politician, but was also a more famous playwright than his father. In 1762 Thomas Sheridan published *A Dissertation on the Causes of the Difficulties Which occur, in learning the English Tongue, With a Scheme for publishing An English Grammar and Dictionary, upon a Plan entirely New*. This contained tables showing how, in the way that words are spelled in English, each vowel can have several different sounds (to which Sheridan attached numbers from 1 to 5); showing also how the same letters or combinations of letters can be used to represent different sounds, and how the same sounds can be represented by different letters. Sheridan's *Dissertation* promised a dictionary in which the different sounds of each vowel would be distinguished by numbering them. He is said to have started work on it in 1760, and Boswell discussed it with Johnson in 1772:

BOSWELL: "It may be of use, Sir, to have a Dictionary to ascertain pronunciation."

JOHNSON: "Why, Sir, my Dictionary shows you the accent of words, if you can but remember them."

BOSWELL: "But Sir, we want marks to ascertain the pronunciation of the vowels. Sheridan, I believe, has finished such a work."

JOHNSON: Why, Sir, consider how much easier it is to learn a language by the ear, than by any marks. Sheridan's Dictionary may do very well; but you cannot always carry it about with you: and, when you want the word, you have not the Dictionary. It is like a man who has a sword that will not draw. It is an admirable sword, to be sure: but while your enemy is cutting your throat, you are unable to use it. Besides, Sir, what entitles Sheridan to fix the pronunciation of English?

If Sheridan's Dictionary was indeed finished by 1772, he was very dilatory in getting it

printed, for it was not published until 1780. By then, various other pronouncing dictionaries had appeared.

In 1766, James Buchanan, author of the 1757 pronouncing dictionary, published an *Essay towards Establishing ... an Elegant and Uniform Pronunciation of the English Language*. During the years that had passed since the publication of his earlier dictionary, Buchanan had changed his mind about the best way to teach pronunciation and now believed that numbering vowel sounds was not satisfactory, because the writer was not present to demonstrate the sounds to the reader. As Buchanan explained in the Preface to his *Essay*, respelling was the better way:

If I signify in writing, that [a] has five different sounds; and that 1. it sounds long in same, fair, compare, profane, &c. 2. broad, like German [a] in call, war, bald, ward, water, &c. whoever has not been taught these sounds *vivâ voce*, or considered them abstractedly, has received no instruction. But let these sounds be properly represented in combination, and a child that can read a little will readily pronounce them thus, saim, fair, compair, profain, kaul, waur, wauk, bauld, waurd, wautĭr, &c.

That is not a sound argument. Both ways of attempting to teach sounds by means of written comparisons are open to the same objection. If I say that *eight* is pronounced with the first sound of *a* as in *hate*, it does not help someone who does not know how to pronounce *hate*, nor does it correct the speech of a reader who pronounces *hate* with a sound that is not the same as the one that I recommend. Equally, if I say that *eight* sounds as if it were written *ate* or *ait*, I am assuming that my readers know how I want those words to be pronounced. Buchanan, however, had come to believe that respelling was the only answer, and his *Essay* of 1766 is a pronouncing dictionary in the way that Dyche's was a spelling dictionary — a dictionary without definitions. The greater part of the book is a word-list in parallel columns; the left hand column contains an alphabetical list of words in conventional spelling, with an accent marking the primary stress; the right hand column has the same words respelled in a manner which, together with long and short accents, was intended to indicate the pronunciation favored by Buchanan.

Buchanan's Preface refers to another book that had appeared the previous year, *A Spelling and Pronouncing Dictionary*, by a Mr. Johnstone. I have not seen a copy, but this need not trouble us, because Webster never saw it either. I mention it only because Johnstone's dictionary would be referred to in the correspondence that followed the publication of Webster's spelling book.

The next notable pronouncing dictionary was William Kenrick's *New Dictionary of the English Language*, which appeared in 1773. Kenrick began with a spirited attack on his predecessors, pointing out that those who purported to teach English pronunciation were not themselves English — Sheridan was Irish, and Buchanan was a Scot. "There seems," said Kenrick, "a most ridiculous absurdity in the pretensions of a native of Aberdeen or Tipperary, to teach the natives of London to speak and read.... That they should not have succeeded is no wonder. Men cannot teach others what they do not themselves know." As a demonstration of Buchanan's system, Kenrick wrote out a passage from Johnson's *Idler* respelled in the fashion of Buchanan's *Essay*:

Eezy poeetry iz that in wheetsh nateuril thots air expressed without violins too the lan-gwidsh. Thee diskriminaiting kariktir ov eez konsists prinsipilly in the dikshun, for awl trew poeetry reequirs that thee sentimints bee nateuril. Langwidsh suffirs violins by harsh or by dairing figurs, by unshootibl transpozeeshun, by uneuzyl akseptaishuns ov wurdz, and any lisins wheetsh wood bee avoided by a ritir ov proz.

Kenrick observed that "the English reader will very readily discover, in attempting to decypher the above passage, that the essayist must be a North-Briton [i.e., a Scot], and not a native of England." The rendering of Buchanan's respelling is not quite perfect, but the point is a good one: Pronouncing *which are* as *wheetsh air* is clearly Scottish, and other examples can be found throughout Buchanan's *Essay*. A particularly Scottish enunciation is his rendering of syllables that, farther south, would have been spoken with the "Italian" sound of *a*, as in *father*. Buchanan calls this "its acute sound, which seems to approach to au, but is really short ă, twice, but rapidly pronounced." He denotes this sound by a circumflex accent over the letter, as "fâthĭr, râthĭr, ârmz, ârdŭr, commând, ârmў, &c." Try pronouncing *fathir* with two short *a*s "rapidly pronounced," a short *i*, and a rolled *r*, and you will find that you can smell the

heather and faintly hear the skirl of distant bag-pipes.

Now, it is a valid criticism of Buchanan's book that it teaches its readers to speak with a Scottish accent when they want an English one, but that is not a valid criticism of Buchanan's *system*. Indeed, the very fact that Buchanan's respellings lead to a a recognizably Scottish tone of voice is proof that the system works. Even so, Kenrick did not like it. "Disfiguring the orthography," he thought, "is very prejudicial to the learner; who, in thus being taught to speak and read, will forget, or never learn, how to write." Here, we see the subtlety of his producing the passage of remodelled Johnson: It suggested to the reader of Kenrick's Introduction that Buchanan favored a phonetic respelling *as a way of writing English.* Buchanan did not. The readers of his *Essay* could only find his phonetic respellings by looking up words in their conventional spelling. Kenrick, however, would avoid respelling, and favoured a system of numbering vowel sounds.

The system that Sheridan had set out in his *Dissertation* identified 20 vowel sounds — three sounds of *a,* four sounds of *e,* five sounds of *i,* and so on — but they were not all different. The first sound of *i,* (as in *fit*) for example, sounds the same as the third sound of *u* (as in *busy*). The critical reader might notice, as well, that Sheridan's table contained neither the Italian sound of *a* nor the letters *e* and *o* representing the short sound of *i* in the words *English* and *women.* Sheridan did point out that the same sounds may be represented by many different combinations of letters; for example, the third sound of *a* (as in *hall*) is heard in the words *draw, cause, fall, bald, talk, broad, ought,* and *caught.* For Sheridan, it would be possible to indicate the pronunciation of any of those words by respelling them with $\overset{3}{a}$ to represent the vowel sound. Kenrick, however, could not do that, because he disapproved of respelling. He therefore devised a system in which a particluar number represented a particular sound, *regardless of the letter or letters by which it was represented.* These he set out in a table:

TABLE OF ENGLISH SOUNDS,
OR VOWELS,

Expressed in different Syllables
by various Letters.

Kenrick identified sixteen different vowel sounds, ranging from "No. 1. Example. *Cur, fir, her, monk, blood, earth,* &c." to "16. Ex. *Why, nigh, I, buy, join, lyre, hire,* &c. &c." Some of those words seem out of place, for example rhyming *cur* with *monk,* and *join* with *buy,* but the table gives a true indication of Kenrick's pronunciation. His ear, in fact, was very good, and he deserves particular praise for identifying and indicating the indeterminate vowel sound, which, he said, should be added to the sixteen in his list. It is the sound represented in the modern phonetic alphabet by the symbol ə. Kenrick called it "the indistinct sound, marked with a cypher thus [o], as practised in the colloquial utterance of the particles *a* and *the,* the last syllables of words ending in *en, le,* and *re;* as *a garden; the castle,* &c. also in the syllable frequently sunk in the middle of words of three syllables, as *every, memory, favourite,* &c...."

The body of the dictionary was derived from Johnson, which Kenrick acknowledged, offering the curious suggestion that his work might be regarded as furnishing an index to Johnson's:

> With respect to the etymology, explanation of words, and illustrations of idiom and phraseology, the reader will find that I have generally followed the celebrated dictionary of the learned Dr.Johnson. As the present performance is chiefly calculated to correct and ascertain the orthoepy of our tongue, I thought it might be of some advantage to its readers, to make it at the same time a copious index to a work of very general acceptation, in which the literal authorities, collected from our best writers, may be consulted at large.

That use of the word "follow" is something we shall meet again. If I copy your work, I may be thought a scoundrel, but if I follow your lead, I am a respectful disciple.

The other principal pronouncing dictionary inspired by Sheridan's *Dissertation,* but published before Sheridan's Dictionary, was *The Royal Standard English Dictionary* by William Perry, published in 1775. Perry, another Scot, criticised and improved Sheridan's scheme. His system of numbering the sounds of each vowel was similar to Sheridan's, but he rearranged the tables, and supplied some omissions, in particular putting in the Italian sound of *a.*

Sheridan may have been unaware of Perry's criticism; if he was aware of it, he ignored it.

When his dictionary finally made its appearance in 1780, its scheme for distinguishing the different sounds of the various vowels was exactly as it had been in his *Dissertation*, published nearly twenty years before.

In a moment, we shall follow the development of Webster's first spelling book. One of his principal objects, he would claim, was to provide "some easy guide to the *standard* of pronunciation, which is nothing else but the customary pronunciation of the most accurate scholars and literary Gentlemen. Such a standard, universally used in schools, would in time, demolish those odious distinctions of provincial dialects, which are the objects of reciprocal ridicule in the United States." [5] Webster was addressing the same problem as the compilers of pronouncing dictionaries, and his critics would suggest that with Sheridan, Kenrick, Johnstone and Perry before him, he would have had no great difficulty in solving it. Webster

denied having used any dictionary other than Entick's, but the scheme that he adopted was undoubtedly based on Sheridan's.

Starnes and Noyes, having surveyed the first 150 years in the history of the English dictionary, pointed to "three unsavoury corollaries.... (1) in this early period lexicography progressed by plagiarism; (2) the best lexicographer was often the most discriminating plagiarist; (3) a good dictionary was its own justification, whatever the method of compilation."

Those methods of lexicography did not suddenly go out of fashion in the middle of the eighteenth century. The compilers of the pronouncing dictionaries "followed" Johnson. Webster would produce a good dictionary seventy five years after Johnson, and he, too, employed the traditional techniques. First, however, he compiled the spelling book that is the subject of the next chapter.

4. Webster's *Grammatical Institute*, Part I

We left Webster, early in 1782, teaching school in Goshen and not at all happy about it. He was qualified to practice law, but he had neither capital nor connections, and he knew that he would not be able to get started. He had tried in vain to leave teaching and find "mercantile employment." He deserved something better than schoolmastering. "The principle part of instructors," he wrote soon afterwards, "are illiterate people." The *Memoir* gives a retrospective account of his dismal situation:

His prospects of better employment were not encouraging; it was uncertain when the war would be at an end; and he knew not by what means he could find business better suited to his inclination. He had, in hours stolen from necessary occupations, acquired so much knowledge of Law, as to obtain a license to practice, but he had not made himself acquainted with the forms of proceedings, and could not enter upon the practice with advantage. In addition to these circumstances, his health was impaired by close application, and a sedentary life. He was without money and without friends to afford him any particular aid. In this situation of things, his spirits failed, and for some months, he suffered extreme depression and gloomy forebodings.

In this state of mind, he formed the design of composing elementary books for the instruction of children; and began by compiling a spelling book on a plan which he supposed to be better adapted to assist the learner, than that of Dilworth.

That last paragraph compresses the events of about a year. Webster conceived the *idea* of revising Dilworth in the summer of 1782, but he did not immediately carry it out. The reasons for doing it were clear enough, but so were the risks. Dilworth had obvious faults, even for the English market; it would be even more unsuitable for the schools of the new America.

Webster had the natural vanity of the would-be author. He, Noah Webster Jun., Esq., could teach all of America to read, to write, and to pronounce properly. These were lessons that Webster himself had learned, though to his shame other members of his family had not. It was too late to teach his father and his brother Abraham, but he could teach everyone else. Was it not his patriotic duty to write the book? But what if he wrote it and it did not sell? On the one hand fame and fortune; on the other, ridicule and ruin.

The main motive was money. Here was a business venture that, if it succeeded, might free Webster from the schoolroom forever. Then he realized that the venture could not succeed financially without the protection of a copyright law. America might benefit, but there would be no profit for Webster if others could print and sell his book without paying him. When Franklin invented a new stove, he gave the design free of charge to his countrymen; but Franklin had other irons in other fires. Webster could not afford a gesture of that sort. In a patriotic puff at the end of the Introduction to his spelling book, he would write:

The author wishes to promote the honour and prosperity of the confederated republics of America; and chearfully throws his mite into the common treasure of patriotic exertions.

Humbug! It was the honor and prosperity of Noah Webster that he wished to promote, and he had not the least intention of making a charitable donation of his mite. This is clear from the last paragraph of the advertisement printed at the front of the book:

As the whole will be published under the protection of a law of this State, entitled "An Act for the encouragement of Literature and Genius," all Printers and Booksellers will take notice of this information and not incur the penalties of that Statute.

That, however was still a year ahead. In 1782, none of the American states had a copyright law, and Webster was not about to write his book until there were some. He also wanted to be told that his ideas were good and that the book would sell. On August 25, 1782, he wrote to Barlow (who was still an army chaplain) telling both of his despondency and of his plan for improving Dilworth. Barlow replied:

Camp, Aug. 31, 1782

Dear Webster,

...I most heartily feel for you, my Webster, in everything you feel as a misfortune, though perhaps they are not really such which wear that appearance. Your perseverance will certainly overcome them. You will gain from them experience in the knowledge of human life, and be ready to relish better fortune when it shall appear. We are all a pack of poor dogs and I have worn out half my life in buffeting my destiny, and all I have got for it is the knack of keeping up my spirits, letting the world slide, and hoping for better days. I like your plan about Dilworth; it will be useful & successful in the world at large if you can make it useful to yourself. Your attempting it is an expression of that benevolence to your fellow-creatures that I know you to possess: but it is a work of labor, and you ought to make something by it. You know our country is prejudiced in favor of old Dilworth, the nurse of us all, and it will be difficult to turn their attention from it; you know, too, that printers make large impressions of it, and afford it very cheap.

Now if you make an impression, unless it be very large, you can't afford it so cheap as they do, even if you get nothing for your copy[right]: if it is large the novelty of the book will make it lie upon your hands. If the impression is small, the greatness of your necessary price will be another reason why it will lie upon your hands. I once ventured an impression of Lowth and lost half the cost and all my labor. However, yours is a thing more generally wanted, and the risk may not be so great. I only suggest these facts for your caution. If you contract with your printers upon good terms, or take some other cautious plan, you may make advantage from the design. I wish well to the plan. Dilworth's grammatical plan is much worse than nothing. It holds up a scarecrow in the English language, and lads once lugged into it when young are afraid of all kinds of grammar all their days after. I will help you to what knowledge I can upon the subject you mention. But it appears to me at first thought that the names of places, except a few

of the most noted, will not be useful to be spelled out by children. I would prefer filling a few pages with detached pieces of American History, or some other history, or geography. However, this is by the bye. It is a happy thought, and it comes cheap.

Having now, I would suppose, reached the school summer holidays, Webster decided to set out on a journey, taking with him the plan of his proposed work and some pages that he had already written. Then, as now, embarking on a journey of this sort involved getting letters of introduction from people that one knew at home, to friends of theirs who might be useful in the places one was going to visit. Those people in turn gave one letters to other friends in other places. Webster adapted this system rather ingeniously to suit the two-fold purpose of his trip. First, he wanted to show his plan to academics, to obtain both their approval and the benefit of their suggestions for improvements. These men were members of the class for which Webster felt the greatest respect. He called them "the most eminent literary characters in America" and "literary gentlemen." (The idea of "literary ladies" did not suggest itself). When the spelling book was published, Webster was able to write that its plan had "the approval of some principal literary characters, not only in Connecticut, but in the States of New-York, New-Jersey, and Pennsylvania." This was true, but the sound was more impressive than the reality. He had never been outside those four states; within each of them he had managed to secure the approval of at least one "literary character."

The other people he needed to see were members of state legislatures, who might be able to arrange for copyright protection. What he wanted to show them were not just letters of introduction, but letters from the literary characters saying that his proposed work was a very good idea, and that it deserved to be protected by copyright.

On his first journey, the quest for copyright was a complete failure. The legislatures of New Jersey and Pennsylvania were not in session when Webster was there, and he arrived in Hartford when the Connecticut legislature was sitting, but too late in the session to obtain a hearing. The memorial that he wrote in Hartford, October 24, 1782, shows his intentions at that time, and what he then regarded as the

most significant improvements that he was going to make to Dilworth. It also shows that he was not suggesting a general copyright law for the benefit of all authors, but only a private act for his own benefit. I have reproduced some of the corrections that are in Webster's handwritten draft:

To the honorable the General Assembly of the State of Connecticut, the memorial of Noah Webster, late of Hartford in Connecticut & now of Goshen in Orange County & State of New York, humbly sheweth, that your memorialist has with great labor & expence compiled a work which he proposes to call *The American Instructor* in to be printed in two volumes; the first volume being a proper spelling-book, contains an amendment of those tables and lessons of short easy words in the Spelling-book of Mr. Dilworth, which were liable to exception & which are here rendered more plain for children — Instead of those proper names of places which belong to Great Britain, which we are incapable & unwilling to learn, & which are totally useless in America, your memorialist has inserted those words only which occur in the sacred or other writings, which are of obvious use & difficult pronunciation, together with the names of the Kingdoms of Europe, their capital Cities & the United States of America, the Counties, principal towns & rivers in each seperate State — with other improvements of obvious utility.

Instead of that long treatise of Grammar of Mr. Dilworth, which in the most material points, bears not the least analogy to the nature & idioms of the english language, he has inserted the last volume contains an abridgment of Grammar, extracted from the most approved modern writers upon that subject, with his own observations & some notes pointing out the most common & flagrant errors in speaking & writing, the whole being reduced to the Capacity of children. In addition to this he has inserted a few easy dialogues, calculated to attract the attention of children & which, experience has taught your memorialist are the best adapted to learn teach children to read with propriety, & almost the only method to break ill habits in pronunciation; & also some remarks upon the vices of mankind, designed to inspire youth with an abhorrence of vice & a love of virtue & religion. To close the whole is annexed a short account of the discovery of America — the time of the settlement of each State, with an epitome of their respective constitutions as established since the revolution — which is designed to diffuse a political knowledge of this grand confederation of republics among that class of people who have not access to more expensive means of information.

Your memorialist, ever ambitious to promote the interest of literature & the honor and dignity of the American empire, designs the above-mentioned work for the general use of benefit of youth in the United States. And in order to prevent spurious editions & to enable your memorialist to have the book under his own correction, & especially to secure to him the pecuniary advantages of his own productions to which he conceives himself solely entitled, your memorialist therefore humbly prays that this honorable Assembly would appoint a committee to examine into the merit and usefulness of the performance & upon their favorable report would, by a law passed for purpose [*sic*], vest in your memorialist & his assigns the exclusive right of printing, publishing, & vending the said *American Instructor* in the State of Connecticut for & during the term of thirteen years from the passing of said act, or for such other term of time as this honorable Court Assembly shall in their wisdom see proper. And your memorialist as in duty bound shall every pray.

Notice that Webster had already decided to separate the spelling book and the grammar, which Dilworth had combined into a single volume. A pupil did not need a grammar until he had finished with his spelling book, but a well-used spelling book had probably fallen to pieces. Though the War of Independence was not yet over, Webster's book was very definitely aimed at the schools of the new America, hence the British place names in Dilworth were to be removed, and American names substituted for them. To emphasize this major selling point, Webster had chosen the title *The American Instructor*, just as his great dictionary, 45 years later, would be *An American Dictionary of the English Language*.

One of the manuscript corrections shows that Webster instinctively used the word *learn* in the sense of *teach*, but knew it to be wrong. We shall see him use it again in the spelling book itself. It is also interesting to notice that Webster used the spellings *labor, honor, honorable* and *favorable*, in all of which Johnson would have had a *u*. That is not a sign that Webster was in favor of progressive spelling so early in his career. In fact, those spellings were already established in America and were used by Webster's tutor. Webster used them because he had been taught them, but he did not at this time approve of them, and he would say in the spelling book that Johnson's spelling was correct.

Though he made no progess on copyright at this time, Webster's account shows that he had rather more success in securing testimonials from the literary characters in New Jersey and Pennsylvania:

In Princeton, I waited on the Rev. Samuel Stanhope Smith, then professor of theology in Nassau Hall, and afterward president of that institution, who examined my manuscripts, recommended the works, and expressed his opinion in favor of copy-right laws. The following is a copy of his opinion.
"Mr. Noah Webster having shown to me a plan of reforming the spelling book of Mr. Dilworth, associating with it an abridgment of Mr. Lowth's Grammar and other articles of knowledge, very proper for young persons in the country; and having shown to me a part of the execution; I do conceive that he proposes many useful improvements in a book of that kind; and that he has executed with judgment that part which he has already finished. Every attempt of this nature undoubtedly merits the encouragement of the public; because it is by such attempts that systems of education are gradually perfected in every country, and the elements of knowledge rendered more easy to be acquired. Men of industry or of talents in any way, have a right to the property of their productions; and it encourages invention and improvement to secure it to them by certain laws, as has been practiced in European countries with advantage and success. And it is my opinion that it can be of no evil consequence to the state, and may be of benefit to it, to vest, by a law, the sole right of publishing and vending such works in the authors of them.

SAMUEL S. SMITH"

Princeton, Sept.27, 1782
This paper was afterward signed by Archibald Gamble, of the University in Philadelphia.[1]

In No. 7 of the *Memoir*, Webster recalled the same events:

On his way to Philadelphia, he called on the Rev. Samuel S. Smith, then Professor of Theology in Princeton College, and submitted to him the manuscript of his proposed elementary books. Professor Smith approved the plan and suggested some improvements, which were adopted.... In Philadelphia, N.W. obtained favorable opinions respecting his projected elementary book, and hints for improvements in the plan, which determined him to prosecute his purpose.

In his home state of Connecticut, Webster did not need letters of introduction, but he still wanted recommendations. We have already met the member of the legislature whose aid he intended to enlist, John Canfield, whose daughter had been a pupil at Webster's school in Sharon. The literary character Webster got to write to Canfield is also somebody we have met, Tapping Reeve, who had helped Webster when he was studying law in Litchfield. Reeve

qualified as a literary character because he was "formerly one of the Masters of the College at Princeton." At Webster's request, Reeve wrote to Canfield:

Litchfield, Octo.12, 1782

Sir,

Mr. Webster has this evening shewn me a plan of a new English Spelling-Book and Grammar; informing me, that you wished to know my opinion respecting it. I have perused it sufficiently to form an opinion on the general plan; it appears to be well conceived and judiciously executed. and I apprehend would better answer the purposes of its design, than any thing which I have hitherto seen. I think it well deserves the attention of the public; for (what is of no little importance) the general use of it will go very far towards demolishing all those odious distinctions occasioned by provincial dialects.

Yours, &c.
TAPPING REEVE.

Both Samuel Smith and Tapping Reeve say that Webster showed them "a plan" (which has not survived) of his proposed work; Smith also saw "a part of the execution.": "Professor Smith approved the plan and *suggested some improvements, which were adopted....* In Philadelphia, N.W. obtained favorable opinions respecting his projected elementary book, and *hints for improvements* in the plan, which determined him to prosecute his purpose." Webster, then, was sufficiently encouraged by the responses of Smith, Gamble, and Reeve to continue writing the spelling book: "I then returned to Goshen, and devoted the winter to a revision of my manuscripts, *and the introduction of some improvements, which had been suggested by gentlemen in Princeton and Philadelphia.*"[2] It is reasonabe to suppose that the changes to the spelling book introduced in the winter of 1782-83 were suggested to Webster by the literary gentlemen to whom he had shown his original plan. What were those changes?

In January 1783, Webster prepared fresh memorials to be submitted to the legislatures of Connecticut and New York. That for Connecticut he sent with a cover letter to John Canfield, enclosing Tapping Reeve's letter, a copy of Samuel Smith's "Opinion," and "a specimen of farther improvements in the work I have undertaken." Webster's cover letter

suggests that the advice he had received the previous year had led to a fundamental revision:

I find the plan I now propose will cost me still more labor; I have been indefatigable this winter; I have sacrificed ease, pleasure, and health to the execution of it, and have nearly completed it. But such close application is too much for my constitution. I must relinquish school or writing grammars. I shall not pursue the plan any further, unless it shall meet with public approbation, encouragement, and security. On the decision, therefore, of these two legislatures depends the further prosecution of my design....

"The plan I now propose" was clearly significantly different to the earlier plan, and involved a lot of extra work. By comparing the first part of the petition that he drafted early in 1783 to the legislature of New York with the memorial from 1782 *To the General Assembly of Connecticut* we can see how his plan had developed:

Memorial to Legislature

of N York Jany 18, 1783[3]

To the honorable the Senate & Assembly of the State of New York, the petition of Noah Webster of Goshen, in said state, humbly sheweth: that your petitioner has with great labor & expence composed a new American Spelling Book & Grammar, designed particularly for the youth in the American Empire. The Spelling-Book is framed upon a new and laborious plan; that of reducing the pronunciation of our language to an easy standard; which is effected by the help of figures. All the various sounds of our vowels, which amount to near twenty, are represented by five figures only, & the words arranged in such order that the sounds of the vowels in fifteen or twenty words are often expressed by a single figure — The different sounds of several letters & the silent letters, both vowels & consonants, are distinguished so as to be understood at a glance — with many other improvements, calculated to extirpate the improprieties & vulgarisms which were necessarily introduced by setlers [sic] from various parts of Europe; to reform the abuses & corruptions which, to an unhappy degree, tincture the conversation of the polite part of the Americans; to render the acquisition of the language easy both to American youth & to foreigners; & especially to render the pronunciation of it accurate & uniform by demolishing those odious distinctions of provincial dialects which are the subject of reciprocal ridicule in different States....

The lessons & exercises, designed to teach reading & speaking with propriety, are not left, as is common, without directions for their pronunciation, but the emphatical words are distinguished from the others, & an easy abridgment of the rules of speaking, prefixed to the work. The exercises are such as to inspire youth with a contempt of the unmanly vices of mankind & a love of virtue, patriotism, & religion. Your Petitioner, in pursuance of his own wishes to see America rendered as independent & illustrious in Letters as she is already in arms & civil policy, is collecting & has already collected a considerable part of the names of the counties, chief towns & rivers in the United States....

The "laborious plan ... of reducing the pronunciation of our language to an easy standard, which is effected by the help of figures" was totally new. New, that is, to Webster. Something very similar had been proposed by Thomas Sheridan 20 years earlier, and after that revised by others, particularly William Perry. Sheridan published *Lectures on Elocution* (1762), *Lectures on Reading* (1775), and a *Rhetorical Grammar & Dictionary* (1780). There are striking similarities between Webster's plan (as described in the Introduction to the spelling book) and Sheridan's ideas. Sheridan also hoped to eradicate regional dialects, though in England, not in America, and he anticipated both of Webster's criticisms of Dilworth's method of dividing words into syllables. Webster's earlier memorial, in 1782, had not hinted at any of those ideas, which strongly suggests that later in 1782 Webster had been directly or indirectly influenced by Sheridan.

In January 1783 he still planned just two volumes, a spelling book that was to be an improved version of Dilworth, and a Grammar. The latter was to be a simplification of Lowth's *Short Introduction to English Grammar*, "reduced to the capacity of children," with some exercises in reading, "such as to inspire youth with a contempt of the unmanly vices &c.," tacked on. Soon afterwards, the morally uplifting readings accumulated to such an extent that he decided to put them into a separate volume, a reader. By January 1783, the proposed title had changed from *The American Instructor* to *The American Spelling Book and Grammar*. Later in 1783, however, he discussed his plans with the president of Yale, Ezra Stiles, who suggested that the set of books should be called *A Grammatical Institute of the English Language*. Webster was too much in awe of the Reverend Dr. Stiles to disregard his advice, and the title page of the spelling book therefore described it as

A

Grammatical Institute

of the

ENGLISH LANGUAGE

comprising

An easy, concise, and systematic Method of

EDUCATION,

Designed for the use of English Schools

In AMERICA,

IN THREE PARTS.

PART I.

Containing,

A new and accurate Standard of Pronunciation

The name *Grammatical Institute* was unfortunate in more ways than one. As the title of a spelling book, it was thought (like Webster himself) to be unpleasingly pretentious. For the grammar, a simplification of Lowth, it had the additional disadvantage of being already in use. John Ash had some time before published *Grammatical Institutes, or an easy Introduction to Dr. Lowth's English Grammar.* Webster later regretted that he had taken Dr. Stiles' advice, but he felt unable to drop the name, because the title had been registered to secure copyright.

In examining the spelling book, I want to look first at certain *ideas*, and then at *content*. The main ideas are (1) the method of dividing words into syllables, both the abandonment of the Dyche/Dilworth "classical" rules and the writing of terminations such as *-tion* as a single syllable; (2) the indication of pronunciation, especially the use of numbers placed above the letters to distinguish the different sounds of vowels; and (3) spelling (in the sense of orthography). In each of these areas, I shall show that the same or very similar ideas had earlier been expressed, often more than once, by Thomas Sheridan. Sheridan's ideas were not always right, but, as Juliana Smith observed of Jack Horse, "at least they were all his own, and that is more than can be said of N.W.'s."

When we come to look at content, the aim is similar, but more limited: I want to show that Webster copied quite a lot of material from Dilworth and Fenning and elsewhere.

In Webster's favour, it must be said that his spelling book was in many ways significantly better than Dilworth's, and that the greater part of it was original. If we were concerned with its educational quality, we would have to examine the whole thing, but that is not our purpose. I concentrate on the part that Webster borrowed because I want to show you what he did, in the way of using ideas and materials that came from others. At this stage, we make no moral judgment. Later, when Webster himself defines a standard by his criticism of others, we can measure him against the same standard.

In the text of the *Institute*, p. 24, we see that "spelling" still meant dividing words into syllables:

SYLLABLES.

A Syllable is one letter or so many letters as can be pronounced at one impulse of the voice, as *a, hand.*

Spelling is the art of dividing words into their proper syllables in order to find their true pronunciation.

GENERAL RULE.

The best way of dividing words for children, is to divide them so as naturally to lead the learner into a right pronunciation*.

*This is Dr. Lowth's idea of spelling and the sentiment of several Literary Gentlemen in America, upon whose authority I have ventured to reject all particular rules and to divide the syllables just as the words are pronounced. See the Introduction.

Webster's definition of "syllable" is much better than Dilworth's, because Webster combined Dilworth's "one letter or more than one," with part of Lowth's definition "pronounced by a single impulse of the voice." The sentence in Lowth on "the best way of dividing words for children," says "The best and easiest rule, for dividing the syllables in spelling, is to divide them as they are naturally divided in a right pronunciation; without regard to the derivation of words...."

When Webster wrote, "See the Introduction," he was referring back to a passage that formed part of a sustained attack on Dilworth:

In order to render the sounds of words easy and natural for children, it was necessary to alter the customary method of dividing syllables. This is done with deliberation and diffidence; but with full conviction that both necessity and utility demanded an alteration. Besides this, I am supported by the authority of some of the most eminent literary characters in America, and the best English Grammarians. Mr. Dilworth has endeavoured to establish general and arbitrary rules for division of syllables, and has divided his tables according to them, without any regard to the proper sound of words, which is the

only just rule in this matter. This single circumstance has led learners into more errours in articulation* than all other causes whatever. [Webster's footnote: *"A good articulation consists in giving every letter in a syllable its due proportion of sound, according to the most approved custom of pronouncing it; and in making such a distinction, between the syllables, of which words are composed, that the ear shall, without difficulty acknowledge their number, and perceive at once to which syllable each letter belongs. Where these points are not observed, the articulation is proportionally defective." Sheridan on Elocution Lect.2.]

The words *cluster, habit*, Mr. Dilworth divides *cluster ha-bit*; acording [sic] to which, a child naturally pronounces the vowel in the first syllable, long. But the vowels are all short; the accent is on the first syllable and not only so, but particularly on the consonants *s* and *b*. Here then, according to his plan of dividing syllables, the accent, which is on the first syllable, falls upon a consonant that is joined to the last. Into such monstrous absurdities was he driven by his zeal to establish general rules. In order to obviate this difficulty, he has placed a double accent thus, *clu"ster, ha"bit*. If by double accent be meant a union of two accents, this is not true, for there can be but one. If by double accent be meant, the sound of the consonant repeated — that is, the sound joined to the first and to the last also, that is not true: For if fifty consonants of the same kind were joined together, no more than one could be sounded. I appeal to the most accurate ear, whether, in ordinary pronunciation, there be the least difference in the sounds of these words, *hab-it, hab-bit, habb-bbit*: And if there be not, then double accent is a term without meaning, and the use of it is only an additional circumstance to puzzle children. Had Mr. Dilworth attended to the foregoing rule, he could not have blundered into so gross an errour. But this is not so surprising when we reflect that the authors of dictionaries have made the same mistake. I do not recollect to have seen more than one dictionary, that takes notice of the important distinction between an accented vowel and an accented consonant. Let words be divided as they ought to be pronounced *clus-ter, hab-it, nos-tril, bish-op*, and the smallest child cannot mistake a just pronunciation. The only reason why we divide syllables for children, is to lead them to the proper pronunciation of words; and the easiest and most natural way to do this, in spite of the most venerable authority, must eternally be the best way.

Mr. Dilworth tells us that *ti* before a vowel, sound like *si* or *sh*; but there are so many exceptions to this rule, that it would better have been omitted. There are several hundred words, in which *ti* before a vowel retain their proper original sound. But they do not sound like *si*, for then *nation, motion*, must be pronounced *na-si-on, mo-si-on*. The proper sound of *ti* is that of *sh*. Then if we make three syllables of these

words, they will stand thus, *na-sh-on, mo-sh-on*, and we have one syllable without any vowel and consequently without any sound. But they are not words of three syllables and are not considered as such, except in the old version of the psalms. However they might be pronounced formerly, *tion, tia*, &c. are now by universal consent pronounced in one syllable and so are written by all the poets. In compliance with universal custom and the settled propriety of the language, I have ventured to consider them as one syllable.

That passage contains the definitive statement of the "Webster" system of syllable division, which differs from Dilworth's system in two respects. First, a short vowel is to be indicated by joining the succeeding consonant to it, rather than making the consonant part of the following syllable—*hab-it* rather than *ha-bit*. Second, *-tion* constitutes a single syllable. Notice that Webster's footnote in the above passage is a quotation from Sheridan's *Lectures on Elocution*; Webster would later write, "I never heard the names of Sheridan, Kenrick or Perry till I had prepared my copy for the press, and never consulted their work till I had published my first edition."

Webster claimed that his anti-Dilworth position on the division of syllables was "supported by the authority of some of the most eminent literary characters in America, and the best English Grammarians...." The American literary characters he was referring to were the ones he had visited on his journey in 1782; the the only English Grammarian identified in the text is Lowth, but we know that Webster had also read Fenning, and that Fenning had abandoned the Dyche/Dilworth Rules before Webster did so. Compare Fenning's table heading, "Words divided as they ought to be pronounced," with Webster's sentence in the passage quoted above: "Let words be *divided as they ought to be pronounced*." Furthermore, two of Webster's four examples, *clus-ter* and *nostril*, were in Fenning's table. Webster acknowledged none of this. He wanted to appear to be a courageous innovator, and he therefore compared himself only with Dilworth.

So that he would appear in a yet more favourable light, Webster made Dilworth out to have been even more of an idiot than he really was. Consider, for example, the passage in which Webster explored the possible meanings of

"double accent." He said, "[It is] a term with-out meaning, and the use of it is only an addi-tional circumstance to puzzle children." In fact, as I mentioned in an earlier chapter, Dilworth never puzzled children in this way. He *used* the mark ("), *but he did not call it a double accent.* Nor did he suggest that it indicated either an ac-cent repeated or the consonant repeated. He said the mark showed that the pronunciation of the word would be better shown if the fol-lowing consonant were joined to the preceding syllable, which is exactly what Webster said — but Webster went further. Because he wanted to indicate only pronunciation, he *did* join the consonant to the preceding syllable. In this matter, that is the only difference between them. Actually, in many of these words, dou-bling the consonant would have exactly the same effect on the pronunciation as moving the consonant to the first syllable; the mark (") in *ha"bit* indicates that the word is pronounced with a short *a*, like *rab-bit*, rather than with a long *a*, like *ra-bid*. More simply, the mark indi-cates that the preceding vowel is short.

"If by double accent be meant, the sound of the consonant repeated — that is, the sound joined to the first [syllable] and to the last also, that is not true: For if fifty consonants of the same kind were joined together, no more than one could be sounded." That little sneer caused Webster some trouble later on. An astute critic compared the passage with *Webster's own words* in the first edition of his Grammar: "If the fol-lowing syllable begin with a vowel, we cannot avoid joining to it the last consonant, which is the same as doubling the consonant." "What a curious contrast!" the critic said.

Since Dyche, who invented the mark, *did* call it a double accent, Webster's using the same expression suggests that he had seen Dyche's spelling book as well as Dilworth's and Fen-ning's. This is certainly possible; copies of Dyche printed in London would have been shipped to America, and there was an edition of Dyche printed in New York in 1750.

In August 1783, before the spelling book was published, Webster sent some pages from it to the Reverend Elizur Goodrich (father of Chauncey and Elizur) asking him to show them to the members of the Corporation of Yale at commencement. Not surprisingly, those gen-tlemen were too busy to pay any attention, and

Goodrich sought to make up for this, and for the lateness of his reply, by sending 13 pages of comment on Webster's material. These in-cluded the following paragraph:

Mr. Dilworth followed the rules of spelling long es-tablished: He only improved on a system that had been in being for ages before he was born, and in that method, the double accent you so much cen-sure was a real advantage. Mr. Dilworth does not call it an accent, but only explains the mark, nor was he, as I conceive, the proposer or the author of it. Mr. Dyche had before introduced it and called it a dou-ble accent, whether with propriety I inquire not. He used it as a mark to teach, when the stress of the voice upon the syllable draws the consonant to the preceding vowel, which by the rule of spelling ought to be separated from it, and as an expedient to oblige both the favourers of the old and new method, who by the help of it might use his book according to their several notions. Your zeal against this accent, in my opinion, is rather intemperate....

That concise and accurate summary shows that Dyche's book was familiar in Yale, where Web-ster had been educated.

For another "curious contrast," let us look ahead to Webster's *Compendious Dictionary* of 1806. Consider how the word *logic* should be divided. Webster's anti-Dilworth spelling book rule tells him to make the *g* part of the first syl-lable, to show that the *o* is short; on the other hand, that would suggest that the first syllable is pronounced like the word *log*, with a hard *g*. To show that the *g* is soft, the second syllable, *-gic*, must be kept together. This is just the sort of dilemma that Dyche had tried to solve by means of the double accent, and *in the dictio-nary Webster adopted the same solution.* Here is a sentence from his "Directions for the Pro-nunciation of Words":

A double accent thus, *lo"gic, a"cid, ma"gic,* denotes that the sound of the succeeding consonant belongs to the first syllable ....

Webster's scornful words from the spelling book apply more aptly to that passage from his own dictionary (which *did* call the mark a "double accent") than to Dilworth's *New Guide* (which did not):

Here then, the accent, which is on the first syllable, falls upon a consonant that is joined to the last.... In order to obviate this difficulty, he has placed a dou-ble accent thus, *lo"gic, a"cid.* If by double accent be meant a union of two accents, this is not true, for there can be but one.... double accent is a term

without meaning, and the use of it is only an additional circumstance to puzzle children.

In the matter of *-tion* and similar terminations, Webster was probably right when he suggested that there had been a change in pronunciation, and he was certainly right that a 1783 spelling book should reflect the speech of 1783 and not that of 1740 (Dilworth) or 1707 (Dyche). On the other hand, he once again misrepresented Dilworth, who did *not* say that *motion* should be pronounced *mo-sh-on* in three syllables. What Dilworth said was that *ti* before a vowel was either pronounced *si* (and motion would then be a word of three syllables) or *sh* (when motion would have two syllables). Fenning, as we have seen, was apparently aware of a dilemma in this area, but he did not explain it clearly, and he was not bold enough to resolve it. Sheridan, however, spelled out very clearly both of Webster's objections to Dilworth's method of dividing syllables:

[Children] should be taught to take in all the letters into the same syllable, which are kept together in utterance; which, surely, is the most obvious and rational method. Thus the words *habit, widow, rather*, should not be divided in the usual way, *ha-bit, wi-dow, ra-ther*; but *hab-it, wid-ow, rath-er*. This rule of dividing syllables is so plain and manifestly proper, that nothing but a total neglect in this, as in almost all other articles, of preserving any analogy between writing and speech, could have prevented its taking place.
There is another very improper division of syllables, in general use, in all words where the letter *i* precedes a vowel in the same syllable; such as *question, bestial, region*; or the vowel *e*, as in *righteous, courteous*. For, in all instances of this sort, these vowels coalesce in English, and form diphthongs, so as to make but one syllable. Whereas in the usual mode of dividing them they seem to form two. Thus, instead of *ques-ti-on, bes-ti-al, righ-te-ous*, they ought to be divided into two syllables only, as *ques-tion, bes-tial, righ-teous*, in the manner in which they are pronounced, and always used in metre.[4]

Here we have two consecutive paragraphs in Sheridan that express the same objections to Dilworth's methods of dividing syllables, and in the same order, as Webster's consecutive paragraphs. Both Sheridan and Webster end with an observation to the effect that the terminations such as *-tion* are always "pronounced in one syllable and so are written by all the poets."

Sheridan had made the same points in other books, as well, published both before and after *The Art of Reading*, but all earlier than Webster's *Grammatical Institute*. The one Webster quoted from was *Lectures on Elocution*. This was published in a volume which also contained *Some other Tracts relative to those Subjects*. One of the "tracts" was entitled *A Dissertation on the Causes of the Difficulties Which occur, in learning the English Tongue, With a Scheme for publishing An English Grammar and Dictionary, upon a Plan entirely New*. In the *Dissertation*, Sheridan promised that, in his planned grammar,

Our manner of uniting syllables so as to form words shall be considered, and of distinguishing those syllables from each other in pronunciation, shewing what letters are kept together, and what separated in utterance; often erroneously marked in our grammars and spelling books, whose authors have divided their syllables, by rules that have no reference to pronunciation.[5]

In 1780, Sheridan published the promised dictionary and grammar. Its title describes it as "A Complete Dictionary of the English Language, One main Object of which, is, to establish a plain and permanent Standard of Pronunciation. To which is prefixed A Rhetorical Grammar." In it, as one might expect, the *-tion* and similar terminations are consistently shown as one syllable. Also, in the dictionary,

The syllables of the words are divided according to the mode of pronouncing them; that is, all letters which are united in utterance in the same syllable, are here kept together also in writing, and separated from the rest; which certainly is the natural division, though it be contrary to the fantastic mode followed in our spelling-books and grammars.[6]

In Sheridan's dictionary, the pronunciation of each word is indicated by a combination of division into syllables, marking accents, respelling, and putting little numbers over the vowels to distinguish their different sounds. Sheridan's manner of dividing the syllables is that which Webster later adopted.

In the passage quoted above from Webster's Introduction, there is the sentence "I do not recollect to have seen more than one dictionary, that takes notice of the important distinction between an accented vowel and an accented consonant." Sheridan's Dictionary certainly

takes notice of that distinction. Again, this is anticipated in the *Dissertation:*

Under this head will be laid open the nature and use of our accent, that grand master-key to the pronunciation of our tongue, whose nature has hitherto been little understood, or grossly mistaken. This is evidently shewn in our dictionaries, where the accent is invariably placed over the vowel of the accented syllable. Now nothing is of more moment in our tongue than to know when the accent is on the vowel, and when on the consonant. By placing it constantly over the vowel, there is a rule of error established, which must infallibly mislead provincials and foreigners, in the pronunciation of all words, where the accent ought to be on the consonant.... [7]

Sheridan explained it again in the *Rhetorical Grammar:*

The great distinction of our accent depends upon its seat; which may be either upon a vowel, or a consonant. Upon a vowel, as in the words, glóry, fáther, hóly. Upon a consonant, as in the words hab'it, bor'row, bat'tle. When the accent is on the vowel, the syllable is long; because the accent is made by dwelling upon the vowel. When it is on the consonant, the syllable is short; because the accent is made by passing rapidly over the vowel, and giving a smart stroke of the voice to the following consonant.

Webster observed in his Introduction that "The British writers remark it as one of the follies of their nation, that they have attended more to the study of ancient and foreign languages, than to the improvement of their own"; Sheridan made that remark in his *Lectures on Elocution*. What follows in Webster's Introduction is scarcely more than a précis of Sheridan's *Dissertation*.

Webster then claimed to have devised a system for numbering the different vowel sounds, as a means of promoting uniformity of pronunciation, which is exactly what Sheridan devised, and he set it out both in the *Dissertation* and in his *Grammar and Dictionary*. Both Webster and Sheridan demonstrated the necessity for it by what Webster called a "Scheme, Exhibiting the deficiency, redundancy, and irregularities in the orthography of the English Language." This showed, first for vowels and then for consonants, that the same letter can have several different sounds, and that the same sound can be represented by different letters or combinations of letters. In some respects Webster's scheme is an improvement on Sheridan's, but the similarity of arrangement, and the

number of words that are the same in both, are such that it is impossible to believe that Webster was not using Sheridan's system as his starting point.

Here are two equivalent tables:

Sheridan's:

	First	Second	Third	Fourth	Fifth
A	hat	hate	hall		
E	bet	there	here	her	
I	fit	bite	field	stir	birth
O	not	note	prove	love	
U	cub	bush	cube	busy	

Webster's:

A	fate	hat	halt	ask	
E	here	let	there	her	
I	time	tin	fir	fatigue	
O	note	not	prove	love	gone
U	cube	tub	bush	busy	

Here every vowel has four or five different sounds.

Sheridan says of his first table: "every vowel stands as a mark for three, four, or five different sounds." Webster altered "stands as a mark for" to "has." In the two tables, more than half the words are the same — a proportion which is surely too high to be chance.

In the next table, a similar proportion of the words are identical, but what is more striking is that the *sets of letters being compared* are the same, and they are *arranged in the same order*: -ere, -ove, -ou-, -o-, -oo-, -ea-:

Sheridan:

Different sounds marked exactly in the same way.

There	here		
Grove	prove	love	
Fourth	youth	mouth	tough
Who	go		
Door	noon	blood	
Bear	hear	head	heart

Webster:

There	here		
Rove	move	dove	
Four	your	lour	rough
Who	go		
Door	poor	blood	stood
bear	hear	head	heart

Here different sounds are marked in the same way.

In the following section, as Sheridan described it, "the same sound is marked in four, five, six, seven or eight different ways." Webster's description is "the same sound often

xpressed in six, seven or eight different ways." Here are two of their lists to compare:

Sheridan	Webster	Sheridan	Webster
2d o	1st or long o	3d u	1st or long u
o go	o go	u cube	u cube
ow blow	ow blow	eu feud	eu feud
ew shew	oe foe	ew new	ew new
oe foe	ou four	ue clue	ue true
ou fourth	oo door	iew view	ieu lieu
oo door	oa groan		eau beauty
oa groan			iew view
			ui fruit

In the other lists, fewer of the words are the same, but once again Webster dealt with the same vowel sounds as Sheridan, and arranged them in almost the same order.

Next, both went on to consonants. Here, Sheridan made several mistakes that Webster corrected. To demonstrate the letter *x* sounding like *z*, Sheridan gave the example *Xerxes*— a bad choice because it has two *x*s in it, one of which does not sound like *z*. Webster substituted *Xenophon*.

Sheridan treated the *sh* sound in *social* and *nation* as a sound of the letter *c* or *t*, which is only right if you sound the *i*, as in the word *negotiate*. Webster attributed the *sh* sound to the combinations *ci* and *ti*. Sheridan wrote:

C has three sounds	k	care
	s	cease
	sh	social
F has its sound marked by two	Ph	Philip
different combinations of	gh	laugh
letters		

            &c. &c.

Webster's corresponding passage:

C has 2 sounds	k	as in case
	s	cellar
F is represented	ph	Philip
by 2 other com-	gh	laugh
binations of letters		

            &c. &c.

In the consonants, the sounds that Sheridan dealt with were those of *C, F, G, J, S, T, X, Th, Ch* and *Gh*. Webster chose many different words, but his list of sounds was the same, except that he omitted *Gh* and substituted *ti* and *ci* sounding like *sh*. Sheridan wrote, "This is but

a small specimen, of the irregularities to be found in the state of our written language." And so it is, which makes it the more striking that Webster showed almost exactly the same specimen, and in the same arrangement.

Sheridan set out his "Scheme of the Vowels"—giving numbers to the different sounds of the vowels—several times, in very similar forms. In 1762, it was in the *Dissertation* included with his *Lectures on Elocution*. It reappeared in Lecture I of *The Art of Reading*, published in 1775, and again in the *Rhetorical Grammar & Dictionary*, published in 1780. The tables showing the same letters representing different sounds and the same sounds represented by different letters were in the *Dissertation*, and again, with some variations, in the *Rhetorical Grammar & Dictionary*. All the quotations set out above are from the *Dissertation*, which we know Webster to have seen because he quoted a passage from *Lectures on Elocution* in the same volume. The comparison shows beyond a doubt that Webster based his scheme on Sheridan. Quite apart from the large number of words that are the same, if Webster had devised it himself, he would not have reproduced exactly the content, order, and arrangement found in Sheridan's *Dissertation*.

In the *Dissertation*, Sheridan announced his intention to publish a *Rhetorical Grammar and Dictionary* based on his ideas, but it took him nearly twenty years to do it. In the meanwhile, William Perry published, in 1775, *The Royal Standard English Dictionary*, in which he criticized and improved Sheridan's scheme. The most striking defect in Sheridan's table was that it left out what was known as the Italian sound of a, as heard in *art, ask, charm,* and *father*. Perry corrected this defect. Another alteration he made was to change the order of the columns in the table, so that the first sound of each of the vowels became the long sound, corresponding to the name of the letter; Sheridan had put the short sounds of the vowels (*hat, bet, fit, not,* and *cub*) in the first column. Another innovation in Perry's Dictionary was the printing of silent letters in italics, as in "Dum*b*, Fe*a*ther, *H*our, Su*b*tle." In 1776, Perry published a spelling book, *The Only Sure Guide to the English Tongue*, subtitled *A New Pronouncing Spelling Book*, which claimed to be "Upon the same Plan as The Royal Standard English Dictionary." In Perry's

spelling book, therefore, silent letters were printed in italics. Also, Perry stressed that terminations such as *-tion, -cial, -cient, -tious* and *-geous* were pronounced as one syllable. In *The Only Sure Guide*, "mo'tion" was in the list of "Dysyllables accented on the First Syllable."

Webster certainly used Sheridan's scheme, rather than Perry's, as his basis, and there is no direct evidence to show that he had seen either Perry's dictionary or his spelling book before the publication of the *Grammatical Institute*, but he may have done so. Webster, also, moved the long sound of the vowels to the first column in his table, put in the Italian sound of *a*, and printed silent letters in italics. There are other innovations in Perry's spelling book, such as marks used to distinguish between the two sounds of *s*, of *g*, of *ch*, and of *th*, which are not to be found in Webster.

Both Sheridan and Webster thought that their systems of numbering the different vowel sounds would lead to uniformity of pronunciation. As Webster put it, "Such a standard, universally used in schools, would in time, demolish those odious distinctions of provincial dialects, which are the objects of reciprocal ridicule in the United States." He was quite wrong. It is not possible to eradicate accents in this way. The reason is that children come to school, and to reading, with their accents already in place, and those accents are transparent and consistent. They are transparent, that is to say, from the inside. I speak, myself, with the accent of my own time, place, and education (upper-middle-class England; Eton and Cambridge in the '50s and '60s) but I am not aware, when I speak, that I have any accent at all. If two people with the same accent have a conversation, neither is aware of accent. If two people with different accents have a conversation, each is aware of the accent of the other, but not of his own. The problem of consistency I can demonstrate by an example. If I were to ask a person from the north of England what he was wearing on his head, he would reply ,"A hat," but it would sound to me like "A hut." It would be no use my trying to "correct" his pronunciation by giving him a book saying that "hat" has the second sound of *a* as in *cat*, because he already knew that, and that is exactly how he spoke the word. For him, "*cat*" is pronounced in the way I would say "*cut*"—

"the fut cut sut on the mut"—and any other way of speaking, for him, would be affected and odd.

In the same way that Webster's spelling book could not change existing accents, Dilworth's would not corrupt an existing pronunciation. Because children learn to speak first and to read afterwards, it makes little practical difference whether the syllables in their spelling books are divided in Dilworth's manner or in Webster's. The words whose appearance in print they first learn to recognize are simple words whose sound they already know. They will not pronounce *ha-bit* with a long *a*, or *no-stril* with a long *o*, because they know the words. More complicated words are then made up from smaller pieces that have become familiar. The purpose of dividing longer words is to present them to the eye as a series of recognisable pieces.

To a student of the history of English, the value of Sheridan's and Webster's tables of words is that they show changes in the pronunciation of particular words. Webster, for example, gave five sounds of the letter *o*, exemplified by the words *note, not, prove, love*, and *gone*. I would pronounce *gone* with a short *o*—the same vowel sound as *not*—but for Webster it had the sound of the third or broad *a*, rhyming with *hall, cause, law, groat* and *ought*. A groat was an old English fourpenny coin, which I would pronounce to rhyme with "boat," but Webster did not—in his big dictionary, the pronunciation is indicated by the respelling *grawt*. To me, that sounds Scottish. Such changes in pronunciation over time can corrupt the rhymes in poetry, as in Philip Freneau's 1792 poem commenting satirically on the ostentation of the presidential coach; to maintain the rhyme, one must adopt Webster's pronunciation of "groat":

No matter—(said Samuel) a coach shall be bought—
Tho' puppies may chatter, I care not a groat—
Around it a score of devices shall shine
And mottoes, and emblems—to prove it is mine....[8]

I quoted above an assertion by Webster that he had never heard the names of Sheridan, Kenrick, or Perry, till he had prepared his spelling book for the press. A similar statement, in an earlier letter to the press, was in these terms:

I was wholly unacquainted with those authors [Sheridan, Perry and Kenrick] till after I had published the first edition. Entick's Pocket Dictionary was the only work of the kind that I consulted while I was compiling it.[9]

We have seen what was in Sheridan and Perry; that sentence from Webster's letter prompts us to look at Entick also. Entick's *New Spelling Dictionary* contains "A Grammatical Introduction to the English Tongue," which gives rules for dividing words into syllables, including the following:

division of words into syllables is called *spelling*, and may be reduced to the following rules....
3. When two or three consonants come together in the middle of a word, if they are such as can begin a word, they go together with the latter syllable, otherwise they must be parted; or they may be divided in such manner as may best agree with their most easy and distinct sounds in pronunciation, as *re-store, be-speak, fa-ble, de-spise*: in all which kinds of words, the middle consonants sound, and are therefore best joined, with the latter syllable. But in *mas-ter, whis-per, sis-ter, pub-lish*, the very same consonants must be parted, being naturally pronounced in that manner.

Entick practiced what he preached. In his dictionary, Webster's examples, *clus'ter, hab'it, nos'tril,* and *bish'op*, are all thus divided. We have earlier seen that Bailey had introduced the same system into his dictionary in 1737; the only difference between Bailey and Entick is that for accented vowels, Bailey (who was using capital letters) put the accent after the vowel, where Entick put it over the vowel. In Bailey, we find *BI'NARY* and *BISH'OP*; in Entick, *Bínary* and *Bish'op*.

It begins to look as though Dilworth and his disciples were the only people left who did *not* recommend "Webster's method" of dividing syllables.

The next subject I want to explore is spelling. Over the years, Webster was engaged in many disputes over spelling, and he is often given the credit (or blamed) for the fact that Americans spell the way they do, and in a manner different to the English. That is something we shall examine in detail later on. Looking at the different battles — American v. British, Webster v. Johnson, Webster v.Cobb, Webster v. Worcester — it is easy to imagine that they are all parts of the same war — that Webster consis-

tently represented American spelling, and that his various enemies, Johnson, Cobb and Worcester, represented British. As we shall see, that is not just an oversimplification; it is a serious distortion.

We saw in the previous chapter how Johnson sought to turn back the orthographical clock and undo some of the spelling reforms that were finding favour before the publication of his dictionary. Sheridan took the same view with regard to orthoepy. He wanted to restore the pronunciation of the time of Queen Anne, roughly the first decade of the eighteenth century (and ten years before he was born). English, in his view, should be spoken as it had been spoken by his godfather, Dean Swift:

There was a time, and that at no very distant period, which may be called the Augustan age of England, I mean during the reign of Queen Anne, when English was the language spoken at court; and when the same attention was paid to propriety of pronunciation, as that of French at the Court of Versailles ... But upon the accession of a foreign family to the throne, ... the English language suffered much by being banished the court, to make room for the French. From that time the regard formerly paid to pronunciation has been gradually declining. ... It is to be wished, that such a standard had been established at the period before mentioned, as it is probable, that English was then spoken at its highest state of perfection. Nor is it yet too late to recover it in that very state.[10]

With regard to spelling, Sheridan explained how desirable it would be to have a system in which there was one sound for each letter, and one letter for each sound — a phonetic system — because then there would be no difficulty in knowing how to pronounce words that one had only seen in writing. He too realised, however, that such a system was impossible unless the alphabet were reformed:

it was warmly contended that words ought to be spelt as they are pronounced; and no doubt this opinion might have been supported by such unanswerable reasons, that notwithstanding the power of custom, the force of fashion, and the efforts of pedantry against it, it must in time have made way, and our spelling would have been gradually reformed and moulded by that rule, were there not an unseen obstacle in the way arising from a defective alphabet. The thing was indeed impracticable....[11]

Since a phonetic system could not be established, Sheridan used Johnson's spelling. Johnson's conservative tastes exactly matched his own:

Dr. Johnson's spelling has been implicitly followed in the present Dictionary. It scarce deviates from that used by the writers in Queen Anne's reign; as he has judiciously rejected several innovations attempted since that time by vain and pragmatical writers, who, from an affectation of singularity, have attempted to introduce changes, upon principles which will by no means stand the test of examination: and it might indisputably be proved, that no alterations in that respect, productive of any real benefit, can be made, without new moulding our alphabet, and making a considerable addition to its characters; a point utterly impracticable.[12]

With regard to pronunciation, the Author has laid his reasons before the public of his having followed that which was established at the same æra. Thus, in both these articles, has he in this one work endeavoured to fix two anchors to our floating language, in order to keep it steady against the gales of caprice, and current of fashion.

Having earlier seen the extent to which Webster followed Sheridan, we should not be surprised that he too, in the first edition of his spelling book, favored Johnson's spelling:

In spelling and accenting, I have generally made Dr. Johnson's dictionary my guide; as in point of orthography this seems to be the most approved authority in the language.*

---

*There seems to be an inclination in some writers to alter the spelling of words, by expunging the superfluous letters. This appears to arise from the same pedantic fondness for singularity that prompts to new fashions of pronunciation. Thus they write the words favour, honour &c. without u. But it happens unluckily that, in these words, they have dropped the wrong letter — they have omitted the letter that is sounded and retained the one that is silent; for the words are pronounced onur, favur. They may with the same propriety drop u in pious, virtuous, &c. and a thousand other letters. Thus e is omitted in judgment; which is the most necessary letter in the word; it being that alone which softens g. Into these and many other absurdities are people led by a rage for singularity. Our language is indeed pronounced very differently from the spelling; that is an inconvenience we regret, but cannot remedy. To attempt a progressive change, is idle; it will keep the language in perpetual fluctuation without an effectual amendment. And to attempt a total change at once, is equally idle and extravagant, as it would render the language unintelligible. We may better labour to speak our language with propriety and elegance, as we have it, than attempt a reformation without advantage or probability of success.

Even before the Revolution, the -*or* for -*our* termination was more widely used in America than in Britain. We have seen Webster using it in his Memorials to state legislatures in 1782 and 1783, and it is to be found in an edition of Dilworth's *New Guide* published in Boston in 1772. That, indeed, may be one of the reasons why Webster was against it, in addition to his respect for the literary gentlemen who tended not to favour innovation. When one considers the amount of heat generated by his later very different opinions on spelling, it is curious that Webster started, in 1783, from a position of conservative Johnsonian orthodoxy. We shall see how his views changed over the following sixty years.

Those introductory parts of Webster's spelling book were aimed at teachers. The part directed to children starts, like Dyche's and Dilworth's, with the alphabet in Roman and Italic letters. Webster leaves out Gothic, but includes the names of the letters. Even in 1783, the American book called the last letter of the alphabet "zee," where Dyche and Dilworth both called it "zed."

One of Sheridan's peculiar convictions was that the letters *y* and *w* are pronounced *ee* and *oo*. Perry exposed the fallacy by pointing out that if it were right, the words *ye* and *woo* would be pronounced *ee-ee* and *oo-oo*. Webster, however, was under the influence of Sheridan, and therefore instructed "every Master and Mistress" who used his spelling book that

A LETTER is a mark or character used to form words.

There are twenty-six of these letters or characters in English.

Seven of the letters, viz. a,e,i,o,u,y,w, are vowels: The others are called consonants *

*The letters y and w are sometimes ranked among the consonants; but very erroneously. Neither of them has any property of a consonant; tho' both have every property of a vowel....

Because of that view of *y*, Webster's Table I has one more column than Dyche's or Dilworth's. Where they have

  ba be bi bo bu   ab eb ib ob ub

Webster has

  ba be bi bo bu by   ab eb ib ob ub

and so on. When he gets to three letters, however, Webster has had enough of *y* as a vowel,

and his Lessons V and VI are selected from Dilworth's Table III without addition or alteration,
just as Dilworth had taken his table from
Dyche:

bla	ble	bli	blo	blu		bra	bre	br	bro	bru
cla	cle	cli	clo	clu		cra	cre	cri	cro	cru
pla	ple	pli	plo	plu		pra	pre	pri	pro	pru
sla	sle	sli	slo	slu		gra	gre	gri	gro	gru
sha	she	shi	sho	shu		pha	phe	phi	pho	phu

Webster's Table I contains altogether 182
syllables of two and three letters. Of these 170
are the same as those in Dyche and in Dilworth,
the other 12 being all in the *y* column, from *by,
cy, dy* to *ry, ty,* and *wy*. In three-letter syllables,
Fenning had made a very similar selection from
Dilworth, adding a footnote of his own devis-
ing: "* Let the child be taught to pronounce *ce*
the same as *se,* and *ci* the same as *si*." Webster
copied Fenning's footnote, though once again
adding *y*: "A child should be taught to pronounce *ce, ci, cy,* like *se, si, sy*."

He next devotes three pages to words of one
syllable, starting with three letters, and increasing to four and then to five letters. These
too are arranged in regular columns, with the
instruction "The following columns are to be
read downwards: All the words in the same column being sounded alike." Table II contains
words of three and four letters, divided into
eight lessons. In those lessons there are altogether 263 words, of which only 15 are not in
Dilworth's tables, though Dilworth did not put
them in columns because some of his lists were
longer or shorter. Thus Webster's first lesson in
Table II contains the following words:

Bag	big	bog	bug	den	cap	bit	dot
cag	dig	dog	dug	hen	gap	cit	got
fag	fig	fog	hug	men	lap	hit	hot
gag	jig	hog	lug	pen	map	pit	jot
hag	pig	jog	mug	ten	rap	sit	lot
rag	wig	log	tug	wen	tap	wit	not

The only words in that lesson and not in Dilworth are *cit* and *wen,* neither of which could
be considered essential to a child just learning
to read. A *cit* is a derogatory term for a city-
dweller, and a *wen* is something like a wart. For
each of those sets of like-sounding words, Dilworth's list had at least six in it, Webster's
columns being six words high. Where Dilworth's lists contained additional words such

as *nag, tag, gig, jug* and *rug,* Webster left them
out, because there was no room for them in six-
word columns. Webster's later columns contained fewer words so he could use some of Dilworth's shorter lists. Lists having less than four
words, such as *beg, leg,* he did not use.

Webster's Table III has three lessons on five
letter words; there are 98 words in the three
lessons, and all but four of them are in Dilworth.

Webster's eleven lessons, therefore, contain
altogether 361 words, of which all but 19 were
in Dilworth, the only difference being that Dilworth had them in amorphous masses, whereas
Webster arranged them in neat columns with
the number of the vowel sound at the head of
each column as an aid to correct pronunciation. To avoid mispronunciation of particular
words, he used asterisks and footnotes, for example warning the reader of Table II against
pronouncing *lest, nest* and *jest* as *leest, neest,*
and *jeest*.

Most of the 19 words not in Dilworth are in
Dyche. Dyche's tables are even less organised
than Dilworth's, but similar lists of rhyming
words are there — indeed, it was from Dyche
that Dilworth got them — and Dyche's lists include *cit* and *wen,* and all but three of Webster's
words that were not in Dilworth. Those three
are *grog, bile,* and *rinse*. The first two are very
properly omitted from a book intended for
young children (and "grog" did not exist by that
name when Dyche wrote his spelling book), and
rinse did not belong in Webster's column anyway, where the other words were *mince, since*
and *prince*.

This cannot be regarded as conclusive proof
that Webster used Dyche as well as Dilworth,
not least because there were many different editions of Dilworth, and their word lists are not
always the same. Also, if Dyche included all the
words he could think of with a particular termination, then whatever words of that termination Webster decided to put in his columns
would be in Dyche's lists. On the other hand, *cit*
and *wen* are such unsuitable words in this context that Dilworth or his editor probably left
them out on purpose, and Webster would not
have been likely to have chosen them independently.

A difference in arrangement between Webster and Dilworth has already become apparent

at this stage in the book. Dilworth, as soon as he had his readers spelling out words, started stringing those words together into sentences, whereas Webster leaves sentences to the end. Dilworth's first sentence, "No man may put off the law of God," is on page 15; Webster copied the sentence, but it does not appear until his page 101. This was a mistake he would correct in a later edition; readers preferred to have the indigestible stodge of words leavened by occasional sentences — even the rather serious sentences favoured by Dilworth. We, however, are making our way through Webster, and we must therefore suffer more of the tedium of unconnected words. We proceed to Table IV, which is headed "Easy words of two syllables, accented on the first."

Both Dilworth and Fenning have corresponding tables, and a comparison of the three table headings is instructive. Dilworth is characteristically verbose:

OF DISSYLLABLES.

Some easy words accented on the first syllable, whose spelling and pronunciation are nearly the same.

Fenning derived much of his content from Dilworth, but wrote his heading in a simpler style:

WORDS OF TWO SYLLABLES, ACCENTED
ON THE FIRST SYLLABLE

Webster took the whole of Fenning's heading (save for the redundant last word) adding at the beginning the word "Easy," which came from Dilworth:

Easy words of two syllables, accented on the first.

Webster's table contains 378 words, of which 367, or just over 97 percent, are in Dilworth's table. His having copied from Dilworth is further shown by the fact that Webster (and Fenning too) reproduced a mistake in the alphabetical order in Dilworth's list (*timely* appears before *tidings*). Of the 11 words in Webster that are not in Dilworth, two are in Fenning, and another two differ only by one or two letters from a word in Dilworth's list (*cutter/cutler, dressy/dresser*). That leaves only seven words that Webster may be said to have added to the corresponding tables in Dilworth and Fenning. Of these, three are of particularly American significance: *Congress, Dollar* and *Negro*. This,

however, gives Webster more credit for originality than he deserves, since Fenning's later table of "Nouns Substantive of two Syllables, accented and explained" includes three of Webster's seven words. There we find "Con-gress, *a meeting together*," and "Dol-lar, *a foreign Coin*." Webster's original contribution turns out to be only four words out of 378: *Burgess, Conge, Negro* and *Spirit*.

The syllable-division in Dilworth that Webster objected to does not occur in this table, because it is Dilworth's table of words "whose spelling and pronunciation are nearly the same." There is, therefore, no significant difference here between Dilworth's syllable-division and Webster's. Webster has *jest er* where Dilworth has *jes-ter*, and Webster has *fid ler* where Dilworth spells the word right, and divides it *fid-dler*. The only other difference is in the word *jock-y*, where Webster copies Dilworth's faulty spelling but divides it *joc ky*. Their different ways of dividing these words do not affect pronunciation. In the other 363 words in Webster's table that are also in Dilworth, Webster's spelling and syllable-division are the same as Dilworth's. Furthermore, in those few words where Webster differs from Dilworth, his spelling and division are identical to Fenning's.

Dilworth's second table of disyllables is headed "Words accented on the first syllable; the spelling and pronunciation being different." It contains some words whose division into syllables might suggest a false pronunciation, and in many of these Dilworth employs the "double accent" — Webster's examples of wrong division, *bi"shop* and *ha"bit*, are from this table, which also contains words not pronounced the way their spelling would suggest, such as *daugh-ter, cup-board*, and *haut-boy*. There are, however, many words — such as *bon-fire, dim-ple* and *cheese-cake*— that seem to offer no difficulty at all in pronunciation. Because Dilworth classified words only by their number of syllables and where the stress came, he had many difficult words in this table, much too early in the book for children just beginning to read. Webster sensibly moved these further back. He put them into his Table XIII, which is headed "Words of two syllables, accented on the first." That is exactly the same heading as his Table IV, but without the word "Easy." It is a

very long table, taking up nearly all of pages 51 to 54 of the book. In all, it contains 455 words, and over 90 percent are from Dilworth's second table of disyllables, together with some from the first table that Webster had not already used in his Table IV.

There is no discernible pattern in Webster's choice of words from Dilworth, or any criteria by which he decided which of Dilworth's words to exclude. Looking at the words Webster added, however, it is possible to see his mind at work. Some were words liable to be mispronounced, to which he would provide admonitory footnotes. Thus he put in *chimney* and *carry* so that he could condemn pronouncing them *chimbly* and *kerry*. He did the same thing to some of Dilworth's words as well of course: footnotes to *barefoot, backward, cover* and *dandruff* explain that they should not be pronounced *bowfoot, backard, kiver* and *dander*. Nearly all his other additions were words directly suggested by words in Dilworth's list. Dilworth had *downright, frightful* and *levee*, and Webster added *downwards, frighten* and *level*; *mortal* suggested *mortgage*; *novel, novice*; *pleasant, peasant* and so on.

In following Dilworth's words to their new home in Webster, we have passed by a large chunk of the *Grammatical Institute*. But for that detour, we would have come to Table V, "Easy words of two syllables, accented on the second." Once again, the heading is from Fenning, but the content is taken from Dilworth's Table III. Out of the total of 244 words in his table, Webster contributed just three: *de range, fi nance*, and *huz za*. The last was added to support a footnote condemning the pronunciation *whorra*.

Webster's tables VI to XI contain easy words of three syllables, and then four, accented on different syllables. He continues to rely heavily on Dilworth, though in general as the number of syllables goes up, the proportion of each table taken from Dilworth goes down.

Webster has now finished with easy words. Table XII contains "more difficult and irregular words" of one syllable. Many of the words were in Dilworth's one-syllable section, but Webster rearranged them. Dilworth grouped together words with similar spelling, distinguishing by brackets ones that were pronounced differently

Bar far jar mar tar (war)
Cant pant rant (want)
Horse (worse)

Webster did the opposite, grouping words of similar sound, regardless of their spelling: *war* was in a group, not with *bar, far, jar, mar*, and *tar*, but with *nor, for, cost, lost, tost, halt, salt, fault, form, warm, swarm, corn, warn, sawn, lawn* and *gone*. Reading these lists out loud gives some surprising indications of Webster's pronunciation. One would not expect, for example, among the rhyming list of *drum, come, some* and *dumb*, to find the word *bomb*.

The hard words continue up to Table XX, "Words of five syllables, accented on the third," with a continuation of the earlier trend, a lessening dependence on Dilworth as the number of syllables increases. By this stage, therefore, only about 20 percent is directly from Dilworth, with a further proportion derived indirectly, for example by changing Dilworth's *-tion* terminations. Thus Webster replaced *introduction, regulation,* and *satisfaction* (which Dilworth listed as five-syllable words, but Webster counts as four) with *introductory, regularity* and *satisfactory.*

Webster next addressed the question of "Words ending in *tion, sion,* and *cion,* which sound like *shon* short, or nearly like *shun*; and therefore ought to be considered as one syllable only." Fenning, not wanting to be controversial, had avoided them. Webster would do no such thing. He knew that he was right and Dilworth was wrong, and he wanted to make the point very clearly to all his readers. The following three and a half pages of the *Institute* are entirely filled with such words, growing inexorably from two syllables to five. Webster could no doubt have managed this part without any help from Dilworth, but he didn't have to— Dilworth had such words, they were just in the wrong tables. Nearly half of Webster's *-ion* "Words of four syllables, accented on the third" came from Dilworth's table of words of *five* syllables.

Webster's next substantial borrowing from Dilworth is in his table of "Proper names, divided and accented." Dilworth had separated them according to their numbers of syllables; Webster combined them into one table and left out the British place names, but over 80 percent of his words came from Dilworth.

These include such improbable "proper names" as *Bissextile* and *Thermometer*. The latter is a clear sign that Webster was using Dilworth. Dyche does not include it in his corresponding table (he has *Theodolite* instead) but nearly all Webster's words that are not from Dilworth are in Dyche. The proportion that are in one or the other is over 96 percent

The next table was Webster's own. It contains phonetic respellings to indicate the pronunciation of words "the spelling and pronunciation of which are very different. A considerable part of them are French words introduced into our language and retaining their original pronunciation." Here we find *aidedecamp*, thus written as one word, respelled *aid de cong; entendre* becomes *an tawn der*; and *rendezvous, ren da voo*. Such are the results when an American learns French from a Swiss. Later on, Webster would recommend some of his phonetic respellings as the correct orthography—*opake*, for example, is preferred to *opaque* in his 1806 dictionary, though not *anteek* to *antique*. In some cases, the phonetic spellings were already coming into use, such as the *-er* terminations in *luster*, *meter*, and *specter*, but in this conservative phase, Webster was against them. In giving *risk* as a phonetic respelling of *risque* he was being ultraconservative—the modern spelling was already so well accepted that it was in Johnson.

Webster's next table explains Roman numerals, and is based on both Dilworth and Fenning. Fenning's table is headed

TABLE XVII

Of FIGURES or NUMBERS.

Webster's reads,

TABLE XXXII

Of NUMBER.

Both Fenning and Webster (and Dilworth too) had been using Roman numerals all along in numbering their tables, but only now is any explanation given of how they work. Dilworth's table had only two columns—one for Roman numerals, and the other for the numbers written out in English words. Fenning added the corresponding Arabic numerals, and Webster added ordinals, which he called "Numerical Adjectives." All three gave a year written in Roman numerals as an example, and in each

case it was the year of publication of the edition. Part I of the *Grammatical Institute* was published in 1783, or MDCCLXXXIII. This points to a useful trick: In dating an early spelling book which has been carelessly used and has lost its title page, look at the last figure in the table of Roman numerals, which will often tell you the year the book was printed.

The next table is an old favorite in spelling books—the list of homophones—Webster's heading (copied verbatim from Dilworth) calls them "Words, the same in sound, but different in spelling and signification." Dyche, Dilworth and Fenning all have such lists, and there is one in Entick's dictionary as well. One might ask why homophones need to be "different in spelling"—the answer is, they do not. Dyche's heading describes them only as "Words the same, or nearly alike in sound, but different in signification." Dilworth added the limitation "different in spelling," but he then ignored those words; his table contains several words which have more than one meaning without changing their spelling, such as *cashier, canvass, lie* and *mortar*. Fenning was more careful. He included "different in spelling" in his heading, and he therefore excluded from his list any pairs of words that had the same spelling. Webster, too, gave effect to the description "different in spelling," but he found *three* different ways of doing it. The first, Fenning's way, was just to leave out the words that were spelled the same. *Cashier* was dealt with in that way. The second was to add a word of the same sound, but different spelling. Thus he added "*Lye*, water strained thro' ashes," to Dilworth's two meanings "*Lie*, a falsehood, also to rest on a bed." His third technique was to change the spelling of one meaning but not the other. We can approve his spelling "*Canvass*, to examine" in a different manner to "*Canvas*, coarse cloth"; but the distinction between "*Mortar*, to pound in," and "*Morter*, made of lime" is not supported by Webster's own dictionaries. Indeed, the fact that the spelling of the two words is the same is the subject of comment in the *American Dictionary*:

In other languages, as in English, the orthography of this word and of the last is the same, and perhaps this name is taken from beating and mixing.

In his attempt to avoid including words of the same spelling, Webster once slipped up; he

added "*Bear*, to suffer" to the words in Dilworth and Fenning, "*Bare*, naked," and "*Bear*, a beast."

Webster's postscript, "In this Table I have omitted several words which are found in Dilworth and Fenning …," shows that he relied on those sources for words that he did not omit. This inference is supported by an examination of the content of the table. Despite the omissions, it fills almost five pages, and contains 332 words; they are all taken from Dilworth or Fenning, except *Bear* and *Lye*, the only two words that Webster added. In most cases, he copied Dilworth's or Fenning's explanations of the words as well.

Webster's next table heading is "Of ABREVIATIONS"—itself an unintentional abbreviation of Dilworth's heading. Webster's table contains 113 abbreviations, of which 110 were taken from Dilworth or Fenning. Webster was not so ardent a republican that he felt he should exclude "G.R. George the King"; and in company with the king, we find the queen, a marquis, a lord or lady, a baronet, a knight, and an honourable. As Webster was compiling his book in the last year of the War of Independence, we may be pretty sure that the last abbreviation in his list had not been in any earlier spelling book—it was "U.S.A."

The following ten pages of the *Institute* owe nothing to either Dilworth or Fenning. They constitute the geographical section. First, a page and a half are given to Europe and the West Indies. We learn, for example, that the most populous kingdom of Europe was Germany, with its capital at Vienna. There are then eight pages on America, of which fully a quarter is taken up with information about Connecticut. For each county in that state, the major towns are named, and for each town, Webster gives the number of white inhabitants and the distance in miles from Hartford. For the other states, only the names of counties or towns are given. At first sight, this all looks a bit out of place in a spelling book, but Dilworth would have given the same placenames if he had been writing in America, separated according to their numbers of syllables and arranged in alphabetical order. Webster's system is certainly more instructive and useful than that.

I have already referred to Tommy and Harry, where Webster acknowledged that his story was based on Fenning's; that apart, Webster's last substantial borrowing was in the department of improving sentences. Fenning, like Dilworth, began to introduce these as soon as simple words were available, which is reflected in his heading "Lessons in Words of one Syllable, very easy to spell and read, and by which a Child may begin to know his Duty to God and Man." Once again, Webster's heading was a simplification of Fenning's: "Lessons of easy words to learn children to read and know their duty." Webster was later criticized for the use of *learn* in the sense of *teach*. In his 1806 dictionary, he gave both meanings, without comment. In the *American Dictionary* he insisted that the "popular use" of *learn* to mean *teach* was etymologically justifiable and "found in respectable writers," but honesty compelled him to admit that it "is now deemed inelegant as well as improper."

The first sentence from Webster's table, "No man may put off the law of God," was direct from Dilworth. After that, he mixed up bits of Dilworth, sometimes a whole sentence, sometimes only part of one, with other bits that were not from Dilworth. His second sentence, "My joy is in his law all the day," is Dilworth's third, "My joy is in God all the day," but with Webster giving effect to his stated resolve to avoid excessive use of the name of the Deity. His fourth sentence, "Let me not go in the way of ill men," comes from two of Dilworth's, "Let me not go out of thy way, O God," and "Go not in the way of bad men." Later in the same table, Webster copied large sections of Fenning's lessons, with little alteration. One of those paragraphs is particularly revealing:

Fenning	Webster
When a good boy is at school, he will mind his Book, and try to learn to spell and read well, and not play in School Time; and when he goes to, or comes from School, he will pull off his Hat, or bow to all he meets; and when he goes to Church, he will sit, kneel, or stand still; and when he comes Home, he will read God's word, or some good Book, that God may bless him.	When good boys and girls are at school, they will mind their books and try to learn to spell and read well, and not play in time of school. When they are at church, they will sit, kneel, or stand still; and when they are at home, will read some good book, that God may bless them.

First notice that Webster changed "a good boy" to "good boys and girls." Fenning's Frontispiece shows boys and girls at school (in separate classes — the boys are being taught by a master and the girls by a mistress), but both Dilworth's and Fenning's spelling books are at least subconsciously addressed to boys. Webster deliberately included girls, not because he was a believer in equality of the sexes, but because he believed that girls ought to be educated to fill their proper station in life. A woman's place was in the home, as wife and mother, but she could not perform either of those roles satisfactorily without a good basic education. His spelling book was necessary to all pupils, regardless of their sex.

The only other substantial alteration Webster made to Fenning's lesson was leaving out the description of the good boy on his way to school: "When he goes to or comes from School, he will pull off his Hat, or bow to all he meets...." He left that out because it had given him the idea for an entertaining dialogue, which he put in the *Grammatical Institute* a few pages later on:

How came you so late at school?

I stopped to pull off my hat to a Gentleman.

How long did that hinder you?

A considerable time.

Pray, Sir, how do you make your manners?

I parade myself with my face to the person, take off my hat with both hands, make several bows and scrape with my right foot.

I do not wonder you are late at school; for surely if you meet several persons, it must employ most of your school hours.

It takes some time, indeed; but we must do as we are taught.

But I was taught a shorter way to be mannerly — I was directed not to stop, but to pass on and take off my hat with the hand that is opposite to the person I meet, without turning my head or scraping the ground with my foot....

Well if you are taught the best way to pay your respects to people, I am very happy. But I think that you are faulty in another particular. You run and bawl along the streets, like a mad-man, without any regard to decency....

A year before it was published, Webster had told the Connecticut legislature that his spelling book would contain "an amendment of those tables and lessons of short easy words in the Spelling Book of Mr. Dilworth," Which is exactly what Webster produced — not *Webster's* tables of short easy words, but *Dilworth's* tables, *amended by Webster*. The lessons were partly Dilworth amended, partly Fenning (but that was never acknowledged) and partly Webster. He also took out "the proper names for places which belong to Great Britain" and, where necessary, he changed Dilworth's syllable division to accord with that recommended by Sheridan, Perry, and Entick, which had not previously been applied in consistent manner to any spelling book that he had seen. In the matter of pronunciation, he gave numbers to the different sounds of the vowels and reorganized the content of the tables (which was mostly Dilworth's content) so that the same vowel sounds were grouped together.

Some of Webster's changes were improvements. He replaced Dilworth's English villages with the names of American states, counties and towns, which certainly made sense for American schools. He also introduced nonscriptural readings, which must have been welcome to the children. Some of the changes, however, were not improvements. It was not a good idea to leave all the readings until the end, the absence of any fables was not popular, and some of the lists of words were much too long. Those were mistakes that Webster would later correct. The changes designed to create uniformity of pronunciation probably made no difference in practice, but they may have been seen as improvements, and therefore helped to sell the book. In general, Webster's book succeeded because it was sufficiently familiar not to be alarming — it was still recognizably Dilworth underneath — while at the same time it was sufficiently improved to be worth buying, even though it was more expensive than Dilworth.

In creating a spelling book based on Dilworth's, Webster was doing to Dilworth what Fenning had earlier done, and what Dilworth himself had done to Dyche. This was certainly not illegal, nor was it even immoral, though one would have liked to see Webster giving more generous acknowledgment to those whose work he had used. We can withhold any further moral judgment until we see him denying that he had used their work, and see him criticizing others whose method of working was the same as his own.

5. "Origin of the Copy-Right Laws in the United States"

In 1841, Webster was visited in New Haven by an Englishman, Charles Lyell, who later wrote, "When the lexicographer … was asked how many words he had coined, he replied one only, to demoralize, and that not for his dictionary, but long before, in a pamphlet published in the last century."[1] The pamphlet was a paper that Webster published anonymously in 1794, *The Revolution in France, considered in Respect to its Progress and Effects. By an American*, and it contained the sentence "All wars have, if I may use a new but emphatic word, a demoralizing tendency."

Webster was proud of his word. He included it in the *Compendious Dictionary* in 1806, and in a letter to John Pickering he said that it was "so well-adapted to express ideas not expressed by any other single term that I am persuaded it must maintain its ground."[2]

In the last year of his life, 1843, Webster put together *A Collection of Papers on Political, Literary and Moral Subjects*.[3] They were his own tracts and articles from the previous fifty years, and letters that he had written to important people, with their replies. It was the last book that he published, and he meant it to be a memorial. He wanted to place on record his most significant contributions to American history and learning. The book included what he claimed to be the first printed proposal for a new federal constitution, and his correspondence with Madison on the subject. Here also was his paper on the French Revolution, because it contained his word *demoralize*. This time, the publication was not anonymous, and it had a printed footnote: "This is the first time this word was ever used in English. It is now common in the United States and in England."

What Webster claimed is probably true. The *Oxford English Dictionary* has no earlier citation of *demoralize* than Webster's 1794 tract. He did not use the word in its modern sense of undermining *morale*; he meant corrupting *morals*, but the word is the same. It is my belief, however, that he did not invent the word at all but took it from the French. At the time, Webster was translating items from French newspapers for his own New York paper; coming across the word *démoraliser* and unable to think of an English word of the same meaning, he anglicized it. If that is right, his footnote is a nice example of careful truthfulness: "This is the first time this word was ever used *in English*."

Another paper in the 1843 collection is "Origin of the Copy-right Laws in the United States." Webster wanted to show that he was largely responsible for the existence of those laws, and he succeeded so well that Warfel wrote in his biography, "Webster unquestionably is the father of copyright legislation in America."[4] Similarly, the author of a book on the first English Copyright Act said that "before the first Federal Copyright Act was passed, individual States had enacted their own Copyright law, largely through the strenuous efforts of the lexicographer Noah Webster."[5] Let us discover whether they were right.

This is how his paper begins:

The origin and progress of laws, securing to authors the exclusive right of publishing and vending their literary works, constitutes an article in the history of a country of no inconsiderable importance. The following are the most material facts respecting the origin of the laws on that subject in the United States.

There follow some of the material facts respecting the origin of copyright laws in America, and many other rather less material facts concerning Webster's own activities. Remember, as you read, that in all the petitions that have survived, Webster's efforts in 1782 and 1783 were *not* directed to "securing to authors the exclusive right of publishing and vending their literary works," but only to securing exclusive rights for Noah Webster in his own literary works. He was asking for private acts for his personal benefit, not general acts for the benefit of all authors.

The next section of his paper retells the early history of what was to become the *Grammatical Institute:*

In the year 1782, while the American army was lying on the bank of the Hudson, I kept a classical school at Goshen, Orange County, state of New York. I there compiled two small elementary books for teaching the English language. The country was then impoverished; intercourse with Great Britain was interrupted; school books were scarce and hardly obtainable; and there was no certain prospect of peace.

In the autumn of that year, I rode to Philadelphia for the purpose of showing my manuscripts to gentlemen of influence, and obtaining a law for securing to authors the copy-right of their publications. As the legislatures of New Jersey and Pennsylvania were not then in session, the latter object could not be accomplished. On my way I called on Gov. Livingston then in Trenton, and inquired whether it was probable that a copy-right law could be obtained in New Jersey. The Governor replied that if I would wait till noon, he would consult his council, then in session, and give me an answer. At the time appointed I called again, when the Governor told me the council gave him very little encouragement.

So far, he had tried two states but obtained no copyright.

Webster's paper then gives an account of his visit to Professor Smith at Princeton, who provided a letter of recommendation. Next, Webster presented his first petition to the Connecticut legislature:

In October following, I went to Hartford, with a view to petition the legislature of Connecticut, then in session at that place, for a law *to secure to me the copy-right of my proposed book.* The petition was presented, but too late in the session to obtain a hearing. I then returned to Goshen, and devoted the winter to a revision of my manuscripts, and the introduction of some improvements, which had been suggested by gentlemen in Princeton and Philadelphia.

In the above paragraph, italics have been added to show that Webster was still after a private act, not a general act. In any case, he did not get it. Three states, but still no copyright.

In January, 1783, I prepared another memorial to be presented to the legislature of Connecticut, for the purpose of procuring a copy-right law, which memorial was committed to the care of John Canfield Esq. But *the necessity of it was superseded by the enactment of a general law upon the subject.* This law was obtained by the petition of several literary gentlemen in that state.[6]

Once again, the italics are mine. Webster was asking for a private act, but this became unnecessary because the legislature passed a general act, at the suggestion of the "literary gentlemen" of Connecticut.

In the same winter, I went to Kingston in Ulster County, New York, where the legislature was in session, with a view to present a petition for the like purpose. The necessity of such petition was prevented, by the prompt attention of General Schuyler to my request, through whose influence a bill was introduced into the senate, which, at the next session, became a law.

Webster's petition asked for "the sole exclusive right of printing, publishing, and vending the said new American Spelling Book and Grammar in the State of New York during the term of thirteen years." As in Connecticut, it became unnecessary for him to present it, because the legislature passed a general copyright law. What perhaps happened was that Webster turned up with his petition, and General Schuyler's response was, "What about other authors?" So he procured the passing of a general act.

In the same winter, the legislature of Massachusetts enacted a copyright law; procured probably by the agency of Rev. Timothy Dwight, then a member of the house of representatives.

No credit for Webster there.

As Congress, under the confederation, had no power to protect literary property, certain gentlemen, among whom was Joel Barlow, presented a memorial to that body, petitioning them to recommend to the several states, the enactment of such a law.

In May, 1783, on the report of Mr. Williamson, Mr. Izard and Mr. Madison, Congress passed a resolution, recommending to the several states to secure to authors or publishers of new books not before printed, the copy-right of such books for a term not less than fourteen years.

In December, 1783, Governor Livingston informed me by letter that the legislature of New Jersey had passed a law agreeable to the recommendation of Congress.

When state legislatures passed copyright acts after May 1783, we cannot give credit to Webster, since the recommendation of Congress that a general copyright law be passed by each state must have carried more weight than a petition from an itinerant Connecticut schoolmaster. The New Jersey law was actually passed several months before December 1783, but Webster's paper gives the date of his letter from the governor because that was more important (to him) than the date of the act. New Hampshire and Rhode Island also passed copyright acts in 1783 in response to the recommendation of Congress, but Webster does not mention those states at all, because he had not visited them.

At this stage, three men from Connecticut might be said to share the credit for the spread of copyright laws in America — the old firm of Webster, Dwight, and Barlow.

By mid–1783, Webster had sufficient assurance of copyright protection in the Northern states to complete the preparation of his *Grammatical Institute*. The spelling book was published in October 1783, the grammar in March 1784, and the reader in January 1785. He probably did not at first anticipate selling much outside New England, but sales there were so encouraging that he decided to sell in the South as well. More copyright laws were needed.

In May, 1785, I undertook a journey to the middle and southern states, one object of which was to procure copy-right laws to be enacted. I proceeded to Charleston, but the legislature not being in session, I returned to Baltimore, where I spent the summer.

If this was really an account of the origin of American copyright laws, that last paragraph, in which nothing happened at all, would have no place. In fact, the paper is a description of Webster's journeys in pursuit of copyright, and so it records his failures as well as his successes. In any case, his recollection here would seem to be at fault. By the time he arrived in Charleston, there must already have been a copyright law in force in South Carolina, because an entry in his diary shows that he registered the *Institute* there, on 30th June 1785:

Introduced to Mr. Hutson, Mayor of the City and Intendent in this State. He approves of the first & second part of the Institute. I get a certificate for entering the title of the Institute in the Secretary's office, agreeably to act of Assembly.

From Charleston, he returned to Baltimore, "and as the legislatures of Maryland, Virginia and Delaware were not in session, he continued in Baltimore during the summer."[7]

In November 1785, he set out again on the copyright quest, headed for Richmond, Virginia. On the way, he visited Mount Vernon, where Washington gave him a rather noncommittal letter of introduction:

To his Exc[y]. the Governor; the Speaker of the Senate, & the Speaker of the House of Delegates

From GEORGE WASHINGTON

Mount Vernon 6th Nov[r].1785

SIR,

This letter will be handed to you by Mr. Webster whom I beg leave to introduce to your acquaintance. He is author of a Grammatical Institute of the English language — to which there are very honorable testimonials of its excellence & usefulness — The work must speak for itself; & he, better than I can explain his wishes.[8]

Webster's paper records his receiving that letter:

In November, I visited General Washington at his mansion; he gave me letters to Governor Harrison in Richmond, and to the speakers of both houses of the legislature. The law desired was passed for securing copy-rights.

That statement is entirely neutral — one cannot tell whether the passing of the copyright law by the Virginia legislature was the result of Webster's turning up with a letter from Washington or whether it would have happened anyway. When he next wrote to Washington, however, Webster allowed him some of the credit:

December 16, 1785

Sir,

I have just returned from Richmond where I was happy enough to succeed in my application to the legislature. For this success I acknowledge myself indebted, in some measure, to your politeness.

Should the same success attend me in the states of Delaware and New York, my whole plan will be accomplished; and if on my return to the northern

states I find myself in tolerably easy circumstances, I propose to sit down and devote my attention to literary pursuits....[9]

The next paragraph of Webster's paper shows that he was *not* successful in Delaware:

In December, I visited Annapolis, where the legislature was in session; and in February I visited Dover, in Delaware, for the same purpose. On petition, the legislature of Delaware appointed a committee to prepare a bill for a copy-right law, just at the close of the session, but the enactment was deferred to the next session.

That paragraph implies that the petition in Delaware resulted in a copyright act in mid-1786. Webster says the same thing in No. 16 of the *Memoir*, so this must have been his recollection of the event, but it was mistaken. In January 1787, when he was in Philadelphia, he learned that Delaware had still not passed a copyright law, and he wrote to the speaker of the Delaware House of Assembly, suggesting that they do so.[10] This time, he was asking for a general law, but his strongest argument was that he, Noah Webster, deserved the protection that such an act would give. Notice the characteristic opening sentence of the letter and the "literary characters" popping up towards the end:

Sir,

The importance of this communication must be my apology for addressing a Gentleman with whom I have not the honor to be acquainted.

I am just informed that the legislature of Delaware have not passed the law which I petitioned for, last Jan^y — that they consider it a private matter — & that it will be necessary for some person to attend to draft the form of an act & commit it to the speaker of the house of Assembly. It is impossible for me to attend at present & I have an interest depending on the act.

I have therefore made a rough informal draft of a law securing to authors the benefit of their own publications.

It is not correct, but contains the principles of the acts which have been passed in other States. I beg leave to state a few circumstances & facts & submit the whole to the wisdom of the legislature. Every State in the Union, Delaware excepted, has passed *a general Law* for the benefit of authors, the citizens of the States — Each State must pass the law, before its own citizens can take the benefit of the acts of the other acts — at least of four or five of them — most of the acts make it necessary to register the title of the book in some Office — The penalties are very various — The term of time is different in different

states — some for 20 years unconditionally — others for fourteen years unconditionally, & 28 years, on condition the author himself survive 14 years — In two States, Pennsylvania & Maryland, the operation of the act is suspended, till *all other states* have a similar law — all the states have passed the act except Delaware — all the property I have on earth depends on these laws — & I have expended about 700 dollars, to procure them to be passed in the different States.

You perceive Sir, by these facts, for the truth of which my honor is pledged, how much depends on the hon^{ble} the legislature of Delaware State — I cannot but hope, that so wise a body will grant my petition, and at their present Session — & thus secure, not only in Delaware, but in Maryland & Pennsylvania, the rights of a man, who has devoted the prime of life to the purpose of composing a system of instruction for American youth & which has been honored with the approbation of some of the first literary characters in America.

Your attention to this bill will do a public service & particularly oblige one who has the honor to be

Sir
Your most obedient
humble Servant
Noah Webster jun.

Philadelph^a Jany 24th 1787
The honorable the Speaker
of the House of Assembly
State of Delaware

One sentence in the letter needs correction and explanation: "Each State must pass the law, before its own citizens can take the benefit of the acts of the other acts [states] — at least of four or five of them." That sentence was intended to mean that the acts in four or five states contained a provision requiring reciprocity, as a condition of giving copyright protection to citizens of other states. Thus, if you came from Delaware, you could not register a copyright in New York, because your state did not give protection to the citizens of New York. If you came from Connecticut, you could, because it did. Those provisions did not affect Webster, because he came from Connecticut. As Webster emphasized in his letter to Delaware, however, the continuing absence of any copyright law in that state was more important to him than it might at first appear, because without it, the laws in Pennsylvania and Maryland did not come into effect at all.

Shortly after dispatching his letter to the

Delaware speaker, Webster wrote to the Philadelphia newspapers, staking his claim to a place in history as the instigator of American copyright laws. Already he was making it appear that his applications had been for the benefit of authors in general rather than for his personal benefit, and what he said about Delaware was also inaccurate. The letter appeared in The *Pennsylvania Packet, and Daily Advertiser*, (printed by John Dunlap and David C. Claypoole) on Wednesday March 7th, 1787:

MESSRS. DUNLAP & CLAYPOOLE,

HAVING formed a design, as early as the year 1782, of publishing a small work for the use of schools in this country, I made application to several legislatures for a law of each, securing to authors the exclusive right of printing and vending their own works, for a certain term of time. A resolution of Congress, recommending this measure to the several states, was procured. By this recommendation, by the assistance of my friends, or by personal application, a law of this kind is obtained in every state, except Delaware; in which state my petition is granted and a committee appointed to bring in a bill in form, which will undoubtedly be enacted into a law the next session of the legislature. As there is probably no person in the United States, who has made it his business to acquaint himself with the tenor of the several laws, and as every printer as well as author is interested in these laws, you are requested to publish the following account, which I have taken pains to collect for my own particular benefit.

New Hampshire — Term of years, twenty. Penalty, from £1 to 1000, at discretion of the court. Condition, Proviso, Limitation,

Massachusetts — Term of years, twenty-one. Penalty, from £5 to 2000. Condition, 2 copies of the books to be presented to the library of Harvard College and a certificate from the librarian. Name of the author to be in the title page. Proviso, Limitation,

Rhode Island — Term of years, twenty. Penalty, from £1 to 1000, at discretion of the court. Condition, Proviso, Limitation,

Connecticut — Term of years, fourteen — and if the author survive the first fourteen years, then another term of fourteen years. Penalty, double the value of all copies printed. Condition, registry of the title of the books with the secretary of state. Obligation to furnish the public with books. Proviso, Limitation, the act extends not to citizens of other states — till the states have passed a similar law.

New-York — Term of years, fourteen — and if the author survive the first fourteen years, then another term of fourteen years. Penalty, double the value of all copies printed. Condition, registry of the title of the book with the secretary of state. Obligation to furnish the public with books. Proviso, Limitation, the act extends not to citizens of other states — till the states have passed a similar law.

New Jersey — Term of years, fourteen — and if the author survive the first fourteen years, then another term of fourteen years. Penalty, double the value of all copies printed. Condition, recording the title with the clerk of the council. Proviso, Limitation,

Pennsylvania — Term of years, fourteen — and if the author survive the first fourteen years, then another term of fourteen years. Penalty, double the value of all copies printed. Condition, registry of title with the prothonotary of Philadelphia. A certificate of the registry printed on the back of the title page. Proviso, suspended till all the states shall have passed a similar law. Limitation,

Maryland — Term of years, fourteen — and if the author survive the first fourteen years, then another term of fourteen years. Penalty, all copies of books and two pence per sheet for all copies in possession of the offender — forfeited. Condition, title registered with the clerk of general court for the Western shore, and certificate of it.

Proviso and Limitation, action to be brought within twelve months after the offence. Act suspended till all states have passed a similar law.

Virginia — Term of years, twenty one. Penalty, double the value of all copies printed. Condition, registry of title with clerks of council and certificate. Proviso and Limitation,

North Carolina. — — — Unknown, but by information, the term is fourteen years unconditionally, and twenty eight years conditioned that the author survive the first term, and no other condition.

South Carolina — Term of years, fourteen and twenty eight, on condition the author survive the first term. Penalty, not recollected — Condition, registry of title with the secretary and certificate. Proviso and Limitation,

Georgia — Term of years, unknown. Penalty, not recollected. Condition, registry of title with the secretary and certificate. Proviso and lim,

These are the most material articles in the laws for securing the literary productions of America, to authors and proprietors and their heirs or assigns. I am not certain that I have stated the exact sum which limits the extent of the penalty in New-Hampshire and Rhode-Island; but it is an immaterial defect. I have only to add, that under such restrictions, the acts are all general, extending to all the citizens of the United States.

I am, Gentlemen,

Your most obedient,

Humble Servant,

N. WEBSTER.

Philadelphia, March 1, 1787.

The same letter appeared in the *Pennsylvania Herald and General Advertiser* on Saturday, March 10, 1787, addressed "To the PRINTER."

That was the end of Webster's first copyright campaign. The Federal Constitution was adopted on September 17, 1787, and ratified the following year; Article I, Section VIII, paragraph 8 gave Congress the power "to promote the progress of science and useful arts, by securing for limited times to authors and inventors the exclusive right to their respective writings and discoveries." The Federalist papers urged, among other things, the necessity of federal patent and copyright laws for the encouragement of inventors and authors. Congress sat for the first time under the new constitution in 1789, and a federal copyright act was passed on May 31, 1790, in the second session of the first Congress.

An entry in his diary for April 17, 1789 (when he was in Boston, to be near his fiancée Rebecca Greenleaf) shows that Webster himself drafted a copyright bill at this time:

> April 1...Congress form house of Representatives.
> 6. Senate in Congress formed
> 17. Walk to Cambridge. prepare a copyright bill for Congress.

All that his paper says about the federal act is "In the year 1790, Congress enacted their first copy-right law, which superseded all the state laws on the subject." Webster would certainly have claimed the credit if he had drafted the act, and we must suppose, therefore, that the bill adopted by Congress was not the one mentioned in the diary.

The federal statute, like many of the state acts that it superseded, was modelled on the English Copyright Act of 1709, known as the Statute of Anne,[11] and closely imitated its title:

English: An Act for the Encouragement of Learning, by vesting the Copies of printed Books in the Authors or Purchasers of such Copies, during the Times therein mentioned.

American: An act for the encouragement of learning, by securing the copies of maps, charts, and books in the authors and proprietors of such copies, during the times therein mentioned.

"Copies" in the title of the English act means what would today be called "copyrights." The word "copyright" did not come into use until more than fifty years after that act was passed, and therefore does not appear in the act itself. The American act does use the word "copyright," and its title is somewhat misleading.

The federal statute gave copyright to authors (provided that they were citizens of, or resident in, the United States[12]) for an initial period of 14 years. An author who was still alive at the end of the 14 years (and still a citizen of or resident in the United States) could apply for a second 14-year term. To qualify for the first term, the title of the book had to be registered with the clerk of the court for the area where the author lived, and for this a fee of .60 was payable. The clerk would furnish certificates of that registration, under seal, for a further .60 per copy. The fact of registration had then to be published in a newspaper within two months, for four consecutive weeks, and a copy of the book had to be deposited with the secretary of state within six months of publication. The English statute did not prescribe any formalities for the author to enjoy the second term of copyright, stating that "after the Expiration of the said Term of fourteen Years, the sole Right of printing or disposing of Copies shall return to the Authors thereof, if they are then living, for another Term of fourteen Years." In America, however, the title of the book had to be registered a second time, and another set of advertisements placed:

> If at the expiration of the said term, the author or authors, or any of them, be living, ... the same exclusive right shall be continued to him or them, his or their executors, administrators or assigns, for the further term of fourteen years: Provided, he or they shall cause the title thereof to be a second time recorded and published in the same manner as is herein after directed, and that within six months before the expiration of the first term of fourteen years aforesaid.

A supplementary act in 1802 imposed a further requirement: The copyright certificate had to be printed in full on the title page of every book, or on the following page. It was nearly always put on the back of the title page.

Whether or not Webster deserves to be remembered as "the father of American copyright" is open to question. There is no doubt that he was one of the first Americans to appreciate the importance of copyright to a would-be author

(himself) who hoped to make money by writing books, but the concept was not a new one. The need for patent and copyright protection to encourage creativity was well understood. The copyright acts passed by the several states, and the federal statute of 1790, were generally similar to the first English copyright act, even to the extent of using periods that were multiples of seven years, a feature of Royal Letters Patent. Webster, however, believed that he had played a crucial role in these events. In his later thinking, he had been important to copyright, and copyright was important to him.

6. Webster in Hartford, 1783–1785

Haunted by Dilworth's Ghost and Others

In the interval between his second journey through the Northern states in pursuit of copyright, and his journey to the South, Webster was in Hartford. With help from the faithful Barlow, he saw to the publication of the *Grammatical Institute*, as recorded in No. 9 of the *Memoir*:

In the spring of 1783 N.W. left Goshen, and repaired to Hartford for the purpose of procuring the publication of his first elementary books. Here he had serious obstacles to encounter. Most persons, who were apprised of his design, considered it as visionary, and among his friends, two gentlemen only, John Trumbull and Joel Barlow, ventured to encourage him with the prospect of success. In addition to this discouragement, he was destitute of the means of defraying the expenses of publication; and no printer or bookseller was found to undertake the publication at his own risk. But in the most trying exigencies, his fortitude never forsook him. He received a little aid from Mr. Barlow, whose generosity far exceeded his ability; and N.W. contracted with Hudson and Goodwin his obligation although the future sales only would enable him to fulfill his engagement. But it was not a time to shrink from the execution of his design; he had confidence in its success, and took upon himself the risk.

The first elementary book was published in October 1783; the author being twenty five years of age. The success was better than he had expected; the edition of five thousand copies being exhausted during the following winter.

The second part of the work, of grammar, was published in March 1784, and the third, in January 1785.

During this same period, Webster first became active as a political journalist, writing letters under various pseudonyms to the *Connecticut Courant*. The matter is relevant only because when the *Institute* was attacked soon afterwards by someone calling himself "Dilworth's Ghost," Webster was convinced that his political enemies must be responsible. Alternatively, the attacker might be a bookseller who was finding it increasingly difficult to dispose of his stock of Dilworth's *New Guide*. Those conjectures were both mistaken. Dilworth's Ghost was later identified as a retired schoolmaster called Hughes and there is no reason to suppose that he had any such political or commercial motives — he was just bored, and took delight in teasing Webster, whom he thought cocksure and arrogant.[1] He also recognized the sources of some of Webster's material, and thought it comical that Webster should be warning of his copyright protection, when much of his work had been copied from others.

The Ghost's first letter appeared in the *Freeman's Chronicle*, Hartford, on June 24 1784. It was reprinted in New Haven, in the *Connecticut Journal* (issue No. 870), on Wednesday, June 30:

Mr. N--- W------, A.M. alias Esq.

SIR,

BEING sent by Mercury to visit one of the Schools in the State of Connecticut (for you will be pleased to observe that the Gods employ the Souls of us poor Abecedarians in the "old Way,") I there saw the first and second Part of what you, in the Plenitude of paternal Affection, call "A Grammatical Institute." In which, if I mistake not, (as I have no pretensions to infallibility yet, being only in a State of Probation) there are as many Errours, of one Kind or other, as there were in my "New Guide," when it was first published, and that notwithstanding the Advantages which you must have derived by being in the Body so long after that Book was compiled, as well as since the publication of many other Treatises on the same Subject, some of which are as much superior to yours and mine, as the Gods are to Mortals. Neither are you, by your own Account, a Stranger to several of the best of those Productions. Yet have you not been

able, even to transcribe and compile (for Transcribing and Compiling make the Bulk of your "Institute,") without a numerous Catalogue of Mistakes,
&c.— Tho' at the same Time, you were endeavour-
ing by Implications, &c. to persuade the Inhabitants
of your "New Empire"— that you were capable of
fixing a Standard of Pronunciation, as well as of Diction, Arrangement, &c. for the rising Generation,
and unborn Millions of a "New World."— Such is
the Pride and Vanity of Men whilst on Earth!— Not
considering that Mutability or the Language of Mortals, cannot, like that of the Pantheon, become immutable. Nor is this any Misfortune to those who
use it, but, on the contrary, a very great Advantage.
For, could the Gibberish of their most ancient Ancestors have been rendered permanent, the present
Race, and its Posterity, must have jabbered it as well
as they could.— The Wish of the Gods therefore is,
that it may go on refining till it is as perfect as the Nature of Man will admit; and, that none of your vicious Examples may be adopted by the sensible and
polite of the "New and independent Empire," when
so much better may as easily be obtained, and that
without having Recourse to your "Much celebrated
Grammarian, Mr. Buchanan," who, "by the Way,"
has been very justly ridiculed by his Countrymen, for
attempting what you have since attempted; that is, to
establish that which neither he nor you understood
at the Time you were both imposing your Crudities
on the Public as the most refined Proprieties — for
Proof of which against you, be pleased to recur to
your own Note, in Page 8th, Part the 2nd, where you
promise that "the Powers of the Letters will be examined with Accuracy in the 2nd Edition of the first
Part of the Institute."— Does this not clearly imply
that the first Part was an undigested Performance?
And, if that be the Case with the first Edition, who
can depend that the second will be perfect, or that
their Children may not be obliged to unlearn in one,
what they have learnt in the other? I wish you to
think seriously of this Affair before you irreparably
injure the Innocent.

The Plan which you have adopted for the "Division of Syllables," to use your own Phraseology, has
been repeatedly suggested, and partly formed by several others, the Works of whom I saw when a So-
journer on Earth, and some since.— In a Variety of
Instances you have servilely copied such Parts of
these, which you ought not, and, in other Cases, either from Pride, Inattention, or the Want of Judgment, you have omitted several of the most critical.
Nor will the Manner in which you "divide the syllables," any more lead to a proper Pronunciation, in all
Cases, half a Century hence, no, nor even now, than
the Rules I adopted sixty Years ago, will at this Time,
or did when they were framed.— This, perhaps, may
be a Distinction which you have not attended to, in
every Point of View, Sir.

You accuse me very invidiously, and without
sufficient Cause, of Absurdity and Falsity, and after-

wards adopt what you had censured in me, altho' as
I told you before, you have had the Advantage of a
Number of very eminent Authors on Philology and
the Didactick, since my "New Guide" was first published, besides having a fleshly Tabernacle at a remarkable Era for grammatick Disquisitions, &c. Yet
is your Pronunciation by no Means just, nor your
Style accurate, as you would fain have them thought
to be.— On the contrary, the former is frequently vicious, and the latter is not only inaccurate, but inelegant and bombastick in a Variety of Cases.— Nay,
it is almost every where filled with disagreeable and
useless Repetitions — In one Place, too elliptical — in
another, redundant — here a Want of Concord —
there a wrong Preposition, with bad Arrangement or
aukward Transposition, and, if possible, worse Language, whilst you are exerting your "most laborious
Efforts" to be thought the Pattern of Purity — the
Model of Politeness and good Manners, as well as
Master of the most elegant Diction and harmonious
Composition.

But what outdoes all the Rest of your Outdoings,
is, that you are not only inconsistent with the Authours whom you have transcribed, but with yourself, and that in the very Rudiments of the Science
which you more than simply profess to teach, as you
speak, at Times, like the great Founder of some
mighty Empire, or in the Style Royal; that is, —
"We"— Yet, in giving Rules for constructing Sentences, &c. you frequently violate them before they
are completed, and, in the Midst of a Criticism, you
are guilty of a Solecism.— These, you are very sensible, are Improprieties with which I am not justly
chargeable, in my "New Guide," and therefore you
ought not to have treated my laudable Endeavours
to promote Science, with so much Severity and Contempt — But Spleen, Ambition and Avarice seem to
have been predominant with you.

However, to be candid, (and the Gods allow of
nothing but Candour) it turned out to be a very
pretty Affair, as it went nearly through thirty Editions whilst I was an Inhabitant of your Globe, and
that is more than you can rationally promise yourself from your "Institute," tho' you claim the Benefit
of the Statute, least somebody or other should do as
you have done, which, all Circumstances considered,
is truly a very laughable Affair!

And if mine were "a mere Latin Grammar indifferently transcribed," as you hint that some your Contemporaries have suggested to you, I think that
your's may, with much more Justice, be said to be an
"Institute" very badly copied, and which I cannot,
consistently with the Trust reposed in me, *by the God
of Letters*, &c. call absolutely "A Grammatical Institute," at this advanced Period of Literature, as it contains too many Incongruities, &c. to admit of such
an unqualified Appellation, even if all the Errours of
Punctuation should be imputed to the Press, which
is often the reputed Parent of many legitimate
Issue.— Besides, it is greatly defective in another very

important Respect, notwithstanding you prepared the Mind of the Reader, in the Preface to Part the first, for a Wonder, which, on some Accounts, it really may be termed.

Had you, instead of superciliously setting yourself up as a Pattern of Style and Composition, for the present and future Generation of a vast Empire, adopted the Modesty of some of the Authours whom you have copied and abused, in Part, and published a little Manual on Grammar, for the Use of a few Friends, or a small Circle of Acquaintance, &c. without insulting or traducing others, you might, perhaps, have been entitled to the Pity, Patronage, or Thanks of all who read it. But your Arrogance and Want of Candour have precluded you from either, with those who are competent to judge of such a Performance.

Finally, (for Mercury calls) if the foregoing Assertions should be positively denied, they will, when the Gods permit, be more explicitly treated of—by

DILWORTH'S GHOST.

P.S. As you claim the protection of the Law for that which you *call your own*, your Equanimity cannot be disturbed, should one of Dr. Lowth's Proxies—Ash's,* Sheridan's, or Kenrick's, &c. &c. Agents commence an Action against you for Plagiarism, or *what is really theirs?*—As from A.M. in Part the first, you have risen to Esquire, in Part the second, may it not be expected that you will appear *benighted* in the third Part, and dubb yourself Sir N—h, &c. or, perhaps, from "We," to "We ourself," which must undoubtedly entitle you to all the Respect that can be due to an imperial, pedantick Despot.

D.G.

*This Gentleman's Errours concerning Accent, Quantity, &c. you have adopted as your own, tho' they were some time before your "Revolution" detected and exposed by a very ingenious Writer of Great-Britain.

Webster's diary shows that he was away from Hartford when that letter appeared, and indeed for the whole of June 1784. While he was still away, a letter appeared in the *Freeman's Chronicle* defending him, the writer calling himself "Thomas Dilworth." That letter, like the Ghost's, was reprinted by the *Connecticut Journal* in New Haven, appearing on July 14:

To the PRINTERS.

AS a certain inhabitant of your globe, who by his veneration for the gods is most evidently an heathen, has had the assurance to assume the name of Dilworth's Ghost (No. 870) and pretended to appear in my shape, I beg you to publish my protest against him in your next....

This mimic of a ghost seems greatly vexed to find

a Spelling-book and a Grammar, that is not in every part of it perfectly new. He might as rationally quarrel with Dr. Johnson's Dictionary for having no words in it that are not in Bailey's. I take liberty to assure him, that every work of this kind can only be progressive, and an improvement on former writers; and that altho' Lowth, Ash, Sheridan, Buchanan and Perry, had made many judicious remarks on the English language, and hinted a variety of improvements in the mode of education since my day, no one had attempted to reduce their observations to use for the benefit of schools, or to compile a Spelling-book on a similar plan, before the author of the Grammatical Institute. My impostor's observations on the style of that author, I shall not further notice, than to desire him not to attempt to criticize others, till he can himself write in a style, that shall at least bear some faint resemblance to grammar and good sense, nor to find fault with the arrogance of any writer, while he shows himself to be as abusive a scribbler as ever disgraced the annals of literature.—And I shall conclude by informing him, that it is the opinion in these parts, that he is some petty schoolmaster, who rails at a work he cannot understand, and that I have the honour to be, with the greatest contempt, his Master,

THOMAS DILWORTH

I do not know of any authoritative identification of "Thomas Dilworth," but the person most likely to have had both the inclination and the information to defend Webster was Barlow. He was certainly on the spot, since he and his partner Elisha Babcock launched their own newspaper in Hartford, the *American Mercury*, a few days later. The first issue came out on July 12, 1784, and contained an advertisement for Webster's "Spelling Book and Grammar." "Thomas Dilworth" used the same words, only once referring to it as the *Grammatical Institute*, the title the Ghost had mocked. The defense offered by "Thomas Dilworth" was moderate and entirely reasonable—first, any spelling book or grammar was bound to be based upon what had gone before; second, though Sheridan and others had "hinted a variety of improvements in the mode of education, ... no one had attempted to reduce their observations to use for the benefit of schools, or to compile a Spelling-book on a similar plan." That sentence shows that the writer of the letter knew that what Webster had done in making his spelling book was (as we have seen) to modify earlier spelling books by applying to them the lessons he had learned from Sheridan.

Webster would deny that he had done anything of the sort.

Webster's first response to the Ghost was a rather tedious letter published in the *Freeman's Chronicle* on July 8, in which he refused to answer a letter signed with a pseudonym. This was a curious attitude for him to adopt since he was himself writing his political articles under a variety of pseudonyms, believing that people would not take them seriously if they knew who the writer was. This was Webster's letter:

MR. PRINTER,

I have been informed that during my absence on a journey Mr. Dilworth's Ghost has made his appearance in this city and has made some remarks upon the *Grammatical Institute*. I have likewise been informed that Mr. Dilworth himself has since sent word that the Ghost was an impostor and by no means authorised to appear in his name....

Now, Mr. Printer, if the Ghost you have introduced to this city be really Mr. Dilworth's, I suspect that some petty schoolmaster or bungling printer, who has a large number of Dilworth's books on hand and finds them less saleable than formerly, had called up his Ghost to defend the books and help the sale; in this case he may say with propriety, "The Lord hath departed from him." But I am inclined to think the Ghost is an impostor for the following reasons.

First, Mr. Dilworth was a scholar and a respectable character when living, and unless he is much degenerated since his death, his Ghost could not have been the author of such an awkward title or such indecent remarks; much less could his Ghost risque his reputation upon the proof of his assertations. In the next place, Mr. Dilworth, since he is dead, can have no interest in doing me an injury. In the last place, he had, when alive and probably his Ghost has still, too much prudence to contradict the decided opinions of the best grammarians in two nations. That the publication referred to is the production of a Ghost I have no doubt, for no being on this earth, I am sure, is capable of such a ghostly performance.

But the probability is that it is the Ghost of the late Convention, for the style and spirit of the remarks exactly resemble those of their writers, and they seem to be produced in a fit of peevishness.[2] But let the Ghost be Dilworth's or any other person's, I take this opportunity of declaring to the world that no publication of any kind will be noticed by me but such as have the following qualifications.

1. The author's REAL name must be subscribed to it. A man of honor, courage, and candour will be willing to meet his antagonist in the open field; none but cowards will skulk or attack a man behind the curtain. I have hazarded my reputation upon the merit of what I have published; any person that dare not do the same is exposed to suspicion and deserves no notice.

2. The sentiments must be cloathed in a decent style. I care very little how severe remarks are, but I despise scurility.

3. The language must be grammatical. A GRAMMARIAN will express himself with propriety — and a man who is not a GRAMMARIAN has no right to criticise upon GRAMMAR.

These, Mr. Printer, are the qualifications that entitle any remarks upon my works to an answer; and as the ghostly publication which lately appeared in the *Chronicle* wants all these requisites, His Ghostship will excuse my silence upon the charges alledged against the Institute.

I am, Mr. Printer, Your's and his Ghostship's most humble Servant,

N.WEBSTER, Jun.

It is my belief that Webster had no intention of leaving Dilworth's Ghost unanswered, and that his reason for writing as he did was to provoke the Ghost into disclosing his identity. If that was his purpose, he failed. The Ghost did not respond to Webster's letter. That left Webster with a problem — he had publicly said that he would not answer anonymous allegations, but he wanted to tell his answers to the world. His solution was to make the Ghost repeat his allegations elsewhere. Webster sent a copy of the Ghost's letter in the *Connecticut Journal* to Elizabeth Holt, proprietor and publisher of the *New York Journal and State Gazette*, with a request that she reprint it. This she did, on July 15, 1784. On July 22, Webster wrote a long and detailed response, which he sent to the New York paper.

I am speculating when I say that it was Webster who sent the Ghost's letter to Mrs. Holt, but I think it likely. She did not just see the letter in the *Freeman's Chronicle* or the *Connecticut Journal*— somebody sent it to her and asked her to print it. When she did so, it was under the heading:

From the CONNECTICUT JOURNAL
(Inserted by Desire)

Who would have desired to see it reprinted in New York? There was no reason for Dilworth's Ghost to want it; apart from anything else, the *Grammatical Institute* had not at that time been sold in New York. For Webster, on the other hand, that was a good reason for provoking a lively exchange in the New York papers; people who saw his books being attacked and defended would want to read them, and

that could only be good for sales. The strength of his position was that, even if he had borrowed ideas from Sheridan and tables from Dilworth and Fenning, his spelling book was, for American schools at least, unquestionably better than theirs. So, he sent off his long reply to the Ghost's letter, and waited for it to appear in the *New York Journal.*

Eight weeks he waited, and still his letter did not appear. That was not part of his plan, but he saw a way of turning it to his advantage — he would get Mrs. Holt to publish not only his letter but a free advertisement for the *Institute* as well. He made copies of some of the best recommendations he had received, and sent them off to her, with a letter dated September 13, 1784:

I find by your Papers, that the Remarks I sent you in answer to Dilworth's Ghost, have not been made public. — The Institute has the sanction of the first characters in America. — It has taken place generally of all other school books wherever it is known. — If it be a valuable work, every friend to his country ought, from motives of pride and interest, to encourage it in preference to British productions. — I find it difficult in many places to get the books advertised, even when I pay for it; — I hope you are incapable of being actuated by such motives as I find some Printers are — I beg you would insert without delay the remarks I sent you some weeks since, and the foregoing recommendations directly under them....

Mrs. Holt did as Webster asked. In the *New York Journal* for Thursday, September 23 1784, she published that excerpt from Webster's letter to her, with her reply:

Mr. Webster may be assured, that the ruling principles which actuate us would never admit of any acts of partiality; — his answer would have appeared before now, but that several very lengthy public advertisements occupied the principal part of our paper.

Webster's answer to Dilworth's Ghost followed:

Mrs. HOLT,

In your paper No. 1967 I perceive you have inserted from the *Connecticut Journal* some remarks upon me and my *Grammatical Institute* under the signature of Dilworth's Ghost....

The writer of the *ghostly* remarks ridicules the idea of fixing a standard of pronunciation because language is mutable. This proves that, however he may be acquainted with affairs in the world of spirits, he is totally ignorant of the history of this. The Greek language from the age of Hesiod to that of Polybius

remained in a fixed state, nor was there any perceptible variation in the orthography: Every letter had a determined sound, and every word was composed of the same letters during a period of near a thousand years. The Roman language also suffered little or no variation for a long period.... On the foregoing facts and observations I leave the Ghost to make his own comment.

In that section of his letter, of which I have quoted only a small part, Webster paraded his learning, establishing his intellectual superiority over his antagonist and over the readers of the newspaper. His argument, however, was unsound. What the Ghost was objecting to was the idea that it was possible to fix a standard of pronunciation for English; Webster's response, that other languages had remained unchanged for long periods (even if true) was no answer to that objection; indeed, Webster himself conceded, in a quotation from Home's *History of Man,* that "the English language has not yet acquired all the purity it is susceptible of...."

In reality, Webster had at that time no carefully reasoned theory of linguistic development. His views were influenced by whichever "literary character" he had most recently read or listened to, and in support of those views he would deploy whatever argument came first to mind. If, instead of wanting to fix the pronunciation of English, he had wanted to justify altering the spelling, he would have put forward exactly the opposite argument:

Every man of common reading knows that a living language must necessarily suffer gradual changes in its current words, in the signification of many words, and in pronunciation. The unavoidable consequence, then, of fixing the orthography of a living language, is to destroy the use of the alphabet.

Those are Webster's own words, from the Preface to the 1806 *Compendious Dictionary.* By that time Webster was a proponent of spelling reform, and agreed with the Ghost that "the Language of Mortals, cannot, like that of the Pantheon, become immutable."

Next, Webster addressed the Ghost's allegation of plagiarism. Notice that he only mentioned the grammar, where he felt himself to be on stronger ground than in the spelling book.

I am accused of compiling and transcribing. The accuser ought, however, to remember that every grammar that was ever written is a compilation. The materials of all English grammars are the same, and that

man who arranges the principles of the language in the best form and reduces the ideas to the easiest method compiles the *best* Grammar. Every writer whose works I have seen is liable to the charge of plagiarism. Dr. Lowth borrowed many of his ideas from Bishop Wilkins, Mr. Harris' *Hermes,* Dr. Ward's *Essays,* &c. Mr. Buchanan borrowed from Dr. Lowth, and Dr. Ash borrowed from both. Nay more: Mr. Dilworth borrowed from Latin and Greek grammars several cases and tenses which do not belong to the English language. If, therefore, all English grammarians are under a necessity of compiling from the same materials and, consequently, of transcribing each other's works in a greater or less degree, that man has the best claim to approbation who makes the most judicious choice.

That paragraph is important to our study, because there Webster, when he was the person accused, explained the justification for "transcribing and compiling." But Webster took a very different view when others transcribed from his works. He gave no approbation to people who made a "judicious choice" from his own spelling books and dictionaries.

Whether one is considering the legal wrong of infringement of copyright or the moral wrong of plagiarism, it is important to distinguish between ideas, and the words in which those ideas are expressed. Copyright protects only the arrangement of words in which ideas are expressed, not the ideas themselves. When Webster said "the materials of all English grammars are the same," he was right, if he meant that all grammars divide words into parts of speech and list the same pronouns, cases, tenses and so on. That, however, does not justify a later author in copying the wording of an earlier grammar, which is plagiarism as Webster himself would define it — "introducing passages from another man's writings and putting them off as one's own." The fact that Dr. Lowth "borrowed many of his ideas from Bishop Wilkins," if he did, was not an act of plagiarism unless he also copied the words of Bishop Wilkins in which those ideas were expressed. A worker in any field of scholarship seeks to build on the work of those who have gone before and incorporates into his own work all earlier ideas that he believes to be right — it would be perverse to do otherwise. That is not plagiarism, nor can it be criticized at all if due credit is given to those who originated the ideas.

In the next section of his reply to the Ghost,

Webster failed to give credit to anyone. As we have seen, all his ideas as to the best way of dividing syllables had been put forward earlier, and in books that we know he had read. This was something he was not prepared to admit:

But I am told "that the plan I have adopted for the division of syllables has been repeatedly suggested and partly formed by several others, the works of whom I have in part servilely copied and in part have judiciously omitted." What a bare-faced assertion! I never knew till the Ghost informed me that the attempt had been made. I have never seen any schoolbook upon such a plan, nor can I yet find the authors' names or the works I am said to have copied. I hesitated at first whether to alter the method of dividing syllables or not till I was assured by the most eminent scholars in America, particularly by some of the instructors at Nassau Hall and the University of Pennsylvania, that I might make the alteration with the greatest safety. I shall spend no time in reasoning upon the subject, but just observe that gentlemen who have taught children upon both plans say that the plan I have adopted is inconceivably the best plan....

It seems to be the opinion of the Ghost that I am much indebted to Mr. Sheridan, Mr. Perry, and Mr. Kenrick for a method of ascertaining the pronunciation of words; and possibly a superficial view of our indexes or keys may warrant the opinion. But I presume the writer has not seen the works of those authors and has founded his supposition on my mentioning their names in some of my publications.... I have only to observe on this point that I was wholly unacquainted with those authors till after I had published the first edition. Entick's Pocket Dictionary was the only work of the kind that I consulted while I was compiling it. In the second edition I have introduced some improvements, and by the assistance of those three authors. This I have acknowledged in the Preface and conceive it to be no crime....

What motives dictated the late ghostly attack upon the *Institute* I presume not to determine; and as to its effect upon the minds of men I feel perfectly easy. My attachment to the Revolution, my opposition to the late factious spirit of Connecticut, my endeavours to support the power and measures of Congress and the principles of the Federal Government — a business to which I acknowledge my tongue and my pen have been incessantly devoted — these circumstances have made me some personal enemies who acknowledge my influence by seeking revenge. But if I have been in the least degree instrumental in effecting a revolution of sentiment in a single state that was embroiled with faction, the thought will give me happiness on the verge of eternity, while the sacrifice of a few friendships and the loss of pecuniary advantages will be deemed *trifles* beneath the notice of, Madam, Your most obedient, humble Servant,

N.WEBSTER, Jun.

Immediately below that letter, Mrs. Holt obligingly printed copies of Webster's "Recommendations." The first was the response to some free copies of the spelling book that Webster had sent to Harvard:

Extract of a letter from Dr. Joseph Willard, *President of the University of Cambridge, to the Author, dated Cambridge, February 2, 1784.*

"SIR,

"I Received, some time ago, three copies of your *Grammatical Institute of the English Language.* I have perused it myself, and put into the hands of several friends for their perusal. We all concur in the opinion, that it is much superior to Mr. Dilworth's New Guide; and that it may be very useful in schools.

"I wish you success, Sir, in every endeavour to advance useful knowledge, and hope, in a particular manner, that your exertions to promote an accurate acquaintance with the English language among our youth, will be attended with the utmost advantage.

I am, Sir,

Your humble servant,
JOSEPH WILLARD."

The next "recommendation" was the letter Tapping Reeve, "formerly one of the Masters of the College at Princeton," had written to John Canfield to help Webster in his first copyright campaign. His name was not familiar in New York, and Mrs. Holt called him "Japping Reeve." Since the letter had been written in October 1782 (before the *Grammatical Institute*) Reeve had not seen the book, and only expressed approval of "*a plan* of a new English Spelling-Book and Grammar." That, however, was unlikely to be noticed by a casual reader of the newspaper.

The other recommendations were a letter to Webster from Benjamin West, "an eminent instructor of youth in Providence," and a circular, signed by various Connecticut worthies (mostly Webster's teachers and friends): the Hon. Oliver Wolcott, Esq.; the Rev. Ezra Stiles, D.D., president of Yale College; the Rev. Elizur Goodrich, D.D.; Col. George Wyllys, secretary of state; Col. Thomas Seymour, mayor of New Haven; Col. Samuel Wyllys, alderman; the Rev. Eliphalet Steele; John Trumbull, Esq.; the Rev. Timothy Dwight; the Rev. Nathan Strong; the Rev. Nathan Perkins; Andrew Law, A.B.; Chauncey Goodrich, Esq.; and, of course, Joel Barlow, A.M.

Thinking that his recommendations looked rather well in the *New York Journal*, Webster decided to have them printed in other newspapers. They appeared in Barlow's *American Mercury* for several weeks following October 11, 1784, and also in the *Connecticut Journal* on November 24:

TO BE SOLD
By ISAAAC BEERS,
Webster's Grammatical Institute
of the English Language, First & 2d Parts
(The third is preparing for the Press.)
From a great variety of Recommendations of this work, the following are offered to the Public.

This prompted another anonymous correspondent to join in the fun of teasing Webster. On November 1, 1784, "A Learner of English Grammar" wrote a letter to Barlow's paper, the *American Mercury*, politely asking Tapping Reeve to explain a rule in Webster's spelling book, by which he was puzzled. Barlow was not keen to publish an attack on his friend, but Webster again wanted to know the identity of his assailant, so Barlow printed a small paragraph in his newspaper on December 6:

∴The piece subscribed "A Learner of English Grammar," is received, and will be inserted as soon as the writer will favour the Printers with his name: Which he may do in confidence.

The Learner preferred to maintain his incognito, so he ignored Barlow's invitation, and sent his piece, with a covering letter signed "ENTITY," to Messrs. Collier and Copp, who were about to launch a new newspaper in Litchfield, Connecticut. The first issue of the *Weekly Monitor and American Advertiser* was to be published on December 21, 1784.

Meanwhile, Dilworth's Ghost had been prompted to walk again by the publication of the second edition of Webster's spelling book. The Ghost wrote a long letter, which he sent to the *Connecticut Journal.* He expected that it might appear on December 17, but it didn't; instead, there was a reprint of Webster's letter to the *New York Journal.* The Ghost accused Webster of having "prevailed on Messieurs Greens [the publishers of the *Connecticut Journal*] to reprint a publication of yours, from Mrs. Holt's paper, in preference to some remarks, &c., on your books and conduct, which had been sent them." There is no reason to suppose

that Webster deliberately caused the Greens to exclude the Ghost's letter, but he probably had objected to their delay in publishing his own; they used Mrs. Holt's excuse and printed it under the headline "*The following Reply has been omitted for several weeks, for want of Room.*" Like the Learner of English Grammar, the Ghost then thought of Collier and Copp's new paper, and sent his piece to Litchfield.

What followed was a remarkable chapter in the history of American journalism. For a period of 12 weeks (the first 12 weeks of its publication) the Litchfield *Monitor* was dominated by a discussion of Webster's *Grammatical Institute*. In its very first issue, December 21, 1784, the letter from The Learner took up three-quarters of the front page. The following week, there was a reply from a gentleman signing himself "A.B." Dilworth's Ghost's second letter then occupied the whole of the front page for two weeks, and the second of those issues, January 11, 1785, also had a reply from the Learner of English Grammar to A.B. On January 13, Webster's diary records, "Write an answer to the second Ghost, who has attacked the Institute." The "second Ghost" was the Learner, and Webster's answer to him filled the front page of the *Monitor*, and part of page 2, on January 18. The following day Webster wrote an even longer reply to the first installment of the Ghost's second attack. His diary entry says, "Write another answer to the Ghost. I have exposed myself to malice, envy, criticism &c. by my publications. I knew I should when I began and I am prepared for an attack on all sides."

On January 25, the *Monitor* acknowledged having received Webster's second letter, and also A.B.'s reply to the Learner, but it did not print them that week, because all the available space was occupied by another letter from the Ghost. Webster's letter appeared the following week, taking up a page and a half, and A.B.'s had most of the front page the week after that. The following week, Webster's reply to the Ghost's second installment was confined to a page and a half only by printing the part on page 2 in smaller type.

At this time, two of Webster's classmates were editing local newspapers: Barlow (with his partner Babcock), at the *American Mercury* in Hartford, and Josiah Meigs at the *New Haven Gazette*. On February 21, Barlow published a letter from Webster, referring to the fact that his work had become "a subject of great speculation especially in Litchfield County" and begging leave "to submit to the public a few remarks on the two schoolbooks that have been most used and esteemed in Connecticut, viz., Dilworth's *New Guide* and Dr. Lowth's *Introduction.*" Meigs published the same letter on March 3. Webster had come to realize that writing to the papers was an effective and inexpensive way of bringing his works to the notice of the public.

Meanwhile, back in Litchfield, Webster's supporters had burst into verse. On March 1, the *Monitor* had a Poet's Corner (something it had not done before, though the *New York Journal* often had one). It contained a poem addressed "To Dilworth's Ghost," and signed Philodilworth. Mrs. Ford writes, "probably by Mr. Barlow."[3]

By March 8, Messrs. Collier and Copp clearly thought the whole thing had gone on long enough. They printed a final salvo from Dilworth's Ghost, but all in small type, and not on the front page. They found room, however, for a second poem, a very bad one, attacking Webster's various critics.

No doubt the citizens of Litchfield found it entertaining to read these mutually abusive exchanges, but we have space for only a small selection, and must pass over those parts where each side amused itself by criticising the grammar of the other. Let us start with the first letter from the Learner:

OBSERVING a note in one of Messieurs Barlow and Babcock's papers, from Tapping Reeve, Esq. of Litchfield, to John Canfield, Esq. of Sharon, concerning the plan and execution of Mr. Webster's "Institute," which the former seems to think "well conceived and judiciously executed;"—As Mr. Reeve's literary abilities, as well as his veracity and philanthropy, are universally acknowledged, I wish you to let him know, by inserting this in your next paper, that, in consequence of his recommendation, I have been induced to peruse the first part, of the first edition, of what Mr. Webster calls his "Grammatical Institute," and observe in a "N.B." at the bottom of page 50, the following words—"That no vowel is long, but in an accented syllable, and that only when the accent falls upon the vowel—And likewise, that when the accent falls upon a consonant, *all* the vowels in that word are necessarily short."—According to which, I find myself something at a loss to pronounce a great number of words which I have been taught, and by those who were esteemed tolerable

good speakers, to utter otherwise — And, therefore, entreat his candid interposition towards reconciling the foregoing rule with the common or received manner of pronouncing the following catalogue of words, which might very easily have been increased.

As Mr. Reeve acknowledges that the demolishing of odious distinctions, which have been occasioned by provincial dialects, is a matter of no little importance, it is confidently expected that he will bestow a few moments on the investigation of an affair, in which the youth of the present day are so much interested, especially those who are designed for the bar and the pulpit. — Nay, there is a national point of view in which it cannot be too accurately ascertained — For how ridiculous must a Delegate, or Ambassador, appear before an improved and refined audience, at one time drawling out long, aukward syllables, without any accents at all; and then, at another, misplacing of them, when he ought to acquit himself with volubility & propriety upon every exigence.

If it be inquired why Mr. Reeve is called upon to reconcile the foregoing rule with the received manner of pronunciation; the subscriber begs leave to refer to the specification of this gentleman, over his letter to Mr. Canfield, as it lately appeared in Messieurs Barlow and Babcock's paper — Whence it immediately occurred, that, if Mr. Reeve had been a master in that very respectable seminary of polite literature at Princetown, he must, of course, have made pronunciation a part of his study, at least, besides his practice in common with the gentlemen of the robe, whose profession leads them to cultivate elocution.

There followed a list of 112 words said to contradict Webster's rule, being words with a long vowel in an unstressed syllable. The list included words such as *antidote, bonfire, cargo, museum, utopian,* and *humane.*

The rule that the Learner of English Grammar quoted from page 50 of the first edition of the spelling book was Webster's restatement of a rule found on pages 258–59 of Sheridan's *Lectures on Elocution*:

[W]henever the accent is on the consonant, the sound not only of the preceding vowel is always shortened, but no other vowel in the word has ever its full long sound; and whenever the accent is on the vowel, that vowel has always its full long sound, and all the other vowels in the word are pronounced short.

In calling himself Entity, the Learner was claiming to be a person of more substance than Dilworth's Ghost. Webster's letter in the January 18 *Monitor* labored the same joke:

The Ghost now appeared in a different shape. From a substantial spectre in a state of probation, he has transmigrated into an *Entity*, a mere physical existence. Probably the third form which he will assume, will be a *non-entity*; and this will no doubt be his finishing metamorphosis.

The same letter contained Webster's reply to the question the Learner had put to Tapping Reeve:

With respect to the pronunciation of the words mentioned by our *Learner of Grammar*; whether Mr. Reeve should take notice of the request or not, I shall only observe; that I fully adopt the opinion of Dr. Ash, Mr. Kenrick, and Mr. Perry, with regard to a plurality of accent. If the writer denies this, I can have no dispute with him; for my plan of pronunciation is built upon this idea. If a man will deny that there are two accents on such words as *gratitude, unanimity, exaltation,* &c. I will leave him to enjoy his opinion without attempting to convince him of his error. This idea resolves the difficulty with repect to the greatest number of words in our writer's catalogue. The two words *antidote* and *commodore*, have two accents; the full or strong accent on the first syllable, and a weaker accent on the third. The first accent falls on the consonants *n* and *m*, and the vowels that precede, are *short*. The second accent falls on the vowel *o*, in the last syllables, and that vowel is of course *long*. With respect to such words as *priority, utility, location*; the vowel in the first syllable has its first sound; but good speakers will not dwell on it so long, or pronounce it with so much force, as they do an accented vowel. To dwell on the first vowel in *location*, as long as you do on the second, would be the same fault of *drawling aukward syllables*, which our critic represents as so ridiculous in a Delegate or Ambassador.

These remarks and rules will apply to every word in our *learner's* catalogue, and every similar word in the language. The very idea of *accent* implies a force or continuance of voice on a vowel, without which it is necessarily short. I defy every grammarian on earth to find a vowel in any language that can be properly called long, without some degree of accent. Should this be denied, I can produce a group of authors of established reputation to support the sentiment....

Webster's next letter was a reply to Dilworth's Ghost, but it referred to the Learner's question as if the Ghost had asked it:

Some people find fault with your criticisms. They say you have filled several papers with remarks that are nothing to your purpose; that the only thing which respects the merits or demerits of the work is your enquiry proposed to Mr. Reeve concerning my rule, "That all vowels in unaccented syllables are short."

That response to the Learner is superficial, eva-sive, and intellectually dishonest. For the mo-ment, let us accept Webster's restatement of his rule: *All vowels in unaccented syllables are short.* He now says that every long vowel is accented. Whether that is true or not, it is completely use-less as a guide to pronunciation, because you have to know the pronunciation to apply the rule. The Master-Student dialogue would go like this:

> MASTER: If a vowel is in an *unaccented* syllable, you must pronounce it *short*.
> STUDENT: How do I know which are the unac-cented syllables?
> MASTER: They are the ones with *short vowels*.

Next, Webster's explanation ignores his own teaching in the spelling book. The word *anti-dote* is in his table of "Easy words of three syl-lables, accented on the first." The words *ani-mate, appetite, altitude, actuate, agonize* and *anecdote* are likewise all said to be accented on the first syllable, yet all have a long vowel in the third syllable. None of those words is said to be accented on both the first syllable and on the third. This is not because Webster had not thought of the idea of secondary stress, which he describes in detail in the spelling book in re-lation to words of four syllables or more. Those four-syllable words do not save his rule either, since their weakly stressed syllables (such as the third syllable in *caterpillar*) generally do not have long vowels.

Furthermore, Webster was able to put for-ward his answer to the Learner only by disre-garding the words in the spelling book which immediately preceded those the Learner quoted:

I would therefore have it impressed upon the minds of learners, that the greatest stress of voice is to be laid on *one syllable*, and that the others must be dis-tinctly sounded but with more rapidity.

Finally, and most seriously, Webster was not telling the truth when he said his rule was "That all vowels in unaccented syllables are short." He was deliberately leaving out the second half of the rule, the part that had puzzled the Learner: "When the accent falls upon a conso-nant, *all the vowels in that word* are necessarily short." Webster himself had taught, and re-peated in his letter to the Learner, that the *a* in

antidote is short because the accent falls on the *n*. Similarly, in the words *animate, appetite,* and *altitude,* the initial *a* is short because the stress falls on the following consonant. Therefore, if Webster's rule, (Sheridan's rule, that is to say) were sound, the other vowels in all those words should be short. Since they are not, there must be something wrong with the rule. Webster did not try to justify that part of the rule because he could not—he just pretended it was not there.

The Learner of English Grammar was not the only one to have noticed Webster's recom-mendations reprinted in the newspapers. The Ghost had seen them as well, and in the second part of his second letter, he pointed out that no matter how many "certificates" Webster ob-tained, they would not cure his errors of gram-mar:

Did not Dilworth's Ghost tell you that you were in-consistent with your pretensions, as well as with the authours you had transcribed?—What will it avail you to beg certificates?—Facts will speak louder than anything you can obtain, even from the State itself.—You have many already, and some from as respectable characters as any in the State—Men of sense, learn-ing and veracity—Yes, and sacred characters too—But can any, or all, of these gentlemen, by their char-acters, weight, or influence, alter the nature of things?—I am very confident that they have too much good sense to think of offering so gross an in-sult to the understanding of the publick.—Can num-bers, riches, learning, respectability of character, or office or even sacredness itself, make *false concord pass for true?* Can they jointly, or separately, hide from the eyes of the impartial reader, one repetition, or reconcile inconsistencies?—Can they supply deficiencies, where you have been too elliptical, or make bad arrangement, good?—Or do you imagine, that certificates will make any person who has read Sheridan's lectures, rhetorical grammar and dictio-nary—with Kenrick's do.—Johnston's pronouncing dictionary and Ash's, as well as Lowth's and Ash's grammar, &c. believe, that the plan is your own, or that it cost you much 'labour,' unless you were trou-bled with a costiveness of the brain, at the time?

As before, Webster's first response to a sug-gestion that he had copied from others was to discuss the grammar, rather than the spelling book:

As to your charge of plagiarism I have only to inform you that it was my original plan to take the principles of Dr. Lowth, so far as they are vindicable, and throw them into a more familiar method for beginners.

This I have endeavoured to do, and I claim nothing of Dr. Lowth's as my own. In two important branches of grammar I have attempted some improvements....

As to the first part, the plan, I solemnly declare, was my own. I never heard the names of Sheridan, Kenrick, or Perry till I had prepared my copy for the press, and never consulted their work till I had published my first edition. But I acknowledge myself much indebted to them for the improvements in the last editions....

Webster's assertion that he had never heard the name of Sheridan until he had prepared his copy for the press is quite clearly inconsistent with the fact that the first edition of the spelling book contains a quotation from Sheridan's *Lectures on Elocution*. Furthermore, the comparison we have made between Sheridan's scheme and Webster's leaves no doubt that Webster had made use of Sheridan. Here, therefore, we have to conclude that Webster was not telling the truth.

The poem "To Dilworth's Ghost" by "Philodilworth" contains nothing that is relevant to our study, but I cannot resist quoting some of it:

> The friendly banner of a Ghost,
> Defends from harm, worst come to worst.
> But such as bravely stand it out,
> And scorn to answer, scold and shout,
> And think, as some affect to do,
> Tho' from a wrong, or partial view,
> That truth will stand without a prop,
> And merit needs no shoring up, —
> Deserve to be severely used
> By nameless critics, and abused.
> Authors of this uncouth complexion,
> Are sure to meet your just correction.
> Besides, the method you pursue
> Deserves my commendation too;
> For Ghosts and Goblins strike with terror,
> Most likely to reclaim from error!
> And all the windings you devise,
> Proclaim you candid, prudent, wise.
> Your language too is energetic,
> Harmonious, pointed, strong, pathetic.
> What a rich COPIA of words
> Your pleasing eloquence affords!
> Your stile — how easily it flows!
> How gracefully your periods close!
> The whole, such elegance and ease
> Pervade, it cannot fail to please.
> Smooth as the rattling of a cart,
> Correct as Nature, spoil'd by art.

More poetry, appeared the following week, closing the Litchfield correspondence:

> Here Dilworth's Ghost comes piping hot,
> But from what world he tells us not;
> He leaves conjecture to her guesses,
> Form'd on the temper he expresses:
> He throws out arguments as swinging   )
> As rage in marble — and convincing,   )
> Or tomahawk in hand of Indian.   )
> In lore pedantic makes a pother,
> Inveighs against Institute and Author:
> Deals scandal with illib'ral sneer,
> Genius attacks, front, flank and rear:
> The bully plays in all his movements,
> And wages war 'gainst all improvements:
> On an imaginary blunder   )
> Pours out his rage in magic thunder,   )
> And makes himself the world's last wonder.)
> Bedaubs mankind with dirt and mud,
> But spills, at last, more ink than blood.
> He Dilworth's Ghost? 'Tis all a fiction!
> To this his deeds speak contradiction.
> Could Dilworth see his name thus stole
> And thus traduced, 'twould mad his soul.
> His speed the lightning's glare would distance,
> His wrath sink Entity to non-existence
> And strike the grammar learning dabster,
> A deadlier blow than he struck Webster.

That was the end of the matter in the *Monitor*. None of Webster's critics ever drew attention to his unacknowledged borrowings from Fenning, or to the fact that the first edition of the spelling book contained a quotation from Sheridan, whose name Webster claimed never to have heard.

On balance, it seems likely that the notoriety resulting from this correspondence did Webster nothing but good. On 17 January 1786, Hudson & Goodwin advertised for sale

At their Printing Office, near the Bridge, Hartford, WEBSTER'S Grammatical Institute, Part I, II and III, By the groce, dozen or single. So great has been the demand for this valuable work, in this and the neighbouring states, that upwards of FORTY THOUSAND have been disposed of in about TWO YEARS.

Webster had not been idle while the Litchfield correspondence was going on. He had returned to the study of law, and actually conducted a few cases — his first before a jury was a dispute between two of his father's cousins, the brothers Ebenezer and Medad Webster. Business at the bar, however, was not sufficiently brisk to afford him a living, and he continued with the preparation of his educational works, as well as with political writing. Some of his reading in 1784 is recorded in his diary:

October   1. Finished reading Betsy Thought-
              less. Novels will not bear reading
              but once. It would be well if people
              would not permit children to read
              romances, till they were arrived to
              maturity of judgement.
          28. Read Belisarius, a work that deserves
              to be engraven on the heart of every
              Legislator.
November 29. Finished reading Mr. Barlow's
              Columbus.

He must have borrowed Barlow's manuscript, since *The Vision of Columbus* was not
published until 1787. Presumably he liked it,
since he included excerpts in the reader, the
third part of the *Grammatical Institute,* which
was published by Barlow & Babcock early in
1785. It also included bits of Dwight's *Conquest
of Canaan.*

Webster's diary records that he finished
compiling the Reader on February 5, 1785. Later
that month, he wrote a political pamphlet,
Sketches of American Policy, of which the *Memoir* contains this account:

In the first sketch, the author treats of the theory of
government. This was written soon after reading
Rousseau's *Social Contract*, from which he had im-
bibed many visionary ideas, which subsequent
reflection and observation induced him to reject.

The second sketch contains a brief view of the
governments on the eastern continent.

The third sketch contrasts the condition of the
United States with that of European States, in regard
to the forms and principles of government.

The fourth sketch purports to describe a plan of
policy for improving the advantages and perpetuat-
ing the union of the American States. He laid it down
as a fundamental principle, that there must be a
supreme power at the head of the union, vested with
authority to make laws that respect the United States,
and to compel obedience to those laws — a supreme
head having as ample power to enforce its laws, as the
legislatures of the several states have to make and
enforce laws, on their citizens, in matters of their
own police; that so long as a single state could defeat
or control the measures of congress of the twelve
other states, our union was but a name, and our confederation a cobweb....

The ex-Chancellor Kent of New York has repeatedly said that this pamphlet contains the first distinct proposition for the formation of a new Constitution that was made or published.

When Webster set out from Hartford on
May 2, 1785, in pursuit of copyright protection
in the Southern states, it was with copies of that
pamphlet in his pocket.

7. Itinerant Lecturer and Spelling Reformer

His first day's journey took him only as far as New Haven, where he saw a hot-air balloon rise several hundred feet, thanks to the "ingenuity of Mr. Meigs." He also made a contract with a Mr. Fitch, for the printing of an edition of the second part of the *Institute*.

From New Haven, he sailed to New York, arriving on May 4, 1785. The following day, he took tea with Mrs. Aaron Burr, whose children had been pupils at his school in Sharon, four years before. From New York, he sent his baggage by ship to Charleston (including copies of parts of the *Institute*) and he himself set out on horseback for Baltimore, stopping for a day in Philadelphia on the way.

In Baltimore, Webster was introduced to Dr. Moyes, described in his diary as "the celebrated Scotch lecturer or Natural Philosopher, blind but sensible." Dr. Moyes was on a lecture tour of America, and during May Webster attended six of his lectures, on subjects such as light, phosphorus, sounds, and electricity. Part way through the series, he made his first foray away from Baltimore in pursuit of copyright:

[May] 19.... set out for Alexandria arrive at 8 o'clock — 50 miles.

20. Visit Dr. David Stuart, a member of the legislature; lay before him my wishes for a copyright law; he promises his assistance[1]; he introduces me to Col. Symms, another member from Alexandria. Afternoon I proceed to Gen[l].Washington's seat, 9 miles from Alexandria, down the River Potowmack, an elegant situation on the bank of the river; treated with great attention; continue with him the night. Play whist with the Gen[l] and his Lady, who is very social.

Webster's excuse for calling on Washington was that he wanted to give him a copy of *Sketches of American Policy*. Why the General should, in exchange, have given Webster dinner, a game of whist, and a bed for the night, is unclear; perhaps it is an example of Southern hospitality.

Back in Baltimore, Webster thought of opening another school, and placed an advertisement:

To the Inhabitants of Baltimore

It is a very common and a very just complaint that no Branch of Education is neglected so much as the Study of our native Language. From what Cause this Neglect proceeds, it is needless to examine, as the Fact is generally acknowledged and lamented. It is a Fact equally to be regretted, that the Instruction of a School has in many Places been accounted a disreputable Employment, and of course committed to Men of indifferent Characters and Abilities. The Good sense of Baltimore seems to have prevailed over these Prejudices, and it is sincerely to be wished that a total Reformation may be wrought in our Method of Education. The Subscriber, having employed several years in improving the English Grammar, and with very unexpected Success, offers, at the Solicitation of his Friends, to open a School in Baltimore, for the Instruction of young Gentlemen and Ladies in Reading, Speaking and Writing the English Language with Propriety and Correctness. He will also teach Vocal Music in as great perfection as it is taught in America. He expects as an indispensable condition that the School should be patronized by Families of Reputation, and he himself will be responsible for the success of the undertaking. For particulars inquire of the Subscriber, at his Lodgings at Mrs. Sandersons', opposite South Street.

May 25, 1785   NOAH WEBSTER

Without waiting for a response to that advertisement, Webster made arrangements for another journey, down the coast to Charleston. He set sail on June 1, but did not arrive until the

26th. Adverse winds, fierce squalls, and periods of windless calm prolonged the journey so much that fresh food on the boat ran out, and water had to be rationed.

The box of books that he had sent from New York had arrived before him, and on June 27 his diary records, "Open my books at Mr. Timothy's & advertise them." On June 30, he registered the title of the *Institute* to secure copyright.

As a way of bringing the *Institute* into use, and thus promoting future sales, Webster would often give free copies to a local school. This he did in Charleston, though not until after the July 4 celebrations:

> July 1 and 2.   Nothing particular, the weather is hot & the Musketo's troublesome.
>   3. Sunday, Read Beattie's Theory of Language, lent me by Mr. Sam¹ Baldwin.
>   4. Independence Celebrated with Cannon, musquetry, fire works &c. a balloon set off, takes fire, falls on the market, but the fire extinguished. I ascend the steeple to take a view of the town from the steeple; Charleston is very regular; the most regular of any in America, except Philadel & New Haven. They have a good chime of bells.
>   5. Wait on Mr. Hutson with a note, presenting the Mount Sion Society 200 first part & 100 2d part of the Institute; for the benefit of Winnsborough College....

There was nothing more to be done in Charleston, so he returned to Baltimore, the journey this time taking only a week. He could not pursue copyright further because the legislatures of Maryland, Virginia, and Delaware were not in session, so he stayed in Baltimore for the rest of the summer. One of the first things he did when he got back there was to write to Washington, asking him to endorse the *Institute:*

Baltimore — July 18th, 1785

Sir,

If the request I am now to make should need any apology but such as will naturally be suggested by its own importance, I am sure it will find it in your candour. The favourable reception of my grammatical publications in the northern States, has induced me to offer them for sale in the Southern; and I am happy to find they meet with the approbation of those literary Gentlemen, with whom I conversed on my tour to Charleston. The performance may possibly appear, at first thought, trifling; & yet as containing the rudiments of our native language, the foundation of our other scientific improvements, it doubtless ought to be considered as extremely important. If you, Sir, view it in the latter point of light & have taken the trouble to examine the general plan & execution, your name, as a patron of the Institute, would be very influential in introducing it to notice in these States. I should be very unhappy to make any request, a compliance with which would require the least sacrifice from so distinguished a character, but if it can be done, consistently with the sentiments of your heart and the delicacy of your feelings, the addition of your name, Sir, to the catalogue of patrons, will, I vainly hope, be a continuation of your public utility — & will certainly be esteemed a singular favour conferred on one who is anxious to improve the literature & advance the prosperity of this country.

> I have the honour to be,
>   Sir,
> with the highest respect,
>   your most obedient
> most humble Servant
>   Noah Webster

P.S. I shall probably remain here till October.

As it turned out, Webster did "vainly hope" for Washington's endorsement. On July 30 the general politely replied that he did not feel able to give the *Grammatical Institute* his approval because he had not had time to read it, and even if he had read it, he would not have been qualified to judge its merits.[2]

Perhaps because he had not been in Baltimore to answer any inquiries, Webster's proposed school never opened, though he did take on some pupils for instruction in vocal music. For his singing school, he used Dr. Allison's church, and in exchange he provided the church with a choir made up from his students. He also returned to the study of French, having on July 18 procured "Telemachus in English & French & a master to teach me." On July 27, we read in his diary "Begin French"; on August 1, "Teaching Music & learning French"; and on September 4, "Sunday. Begin to sing in church; astonish all Baltimore with ten scholars." On October 4, he got into an argument with one of his singers, a Mr. Hall, writing, "People in Baltimore have not been accustomed to my rigid discipline."

Teaching singing to ten scholars was not enough to keep Webster busy or to afford him a living, and he had to think of something else to do. What came into his mind were

Dr. Moyses' lectures; if a blind Scottish scientist could lecture on light, could not Noah Webster, who was anything but dumb, lecture on language?

He began writing his "remarks on the English Language" in the last week of August, and by October 6 had completed five "Dissertations," despite having taken time out on September 27, with two friends, to count the houses in Baltimore. The first person to hear his "remarks" on language was Dr. Allison. This, and the first public readings were recorded in his diary:

[Oct.] 10. Wait on Dr. Allison.
11. Take tea with him, & read my Remarks to him.
12. Breakfast with him again; he concludes to permit me to read them as Lectures in his church.
19. Read my first Lecture, to a small audience, the weather very bad.
21. Read my 2d Lecture.
22. Read my 3d to a larger audience.
24. Read my fourth Lecture.
25. Repeat my first.
26. Read my fifth & last Lecture & close my school. The Lectures have recd so much applause that I am induced to revise & continue reading them in other towns.

Two years before this time, a Colonel Timothy Pickering of Philadelphia had sat up all night in camp in Newburgh, reading the first edition of Webster's spelling book. He liked it so much that he sent it to his wife, to be used in the education of their son John. It was, he told her, "the very thing I have so long wished for, being much dissatisfied with any spelling book I had seen before."[3] Pickering had now seen the second edition of the spelling book and he wrote to Webster suggesting some improvements that he thought might be made to it, commenting on the pronunciation recommended in Sheridan's dictionary and inviting Webster to visit him, "if business should lead you to Philadelphia." Webster later wrote, "This letter commenced my acquaintance & correspondence with the writer, who has proved a most valuable Friend." As we shall see, the view of Webster that Pickering later expressed, sometimes to Webster himself, was not one of uncritical admiration. Webster replied to his letter on October 28:

I have read a short course of lectures in this town, which I have just finished. My criticisms have the approbation of the best judges in this town, who attended the Lectures and who advise me to proceed in my plans. My remarks extend to Bishop Lowth and to other Grammarians as well as to Mr. Sheridan. Their works appear to me capable of improvement and in many instances of great corrections. My criticisms are new and no person here is capable of disproving my remarks. I have begun a reformation in the Language and my plan is yet but in embryo.

I have some business in Richmond, Virginia, where I shall travel in a few days; on my return, I shall make some stay in Philadelphia. I hope to be there by the first of December, and probably shall read my Lectures in that city. As I am the first American, who has entered on such important plans and a youth, as well as a Yankee, I shall need the countenance of Gentlemen of your established Character....

Webster did indeed set off for Richmond a few days later, spending the night of November 5 at Mount Vernon. The next morning, Washington gave him the letter of introduction to gentlemen in Richmond that we have already seen. During this visit, Washington told Webster that he was writing to Scotland to seek a secretary who would also act as tutor to Martha Washington's grandchildren. Webster told him that it would be very bad for America's reputation abroad if it became known that no appropriately qualified person could be found at home, and he undertook to find a suitable candidate when he returned to the North.

Thinking the matter over while he was in Richmond, it occurred to Webster that being Washington's secretary and tutor to the young Custises would be not at all a bad job — and perhaps he could do it himself. He was also considering writing a history of the war, and Mount Vernon would be the ideal place for that. Stopping in Alexandria on his way back from Richmond, he wrote to Washington on December 16, 1785:

I have just returned from Richmond where I was happy enough to succeed in my application to the legislature. For this success I acknowledge myself indebted, in some measure, to your politeness.

Should the same success attend me in the states of Delaware and New York, my whole plan will be accomplished; and if on my return to the northern states I find myself in tolerably easy circumstances, I propose to sit down and devote my attention to literary pursuits. This has long been my plan, and to this I direct all my views. Within a few days past, a new idea has struck me and made so great an

impression on my mind that I have determined to write to you on the subject.

I have thought, Sir, that it might be possible for me to answer your views in the superintendence of your children's education and at the same time to pursue my own designs. Could these two points be reconciled, Mount Vernon would furnish an agreeable philosophical retreat. The particular motive which has influenced me to mention this is that a part of my plan would probably be a work in the execution of which I should have occasion for letters and other papers in your possession. At any rate I should want many articles of intelligence which I could not obtain in any way so well as by the assistance of your letters.

If your wishes could be gratified in a person of my character and abilities, I should expect no compensation for any services but your table and other domestic conveniences.

It is uncertain whether I could adopt such a plan myself, even if I should prove agreeable to you and your family; besides, Sir, I can start objections even on your part. No consideration, however, could prevail on me to suppress this communication.

If any material objection should at once oppose itself to this idea, a line from you, Sir, will satisfy me. If, on the other hand, the plan should strike your mind favourably, I should wish for a more particular explanation before I proceed on my journey, as I must, within five or six days ...

Washington's reply, on December 18, was polite but puzzled:

On the footing you have placed your offer, though I feel myself obliged by it, I am unable, from the indecision of it, to return a satisfactory answer. It would by no means suit me to await the determinations of the assemblies of those states (which are mentioned in your letter) on the applications you are about to make to them; and afterwards, a consultation of your circumstances & convenience, before you could resolve on what plan to fix. Nor indeed, does your offer go to more than one point, whilst I have three objects in view, namely, the education of the children, aiding me in my corrispondencies, and keeping my accounts. The last of which, I believe might be dispensed with, or, at any rate, when they are once digested, and brought into order (which is the present employment of Mr. Shaw) they will require very little attention; but the other two are essential to my purposes....

Webster wrote back on the same day, but already he had seen another objection to his accepting the post, one that he had not previously mentioned. He was 27 years old, and it was time for him to think of getting married:

If I understood you, Sir, it is your wish to find a suitable person and employ him for a number of years.

I am so far advanced in life and have so far accomplished my wishes, that I have no idea of continuing single for any long period: my circumstances do not require it and my feelings forbid it. You will perhaps smile, Sir, at the expression; but if I am frank, I am certainly not singular. This circumstance may probably be an insuperable objection; it almost prevented my writing to you on the subject....

Thus Sir, I have been explicit, tho' I have little expectation that the plan can be reconciled to your views....

Webster continued his tour, reading lectures, applying for copyright, and counting houses. A sixth lecture was added to the original five. Their content is described in an advertisement placed in the *Massachusetts Centinel* on July 12, 1786:

To-morrow evening, At half after seven o'clock, in Mr. Hunt's School-House, Mr. Webster will begin a short Course of LECTURES on the *English Language*, and on *Education*. The course will consist of Six Lectures; the heads of which are the following.

    I. Introduction. Origin of the English Language. Derivation of the European Languages from the ancient Celtic. General History of the English Language. Its Copiousness. Effect of this. Irregularity of its Orthography. Causes of this.

    II. Elements of the English Language investigated. Rules of Pronunciation. Different Dialects of the Eastern, the Middle and the Southern States.

    III. Some Differences between the English and Americans considered. Corruption of Language in England. Reasons why the English should not be our Standard, either in Language or Manners.

    IV. Prevailing Errors in the use of Words. Errors of Grammarians in the Arrangement of the Verbs. Consequences of these in the most correct Writings.

    V. Poetry. Principles of English Verse explained. Use and effect of the several Pauses. Effects of different poetic Measures illustrated by Examples.

    VI. General Remarks on Education. Defects in our mode of Education. Influence of Education on Morals, and of Morals on Government. Female Education. Connection between the Mode of Education and the Form of Government. Effects of an European Education in America. Tour of America a useful Branch of Education. Conclusion.

☞ Tickets to be sold at the Post-Office, and at Mr. Battelle's Book-Store in Marlborough Street, at 12s. the course, for Gentlemen, 6s. the course for Ladies, and 3s. a Ticket for an evening.

After the course shall be finished, a lecture will, if desired, be delivered for the benefit of the poor; consisting of remarks on the population, agriculture, literature, climate and commerce of the United States, taken mostly from actual observation. ...

Those who purchase a Ticket for the first evening may afterwards take a Ticket for the course at 9s.

Webster failed to keep to the timetable he had outlined to Colonel Pickering, and on January 20, 1786, he wrote again, saying that he was back in Baltimore, but expected to be in Philadelphia by February 10. He actually arrived there on February 14, by which time he had delivered his lectures in seven towns. The following day, he dined with Pickering, described in his diary as "one of the best of men." Webster was just as pleased with him when he wrote an account of this visit in No. 16 of the *Memoir*:

In Philadelphia, N.W. found a most benevolent and disinterested friend in Col. Timothy Pickering, whose kindness he often mentioned in subsequent periods of his life. Here he also became acquainted with Dr. Rush, whose attachment to him was manifested to him during life. He waited on Dr. Franklin, president of the trustees of the University, and obtained permission to read his lectures in an apartment in that building. He read one lecture in the University Hall for the benefit of The Pennsylvania Hospital, and a handsome sum was received. He was introduced to Mr. Rittenhouse, and many other distinguished citizens. Among other acquaintances made at this time, was Thomas Paine, to whom Col. Pickering introduced him, for the purpose of seeing his model of an iron bridge in miniature. While in this city he registered his Institute under the copyright law of Pennsylvania.

He gave his first lecture in Philadelphia on February 28, "to an audience of about 100 reputable characters." This was many more than he had been able to attract in the South. David Rittenhouse, America's leading astronomer, was described in Webster's diary as "a plain, modest man." Tom Paine at this time had abandoned politics and had designed an iron bridge, by which he hoped to span the Shuylkill River without the use of piers, and make his fortune. The following year, he returned to Europe to interest people in his bridge (for which he was granted a patent in England) only to be drawn back into politics by the need to answer Burke's *Reflections on the Revolution in France*.

On March 20, Webster left Philadelphia for New York, stopping at Trenton on the way to secure copyright in New Jersey for the *Institute*. On March 31, he wrote to Washington from New York, sending him a copy of *The Conquest of Canaan*, which had been published the previous year, and referring to discussions he had had in Philadelphia with Benjamin Franklin:

I am happy in the opportunity, which Mr. Lee's politeness has offered, of presenting your Excellency a copy of Mr. Dwight's Poem. Whatever faults may be found in this performance, its merit cannot fail to recommend it to every friend of America and of virtue.

I flatter myself that in three or four weeks I shall be able to furnish you with an instructor, as several gentlemen will assist me in procuring a man of worth.

Reading lectures in several towns has detained me longer than I expected; but I am encouraged, by the prospect of rendering my country some service, to proceed in my design of refining the language and improving our general system of education. Dr. Franklin has extended my views to a very simple plan of reducing the language to perfect regularity. Should I ever attempt it, I have no doubt that I should be patronized by many distinguished characters....[4]

In the end, the post in Washington's household was offered to Tobias Lear of New Hampshire, on the recommendation of General Lincoln. Lear's subsequent history is summed up by Mrs. Skeel in a depressing footnote: "He accepted the offer and acted as General Washington's Private Secretary for many years, and later became Consul General at Santo Domingo and at Algiers. Returning to the United States he held a subordinate position in the Treasury Department, and killed himself."[5]

On April 6, 1786, Webster delivered his first lecture in New York, and somebody who heard it said that he should try talking slower and lower. A squeaky voice was not agreeable in a lecturer. This was not the first criticism he had received; Pickering, too, had told him that he was not good at reading. Then, on April 11, the *Daily Advertiser* printed unkind remarks about his first lecture. Webster replied,

That my delivery was ungraceful may be true. I was never taught to speak with grace. I know of no institution in America where speaking is taught with accuracy. My subject will not admit of animation in a great degree. I had the misfortune on the first evening to pitch my voice on a key too high for the audience, and was so much indisposed that I could scarcely speak at all....

On 25th April, he wrote to Pickering:

I am improving my Lectures. I have added another. I have regularly about the same number as attended in Philadelphia, among [whom] are many of the first characters in Congress and the Citizens. The design is well received.

I am surprised that you never told me of my great

fault in speaking, pitching my voice on too high a key. It was almost the sole cause of the other fault which you took so much pains to correct. They cured me here the first evening. And I speak now so as to please myself tolerably well, which I did not in Philadelphia. This week I finish. I have received requests to read Lectures in Boston and Portsmouth. I propose to read in Hartford, in May, during the Session of the Legislature, in New Haven, the beginning of June, and then proceed to Boston....[6]

Writing to his nephew, John Gardner, Pickering gave a dispassionate assessment of Webster, his lectures and his letter:

With respect to Mr. Webster, you must have noticed that with a competent share of good sense, he possessed a *quantum sufficit* of vanity, so that he really overrated his own talents. He imagined that he was a good reader, but I had so much friendship for him as to point out his defects; and though it was evidently a little mortifying, he thanked me then, and has since made his acknowledgments by letter. He was particularly defective in reading poetry, and this perhaps as much as anything disgusted his audience. In truth there was so much of egotism, especially in a young man, apparent in his communications, as to prevent his hearers receiving the satisfaction that might otherwise have been derived from many ingenious observations. For my own part I esteem him for his ingenuity, learning and industry.... I have taken the liberty in a letter since his departure to tell him that diffidence in a public lecturer, especially in a young man, was essential to the art of pleasing. As to the encouragement he met with, I do not think it was to be boasted of; at the same time, bating the truly dispeasing marks of vanity, I think the encouragement he received was less than he deserved....
Mr. Webster has repeated his lectures at New York, and he wrote me to an audience, about as numerous as that in Philadelphia. He said that Dr. Ramsay and other members of Congress patronised his design, and his execution of it thus far, and encouraged him to go on, particularly to attempt a reform of the English alphabet, so as to give a distinct character to every distinct sound, and to let no one sound be signified by more than one character. This would introduce some new letters and expunge several of the old ones. Dr. Franklin wrote a paper some years ago which he showed to Mr. Webster. By the way, the Dr. treated Mr. Webster with respect, and expressed himself thus on his Sketches of American Politics, that it was very well written. This remark regarded that part of the pamphlet which in a forcible manner pointed out the necessity of altering the Federal government, and enlarging the powers of Congress. Mr. Webster has since written to the Doctor, submitting to his censure a plan for a reformed alphabet, and requesting the Doctor's permission of dedicating to him his lectures, which he intends to publish.

I believe you did not hear Mr. Webster's lectures. Among other things he showed the glaringly improper pronunciation of many words in all the States, but there seemed to be fewer in New England than elsewhere. The lectures were, I believe, never intended as a catch-penny scheme, but they served to explain and recommend the principles on which his "Grammatical Institute" was founded.[7]

Pickering was absolutely right to make the association between Webster's lectures and the *Grammatical Institute*. The journey to the South was a book promotion tour before it was a lecture tour, but the lectures fitted nicely into the strategy. Webster was able to tell his audiences what was wrong with previous methods of education and to promote his own. The people who decided which spelling book the local school would use were likely to come to the lectures, and even if they did not, they would know that Webster's *Grammatical Institute* had been written by an expert who gave lectures on language. He continued lecturing until December 1786, but we need not follow him round the country, counting houses as he went, because by now all the important connections had been made. When he looked back on those lectures, in No. 13 of the *Memoir*, Webster gave a realistic assessment:

Lectures on Language were not very interesting to a popular audience; his hearers were not numerous, but always respectable. The proceeds of tickets furnished the means of traveling; during the years 1785 and 1786 he had opportunities of becoming acquainted with many literary gentlemen, in the principal cities and towns, between Baltimore and Portsmouth in New Hampshire, and of extending his knowledge of books treating of the subject of philology.

The most interesting of his new acquaintances was Benjamin Franklin, to whom he wrote on May 24, 1876:

Dear Sir,

When I was in Philadelphia, I had the honor of hearing your Excellency's opinion upon the idea of reforming the English Alphabet. I had repeatedly revolved, in my mind, the utility of such a plan, and had arranged some ideas upon the subject, but had not ventured to hope for success in an undertaking of this kind. Your Excellency's sentiments upon the subject, backed by the concurring opinion of many respectable gentlemen, and particularly the late chairman of Congress, have taught me to believe the reformation of our Alphabet still practicable. I know

that several attempts to effect it in England have proved fruitless; but I conceive they failed through some defect in the plans proposed, or for reasons that do not exist in this country.

Enclosed is a plan for the purpose of reducing the orthography of the language to perfect regularity, with as few new characters and alterations of the old ones as possible.

It is probable that a great number of new and unusual characters would defeat the attempt.

I know not whether your Excellency will be able to understand the characters fully; for it is very difficult to convey sounds on paper, and particularly for me, who am no penman, and cannot form the characters exactly as I wish. But this rough draft will, perhaps, give a sufficient idea of my plan, and it is submitted to your Excellency for adoption, amendment, or rejection....

Should this or any other plan be adopted, it is desired that your Excellency would lay it before Congress for their critical consideration. The advantages of adopting a reformation in this country, whether political or literary, will readily occur to an attentive mind, and it would be arrogant and superfluous for me to state them to one who is so accurately acquainted with the elements of language and the interest of America as your Excellency.

General Washington has expressed the warmest wishes for the success of my undertaking to refine the language, and could he be acquainted with the new alphabet proposed, would undoubtedly commence its advocate.

A few distinguished characters might give such weight to an attempt of this magnitude as to crush all the opposition that would be made by the enemies of our independence.

The minds of the people are in a ferment, and consequently disposed to receive improvements, — once let the ferment subside, and the succeeding lethargy will bar every great and rapid amendment. The favorable reception my lectures have generally met with, encourage me to hope that most of the Americans may be detached from an implicit adherence to the language and manners of the British nations....

P.S. It would be esteemed a singular favor, if your Excellency would publicly recommend the Institute — it would facilitate its introduction, and confer a particular obligation on me.

I must also beg permission to inscribe my lectures to your Excellency, when I publish them, as it is probable I may do within a few months.

To this Franklin replied on June 18, 1786:

I received the Letter you did me the honour of writing to me the 24th past, with the scheme enclos'd of your reformed Alphabet. I think the Reformation not only necessary but practicable. But have so much to say to you on the Subject, that I wish to see and confer with you upon it, as that would save much Time and Writing. Sounds, till such an alphabet is fix'd, not being easily explain'd or discours'd of clearly upon Paper. I have formerly consider'd this Matter pretty fully, and contriv'd some of the means of carrying it into Execution, so as gradually to render the Reformation general. Our Ideas are so nearly similar, that I make no doubt of our easily agreeing upon the Plan, and you may depend on the best Support I may be able to give it as a Part of your Institute, of which I wish you would bring with you a compleat Copy, having as yet seen only part of it: I shall then be better able to recommend it as you desire. Hoping to have soon the Pleasure of seeing you, I do not enlarge, but am, with sincere Esteem ...

Franklin's letter was addressed to Webster in New York, which Webster had already left; nevertheless, he received it in New Haven only four days after it was written, and sent his answer on the following day, June 23, 1786:

I am happy that a plan of reforming our Alphabet is so well received by a gentleman who thoroughly understands the subject; and am more and more convinced from the present sentiments and spirits of the Americans, that a judicious attempt to introduce it needs but the support of a few eminent characters to be carried into effect.

I feel the necessity of conferring with your Excellency on the subject, and would do myself the honor of waiting on you immediately, had I not made arrangement, or rather engagements, to read lectures in Boston and Portsmouth this summer. Every circumstance with me renders this the most eligible plan; for the lectures have their effect in preparing the minds of people for any improvements, and my business will require me to be at Philadelphia in September or October. If this would answer your Excellency's wishes, it would be more convenient to me; otherwise I will come to Philadelphia immediately. I shall be in New Haven about ten days, and then proceed to Boston, unless I have further information.

Franklin did not think that the reform of the alphabet was a matter of such urgency as to justify Webster in breaking his engagements; he wrote back on July 9:

I think with you that your Lecturing on the Language will be of great use in preparing the Minds of People for the Improvements proposed, and therefore would not advise your omitting any of the Engagements you have made, for the sake of being here sooner than your business requires, that is in September or October next. I shall then be glad to see and confer with you on the Subject....[8]

Once again, Webster found that he was going to be late arriving in Philadelphia. On October 28, he wrote to Franklin from Hartford, where

he had just arrived "after a Lecturing Tour thro' the Eastern States, in which my success equalled my expectations." Webster continued,

The time is expired, that I proposed for my journey to Philadelphia; and altho' I am determined not to be disappointed by common accidents, yet I labor under some embarrassments which I take the liberty to mention to your Excellency. The profits on the sale of my books which amount now to about £100 per ann. are all appropriated to reimburse the expenses I have incurred in prosecuting my designs, so that I cannot with propriety expect any assistance from them for the coming year. My Lectures which have supported me hitherto are closed & I have nothing to depend on for subsistence this year, but my further exertions in some business. I can hardly bear my expenses to Philad^c, much less can I support myself there without some business which is not ascertained.

Possibly a subscription may be obtained for a repetition of my Lectures in Philad^l. I have thought of instituting an oratorical academy in that city or New York, or to open public reading[s] after the plan of Mr. Sheridan in London. I was asked when in Philad^l by President Ewing, whether I would accept the professorship of Oratory in the University. This I could not do then & I do not know whether I should now be willing. I know not the emoluments of it, nor indeed the business. If it requires the attention of a man, like a school, as I suspect from a little acquaintance with Mr. Gamble, the late professor, I should not — I could not take it. If the business consists in reading Lectures at stated times, or in hearing the lessons of a class, as the instructors practice in New Haven or Cambridge, it is probable I should be glad of the place.

I wish for business — it is my life — it is my pleasure, as well as my support. But I began a vast design without without a shilling, and I know the world too well to ask pecuniary assistance from any person. I want none, I will take none, but what I earn. I wish, if possible, to have business which will afford me some leisure, for my lectures must be prepared for the press as soon as possible, & my Institute stands in need of improvement.

If your Excellency can furnish me with any prospects in either of the ways mentioned, or in any other, it would be a satisfaction to me & enable me to make such arrangements here as will be necessary, if I leave this State....[9]

Franklin did not come up with the offer of a job, and so Webster left Hartford on November 23, 1786, "to seek a living". He arrived in Philadelphia on December 26, delayed by snow, and by the need to give a few more lectures on the way. Webster shows in No. 17 of the *Memoir* that he felt himself to be conferring something of a favor on Franklin in making the journey:

In the autumn of 1786, N.W. went to Philadelphia, at the request of Dr. Franklin who wished to consult with him on a plan for reforming the orthography of the English Language. Dr. Franklin had, many years before, formed the scheme of a new alphabet, and had types cast for printing his new characters, specimens of which are seen in his works. It was the Doctor's desire that N.W. should take these types and prosecute the plan....

Where Webster speaks in that passage of "reforming the orthography of the English Language," he is attempting a little rewriting of history. In fact, as we have seen, he was at this time not just thinking of changing the spelling of English, but of changing the alphabet itself. Pickering's letter to his nephew referred to Webster's plans for "a reform of the English alphabet, so as to give a distinct character to every distinct sound, and to let no one sound be signified by more than one character, [which] would introduce some new letters and expunge several of the old ones." Webster's diary for May 25, 1786, says ,"Form a plan of a new Alphabet & send to Dr. Franklin...."; his letters to Franklin, in May and in June 1786, both referred to reforming the alphabet. On February 24, 1787, two months after his arrival in Philadelphia, he read a lecture (according to his diary) on "Reforming the English Alphabet." Of course it is not politically possible to carry out such a reform, and Franklin, a wily old politician if ever there was one, knew that perfectly well. At the same time, he had amused himself by working out a theoretical system, and he had some type cast for printing it because he was, by training, a printer. When retelling the story later on, Webster preferred a different version, in which Franklin was the impractical dreamer and Webster the hard-headed realist who knew all along that Franklin's scheme was not feasible. He writes in No. 17 of the *Memoir*,

This desire of the Doctor was somewhat embarrassing to N.W., for he was then and has ever been of the opinion that any scheme for the introduction of a new alphabet, or new characters, is and will be impracticable. Nor did he think any scheme of this kind necessary for the purpose; being persuaded that the characters we use, with a few points attached to them, to designate different sounds, may be made to answer all essential purposes of a perfect alphabet.

Accordingly, he declined the Doctor's offer of the use of his types, alledging that he could not risk the expense of the undertaking, especially during the troubles of the times.

Contrast Webster's excuse here (written many years later) that he could not attempt a reform of the alphabet "especially during the troubles of the times" with what he wrote to Franklin in May 1786. What he said then was that he believed "the reformation of our Alphabet still practicable," and that the *ideal* time to make the attempt was when "the minds of the people are in a ferment."

If Webster did indeed have plans to "introduce some new letters and expunge several of the old ones," he had swung to the opposite extreme from the Johnsonian conservatism of the first edition of the spelling book. He did not long remain at that extreme, for he soon realized that he did not have the political weight necessary to carry through a reform of the alphabet, however desirable it might be. Spelling reform, however, was not nearly so difficult, and that is what Webster next embraced. He became an advocate of more or less phonetic spelling, using the existing alphabet. Here, his position is well documented, for when his revised lectures on language were eventually published as a book, in 1789, he added as an Appendix, "An Essay on a Reformed Mode of Spelling." The book was called *Dissertations on the English Language: with Notes Historical and Critical; By Noah Webster, Jun. Esquire.* In the following year, 1790, he published *A Collection of Essays and Fugitiv Writings*, where the deliberately provocative title gave promise of some even more unorthodox spelling within.

In a paragraph and footnote that Webster evidently wrote with Johnson's Dictionary in front of him, the Appendix to the *Dissertations* refers to earlier proposals for reform:

Several attempts were formerly made in England to rectify the orthography of the language..... *

*The first by Sir Thomas Smith, secretary of state to Queen Elizabeth; Another by Dr. Gill, a celebrated master of St. Paul's school in London; Another by Mr. Charles Butler, who went so far as to print his book in his proposed orthography; Several in the time of Charles the first; and in the present age, Mr. Elphinstone has published a treatise in a very ridiculous orthography.

That is an unacknowledged précis of a paragraph in Johnson's grammar (at the front of his dictionary). Here are some of Johnson's own words:

There have been many schemes offered for the emendation of our orthography. One of the first who proposed a scheme was Sir Thomas Smith, secretary of State to Queen Elizabeth. Another by Dr. Gill, the celebrated master of St. Paul's school in London. Dr. Gill was followed by Charles Butler, who printed his book according to his own scheme. In the time of Charles I, there was a very prevalent inclination to change the orthography....

Webster goes on:

But I apprehend their schemes failed of success, rather on account of their intrinsic difficulties, than on account of any necessary impracticability of reform. It was proposed, in most of these schemes, not merely to throw out superfluous and silent letters, but to introduce a number of new characters. Any attempt on such a plan must undoubtedly prove unsuccessful. It is not to be expected that an orthography, perfectly regular and simple, such as would be formed by a "Synod of Grammarians on principles of science," will ever be substituted for that confused mode of spelling which is now established. ...

The "Synod of Grammarians" is a direct quotation from Johnson. The quotation marks acknowledge that it was borrowed, though without identifying the source.

Next, Webster summed up his own proposals:

The principal alterations, necessary to render our orthography sufficiently regular and easy, are these:
1. The omission of all superfluous or silent letters; as *a* in *bread*. Thus *bread, head, give, breast, built, meant, realm, friend*, would be spelt, *bred, hed, giv, brest, bilt, ment, relm, frend*. Would this alteration produce any inconvenience, any embarrassment or expense? By no means. On the other hand, it would lessen the trouble of writing, and much more, of learning the language; it would reduce the true pronunciation to a certainty; and while it would assist foreigners and our own children in acquiring the language, it would render the pronunciation uniform, in different parts of the country, and almost prevent the possibility of changes.
2. A substitution of a character that has a certain definite sound, for one that is more vague and indeterminate. Thus by putting *ee* instead of *ea* or *ie*, the words *mean, near, speak, grieve, zeal*, would become *meen, neer, speek, greev, zeel*. This alteration could not occasion a moments trouble; at the same time it would prevent a doubt respecting the pronunciation; whereas the *ea* and *ie* having different sounds, may give a learner much difficulty. Thus *greef* should be substituted for *grief; kee* for *key; beleev* for *believe; laf*

for *laugh*; *dawter* for *daughter*; *plow* for *plough*; *tuf* for *tough*; *proov* for *prove*; *blud* for *blood*; and *draft* for *draught*. In this manner, *ch* in Greek derivatives, should be changed into *k*; for the English *ch* has a soft sound, as in *cherish*; but *k* always a hard sound. Therefore *character, chorus cholic, architecture*, should be written *karacter, korus, kolic, arkitecture*; and were they thus written, no person could mistake their true pronunciation.

Thus *ch* in French derivatives should be changed into *sh*; *machine, chaise, chevalier*, should be *written masheen, shaze, shevaleer*; and *pique, tour, oblique*, should be written *peek, toor, obleek*.

3. A trifling alteration in a character, or the addition of a point would distinguish different sounds, without the substitution of a new character. Thus a very small stroke across th would distinguish its two sounds. A point over a vowel, in this manner, *à*, or *è*, or *ī*, might answer all the purposes of different letters. And for the dipthong [sic] *ow*, let the two letters be united by a small stroke, or both engraven on the same piece of metal, with the left hand line of the *w* united to the *o*.

These, with a few other inconsiderable alterations, would answer every purpose, and render the orthography sufficiently correct and regular.

Webster has here moved away from the extreme position described by Pickering, and not merely by abandoning the idea of introducing new characters. Then, he was considering a reformed alphabet in which (1) there would be one character for each sound, and (2) there would be one sound for each character. He is still trying to retain the second of those conditions, to avoid uncertainty with regard to pronunciation, but the first condition is no longer enforced. For example, each of the words karacter, kolic, and arkitecture, has retained a letter c which has the same sound as the letter k that Webster introduced.

Webster has already said, and he repeats, that phonetic spelling would make it easier for children and foreigners to master both the writing and the pronunciation of English. He then points out two less obvious advantages:

3. Such a reform would diminish the number of letters about one sixteenth or eighteenth. This would save a page in eighteen; and a saving of an eighteenth in the expense of books, is an advantage that should not be overlooked.

4. But a capital advantage of this reform in these states would be, that it would make a difference between the English orthography and the American.... The alteration, however small, would encourage the publication of books in our own country.... Besides

this, a *national language* is a band of *national union*. Every engine should be employed to render the people of this country *national*; to call their attachments home to their own country; and to inspire them with the pride of national character....

There is a footnote to this page in the Appendix, in which Webster writes:

I once heard Dr. Franklin remark, "that those people spell best who do not know how to spell;" that is, they spell as their ears dictate, without being guided by rules, and thus fall into a regular orthography.

The assertion that bad spelling is good is a typical Franklin paradox. He had said the same thing in a letter to his sister Jane Mecom, on July 4, 1786: "You need not be concern'd in writing to me, about your bad Spelling, for in my Opinion, as our Alphabet now stands, the bad Spelling, or what is call'd so, is generally the best, as conforming to the Sound of the Letters and of the Words." This is certainly true if a sensible phonetic system of spelling is adopted, for then what is now condemned as bad spelling would become correct. Spelling reform would help those who do not know how to spell.

When she was editing her mother's book, Mrs. Skeel had to decide whether or not to interfere with the spelling of Webster's manuscript material. She had correspondence on the subject with Charles Evans, compiler of the *American Bibliography*, and this is what she wrote:

The only corrections I have not accepted, concern spelling or punctuation. In the list of life's ironies I should suggest that my forbear became a reformer of orthography because he was not a *born* speller — he to the end of his middle life retaining what the Virginian called "private ideas on that subject." It has not seemed to me that his editor should be a purist for him, but should give his "first" or even his second "fine careless rapture" free scope. In this my brother disagrees with me as he thinks that the reader's eyes and time should be considered. But I prefer to print the diary verbatim, like the letters, so that April *wether* did actually differ from May *weather*, as described by Webster.[10]

Mrs. Skeel was absolutely right to leave Webster's spelling untouched, but I believe her analysis to have been precisely wrong. There is probably no such thing as a "born" speller, but Webster was no worse at it than most other educated men. When she saw him write *wether*, Mrs. Skeel supposed that he was doing what

came naturally, and that when he wrote *weather*, he was remembering how the word ought to be spelled. I think it was the other way round. Webster's education had taught him how to spell conventionally, and his natural instinct was therefore to write *weather*: at the same time, his "private ideas" on the subject led him to favor dropping the silent *a*. He recommended the spelling *wether*, but he did not always remember to practice what he preached.

We can see this when we look at an example of the reformed spelling in use. Here is the final part of the Preface to Webster's *Collection of Essays and Fugitiv Writings*:

The reeder wil obzerv that the orthography of the volum iz not uniform. The reezon iz, that many of the essays hav been published before, in the common orthography, and it would hav been a laborious task to copy the whole, for the sake of changing the spelling.

In the essays, ritten within the last yeer, a considerable change of spelling iz introduced by way of experiment. This liberty waz taken by the writers before the age of queen Elizabeth, and to this we are indeted for the preference of modern spelling over that of Gower and Chaucer. The man who admits that the change of *housbonde, mynde, ygone, moneth* into *husband, mind, gone, month*, iz an improovment, must acknowlege also the riting of *helth, breth, rong, tung, munth*, to be an improovment. There iz no alternativ. Every possible reezon that could ever be offered for altering the spelling of wurds, stil exists in full force; and if a gradual reform should not be made in our language, it wil proov that we are less under the influence of reezon than our ancestors.

That paragraph is followed by an indication of the time and place when it was written — "*Hartford, June* 1790.," which is an example of American phonetic spelling that owes nothing to Webster. The place where he was born and raised took its name from Hertford in England, but wrote the word as it sounded. In the same way, Barlow's hometown, Redding in Connecticut, has the pronunciation, but not the spelling, of Reading in Berkshire.

The excerpt from Webster's Preface shows that he was neither thorough nor consistent in applying his own principles. He should, for example, have replaced *ph* by *f* in *orthography*: also, if *s* with the sound of *z* is to be replaced by *z* in *obzerv, iz, waz* and *reezon*, it should also be replaced by *z* at the end of plurals such as *essays* and *wurds*. Similarly, *c* sounding like *s* should

be replaced by *s*—*ancestors* should be written *ansesterz*. Webster remembered to remove the initial *w* from *ritten* and *riting*, but left it on *writers*. It might be said, indeed, that the very title of his book reflected the tentative nature of his reforms: He chopped the *e* off *Fugitiv*, but left the *W* on *Writings*.

The experimental phonetic spelling in the *Fugitiv Writings* excited almost universal ridicule, and Webster did not persist in any wholesale attempt to convert America. At the same time, he was himself so fully convinced of the good sense of his proposals that he could not bring himself to abandon them entirely. Those that were most extreme he abandoned straight away, others more gradually, and some he never abandoned at all. In broad terms, he stopped trying to introduce phonetic respellings, but went on trying to expunge silent letters — but there are exceptions to both those generalizations.

That attitude of mind would have a profound effect later, when he began to compile dictionaries. Many lexicographers have been in favor of spelling reform in theory, and some of them have written articles and sat on committees whose aim was to persuade people to adopt reformed spelling in practice. At the same time, they have not allowed their dictionaries to reflect those views, believing that the purpose of a dictionary is to describe what the language is, not to prescribe what it ought to be. Webster had no such scruples, perhaps because he could not stop himself telling people when he believed them to be wrong. As we shall see, he introduced a number of reformed spellings into his dictionaries — spellings that were not in use, and often never had been in use, but which he believed ought to be used. It was the characteristic of his dictionaries that his critics most objected to.

One of those critics was Oliver Wendell Holmes, whose father, Abiel Holmes, was a Congregationalist minister and a friend of Webster's. Holmes (the son) was a man who liked dictionaries. On the occasion of the Autocrat's first visit to the Breakfast Table in *The New England Magazine* in 1831, he said,

When I feel inclined to read poetry I take down my Dictionary. The poetry of words is quite as beautiful as that of sentences. The author may arrange the gems effectively, but their shape and lustre have been

given by the attrition of ages. Bring me the finest simile from the whole range of imaginative writing, and I will show you a single word which conveys a more profound, a more accurate, and a more eloquent analogy.

It seems unlikely that the Dictionary he used to take down was Webster's. Believing that words were shaped "by the attrition of ages," Holmes disliked Webster's attempts to speed up the process and shape them himself. In the second chapter of *The Professor at the Breakfast Table*, Holmes likened this to interfering with the free movement of a weathervane:

The little gentleman ... shocked the propriety of the breakfast table by a loud utterance of three words, of which the two last were "Webster's Unabridged," and the first was an emphatic monosyllable.—

Beg pardon — he added, — forgot myself. But let us have an *English* dictionary, if we are to have any. I don't believe in clipping the coin of the realm, Sir! If I put a weathercock on my house, Sir, I want it to tell which way the wind blows up aloft, — off from the prairies to the ocean, or off from the ocean to the prairies, or any way it wants to blow! I don't want a weathercock with a winch in an old gentleman's study that he can take hold of and turn, so that the vane shall point west when the great wind overhead is blowing east with all its might, Sir!

8. Webster in Philadelphia, and in Love, 1787

Webster arrived in Philadelphia on December 26, 1786, and lost no time in reestablishing contact with his influential friends. He visited Franklin on the 28th and dined with him two days later. On New Year's Eve, he dined with Colonel Pickering.

During the first week of January 1787, he read two important books on language, probably borrowed from Franklin, and he made arrangements for a new series of lectures:

January 1st 1787. Read Horne's Diversions of Purley, a new & useful Theory of language.
2. Publish subscription papers for a course of Lectures. Wait on Dr. Ewing.
3. Breakfast with Mr. Brown, Master of the Ladies Academy. Pass the evening at Dr. Sproats, obtain permission to use the University for lecturing.
4. Read Bishop Wilken's Real Character. Evening at Mr. Austin's.

What Webster was reading on New Year's Day was the first edition of Part I of ΕΠΕΑ ΠΤΕΡΟΕΝΤΑ, by John Horne, which had been published in London the previous year — an indication that Philadelphia was by no means out of touch with European learning. Part II was published in 1805, and Part III was never published at all; the author burned the manuscript not long before he died. There was no American edition until 1806. ΕΠΕΑ ΠΤΕΡΟΕΝΤΑ means "Winged Words," a reference to Hermes, who is Language, the divine messenger. The frontispiece shows Hermes strapping on his winged sandals. Because the average English reader was not comfortable in Greek, Horne provided an alternative title by which his book is more usually known, *The Diversions of Purley*. Purley, near Croydon in Surrey, was the home of William Tooke, and the "Diversions" were imaginary conversations that took place there between (in Part I) "B," "T" and "H." "B" was Dr. Beadon, a clergyman and academic, afterwards bishop of Gloucester; "T" was Tooke himself; and "H" was the author of the book, John Horne, who in the course of these conversations set out his theories of language and etymology, and a good deal of politics as well. Horne, argumentative, radical, antiestablishment and pro–American, was an extraordinary man. He first got into trouble with the authorities in England by raising money to help the dependents of Americans killed at Lexington. Later, he was tried for treason, and Part II of the *Diversions* is dedicated to the members of the jury that acquitted him. Tooke was his benefactor, and Horne in gratitude, (and in the expectation of a legacy he did not receive), took his name, so that he is generally known as Horne Tooke. He so over-emphasized the connection between English and Anglo-Saxon that it took English scholarship fifty years or more to recover. As a result, much of the historic work on the etymology of the English language was done by Germans and Scandinavians.

The other book Webster read in that week, Bishop Wilkins' *Towards a Real Character,* was less influential than *The Diversions of Purley,* but no less interesting. It attempted to construct a universal language by drawing a map of meanings. Wilkins divided the class of all meanings into subclasses, sub-subclasses and so on, until the final subdivision left only a single meaning. The model is a biological one of genus, species, subspecies and so forth, with, for animals, a final division into male and female. Thus, a particular location on the lan-

guage map represents the meaning "male sheep"; in English, this is indicated by the word "*ram*"; in other languages, the word will be different, but the meaning, and the location on the map, will be the same.

The first of Webster's new series of lectures, on "Manners," was read "to a small audience" on January 27. He lectured on "Government" on February 6, and on "Reforming the English Alphabet" on February 24. The lectures were not a success, but they helped to pass the time until March 1 when he went to visit "Mr. Ingraham's family" and there met "Miss Greenleaf." Duncan Ingraham and his wife Suzanna (Sukey) had lived for some years in Holland, but had recently returned to Philadelphia. Miss Greenleaf was Sukey's younger sister, Rebecca, who was on a visit from Boston, and Webster quickly fell in love with her.

Within a week he described her in his diary as "the sweet Miss Greenleaf"; on March 15, "Miss Greenleaf, the black-eyed beauty"; on March 22, she was "the lovely Becca," and they went to a concert together. After that, he was at the Ingrahams two or three times a week, and his diary records, "I am at my favorite place," and "With my heart."

In this situation, Webster could not think of leaving Philadelphia, but neither could he remain there without earning some money. Once again, he had to fall back on teaching. On April 10, 1787, he was interviewed by the trustees of the Episcopal Academy, and agreed to "accept of a place there 6 months—@ 200£ a year—Currency." He started in the Mathematical Department, on April 13.

Clearly Philadelphia was no place to keep a secret, for only five days later, on Wednesday, April 18, the following letter appeared in the *Freeman's Journal:*

The uncertainty of all human affairs never appeared more manifestly than in the case of NOAH WEBSTER, jun. esq. whose extraordinary abilities and unparelleled [sic] knowledge of the English language, have enabled him to write that masterpiece of instruction, his *Grammatical Institute.* His consciousness of his own great learning and genius, had justly led him to imagine, that, by his becoming an itinerant lecturer though the United States, he would, by this means, be one of the most valuable citizens of our new empire, and have his name ranked among the great men of this western world.— But, alas! all his well-digested plans and schemes have vanished

into smoke, his LEARNED and USEFUL LECTURES have been neglected, and he himself suffered to starve, or to join one of the most Herculian [sic] pieces of labor that ever any poor man engaged in, to wit, that of a schoolmaster.

This learned man, whose extraordinary knowledge and abilities gave him good reason to expect at least *one thousand guineas* a year of clear profit from his lecturing, is now obliged to accept of *two hundred pounds* a year of paper money, which at present, allowing for discount, is scarcely one hundred pounds sterling. But what is still worse—to aggravate the misfortune, he is to be under the Principal of the Protestant Episcopal academy, a man whose temper has already sent off above half a dozen of teachers, and in a short time must break up the academy. This is surely a strange reverse of fortune on the part of Noah Webster, esq. Would God that he may have magnanimity of mind sufficient to bear all this!

SETH

Webster correctly identified "Seth" as one Thomas Freeman, who had previously taught at the academy, and had been dismissed. Freeman greatly disliked the principal of the academy, the Rev. Dr. Andrews, but it is unclear whether he had been dismissed because he disliked the principal, or disliked the principal because he had been dismissed. Either way, he managed to touch Webster on a tender spot. Webster had himself said in the Introduction to his spelling book that "the principal part of instructors are illiterate people," and he would certainly have preferred some more prestigious employment. It would have been more sensible to have ignored Seth, but a young man in love wants to be seen putting up a manly defense when he is attacked, and Webster wrote a vigorous but ill-judged reply, signed "Adam," containing a catalogue of his own virtues. It appeared in the *Freeman's Journal* for April 25, 1787:

"*Si inveniretur aliqua civitas, in qua nemo peccaret, supervacuus esset inter innocertes orator, sicut inter sanos medicus.*" *Tacitus, De Orat. Dial.*

The English of this passage, adapted to my present purpose, is simply this—"If there were no officious scribbling fools on earth, the lash would be useless."

Your correspondent Seth, or rather *Freeman*, in a pathetic apostrophe, has published his amazement at an event which has lately taken place in the Episcopal Academy. A young gentleman, who has been flourishing through the United States with lectures and a new grammatical publication, has suddenly sunk into the humble office of a teacher of children!

What is *Seth's* conclusion from this? Why, that the man is a poor starved wretch. Seth, poor fellow, was bred in a country where the instructors of children are no company for gentlemen; and he, by masterly reasoning, deduces this consequence from the fact in that country that in this country a *gentleman* will not teach a school. But the gentleman alluded to was bred in a part of America where no men but of the best character and education are permitted to take schools; and he has a whimsical opinion of his own that this practice is right and laudable. He thinks it happy that America has not arrived to that pitch of refined taste which places the *first* business of society in the worst hands, and directs that *drunkards* and *clowns* should form the minds of youth for good citizens and legislators.

Suppose *Seth* should be informed (and he wants either information or honesty) that the gentleman who is so degraded by his acceptance of a place in the Academy is a descendant of the oldest and most respectable families in America, and that his ancestors governed provinces fifty years before Pennsylvania was settled; that he has received as good an education as America can afford, and improved it by a personal acquaintance with the greater part of the principal literary gentlemen in the United States; that his grammatical publications are received into use in one half the States and are spreading in the others as fast as they can be published; that his neglected lectures have been, and still are, under the patronage of the first characters in America; that his political writings have been the acknowledged means of restoring federal measures of great consequence; that for this service he received the thanks of that great and good man, the late Governor TRUMBULL; that for his services to the army, he received the thanks of a Major-General, both for himself and the army[1]; that this gentleman is a lawyer, a regular practitioner at the bar in any of the courts of a neighboring state; that he is possessed of a property which neither *one* nor *two* thousand guineas can purchase. Nay more, suppose *Seth*, who seems to think that an instructor must be a low character, should be informed that this gentleman's reputation is not stained with one dishonourable action. What then! Why, it is a *strange thing* that he should undertake to "Teach the young idea how to shoot."

This may be strange to Seth; and it is the character of blockheads to be gazing, and staring, and gaping at what they suppose *wonderful things* but which appear to other people very common objects. It is probable that *Seth* would be astonished to hear that antient kings and sages taught children and schools — yet it is true — and the different practice of the moderns is a proof of their corruption.

The gentleman has motives for teaching in the Academy which are the noblest that can actuate the human mind. These motives are known to his particular friends; this is sufficient for him and them:

if *Seth* is not satisfied, let him feed upon his wonder.

Seth thinks £200 a year, and paper money too, is a poor pittance. Well, what will he think when he is told that the gentleman refused any stipulation, even for a farthing; and when he accepted the offer, declared to the committee that it should be wholly at their option whether to make him the least compensation or not? Why, this is more amazing still, especially to *little minds!* What is the result of all this? Why, nothing of consequence: A certain stupid fellow, who calls himself *Seth*, ... has published a few impertinent falsehoods, which are as harmless as the author is contemptible. In future, when he has an itch to intrude into other men's business, and display his talents at writing, he will give less offence by confining his exhibitions to his pot-companions at the Derby Ram, for the public wish not to be troubled with them.

But *Seth* aims his most deadly weapons at the Episcopal Academy. He insinuates that the *Principal* is a man of severe temper, and asserts that he has injured the institution by exercising it in dismissing the teachers. Every person in Philadelphia who has kept good company knows that gentleman is possessed of a temper the most unexceptionably mild and amiable. The insinuation is ridiculous, because there is not the most distant probability that any person will believe it. The only fault of the *Principal*, if he has committed any, was that he did not dismiss some of his teachers sooner and supply their places with men of more respectability. If this is a fault, it must be ascribed not to the severity, but to the mildness of his temper. But a change has taken place, which will probably prevent all future complaints on this head.

ADAM[2]

The bit about Webster "refusing any stipulation" is odd, since he certainly did not offer his services to the academy free of charge. The trustees probably asked him how much he expected to be paid, and he sensibly replied that he was happy to leave that to them. After all, if they had a figure in mind and he named a higher sum, they might have rejected him; if he suggested less than they were prepared to pay, they would have agreed to it.

As he was being teased by a former teacher at the academy, Webster's diary entry for April 30, 1787, is relevant here. He wrote, "Busy enough with the Boys of the Academy. They have been managed, or rather not managed, by poor low Irish Masters. O habit! O Education! Of what Importance that our first examples be good, & our first impressions virtuous."

The same issue of the *Freeman's Journal* that

contained Webster's reply to Seth, signed "Adam," had another letter provoked by Seth's, which was signed "Lamech." These names have biblical overtones that would have been familiar to the eighteenth century reader. Seth was an ancestor of Noah, just as Freeman had preceded Webster at the Episcopal Academy. Webster used the name "Adam" as an indication of seniority, because Adam was the father of Seth. Lamech (son of Methuselah) was Noah's father. Reading Seth's letter, Lamech had been struck by the reference to "Noah Webster Jun. Esq.,"

Sir,

Upon hearing a humorous piece read in your paper of Wednesday, signed Seth, I conceived that the writer, through a fit of mirth, had been applying titles to Mr. Webster's name which were only of his own invention, and which Mr. Webster had no pretensions to; but as soon as the gentleman who read the piece let me look at the title page of Webster's Grammatical Institute, which he happened to have in his pocket, I found that the matter was just as Seth had represented. "Well," said I, "if Mr. Webster had considered in his mind the value of this noble maxim, that *humility leads to honor*, I am certain he would not have joined the title Esquire to his name, for such a conduct tends to expose a man's vanity, and to lay him open to the attacks of his enemies; besides, sir, gentlemen of real rank and fortune have all the right in the world to be offended at him for assuming a title to himself which only belongs to them; for who in his senses ever used the appellation esq. to a schoolmaster, a *flagellator anorum* to be called esq.! fie! fie! such a contradiction of terms! we might with equal propriety call a Hottentot, a Yankee, or a Savage a refined Frenchman." "Not so fast neither," says the gentleman, "for I am his countryman, and was bred up in the same college with him; I can prove by pure logic that he has a right to the title esq." "Pray, sir," said I, "let us hear your pure logical demonstration of this matter; for I have often heard, that the logic of New-England was confined to one single principle, namely, *I shall not cheat you, but I will outwit you if I can.*" "You are altogether mistaken, sir," replied he, "for I shall demonstrate my thesis by a concatenation of syllogisms, which is the only method of proving truths that the literati ought to admit of; first, then, every man born in New-England has a right to a title, *quia nobilis natu*, but Noah Webster was born in New-England, *ergo*, Noah Webster has a right to a title. Again, every man who conceives that a title should be joined to his name, has a right to one; but Noah Webster conceives that a title should be joined to his name, *ergo*, Noah Webster has a right to a title. Moreover, every-one who has written a spelling-book, and has a right

to a title, should be called esq. but Noah Webster has written a spelling-book, and has a right to a title, *ergo*, Noah Webster should be called esq. Now, sir," says he, "I hope you are convinced of the truth of my proposition." "Yes," said I, "but a man convinced against his will, is of the same opinion still. However, setting this matter aside for the present, I would be glad to know by what kind of logic you can demonstrate that he had a right to realise a thousand guineas a year of clear profit from his lecturing, which Seth tells us he expected to do; for this sum, if we reckon it in solid sterling coin, is nearly equal to the salaries of the four governors of the New-England States; now, in my opinion, sir, before he commenced itinerant lecturer, he must have known very little of the state of learning and refinement in these United States, for in every city, and indeed in every part of the country that he would go to, I am well convinced that he might find men of infinitely superior abilities to himself, even in that part which he pretended to have such a profound knowledge of; and has not his success proven this to be the case?" "In regard to the 1000 guineas a year," answered the gentleman, "I can say but little, for the sum is so much above any thing that ever I have heard in New-England, that I know of no syllogism whereby I could demonstrate his having a right to expect such an astonishing heap of wealth from his lecturing; but I imagine that the mistake lay in his want of a proper knowledge of arithmetic, by which he must have placed two cyphers more to the sum than he ought to have done." "Bless me," said I, "take away two cyphers from 1000, and you will but leave him 10 guineas a year." "A very good salary," rejoined the gentleman, "in New England; I am sure there are at least five hundred schoolmasters in that country who have not so much; in short, I recollect that Noah's schoolmaster and mine received but twelve pounds currency from the parish, and we have often thought that his salary was a very large one; and I can prove by logic, that our old master's income was more than either Noah or any of his scholars ought to propose for themselves." "You may save yourself the trouble, sir, said I, for this matter appears sufficiently plain to me without your syllogisms, therefore, I shall take it for granted, that ten guineas a year was the sum he proposed to himself, and not a thousand; so that I find he has advanced himself amazingly, by becoming a teacher in the Episcopal academy, instead of being depressed, as Seth seems to think. Seeing then, sir," continued I, "he has bettered his circumstances so much, by getting into the academy, how is he to keep his place; for if the principal be such an overbearing man as Seth seems to insinuate, I am afraid that he will have him out in a hurry." "Never trouble yourself about that matter," says he, "for I can prove by a single syllogism, that the principal stands a greater chance to be ousted by Noah, than Noah by the principal." He was just about to begin his syllogism, when I interrupted him, by saying, "Plague on

your logic, and your syllogisms. Let us have done, and suppose the rest."

LAMECH

The next week, on May 2, 1787, Seth replied to Adam:

"Si inveniretur aliqua civitas, etc." TACITUS

Which, to answer my present purpose, I English thus — "If there were no vain pedants, no frothy pretenders to nobility, ridicule in this respect would be useless." I remember to have read an old moral in Dilworth's spelling- book, *Evil be to them that evil think,* also, *Throw a crust to a surly dog and he will bite you.* How prophetic and well adapted to the present purpose is this saying! *Adam,* or rather WEBSTER, instead of taking good counsel from me, poor Seth, who wished to do him a good turn, by putting him on his guard, that he might know how to please and flatter the Principal of the Academy, in order to keep his place, makes at me with all his force, and lays me such a number of gubernatorial thumps, that, had my head been anything else but a block, it must have been pounded to a mummy by them; but, thanks to my stars, my head is still sound — poor Seth is of a good temper, and notwithstanding the maltreatment which he has received from the governor, is not in the least angry; and in this respect he seems to differ much from his honor the 'squire, who must needs get into a passion, about "a few harmless things published by a contemptible author." Has not poor Seth all along observed good decorum, in giving this illustrious personage his title? Yes, because he knew that he had an indisputable *title to titles* Has not his honor the 'squire certified to us, that he is a twig guberbatorial? — That his ancestors governed, not a province only, but provinces, fifty years before Pennsylvania was settled? No doubt but they were governors as many years before Noah's flood; and its likely that the 'squire's great modesty prevented him from giving us so vast a retrospective view of his primæval grandeur. Our ideal governor is rather indefinite respecting these provinces — perhaps he knows that we must naturally find them out to be in the mountains of the moon. He has not told us whether his ancestors held their governments by hereditary right — which were monarchical, aristocratic, or democratic; or what other form of government they had, or whether they had any at all. But we hope he will satisfy our curiosity in these particulars, in some of his future publications. It is one thousand leagues from being either queer or droll, to observe that the innate *modesty* and *liberality* of those who are nobly born — 'Squire Webster's whole performance is a proof of his modest humility; and his liberality is conspicuous, in his plunging all his brother chips of a certain kingdom into clownism, without a single exception. — Oh rare Noah Webster, esquire! — These are sentiments consistent with gubernatorial sublimity! Will your honor the 'squire be graciously pleased to answer me one question, Is it not a little odd that a regular bred lawyer should become a schoolmaster, supposing him to have "a whimsical opinion of his own that this practice is right and laudable"? I fear there are some who may say, that he must have been only a poor pettyfogger at the bar (altho' Seth thinks very differently); if not, why did he not return to his profession when lecturing failed him — when his pressing invitations to an antient godly jig only cleared him threepence halfpenny? Would it not be advisable for him to take a few instructions from the Jewish high priest, before attempting another lecture of this kind?

One question more to your honor, and then I shall have done. How did you find out that Seth was a poor *stupid fellow*? For Seth thinks that your information invalidates itself; in short, it looks as if it had been both *tarred* and *feathered.* — Expect a little more next Wednesday.

SETH

As he promised, Seth's next letter appeared the following Wednesday, on May 9:

Nosce te ipsum

When a man exposes himself to ridicule by his vanity, and justly deserves by his thrasonical pretensions to superlative merit, it would be really wrong to let him escape; and for this obvious reason, that it has a greater tendency to cure him of his folly, than the most serious and solid reasonings of the ablest philosophers in the world. — So much by way of preface, and now to my subject. — I notified N--H W-B---R, Esq. in the Freeman's Journal of last week, that he should hear more from me to-day, and I mean to be as good as my word. I made a few remarks on the modest performance of the 'squire in my last, and am just about to add half a score or so more to them, as there is abundance of room still left; and now I come point blank to his serious hypothesis and my respondentia. — First, then, his honor saith, *that he has received as good an education as America can afford;* — upon my ruffles, with all due deference to the 'squire, I doubt it a little: I will bet two and twenty pence against a copy of his Institute, of the second edition, that I shall find twenty or thirty folks in this city (and that is but a small part of North and South America) who can *learn** [Seth's footnote: * Webster, in his spelling book, uses *learn* for *teach;* in page [blank] he says, "Easy lesson to *learn* children to read and to know their duty."] him some little nick-nacks yet which belong to a good education. Old Mr. Dilworth judiciously remarked in his spelling book, that,

"He who thinks himself already wise,

"Of course all future knowledge will despise."

There is a good deal more to the same tune, which one may find by turning towards the latter end of the

same book.— He further saith, *he has a property which neither one nor two thousand guineas would purchase*; but he neither tells us whether this property consists in lands, cash, or in bales of unbound spelling books, or packages of literature stored up in the garrett of his terrestrial fabric, nor what else it consists in— he is a little obscure sometimes, and that is a great pity.— He again saith, that *I aim my most deadly weapons at the Episcopal Academy*; but this really is not so; (for Seth cares not whether the Academy consists of 5000 or only of 5 boys) it is true, I took aim at a certain mark thereabouts, for some reasons which I shall show in less than a century, and some confounded obliquity or zigzagity happened just to touch a tumour on or near the noddle of a certain itinerant 'squire who was unluckily in reach; this must put him in a great passion at me, for which he calls me a blockhead— dull— stupid, and all to that; so this is the whole of it.— Again, he saith, he *joined the Academy from motives the most noble that can actuate the human mind.* I have nothing to say about the most nobleness of his motives— I believe they were right laudable motives, and motives that would make any man skip; namely, to prevent starvation. But he saith he *refused every stipulation*, and teaches purely for God's sake. Well, now, your grandees, when they become schoolmasters, are the most eccentric schoolmasters under the moon. Really they like to say and do every thing in a queer out of the way manner. Could he not as well have lectured gratis, and continued at that business, as to teach for nothing in the Academy? Would he not thereby have benefitted hundreds or thousands who could not well spare half a dollar a ticket. His honor informeth us in a later publication, that he hath got a refined education, which is rarefied, purged, and purified from all manner of dregs and excrementious matter; but I fear the 'squire's ipse dixit won't convince every body that his education is entirely refined yet, till the froth totally disappears, and every windy particle takes to its heels and scampers off.— He addeth, that *in the part of America where he was bred, none but men of the best character and education take schools.* Well, this same part of America is a glorious place, where the character and education of all schoolmasters are in the superlative degree; but as this is a degree of comparison which he seems to be very fond of, perhaps he compares some of his adjectives the wrong way. Be that as it may, there is no doubt, but in his Utopia the schoolmasters are all the legitimate breed of Stadtholders. It appears strange to me (and "it is the character of blockheads to be staring and gaping at what they think wonderful things") that he has not certified us, in the pompous display of his nobility and intellectual worth, whether he took a degree or not; perhaps his modesty restrained him from it, or perhaps he thought that Esquire and A.B. would snarl and cuff and bite one another in the title page of his Institute; Now, I guess, to prevent strife of that kind, he discarded poor A.B. and retained the Esquire for his gentleman usher.— Here follows a long rigmarole of his consequence and respectability, which would jade the brains of any sinner living to animadvert upon; as that of the almost universal spread of his spelling books; the respectable patronage of his neglected lectures; the tranquillity that nestled in the profundity of his political writings, that Governor Fiddlestick received the thanks of Governor Bull; that for his service to the army (perhaps standing fugleman on field days) he received the thanks of a Major General of the army, to be distributed in rations to the men, with only a knapsackful or so reserved to himself; Now, whether that be so or not, what, in the name of puffology, is that to us? I wish he would not bother us, nor slap his merits in our teeth. Indeed, had these *wonderful things* come from any other quarter well authenticated, even I, poor Seth, (by his honor sir-named the Stupid) would have thought him a respectable character; but as they come from himself, and want a certain stamp, it had been full as prudent to let them rest snug in his brainpan till some future occasion.— Perhaps his honor may hear next Wednesday again from

SETH

In the same paper as Seth's second letter there was the first installment of an attack on Webster's grammar by one James Kidd, who would seem to have aspired to write a review that was longer than the grammar itself. Webster did not mind this. The discussion of dry points of grammar was very much to his taste, and their dialogue continued until Webster left Philadelphia.

While all this was going on in the *Freeman's Journal*, Webster had been attacked in *The Independent Gazeteer* by someone signing himself "A Pennsylvanian." Webster's reply, under his own name, appeared on May 10, 1787, the day after Seth's second letter. We are not concerned with that argument, which was on an unrelated topic, but one paragraph of Webster's letter must be quoted because it particularly appealed to Seth:

Had I not a thousand testimonials of my patriotism, love of government and justice; had I not written the substance of volumes in support of the Revolution and of federal measures; had I not crushed, almost with my single pen, a state combination against those measures; did not almost every weekly or other periodical publication in America contain proofs of my sentiments, which at any moment can be laid before the world; nay, had I not received an honorary reward for my patriotism, even in this city, I might have had some apprehensions from the malevolent charges and suspicions of the *Pennsylvanian*.

The following week in the *Freeman's Journal*, James Kidd continued, but came nowhere near finishing, his attack on Webster's grammar. The week after that, May 23, Webster replied to Kidd's first installment; Kidd's further remarks had to be postponed for want of room; and Seth had another go:

Charge me not, gentle readers, with tediosity in finishing my reply to his honor the 'squire, for to set your hearts at ease, I am drawing near to a conclusion. My direct view in appearing in print once more, is to thrash the jacket of *Vainglory* wherever I catch him — whether he be the associate of a governor, 'squire, lawyer, pedant or schoolmaster; because he is a sorry scrub, and does more harm than one would think for. Now, know ye, whom it may, and whom it may not concern, that I, poor Seth, do believe and suppose, that his honor 'squire Web r, alias the *trot-about pedagogue*, hath been a constant mess-mate of this same Vainglory ever since he could distinguish a noun adjective from a verb; however, as to that, I cannot be positive; but certes, at any rate, they seem to be cronies of a pretty long standing. Whoever doubteth what I say, let them take a peep at his honor's piece signed Adam, and if that won't convince them, let them take another at his piece signed Noah Webster, of last Wednesday, and that puts the matter beyond an *if* or an *an*; for he tells you of such a huge budget of testimonials as would almost break the back of an ass to stand under them, all relating to his patriotism, love of government, and justice — Ferrule me such tumid puffers, say I. The maimed limb of one worthy officer or soldier, who bravely fought in defence of his country, is a more noble testimonial than his whole thousand. As to his love of government, that's likely enough — he has that by *hereditary right*; but his crushing a combination almost with his single pen, shews him to be a man of considerable spunk undoubtedly. Now to me it appears among the class of *wonderful things* that a *literary bruiser* who could knock me up the heels of a combination, insurrection or dangerous rebellion and lay it flat on its crupper; or whack it so with his potent pen, that it turned as mute as a "mouse in the hole in the wall;" I say it appears wonderful, that the good people of that State did not seize upon such a tip top *"influential man"* per force, and make a governor of him in good earnest. Faugh! how merit can be so much overlooked! — but this corresponds with some saying in a very good old book, namely, that "a prophet hath no honor in his own country." If what he says be true, God pity the State where such a *nerveless Thraso* must have been the first-rate character. If it be not true, he is certainly moon-struck, so that is an end of the matter. He next adds that almost every weekly and other publication contained proofs of his sentiments, that they can be laid before the public at a minute's warning, and that he hath re-

ceived an honorary reward in this city, &c. Now I'll be ferruled on the fingers if ever I heard one single syllable of his *pen* and *ink-istical* prowess, *high birth, rewards*, &c. &c. &c. before April the 25th and May the 10th 1787, either in conversation, newspapers, or otherwise, and I am much of opinion nobody else in this city has heard any thing of the matter. But the moment they are laid before the public, well attested, all our doubts will scud off like fun. Indeed, a piece has appeared since, said to be written by that patriotic character, something to the tune of "What the devil ails you." I suppose this is one culled out the testimonial wallet, as the *prime combination bruiser*, and really if this strong nerved shaver did not send the mob helter-skelter, the devil was in them indeed! though he neither mentions the town nor the paper in which it got a typographical squeeze (particulars necessary to satisfy scrupulous persons), yet it would be uncandid not to believe him as the author of this piece. If his view in this publication be to vindicate his political character, it answers the end well enough with me; but if to establish his *literary character*, it can have no effect; because, with all my *dulness* upon my head, it has, *I affirm that*, scarce a claim to mediocrity. Whatever others may think, I know not, but to me it appears as plain as can be, that if we had so able a political writer a few years ago in this State, our citizens would not have been divided into two parties, to wit, republicans and constitutionalists, alias skunks. God help us, such a lucky cast was not allotted for us; perhaps we were unworthy of it. For my part I never meddle with politics, *pro* or *con*, no more than I would with the jaws of a hungry shark, for two weighty reasons, first and foremost, because I *Seth, ycleped the stupid* by his worship, am but a poor hand at such things; and secondly, because I think that the good people of Pennsylvania, *"backed"* by their rulers and sages, are quite competent to the task of legislation, and all other political concerns, when they fall cleverly about it, without the interference of my pen, or indeed the tongue or pen of any conceited half-learned pedagogue from New-England. Vanity is really a silly passion, and I believe that there never were half a dozen of men of real merit and abilities slaves to it, since the creation of the world; it is a *sore place, a confounded gangrene*, which makes the unfortunate owner of it, winch and growl whenever it is touched. The word *schoolmaster* grated upon his honor's ears like a rasp; and so he tells us that kings &c. taught schools in days of yore. I remember to have heard of one king, Dionysus, the tyrant of Sicily, who after being banished, went to Corinth, where he lived poor and mean, and was obliged last of all to turn schoolmaster, so that when he could not overrule men, he might tyrranize over children; now whether he taught a private school, or was under the principal of an academy is uncertain; but if he was, and happened to have over him a mean, over-bearing dolt-headed principal, who would treat him, on several occasions before the

boys with pointed indignity, I say, if he had such a one as this over him, he must have been under the necessity of cringing, or budging off with himself. His honor the 'squire, near to the toe of his epistle to the public, gives us a specimen of his good sense and knowledge of the human heart, where he "takes God *Almighty* to be his witness, that not an action of his life proceeded from a bad principle." Ah! how happy it is, to be in a state of sinless perfection! Oh 'squire, thou art a true saint ingrain, and certainly in a most trim condition! We know of none who have any pretensions like thyself, as to moral rectitude, except thy country-woman, the she Messiah, Jemimah Wilkinson, a right heavenly lass, who we think would be a most eligible rib for thee, if thou art disposed to a matrimonial union; should this happen, we would have a fair prospect of the Millenium upon earth directly. Time will tell whether his honor the 'squire shall or shall not hear again from

SETH

Seth did not write again, but to make up for it there were two letters from Kidd the following week. One was the continuation of his remarks on Webster's grammar, the other his reply to Webster's letter. One passage, though primarily a criticism of Webster's own writing, made an accusation of plagiarism:

You endeavor to defend your absurdity in putting the verbs of the following sentence in the present time — "But we should reflect that languages are not framed by philosophers. On the contrary they *are* spoken long before they *are* written; and spoken by barbarous nations, for many ages before any improvements *are* made in science." — but this you cannot do, for the sentence is a plagiarism from the Preface of Johnson's dictionary, which you corrupted, in order to make it your own: please to read the sentence as it stands in that author. "As language was at its beginning merely oral, all words of necessary or common use *were* spoken before they *were* written; and while they *were* unfixed by any visible signs, must have been spoken with great diversity," &c. See, sir, with what propriety Johnson used the verbs in the past time, which you abused in the present....

A similarity between a part of one of Webster's sentences and a part of one of Johnson's, with the tenses changed, is not sufficient to convict Webster of plagiarism. Kidd's accusation, indeed, was self-defeating, since it started by criticizing Webster for having changed Johnson's words. The idea that both of them expressed is commonplace, but even if it had been Johnson's idea originally, Webster would have been entitled to express it in his own words. Webster's defense, however, went much further

than that; he denied having any recollection of Johnson's Preface:

Mr. Kidd, it is disagreeable to accuse any man of *lying*; but you should have qualified your expression with an *I believe*, or *I suppose* or something equivalent. Your assertion is unqualified, and it is a falsehood. I have not read that Preface these seven years past — I never copied a word of it, and I do not recollect a sentence of it.

Seven years earlier, Webster had been studying law in Litchfield, and had not even thought of writing a spelling book and grammar. If he was telling the truth, therefore, he had previously been sufficiently interested in Johnson's dictionary to have read the Preface, and we have seen that he had the book before him later, when he wrote his "Essay on a Reformed Mode of Spelling," but he did not look at it while he was compiling the *Grammatical Institute*.

On Saturday May 24, Webster was kept at home by a headache — a fortunate circumstance as it turned out, because that was the day George Washington chose to pay him a visit. Washington had come to Philadelphia for the Constitutional Convention. Webster knew several of the delegates to the convention, including Oliver Ellsworth from Connecticut and Barlow's brother-in-law Abraham Baldwin, who was representing Georgia. On June 6, Webster transferred to the English Department in the Episcopal Academy; on June 24, he said goodbye to Rebecca Greenleaf, who returned to her family in Boston.

Webster had to stay in Philadelphia, because he was committed to teaching at the Episcopal Academy until October. He therefore occupied himself with further revision of the *Grammatical Institute*. In the spelling book, he made fundamental changes, some of which, as Monaghan says, "seem to have been motivated by suggestions from [his] friends and some by his own reactions to the criticisms he had received from those who were not so friendly to him."[3]

The most obvious change to the speller was that Webster adopted the title he had included in his memorial to the legislature of New York back in 1783, calling it *The American Spelling Book*. Monaghan is mistaken, however, to say that he "abandoned President Stiles' unfortunate title, *A Grammatical Institute*." In 1785, Webster had told Dilworth's Ghost that it was too late to alter the title, because "the title page

is registered with the Secretary of State to secure the copyright." That was still the position in 1787, because Webster could not conveniently tour the states again, to deposit a different title. Instead, he added the new title to the old one and the speller became "The American Spelling Book: containing an easy Standard of Pronunciation. Being the First Part of a Grammatical Institute of the English Language." So that Stiles would not be offended at the reduced emphasis given to the title he had suggested, Webster dedicated the book to him.

A number of improvements were made in the new version. Sheridan's rule that had puzzled the Learner of English Grammar disappeared, and Webster now showed both primary and secondary stress in polysyllables. The improving sentences were moved forward, so that "No man may put off the law of God" was once again among the tables, where Dilworth had it. The story of Tommy and Harry was taken out, but the debt to Fenning was not reduced, because Webster stole the first of his fables:

Of the Boy that stole Apples

An old Man found a rude Boy upon one of his Trees stealing Apples, and desired him to come down; but the young Sauce-box told him plainly he would not. Won't you? said the old Man, then I will fetch you down; so he pulled up some tufts of Grass, and threw at him; but this only made the Youngster laugh, to think that the old Man should pretend to beat him out of the Tree with grass only.

Well, well, says the old Man, if neither words nor grass, will do, I must try what virtue there is in Stones; so the old man pelted him heartily with stones; which soon made the young Chap hasten down from the Tree and beg the old Man's pardon.

MORAL

If good words and gentle means will not reclaim the wicked, they must be dealt with in a more severe manner.

Fenning's spelling book contained four fables; Dilworth had twelve. Webster took a middle course and put in eight. Apart from the first, none of them was taken from either Dilworth or Fenning, but that does not mean that Webster wrote them himself—he took them from Dodsley's *Select Fables of ESOP and other Fabulists.* Later, though indirectly, Webster would owe Dodsley a much greater debt, for all Webster's dictionaries were based, directly or indirectly, on Johnson's, and as we have seen, without Dodsley, Johnson would never have written his dictionary.

Dodsley's *Select Fables* is in three parts: Book I, *From the Ancients*; Book II, *From the Moderns*; and Book III, *Newly Invented* or *Original Fables.* The fables used by Webster are in Books I and II, which were not originated by Dodsley, and one has therefore to ask whether Webster found them in Dodsley's collection or in whatever was Dodsley's source. In one of them, however, "The Fox and the Swallow," Dodsley has a note that "Instead of the Swallow, it was originally a Hedge-hog; but as that creature seemed very unfit for the business of driving away flies, it was thought more proper to substitute the Swallow." Webster's third fable is "The Fox and the Swallow," not "The Fox and the Hedge-hog." Furthermore, between Dodsley's original 1761 edition, and that of 1776, minor alterations were made in the wording of some of the fables; for example, in the 1761 version of "The Bear and the two Friends," two friends set out together upon a journey which led through "a dangerous desert". In the 1776 edition, the desert has been replaced by "a dangerous forest." Webster's fable has the "dangerous forest," and other changes from the 1761 version. We may be certain, therefore, that Webster's fables came from an edition of Dodsley other than the original edition. Probably, it was the edition printed in Philadelphia in 1786. In the seven fables that he took from it, he made no significant changes.

The revised spelling book, the seventh edition altogether and the first in Philadelphia, was finished in mid–July 1787, by which time James Kidd was about halfway through his "remarks" on Webster's grammar. On September 22, Webster entered in his diary, "Write an answer to Mr. Kidd." A week earlier, he had been invited to write in support of the proposed new Federal Constitution, as described in No. 18 of the *Memoir*:

During the summer of this year, was held the Convention of delegates, which formed the present Constitution of the United States. Their deliberations were closed and the form of the Constitution published in September. On the 15th of that month, two days before the close of the proceedings, Mr. Fitzsimmons, one of the delegates of Pennsylvania, wrote a note to N.W. requesting him, if he should approve of the form of the constitution, which was to be proposed to the people, to give it his support.

Webster could not start on this task until after October 4, "Quarter day which releases me from the Episcopal Academy." What he then wrote, *An Examination into the Leading principles of the Federal Constitution*, took him just two days. It was published, dedicated to Franklin, on October 17. Webster was proud to have been asked to write it, but he was not pleased with the result, as he later wrote, "This pamphlet was written in haste, and was not satisfactory to himself or to friends of the Constitution."[4]

Webster's last contribution to his ongoing dialogue with James Kidd was in two parts. The first appeared in the *Freeman's Journal* on the day his pamphlet was published, October 17; the second part was published the following week. "I have now finished the business which detains me in Philadelphia;" he wrote, "and notwithstanding the dryness of the controversy, which offends the bulk of readers, I must do you the justice, before I leave the city, to offer my sentiments upon your remarks...." Kidd had not actually finished his remarks; there were more of them in the paper on November 7 and yet more on November 14, but Webster was not there to read them. He had left Philadelphia on October 25, 1787.

9. Webster in New York, 1788

The American Magazine

On his way north from Philadelphia at the end of October 1787, Webster spent a few days in New York. He then went on to Connecticut, visiting friends and relations. During this period he decided on his next career move: He would publish a literary magazine, to be called the *American Magazine,* in New York. He went back there at the end of November to make the arrangements:

November 28. Embark for New York
   29. Arrive at evening.
   30. Take lodgings for the year at Mrs Vandervoorts at £80-0.0.
   December 3. Making a contract with Mr Loudon, where I take tea.
   4. Make the bargain for printing the American Magazine & get the paper on Shore.

The adjective *American* in the magazine's title shows Webster's nationalism, but it also indicates that he was aiming for a national circulation. He did not achieve it, and the magazine lasted only a year. In its content during that year, it contained a certain amount of material that is relevant to our study.

Many articles were copied from other magazines, both European and American. That was the way that most American newspapers and magazines filled their pages. Each had only a local circulation, and the same amusing anecdotes and shocking stories did the rounds of periodicals all over the country. It would not be right, therefore, to regard that sort of borrowing as plagiarism, or as being in any way improper.

Though Webster's magazine was published in New York, much of his outside help in gathering material came from Connecticut. He wrote long letters about American antiquities to Ezra Stiles, so that he could publish his letters and Stiles' replies. Josiah Meigs, whose *New Haven Gazette* had folded two years before, was still publishing books, and he sent copies to Webster for review. In two installments, in the second and third issues of the magazine, Webster reprinted Dwight's "Valedictory Address to the Young Gentlemen who commenced Bachelors of Arts at Yale College, July 25th 1776." In other issues, he included some of Dwight's poems, a chunk of Barlow's *Vision of Columbus,* and a slice of Trumbull's *The Progress of Dulness.* He also defended his friends, in his own way, against the attacks of others. In one issue, he reprinted a more or less favorable review of *The Vision of Columbus* from the *Critical Review* of January 1788. In another, he castigated one Peter Markoe, whose poem, *The Times,* had commented on the soporific effect of reading Barlow's poem. Webster wrote that Markoe's "attack on the author of the *Vision of Columbus* is, in a high degree, illiberal and unmerited. The author of the Vision, whether we consider him as a man, a patriot, or a scholar, is far superior to his satirist, yet his poem is represented as an opiate, that produces dulness and sleep in the reader.... But all invectives cast upon so amiable and respectable a character as Mr. Barlow, must prove harmless to any man but the author."

I mentioned in an earlier chapter that Webster filled some space in *The American Magazine* with his own undergraduate effusion, "Hail, rising genius," addressed "To the Author of the Conquest of Canaan." That was two years after he had sent a copy of Dwight's poem to Washington, with a letter acknowledging its faults. When he had the idea of publishing his own poem, Webster was faced with a bit of a problem: He was happy to flatter Dwight (who

was an influential man, and a top "literary character"), but at the same time, he did not want to appear blind to the shortcomings of Dwight's poem. Everyone who tried to read it found it hard going. Webster solved the problem by publishing his poem anonymously, and concealing its authorship (and excusing its uncritical flattery) by describing it as "Written by a Youth of Nineteen." As Webster was then approaching thirty, who would have supposed that he might have written it himself, years before the *Conquest* was published?

In a later issue of the *American Magazine*, Webster expressed a less flattering opinion of *The Conquest of Canaan*. He was actually defending Dwight, or rather, he was attacking the authors of the *London Review* for their criticisms of *The Conquest*. They had supposed the poem to be an allegory, in which the campaign of Joshua to capture the Promised Land for the Children of Israel represents Washington's liberation of the American colonies.[1] Webster's answer included a letter written by Dwight himself, in which he said, "That Gen. Washington should be supposed to resemble Joshua is not strange. They are both great and good characters, acting at the head of armies, and regulating the chief interests of their countrymen." Nevertheless, the supposed allegory could not have been intended, because "the Poem was begun in the year 1771, and written out, several times, before the year 1775: — all the essential parts were finished, before the war was begun." When it came to the quality of Dwight's poetry, however, Webster could not bring himself to disagree with the English critic:

Many of Dr. Dwight's friends will however acknowledge the propriety of the following criticisms — "That in some passages there is a strange confusion of ideas and language — that in others, there is a want of perspicuity — that there is too much bustling and killing — that the descriptions are too long, and often abound with repetitions of the same imagery." — To these faults or others must we ascribe the fatigue of reading the Poem, which is generally complained of in America.[2]

One other review in the *American Magazine* must be mentioned. In 1788, a poem called *The Triumph of Infidelity* was published anonymously, "Addressed to Mon. de Voltaire." It told how Satan went around the world spreading skepticism — disbelief, that is to say, in the fundamentalist Calvinism of the Connecticut Congregationalists. The poem attacked papists, deists, unitarians, and the Chinese. Having first visited Scotland and France (to inspire Hume and Voltaire) Satan confronted his greatest challenge, America. For the poet, Satan's most potent weapon against the true religion as taught by Jonathan Edwards, was the Rev. Charles Chauncy of Boston. This was not a personal attack, since Chauncy had died the year before, but an attack on his doctrine of universal salvation.

In 1788, when Webster was reviewing the poem, his own religious reawakening was still twenty years ahead. At this time, he was much nearer to the free-thinking tolerance of his undergraduate days. Also, he had no idea that the author of *The Triumph of Infidelity* was none other than the Rev. Dr. Timothy Dwight. Webster's review commented condescendingly on the poet's skill and complained of obscurity:

The poem is not destitute of poetic merit. The versification is generally correct, and variegated but intolerably harsh. The irony of the piece is indifferently well supported thro' the whole, and here and there we find a severe sarcasm. We cannot however consider the satire as uniformly natural and severe. A jumble of words, forced conceits and far-fetched ideas will never pass for wit or satire. What does the author mean by *undeifying the world's Almighty Trust?* Why neither more nor less than the Socinian doctrine which denies the divinity of Christ. But who could suspect the meaning without a context or comment?

> "This M----- proves, in whom my
>   utmost skill
> *Peer'd* out no means of mischief,
>   but the will."

This passage follows a short account of Dr. Chauncey and his opinions; from which circumstance, and *from nothing else*, we judge the writers meaning to be this, that Satan with all his skill could not furnish Murray with any abilities or means of doing mischief, *equal* to Chauncey's, except his will. But the writer, with *all his skill in obscuring his ideas*, in which he appears to be an adept, could have hardly found another mode of expression so little calculated to convey his real meaning.

Webster next came to the defense of the Chinese, who he thought, had been subjected to "the most illiberal abuse." He was surprisingly keen on the Chinese, saying they were "a nation

... celebrated thro' the world for the most perfect system of ethics and civil government ever carried into execution — and for improvements in philosophy and the arts that vie with those of ancient Greece and Rome." It was not fair, he thought, to abuse them "merely because they are not *christians.*"

Webster's assessment of Dwight's theology was accurate, but not polite:

In short the author appears to be a theological dogmatist, who has found the right way to heaven, by creeds and systems; and with more imperiousness than would become infinite wisdom and power, damns all who cannot swallow his articles of faith. A man who can groupe together such men as *Shaftesbury, Priestley, Chauncey* and *Allen* and stigmatize these and many of the first philosophers promiscuously as fools and knaves, can hardly be a candidate for that heaven of love and benevolence which the scripture informs us is prepared for good men.

Then Webster accused the author of plagiarism:

Nor can we think the writer more remarkable for his poetic talents than for his liberality. He can indeed borrow lines without giving credit; but he should not borrow from such a smooth versifier as Pope — the contrast between his own lines and those borrowed immediately detects the plagiarism. Witness the following from Eloise and Abelard.

> "Oh write it not, my hand!
> the name appears
> Already written: Wash it out, my
> tears:"

Compared with the two succeeding lines of the author's —

> "Still, oh, all pitying savior!
> let thy love
> Stronger than death, all heights
> and heaven above, &c."

The harshness of these lines is nothing singular — one half the poem is a jumble of unmeaning epithets, or an unnatural association of ideas. What does the writer mean by *pinions rising above the arches of a thousand skies?* We have heard of the *third heaven,* and Dionysius, the divine, has dreamt of *nine orders* of angels; but we do not recollect to have seen any account of a *thousand skies.* Yet *thousand* is a favorite word.

> "The pagan fabric of a *thousand*
> years."

The writer has abused Dr. Chauncey freely for his purgatories; yet he talks about a *lowest hell*; and although the number of hells is not mentioned, yet Satan was once *plunged beneath the lowest.* Query, where did he stop?

That review, like so much of Webster's work, infuriated people so much that they wrote to the papers about it. They did not write to Webster's *American Magazine,* because it was a monthly publication, and a dialogue at monthly intervals is too slow to be satisfactory. The correspondence appeared in the *New York Daily Advertiser.* The first contributor was "Benevolus," on Saturday August 9, 1788. He had spotted in the review a trick that we have seen Webster using against Dilworth — asserting a general weakness in his adversary, and giving two "examples" (as if they were typical of many) when in fact there were no instances apart from those two. "Benevolus" pointed out that

of obscurity, two instances in the Poem are produced, which are now kindly explained to us, through wonderful skill and sagacity. For these two, in a poem of considerable length, the author is called an adept in *obscuring his ideas.*— Just as candid is the remark on *a thousand skies* and *a thousand years,* as though it was a favorite word, when it is only twice thus used.

Because readers of the *New York Daily Advertiser* probably did not subscribe to the *American Magazine,* Webster's review was reprinted immediately following the letter from "Benevolus." This caught the attention of "J.M.," whose letter appeared in the *Daily Advertiser* on August 27. Webster's review had been anonymous, but J.M. knew who had written it, and thought that someone with Webster's credentials should have understood the meaning of "*peer*":

The author of a new Spelling Book, and of a new Grammar of the English language, ought to have understood English so well as to know, that *to peer* does not signify *to furnish.*

J.M. found the verb "*to peer*" even in Entick's little dictionary. He also pointed to another instance of the "two example" trick, when Webster accused the author of the poem of borrowing lines without giving credit. More significantly, J.M. explained that the two lines in question were not *stolen,* but *quoted,* and would be recognized as lines of Pope by any educated reader:

In the next paragraph, the Poet is censured for borrowing lines without giving credit for them: In the whole compass of the Poem, as far as I can judge from my own reading, two lines, and two only are borrowed; and these are lines of such notoriety to

every person who has read poetry at all, that to have given credit for them, instead of being necessary to prevent the charge of plagiarism, would have been justly esteemed superfluous and trifling.

Dwight did, perhaps, make another reference to a line of Pope. At the end of the poem, Satan pushes off in a huff, not because he has failed to conquer the virtuous citizens of America, but because they are all infidels already and there are no virtuous citizens left:

> From a dim cloud, the spirit eyed
>   the scene,
> Now proud with triumph, and now
>   vex'd with spleen,
> Mark'd all the throng, beheld them
>   all his own,
> And to his cause NO FRIEND OF
>   VIRTUE won:
> Surpriz'd, enrag'd, he wing'd his
>   sooty flight,
> And hid beneath the pall of endless
>   night.

"NO FRIEND OF VIRTUE" (in capitals in the second printing of Dwight's poem) would have brought to the mind of the educated reader a line in Pope's *First Satire of the Second Book of Horace, Imitated*, where Pope describes himself, wielding his satirical pen, as "TO VIRTUE ONLY AND HER FRIENDS, A FRIEND."

To complete Webster's discomfiture, J.M. gave biblical chapter and verse, twice over, for "lowest hell."

On September 5 Webster's reply to J.M. appeared, signed The Reviewer. It was not one of his better performances. When he wrote it, he had just returned from Boston and Rebecca Greenleaf, where he had received her father's formal consent to their betrothal. He had other things on his mind than J.M. Nevertheless his letter affords some entertainment. To begin with, he supposed that J.M. might be the author of *The Triumph of Infidelity*, and he called up against him, and in support of the opinions expressed in his review, "a host of literary gentlemen, and ... some of the most respectable clergymen in this country." This is rather comical because there can be little doubt that if Webster had drawn up lists of the most distinguished "literary gentlemen" and "respectable clergymen" in America at the time, Dwight would have been near the top of both lists.

Some of J.M.'s best points, including his an- swer to the charge of plagiarism, Webster did not comment on at all, merely suggesting that they were matters of opinion. He did attempt to justify his attack on the expression *peer'd out*, but he did it so badly that he only made his position worse. He agreed that "*to peer*" was defined in Entick. "I have consulted," he said, "half a dozen authorities, superior to Entick, and find the definition the same." Webster, however, disagreed with all of them. In his opinion, "peer is a word not known — not used in America — nor in any English writer that I have seen." If it had any meaning, it was a con- traction of "*appear*," and the line "*Appeared* out no means of mischief but the will" did not make sense. This is disappointingly weak stuff.

Most of Webster's letter was a defense of the Chinese, which is not a subject that concerns us, but one aspect of it is too remarkable to be passed over. J.M. thought the Chinese open to criticism because some of their priests, known as Bonzes, went about the country without any clothes on. Webster replied that this was no worse than having naked people wait at tables, which happened in parts of America! First, he quoted from J.M's letter:

But, "a vast number of persons under the name of Bonzes, traverse the country, naked as they were born, and under the shield of sanctity, thrust them- selves into all companies of men and women &c." To us, this is shocking, yet custom there, if this practice really exists, has rendered it familiar. But I question, whether some American customs would not appear to other nations equally shocking. It is a custom in some parts of America for servants to traverse the country naked as the day they were born — nay, for naked domestics to wait on gentlemen's tables. Ladies, habituated to the custom, think nothing of it; altho' a northern lady would at first sight of it, be frightened out of company.[3]

Only with the information given above is it possible fully to appreciate the following defini- tion, taken from Webster's *American Dictio- nary*:

BONZE .... In China, the Bonzes are the priests of the Fohists, or sect of Fohi. They are distinguished from the laity *by their dress*....

Early in this book, I said that it was a charac- teristic of Webster always to believe he was right. In the last paragraph of his letter to the *Daily Advertiser*, he claimed exactly the opposite. To

be fair to Webster, I will set out the paragraph in full:

I have only to remark further, that altho' I see and converse every day with men whose sentiments are totally different from my own, yet I love them as well as any persons of my own persuasion. It is an article of my belief, that my own opinions may be *wrong*— that those of my neighbor may be *right*. In consequence of this persuasion, I can take by the hand, persons of all religions, and all nations — I can embrace the Mandarins of China, and the author of the Poem which abuses them, with equal and cordial affection. I believe that all men are my brethren — I believe in that religion which teaches that *God is Love*, and that men approach to perfection, in proportion as they cherish the heavenly principle.

The last sentence shows that Webster was at this time some way removed from the Congregationalist orthodoxy in which he had been brought up. This was spotted by the last contributor to the controversy, who signed himself "A Believer of Revelation." His letter, in which Webster (the reviewer) is referred to as "the R," appeared in the *Daily Advertiser* on September 15, 1788:

.... Upon the whole, it is apparently evident, from the general tenor of the R's strictures on the poem in question, that he considers its design as levelled against his own favorite sentiments, and is therefore, by natural consequence, entirely wrong, both in design and execution. In a word, he has implicitly told the world, what perhaps will do him no honor — that he himself does not believe in the doctrine of Divine Revelation.

To round it off, as the Dilworth's Ghost correspondence had been rounded off three and a half years earlier, I shall give you some excerpts from a very inferior poem. It actually appeared in the *Daily Advertiser* a few days before the letter from A Believer of Revelation. The poet, like J.M., had identified Webster as the author of the review of Dwight's poem:

I wonder what the good man thought,
When he the Devil this way brought,
To put the Reviewer in a passion
And bring the *Great Grammarian's* lash on.

He was careful to avoid a charge of plagiarism:

I know you'll stare, Tom, when you see
This rhyming jingle sign'd by me;
I always knew I was a Poet,
"If I'd but wit enough to show it."
The last line, Tom, you see I borrow,

I mark it too, lest to my sorrow,
Some mighty Critic should review me,
And cut and slash, and hack and hew me,
And finding nothing else to bark at,
Says, "you could borrow and not mark it."
For your sore Critic grasps at all things;
At somethings, nothings, and at small things;
At any thing, and things of all kinds,
So apt to snarl and growl are small minds.

The poet's opinion was the same as mine, with regard to "peer out," that Webster had only made things worse for himself by his reply to J.M.:

You may have seen the answer too,
To this well judg'd and learn'd review;
By mild BENEVOLUS and J.M.
The first to stew, the last to fry him;
Finding the heat approach him nigher,
He springs from frying pan into fire;
For waspish still, as sure as you are
A friend to candour, this Reviewer
In Child's paper answer makes,
And plays a thousand merry freaks;
Of language talks, in which he's ne'er out,
Excepting that he cannot "peer out"
What Johnson says concerning peering;
And surely Tom, he must be sneering,
When he informs us peer is not known,
Or peering faculties he's got none;
He tells us, Tom, that many others,
Among his right *religious* brothers,
Who "*pass*" like him for men of sense
And learning, Thomas, most immense,
Could not discover, or make clear out,
The meaning of the words to "peer out."

After a good deal more mockery of this sort, the poem ends:

He shews us, Tom, by proof prodigious,
That he himself is right religious;
That he is meek — that he is humble -
In short, that he's "a perfect jumble"
Of good ingredients, sweet and strong,
And silent — as a Chinese *Gong*.

THE PHILOLOGICAL SOCIETY

In 1788, Webster was still a firm believer in a distinct American language, as an emblem of American independence, and he promoted this belief through the medium of the Philological Society. His diary entry for March 17 may be the first mention of that society: "Admitted & take my seat as a member of the Society for promoting a knowledge of the English Language." If it is, the description is rather loose, since the aim of the Philological Society was consistently

expressed as "improving the *American* tongue," rather than "promoting a knowledge of the *English* Language." An example is the first public announcement about the society, in the April issue of the *American Magazine*:

A Number of Gentlemen in this city have formed themselves into a Society, by the name of the PHILO-LOGICAL SOCIETY, for the purpose of ascertaining and improving the American Tongue. Since the separation of the American States from Great-Britain, the objects of such an institution are become, in some measure, necessary, and highly important.[4]

Several entries in Webster's diary for April 1788 are relevant here:

April 7. At Evening form a Constitution for the Philological Society.
    17. I take tea with Mr. Hazard.
    21. Attend Philolological Society. finish the Laws.
    28. Sick, but at evening attend the philological Society, & read a Dissertation. ordered to be published.

April 7, 21, and 28 were all Mondays; the meetings of the society were usually held on Monday evenings.

Ebenezer Hazard, with whom Webster took tea on April 17, wrote to his correspondent in Boston, Jeremy Belknap, a few months later:

I do not know all the members of the Philological Society, though I have understood that they are not numerous. The Monarch [Webster] reigns supreme, and some of his subjects (I am told) have had only an English education. How they will succeed in establishing a 'Federal Language' time must determine.[5]

Hazard also told Belknap his opinion of Webster:

He certainly does not want understanding, and yet there is a mixture of self-sufficiency, all-sufficiency, and at the same time a degree of insufficiency about him, which is (to me) intolerable.

The "Dissertation" that Webster read to the society on April 28 was on "The Influence of Language on Opinions and Opinions on Language." It was published, as directed by the society, in the May issue of the *American Magazine*,[6] and Webster later included it in his *Collection of Essays and Fugitiv Writings*. In the magazine, the introductory paragraph contained references to the society, that were omitted in the book:

In the infancy of an institution, founded for the particular purpose of ascertaining and improving the American tongue, it may be useful to examine the importance of the design, and show how far truth and accuracy of thinking are concerned in a clear understanding of words.... We cannot hesitate a moment to conclude, that grammatical enquiries are worthy of the labor of *men*, and particularly of the members of this society.

Webster spent most of May 1788 in Connecticut, but he returned to New York in time to say goodbye to Barlow, who sailed for France on the 25. Until she was able to join him, Barlow's wife Ruth went to stay with her brother Dudley, who was a lawyer in Greenfield Hill. There, they were members of the congregation of Barlow's old friend and mentor, the pastor, master, poet and farmer, the Rev. Timothy Dwight, who was awaiting the call to return to Yale as president. Barlow was going to France as agent for the Scioto Land Company, seeking to borrow money in Holland, and to find purchasers in Europe for land in Ohio. The scheme has been denounced as fraudulent since the promoters did not own the land—but that is not quite fair to the promoters, because they did have an option to buy the land. If sufficient money had been borrowed, and if enough purchasers had been found, they would have been able to exercise that option. They would then have made an enormous profit and been applauded for their business acumen. Like gambling with someone else's money, there's no problem if you win. As it was, they lost. Not enough purchasers were found; those who did buy discovered that the company could not give them title to the land they had paid for; and the principal promoter, William Duer (an old-Etonian), ended up in jail. Barlow found himself stranded in Europe in the middle of the French Revolution and did not get back to America for seventeen years.

Webster had no such excitement. The day after Barlow sailed, he took tea at Mr. Child's, and attended another meeting of the Philological Society. The next week, on June 2, he read "a Philological Dissertation" before the society. He read his "2d Lecture" on June 26, and his "4th Lecture" on July 8. It appears that he was subjecting the members of the society to the lectures on language with which he had toured and bored America two years

before. Not all their meetings, however, were
so dull. On June 30, Webster recorded "Hear
Mr. Dunlap's *Love in New York* a new Comedy,
read — it is ingenious." The young William
Dunlap, like many Americans who showed
some talent for painting, had been sent to London to study with Benjamin West. West painted
uncommonly large canvases, was much admired by George III, and became President of
the Royal Academy. Dunlap neglected his studies, spent too much time going to parties with
West's son Raphael, and returned to America
thoroughly ashamed of himself and resolved to
lead a more serious life. Meanwhile, he was trying to make a living in the theater. His association with the members of the Philological Society had a suitably sobering effect, as he later
wrote:

It was my good fortune, soon after my return, to become a member of a literary society formed by young
men for mutual instruction and improvement. My
friend Samuel Latham Mitchill, Noah Webster (then
editing a magazine in New York), and others afterwards known in American literature, were members.
This led to a more regular course of study than I had
ever known....[7]

Dunlap also interlocks with other pieces
of our jigsaw puzzle; he married Elizabeth
Woolsey, whose sister was the wife of Timothy
Dwight. Dunlap thus spent some of his happi-
est hours with Dwight at Greenfield Hill, where
Ruth Barlow was staying with her brother Dudley.

The play that the Philological Society heard
read, *Love in New York*, has not survived, but in
another of Dunlap's plays, written a few months
later, there is a description of Webster:

> When first I join'd them how oft did I
>   hammer
> Night after Night, to teach the dunces
>   Grammer
> My Rules, my lectures, evr'y nigh
>   repeated
> Began to talk sometimes, ere they were
>   seated
> To shew my zeal I ev'ry night held forth
> And deep imprest th' Idea of my worth
> Not soon forgot.[8]

Dunlap was responsible for the accounts of
the society. The President was Josiah Hoffman,
who, on behalf of the society, signed a recommendation for Webster's spelling book:

New York July 4, 1788

The Committee of the Philological Society, appointed to examine the First Part of Mr. Webster's
Grammatical Institute of the English Language, beg
leave to report to the Society, That we approve of the
plan and execution of the work, and recommend it
to the use of schools in the United States, as an accurate and well digested system of principles and
rules, calculated to destroy the various false dialects
in pronunciation in the several states, an object very
desirable in a federal republic.

In Society. *Resolved, that the Society do accept of the
foregoing Report.*

Test,   JOSIAH O. HOFFMAN,
President.

Just a week after Webster's arrival in New
York, December 6, 1787, he entered in his diary,
"Delaware Ratifies Constitution" (which actually happened the following day). On December 12, the correct date this time, he wrote,
"Pennsylvania ratify New Constitution." He
took a keen interest in the new Constitution,
because he felt that he had brought it about.
The first written suggestion for it had been
contained, so he believed, in his *Sketches of
American Policy*; the first document recommending it to the people was his *Examination
into the Leading Principles of the Federal Constitution*. The condition for its adoption was
that it should be ratified by nine of the thirteen
states, and this was achieved on June 21, 1788.
Webster heard the news on June 25, and wrote,
"Hear that New Hampshire has ratified the
Constitution. Great joy at the Ninth." Virginia
ratified the following day. At this time, the convention for the state of New York had not
resolved on ratification, and the people of the
city (which was largely Federalist) decided to
apply a little pressure by organizing a huge procession to celebrate ratification by the first ten
states.

The Philological Society was to participate in
the procession, and Webster found himself involved in frequent meetings:

July 7. At evening attend Philological Society. choose
officers.
   8. Attend the same & read my 4th Lecture. Appointed one of the committee to arrange matters for
the procession.
   9. Wait on the Federal Committee for the purpose.
   10. Assist in forming the arms of the Philological
Society.
   11. at evening Read my 4th Lecture & finish it.

14. At evening attend Society.

17. Meet the Committee of arrangement for the Philological Society, & order the Procession for the 23d Inst.

21. Prepare for Procession. attend Society.

23. The Grand Procession in New York to celebrate the Adoption of the Constitution by 10 states. Very brilliant but fatiguing. I formed a part of the Philological Society, whose flag & uniform black dress made a very respectable figure.

Whether or not the grand procession influenced their decision, the New York Convention voted to ratify the Constitution three days later. Webster's diary recorded "News of the Convention's adopting the Constitution received, & great joy testified. Mr. Greenleaf's windows broken." Thomas Greenleaf was a printer opposed to the Constitution.

Webster had been asked by the Committee of Arrangements to write a detailed account of the procession, which he did on June 26 and 28, and it was published in the *New York Daily Advertiser* on August 2. The procession was led by a band of music, followed by members of different trades and professions, carrying banners decorated with significant emblems. Altogether, "the line of procession, containing nearly five thousand people, extended upwards of a mile and a half...."

The arms of the Philological Society, which Webster had helped to devise, are explained in detail in his description of the society's part of the parade:

The secretary, bearing a scroll, containing the principles of a *Federal* language.

Vice-president and librarian, the latter carrying Mr. Horne Tooke's treatise on language; as a mark of respect for the book which contains a new discovery, and as a mark of respect for the author, whose zeal for the American cause, during the late war, subjected him to a prosecution.

Josiah Ogden Hoffman, Esq. the president of the society, with a sash of blue and white ribbons. The standard bearer, Mr. Willliam Dunlap, with the arms of the society, viz.—Argent, three tongues, gules, in chief; emblematical of *language*, the improvement of which is the object of the institution. Chevron, or, indicating firmness and support; an *eye*, emblematical of *discernment* over a pyramid, or rude monument, sculptured with Gothic, Hebrew, and Greek letters. The Gothic on the *light* side, indicating the *obvious* origin of the American language from the Gothic. The Hebrew and Greek, upon the reverse or *shade* of the monument, expressing the remoteness and *obscurity* of the connection between those languages and the modern. The *crest*, a cluster of cohering magnets, attracted by a key in the centre; emblematical of *union* among the society, in acquiring *language* the *key* of knowledge; and clinging to their *native* tongue in preference to a *foreign* one. The *shield*, ornamented with a branch of the oak, from which is collected the *gall*, used in making ink, and a sprig of *flax*, from which *paper* is made, supported on the dexter side, by CADMUS, in a robe of Tyrian purple, bearing in his right hand, leaves of the rush or flag, *papyrus*, marked with Phoenician characters; representing the introduction of letters into Greece, and the origin of writing. On the sinister side, by Hermes, or Taaut, the inventor of letters, and god of eloquence, grasping his caduceus or wand. Motto—*Concedat Laurea Linguæ*— expressive of the superiority of *civil* over *military* honors. The flag, embellished with the Genius of America, crowned with a wreath of 13 plumes, ten of them starred, representing the ten States which have ratified the Constitution. Her right hand pointing to the Philological Society, and in her left, a standard, with a pendant, inscribed with the word, CONSTITUTION.

The members of the Society in order, clothed in black.

Rebecca's reputedly rich brother, James Greenleaf, had been in New York at this time, and Webster felt some satisfaction in having introduced him to a Mr. James Watson, with whom Greenleaf formed a partnership. On August 1, however, brother James sailed for Amsterdam on business, and Webster decided it was time for him to visit Rebecca. He set out by boat for Providence on August 8, spending a night at Newport on the way, and then rode from Providence to Boston, arriving on August 11. While he was on this journey, the letter signed "Benevolus" appeared in the *New York Daily Advertiser*. On August 14, Webster asked for and obtained the consent of Rebecca's father to their betrothal. After that, he did the rounds of Rebecca's relations, and he left Boston to return to New York, on August 25.

In December 1785, Webster had told Washington, "I have no idea of continuing single for any long period. My circumstances do not require it..." Now, nearly three years later, he had found the lady, and she had accepted him; but a realistic assessment of his circumstances showed that he could still not afford to marry, because *The American Magazine* was losing money. Summing it up in No. 19 of the *Memoir*, Webster wrote:

In the impoverished and distracted state of the country, no adequate encouragement was found, and at the close of the year, the publication was discontinued. In this undertaking a considerable pecuniary loss was incurred.

The decision to discontinue the magazine had been taken by October, for on his 30th birthday, October 16, 1788, he recorded in his diary, "I have read much, written much, & tried to do much good, but with little advantage to myself. I will now leave writing & do more lucrative business...."

The last reference to the Philological Society in Webster's diary is in the entry for November 3, and it appears that the society may have folded after his departure from the city on December 20. On that day, he wrote, "Sail to New Haven. Happy to quit New York."

10. Brother James'
Beneficiary, 1789–1798

Webster did not immediately put into effect either part of the resolution he had entered in his diary on his 30th birthday, to "leave writing & do more lucrative business." He had still some books he wanted to publish, and anyway he could not embark on the practice of law (which he hoped would be lucrative) until he knew where he was going to live. The choice was between Boston and Hartford. Rebecca's family and friends were in Boston; it would be agreeable for her to be among them, and they might be useful to him in getting work. On the other hand, his contacts were in Connecticut, and it might be embarrassing for Rebecca to be married to a struggling lawyer in Boston, when other members of her family lived in the same city in more affluent circumstances. Webster had some income from his publications, but scarcely enough to live on. Indeed, he did not have enough money of his own to get married on, but he was relying on James Greenleaf, his future brother-in-law, to cover the cost of setting up his new home.

Because he had to consult with Rebecca about where their home was going to be, Webster went to Boston when he left New York, stopping on the way in Hartford to spend Christmas with his parents. He arrived in Boston on December 31, 1788. Immediately he was welcomed by Rebecca's large family. His diary records his taking tea or dinner, sometimes three or four times a week, with her parents, with her brothers, and with her brothers-in-law Thomas Dawes and Dr. Nathaniel Appleton.

At this time also, he was able to return to a project that had been put on one side while he was busy with the *American Magazine*—that of turning his lectures on language into a book. The book was published in 1789 as *Dissertations on the English Language, with Notes, Historical and Critical.* Once again, we find Webster borrowing from another man's work. This was pointed out much later, in a letter which appeared in the *Salem Gazette* (published by William Carlton) on November 24, 1795:

a late Lecturer upon the English Language… printed in his syllabus that the Language was of Celtic origin. A Friend suggested his doubts. The Lecturer for the first time wished to think upon the subject. But how should he begin. Dr. Percy was put into his hands to prove the language of Teutonic origin. The Lecturer was puzzled, because he had written it another way. But at length, rich in expedients, to acquit himself with honour, he publishes a Dissertation, and profits from the hint, by borrowing the Doctor's 20 pages without paying him a compliment for them, and concludes that the language, that he might have something of his own and not go too deep into the puzzle, was… both Celtic and Teutonic.

M.D. Esquire

The book referred to as "Dr. Percy" is *Northern Antiquities* by Paul Henri Mallet, translated from French into English by Percy and published in London in 1770. Webster made several references to Mallet in his *Notes Historical and Critical*, deriving from him such information as the Nordic origin of the words *Yule, Tuesday, Wednesday, Thursday* and *Friday.*[1] Mallet was duly credited with having furnished that information. What "M.D. Esquire" was referring to, however, was quite a different matter. Pages 340 to 349 of Webster's book (10 pages rather than 20, but Carlton may have misread M.D's handwriting) were transcribed directly from the Preface that Percy added to *Northern*

Antiquties. For this, as M.D. said, Webster did not pay Percy so much as a compliment. Those pages mainly contain the Lord's Prayer in various ancient languages, which Percy had not originated but had collected from sources he (and Webster copying him) acknowledged. Webster, however, made it appear that this was his own work, copying Percy's paragraph beginning "I am not able to produce any specimen of the Celtic…," without showing that he was quoting. That was plagiarism within Webster's own definition: "introducing passages from another man's writings and putting them off as one's own."

On February 1, 1789, Webster wrote to James, who was still in Holland, reminding him that his sister's wedding could not take place without the financial provision that James had promised:

Since my last, I have exchanged my residence. You will hear of me in future in Boston. My clear loss by business the last year was about £100, with my time and expenses, or about £250 in the whole. This hurts me sensibly, as it affects my best friends and benefactors. Still I have resources, and I shall exert myself to call them forth to repay their generosity.

I still adhere to my resolution of following a profession. It is my best, my only resort. I am correcting my book, which is now in the press and will be finished in April or May. When it is done, I will send you a dozen copies. If this work should sell well, it will help me; if not, it will be a further embarrassment.

But I have done with making books. I shall enter upon the pursuit of law immediately and practise either in Hartford or this town, for my license will introduce me here, and Mr. Dawes will assist me. This remains to be determined. The little property I have will go further in Connecticut than in Boston. But my affection for your amiable sister inclines me to remain here. Her friends are here, and although she is willing to go where my interest calls me, yet I know she will be happier here. My wishes are hers, and if there is a prospect of getting subsistence by business in Boston, this shall be preferred.

I am as happy as the heart of the loveliest of her sex and the kindness and esteem of all your connections can make me. Still a union of a more sacred and enduring nature is my ardent wish. In this wish I am not alone; but whatever may be our desires, your sister and myself must postpone a nearer union till she can be furnished and I can begin business.

Your sister depends upon you for provision for furniture, and I must depend upon my own exertions. I shall try to make it convenient to marry in the course of this year, but it depends partly on your

assistance and partly on the events that are not altogether in my power.…

With anxious wishes for your welfare and prosperity, I am, my worthy friend,

Yours cordially,

Noah Webster.

On February 14, Webster received a letter from James, bringing the news that he had the previous year married a Dutch lady, Antonia Scholten, and that he was as a result utterly miserable:

My Domestic situation it imports but few to know of. I am far from being happy, but the idea of having it in my power to insure my family from want, throws from time to time a ray of sunshine upon my mind which in some measure reconciles me to life, & indeed is all I have to render life supportable to me.…

Webster's *Dissertations* were published in Boston, but did not sell. The *Memoir* records the event, as well as a series of later unprofitable publishing enterprises:

The winter of 1788-89, N.W. spent in Boston, superintending the publication of his *Dissertations on the English Language.* By this publication he incurred a heavy pecuniary loss.…

In 1790, N.W. prepared for the press and published a volume of essays and fugitive pieces; but the work produced no profit.

In this year also N.W. abridged his grammar, and published it with the title of *The Little Reader's Assistant.* In this little book, he introduced what was called a *Federal Catechism,* or explanation of the Constitution of the United States and the principles of government and commerce. This was the first attempt of the kind, and much applauded by particular persons; but the book did not continue long in use in schools.

In this year also N.W. published Governor Winthrop's Journal.… A small edition only of this valuable work was published, and the whole was sold; but it afforded no profit to the Editor.

Meanwhile, the decision on Webster's place of residence had been taken in favor of Hartford, as Webster had written to James on February 15:

The place where I shall reside has been something uncertain; but on consulting all opinions, Hartford is recommended as the most eligible. Your sister wishes to be with her friends; and my wishes are always with hers. But Mr. Dawes is clear that it would be much better for me to reside in Hartford, where I am more known and where property will go much farther in supporting a family than in

Boston. So it is determined and your sister consents with cheerfulness. She is most amiable and deserving, our hearts are one, your friends appear to be pleased, and Becca shall be happy if I can make her so....

He returned to Hartford in May 1789 and recorded in his diary, "take lodgings at Mr. Trumbulls at 10/ a week." John Trumbull was an old friend, a lawyer, and author of the satirical poem *McFingal*. Oliver Ellsworth, who had been elected to the Senate, wrote Webster a friendly letter from New York, offering him rooms in his Hartford house, where Webster had boarded ten years earlier:

I congratulate you & the City of Hartford on your settlement there in the practice of the Law. Should you like a tenement of my house, by & by when you can see what the accomadations [sic] will be, I shall be glad to engage it to you....[2]

On June 6, 1789, Webster wrote to James: "I think it prudent and best to marry as soon as a house can be obtained and furnished. For this we depend wholly on your goodness; and the sooner you can make it convenient to assist your sister, the sooner you will make us happy." James obliged by providing $1000 for furnishing the house, and later added another $200 for Webster to buy a law library. To judge from his diary, Webster did scarcely any legal work in 1789, but that was in keeping with the forecast that he had sent to James on October 12:

in law as in physic, a young man must make slow progress in business; his abilities must be tried, before he can be much trusted with important business. The progress of young lawyers is nearly ascertained in this town. The first year they get but little business — the second, more — the third, may nearly support themselves — the fourth, perhaps make a little money, and after that they have generally pretty full practice and make one, two or three hundred a year. I have as good a prospect as my neighbors; better I cannot expect. I believe however my talents for speaking, notwithstanding Mr. Watson's opinion, are rather superior to most of our young men's....

In spite of his expectation that only in the third year would he be able nearly to support himself, Webster was resolved to marry as soon as James' money became available. He set out for Boston on this "important errand" on October 19, 1789, three days after his 31st birthday.

He and Rebecca were married on October 26, just as Webster was getting over a nasty bout of the flu:

October 23. Taken with the Influenza.
24. President Washington arrives in Boston, and all the world is collected to see him. I am almost confined with the Influenza. This differs from a common cold, by affecting the eyes & taking away all taste. The head appears to be fastened with chains, and the disorder is attended with a cough. The best remedy is hot liquors to produce perspiration, or a sweat brot on by violent exercise in a warm room. But if the stomach is disordered & refuses diet, a puke is necessary.
25. Sunday. Confined, but my disorder has come to its crisis.
26. Much better. This day I become a husband. I have lived a long time a bachelor, something more than thirty one years. But I had no person to form a plan for me in early life & direct me to a profession. I had an enterprising turn of mind, was bold, vain, inexperienced. I have made some unsucessful attempts, but on the whole hav done as well as most men of my years. I begin a profession, at a late period of life, but have some advantages of traveling and observation. I am united to an amiable woman, & if I am not happy, shall be much disappointed.
November 1. Sunday. Design to go to church, but my hairdresser defeats my plan & Mrs Webster goes with the family to attend Sacrament. To punish my hairdresser I keep back part of his due. But I attend afternoon. dine at brother Daniels.
2. Mrs Webster & her Sister Priscilla with myself set out for Hartford....

Webster took his bride (and her sister) back to his lodgings with Trumbull, while their new furniture (paid for by James) was set up in a house that Webster was renting from Jeremiah Wadsworth. They moved in there on November 7, 1789, and the next day it was Rebecca's turn to go down with the flu. She wrote to her family in Boston that she was "terrible homesick," and Trumbull wrote to Oliver Wolcott:

Webster has returned and brought with him a very pretty wife. I wish him success, but I doubt in the present decay of business in our profession, whether his profits will enable him to keep up the style he sets out with. I fear he will breakfast upon Institutes, dine upon Dissertations, and go to bed supperless.

There is a difference of opinion between Mrs. Ford and Warfel as to whether Trumbull's fears

were realized. According to the family folklore, Webster had plenty of business, "supported his family well, assisted his aged father, bought a farm in western New York for his brother Abraham as a free gift, educated his nephew Nelson Webster, and later had something to invest in his new publishing enterprise in New York."[3] Warfel, on the other hand, says that "his business had not kept pace with his ambition or needs. In July, 1793, he found himself still in debt to the extent of $1815, a clear loss of $400 on the *Dissertations* having increased the sum he owed for his college expenses and lecture tour. This sum, it might be said, did not include the gifts, for so the loans became, of James Greenleaf.... In the general decay of legal business he had suffered with the other young lawyers. He had to look about for a new business."[4] Warfel's figures come from a letter that is included in Mrs. Ford's book,[5] in which Webster gave James a list of his debts, perhaps in the hope that James might pay them off. They did not include the money that James himself had provided. It seems that if Webster had been as successful as Mrs. Ford suggests, he would have continued in the practice of law. Webster's own account, in No. 26 of the *Memoir*, supports Warfel:

In 1793 N.W. found that his professional business, with small emoluments of his office of Notary Public, was not adequate to the support of his family; and the proceeds of the sale of his copyrights in the eastern states, were exhausted. He then began to contemplate a change of business....

By this time, Webster had more than just himself and Rebecca to provide for. Their first child was born on August 4, 1790, and named Emily Scholten, "in Honor of the family into which brother James has married in Amsterdam." Since Webster knew that the Baroness Scholten had made James very unhappy (and they later divorced), this was not the most sensitive acknowledgment of James' generosity that Webster could have contrived. The Websters' second child, Frances Juliana (Julia) was born on February 5, 1793, and a few months later Webster started looking for other employment.

It was at this time, about the end of April 1793, that brother James returned from Amsterdam (without his wife). The following June,

Webster wrote to him, discussing the possibility of setting up in the book trade, or perhaps taking up farming. Once again, he was relying on James to come up with some money:

Dr. Appleton writes me to think of Boston. The Boston Book Store, he thinks, from the declining health of Mr. Blake, will soon be disposed of, and it is a good stand. To this plan there are objections. ... Boston is not so good a place for business, and you will perhaps hardly believe it, but Becca seems not to wish to return to Boston. This, *entre nous*, may be pride, but is it not laudable? Certainly, if she cannot live as her sisters do—which perhaps she ought not to expect at present. At any rate Boston must be given up—at present.

I should not be very apprehensive of beginning business alone, but I believe it to be ineligible for several reasons—however much will depend on your opinion—and more still on your assistance, which, as it will be proportioned to your generosity, will probably exceed your ability....

Once again, James came to Webster's aid. As Warfel describes it:

In July Greenleaf went to New York, and there in consultation with James Watson arrived at the conclusion that Webster might undertake a newspaper. Alexander Hamilton, Rufus King, John Jay, and other supporters of Washington, wished a sound Federalist paper conducted in that city and were willing to advance money for its establishment....

James and his partner Watson were the instigators of the scheme and were among the financial backers. James also found Webster a house, No. 168 Queen Street, which was large enough to hold not only Webster, Rebecca, and their two children, but also James himself, and his convivial French friend Charles Nicolas de Lagarenne. James wrote to Webster on October 7, 1793:

My first object since my return has been to look out for a Home for you, & I have happily succeeded. Our Dear Becca (for New York) will be lodged like a little queen, the house is now occupied by Tommy Franklin, & will be empty first of next month, so that you need lose no time in making arrangements for moving. The House is in excellent repair, & is large enough to allow of your lodging my friend Lagarenne & me, I shall have of my own a good deal of furniture to put into it....[6]

Webster and his family moved into the house on November 15, and on the 18th he noted in his diary, "Mr. Lagarenne & James

Greenleaf take lodgings with us." The first issue of the new paper came out three weeks later.

Webster's concerns at this time were not in any way linguistic, philological, or lexicographic, and there is no need for us to follow his career as a newspaper editor in any detail. It is sufficient to extract a summary from the pages of the *Memoir*:

> In December [1793], he published the first paper, called the *Minerva*, a daily paper. In a few months afterward, he formed the plan of a paper for country subscribers, to be printed ... with the same columns, without the composition. This saving of labor enabled him to furnish a large paper at a small price. This mode of publishing newspapers for the country with the contents of the daily papers ... has since been extensively adopted.
>
> The first semi-weekly paper for the country, called the *Herald*, was published in June 1794. The titles of the papers were afterward changed; and they are now published under the titles of the *Commercial Advertiser* (daily) and the *New York Spectator* (semi-weekly).... The labor or selecting matter for the daily paper, of correcting proofs, and of keeping the accounts of the office, in which no clerk was employed, with the additional labor of writing or translating from French papers, very soon impaired his health. But his zeal was not limited to the course of business: in the winter of 1793-4 he increased his labors by writing matter for a pamphlet, which was published with the title of the *Revolution in France*....
>
> During this winter, his strength was exhausted; in two instances, his pulse was scarcely perceptible in the radial artery; but he revived.
>
> In 1796, the papers affording a handsome profit, N.W. gave the immediate superintendance of them to a partner and a clerk and took a house at Corlaer's Hook, where he resided till he left New York. Here he kept a horse, and riding into the city daily, to attend to his papers, in the hours of business, and returning in the afternoon, he gradually recovered firmer health....
>
> Being weary of the drudgery of superintending the publication of a newspaper, he determined to remove his family to New Haven, where he could enjoy more leisure and have better advantages for educating his children than he could enjoy at Corlaer's hook. On the last day of March 1798, he left his residence with his family, embarked on board a ship commanded by Capt. John Miles and landed in the evening at New Haven. He took the house built by Benedict Arnold which had been forfeited and sold to a Mr. Sloan. This house, which was unfinished, he afterward purchased and completed.

In a moment, we shall follow Webster to New Haven, in company with Rebecca and their three children (a third daughter, Harriet, had been born on April 6, 1797). First, however, I must show you how Webster demonstrated his gratitude to James. At the same time, we can examine an interesting example of how Mrs. Ford sometimes created a rather distorted image by interweaving a warp of truth with a weft of family gossip. Referring to Webster's move from the large house on Queen Street, she writes,

> For some reason the Webster family removed from the thickly settled part of New York, leaving their large residence in Queen Street and went up 'to the country at Corlaer's Hook,' which at that time was given over to detached villas with land about them. ... it may have been due to the falling of Mr. James Greenleaf into pecuniary difficulties — through over-investment in the budding city of Washington — which perhaps left too spacious a house on Webster's hands....[7]

It is quite true that James "fell into pecuniary difficulties through over-investment in the City of Washington" but this happened some time after his departure from Webster's house in New York. When he returned to America from Amsterdam in 1793, James saw the city of Washington as an exciting financial opportunity. He hoped to make a great deal of money by developing large areas of the nation's future capital. At the same time he hoped to do a bit of good for another of his brothers-in-law, Nathaniel Appleton, to whom he offered a job. Appleton wrote to Webster from Boston on November 23, 1793 to tell him about it, and ask his advice:

> Our good friend & Br° James has in the goodness of his Heart & in the Assiduity of his business, made a proposition to me, by the last mail, with which it is not impossible you may be already acquainted. It is for me to quit all my business, family & other connexions, & remove with my Wife & Children to the New City of Washington, where, as you have doubtless been informed he is a very great proprietor, probably the largest of any man in the U.S. he wishes me to reside there as his Agent & is willing to *guaranty* to me a certain sum for a certain term of years. Such a proposition from most men would appear to me to be visionary, but relying on his judgment I do not conceive this to be so. In so important a concern as you may easily conceive this to be I am desirous of the best judgment of my best friends, among these I rank you as one very dear to me. Y[ou] will therefore please by the *return of this Mail*, give me your friendly advice on the subject. Do you think

the Climate would probably agree with my Health, which is always the poorest in the Months of Aug^t & Sep^r? do you think me competent to do what would be expected of me — would it not be a constant round of great fatigue of body and mind? Do not Br^o James' prospects depend very much on the *contingency* of that place being the seat of Govern^t at the time proposed?...[8]

Appleton accepted James' offer. Unhappily, all his worst fears turned out to be justified, both about his own frailty and about the precarious nature of James' investment. Soon after his arrival in Washington, Appleton came down with what is said to have been malaria, and in December 1794 he returned to Boston as an invalid. He died the following April. James had managed to unload a large part of his investment onto the firm of Morris and Nicholson, but they also got into difficulties and were unable to pay him. The property boom in Washington arrived too late, and they all went bust. To make matters worse, James had given Appleton's job to his newest brother-in-law, William Cranch, and Cranch was bankrupted too.

According to Mrs. Ford, James, "after his financial calamities," went to live with his youngest sister Nancy and her husband, William Cranch. She paints a moving picture of the three of them in later years:

It is said that he [William] and his Nancie were lovers till their last moment together, and that her brother James Greenleaf, who had taken refuge with her after his financial calamities, was equally fond of her; often she sat, a lively old lady, on the sofa with her husband and her brother, each holding her hands and enjoying her sweetness and repose. James Greenleaf often said he hoped he should never live an hour after his sister Nancie's death. He almost had his wish, she dying in the morning and he at night, almost as much from grief as disease....[9]

In this account, fact and fancy are intertwined. James' leaving Webster's house had nothing to do with his financial difficulties. At that time he thought he had plenty of money.

From New York, he moved to Pennsylvania and bought Lansdowne, Governor Penn's country house by the Schuylkill, with two hundred acres. He also bought a large town house in Philadelphia that had belonged to General Dickinson. Two years later, in 1797, both houses were repossessed. James later managed to refloat himself by marrying a lady with money. William Cranch was kept afloat by his influential relations. When he got into financial difficulties, his uncle John Adams was the president, and provided a judicial appointment to keep him off the breadline. One of the first problems that confronted Jefferson when he succeeded Adams in 1801 was deciding what to do about the "midnight judges" that Adams had appointed just before he left office — William Cranch was one of those judges. He was allowed to remain on the bench, and administered the oath of office to Madison, when the latter became secretary of state.

In old age, James did not live with his sister Nancy and Judge Cranch, but in his own house, which was round the corner from theirs. He did die on the same day as his sister, but as he was 78 and had been very ill for some time, the most that can be said is that the news of her death may have hastened his passing.

That leaves unanswered the question, why did Webster move from the large town house on Queen Street to live in the country at Corlaer's Hook? I am not sure of the answer, but I do know why James moved — Webster drove him away. Webster, who owed his wife and family, his house and his job to James' generosity, attacked James for disrupting his domestic peace. James left in a huff, and they were never friends again. James had committed the unpardonable offenses of inviting unexpected guests to dinner, and being altogether too cheerful. Perhaps Webster moved into a smaller house because he wanted to live in one that did not have room for James.

11. Webster in New Haven, 1798–1807

Webster left New York for New Haven on April 1, 1798, and a few days later, on April 10, he started writing *A Brief History of Epidemic and Pestilential Diseases*. The subject of yellow fever had interested him since his time in Philadelphia, where he had become a friend of Dr. Benjamin Rush. Philadelphia was periodically ravaged by outbreaks of the disease, and argument raged between its medical men as to whether the infection was of local origin or carried from place to place. A system of quarantine might prevent its arrival if it were imported but would otherwise be a useless inconvenience and an impediment to trade. Webster entered enthusiastically into the argument on the side of Dr. Rush and local origin and against Dr. Currie and importation. Webster's *Pestilential Diseases* is interesting to us because it has similar flaws in method to those in his later work on the roots of language. In both, a superficially scientific study was supposed (and was believed by Webster) to prove the correctness of his own previously held unscientific beliefs.

Many supporters of the "local origin" faction thought that epidemics were associated with tainted air. A particularly unpleasant smell, such as might come from a pile of rotting fish or the excrement discharged at the quayside from slave ships, either caused disease, or promoted its spread. The theory has left a fossilized footprint in our language, for *malaria* means "bad air." Webster subscribed to a modified version of that creed, believing a localized nasty smell to be the *secondary* cause of an epidemic, the *primary* cause being "a quality of the atmosphere, extending *usually over one hemisphere*, sometimes *over the globe*."[1] This "quality of the atmosphere" was caused, he suspected, by comets passing overhead, or by volcanic eruptions, earthquakes, or tornadoes. "In a few instances, this general cause, with the season, has produced true plague, without the least operation of noxious exhalations. In most cases, however, the plague is not produced without the co-operation of local vitiation of the air."

Webster collected a vast amount of information. He scoured libraries for accounts of plagues from remotest antiquity, which he correlated with eruptions and the passage of comets. He placed advertisements in periodicals, and he wrote letters to doctors around America, asking for particulars of epidemics and associated climatic events. This gives his study the appearance of respectable research, but all that he was able to see in the mass of material that he accumulated was the confirmation of his own preconceived ideas. In November 1799, he wrote to Rush: "I feel a good degree of confidence in my proofs that epidemic diseases of all kinds proceed from chemical changes in this fluid in which we live, & whose vivifying & elastic powers constitute the source of life."

The mosquito that actually carried yellow fever was identified nearly a hundred years later by a doctor in Havana called Charles (or Carlos) Finlay. Nobody took much notice until, several years afterwards, mosquitoes were implicated in the spread of malaria. Finlay's theory was then confirmed by a foolishly courageous research program in which Dr. Walter Reed and members of his team allowed themselves to be bitten by infected mosquitoes. The breeding places of the mosquitoes around Havana were immediately attacked by draining them, or by pouring oil on stagnant waters, which led to a swift and startling reduction in the death toll from the disease.

Strangely enough, when Webster had trawled the American waters for information, one little fish that lay almost unnoticed in his net was the fact that yellow fever epidemics were associated with mosquitoes. In December 1798 a certain Charles Holt wrote telling him that a curious observer of natural phenomena had remarked to Holt on "the astonishing number of flies, moschetoes, etc.," which particularly attracted his attention, and said "I am afraid we are going to have the pestilence & Yellow Fever here." "It was an expression," Holt commented, "which succeeding circumstances [i.e., a yellow fever epidemic] have forcibly brought to my recollection." Webster's conclusion was that the same state of the atmosphere that promoted the spread of disease must also cause mosquitoes to breed. This is his account of the incident, which affords an example of his deductive reasoning:

Considerable quantities of salted fish, which lay in certain stores in New-London, and which had not been well cured with the usual quantity of salt, became fetid and offensive, altho not putrid, and assumed a red cast with a slimy feeling — it also lost its texture and firmness. This was opened and spread in the streets for the purpose of being dried: and from its offensiveness and vicinity to the place where the disease first appeared, it is supposed to have been an exciting cause of the fever. This opinion has doubtless some foundation: but putrid fish will not always occasion disease. It is probably true that the bad state of the fish was partly owing to a previous bad state of the air: altho it afterwards became a *cause* of a *worse state* of the air.

What seems to put this beyond doubt, is, the unusual number of musketoes, in the adjacent country, and the multitudes of flies of uncommon size, exceeding what had been before observed. With these phenomena before our eyes, we can be at no loss to account for the pestilential fever in New-London.[2]

In order to pursue his researches, Webster had been compelled to study science, and here he found little help in Johnson's Dictionary. Johnson claimed that he had included "terms of art ... such as could be found either in books of science or technical dictionaries," but his interests were more literary than scientific, and in any case, the number of technical dictionaries available to him before 1755 was not large. When Webster wrote *Pestilential Diseases* he had not yet acquired his own copy of Johnson (the eighth edition, published in London in 1799) but it would have made little difference which edition he consulted because Johnson's scientific vocabulary was not brought up to date. The later dictionaries did not help either, since they were largely derived from Johnson's. Since the publication of the *Grammatical Institute*, two more of these had appeared in England: the pronouncing dictionaries of John Walker and Stephen Jones.

Walker produced his in 1791, following in the footsteps of Sheridan, Kenrick, and Perry. There is an account of its publication in the Preface to yet another pronouncing dictionary, that of James Knowles, published in 1835. Knowles was Sheridan's nephew, and to maintain his family pride he felt obliged "to state the circumstances that led to the publication of Mr. Walker's Dictionary: circumstances which, I suspect, are unknown even by the successors of the Booksellers, whose names I am about to mention."

Mr. Sheridan commenced his Dictionary in 1760: but did not publish it till 1780. He died at Margate, in Kent, in 1788, on his way to Lisbon for the recovery of his health, attended by his younger son, the late R.B. Sheridan, leaving his Dictionary in the hands of his younger daughter, and his Booksellers, and Publishers, Dilly in the Poultry, Dodsley's Pall Mall, and Wilkie in St.Paul's Church Yard, between whom, differences arising, which could not be accommodated, the publication of his Dictionary was discontinued.

Mr. Walker was at that time a Teacher of Elocution in the Academies in and near London: and was encouraged by the Booksellers, whose names appear to the first edition of his Dictionary published in 1791, to take Mr. Sheridan's work, and form another upon it. This he did, by merely copying it in the mass: carefully omitting any notice of the masterly, and complete developement of all the simple and compound elementary principles of pronunciation, Accent, Emphasis, Rules of English Versification, &c. which precede the Dictionary, and substituting in their room "599 Rules, or Principles of Pronunciation," and, from them deducing a key-line of the vowel sounds, which runs along the head of every page of his Dictionary....

The circumstances described by Knowles would certainly have been unknown to the booksellers, because they never happened. Walker's dictionary could not have been intended to fill the gap left by the disappearance of Sheridan's, because Sheridan's dictionary did not disappear. The original publishers may have had a disagreement after Sheridan's death, but one of them, Charles Dilly, published a second

quarto edition in 1789, and later editions in two volumes octavo in 1790 and 1797. Sheridan's dictionary also provided the groundwork for the popular *General Pronouncing and Explanatory Dictionary* of Stephen Jones, which was subtitled *Sheridan Improved*. More probably, other publishers were seeking a compiler for a pronouncing dictionary to compete with Sheridan's, and Walker would have been the obvious candidate. He was a former actor who had been lecturing on elocution since 1771, and he was considered the leading authority on polite pronunciation. He had also proposed such a dictionary in 1774. The early editions of his dictionary closely resembled Sheridan's, being of the same quarto size, of comparable thickness, and similarly printed in three columns. Much of the content was similar too, because both were "following" Johnson. Sheridan said that he had "In the explanatory part ... chiefly followed Dr. Johnson," and Walker that, "With respect to the explanation of words, except in very few instances, I have scrupulously followed Dr. Johnson." Walker's "Principles of English Pronunciation" (of which Knowles got the number wrong — there were 598, not 599) owed nothing to Sheridan.

Walker's customers were people who wanted to conceal their foreign, provincial, or lower class origins, in order to get by in polite society. He therefore included "Rules to be Observed by the Natives of Scotland, Ireland, and London, for avoiding their respective Peculiarities, and Directions to Foreigners, for acquiring a Knowledge of the Use of this Dictionary." Pronunciation was indicated by a combination of respelling and numbered vowels, together with references to the numbered sections of his 598 Principles. In addition, little pointing hands within the text indicated especially interesting or disputed questions of pronunciation. One which particularly irritated Webster was in the entry for *garden*:

☞ When the *a* in this and similar words is preceded by *G* or *K*, polite speakers interpose a sound like the consonant *y*, which coalesces with both, and gives a mellowness to the sound: thus *a Garden* pronounced in this manner is nearly similar to the two words *Egg* and *Yarden* united into *eggyarden*, and *a Guard* is almost like *eggyard*.

Under *guard*, Walker was even more didactic, but forgot that *egg* in such words includes the indefinite article:

☞ This word is pronounced exactly like the word *yard*, preceded by hard *g*, nearly as *egg-yard*. The same sound of *y* consonant is observable between hard *g* and *a* in other words. Nor is this a fanciful peculiarity, but a pronunciation arising from euphony and the analogy of the language.

In *guilt*, it is an *e* that is interposed, but to the same effect:

☞ It is observed in Principles, No. 92, that, when *g* comes before short *a*, the sound of *e* so necessarily intervenes that we cannot pronounce those letters without it: but that when the *a* is long, as in *regard*, we may pronounce these two letters without the intervention of *e*, but that this pronunciation is not the most elegant. The same may be observed of the *g* hard, and the long and short *i*. We may pronounce *guide* and *guile* nearly as if written *egg-ide* and *egg-ile*, though not so properly as *egg-yide* and *egg-yile*, but that *gild* and *guilt* must necessarily admit of the *e* sound between hard *g* and *i*, or we cannot pronounce them.

"Egg-yarden is a lovesome thing" sounds quite absurd, of course, but some old fashioned English gentry, even today, pronounce words such as *gap* with a slight sound of *y* after the *g*. They are unaware of it, and might even deny it, but they really do say "The fyat cyat syat on the myat." There are other words in which the *y* is, in every sense, more pronounced. A *tutor* of *elocution* in London today will tell his *pupils* that the sound of *y* should be interposed before the *u* in those words, and in many others such as *duty*, and after *T* every *Tuesday*. The *student* who fails to learn this simple lesson will be thought *obtuse*. Where *t* comes before *u* in such words, sounding the *t* as if it were *ch* is common but is not considered correct. *T* does, however, make the sound of *ch* in words like *nay-cher* and *jess-cher*. It is said that the *yoo* sound in English is an attempt at a French *u*, but one does not make the sound with any consciousness of that fact. This interposed *y* is much more common in England than in America, but there are a few words in which an American will sound it where an Englishman would not. In England, for example, everyone says *figger*, but many Americans pronounce the word *fig-your*. Pronunciation, like dress, is a matter of fashion and convention, and that which is familiar is generally assumed to be correct.

Walker, certainly, was assumed to be correct. At least, his name became associated with

the idea of correct pronunciation, and very large numbers of his dictionary were sold, mostly in octavo size. In addition, it was thought a useful selling point to incorporate Walker's pronunciation into other dictionaries. Johnson's abstract edition was "improved by the Standard of Pronunciation established in the Critical Pronouncing Dictionary of John Walker," and was published in that form by Jacob Johnson & Co. in Philadelphia, in 1805.

Pronunciation was a subject that interested Webster, but none of these general dictionaries was of much use to him in the study of science. The only dictionaries that had been printed in America were even less useful, though there was a considerable demand for them. A nation of immigrants, especially one with a cultural inferiority complex and an insatiable appetite for self-improvement, provides a ready market for dictionaries. In 1796, the London bookseller Henry Lemoine contributed an article to the *Gentleman's Magazine* on the book trade in North America,[3] in which he said that "novels and useful histories are the best articles to be considered here, *after Dictionaries.*" He was offering advice on what English books could profitably be shipped to America, but the existence of such a demand had already led to the reprinting of British dictionaries in America, and would soon prompt Americans to compile dictionaries of their own.

The first dictionary to be printed in America was an edition of Perry's *Royal Standard English Dictionary*, published by Isaiah Thomas in Worcester, Massachusetts, in 1788.[4] It must have been popular, since by 1802 six more editions had been issued, and Ebenezer Merriam printed the same book in Brookfield five times between 1801 and 1813. These were little square octavos. Similar pocket editions of Sheridan's dictionary were printed in Philadelphia in 1789 and in 1796, and American reprints of Walker began to appear in 1803.

The first homegrown American dictionary was the duodecimo *School Dictionary*, compiled by Samuel Johnson Jr., which was published in New Haven in 1798. The Preface explained that his object was "not ... to afford either entertainment or instruction to persons of Education," but rather "to furnish Schools with a dictionary which will enable youth more easily to acquire a knowledge of the English Language." He admitted that "the principal part" of the book had been collected from "Authors of established reputation," but that admission conceals rather more than it discloses. In fact, almost all the *School Dictionary* came from Perry's *Royal Standard English Dictionary*, with very little alteration to the definitions. Johnson merely left out most of Perry's words to produce a much shorter and cheaper book. *Lamellated* to *laud*, a typical page of the *School Dictionary*, contains 21 words; the same section of Perry has 122 entries.

Samuel Johnson Jr. next embarked on a joint work with John Elliott, "Pastor of the Church in East-Guilford." It was called *A selected, pronouncing and accented Dictionary,* and was published in Suffield, Connecticut, in 1800. Several recommendations were printed at the beginning, among them an extract of a letter from Noah Webster, Junr. Esq.:

Mr. Elliot [sic], I have not time to examine every sheet of your manuscript, but have read many sheets in different parts of it: your general plan and execution I approve of, and can sincerely wish you success in your labors, I am, Sir, with much respect, your obedient servant,

NOAH WEBSTER, Junr.

Webster there used the spelling *labor*, though the dictionary itself has *labour*. Elliott and Johnson are inconsistent in their use of these terminations (as was the *School Dictionary*) using *-or* in *arbor, ardor, dolor, fervor,* and *tenor,* but *-our* in *colour, honour, odour, parlour,* and *vigour*. The spelling *armor* is used in the definition of *armory,* but in *breastplate* they use *armour*. It looks as though they were using both an edition of Entick's *New Spelling Dictionary* that mostly had *-or*,[5] and Perry, who favored *-our*. Some inconsistencies, such as *arbour* in the definition of *bower,* and *armour* in *Breastplate,* were mistakes copied directly from Entick. In the word list, Elliott and Johnson changed Entick's spelling from *color* to *colour,* but they failed to change it in the definition of *blowzy* ("high colored") or in the table of homophones (*blue,* "a kind of color"). The fact that they were working from a dictionary that used the spelling *color* is most clearly shown by the fact that they failed to move the entry in the dictionary itself. The definition of *colour* ap-

L A N   L A R   245

Lăm'ĭ-nat-ĕd, *a.* plated

Lămm, *v. a.* to beat soundly

Lăm'măs, *s.* the first day of August

Lamp, *s.* a light made of oil or spirits

Lamp'black, *s.* a substance made by holding a torch under the bottom of a bason, and as it is furred, striking it with a feather into some shell placed on purpose

Lăm-pôon', *s.* personal satire, abuse, censure : *v. a.* to abuse with personal satire

Lăm-pôon'ĕr; *s.* a writer of personal satire

Lăm'prey, *s.* an eel

Lănce, *s.* a long spear : *v. a.* to pierce, open chirurgically

Lăn'cĕt, *s.* a chirurgical instrument to let blood

Lănch, *v. a.* to cast as a lance, dart

Lănd, *s.* a country, earth, ground : *v. a.* and *n.* to set on shore, to come on shore

Lănd'ĕd, *a.* ashore; having an estate in land

Lănd'fŏr-cĕs, *s.* soldiers who serve on land

Lănd'grăve, *s.* a German title, a Count

Lănd'hōld-ĕr, *s.* one who possesses land

Lănd'jŏb-bér, *s.* who buys and sells land

Lănd'ing, *s.* top of stairs ; place to land at

Lănd'la-dy, *s.* the mistress of an inn

Lănd'lĕss, *a.* without property or fortune

Lănd'lŏck-ĕd, *a.* hemmed in by land

Lănd'lŏrd, *s.* the master of an inn ; one who owns lands or houses, who has tenants

Lănd'màrk, *s.* a fixed mark of boundaries

Lănd'scăpe, *s.* a prospect of a country ; a picture representing an extent of place with the various objects around it

Lănd'tăx, *s.* a tax upon land and houses

Lănd'wāit-ér, *s.* one who watches the landing of goods

Lănd'ward, *ad.* towards land

Lăne, *s.* a narrow street or passage

Lăn'gûage, *s.* human speech ; style, tongue of one nation ; the manner of expression

Lăn'gûag-ĕd, *a.* knowing various languages

Lăn'gûage-màs-ter, *s.* a person who professes to teach languages, a linguist

Lăn'gûĕt, *s.* a weaver's leaden tongue

Lăn'gûid, *a.* faint, heartless, infirm, dull

Lăn'gûid-ly, *ad.* feebly, infirmly, weakly

Lăn'gûid-nĕss, *s.* feebleness, weakness

Lăn'gûish, *v. n.* to lose strength, to pine: *s.* an appearance of softness and tenderness

Lăn'gûish-ing-ly, *ad.* faintly, dully, sadly

Lăn'gûish-mĕnt, *s.* softness of mien

Lăn'gûór, *s.* heaviness of spirit

Lănk, *a.* faint, languid, slender, meagre

Lank'nĕss, *s.* a want of flesh, slenderness

Lăns-quĕn'ĕt, *s.* a well-known game at cards ; a common foot-soldier

Lăn'tĕrn, *s.* a case for a candle, a light-house

Lăn'tĕrn-jāws, *s.* a thin meagre vissage

Lăp, *s.* a seat on the thighs; a fold or plait : *v. a.* to wrap round, lick up

Lăp'dŏg, *s.* a little dog for the lap

Lăp'fûl, *s.* as much as the lap can hold

Lăp'ĭ-cide, *s.* a stone-cutter

Lăp'ĭ-da-ble, *a.* worthy of being stoned, fit to be stoned

Lăp'ĭ-da-ry, *s.* who deals in stones or gems

La-pĭd'e-oŭs, *a.* stony, of a stony nature

Lăp-ĭ-dĕs'cĕnce, *s.* concretion of a stone

Lăp-ĭ-dĕs'cĕnt, *a.* burning or changing to stone, forming into a concretion of stone

La-pĭd-ĭ-fĭ-ca'tion, *s.* act of forming stones

Lăp-ĭ-dĭf'ĭc, *a.* forming into stones

Lăp'ĭd-ĭst, *s.* a lapidary, a dealer in jewels

Lăp'pér, *s.* who wraps or laps up

Lăp'pĕt, *s.* part of a woman's head-dress

Lăpse, *s.* a small errour ; a fall, a flow, a glide: *v. n.* to lose the proper time, to fall,

Lăp'wing, *s.* a noisy bird   [glide

Lăp-wórk, *s* one thing wrapped in another

Làr'bōard, *s.* the left-hand side of a ship

Lăr'ce-ny, *s.* theft, a petty theft

*21

A page from Perry's *Royal Standard English Dictionary*, the source of most of the *School Dictionary* definitions.

pears before *colossus,* where it should be if the spelling *color* were used. Similarly, *honour* and *honourable* appear before *honorary.* In one important respect they followed Perry rather than Entick, separating the initial letters *I* and *J* in the alphabetical list, and the letters *U* and *V.* The final *k* is absent from such words as *music* and *public,* but there they were following the example set by both Perry and Entick, and they

restored the *k* to *bishoprick.* Overall, Elliott and Johnson is little more than an enlarged version of Johnson's *School Dictionary* (it has 50 entries between *lamellated* and *laud*), with material taken from Entick as well as from Perry.

Joseph Friend cited the listing of well-established borrowings from American Indian languages, such as *tomahawk* and *wampum,* as an indication of the "Americanism" of the

Elliot-Johnson dictionary.[6] There are a few additions of that sort, but many of those words were so well-established that they were already in the English dictionaries. Both *tomahawk* and *wampum* were in Entick. Similarly, most of the homophones that Friend takes as indicative of New England speech at the end of the eighteenth century are also to be found in Entick's "Table of Words that are alike, or nearly alike, in Sound, but different in Spelling and Signification."

In their Preface, Elliott and Johnson mentioned certain shortcomings of earlier dictionaries:

Serious objections lie against those in common use, arising from their price, but more especially from their want of delicacy, and chastity of language. Many words, there found are highly offensive to the modest ear, and cannot be read without a blush. To inspire youth with sentiments of modesty, and delicacy is one of the principal objects of early instruction: and this object is totally defeated by the indiscriminate use of vulgar, and indecent words.

Before Bowdler, the process of removing the rude bits from books was known as "castration." Elliott and Johnson duly snipped out Entick's *fart* and *turd*, and

ɪ ɪ 2	L A

Lăm el la ted, *a.* covered with plates
Lăm i na, *ſ.* thin plate; one coat laid over another
Lam poôn, *ſ* perſonal ſatire, abuſe, cenſure: *v. a.* to abuſe with perſonal ſatire
Land grave, *ſ* a German title, a count
Lan guid, *a.* faint, heartleſs, infirm, dull feeble
Lan guid neſs, *ſ.* feebleneſs, weakneſs
Lan guiſh, *v. n.* to loſe ſtrength to pine: *ſ.* an appearance of ſoftneſs or tenderneſs
Lan guiſh ment, *ſ.* ſoftneſs of mien: ſtate of pining
Lan guor, *ſ.* heavineſs of ſpirit
Lap i da ry, *ſ.* who deals in ſtones or gems
Lap i dif ic, *a* forming into ſtones
Lăp id iſt, *ſ.* a lapidary, who deals in jewels
Lar ce ny, *ſ.* theft, a petty theft
La ſcĭv i ous, *a* lewd, wanton fond
La ſciv i ouſ neſs, *ſ* loſeneſs, wantonneſs
La ſſi tude, *ſ.* fatigue, languor, weckneſs
La tent, *a* concealed, hidden, ſecret
Lat er al, *a.* on or near the ſide, parallel
Lat i tu di nā ri an, *ſ.* who departs from orthidoxy; *a.* unconfined, unlimited
Lăt tice, *a.* a window of grate work
Laûd, *v. a.* to extol, praiſe, celebrate

A page from *The School Dictionary* (1798) by Samuel Johnson Jnr.

thereby began a remarkable tradition. Those harmless words were banished from American dictionaries (though not always from American reprints of English dictionaries) for more than a hundred years. Elliott and Johnson did not, however, snip out enough to satisfy the critic of the *American Review*. He examined their dictionary closely, and found a word

to which, at first, we thought these gentlemen had

the exclusive right. We cannot soil our page with a transcription of it: it is to be found under the letter F, and is called *French*, but we were sure no *French* dictionary would admit a word so shockingly indecent and vulgar.... Nor did we think it possible that it should find its way into any English dictionary: but turning to Ash, whose purpose it appears to have been to insert every word written or spoken in our language, we there found it. We hope, however, that neither the authority of the reverend pastor, or even of his learned colleague, will be sufficient to give it

currency. Observing, from the definition of this word in Ash, which they have literally copied, that he does not understand the meaning of the term, we sincerely hope that they may have the same apology: for ignorance would here afford them some excuse as men of decency and piety, though none as lexicographers.[7]

What was the word? In 1934, Allen Walker Read of the University of Chicago published an article, *An Obscenity Symbol*, in the journal *American Speech*. It was an examination of taboo in language, and particularly a study of the word *fuck*, with special reference to its appearance in dictionaries.[8] This was a courageous thing to do, though the publishers of *American Speech* were not so bold as to allow the word anywhere in the article, describing it instead as "the most disreputable of all English words — the colloquial verb and noun, universally known by speakers of English, designating the sex act," and thereafter referring to it as "our word." Read knew, of course, that Ash had defined *fuck*, and he assumed (not having the opportunity to examine Elliott and Johnson) that the *f-word* complained of in the *American Review* was "our word." Well, it wasn't. Elliott and Johnson were not using Ash: they were using Entick and Perry, and neither of them contains "our word." Not long afterwards, Eva Mae Burkett was writing her doctoral thesis on *American Dictionaries of the English Language before 1861,*[9] and she searched Elliott and Johnson for something rude beginning with *f.* She did not find *fuck*, because it is not there. In fact, the only remotely blushworthy thing she found was *feme covert*, a French law term meaning "a married woman." Could that have been what upset the 1801 reviewer? No, it wasn't that either. The word the critic was complaining about was *foutra*, which Johnson's Dictionary said was "[from *foutre*, French.] A fig; a scoff: a word of contempt. Not used." Johnson gave a quotation from Shakespeare's *Henry IV*, which was probably his reason for including the obsolete word in his dictionary. Ash took his definition from Johnson, just changing "word of contempt" to "act of contempt." But what *was* the act? To find the answer, we have to follow the clue Johnson provided by the word *fig*, which leads us back to his entry "*fico* [Italian.] An act of contempt done with the fingers, expressing *a fig for you.*"

Elliott and Johnson's definition was "Foutra *(Foo tre)* a scoff, an insult, a gibe," which came mostly from Perry ("a scoff, an insult") with the word *gibe* added from Entick ("a scoff, gibe, sneer, fig, mark of contempt"). Elliott and Johnson did not, as the critic said, call the word French — he was thinking of Ash, no doubt — nor does it appear that Ash misunderstood the word. Rather, it was the critic who was being too clever by half. *Foutra* is derived from the French word *foutre* (meaning *fuck*) but it has no more directly sexual implication than telling someone to "bugger off." The critic was also wrong to suggest that such a word should not be in any English dictionary. It is a bit out of place in this one, however. Elliott and Johnson were compiling a school dictionary that was to include less than half the words in Perry or Entick. They left out *fico* (which was in both). Why on earth did they include *foutra?*[*]

One other American dictionary was published in 1800: Caleb Alexander's *Columbian Dictionary of the English Language.* I have not examined a copy, but Krapp did so, and his examination did not bear out Alexander's claim on the title page to have included "many new words of general use, not found in any other English dictionary."[10] *The Columbian Dictionary*, however, is said to be the first that defined the word *telegraph.*

In this situation, Webster saw a business opportunity. There was a need for a general dictionary that explained terms of science. Indeed, there was a market for dictionaries of all sizes, which he was well qualified to supply. From the very beginning, he had it in mind to produce not just one dictionary, but a whole series. This was announced (by Webster, of course) in the New Haven newspapers six months after the publication of *A Brief History of Epidemic and Pestilential Diseases*:

> Mr. Webster of this city, we understand, is engaged in completing the system for the instruction of youth, which he began in the year 1783. He has in hand a Dictionary of the American Language, a work long since projected, but which other occupations have delayed till this time. The plan contemplated extends to a small Dictionary for schools, one for the counting-house, and a large one for men of science. The first is nearly ready for the press — the second and third will require the labor of some years.

The announcement went on to explain that *Dictionaries of the American Language* were

---

It was also in Samuel Johnson Jnr's School Dictionary, *but nobody complained.*

needed because the language of America would inevitably diverge more and more from that of England. Webster later came to believe that the language of England and that of America should stay the same, even though some words might be different: his 1806 dictionary did not call itself a dictionary of the American language, but *A Compendious Dictionary of the English Language*. Before he could concentrate on it, however, he had to attend to the source of his bread and butter. He revised the spelling book.

Webster had brought out a revised edition of the speller, the first one with fables, in 1787, while he was still in Philadelphia. It was not immediately the subject of a new copyright, because there was then no federal copyright act and Webster was not in a position to make another tour to register the new edition in the separate states. He still relied, therefore, on his original registrations of Part I of the *Grammatical Institute*.

Under the federal act of 1790, it made no difference whether a work had already been published or not, or whether it was already protected by state copyrights. If the title of the work was deposited in the clerk's office of the district court where the author or other proprietor of the copyright lived, then (subject to certain other statutory conditions) the work would enjoy copyright throughout the United States for 14 years. The other conditions at that time were that within two months of the deposit of the title, the proprietor had to cause a copy of the copyright certificate "to be published in one or more of the newspapers printed in the United States, for the space of four weeks," and that within six months of publication, a copy of the book had to be delivered to the secretary of state. If the author was still alive at the end of the first term of copyright, he could qualify for a second 14 year term by depositing the title again during the last six months of the first term and again publishing the copyright notice for four weeks in one or more newspapers. The requirement that the copyright notice be printed in the title-page of a book, or in the page immediately following, was added in 1802.

The 1790 act was passed on the last day of May, and within a month Webster had registered the three parts of the *Institute*.[11] The title that he deposited in June 1790 was that of the revised version, the Philadelphia speller of 1787. It was called *The American Spelling Book, containing an easy standard of pronunciation, being the first part of a Grammatical Institute of the English Language, in three parts, by Noah Webster, jun. Esq.*

Webster had been aware of the importance of copyright even before he had sold a single book, but at the beginning the success of the work was uncertain, and he probably gave little thought to what he was going to do when his copyright expired. Later, when the spelling book proved to be a best-seller, he devised a strategy intended to prolong the copyright indefinitely — whenever copyright was due to expire, he would produce a revised edition, and deposit a new title. The term of copyright would start afresh.

Put thus simply, the plan sounds quite convincing, and *emotionally* Webster seems to have believed that it worked. *Intellectually*, he must have known that it did not. In reality, that strategy would not prolong copyright at all. When he registered a new title to secure copyright in a new edition, only the new material would be protected. When the copyright in the old edition expired, the whole of that edition fell into the public domain, and anybody was free to reprint it, or to use it as the basis for his own speller. Webster was never comfortable with this, and he continued to complain, long after the expiry of his early copyrights, that others had taken unfair advantage of him by compiling spelling books which incorporated "his" improvements.

Commercially, he had no reason to complain. His spelling books were vastly more successful than those of his competitors, and though there was a certain amount of printing of earlier editions that were out of copyright, Webster was generally successful in meeting that competition by advertising his succeeding version as new and improved. People did not want to buy the old one if it was outdated and inferior.

In June 1804, the first 14 year term of copyright in the *Institute* under the 1790 Act came to an end. Webster was entitled to register again for another 14 years, but he had already decided on a further revision of the book. What he produced in 1804 was called *The American Spelling Book; containing the Rudiments of the English*

Language, for the use of Schools in the United States. He finally dropped the name *Part I of the Grammatical Institute*, which did not appear even as a subtitle. According to Mrs. Skeel's Bibliography "Application for copyright was made in the Connecticut District on November 1, 1803";[12] but all the copies of the spelling book that I have seen refer to a registration in Connecticut on March 14, 1804, for the first term, and to re-registration for the second term on September 15, 1817. That spelling book remained in use without substantial alteration from 1804 until 1829. In it, the trick of telling the year of printing by looking at the last entry in the table "Of Numbers" no longer works — the last number stayed at 1804, MDCCCIV, throughout the life of the 1804 *American Spelling Book.*

One then asks whether Webster bothered to renew the copyright in the old spelling book, the Philadelphia revision, when its first term expired in June 1804. He would have had to do it during the previous six months. The Copyright Act obliged the clerk of the federal district court to record titles "in a book to be kept by him for the purpose," but it is not possible to consult the book in which this entry would have been made, because it is lost; there are no surviving copyright records for Connecticut earlier than September 1804. The usual indication of a copyright registration after 1802 is the copyright notice printed on the back of the title page, but that is not available to us either, because Webster did not reissue the old speller after 1804. What we see appearing at that time is the new *American Spelling Book,* with a different title, and with a copyright notice referring to its registration in March 1804. That was what his competitors saw as well, and at least one of them was advised that the old copyright must have expired, so that they were free to reprint the old book. In 1804, E. Merriam & Co., printers and booksellers of Brookfield, Massachusetts, issued an unlicensed edition of Webster's speller. "E" was Ebenezer Merriam, and "Co." was his brother Daniel. They were respectively the uncle and the father of George and Charles Merriam, who would take over the publication of the *American Dictionary* forty years later. In Leavitt's words, Ebenezer and Daniel "innocently took the advice of mistaken counsel that anyone could print a *Blue-Back*

Speller, and had unknowingly started to run off printings of Webster's work..."[13]

The person most affected by a competing Webster speller appearing in Massachusetts would have been Webster's licensee in Boston, John West, and on December 21, 1804, Webster wrote to him, reporting that he had put a stop to the Merriams' infringement:

I directed a prosecution of the Merriams, which bro^t them to a settlement — & upon their paying me a considerable sum in damages, I acquitted them, on condition they send the books out of N. England.[14]

Webster had clearly been able to persuade the Merriams that he had renewed the 1790 copyright. He also told his counsel that he had done so, when he sought legal advice in the matter of Bonsal and Niles. By an agreement made in 1797, Webster had sold Bonsal and Niles the right to print and publish his speller in Pennsylvania and Delaware, from the date of the agreement up to June 1 1804. Bonsal and Niles were interested in securing a renewal of that contract, and corresponded with Webster on the subject in 1803. In a letter dated November 24, 1803, Webster told them that he intended to impose more onerous terms than under the old agreement, and that "the business of printing this book will hereafter be placed on a different footing." This was not acceptable to Bonsal and Niles, and they decided to build up a large stock of spellers while their licence remained in force. They printed an extra 50,000 copies before June 1, 1804, which they continued to sell after the end of the agreement. Their argument was that they were licensed to *print* up to June 1, 1804, and it must have been intended that they could sell books that had been printed under licence. Webster took the advice of counsel, Mr. Charles Chauncey of Philadelphia, asking the question "Have Bonsal & Niles invaded the rights of N. Webster, secured by the Act of Congress, or have they violated their contract ... by publishing the work since their term?" Chauncey advised that the contract gave Bonsal and Niles the right to "*print and publish* till the 1st of June 1804," not the right to *print* until that date and *publish* what they had printed indefinitely thereafter. As an interpretation of the contract, that must surely be correct, but Webster's right to object to continued sale did depend on his

1790 copyright having been renewed. Chauncey's opinion included this among the facts Webster had given him: "On 22d June 1804, Mr. Webster's copyright of the book expired, and was continued for 14 years, under the Act of Congress." If the copyright had not been renewed, Bonsal and Niles need not have restricted themselves to selling spellers printed before June 1; as soon as the copyright expired, they would have had an unfettered right to print and sell the old spelling book.

Webster did not sue Bonsal and Niles, because their stock of spellers was exhausted by the time he received Chauncey's opinion at the end of July 1805. He considered their conduct fraudulent, however, and had no further dealings with them. By contrast, he accepted that the Merriams had acted innocently, and since they paid up promptly, he formed a very high opinion of them. Not long before he died, he wrote: "The Merriams in Brookfield are old fashioned booksellers — men who make good work & want to be paid for it. I wish all booksellers and book publishers were of the same sort."[15]

The confirmation of Webster's renewal of his 1790 copyrights is to be found in the newspaper advertisements of the copyright notices. These show that on January 12, 1804, he renewed the copyright in the three parts of the *Institute* by depositing two titles in the Connecticut district: the first included both the spelling book and the grammar, the other the reader, with a bit of self-advertisement added. The titles were *The American Spelling Book, containing an easy standard of pronunciation, being the first part of a Grammatical Institute of the English Language, in three parts, by Noah Webster, jun. Esq.— Also, Part II, containing a plain and comprehensive Grammar, grounded on the true principles and idioms of the language."* and *An American Selection of Lessons in Reading and Speaking, calculated to improve the minds and refine the taste of youth: to which are prefixed Rules in Elocution and Directions for expressing the principal passions of the mind: by Noah Webster, jun. Author of Dissertations on the English Language, Collections of Essays and Fugitive Writings, the Prompter, &c.* The newspaper announcement of both those title deposits appeared in the *Connecticut Courant* (Hartford), on February 29, 1804, and in the three suc-

ceeding weeks. That is the newspaper one might have expected Webster to use, as it was published by Hudson & Goodwin, who had been printing the speller ever since the first edition in 1783.

Meanwhile, according to the back of its title page, the title of the new *American Spelling Book* had been deposited in the Connecticut court on March 14, 1804; one therefore looks for the announcement of that deposit in the *Connecticut Courant* during the following two months. It is not there. There is no trace of it (or of a deposit on the earlier date mentioned in the *Bibliography*, November 1, 1803), but at the time when an announcement might have appeared, from March 28 to April 18, there is a second set of notices referring to the old speller and grammar, and the reader. These do not say that the titles were deposited on January 12, 1804 (as in the earlier notices), but on January 30, 1804.

Why should Webster deposit his titles to renew copyright on January 12, and then deposit them a second time on January, 30? It was because the certificates that he received the first time contained a mistake. The first set of advertisements begin "BE IT REMEMBERED, That on the twelfth day of January in the twenty-ninth year of the Independence of the United States of America...." The first year of American Independence was 1776, and 1804 would therefore have been the twenty-ninth year; but the year of independence did not start on January 1. If you start from July 4, 1776, January 1804 was not in the twenty-ninth year of American Independence, but in the twenty-eighth year. In the second set of advertisements, the number has been changed to twenty-eight. If Webster noticed this mistake in his certificates soon after January 12, 1804, it would explain why he returned to the court on January 30 to deposit his titles again. Though the old spelling book was not reissued, the reader continued to be published after 1804; and in a copy printed in 1805 the copyright notice bears the date of the later certificate, January 30, 1804, and refers to the twenty-eighth year of independence.

If that is the explanation, it must surely have been unnecessary for Webster to publish the first set of certificates in the *Connecticut Courant*, as well as the second set; perhaps he was in doubt as to which registration was correct, and

wanted to be able to rely on either one. There can be no doubt, anyway, that he did renew the 1790 copyrights, and that when he threatened Ebenezer Merriam with legal proceedings, he was not merely bluffing.

The absence of any advertisement in the *Connecticut Courant* of the deposit of the new *American Spelling Book* is curious. It is possible that advertisements were placed in a different newspaper, but that seems unlikely, and I have not found them in any of the other Hartford or New Haven newspapers. If Webster forgot to place the advertisements, the 1804 spelling book was not covered by copyright during its first term. That, however, would not have been apparent to a would-be competitor or to a licensee, since Webster was able truthfully to assert, and print in the book itself, that its title had been deposited in the Connecticut district on March 14, 1804. When that copyright came up for renewal, Webster was living in Amherst, and it was therefore in the Massachusetts District Court that he deposited the title the second time. It was perhaps because his copyright was defective during the first term that Webster secured the renewal on the first possible day — September 15, 1817.

In fact, between 1804 and 1818, it would have made very little difference whether the new *American Spelling Book* was protected by copyright or not, because the greater part of it was exactly the same as the old *American Spelling Book* — the Philadelphia revision. Anyone who printed the new one without permission, or any substantial part of it, would have infringed the earlier copyright, which had been properly renewed. That was the situation until the second term of copyright in the Philadelphia speller expired, in June 1818. After that, Webster would have had to rely on the second term of copyright in the 1804 speller, which would actually have given him very little protection, since it only covered the relatively small amount that he had added to the spelling book in 1804.

One person who took advantage of this situation was Elihu F. Marshall, who brought out *Marshall's Spelling Book of the English Language, or The American Tutor's Assistant*, in 1826. Webster wrote to Fowler that Marshall's book is little less than a copy of mine ... it contains almost all my tables, with no alteration except the transcription of a few words. And this work is ushered into the world under a different name and recommended by distinguished characters, who probably did not know they were recommending my book as the work of another man, and a book published in violation of the copy-right law of the United States!

Webster was quite right that Marshall had taken almost all the tables from the *American Spelling Book*: Webster's lists of syllables and words were copied almost in their entirety, amounting to perhaps a hundred pages altogether. This was even more distasteful to Webster because Marshall had changed Webster's spelling and pronunciation to accord with those of Walker's *Critical Pronouncing Dictionary* — and Walker was one of Webster's pet hates. Worse still, Marshall had in some ways improved Webster's spelling book. Both used little numbers over the letters to distinguish the different sounds of the vowels, but Webster's readers were expected to learn his system from a table at the beginning of the book. For Marshall's readers such memorizing was unnecessary because he copied from Walker's Dictionary the idea of printing a line of pronunciation reminders across the top of each pair of pages:

$$\text{F}\overset{1}{\text{a}}\text{te, f}\overset{2}{\text{a}}\text{r, f}\overset{3}{\text{a}}\text{ll, f}\overset{4}{\text{a}}\text{t} - \text{m}\overset{1}{\text{e}}, \text{m}\overset{2}{\text{e}}\text{t, p}\overset{1}{\text{i}}\text{ne, p}\overset{2}{\text{i}}\text{n}$$
$$\text{n}\overset{1}{\text{o}}, \text{m}\overset{2}{\text{o}}\text{ve n}\overset{3}{\text{o}}\text{r, n}\overset{4}{\text{o}}\text{t} - \text{t}\overset{1}{\text{u}}\text{be, t}\overset{2}{\text{u}}\text{b, b}\overset{3}{\text{u}}\text{ll}$$

Marshall also made the book easier to use by breaking up Webster's long lists of words into shorter sections, with sentences or stories in between. For the most part, those sentences were not taken from Webster. The ones he did copy, "No man may put off the law of God," "A good child will not lie swear or steal," and so on, were very old and therefore out of copyright. They were in the *American Spelling Book* (under the heading *Lessons of easy words to teach children to read and know their duty*),[16] but they had earlier appeared in the Philadelphia revision, and before that in the first edition of *Part I of the Grammatical Institute*. Many of them had been taken by Webster from Dilworth or Fenning.

Webster was not exaggerating very much when he said that Marshall's speller was *his* book. He was mostly mistaken, however, when he said that Marshall's book was "published in violation of the copy-right law of the United States." Marshall took very little from the

American Spelling Book that had not been in Webster's speller before 1790. Since the 1790 copyright had expired in 1818, all that earlier material was in the public domain when Marshall used it. It would have been more polite had Marshall acknowledged his debt to Webster, but that is a moral judgment, not a legal one. Marshall infringed Webster's copyright only to the extent that he copied material that Webster had added to his spelling book in 1804.

One thing that Webster included in the speller for the first time in 1804 was his own family. When he made the first major revision of the speller back in 1787, he had been a single man, having only just met Rebecca Greenleaf. By 1803, when he was compiling the new edition, they had five children, and another on the way. In March 1804, when the title of the new *American Spelling Book* was deposited, their eldest daughter Emily was 13, Julia was 11, Harriet almost 7, Mary 5, William 3, and Eliza was 3 months old. The four oldest girls appear in a section of the book headed "The Sisters," where each recites a poem:

THE SISTERS

Emily, look at the flowers in the garden. What a charming sight. How the tulips adorn the borders of the alleys, dressing them with gayety.... Come, my child, let me hear your song.

The Rose

> The rose had been wash'd, lately washed
>   in a show'r,
> That Julia to Emma convey'd;
> A plentiful moisture encumber'd the flower,
> And weigh'd down its beautiful head. &c.&c.

Julia recites "The Lamb," which begins

> Young feeble Lamb, as Emily passed,
> In pity she turn'd to behold;
> How it shiver'd and shrunk from the
>   merciless blast
> Then fell all benumb'd with the cold.
>
> She rais'd it, and touch'd with the
>   innocent's fate,
> Its soft form to her bosom she prest;
> But the tender relief was afforded too late,
> It bleated, and died on her breast.

Harriet's poem is "The Bird's Nest":

> Yes, little nest, I'll hold you fast,
> And little birds, one, two, three, four;

> I've watched you long, you're mine at last;
> Poor little things, you'll 'scape no more.
>
> Chirp, cry, and flutter, as you will,
> Ah! simple rebels, 'tis in vain;
> Your little wings are unfledg'd still,
> How can you freedom then obtain?

It has six more stanzas just as bad. Mary, asked to repeat some verses, recites "On a Goldfinch starved in his Cage."

Webster does not actually put his name to these poems, but nor does he attribute them to anyone else. It might be said that the context, in which Harriet was asked to show her "little volume of poems," suggests that "The Bird's Nest" at least was copied from some other book. If so, the suggestion was too subtle for Warfel, who included all four poems in the book of Webster's verse that he and his wife published. In fact, the first poem and the last are both by Cowper. In Cowper's poem, the rose was conveyed by Mary to Anna, who were his friends Mrs. Unwin and Lady Austen. Webster substituted the names of his two elder daughters. I have not been able to find an earlier source for the second and third poems, so Webster may have written them himself, but Mrs. Skeel's *Bibliography* attributes only the first two to Webster, suggesting that she was aware of a non-Webster source for the third.

William also appears in the *American Spelling Book*. He loves fruit: "See him picking strawberries — bring him a basket — let him put the berries in a basket — and carry them to his mamma and sisters." While the girls are busy with flowers, lambs, little birds, and sewing, William is quizzed about the coins of the United States, both the new currency of mills, cents, dimes, dollars and eagles, and the old pounds, shillings, pence and farthings. Of these he has, for a 3-year-old, a surprising grasp. This is a curious irony, since his elder sisters would later accuse the adult William of being completely incompetent in matters of money.

Not long after the publication of the January 1804 copyright certificates in the *Connecticut Courant*, the newspaper's readers were given an account of Webster's recent and future activities. The style and content, particularly the reference to "the friends of American Literature" all point to Webster as the author:

LITERARY NOTICES

WEBSTER'S American Spelling Book, an elementary work now more generally used in schools in the United States, than any other, and in some States, exclusively, has been lately revised by the author, and received numerous valuable improvements, particularly calculated for the citizens of this country. The first impressions will appear in a few weeks.

In compliance with repeated solicitations from the friends of American Literature in various parts of the country, who urge the utility of a complete system of books for the instruction of youth in our language by a *single hand*, the same author has prepared a *Compendious Dictionary* of our language, upon the latest edition of Entick improved — correcting the more palpable mistakes, and adding three or four thousand words with which the vast improvements in Chemistry, Natural History, and other sciences, have, within half a century, supplied the language. This work will be put to press in a short time, and an elegant edition may be expected in the course of the summer.

The second Volume of *Elements of Useful Knowledge*, completing the History and Geography of the United States, by the same author, is in the press and will be published in a few days by I.Cook & Co. New-Haven, and Hudson & Goodwin in Hartford.

A *complete Dictionary of the English Language*, with the addition of several thousand words, not introduced into any English works of this kind, and with every thing essential in the various English Dictionaries, compressed into a less expensive size, is begun by the same author upon a plan of precision in the definitions, not before attempted, and will be completed as soon as the great labor of the compilation will permit.

That announcement marked a significant turning point in Webster's working life, the point when he began to concentrate on dictionaries. The spelling book remained important because it provided him with funds, but when the next major revision became due he would pay somebody else to do it for him. As usual, he greatly underestimated the time it would take to complete the dictionaries. The *Compendious*, based upon Entick, appeared in 1806, not in the summer of 1804; the "complete" dictionary, which was to contain more words than Johnson but "compressed into a less expensive size," would take another twenty years to finish.

Webster's *Compendious Dictionary of the English Language* was altogether more ambitious than any of its American predecessors. Whereas they had been intended to fill a gap at the bottom end of the market, being smaller and cheaper than Perry or Entick, Webster aimed at producing something that would appeal to his countrymen because it was American, as well as being bigger and better than the English pocket dictionaries. It was, he said, "an enlargement and improvement of Entick's spelling dictionary, which public opinion, both in Great Britain and the United States, has pronounced the best compilation of the kind."[17] If his only aim had been to produce an enlarged and improved version of Entick, his dictionary would have been a lot less controversial than it turned out to be, but Webster had another aim: he was still determined to persuade Americans to change their way of spelling. Previously, he had been motivated only by his enthusiasm for phonetic spelling, but now another unsettling factor was added: He had been studying Anglo-Saxon, and he had discovered a number of common mistakes that needed to be put right.

Reading *The Diversions of Purley*, back in 1787, had shown him the necessity for a student of English etymology to have some knowledge of Anglo-Saxon, so he bought Lye's *Dictionarium Saxonico et Gothico-Latinum* and a couple of Anglo-Saxon books on law and history, and set about teaching himself the language. When he had finished with them, Webster gave the books to Yale, and they are still there. By a careful study of handwritten marginalia, his progress has been followed, and it is the subject of an article by Professor Charlton Laird, "Etymology, Anglo-Saxon, and Noah Webster."[18] These are Professor Laird's conclusions:

The books that Webster bequeathed to Yale ... testify that he made a serious effort to learn Anglo-Saxon; that he examined the texts critically, comparing one with another, noticing grammatical structures which appealed to him as strange and significant; and that he had an eye for words revealing of etymology. The books do not permit us to assume that Webster had extensive knowledge of the language, or any deep understanding of it. Certainly, they do not support Professor Warfel's generous statement that 'he studied, as far as American libraries could supply him with books, Anglo-Saxon.' He seems, on the contrary, to have been far from exhausting the facilities of his private library, having gone through two texts but once, neglected the most difficult, and used his excellent dictionary but scantily....

Thus, if the evidence we have examined can be taken at something near its face value, we might have an estimate like the following. Webster appreciated that Anglo-Saxon had great importance for the study

of the mother tongue, even though he deprecated the study of Middle English. He made an honest effort to learn the language, and did learn to read prose with some facility, although he was far from mastering Anglo-Saxon. His original investigations did not lead him to new and important conclusions, although they did help him to amplify ideas which had grown from his reading of Tooke. In this we have an interpretation not at variance with what we know of Webster as a man. That he undertook the study of Anglo-Saxon when he was perhaps fifty years old, does him credit; that he made amusing blunders is not to be wondered at, especially when one remembers that he was working in pioneer country, that he was associated with no institution where colleagues could provide him with friendly counsel; but to assume that Webster was more than a mediocre student of Anglo-Saxon is perhaps to accept his professions too credulously.[19]

Professor Laird may not have been impressed by Webster's knowledge of Anglo-Saxon, but Webster himself was very proud of it, and his pride shines through the Preface to the *Compendious Dictionary*. The Preface starts by saying that the "eminent classical scholar and divine, the late Dr. Goodrich of Durham" had suggested, on the first publication of the *Grammatical Institute*, that Webster should compile and publish a dictionary. He could not undertake it at that time, but …

My studies however have occasionally had reference to an ultimate accomplishment of such a work: and for a few years past, they have been directed immediately to that object. As I have advanced in my investigations, I have been, at every step, more and more impressed with the importance of this work: and an acquaintance with the Saxon language, the mother tongue of the English, has convinced me, that a careful revision of our present dictionaries is absolutely necessary to a correct knowledge of the language.
To men who have been accustomed to repose almost implicit confidence in the authors of our principal dictionaries and grammars, it may appear at first incredible, that such writers as Johnson and Lowth, should have mistaken many of the fundamental principles of the language. But that such is the fact will appear certain to any man who will read a few pages in a Saxon author.

He then gave examples of errors in the works of Johnson and Lowth, and in Murray's grammar, explaining that those authors would never have made such mistakes if they had been more familiar with Anglo-Saxon. "These examples are sufficient to demonstrate the importance of

investigating the original of the English Language: and how much mischief has been done by men who have compiled elementary books, without qualifying themselves by such previous investigation." His readers were left in no doubt that Webster was now better qualified to compile elementary books than his competitors because he had studied Anglo-Saxon and they had not. Of course the whole of the *Grammatical Institute* had been published before he had begun his study of Anglo-Saxon, and the second part, the grammar, was largely taken from Lowth, but Webster openly acknowledged his own previous fault:

From the censure implied in this remark, I am not myself wholly free, having relied too much on certain modern authorities of eminent literary attainments. Since I have explored the more remote sources of our language, so many mistakes in our present systems of grammar have been detected, that I have declined to alienate the copy right of my own grammar, and shall not consent to a republication of it, until revised and amended.— the grammars of our language now taught in our seminaries of learning, are rapidly banishing from books, some of its best established and most legitimate idioms.

Webster had discovered that some of the usage condemned by grammarians as bad English was actually good Anglo-Saxon. He also found instances of accepted usage which he felt compelled to condemn because it was not good Anglo-Saxon. One such word was *island*:

The Saxons wrote the word *igland, ealond,* and *ieland,* which, with a strong guttural aspirate, are not very different in sound. It is a compound of *ea* water, still preserved in the French *eau,* and *land* — *ealand,* water land, land in water, a very significant word. The etymology however was lost, and the word corrupted by the French, into *island,* which the English servilely adopted, with the consonant *s,* which no more belongs to the word, than any other letter in the alphabet. Our pronunciation preserves the Saxon *ieland,* with a trifling difference of sound: and it was formerly written by good authors, *iland.*

For similar Saxon reasons, *acre* should be *aker,* and the plural of *woman* should be written *wimmen.* In the section of the Preface headed "Orthography," there are more examples where Webster contrasts corrupt modern orthography with Saxon originals:

Thus the present orthography of leather, feather, weather, stead, wealth, mould, son, ton, wonder, worship, thirst, &c. is corrupt.… The true orthography

from the first Saxon writings to the 12th century, was
lether, fether, wether, sted or stede, welga, mold,
suna, tunna, wundor, wurthscipe, thurst.

Broad was written *brade, brede,* and *braed.* We
have preserved the first in the adjective *broad,* but the
pronunciation of the noun *bredth* we take from the
second, and the orthography most absurdly from the
last.

Tongue, was in Saxon written tung, tonge or
tunga, which we pronounce correctly tung, omitting
the last letter as in other Saxon words, and yet we
write the word most barbarously *tongue....*

Though is also a vitious orthography: *tho* being
much nearer to the original word.... *Drought* and
height are corruptions of *drugothe, heatho:* which the
Saxons formed from *dryg* and *heh* or *heah, dry* and
high, by adding the termination *th; ...* The Saxon
termination *th* is universally preserved in the popular pronunciation of this country: and so far is it
from being an error or corruption, that it is the very
essence of the nouns, drouth and highth....

We have seen in an earlier chapter how Webster embraced the idea of phonetic spelling, and
in 1790 had put it into practice in some of his
Essays and Fugitiv Writings. Not surprisingly,
he was accused of trying to introduce hideous
innovations. Now, he was able to defend many
of the same spellings by showing that they were
not innovations at all, but were corrections of
an orthography that had become corrupt. The
practical arguments in favor of having spellings
that match sounds are still valid, of course, but
Webster will hereafter always support his proposals by showing that they have the sanction
of ancient and respectable authority. This is the
theory:

ORTHOGRAPHY

The orthography of our language is extremely irregular: and many fruitless attempts have been made to
reform it. The utility and expedience of such reform
have been controverted, and both sides of the question have been maintained with no inconsiderable
zeal.

On this subject, as on most others which divide
the opinions of men, parties seem to have erred by
running into extremes. The friends of a reform
maintain that our alphabet should be rendered perfectly regular, by rejecting superfluous characters,
and introducing new ones to supply defects; so that
every sound may be represented by a distinct letter,
and no letter have more sounds than one. This
scheme is impracticable, and not at all necessary.*

[Webster's footnote: *In the year 1786, Dr. Franklin
proposed to me to prosecute his scheme of a Reformed
Alphabet, and offered me his type for the purpose. I
declined accepting his offer, on a full conviction of

the utter impracticability, as well as inutility of the
scheme. The orthography of our language might be
rendered sufficiently regular, without a single new
character, by means of a few trifling alterations of the
present characters, and retrenching a few superfluous
letters, the most of which are corruptions of original
words.]

The opposers of a reform, on the other hand, contend that no alterations should be made in orthography, as they would not only occasion inconvenience, but tend to render old books useless, and
obscure etymology. It is fortunate for the language
and for those who use it, that this doctrin did not
prevail in the reign of Henry the fourth: for it was as
just then as it is now: and had all changes in spelling
ceased at that period, what a spectacle of deformity
would our language now exhibit! The doctrin is as
mischievous in its consequences, as the reasons on
which it is founded are false. Every man of common
reading knows that a living language must necessarily suffer gradual changes in its current words, in the
significations of many words, and in pronunciation.
The unavoidable consequence then of fixing the orthography of a living language, is to destroy the use
of the alphabet. This effect has, in a degree, already
taken place in our language: and letters, the most
useful invention that ever blessed mankind, have lost
and continue to lose a part of their value, by no
longer being the representative of the sounds originally annexed to them. Strange as it may seem, the
fact is undeniable, that the present doctrin that no
change must be made in writing words, is destroy-
ing the benefits of an alphabet, and reducing our language to the barbarism of Chinese characters insted
of letters. What is still stranger, this doctrin is per-
tinaciously maintained by the men who make pre-
tences to exquisit taste and refinement in polite literature. And if any thing can add to the
contradictions which such a principle involves, it is
that the same men, who object to the minutest alterations of orthography, are the most active in
effecting changes of pronunciation: thus aiding to
destroy the use of letters, by creating new differences
between the written and spoken language.

The correct principle respecting changes in orthography seems to lie between these extremes of
opinion. No great changes should ever be made at
once, nor should any change be made which violates
established principles, creates great inconvenience,
or obliterates the radicals of the language. But gradual changes to accommodate the written to the spoken language, when they occasion none of these evils,
and especially when they purify words from corruptions, improve the regular analogies of a language
and illustrate etymology, are not only proper, but
indispensable.

On this general principle have all learned and civilized nations proceeded in refining their languages
and preserving the use of alphabetical writing....
This principle also prevailed universally in the

English nation, from the revival of letters to the last century, when certain eminent authors adoped an idea, as absurd as incompatible with improvement, that a living language can be fixed beyond the possibility of change: and to the prevalence of this error, we may ascribe many of the irregularities of our present orthography.

Webster then set out various classes of words in which he had departed from Johnson's spelling, but emphasised that he was not innovating:

I have made no material alterations in the orthography of words, except to correct most palpable errors. In a few instances, I have preferred the orthography of Newton, Prideaux, Hook, Dryden, Whiston, &c. to that of Johnson, as being more analogical and purely English, as in *scepter, sepulcher.* In omitting *u* in *honor* and a few words of that class, I have pursued a common practice in this country, authorized by the principle of uniformity and by etymology, as well as by Ash's dictionary. In omitting *k* after *c*, I have unequivocal propriety, and the present usage for my authorities. In a few words, modern writers are gradually purifying the orthography from its corruptions. Thus Edwards in his history of the West-Indies, and Gregory in his Economy of Nature, Pope, Hoole, &c. restore *mold* to its true spelling: and it would be no small convenience to revive the etymological spelling of *aker.* Cullen in his translation of Clavigero, follows Bacon and Davenant in the true Saxon orthography of *drouth,* and the elegant Blackstone has corrected the orthography of *nusance* and *duchy.*

The dipthongs in words borrowed from the Latin language, have gradually been sinking into desuetude for a century: the few which remain, I have expunged. ...

The part of the Preface where Webster discussed pronunciation was mainly devoted to exposing the inconsistencies between Sheridan, Walker, and Jones. Since they disagreed so much amongst themselves, Webster drew the conclusion that it was not safe to rely upon any of them. Walker came in for particular criticism for giving *ch* its French sound in such words as *Bench,* respelled as *Bensh.* Here, Sheridan and Jones both got it right, recommending *Bentsh.* Other "examples of variance" were set out in a table showing the recommended pronunciations of words containing the letter *u:*

SHERIDAN.	WALKER.	JONES.
Accentuation	Accenchuation	Accentuation
Gratulation	Grachulation	Gratulation
Habitual	Habichual	Habitual
Furnitchur	Furneeture	Furniture

Multichood	Multeetude	Multitude
Protrood	Protrude	Protrude
Prochooberant	Protuberant	Protuberant
Shooperb	Superb	Superb
Chooter	Tutor	Tutor
Choomult	Tumult	Tumult

Webster also condemned giving to *u* the sound of *eu* or *yu,* "except in a few words, as measure, union, &c. in which the sound is changed, for the sake of easy utterance."

Webster had orthoepical oddities of his own, of course. One was his insistence that *slavery* and *bravery* are both two-syllable words, because the letter *e* has already been used up in making the words *slave* and *brave,* and it could not be used again as a middle syllable. A similar analysis appears in the Preface to the *Compendious Dictionary* concerning the *sh* sound of the letters *ti.* In his spelling book, Webster had boldly departed from Dilworth's practice of counting -*ti*- as a separate syllable in such words as *nation* and *partial.* That was certainly correct because it reflected the pronunciation of those words, but it now led Webster to the more dubious conclusion that, since the letter *i* had been used up in making the sound *sh,* it could not be sounded again in derivatives of such words. If *partial* is pronounced *parshal,* it follows that *partiality* must be pronounced *parshality.* Similarly, *substanshate* and *offishate.* He also insisted that the word *deaf* should be pronounced to rhyme with *beef* and that *angel* and *ancient* should have a short *a,* like *angelic, antiquity* and *anguish:* "In these and many other words, the pronunciation in this country is more correct than that of the English: and it would be reprehensible servility in us to relinquish a correct practice and adopt an English corruption."

Webster's belief was that his own pronunciation, "the common unadulterated pronunciation of the New England gentlemen," was how English had been spoken by "the body of the British nation," before the language was corrupted by Sheridan and Walker. That view of the superiority of Connecticut was not always accepted, even in New York, as we see from the description of the Yale-educated schoolmaster Jason Newcome (a parody of Webster) in Fenimore Cooper's *Satanstoe:*

Jason was the son of an ordinary Connecticut farmer, of the usual associations, and with no other pretension to education than such as was obtained in a

common school, or any reading which did not include the Scriptures, some half a dozen volumes of sermons and polemical works.... As the family knew nothing of the world beyond the limits of its own township, and an occasional visit to Hartford,... Jason's early life was necessarily of the most contracted experience. His English, as a matter of course, was just that of his neighborhood and class of life, which was far from being either very elegant or very Doric. But on this rustic, provincial, or, rather, hamlet foundation, Jason had reared a superstructure of New Haven finish and proportions.

As he kept school ... after he left college, the whole energies of his nature became strangely directed to just such reforms of language as would be apt to strike the imagination of a pedagogue of his caliber. In the first place, he had brought from home with him a great number of sounds that were decidedly vulgar and vicious, and with these in full existence in himself, he had commenced his system of reform on other people. As is common with all tyros, he fancied a very little knowledge sufficient authority for very great theories. His first step was to improve the language, by adapting sound in spelling, and he insisted on calling angel, *angel*, because a-n spelt an: chamber, *cham*-ber, for the same reason: and so on through a long catalogue of similarly constructed words.

The defining part of the *Compendious Dictionary* does not generally indicate pronunciation, except by showing the position of the accent, but Webster's *American Dictionary* does indeed say that pronouncing *chamber* with a short *a* is "most analogous and correct."

The section of the *Compendious Dictionary* Preface dealing with pronunciation is followed by one on etymology that affords Webster further opportunities for pointing out Johnson's mistakes and displaying his own Anglo-Saxon. As I have earlier mentioned, Webster also describes the use of the double accent that he had so roundly condemned when Dilworth used it:

A double accent thus, lo"gic, ma"gic, a"cid, denotes that the sound of the succeeding consonant belongs to the first syllable, *c* and *g* in such cases being soft, as lojjic, majjic, assid. Posi"tion is pronounced *posishun*.

In reality, the Preface to the *Compendious Dictionary* has less to do with the *Compendious* than with the *American Dictionary*. The Preface was written some time after the main part of the *Compendious*, and does not describe the content of that work. Rather, it is a declaration of intent, heralding the complete dictionary

that was to come. That is why it attacks Johnson, not Entick. Webster explained his commercial plan in a letter that he wrote on August 18, 1805, to John West in Boston:

I have in the press a Dictionary founded on Entick, with the improvements introduced into the Language since the date of Johnson's, which is the source of all the modern compilations. The addition of 6000 words will swell the book to a size & price beyond what will be proper for *common English* Schools. It will suit the higher schools, the counting house, travellers, private gentlemen &c. It is therefore judged best to publish an abridgment of it; & I have chosen Johnson's in Miniature as a model of the size.

But we have no press except Mr. Babcock's which can do the work — and that will not be able to complete the present volume, till November, which will put it out of our power to furnish an abridgment until the ensuing winter.

I have thought best to propose to you & your associates in business, to undertake a small impression, say 3000, or more if you chuse. It may then be printed as soon as the principal work, and be in market before winter. The expense will not be great, & the experiment will be worth trying. If it should succeed, it will be of great use in supporting the Spelling Book. I am deeply engaged in this undertaking, & am actually compiling a large work, which is intended as a substitute for Johnson's folio & quarto, with what I believe to be valuable improvements. In this undertaking, I want the aid of Booksellers, & as far as their interest will permit I trust I shall have it.

If you consent to undertake this job, I will abridge the work as the sheets are published, & send you the copy. The work is done on minion, and the type should be good. I shall ask nothing for the copyright of an impression of 3000, except a few copies, say 25.[20]

Babcock's printing of the *Compendious* proved to be even slower than Webster had expected. It was not completed until several months after his letter to John West, in January 1806, which was when he wrote the Preface.

The body of the dictionary is exactly what Webster said it would be — an enlargement of Entick, with many scientific terms added. It has the same one-line definitions, and even smaller printing, so that it is not a joy to use. Unlike Entick, it separates the letters *I* and *J*, and *U* and *V*, which was certainly sensible, and probably would have been done more widely in England if it had not been for the conservative influence of Johnson. Friend calls this "a Websterian innovation," but it had already been done in England by Perry and in America by

Elliott and Johnson. Webster sometimes forgot that he was doing it: *maiz* [sic] appears after *majority;* the entries from *clove* to *clovered* appear before those from *clough* to *clouted; never* is before *neuter;* and *drove* and *drover* are before *drought, drouth.* That last is, of course, one of Webster's Saxon spellings, and the main interest of the *Compendious* is that it provides a snapshot of Webster's ever-changing ideas on orthography. Other Anglo-Saxon oddities anticipated in the Preface are "Wimmen, *n.pl.* of *wimman, the old and true spelling,*" "Island, *more correctly* Ieland or Iland," *mold, plow,* and *welth* (as an alternative).

Generally, it is possible to judge how confident Webster was in his departures from Johnson's spelling by looking to see whether he gave one spelling or two. When he was making suggestions that were unlikely to be controversial, he usually gave only one spelling. Thus he did not offer *-our* as an alternative to the *-or* termination, because *-or* was already widely accepted in America. He even gave *savior,* which the editor of Entick had not changed, feeling that it might be sacrilege to tamper with the name of God. Similarly, Webster was sufficiently confident to offer no alternative to *-er* in words such as *saber* and *theater,* except that where Entick had "Orchestra or Orchestre," Webster changed it to "Orchester or Orchestra [ch as k]." *Massacre* and *lucre* were unchanged, because the spelling *-cer* would suggest that the *c* is soft. *Luster* was changed, but not moved, appearing after *lustrate* and *lustration. Neger* and *zeber* were offered as alternatives to *negro* and *zebra.* Another partly changed class was that of words in which a French *-que* was being replaced by *k.* Already in Johnson, *mask* and *risk* had their modern spelling. Webster's notable contribution here is *opake. Grotesk* was offered as an alternative spelling, but only the conventional spelling was given for *burlesque* and *antique.* The final *k* was removed from such words as *public* and *music,* which was by then well accepted, but the spelling *burdoc* was unusual, and the *k* remained on *almanack, frolick, havock* and *traffick.*

Another reform that Webster usually implemented without giving any alternative was chopping the silent *e* off the end of words such as *doctrin, disciplin, examin, gillotin, granit, hypocrit, imagin, libertin, opposit* and *requisit.*

Favorite, however, retained its *e,* and *definite* was given both ways, but "more correctly Definit." Surprisingly, after the title of his book of essays, the *e* was not removed from words ending in *-ive,* such as *fugitive.*

Other entries show differing degrees of confidence and consistency. The silent *a* in such words as *feather* is not omitted in the word list. The alternative spellings *fether* and *wether, thred* and *thret* are given, and *leather* is "more correctly, Lether," but the entries appear in the correct place for the conventional spellings, which are given first. Webster also used the conventional spelling in derivatives of *leather* such as *leatherseller,* and in their definitions, but *lether* is used in the definitions of *shamois* and *tanner,* and there is an entry for *shammylether.* The entries under *ton* and *tonnage* only say "see Tun" and "see Tunnage." *nuisance* has a definition, but then says "see nusance," where there is a slightly longer definition. The entry for *tongue* says "or more correctly Tung," and there is a separate shorter entry under *tung. Breadth* and *bredth* are given as alternatives, as are *height* and *highth,* and there is a separate entry for *highth.* Similarly we find "Ache or Ake" defined, but there are also separate entries for *ake* and *aking.* Entick preferred *ach,* and his spelling slipped in unchanged in *headach, heartach,* and *toothach.*

Webster changed Entick's *defence* to *defense,* but did not move the word — it still appears before *defend.* Similarly, *pretense* is before *pretend. Offense* was both changed and moved. One feature of modern American spelling is not present in this dictionary — it has a double *l* in such words as *libeller, modeller,* and *traveller,* and a double *p* in *worshipper.*

Webster did not include his most extreme oddities in the spelling books, but it is nevertheless possible to trace the development of his ideas on orthography in his spelling books, from Philadelphia in 1787 to New Haven, twenty years later. The first one to be called the *American Spelling Book,* the Philadelphia revision of 1787, was prepared at the time when Webster was under Franklin's influence. He had abandoned Johnson's spelling, and he hoped that it might be possible to introduce a logical phonetic system into America. He would try out such a system (though not very thoroughly) in his *Essays and Fugitiv Writings,* but he did

not use it in his personal correspondence, his magazine, his newspapers, or in the spelling book. At this time, therefore, he had two quite distinct ways of spelling: in *theory*, a very odd-looking phonetic system; in *practice*, the conventional American spelling of the time. He explained his views in the Preface to the Philadelphia revision, here copied from a spelling book of 1789, the 8th Connecticut edition:

As the orthography of our language is not yet settled with precision, I have, in this particular, generally followed the most approved authors of the last and present century. In some classes of words, the spelling of Ash is preferred to that of Johnson, which is less correct.... The spelling of such words as *publick, favour, neighbour, head, prove, phlegm, his, give, debt, rough, well,* instead of the more natural and easy method, *publik, favor, nabor, hed, proov, flem, hiz, giv, det, ruf, wel,* has the plea of antiquity in its favour; and yet I am convinced that common sense and convenience will sooner or later get the better of the present absurd practice.... It is the work of years to learn the present spelling of our language — a work, which, with a correct orthography, might be performed in a few months.

Webster's claim to have "followed the most approved authors" echoes words in the title page of *Lingua Britannica Reformata*, where Benjamin Martin said that his orthography was "according to the usage of the most Approved Modern Authors." Many of Webster's spellings had been recommended by Martin also, though Martin was generally more consistent about it than was Webster. In that passage from his Preface, for example, Webster used the word *favour*, while expressing a preference for the phonetic spelling *favor* which he used in the spelling book itself. He used the *-or* termination in other words of the same class as well, though *clamour* appeared in one table, and *neighbouring* in one of the fables. Johnson's spelling of *publick* was changed also, of course, but to *public*, rather than *publik*. Those "modern" spellings were already commonplace, particularly in America, before Webster started advocating them: Both are in Ash's Dictionary, and they are to be found, for example, in the letters written by "Seth" and James Kidd to the Philadelphia newspapers, before Webster's new spelling book appeared. The spelling *center*, which Martin approved, is said by Ash to be "common but incorrect." Webster thought the

-er termination was correct (except after *c*) and so he used it in the spelling book. It was put forward, of course, as a correction, not an innovation.

Lopping the final *e* from words which normally end in *-ine* is less easily seen as a correction, and perhaps for that reason Webster seems to have been unable to make up his mind whether to do it or not. There are enough missing *e*'s in the Philadelphia revision for them not to be misprints — in *medicin, genuin,* and *determin*— but the final *e* is retained in *libertine, doctrine* and *imagine*.

Some time after the Philadelphia revision, Webster abandoned the attempt to persuade America to use his phonetic system. His personal spelling, however, became more eccentric rather than less, as he adopted a number of unconventional "corrections" prompted by his study of Anglo-Saxon.

There can be little doubt that a spelling book full of eccentric spellings would have been a commercial disaster. Fortunately for Webster's finances, the 1804 *American Spelling Book* largely escaped them. They were not deliberately excluded so that the book would sell — Webster was too much a man of principle to make money by teaching children to spell in a way that he believed to be wrong — but the 1804 *American Spelling Book* was largely a reprint of the Philadelphia revision, and it would have been very troublesome to make changes to material that was already in print. His attachment to his reforms can be seen from the fact that they appeared in large numbers in his *Elements of Useful Knowledge*. In a copy of Volume I printed in 1807, I found *picturesk, oblikely, trecherously, bredth, highth, drouth, fether, lether, crouded, meddows, heffers, strait, akers, vinyard, vallies, turkies, hords, famin, doctrin, determin, examin, opposit, maiz, threds, plow, coco, cloke, ancle,* and *molded*. Webster's use of those spellings in a schoolbook shows that he intended them to be learned by children, and that he no longer regarded them as experimental. His brother-in-law Thomas Dawes said of the book that "it would have been in every schoolboy's hands had its author sacrificed such trifles to the common notions of people as to retain the *a* in breadth &c."[21]

Webster's reluctance to change his existing spelling book was not mere laziness. The book

was printed by licensees in different parts of the country, and communication with them was slow. Before the introduction of stereotyping, it was very difficult to achieve consistency between their various editions, and it would have been impossible to persuade all the printers to make numerous changes to the orthography. Some oddities did get in, however; *strait, highth* and *drouth* are there, as well as *imagin.* At the same time, some old-fashioned spellings slipped in, either because Webster himself used them by mistake, or because a printer did so. Variations between one printer's version and another's often continued for several years. In an *American Spelling Book* printed in Bennington, Vermont, in 1807, one can find *honourable, labour, behaviour, neighbouring* and *theatre.* It even has *drought* on one page, and *drouth* on the very next page. All of those words except *behaviour* have Webster's corrected spellings in the Hartford edition of the same year. In Vermont, however, the uncorrected forms are still there in an 1813 printing of the *American Spelling Book.*

One criticism made of Webster after the publication of the *Compendious Dictionary* was that he had included too many vulgar words. "Vulgar" here, in Webster's own definition, means "common, ordinary, mean, low, trivial." It is a broader category than "obscene," but obscene words are included within it. This was Webster's reply:

It is questionable how far vulgar and cant words are to be admitted into a Dictionary: but one thing must be acknowledged by any man who will inspect the several dictionaries in the English language, that if any portion of such words are inadmissable, Johnson has transgressed the rules of lexicography beyond any other compiler: for his work contains more of the lowest of all vulgar words than any other now extant, Ash excepted…. Let the admirers of Johnson's Dictionary be a little more critical in comparing his vocabulary and mine and blush for their illiberal treatment of me! Instead of increasing the list of vulgar terms, I have *reduced* it by expunging *two thirds* of such words inserted by Johnson! Any person who will have the patience and candor to compare my dictionary with others will find that there is not a vocabulary of the English language extant more free from *local, vulgar,* and *obscene* words as mine![22]

Webster was there mainly criticising Johnson for including in his dictionary such cant words as *fishify, jiggumbob* and *conjobble,* rather than

obscene words. Johnson did not include words that he considered to be obscene. He did include *foutra,* of course, and Webster, knowing of the attack made on Elliott and Johnson, was careful to leave it out, along with Johnson's *arse, bum, fart* and *turd.* He did not, however, object to *piss,* nor to the "house of office" in which you may do it, the *boghouse* or *jakes.* In one area, Webster was actually less inhibited than Johnson, including definitions of *buggery, sodomy* and *catamite,* defining the latter as "a boy that is kept for vile purposes."

At the end of the *Compendious Dictionary,* there are a number of lists or tables which, according to the title page, were "added for the benefit of the Merchant, the Student and the Traveller." They give details of the currency of most of the commercial nations in the world, of weights and measures (ancient and modern), and of the divisions of time amongst the Jews, the Greeks and the Romans. The populations of the various states in 1790 and in 1800 are listed (blacks separately), and the values of their exports, and there is a catalogue of the post offices in the United States with their distances from Washington. Finally, there are three chronological tables, the first one being "remarkable Events on the Eastern Continent," from the creation of the world in 4004 B.C., to the battle of Trafalgar on October 21, 1805. This is an unusual selection of added matter, but it was common to add something to the bare dictionary. Entick had a grammar, a table of homophones, a list of "Most usual Christian Names of Men and Women," "A Succinct Account of the Heathen Gods and Goddesses, Heroes and Heroines &c.," and a "List of All the Cities, Boroughs, Market-Towns, and remarkable Villages in England and Wales," with the days on which their markets were held, and their distances from London.

The following year, 1807, Webster published *A Philosophical and Practical Grammar* (to replace the one that he had withdrawn) and also the school dictionary that had been anticipated in his letter to John West. It was printed at the same New Haven press as the *Compendious Dictionary.* It is smaller than the *Compendious,* and in even smaller type, though neither the book nor the type is quite as small as in the miniature editions of Johnson. The content is a selection from the *Compendious* with very little amendment. One change is that the spelling *fether* is

used in definitions. Thus it has "Featherless, *a.* having no fethers, naked," where the *Compendious* used the spelling "having no feathers." This must have been a deliberate alteration, though Webster did not do the same thing in *leather*. Two etymologically corrected spellings that would later subject Webster to cruel mockery were *bridegoom* and *nightmar*. Neither of them appears in the *Compendious,* but *nightmar* makes its first appearance in the 1807 school dictionary.

As mentioned in his 1805 letter to John West, Webster had started work on his "substitute for Johnson's folio & quarto," even before the publication of the *Compendious*. In 1807, he settled down to it in earnest. Once again, his first problem was money. To compile the intended dictionary would take several years of uninterrupted work — uninterrupted, that is to say, by the need to earn a living. He tried to solve the problem by sending out a begging letter, as described in No. 42 of the *Memoir*:

As early as February 1807 he issued a Circular informing the public of his design and of the general plan of the work; accompanied with commendations from the faculty of Yale College, of Nassau Hall in New Jersey and of Williams College in Massachusetts and of President Wheelock of Dartmouth College. In August of that year he issued a paper to obtain subscriptions for the proposed dictionary, in *advance*, as his own resources were not deemed adequate to the object; but the success was inconsiderable. Indeed his plan was not fully digested at that time; but was afterward much enlarged.

Webster's "Circular" of February 1807 invited "Friends of Literature in the United States," both individuals and societies, to send him gifts of money, which Webster promised would be "gratefully received and faithfully applied to the proposed object."

Not surprisingly, the invitation to contribute to the support of an indigent lexicographer was largely ignored. What Webster really needed was a wealthy patron, and every time he wrote to a rich man, he dropped heavy hints — but no patron appeared. The alternative was a subscription list, to get people to pay in advance for copies of the dictionary. For this purpose, a second circular was printed and distributed:

To the Friends of Literature in the United States

───────────────────

HAVING been several years engaged in researches into the history and structure of the English Language, I have ascertained that this field of Literature has been very imperfectly explored; and that no subjects are less understood, than the origin and combination of words, on which their definitions depend; still less is understood the affinity between the several languages of Europe and Asia. It is probable that on these branches of philology as much remains to be done, as all that has heretofore been done, towards elucidating the history of LANGUAGE, the instrument of all other human improvements. The imperfections and inaccuracies of the best English Dictionaries have been long known and regretted by men of letters in Great-Britain, and some partial attempts have been made and are still making to supply the defect; but on a plan inadequate to the purpose, or by men incompetent to the task. By long and laborious investigation, I have collected many valuable materials on this subject; and I purpose, with the advice of the Faculty of several Colleges, and other good judges, to compile a Dictionary of the English Language, which shall contain every thing valuable in the present Dictionaries, with all the improvements which late discoveries in philology require. And as Johnson's Quarto Dictionary is so large and expensive as to prevent its general use in this country, one great object, in the present work, will be retrench or modify his exemplifications of definitions, in such a manner as to reduce it to about one half the size and cost of that work.

BUT the expences attending the compilation and publication of this work exceed my resources; and without pecuniary aid, it must be abandoned or imperfectly executed. Undertakings of similar labor, in Great Britain, have often been supported by contributions from gentlemen in that country, and sometimes from Germany and other countries on the Continent. It is presumed the friends of learning in the United States will not decline to afford encouragement to a like arduous undertaking on this side of the Atlantic. Among many thousands of gentlemen in this country, who can advance a few dollars each, without sensible inconvenience, it is believed a considerable number may be found, who will cheerfully make the advance.

EVERY gentleman advancing *ten dollars* on subscription, shall be entitled to a copy of the Dictionary, on fine paper and in elegant binding. Booksellers advancing money for ten copies or more, shall have a discount of twenty-five per cent.

N.WEBSTER

New-Haven, August, 1807.

Opposite: Webster's February 1807 circular, ***To the Friends of Literature in the United States.*** Noah Webster Papers, 1764–1843. Manuscripts and Archives Division, New York Public Library.

Circular.

TO THE FRIENDS OF LITERATURE IN THE UNITED STATES:

WHEN I first contemplated the publication of an English Dictionary, my design was chiefly limited to the correction of a few palpable errors in orthography and definition, and the insertion of a great number of legitimate words and significations, not found in any British work of the kind. Being led gradually and almost insensibly, to investigate the origin of our own language, I was surprised to discover that this field of inquiry had never been explored with due attention and success; and that the origin and history, not only of the English, but of the Greek, Latin, and other European languages, are yet involved in no small degree of obscurity. The learned men on the continent of Europe, Vossius, Scaliger and others, who diligently studied the elegant languages of Greece and Italy, neglected to resort, for the radical words, to some of the best sources of correct knowledge, the Celtic and Teutonic dialects, which, next to the Hebrew, are the purest remains of the primitive language. Hence much of their labor was spent in vain. They wandered into the field of conjecture, venturing to substitute opinions for evidence, and their mistakes have led subsequent writers into error. Some English investigators of the subject have been more successful; but they have left no small part of the field unexplored. In consequence of these ill-directed and imperfect researches, the English Dictionary of Johnson, the Latin Dictionary of Ainsworth, and the Greek Lexicons, now in use, which are deemed the highest authorities, and which are books of instruction in our seminaries of learning, contain material errors in the deduction of words from their originals. Were these errors a few mistakes only, " quas incuria fudit," the imperfections incident to every human production, the evil might be permitted to exist, without essential injury to literature. But they are very numerous and important. In our own language, the primitive senses of words are, in some cases, totally lost or greatly obscured, which renders the definitions imperfect; and some of its idioms are scarcely explicable, without resorting to the original ideas of the words. To this ill consequence it may be added, that the origin and progress of language, one of the noblest gifts of God to man, the instrument of most of his social enjoyments and all his improvements, lie covered with darkness.

This state of our language has long been lamented by men of erudition in Great Britain; tho none of them appear, from their writings, to have known the extent of the evil; much less has any man manifested the courage to attempt an effectual reformation.

From an examination of all the radical words in the Hebrew, and a great part of those in the Celtic and Teutonic languages, I can assure the friends of learning, that much new light may be thrown on this subject. The wonderful structure of language, and its progress from a few simple terms, expressive of natural objects, which supplied the wants or affected the senses of unlettered men, thro a series of ingenious combinations, to express new ideas, growing with the growth of the human mind, to its highest state of refinement, are yet to be developed and elucidated; numerous facts respecting the origin, migration and intermixture of nations, are to be unfolded or illustrated; and the common origin of all the nations of Europe, and those of Asia, at least on the west of the Ganges, may be confirmed beyond the possibility of a reasonable doubt, by the affinity of their languages. Equally useful are these inquiries in disentangling the difficulties of the heathen mythology, which have perplexed and confounded the ablest writers.

Having devoted some years to the investigation of this subject, and made discoveries which are deemed interesting to literature, I purpose to compile a complete Dictionary of the English Language, inviting to my assistance the instructors of the principal seminaries of learning, with whom I can most conveniently correspond. At the same time, I would exhibit correct etymologies of many Greek and Latin words, which, if it should be thought advisable by good judges of the subject, might be inserted in new editions of the lexicons of those languages. A few corrections of the same kind would also be noted in the Hebrew Lexicon of Parkhurst. As I make a practice of noting the affinities of other languages, a Dictionary of the German, of the Dutch, French, Spanish and Italian languages, in which these affinities are noted, will be deposited in some public library for the use of future inquirers.

Having advanced far in this design, and amassed a large part of the materials for its execution; materials which no other person could use to advantage—I consider it my duty, as it is my wish, to proceed to the accomplishment of the work. This is also the wish of the gentlemen of literary eminence, who best know my views, and the progress I have made, and who, from their own knowledge of the nature of this subject, are best qualified to appreciate the merit of the undertaking. Whatever differences of opinion on particular points of practice, may exist among men of letters, there seems to be but one opinion on the utility and importance of my general design.

But this work has enlarged so much upon my hands, that the state of my own property will not justify the prosecution of it, entirely at my own expense. The incessant labor of eight or ten years, including the time already devoted to the subject, is of itself a great sacrifice; but to this are to be added the expences of a numerous family, and the cost of many books. My own property is not adequate to these expenditures. Similar undertakings in Great Britain have been supported by contributions; and can there be a question, whether the lovers of learning in the United States, will aid, by like means, any design which promises to enlarge the sphere of knowledge. It is judged proper to make the experiment.—There are two modes in which the friends of this undertaking may assist me; by contributions in money, and by extending the use of the books which I have published for the use of schools, which would augment my own resources. The certificates and communications annexed have reference to both these modes. The contributions of individuals and of societies will be gratefully received, and faithfully applied to the proposed object.

Gentlemen, who receive several copies of this address, are respectfully desired to give them an extensive circulation, in the towns in which they reside and the vicinity, and to take such measures to promote the general object, as they shall deem most expedient,

NOAH WEBSTER, jun.

New-Haven, February 25, 1807.

YALE-COLLEGE, *February 23, 1807.*

NOAH WEBSTER, Esq.

SIR,

THE Faculty of Yale College coincide with you in the opinion, that the improvement of the Lexicography of our language, by tracing its etymological connection with the Teutonic and Celtic tongues, is a

There was then a space for gentlemen to sign their names, put their "places of abode" and enter the number of copies for which they wished to subscribe, and the sums they had paid.

The problem with that invitation was that it did not give potential subscribers enough information. They wanted to know how much money Webster needed, and when the dictionary would be finished. The circular suggested that if not enough money were raised, Webster might not be able to finish it at all, which made it sound rather a dubious investment. Oliver Wolcott took soundings in New York, and reported to Webster in an unencouraging letter dated September 19, 1807:

It is very generally objected to your proposal, that the size of your Dictionary, & the manner in which it is to be published, & the sum required, are not ascertained, & (on account of impositions which are said to have been practiced) it is said that no payments ought to be required in advance, till the subscription is filled.

My experience of the world has satisfied me that it is in vain to reason with the greatest part of mankind, if they have to pay Ten Dollars, in consequence of being convinced. If as I presume a considerable sum is wanted, I cannot encourage you to expect success by means of a popular subscription....

Wolcott explained that there were able, generous and learned people in America, but they were were not wealthy: there were wealthy people too, but they were not literary.

Webster next had a go at his old friend Joel Barlow, whose tedious epic *The Columbiad* had just been published. Tacked on at the end of the poem and notes, it had a Postscript in which Barlow defended his own unorthodox orthography, and at the end of the Postscript there was a kind word for Webster:

Noah Webster, to whose philological labors our language will be much indebted for its purity and regularity, has pointed out the advantages of a steady course of improvement and how it ought to be conducted. The Preface to his new Dictionary is an able performance. He might advantageously give it more development, with some correction, and publish it as a Prospectus to the great work he now has in hand.

Barlow had returned to America in 1805, after an absence of seventeen years. In London, he had mixed with radicals, and published *Advice to the Privileged Orders*. He had been made an honorary citizen of the new French Republic, and had made a fortune in France. He was a friend and supporter of Jefferson, so that his political views were now precisely opposed to those of old-fashioned federalists like Webster and Dwight. He was also suspected of being, like Jefferson, a deist. Indeed, he had been the confidant of the arch infidel Tom Paine, and it was to Barlow that Paine, when he was arrested in Paris, had entrusted the manuscript of the first part of *The Age of Reason*. Barlow was responsible for the publication of that monstrous work. To the Christian fundamentalists, one passage in the *Columbiad*, and one of the plates, showed clearly that Barlow too had become an atheist. This was the passage:

> Beneath the footstool all destructive
>   things,
> The mask of priesthood and the mace
>   of kings,
> Lie trampled in the dust; for here at last
> Fraud, folly, error all their emblems
>   cast.
> Each envoy here unloads his wearied
>   hand
> Of some old idol from his native land;
> One flings a pagod on the mingled heap,
> One lays a crescent, one a cross to sleep;
> Swords, sceptres, mitres, crowns and
>   globes and stars,
> Codes of false fame and stimulants to
>   wars
> Sink in the settling mass; since guile
>   began,
> These are the agents of the woes of man.[23]

The illustration "The Final Resignation of Prejudices" showed a statue of Genius with a pile of abandoned emblems at its feet — including a cross and a mitre. With remarkable insight, the Edinburgh reviewer saw that this might provide the basis for an attack on Barlow, and he set out what was, indeed, Barlow's defense. The review printed the above passage with the word *cross* in italics, and explained in a footnote:

We have put this word in italics, not to insinuate any charge of impiety against Mr. Barlow, but to guard him against that imputation. From the whole strain of his poem, in which he speaks with warm approbation of reformed Christianity, — specifies the purity and evangelical charity of the priesthood as one of the prime blessings of the millennium, — and breaks out into a holy rapture on the prospect of the coming of the Redeemer, — we are satisfied that he

here speaks of the cross merely as the emblem of the low and persecuting superstition of the crusaders, papists, and other sectaries, who make the crucifix an object of idolatrous veneration.[24]

By the time the review appeared, the anticipated attack on Barlow had already been made. Webster, however, was not concerned with political differences or with religious prejudices. He was getting to work on his big dictionary, and he hoped that if he dropped a hint or two Barlow might offer him some money. On October 19, 1807, Webster wrote to him:

Your favor of the 12th has given me much pleasure: not merely on the score of former friendship, but because it informs me of your favorable opinion of my Dictionary and of my further designs. The approbation of classical scholars is the most flattering reward that I can receive....

A few gentlemen of this character like yourself duly appreciate the merit of my labors, but the number is small: my hope and expectations are that it will increase. You will recollect that Judge Trumbull and yourself were the only friends who in 1783 ventured to encourage me to publish my *Spelling Book*. The attempt to correct English books was thought a rash undertaking, yet more than 200,000 copies now sell annually. My *Grammar* had its run, but has been superseded by Murray's. Both are wrong. I have lately published one on Horne Tooke's plan, which President Smith of Princeton pronounces the best analysis of the language ever published. If I can, I will send you a copy.

I have published three books of *Elements of Useful Knowledge*, containing a brief history and geographical view of America and the Eastern Continent. This is getting into use extensively with us, and if I can give it circulation in the middle and southern states, the profits will enable me to bear the expenses of my great work....

I have in the press an abridgement of my *Compendious Dictionary* for common schools, omitting obsolete, and technical terms, and reducing it to a dollar book. With the profits of these I hope to be able to finish my Complete Dictionary. If I could get two or three hundred subscribers to advance the price of it, this would be all I should want: but I have no expectation of such patronage, though I am confident there would be no hazard to the subscribers except that of my life. It will require the incessant labor of from three to five years.... I agree with you that we ought to correspond and understand each other. Dr. Mitchill often suggests this union as important. I will cheerfully accord with any scheme of this kind that shall be deemed prudent and advantageous....

Barlow did not take the hint, and Webster may have feared that his pride in the sales of his

spelling book and *Elements of Useful Knowledge* had made him appear too well off. Within a month he wrote to Barlow again, explaining more clearly his need for funding for the dictionary:

The outline was drawn more than twenty years ago, but my circumstances compelled me to suspend the execution of it, for the purpose of getting bread by other business, until within a few years last past. Even now my resources are inadequate to the work: my income barely supports my family, and I want five hundred dollars' worth of books from Europe which I cannot obtain here, and which I cannot afford to purchase. I have made my wishes known to men of letters by a circular accompanied by certificates, and have isued a subscription paper, but I have not any encouragement that one cent will be advanced by the wealthy citizens of my country. I must therefore drudge on under all the embarrassments which have usually attended like undertakings. It is important that the friends of this species of improvement should be united and aid each other.

It was at just this time, the winter of 1807, that the Rev. Moses Stuart was leading a religious revival in New Haven. Webster's two eldest daughters, Emily and Julia, were among the first to be affected, and Webster took up the study of the Bible, initially with a view to persuading them that they were wrong. Instead, he found himself convinced that they were right, and he made a public profession of his faith in April 1808. Unhappily, this placed him in the camp of Barlow's enemies, and Webster rejected his oldest friend. He claimed that this was because Barlow had forsaken his religion, but that was nonsense. Barlow's beliefs had certainly not changed since Webster's letters in October and November 1807, nor had Webster's knowledge of them. All that had changed was Webster's own viewpoint. His last letter to Barlow was dated October 13, 1808:

Sir:

I had intended to give to the public a short review of your 'Columbiad' before this time, but two causes have prevented me: first, a feeble state of health and much occupation during the summer past, and, secondly, a doubt whether I can execute this purpose in a manner to satisfy you and my own conscience at the same time. Of the poem, as a poem, I can conscientiously say all, perhaps, which you can expect or desire, but I cannot, in a review, omit to pass a severe censure on the atheistical principles it contains. The principles of irreligion you avow, of which I saw a specimen in a letter you wrote to Royal Flint in

1792 or 1795, form the partition-wall which has separated you from many of your old friends. No man on earth not allied to me by nature or by marriage had so large a share in my affections as Joel Barlow until you renounced the religion which you once preached, and which I believe. But with my views of the principles you have introduced into the 'Columbiad' I apprehend my silence will be most agreeable to you, and most expedient for your old friend and obedient servant,. ...

Barlow did not reply.

12. Webster Moves to Amherst

The Synopsis of Radical Words in Twenty Languages

Webster's attempt to raise funds by finding subscribers for the dictionary was not a success. John Jay heard of it some years later and asked if the list was still open. Webster replied, May 13, 1813:

In answer to your inquiry, I would inform you that there are subscription papers for my Dictionary in New York, & one, I believe, in the hands of Whiting & Watson, but no attempts have been made for nearly two years to procure names.

Finding my own resources would not be adequate to the support of my family, while I was engaged in the execution of the work, I made a serious effort to raise money by subscription, and an advance of part of the money. I visited New York, Philadelphia, Boston, Salem, Newburyport &c and laid before many principal literary Gentlemen, not only my proposals, but a specimen of the work. I every where received assurances of liberal support, but on trial no names were procured except a few in New York and New Haven.

Jay ignored the subscription list, and sent $50 directly to Webster. He was one of very few who responded to Webster's appeals with disinterested generosity and encouragement. In 1821, he sent another $50, but so that it would not have the appearance of charity, he said that he wanted each of his two sons to have a copy of the dictionary. At the same time, he made it clear that he did not expect to be repaid, even if the dictionary was never completed.

In his letter to Jay, Webster referred to a visit he had made to Salem, in 1809, which was the subject of a letter from Simeon Colton to his uncle, Simeon Baldwin:

Mr. Webster has just been in this town and in the neighboring towns soliciting patronage for his Dictionary to be published at some future day. In this town he applied to John Pickering, jun., son of the Colonel.... I know him and through him the opinion of the literary men in the neighborhood concerning Mr. Webster....

In this quarter every thing contrary to the opinion of Cambridge University [Harvard] is rejected by the principal characters; consequently, Mr. Webster would be much less popular here than if he paid more respect to that institution. Again Mr. Webster seems determined to run down Johnson and build upon his ruin; nothing could be more fatal to him in this quarter, for our litterati will never believe that he is superior to this great English lexicographer, and by this means will withhold the support they would grant were he more modest in his pretensions.

But there is another capital defect in Mr. Webster's proposition. He proposes that the subscribers should advance 10 dollars each. This I am certain will never succeed in this quarter, for their opinion of the man is not good enough to induce them, hardly, to become obligated to take his books after they are printed. He must devise some other plan or he will get but few subscribers within the atmosphere of Cambridge.

Another thing which has been noticed is his peddling his own productions in person; had he addressed the public thro the medium of the papers, or in handbills, with a specimen of his work, he would have been more successful, and nothing would be more efficacious than the publication of a specimen. But the great and capital defect is the unbounded vanity of the man.... I wish for the honor of our Alma Mater, for the good of the public, and the credit of the man himself, he were not so confident in his own merit, but would be content to address the public as though there were some equal to himself. I suppose Dr. Morse and friends encouraged him, but their opinion would not weigh much with the greater part of the people in Boston and other large towns this way. I would not be censorious on this subject, for I wish the man success, but I wish he would be content to use the ordinary means to obtain it.

Colton's reference to "the honor of the Alma Mater" points to the fact that both he and

Webster, as also Jedidiah Morse, were gradu- ates of Yale. The hostility encountered by Web- ster, however, was due to more than intercolle- giate rivalry: There was religious rivalry in it as well. Harvard was the Unitarian stronghold, Yale was Congregationalist; and the previous year Webster had very publicly embraced the Calvin- ist doctrines of the Congregationalist church. In the past, he had suggested that critics of the *Grammatical Institute* were politically motivated, and he was almost certainly mistaken. Now, he would believe that opponents of his lexicogra- phy were opponents of his doctrine, and to some extent he was probably right. It is certainly true that his new-found faith had a profound effect on the content of the *American Dictionary.*

Webster's religious awakening took place in April 1808. His letter to Judge Dawes, the one which referred to his "falling into vicious com- pany at college" was written in December of that year. In February 1809, he sent Dawes "Reasons for Accepting the Christian and Calvinistic Scheme," which was published in *The Panoplist; or The Christian's Armory* the fol- lowing July. This magazine, which had been founded by Morse in 1805, became Webster's mouthpiece for lexicographical as well as reli- gious pronouncements, and the opposing camp attacked him in *The Monthly Anthology.*

Another of Webster's public letters "To the Friends of Literature" appeared first in *The Panoplist,* then in the *Monthly Anthology,* and later in a curious little weekly magazine in Boston called *Something,* edited (and mostly written) by an old Etonian actor called James Fennell. He used the *nom de plume* Nemo No- body, and he chose the title of his magazine, so he said, because he knew that people did not like to leave a shop without buying *something.* Webster's letter appeared in *Something* on April 7, 1810. In it, he said that if he did not receive financial support for his dictionary from gen- tlemen of talents and property in America, he would either abandon the undertaking, or "apply to the liberality of English gentlemen for the necessary means to enable me to accom- plish the work I have begun." So far as I know, he never made such an application, which was probably just as well since his grammatical works had not been well received in England.[1] The letter also shows that Webster was study- ing the origin of language:

In my contemplated Dictionary, I design to offer a new illustration of the origin and progress of lan- guage; altogether different from anything that has yet appeared. I offer this in confidence, not that my work will be perfect, but that the fruits of my inves- tigations will be a valuable acquisition to the repub- lic of letters; and not to the English nation and their descendants only, but to most of the nations of Eu- rope. After making due allowance for the partiality of every author for his own productions, I am per- suaded that the improvements I contemplate, will appear to deserve encouragement, and to be an ample equivalent for the expense of a new work. These are my real views — such and no other are my motives.[2]

One of the most peculiarly impersonal para- graphs of the *Memoir* describes how his work on the dictionary began:

At what particular time, N.W. began to think seri- ously of attempting the compilation of a complete dictionary of the English Language, is not known. But it appears that soon after leaving New York in 1798, he began to enter particular words and au- thorities on the margin of *Johnson's Dictionary,* to be used, if occasion should offer.

He left New York in April 1798, and cannot then have had his copy of Johnson's dictionary, because it was not published until 1799. It is the eighth London edition, in two quarto volumes, and can be found today in the Rare Books Room in the New York Public Library. The marginal notes show Webster's interest in the origins of language, one of the works most commonly referred to being "Whiter" — that is to say, Walter Whiter's *Etymologicon Magnum, or Universal Etymological Dictionary,* published in 1800. It was Whiter who taught Webster his method of etymological research, which starts from an understanding of the idea of cognate letters:

In our earliest stages of acquiring knowledge, we learn that "Inter se cognatæ sunt Π, Β, Φ, — Κ, Γ, Χ, — Τ, Δ, Θ," — P, B, F — K, G, Ch — T, D, Th; and that these letters are called cognate, because they are changed into each other in the variations of the same word…. The *sameness* (if I may so express it) of the word does not consist in the vowels, or rather, the vowels have nothing to do in determining the *same- ness* or *identity* of a word. We observe, however, that the same idea is expressed by the *same consonants,* or by those, which Grammarians have considered as *cognate* or of the *same kind.*

In the Introduction, Whiter gave instruc- tions that Webster would carefully follow:

If the Etymologist is desirous of tracing out the same word ... through different languages, or amidst various modes of writing and pronouncing that word in different periods or dialects of the same language — or if he is desirous of discovering, what words, conveying similar ideas, are derived from each other — belong to each other or are successively propagated from each other; he must seek this affinity or relationship among words possessing the *same cognate consonants;* and to this test only it is his duty perpetually to appeal. He must totally disregard all difference of appearance in the words, whose affinity he examines; as that difference arises from the adoption of different vowels in different places; or as that difference arises from consonants bearing a different form and called by a different name. He must regard only the existence of the *same cognate consonants—* of *consonants* invested with the *same power — consonants* of the *same kind,* which he has seen — known and acknowledged in the most familiar instances to be perpetually changing into each other, in expressing the same or similar ideas. He should acquire the habit of viewing words in their abstract — simple state, as belonging only to these cognate Consonants, and freed from those incumbrances, by which their difference of appearance is produced, and under which disguise their mutual affinity to each other has been concealed.

The whole of the first volume of the *Etymologicon Magnum,* more than five hundred quarto pages (which was all that Whiter produced at that time), deals with just one root, with *C* (or cognates *G* or *K*) for its first letter, and *B,* F, *P* or *V* for its second.

Webster found this subject so intriguing that he stopped work on the main part of the dictionary to concentrate on it:

My original design did not extend to an investigation of the origin and progess of our language; much less of other languages. I limited my views to the correcting of certain errors in the best English Dictionaries, and to the supplying of words in which they are deficient. But after writing through two letters of the alphabet, I determined to change my plan. I found myself embarrassed, at every step, for want of a knowledge of the origin of words, which Johnson, Bailey, Junius, Skinner and some other authors do not afford the means of obtaining. Then laying aside my manuscripts, and all books treating of language, except lexicons and dictionaries, I endeavored, by a diligent comparison of words, having the same or cognate radical letters, in about twenty languages, to obtain a more correct knowledge of the primary sense of original words, of the affinities between the English and many other languages, and thus to enable myself to trace words to their sources.[3]

Students of language had long supposed that human speech had its origins in the animal sounds made by primitive man, in exclamations of joy, rage and pain, and in imitations of the sounds of other creatures. Notable here were Condillac in France and Lord Monboddo in Scotland. Monboddo was a particularly pleasing eccentric, whose six volume work *On the Origin and Progress of Language* was published in Edinburgh between 1774 and 1792. He is remembered for having identified a nation of savages who had been found not to have the use of speech — they were called the *Orang Outangs.* "They are exactly of the human form," he wrote, "walking erect, not upon all-four, like the savages that have been found in Europe; they use sticks for weapons; they live in society; they make huts of branches of trees, and they carry off negroe girls, of whom they make slaves."[4] That the "negroe girls" were more than slaves to their hairy captors is clear from Thomas Jefferson's observation in *Notes on the State of Virginia,* that blacks show a (sexual) preference for whites, "as uniformly as is the preference of the Oran-ootan for the black women over those of his own species." "Nothing can be more curious and interesting," commented the *Quarterly Review,* "than this nice gradation of ambitious gallantries." Monboddo and his monkeys became great figures of fun, Johnson drily observing that "Monboddo does not know he is talking nonsense," and dismissing his speculations as "all conjecture upon a thing useless, even if it were known to be true."

The other line of linguistic research involves a comparison of modern languages within the same family, usually the Indo-European, in an attempt to reconstruct some parts of a vanished parent language. Most people accept that these two lines of inquiry, forward from the cradle of mankind, and back from the languages of today, can never hope to meet; between the two there are hundreds of thousands of years of linguistic development of which no certain traces now remain. That analysis, however, rests upon an acceptance of a geological scale of time. It was an understanding of the age of the earth that started Darwin thinking about evolution. He was a pigeon fancier, and saw the many varieties of pigeon that man, by selective breeding over quite a short period, had been able to produce. Given enough time, and competition

for scarce resources, could not nature have produced all the varieties of living things? For Webster, after his religious awakening, that span of time did not exist. He believed in Ussher. James Ussher, Archbishop of Armagh and Primate of All Ireland, had made a careful study of biblical chronology, and had calculated that the beginning of time "fell upon the entrance of the night preceding the twenty third day of Octob. in the year of the Julian Calendar, 710."[5] The first day of the world was Sunday, October 23, 4004 B.C., and the first Sabbath fell on Saturday , October 29. Even before his public affirmation of faith, Webster had included some of Ussher's dates in one of the chronological tables at the end of the *Compendious Dictionary*. "The creation of the world and Adam and Eve" was in 4004 B.C., and in the year 2247 B.C., Babel was built, and languages confounded.

The fourth of Webster's *Dissertations on the English Language* started with "Remarks on the formation of language," which mention various writers, including Condillac. That was back in 1789, when Webster had been prepared to accept that language had probably been developed by primitive man from animal grunts:

The invention and progress of articulate sounds must have been extremely slow. Rude savages have originally no method of conveying ideas, but by looks, signs, and those inarticulate sounds, called by grammarians, *Interjections*. These are probably the first beginnings of language. They are produced by the passions, and are perhaps very little superior, in point of articulation or significancy, to the sounds which express the wants of the brutes.

After his religious awakening, Webster had to abandon that sort of theory. Language was not invented by man at all but was given to man by God. There must have been a language in the Garden of Eden, because God had spoken with Adam and Eve there, when they discussed the unfortunate business of the apple. Since those events, less than six thousand years had passed. The original language would have been quite simple and over so many years it would have changed a great deal, but some traces of it might still be found, particularly as languages two thousand years old or more were still accessible.

Webster was fascinated by his linguistic investigations. He later wrote, "I was often so much excited by the discoveries I made, that my pulse, whose ordinary action is scarcely 60 beats to the minute, was accelerated to 80 or 85."[6] It is characteristic of Webster that when he was most excited, he took his own pulse to see just how excited he was.

He would have said that his study of language was similarly conducted in a spirit of scientific detachment, but in reality it was nothing of the sort. As with the yellow fever, he knew the answers before he began. He knew that mankind had started with one couple, and one language, soon after the Creation. He looked for, and thought he found, evidence to support that view. Though it does not match the account in "Dissertation IV" of the development of language from interjections, even in 1789 Webster had said in the Notes at the end of the *Dissertations* that "profane history and etymology furnish strong arguments to prove the truth of the scripture account of the manner in which the world was peopled from one stock or family."[7] He said the same thing in the Preface to the *Compendious Dictionary*— that the study of etymology would "confirm, in no small degree, the scripture account of the dispersion of men." In July 1809, in a progress report he sent to Thomas Dawes, he claimed to have found that confirmation. His letter was published in *The Columbian Centinel* in Boston, August 2, 1809:

I am often asked what progress I have made in the compilation of my proposed Dictionary and when in all probability it will be completed. To these questions I am not able to give precise answers, as the field enlarges with every step I take. I deem it proper, however, to state to my friends that new discoveries of important facts, of which I had not the slightest suspicion when I began the investigation, add almost daily new incentives to my zeal and very much increase in my apprehension the value of researches into the origin and progress of languages. It is a common opinion that etymological investigations are dull and uninteresting in the prosecution, as they are useless in practice. But I find this to be a great mistake that must have arisen from an entire ignorance or imperfect views of the subject. In opposition to this opinion I can affirm that few studies are more interesting, either as furnishing a gratification of curiosity or real improvement of the mind.

It seems to be taken for granted by men who are reputed scholars, and who are really so in most branches of literature, that *language* is a subject perfectly well understood, even so well as to preclude the

necessity of further investigation. Indeed, many seem to think that our language in particular is so perfect, so clearly understood and defined, that it cannot be improved. The student is so well satisfied with the works of VARRO, VOSSIUS, CAMDEN, HICKES, SKINNER, JUNIUS, HARRIS, LOWTH and JOHNSON, that he scarcely thinks of examining HORNE TOOKE, WHITER, and GEBELIN; and even conceives it a species of sacrilege to violate the remains of those giants in literature with the unhallowed spirit of inquiry and scepticism. I was once a slave to this prejudice myself; I say to this *prejudice*, for I am now persuaded it deserves this appellation and that this prejudice now interposes an immense obstacle to the progress of truth and improvement in this country.

In opposition to this opinion, the discoveries that I have already made enable me to state with confidence that scarcely anything belonging to man and his works is so little understood as the *origin* and *structure* of language, and that the English writers above-named, whose works are considered as standard authorities in the language, barely entered the threshold of the subject. I feel the responsibility attached to this remark; but my conscience bears me witness that it is not dictated in the smallest degree by vanity but by deliberate judgment, and that I am possessed of all the means of establishing the truth of the observation.

In addition to the advantages of ascertaining the true orthography and signification of words, advantages well understood and universally admitted, etymological investigations are extremely useful in illustrating history, and probably to an extent not generally believed. Of the following points, however, I have already obtained most satisfactory evidence:

1. That the opinion of the descent of all nations from one pair is well founded and susceptible of new and satisfactory proof.

2. That whatever differences of dialect might have been introduced at *Babel*, languages entirely different were not formed, as the radical words in the principal languages of *Asia*, *Africa*, and *Europe* are still the same.

3. That although the oldest writings extant are in the *Hebrew* language, yet the Hebrew language is not older than the *Arabic*, *Celtic*, and *Teutonic*; and so far is it from being the most ancient and the original language from which the other *Assyrian* dialects — the *Chaldaic, Arabic,* and *Phoenician* — and the *Greek, Latin*, and other European languages are derived, that it is only of cotemporaneous origin with the other primitive languages, and many of its words which are supposed to be *radical* are in fact formed on roots which are now to be found in the *Celtic* and *Teutonic* dialects in the west and north of *Europe*....

The families of men which first peopled the earth migrated in diverging courses. Their progress from the center of *Asia* may be distinctly traced by their languages; and their progress or courses being ra-

diuses of a circle, and the first races or families removing to the greatest distances as they were invited by the conveniences of hunting or impelled forward by succeeding tribes, their descendants and their languages are now to be found at the periphery of the circle in the north and west of *Europe*, etc. These languages retain many primitive words which are lost or disguised in the Greek and Latin; and an inattention to this circumstance has retarded the progress of this kind of enquiries more than any other circumstance.

But nothing amuses me more than a development of the process by which mankind have formed abstract terms or rather applied the names of visible objects and action to express abstract ideas. I cannot, however, enlarge on this subject in a letter.

I have accumulated such a mass of materials for a Dictionary, materials which no other person could use to advantage, that I think it my duty, as it is my pleasure, to prosecute the work....[8]

Given the failure of his subscription, Webster's decision "to prosecute the work" was really extraordinarily brave. When that letter to Dawes was published in August 1809, Webster was the sole support of a wife and seven children. His eldest daughter, Emily, had her 19th birthday two days later; William was nearly 8, and the other children ranged in age from Julia who was 16, to little Louisa who was just 16 months. Louisa had been born a few days after Webster's religious awakening, so that Rebecca was not with him when he made his public profession of faith. He was accompanied by Emily and Julia, but "Mrs. W was confined at the time and could not be a witness of this scene."[9]

In 1810 or early 1811, Webster was running short of money, and had the idea of moving to the country to reduce his expenses. This is mentioned in a begging letter he wrote to Josiah Quincy on February 12, 1811:

My own resources are almost exhausted, and in a few days I shall sell my house to get bread for my children. All the assurances of aid which I had received in Boston, New York etc. have failed, and I am soon to retire to a humble cottage in the country.... A few thousand dollars, for which I can give security, would place me in a condition in the country to live with comfort and pursue my studies; but even this cannot be obtained until the measures of Congress assume a more auspicious aspect....

Quincy did not take the hint, but Webster was able to postpone his retirement to the humble country cottage, because a few of the wealthier citizens of Connecticut undertook to

contribute towards his maintenance for three years. In the first year of this arrangement, Webster's benefactors, each paying either $100 or $50, gave him altogether $1,000. Unfortunately, all but one of the backers then backed out — only William Woolsey made a further payment — and Webster was forced to rely once again on his own resources. His earlier plan of moving house was then put into effect:

At this period, he had to encounter great obstacles. His family was large and apprehensive, and for a period, his income was not sufficient to furnish subsistence for them in New Haven.... A few friends made liberal advances to aid him for a time; but he was compelled at last to yield to circumstances. In July 1812, he sold his house in New Haven, and purchased one in Amherst in Massachusetts ... to this he removed his family, the first week in September following; and here he resided for the ten succeeding years.[10]

Living was cheaper in rural Amherst, and Webster had several acres of land, on which he was able to grow vegetables and fruit to help feed his family. The move was not agreeable to Emily and Julia, however, because both had left boyfriends behind in Connecticut. Emily stayed in Amherst only a year. In September 1813, she married William Wolcott Ellsworth, a young lawyer in Hartford. He was the son of Oliver Ellsworth, who had given Webster lodgings in Hartford, back in the summer of 1779.

Louisa, who was both mentally and physically handicapped, took up much of Rebecca's time and attention. That left Eliza (who was nearly 9 when they moved to Amherst) to be looked after mainly by Julia until 1816, when both Julia and Harriet were married. On May 22, Harriet married a Mr. Edward Cobb of Portland, Maine. Julia married Chauncey Allen Goodrich on October 1. He was the son of Webster's friend Elizur Goodrich, and had been in the same class at Yale as William Ellsworth. It was his grandfather (Elizur Senior) who had made the first suggestion to Webster that he compile a dictionary.

Getting three daughters married off cut down Webster's domestic expenses, and soon afterwards he hatched a scheme for getting rid of William as well: he would transfer William to the Hartford firm of Hudson & Co., (successors to Hudson & Goodwin) together with rights in the *American Spelling Book*. In the past, Webster had sold to various publishers the right to print his speller in a limited area for a period of years. He generally did this because he needed a lump sum immediately, and could not afford to wait for royalties to come in. The result was that he often saw publishers selling very large numbers of his books, when he was getting nothing out of it. In 1804, therefore, he adopted a standard form of contract for all the licensees of his speller, that made his income depend on the number of copies sold. It was this contract that specified that the books be covered in blue paper, and it gave him a royalty of one cent per copy. This provided much-needed income, but it had not proved sufficient to maintain Webster and his family in New Haven, so he had moved them to Amherst in 1812.

By 1816, he had decided that his new system of licences was not satisfactory either. Having a royalty that depended on the numbers of copies sold meant that Webster had to worry about promoting sales, and he found himself constantly keeping accounts. To free himself from all these troubles, he made an agreement on April 19, 1816, with Hudson & Co. for a fixed annual sum. They agreed to pay him $3,000 a year during the second term of copyright — fourteen years from March 14, 1818 — in exchange for the exclusive right to print and sell the *American Spelling Book* throughout the United States. In addition, they agreed to take William as an apprentice or clerk, teaching him bookkeeping and the business of bookselling, with a view to his becoming a partner in the business when he reached the age of 21.

No part of that agreement operated as originally planned. The payment system was changed even before it was due to start; William's apprenticeship came to a premature end, and Webster introduced a new spelling book while Hudson's licence was still in force.

On February 17, 1817, William wrote to his father from Hartford:

I have just seen a letter of Mr. Hudson's to you. In that he says that I take no interest in the business of the store, & that I am taken up with pleasure more than in business.... as to my spending money foolishly I am really afraid that I bought too many sweet things, but very few at a time. I am very sorry to find that Hudson & Co. find so much fault with me, & if it should be your pleasure now that I should have an

education, I am quite willing, or am willing to stay. I should like to know soon your mind respecting this affair. I hope you will not think hard of me. I am young, and have suffered a great deal of anxiety, since I found that he was discontented with me. He attributes my uneasiness to a regret of parting with my studies. I *was* at first a little *home sick* when I found that I must stay here from seven oclock in the morning to nine in the evening, but I mentioned it to noone. I hope it will be settled soon to the satisfaction of every one...

Six months later, William needed money:

I found when I returned from Amherst that two of my silk handkerchiefs were missing and have not been found. I should be glad of another, and if convenient a little *pocket money* for mending &c....

Three months after that, in November 1817, things were no better:

I am very lonesome now Barnes is gone. I am confined as close as a prison from morning 'till 9 oclock in the evening, & should be glad of an evening or two in a week. We do nothing in the evening except one or two in a week. Mr. Hudson writes letters for me to copy. One of Mr. Hudson's nephews sleeps with me in the compiling room....

William is often portrayed as something of an idiot, on the basis of his later business failures, his sisters' criticism, and his own self-deprecating confession that he "suffered from a native imbecility of mind." In fact he was not stupid, but he was nauseatingly sentimental, and wallowed in self-pity when things went against him. I feel some sympathy, however, for William the unenthusiastic apprentice; when he was criticized for his lack of interest in Hudson's business and for spending too much money on candy, he was only 15. Eventually Webster changed his mind and William got some education. In 1819 he was a student at Amherst, and in 1820 he enrolled at Yale, under the watchful eye of his brother-in-law Goodrich.

With regard to the payments due from Hudson & Co., Webster changed his mind also, just when their rights began. On April 20, 1818, Hudson & Co. paid him $20,000 in a single sum, instead of the $3,000 a year for 14 years that had originally been agreed upon.

We are here still in the period when Webster had put aside the manuscript of his dictionary (having only got as far as *B*), "and all books treating of language, except lexicons and dictionaries," and was making "a diligent comparison of words." Thanks to Eliza, we can actually watch him at work:

In the second story of his new home, in a large room, with windows looking to the south and east, Webster set up anew the large circular table which he had used for some years at New Haven. This table was about two feet wide, built in the form of a hollow circle. Dictionaries and grammars of all obtainable languages were laid in successive order upon its surface. Webster would take the word under investigation, and standing at the right end of the lexicographer's table, look it up in the first dictionary which lay at that end. He made a note, examined a grammar, considerd some kindred word, and then passed to the next dictionary of some other tongue. He took each word through the twenty or thirty dictionaries, making notes of his discoveries, and passing around his table many times in the course of a day's labor of minute and careful study.[11]

So far as I know, that is the only more or less first-hand description of Webster working on the *Synopsis of Words in Twenty Languages*. If it is, the accounts given by later biographers must all have been derived from it. Each borrowed from those who had gone before, each adding his own inventive touches. In 1936, Warfel cut Webster's table in half:

Webster's method of work was this: On a semicircular table, two feet wide, he placed his books; beginning at the right end of the table, he would thumb grammars and dictionaries while tracing a given word through the twenty languages, making notes of his discoveries. Many times a day did he follow this pendulum movement.[12]

In 1975, Morgan copied from Warfel, but added a chair mounted on casters:

In his upstairs study ... he had a semicircular table two feet wide, on which he put his reference books. Starting at the right end of the table, he would go through his grammars and dictionaries while tracing a particular word through 20 languages, all the time writing notes on his discoveries. He sat in a chair mounted on casters so that he could move from one end of the table to the other more easily.[13]

Monaghan, in 1983, cites only Warfel, but her first sentence is taken from Morgan, and she, too, mentions the chair:

He had a semicircular table, two feet wide, on which lay his reference books. Working from right to left, swivelling on a chair with casters as he did so, he would methodically trace an individual word in each of twenty languages, making notes as he went along.[14]

Most writers after Warfel have called the table "semicircular," though Rollins is here an honourable exception. Eliza (if it was Eliza) described it as "a large circular table ... built in the form of a hollow circle." It seems to me that she would not have used those words of a table that was semicircular. Its purpose was surely to enable Webster to surround himself with books, all of which would be within easy reach; the circle was hollow so that Webster could put himself in the middle. Furthermore, Warfel's description of Webster's "pendulum movement" does not sound right. His basic movement, repeatedly going through the whole series of dictionaries, would have been round and round, rather than to and fro. That, indeed, is what Eliza said; she referred to Webster "passing around his table many times in the course of a day's labor."

Then there is the chair. The ideal arrangement for a seated researcher would be a fixed chair and a table that could rotate, like sitting inside a dumb waiter, but that would be mechanically complicated. Morgan must have reasoned that with a fixed table, a chair on casters would be not merely sensible, but necessary. Webster, however, was not a seated researcher—he liked to work standing up. This is the advice that he gave in his "Address to Yung Gentlemen":

Whether you reed or rite, accustom yourselves to stand at a high desk, rather than indulge an indolent habit of sitting, which always weekens, and sometimes disfigures the body. The neerer you can keep every part of the body to an eezy strait posture, the more equable wil be the circulation of the fluids; and in order to giv them the most unconstrained flow to the extremities of the lims, it iz very useful to loosen those parts of dress that bind the lims closely.[15]

Eliza's account confirms Webster's opposition to the indolent habit of sitting; she said that he started off his investigation of a word, "*standing* at the right end of the lexicographer's table." Morgan's chair was imaginary.

What about the books on the table? In Webster's own words, he had put aside "all books treating of language, except lexicons and dictionaries." Eliza said there were grammars on the table, and in this she was followed by Warfel and by Morgan. Monaghan, more cautiously, just said that there were "reference books." As I shall shortly explain, I think the grammars were imaginary too.

There is further biographical fiction in the way that Webster has been credited with the mastery of many languages. Warfel started that as well. First, he gave a fanciful account of Webster's studies when he was running a school in Sharon, in 1781:

To his onerous school duties, he had added an ambitious program of study. Under the Reverend Mr. John Peter Tetard, a learned Genevan Huguenot pastor, Webster began studying French. The fascination of comparative modern grammar took hold of him, and soon the German, Spanish, and Italian tongues unlocked their mysteries.... Tom Paine's stirring essays, *The Crisis*, took on new meaning when Webster received from Tetard a copy of Rousseau's *Social Contract*....[16]

Rollins swallowed all of that except the Italian, and regurgitated it into *The Long Journey of Noah Webster*, slightly chewed but wholly undigested:

One Sharon resident fascinated the young schoolmaster: the Reverend John Peter Tetard, a learned European and a Huguenot. With Tetard he studied French, German, Spanish, and Latin, as well as history. Reading Tom Paine's *The Crisis* sharpened his democratic and nationalistic tendencies. In September he dashed back to New Haven ... and returned to discuss Rousseau's *Social Contract* with Tetard.[17]

The fictitious nature of that account can be demonstrated from Webster's own writings. In No. 6 of the *Memoir*, Webster says of Tetard that he was "an accurate classical scholar, and with him N.W. commenced the study of the French language." In the margin of an autobiographical fragment now in the New York Public Library, Webster wrote, "In Sharon, I studied French under the Rev. Mr. Tetard ... an excellent scholar and Christian...." So far as I know, those two references are the only evidence of his studies in Sharon. If he had studied German, Spanish, Italian or Latin with Tetard, why would he only mention French? The bit about discussing Rousseau with Tetard is fiction too. In the *Memoir*, No. 12, Webster refers to his pamphlet *Sketches of American Policy;* the first sketch, he says, was written "soon after reading Rousseau's Social Contract." His diary shows that the pamphlet was written in February 1785—nearly three years after his final departure from Sharon.

This is how Warfel describes Webster's later progress in the study of languages:

In 1807 Webster had mastered twelve languages…. By 1813 he had learned twenty languages, seven of them being Asiatic or dialects of the Assyrian; these were: Chaldaic, Syriac, Arabic, Samaritan, Hebrew, Ethiopic, Persian, Irish (Hiberno Celtic), Armoric, Anglo-Saxon, German, Dutch, Swedish, Danish, Greek, Latin, Italian, Spanish, French, Russian, and, of course, English. Later he added Portuguese, Welsh, Gothic, and the early dialects of Englsih and German.[18]

Now, it is true to say that Webster did not mind giving the impression in lectures and writings that he had the gift of tongues, but he did not actually claim it, and he certainly did not have it. At Yale, he would have studied Latin and Greek, but no other foreign languages, ancient or modern. In 1781, he began the study of French (and only French) with Tetard. He had more tuition in French when he was in Baltimore in the summer of 1785, so that when he was publishing a newspaper in New York, between 1793 and 1798, he was able to include articles that he had translated from French papers. He found this extremely hard work, because he was not fluent in the language and had to make use of a dictionary. In the previous chapter we saw Professor Charlton Laird's assessment of Webster's proficiency in Anglo-Saxon. The only other language he can be shown to have attempted is Hebrew. In the Preface to his 1833 version of the Bible, Webster wrote:

A few errors in translation, which are admitted on all hands to be obvious, have been corrected; and some obscure passages, illustrated. In making these amendments, I have consulted the original languages, and also several translations and commentaries….

Reading the Bible in a foreign language is not like reading a newspaper, because you already have a translation to hand (and working with a crib and a dictionary is not evidence of profound scholarship), but let us say that Webster was probably able to read Hebrew to some extent. He certainly had a copy of *Stuart's Hebrew Grammar*, for when he divided up his library it was included in the list of books presented to Amherst College. His copy of *Parkhurst's Hebrew Lexicon* went to Middlebury College, and a Hebrew Bible was in the list of books for "C.A.Goodrich, wife & children."

Beyond what I have mentioned, I know of no evidence to support Warfel's statement that "by 1813 [Webster] had learned twenty languages." Indeed, it would have been quite impossible for him to have learned most of the languages in Warfel's list, because he had absolutely no means of taking instruction other than "lexicons and dictionaries." From those, once he had mastered their various alphabets, he could learn *words*, but he could not learn *languages*.

For Webster's purposes, words were all that he needed. His method, as he himself described it, was "a diligent comparison of words, having the same or cognate radical letters." That is why his own description of the books on his circular table, "lexicons and dictionaries," makes more sense than Eliza's "dictionaries and grammars." There was no place on his table for grammars, because all he was doing, for ten long years, was comparing *the outward form of words* in twenty languages.

The result of all that labor was the *Synopsis*, which, Webster told his friend Samuel Latham Mitchill, "will make a quarto volume, and is intended as a book of reference and to form an appendix to the Dictionary."[19] In the end, the *Synopsis* was never printed, but many references to it were left in the dictionary, and the Introduction to the dictionary serves also as an Introduction to the *Synopsis*. It starts by defining language, and then gives this account of its origin:

ORIGIN OF LANGUAGE

We read, in the Scriptures, that God, when he had created man … planted a garden, and placed in it the man he had made, with a command to keep it and to dress it… . We further read, that God brought to Adam the fowls and beasts he had made, and that Adam gave them names; and that when his female companion was made, he gave her a name. After the eating of the forbidden fruit, it is stated that God addressed Adam and Eve, reproving them for their disobedience, and pronouncing the penalties, which they had incurred. In the account of these transactions, it is further related that Adam and Eve both replied to their Maker, and excused their disobedience.

If we admit what is the literal and obvious interpretation of this narrative, that vocal sounds or words wre used in these communications between God and the progenitors of the human race, it results that…. language was bestowed on Adam, in the same manner as all his other faculties and knowledge, by supernatural power…. We are not however to suppose the language of our first parents in paradise to

have been copious, like most modern languages; or the identical language that they used, to be now in existence. Many of the primitive radical words may and probably do exist in various languages; but observation teaches that languages must improve and undergo great changes as knowledge increases, and be subject to continual alterations, from other causes incident to man in society.

Webster divided the languages that he studied into two great families, which he called "Shemitic" and "Japhetic." This is explained in the next part of the Introduction:

A brief account of the origin and progress of the principal languages, ancient and modern, that have been spoken by nations between the Ganges and the Atlantic ocean.

We learn from the Scriptures that Noah, who, with his family, was preserved from destruction by the deluge, for the purpose of re-peopling the earth, had three sons, Shem, Ham and Japheth....

Japheth was the eldest son; but Shem, the ancestor of the Israelites, and the writers of the Scriptures, is named first in order.

The descendants of Shem and Ham peopled all the great plain, situated north and west of the Persian Gulf, between that Gulf and the Indian ocean on the east and the Arabic Gulf and the Mediterranean Sea on the west, with the northern coast of Africa; comprehending Assyria, Babylonia or Chaldea, Syria, Palestine, Arabia, Egypt and Libya. The principal languages or dialects used by these descendants are known to us under the names of Chaldee, or Chaldaic which is called also Aramean, Syriac, Hebrew, Arabic, Ethiopic, Samaritan and Coptic....

These languages, except the Coptic, being used by the descendants of Shem, I call *Shemitic*, or *Assyrian*, in distinction from the *Japhetic*. As the descendants of Japheth peopled Asia Minor, the northern parts of Asia, about the Euxine and Caspian, and all Europe, their languages have, in the long period that has elapsed since their dispersion, become very numerous.

All languages having sprung from one source, the original words from which they have been formed, must have been of equal antiquity. That the Celtic and Teutonic languages in Europe are, in this sense, as old as the Chaldee and Hebrew, is a fact not only warranted by history and the common origin of Japheth and Shem, but susceptible of proof from the identity of many words yet existing, in both stocks....

Onto that ethnographic map, Webster superimposed what he knew from his own or others' observations of the way that modern languages have developed. It is commonplace to identify Latin roots in French or English words.

Many words in Latin and Greek clearly show the same roots. Sir William Jones, in what is certainly his most famous single sentence, and quite possibly his longest, pointed out that Sanscrit was a member of the same family. He too mentioned roots:

The *Sanscrit* language, whatever be its antiquity, is of a wonderful structure; more perfect than the *Greek*, more copious than the *Latin*, and more exquisitely refined than either, yet bearing to both of them a stronger affinity, both in the roots of verbs and in the forms of grammar, than could possibly have been produced by accident; so strong indeed, that no philologer could examine them all three, without believing them to have sprung from some common source, which, perhaps, no longer exists: there is a similar reason, though not quite so forcible, for supposing that both the *Gothick* and the *Celtick*, though blended with a very different idiom, had the same origin with the *Sanscrit*; and the old *Persian* might be added to the same family, if this were the place for discussing any question concerning the antiquities of *Persia*.[20]

What constitutes a root? For Webster, it was generally a pair of consonants; those were the "radical letters" that he spent so much time comparing. Vowels were to be disregarded because they changed so freely. It cannot be denied that the words *sang, sing, song* and *sung* have all the same root, but they have only consonants in common. Webster's view on vowels is set out in the Introduction to the dictionary:

CHANGE OF VOWELS

The change of vowels is so common, as to occasion no difficulty in determining the sameness of words; indeed little or no regard is to be had to them, in ascertaining the origin and affinity of languages. In this opinion I accord with almost all writers on this subject; but I have to combat the opinion of that elegant scholar, Sir William Jones, who protests against the licentiousness of etymologists, not only in transposing letters, but in *totally disregarding the vowels*, and seems to admit the common origin of words only when written with the same letters, and used in a sense precisely the same. *

[* Webster's footnote: Asiatic Researches, vol.3, p. 489]

I am not at all surprised at the common prejudice against etymology. As the subject has been treated, it is justly liable to all the objections urged against it. But it is obvious that Sir W. Jones had given very little attention to the subject, and that some of its most common and obvious principles had escaped his observation. His opinion with regard to both articulations and vowels is unequivocally erroneous.

Webster was rather sensitive on the subject of Sir William Jones, both because Jones was an astonishingly accomplished linguist[21] and because (in the passage Webster was referring to) Jones had poked fun at an etymological method that was exactly Webster's own:

I beg leave, as a philologer, to enter my protest ... against the licentiousness of etymologists in transposing and inserting letters, in substituting at pleasure any consonant for another of the same order, and in totally disregarding the vowels: for such permutations few radical words would be more convenient than CUS or CUSH, since, dentals being changed for dentals, and palatials for palatials [sic], it instantly becomes *coot, goose,* and, by transposition, *duck,* all water birds, and *evidently* symbolical; it next is the *goat* worshipped in *Egypt,* and, by a metathesis, the *dog* adored as an emblem of SIRIUS, or, more obviously, a *cat,* not the domestick animal, but a sort of ship, and, the *Catos,* or great sea-fish, of the *Dorians....* Almost any word ... might be derived from any other, if such licences, as I am opposing, were permitted in etymological histories.[22]

What Webster called the "articulations" were radical consonants. They were changeable also, but Webster knew that they did not change at random — they changed only into what he called "cognates":

CHANGE OF ARTICULATIONS, OR CONSONANTS

The articulations, letters which represent the junctions or joinings of the organs, usually called consonants, are the stamina of words. All these are convertible and frequently converted into their cognates. The English word *bear* represents the Latin *fero* and *pario,* and *fero* is the Greek φερω. The Latin *ventus* is *wind* in English; and *habeo* is *have.* The Latin *dens,* in Dutch, Danish and Swedish is *tand;* and *dance* in English is in German *tanz.*

These changes are too familiar to require a multiplication of examples. But there are others less common and obvious, which are yet equally certain. Thus in the Gaelic or Hiberno-Celtic, *m* and *mb* are convertible with *v;* and in Welsh *m* and *v* are changed, even in different cases of the same word. Thus in Irish the name of the hand is written either *lamh* or *lav,* and in Welsh *maen,* a stone, is written also *vaen.* The Greek ß is always pronounced as the English *v,* as βουλομαι, Lat. *volo,* English *will,* German *wollen;* and the sound of *b* the Greeks express by μß.

In the Chaldee and Hebrew, one remarkable distinction is the use of a dental letter in the former, where the latter has a sibiliant. As כוח cuth in Chaldee is כוש cush in Hebrew; דהב, gold, in Chaldaic, is זהב in Hebrew. The like change appears in the modern languages; for *water* which, in most of the northern languages, is written with a dental, is, in German, written *wasser,* and the Latin *dens,* W. *dant,* Dutch *tand,* Swedish and Danish *tand,* is in German *zahn.* The like change is frequent in the Greek and Latin. φραττω in one dialect, is φρασσω, in another; and the Latins often changed *t* of the indicative present, or infinitive, into *s* in the preterit and participle, as *mitto, mittere, missi, missus.*

L and *R,* though not considered as letters of the same organ, are really such, and changed the one into the other. Thus the Spaniards write *blandir* for *brandish,* and *escolta* for *escort.* The Portuguese write *brando* for *bland,* and *branquear,* to whiten, for *blanch.* The Greek has φραγελλιον for the Latin *flagellum.* In Europe, however, this change seems to be limited chiefly to two or three nations on the coast of the Mediterranean. *L* is sometimes commutable with *D....*

In Latin, *f* and *h* have been converted, as *hordeum* for *fordeum;* and the Spaniards now write *h* for *f,* as *hacer* for the Latin *facere; hilo* for *filum; herir* for *ferire,* &c.

When one disregards vowels entirely, and can change consonants into their cognates, there is considerable scope (as Jones pointed out) for asserting that apparently dissimilar words are derived from a common root. The scope enlarges further when one is free to add "casual" letters and to eliminate others, as Webster demonstrates under the heading:

CHANGE OR LOSS OF RADICAL LETTERS

There are some words which, in certain languages, have suffered a change of a radical letter; while in others it is wholly lost. For example, *word,* in Danish and Swedish is *ord; wort,* a plant, is *urt;* the Saxon *gear,* or *ger,* English *year,* in Danish is *aar,* in Swedish is *år,* in Dutch *jaar,* and in German *jahr....*

One of the most general changes that words have undergone is the entire loss of the palatal letter *g,* when it is radical and final in verbs; or the opening of that articulation to a vowel or diphthong. We have examples in the English *bow,* from Saxon *bugan,* to bend; *buy* from *bycgan; brow,* from *breg; lay,* from *lægan* or *lecgan; say,* from *sægan; fair,* from *fæger; flail,* from the German *flegel,* Lat. *flagellum;* French *nier,* from Lat. *nego, negare.*

The same or similar changes have taken place in all the modern languages of which I have any knowledge.

The loss and changes of radical letters in many Greek verbs deserve particular notice.... What proportion of Greek words have been contracted by the loss of an initial or final consonant, cannot, I

apprehend, be determined with any precision; at least, not in the present state of philological knowledge. It is probable the number of contracted words amounts to one fourth of all the verbs, and it may be more.

Similar contractions have taken place in all other languages; a circumstance that embarrasses the philologist and lexicographer at every step of his researches; and which has led to innumerable mistakes in Etymology....

To show how important it is to know the true original orthography, I will mention one instance. In our mother tongue, the word to *dye*, or color, is written *deagan*; the elements or radical letters are *dg*. To determine whether this and the Latin *tingo* are the same words, we must first know whether *n* in *tingo* is radical or casual. This we cannot know with certainty, by the form of the word itself, for the *n* is carried through all the tenses and forms of the verb. But by looking into the Greek, we find the word written with γ, τεγγω; and this clearly proves the alliance of the word with *deagan*. See *Dye* in the Dictionary.

We have many English words in which a *d* has been inserted before *g*, as in *badge, budge, lodge, pledge, wedge*. In all words, I believe, of this class, the *d* is casual, and the *g* following is the radical letter....

By these various transformations, Webster was able to show that words of similar meaning, but apparently different form, were related. As it happens, he was generally comparing languages that really are related, and his conclusions were often right; his method, however, was fundamentally wrong, for it did not allow him to exclude any accidental similarities.

The next stage in Webster's analysis was altogether more dubious. Here, he sought to show the connection between words of similar form, but of manifestly different meaning. Webster knew, because the Bible told him, that all languages were related, and that they had developed over the course of a few thousand years from the simple language given by God to Adam. During that time, the form of words could change (which we were considering above), but so also could the meaning of words. So, when Webster found what appeared to be the same word in two different languages, but with different meanings, or words formed from the same or cognate articulations, even in the same language, he looked for a "primary sense" of the word in the parent language, from which those different words and meanings might have been derived. This is the most characteristic part of Webster's etymology, and the most unreliable:

CHANGE OF SIGNIFICATION

Another cause of obscurity in the affinity of languages, and one that seems to have been mostly overlooked, is, the change of the primary sense of the radical verb. In most cases, this change consists of a slight deflection, or difference of application, which has obtained among different families of the same stock. In some cases, the literal sense is lost or obscured, and the figurative only is retained. The first object, in such cases, is to find the primary or literal sense, from which the various particular applications may be easily deduced. Thus, we find in Latin, *libeo, libet*, or *lubeo, lubet*, is rendered, to please, to like; *lubens*, willing, glad, cheerful, pleased; *libenter, lubenter*, willingly, gladly, readily. What is the primary sense, the visible or physical action, from which the idea of *willing* is taken? I find, either by knowing the radical sense of *willing, ready*, in other cases, or by the predominant sense of the elements *lb*, as in Lat. *labor*, to slide, *liber*, free, &c. that the primary sense is to move, incline or advance towards an object, and hence the sense of willing, ready, prompt. Now this Latin word is the English *love*, German *lieben, liebe*. "Lubet me ire." I *love* to go; I am inclined to go; I go with cheerfulness; but the affinity between *love* and *lubeo* has been obscured by a slight difference of application among the Romans and the Teutonic nations....

We find by the Saxon, that the English *reck*, to care, and *reckon*, and the Latin *rego*, to rule, are all the same word, varied in orthography and application. To find the primary sense of *reck*, to care, we are then to examine the various derivative senses. And we need go no farther than to the Latin *rectus* and the English *right*, the sense of which is *straight*, for this sense is derived from *straining, stretching. Care* then is a *straining of the mind*, a stretching towards an object, coinciding with the primary sense of *attention*. The primary sense of *reckon* is to strain out sounds, to speak, tell, relate; a sense now disused.

The Saxon *carc*, care, *cærcian*, to care, to cark, is connected in origin with the Latin *carcer*, a prison; both from the sense of straining, whence holding or restraint.

For Webster, the simple language of paradise was made up of these "primary senses," each associated with a primitive root. To develop that simple language into a more complex one, words had to be applied in new senses; but the new senses would be connected in some way, perhaps by way of abstraction or metaphor, with the primary senses. Because all languages had descended from a single parent over a relatively short time span, it was legitimate for Webster to seek the primary meaning of *lubens* by considering the meaning of *liber, labor* and

love; all those words had the same radical letters, *Lb*, or their cognates, and it was therefore probable that they were all related.

Webster's principles, and in particular the identification of cognate letters, are further explained in the Introduction:

ETYMOLOGY

The governing principles of etymology are, *first*, the identity of radical letters, or a coincidence of cognates, in different languages; no affinity being admissible, except among words whose primary consonants are articulations of the same organs, as B,F,M,P,V and W; or as D,T,Th and S; or as G, C hard, K and Q; R,L and D. Some exceptions to this rule must be admitted, but not without collateral evidence of the change, or some evidence that is too clear to be reasonably rejected.

Second. Words in different languages are not to be considered as proceeding from the same radix, unless they have the same signification, or one closely allied to it, or naturally deducible from it. And on this point, much knowledge of the primary sense of words, and of the manner in which collateral senses have sprung from one radical idea, is necessary to secure the inquirer from mistakes. A competent knowledge of this branch of etymology cannot be obtained from any one, or from two or three languages. It is almost literally true, that in examining more than twenty languages, I have found each language to throw some light on *every other*.

That the reader may have more clear and distinct ideas of what is intended by *commutable letters*, and the principles by which etymological deductions are to be regulated, it may be remarked that *commutable* or *interchangeable* letters are letters of the *same organs*; that is, letters or articulations formed by the same parts of the mouth. Thus *b,m* and *p*, are formed immediately by the lips, the position of which is slightly varied to make the distinction between these letters. *F* and *v* are formed by the lips, but with the aid of the upper teeth. Now the difference of the jointings of the organs to utter these letters is so small, that it is easy for men in utterance to slide from one form into another....

Letters formed by different organs are not commutable; hence we are not to admit a radical word beginning or ending with *b,f* or *v*, to be the same as a word beginning or ending with *g,d,t,r* or *s*; nor a word whose radical letters are *m,n*, to be the same as one whose elements are *r,d,* or *s,t....*

We have seen cognate radical letters identified in Whiter, so we know that this was not something that Webster worked out for himself, but we can take it back further. In the Notes to his *Dissertations* published in 1789, he was already contemplating the origin of the "Japhetic" languages, and he quoted a passage from "Rowland's Mona Antiquitata Restaurata, p. 261":

It is to be observed, that letters of one and the same organ are of common use in the pronunciation of words of different languages — as for example, *M, B, V, F, P*, are labials: *T, D, S*, are dentals: *G, Ch, H, K, C*, are gutturals — and therefore if the Hebrew word or sound begins with, or is made of, any one of the labials, any of the rest of the same organ will answer it in the derivative languages.... I shall only exemplify in the letters *M, B*, and *V*, which are of one organ, that is, are formed by one instrument, the lip; and therefore are promiscuously used the one for the other, in pronouncing words of one language in another.

The *Synopsis* has never been published. What is usually described as "the manuscript" is in the New York Public Library, but it is not a coherent manuscript of the whole thing in any final form. There are dozens of thin notebooks (each made from about six to ten sheets of paper, stitched down the centre and folded in half) and they contain parts of the work at various stages of development. The latest are parts of a fair copy written out by Webster's son William, who had not learned foreign alphabets other than Greek, and left gaps for Webster to insert words in Hebrew, Arabic and Ethiopic. Some of those gaps have been filled by Webster; others are still empty. Other parts of the manuscript say on them that they have been revised, but what is there is the old version, not the revised one. In one case, there are two versions of the same section, but neither, I think, would have been the final version. From these various parts of the *Synopsis,* we can see what Webster was doing as he went round and round in his circular table.

First, he selected the root he was going to investigate. Early on, roots were identified by sets of two consonants with a vowel between — for example ,"Root cas, caz, gas." Later, this system was abandoned and each root was assigned to a particular "Class." The class identifiers mostly consisted of just two consonants — for example, "Bd." "Class Bd" contains all words having roots of the form "b... d," with any vowel sound between the consonants, but it is much larger than that, because either the *b* or the *d*, or both, may be replaced by any cognate letter. Thus the words *fade* and *beat* are both in Class Bd, the letter *b* in one, and *d* in

the other, being represented by their cognates *f* and *t*. *Speed* is in the same class, the *s* being a casual addition, and the *b* being converted into *p*. *Feather* (or, as Webster preferred, *fether*) is also in Class Bd, though it contains neither a *b* nor a *d* because both the letters of the root are cognates. Similarly, *pack* and *pick* are both in Class Bg.

Having chosen a class, Webster went through the dictionaries of all the "Shemitic" languages, listing all the words that fell within that class, with their meanings in English. He considered those languages to be sufficiently similar to be disposed of as a group, and he dealt with them first because he thought that they were more nearly descended from the original parent language. To each set of corresponding Shemitic words (a set being the same word in several languages), Webster assigned a number. The members of Class Br, for example, are assigned numbers from 1 to 79. He then looked for connections between the meanings under one number and the meanings under another, and where he fancied that he could see such a connection, he cross-referenced them. A group of such numbers might represent a primary meaning associated with the root in the parent language, and by looking for some common element in the different but related meanings, Webster tried to work out what those primary meanings were.

He then passed to a dictionary of one of the "Japhetic" languages, first the Celtic, and then the Teutonic, and wrote down all the words in the class under investigation, with their meanings in English (unless, of course, the language was English). Then, he traced the affinities that he saw between the meanings of words in that Japhetic language and the meanings of words in the bundle of Shemitic languages of the same Class. Wherever he saw a relationship in meaning, he put the number or numbers that he had assigned to words in the Shemitic list, opposite the word in the Japhetic language. In Hebrew, *brud* means *spotted*; he connected it with the Latin *pardus*, English *pard* or *leopard*, an animal which is unquestionably spotted. In Irish, *bradan* means *salmon*, and salmon are spotted too.

For each class, class after class for ten years, he made lists of words in Shemitic languages, and then separate lists of words in each of his

Japhetic languages, Irish, Saxon, English, German, Dutch, Swedish, Danish, Greek, Latin, Italian, Spanish, French, Persian and Russian, with their meanings, and he traced their supposed affinities with words in the Shemitic languages.

Webster wanted the completed *Synopsis* to be an Appendix to the dictionary, and in a sense that is what it is. The *American Dictionary* as published in 1828 has two quarto volumes, but they are part of a three-volume work. The third volume is the one containing the *Synopsis*, and it is missing from every set because it was never printed. The Introduction at the beginning of the dictionary is described on the title page as "An Introductory Dissertation on the Origin, History and Connection of the Languages of Western Asia and of Europe." It describes the background and methods of Webster's etymological researches (some of which we have looked at above); it gives samples from the *Synopsis*, and it summarises the conclusions Webster had reached. In the dictionary itself, many of the etymologies are based on the supposed affinities between Japhetic and Shemitic words that Webster had identified in the *Synopsis*. Often, there are direct references to the *Synopsis* in the dictionary, identifying the classes to which the words belong, and the numbers that Webster had allocated to the related Shemitic words. There are hundreds of those references scattered through the dictionary, some with long explanations of primary meanings. A simple example is the etymology given for the word *fail*:

FAIL, v.i. [Fr. *faillir*; W. *faelu*, or *pallu* and *aballu*; Scot. *failye*; It. *fallire*; Sp. *falir*, *faltar*; Port. *falhar*; L. *fallo*; Ir. *feallam*; Gr. φηλεω, φηλοω, whence σφαλλω; D. *feilen*, *faalen*; G. *fehlen*; Sw. *fela*; Dan. *fejler*; Arm. *fallaat*, *fellel*, whence *falloni*, wickedness, Eng. *felony*. It seems to be allied to *fall*, *fallow*, *pale*, and many other words. See Class Bl. No. 6. 7. 8. 13. 18. 21. 28.]

Much of that is transcribed from the entry for *fail* in the English section of Class Bl of the *Synopsis*, where the manuscript shows a progressive erosion of certainty. Where Webster had originally written "It is," he crossed it out and put "It seems to be." Similarly, in the sentence "fail and fall are the same word differently applied ," he changed "are" to "may be." In the Shemitic section, we find that these words derive from a

No 6.

Heb. בָּלָה *bhalah* to grow old, to waste away or be consumed; to wear out with age. probably from ~~rubbing, wearing, shipping~~ No. 8. o

Ch. Syr. Sam. id. Syr. also to frighten, confound, throw into consternation. No 1. o pine, languish, &c Par.

Ar. To be foolish, stupid, sottish, weak in mind, timid, heedless, negligent. No 20. 40. 53. 18.

w. Eng. *fool, fail.* Gr. παλαιος old, Fr. *vieil.* Eng. to wilt. ~~Texas~~ No 11. 13. 15

Ch. בָּלָא *bala,* & בְּלָא ~~....~~ a wood. G. *wald.* Saxon *weald* a wold. But this is probably from another root, coinciding with Eng. *wold* as denoting complication, especially the sense of a wood or grove. No 46. 51. 47.

Fail. Fr. *feuiller,* sat *fallo.* It. *allire,* Sp. *faltar,* whence Eng. *falter.* Ir. *feallam,* Gr. φηλεω, φηλοω, whence σφαλλω, D. *feilen, faalen.* G. *fehlen.* Sw. *fylla.* Arm. *fall* weak; *fallaat* to weaken; W. *pill,* a ball, defect, fault; *pallu* to fail. Arm. *falloni,* wickedness, a criminal action, Eng. *felony, villany;* Dan. *fejler,* to fail, false, false; *falmer,* to fail or fade. No 7. 13. 91. 90. It is allied to *fall, foil, bulk.* Indeed, *fail* & *fall* are the same word differently applied & in Sw. the same word is used for both. ~~falta to fall off~~ It is also allied to the words *pale* and *pallco* Eng. as uncertain, *palcuo fallow.* In *beala* to die & in Ar. to grow old, &c. &c.

FAIL, *v. i.* [Fr. *faillir;* W. *faelu,* or *pallu* and *aballu;* Scot. *failye;* It. *fallire;* Sp. *falir, faltar;* Port. *falhar;* L. *fallo;* Ir. *feallam;* Gr. φηλεω, φηλοω, whence σφαλλω; D. *feilen, faalen;* G. *fehlen;* Sw. *fela;* Dan. *fejler;* Arm. *fallaat, fellel,* whence *falloni,* wickedness, Eng. *felony.* It seems to be allied to *fall, fallow, pale,* and many other words. See Class Bl. No. 6. 7. 8. 13. 18. 21. 28.]

Above: Handwritten entries for Class B1, which includes the word *fail,* from the Shemitic (*top*) and English sections of the *Synopsis.* Noah Webster Papers, Manuscripts and Archives Division, New York Public Library, Astor Lenox and Tilden Foundations. *Left:* The etymology of *fail* as published in the 1828 *American Dictionary.*

root, the primary meaning of which has something to do with decay, particularly the sort of decay that accompanies senility — as we become old and *foolish*, we tend to *fall* because our senses *fail*, our memory becomes *faulty* and our steps *falter*. *Felony* and *villany*[23] are moral *failings* (and not particularly associated with old age). All these words are related to the French *vieille*, since *f* and *v* are cognates.

In the final paragraph of the Introduction, Webster explained why references to the *Synopsis* were to be found throughout the *American Dictionary*:

Under the head of etymology, in hooks, [i.e. parentheses] the reader will observe references to another work, for a more full explanation or view of the affinities of the words under which these references occur. These are references to a Synopsis of the principal uncompounded words in twenty languages; a work that is not published, and it is uncertain whether it will ever be published. But if it should be, these references will be useful to the philologist, and I thought it expedient to insert them.

Writers well-disposed toward Webster have given him credit for the fact that "he was right more times in his etymologies than he was wrong,"[24] and that "he was shrewd enough to notice the relationship between Greek, Latin and the Teutonic languages before it was generally recognized."[25] Such kindly remarks will not stand up to critical scrutiny. Some of Webster's observations on "cognate articulations" were sound, but they were not original. Many of the words he believed to be related really were related, but his analysis is devalued because his faulty method led him to associate them with so many words with which they were *not* related. Similarly, "the relationship between Greek, Latin and the Teutonic languages" was not something that Webster "noticed"; it had been demonstrated long before, and by writers when Webster had himself quoted in

Notes, Historical and Critical. His acceptance that those languages were related cannot even be regarded as praiseworthy, when it forms part of a biblical generalization that all languages are derived from that given by God to Adam, and when it stands beside assertions that the Basque is brother to the Gaelic, and that there is a striking resemblance between Arabic and Welsh.

Sir James Murray, editor-in-chief of the *New English Dictionary* (now the O.E.D.), said of Webster that "he had the notion that derivations can be elaborated from one's own consciousness … and he included in his work so-called 'etymologies' of this sort."[26] Friend thought that unjust, because Webster did follow a system and did offer his own kind of evidence. I think it not unjust, if one is considering that part of the sytem where Webster guessed at the "primary senses" of roots in the parent Chaldee by looking for a common thread between the widely different meanings of words of the same "class" in various languages. Even Friend conceded that Webster's "assumption of basic identity between words that show only some likeness of consonantal structure,… makes virtually all his original etymological work no more than a curio testifying to the provincial backwardness of American linguistic scholarship at the time."[27]

The *Synopsis* was Webster's major piece of linguistic research. To the end of his life he believed that its value would one day be recognised, and that it would bring him lasting fame. It is a curious irony that things turned out just the other way around. The *Synopsis*, much of which really was original, disappeared into well-merited oblivion. The *American Dictionary*, which to a large extent was a compilation of other men's materials, was the ancestor of the great family of dictionaries that has made the name "Webster" into a household word.

13. *An American Dictionary of the English Language, 1828*

Including the ten years spent on the *Synopsis*, the *American Dictionary* took up most of Webster's time from 1805 to 1825. In England, two more notable lexicographers came before the public during this period: Henry Todd and Charles Richardson.

Archdeacon Todd revised Johnson's dictionary. The result was published in three, four, or five quarto volumes in 1818. If you find a copy in five volumes, you can be pretty sure that it was made by binding the eleven parts that had been issued over the previous three and a half years. Part XI furnished five title pages. Sets that were not made up from parts have fewer volumes. Todd was an antiquarian — at one time he was the archbishop of Canterbury's librarian at Lambeth Palace — and his additions to the word list tended to be older words than Johnson's, rather than newer ones. He was also a scrupulous editor, indicating by a mark in the text wherever he had added an entry of his own or made a change to Johnson's entry. One word that he added was *sutile*, from the Latin *sutilis*, meaning "done by stitching." It was the sort of classical word that Johnson liked, and it is surprising that he did not include it in the dictionary himself, because it was a word that he used. The circumstances afforded Boswell a joke at the expense of Hester Thrale. In a letter to Mrs. Thrale, Johnson had referred to a certain Mrs. Knowles, "the ingenious Quaker lady," and the needlework for which she was renowned. He described her embroidery as "sutile pictures." When Mrs. Thrale printed the letter, she mistook Johnson's long-*s* for an *f*.

In another addition, Todd retold the story of poor Ash's mistake over *curmudgeon*:

It is a vitious manner of pronouncing *coeur mechant*, Fr., Dr. Johnson says, which he received from an unknown correspondent.... Dr. Ash has transferred this into his vocabulary, as if "an unknown correspondent" was the etymology; distinguishing *coeur* by the interpretation of *unknown*, and *mechant* by that of correspondent; which will always excite both in foreigners and natives a harmless smile! But, to be serious, I doubt the etymology given by Dr. Johnson's correspondent....

An abridged version of Todd's Johnson, corresponding to Johnson's own "abstract" octavo edition, was prepared by Alexander Chalmers, and appeared in 1820.

Our second Englishman from this period is Charles Richardson, who might be thought not to belong here, because his eccentric masterpiece, *A New Dictionary of the English Language,* was not published as a separate dictionary until 1836-1837. Most of the *New Dictionary*, however, had earlier appeared in the "Miscellaneous and Lexicographical" section of the *Encyclopædia Metropolitana*. Richardson's is quite unlike any other English dictionary, then or since. Where a series of words have a regular and obvious family relationship — such as *animadvert, animadversal, animadversion, animadversive,* and *animadvertor* — it does not offer separate definitions. To do so would be quite unnecessary for anyone who is sufficiently familiar with the language to be using the dictionary at all. Instead, each such set of words is bracketed together, given some questionable etymology and (sometimes) a rather rudimentary definition. There then follows a huge helping of illustrative quotations in chronological order. In both definition and etymology, Richardson was at a disadvantage

because he was a disciple of Horne Tooke. He explained in his Preface:

The great first principle upon which I have proceeded in the department of the Dictionary which embraces explanation, is that so clearly evolved and so incontrovertibly demonstrated in the 'Diversions of Purley'; namely, that a word has one meaning, and one only; that from it all usages must spring and be derived; and that in the etymology of each word must be found this single intrinsic meaning, and the cause of the application of those usages.

In the matter of etymology, Richardson was even more extreme than Tooke, believing that each individual letter of the alphabet "was the sign of a separate distinct meaning; it was in fact the sign of a word, previously familiar in speech."[1] He asked himself whether etymology would enable him to discover, in any and what languages, words corresponding to the sounds of individual letters. He answered himself:

I think it possible,
   1. To present words, — not from one language only — corresponding to the simple sounds of every consonant letter.
   2. To shew, that these words, used in the position of prefixes and suffixes, retain the meaning which they possess when used alone.
   3. To shew, that these letters or literal words, interposed among other letters, do (in the instances produced) still manifestly retain the same meaning; and I may then assume the courage to affirm it to be an inference of sound reason that, though cases of interposed letters may be rapidly collected, in which it will be vain to attempt an explanation, yet that these letters, these literal roots, were interposed in their original meaning, or else by analogy, from other words that had been previously so constructed.

We shall not attempt to follow Richardson in the pursuit of single-letter roots. Indeed, he himself did not follow them very far. In the body of the dictionary, most of the etymology is no more than the identification of obviously related words in cognate languages, with a certain amount of Tookean nonsense thrown in from time to time. Richardson's dictionary, however, was greatly admired by Murray for the rich luxuriance of its quotations:

Richardson started on a new track altogether. Observing how much light was shed on the meaning of words by Johnson's quotations, he was impressed with the notion that, in a dictionary, definitions are unnecessary, that quotations alone are sufficient; and he proceeded to carry this into effect by making a dictionary without definitions or explanations of meaning, or at least with the merest rudiments of them, but illustrating each group of words by a large series of quotations. In the collection of these, he displayed immense research....[2]

It was a source of regret to Murray that his *New English Dictionary* (now the O.E.D.) did not have room for quotations anything like as long as Richardson's. As Murray went on to point out, however, Richardson's method does not produce a practical dictionary:

Quotations *will* tell the full meaning of a word, *if one has enough of them*; but it takes a great many to be enough, and it takes a reader a long time to read and weigh all the quotations, and to deduce from them the meanings which might be put before him in a line or two.

Richardson's Dictionary, therefore, is a good book to browse in, but it is not a handy reference work.

In America, one further dictionary appeared that we must notice, John Pickering's *Vocabulary, or Collection of Words and Phrases which have been Supposed to be Peculiar to the United States*, published in 1816. The Preface asserted that "in this country, as in England, we have thirsty reformers and presumptuous sciolists, who would unsettle the whole of our admirable language for the purpose of making it conform to their whimsical notions of propriety." Webster had defined *sciolist* in the *Compendious Dictionary* as "a mere smatterer in any science," and he was in no doubt that he was the American sciolist referred to. What made it even more upsetting was that John Pickering was the son of Webster's old friend Col. Timothy Pickering, and had learned from the copy of the *Grammatical Institute* that his father had sat up all night reading in camp, back in October 1783. He was perhaps rather irritated when Webster later changed his mind and taught that much in that book was wrong. Webster was so nettled by Pickering's *Vocabulary* that he wrote and published a long letter in reply to it, which affords a nice example of his directing at someone else a criticism that with greater justification might have been applied to himself:

The man who undertakes to censure others for the use of certain words and to decide what is or is not correct in language seems to arrogate to himself a dictatorial authority, the legitimacy of which will always be denied.[3]

In his letter to John West in August 1805 Webster wrote that he was "compiling a large work, which is intended as a substitute for Johnson's folio and quarto." For the next twenty years, his aim remained constant. Just as his spelling book had been intended to replace Dilworth, and the *Compendious Dictionary* to replace Entick, Webster's "large work" would replace Johnson. The title showed this: It was Johnson's title, *A Dictionary of the English Language*, with the word *American* added. In content, Dilworth's spelling book had provided the basis for Part I of the *Grammatical Institute* and Entick's dictionary for the *Compendious*; in the same way, the *American Dictionary* would be built on foundations provided by Johnson. And, just as Webster had criticized Dilworth in the Preface to the spelling book, he attacked Johnson in the Introduction to the *American Dictionary*:

> Of Johnson's Dictionary, and of the manner
> in which the following work is executed.

Dr. Johnson was one of the greatest men that the English nation has ever produced; and when the exhibition of truth depended on his own gigantic powers of intellect, he seldom erred. But in the compilation of his dictionary, he manifested a great defect of research, by means of which he often fell into mistakes; and no errors are so dangerous as those of great men. The authority created by the general excellence of their works gives a sanction to their very mistakes, and represses that spirit of inquiry which would investigate the truth, and subvert the errors of inferior men. It seems to be owing to this cause chiefly that the most obvious mistakes of Johnson's Dictionary have remained to this day uncorrected, and still continue to disfigure the improved editions of the work recently published.

In like manner, the opinions of this author, when wrong, have a weight of authority that renders them extremely mischievous.... And hence, whenever a proposition is made to correct the orthography of our language, it is instantly repelled with the opinion and *ipse dixit* of Johnson. Thus while the nations on the European continent have purified their languages and reduced the orthography to a good degree of regularity, our enemies of reform contend most strenuously for retaining the anomalies of the language, even to the very rags and tatters of barbarism. But what is more extraordinary, the very persons who thus struggle against the smallest improvement of the *orthography* are the most ready to innovate in the *pronunciation*, and will, at any time, adopt a change that fashion may introduce, though it may infringe the regularity of the language, multiply anomalies, and increase the difficulty of learning it. Nay, they will not only innovate themselves, but will use their influence to propagate the change, by deriding those who resist it, and who strive to retain the resemblance between the written word and the spoken language.

A considerable part of Johnson's Dictionary is however well executed; and when his definitions are correct and his arrangement judicious, it seems to be expedient to follow him. It would be mere affectation or folly to alter what cannot be improved.

The principal faults in Johnson's Dictionary are

1. The want of a great number of well authorized words belonging to the language. This defect has been in part supplied by Mason and Todd; but their supplemental list is still imperfect even in common words, and still more defective from the omission of terms of science.

2. Another great fault, that remains uncorrected, is the manner of noting the accented syllable; the accent being laid uniformly on the vowel, whether it closes the syllable or not. Thus the accent is laid on the *e* in *te'nant* as well as in *te'acher*, and the inquirer cannot know from the accent whether the vowel is long or short. It is surprising that such a notation should still be retained in that work.

3. It is considered as a material fault, that in some classes of words, Johnson's orthography is either not correct upon principle or not uniform in the class. Thus he writes *heedlessly*, with *ss*, but *carelessly*, with one *s*; *defence*, with *c*, but *defensible*, *defensive*, with *s*; *rigour*, *inferiour*, with *u*, but *rigorous*, *inferiority*, without it; *publick*, *authentick*, with *k*, but *publication*, *authenticate*, without it; and so of many other words of the same classes.

4. The omission of the participles or most of them, is no small defect, as many of them by use have become proper adjectives, and require distinct definitions. The additions of this kind in this work are very numerous. It is also useful both to natives and foreigners, to be able, by opening a dictionary, to know when the final consonant of a verb is doubled in the participle.

5. The want of due discrimination in the definitions of words that are nearly synonymous, or sometimes really synonymous, at other times not, is a fault in all the dictionaries of our language, which I have seen......

6. There are in Johnson's Dictionary, some palpable mistakes in orthography, such as *comptroller*, *bridegroom*, *redoubt*, and some others, there being no such legitimate words in the language. In other instances, the author mistook the true origin of words, and has erred in the orthography, as in *chymistry* and *diocess*.

7. The mistakes in etymology are numerous; and the whole scheme of deducing words from their originals is extremely imperfect.

8. The manner of defining words in Johnson, as in all other dictionaries, is susceptible of improvement. In a great part of the more important words, and particularly verbs, lexicographers, either from

negligence or want of knowledge, have inverted the true order, or have disregarded all order in the definitions. There is a primary sense of every word, from which all the other have proceeded; and whenever this can be discovered, this sense should stand first in order. Thus the primary sense of *make* is to *force* or *compel*; but this in Johnson's Dictionary is the *fifteenth* definition....

9. One of the most objectionable parts of Johnson's Dictionary, in my opinion, is the great number of passages cited from authors, to exemplify his definitions. Most English words are so familiarly and perfectly understood, and the sense of them so little liable to be called in question, that they may be safely left to rest on the authority of the lexicographer, without examples. Who needs extracts from three authors, Knolles, Milton and Berkeley, to prove or illustrate the literal meaning of *hand*? Who needs extracts from Shakspeare, Bacon, South and Dryden, to prove *hammer* to be a legitimate English word, and to signify an instrument for driving nails? So under *household,* we find seven passages and nearly thirty lines employed to exemplify the plain interpretation, *a family living together.*

In most cases, one example is sufficient to illustrate the meaning of a word; and this is not absolutely necessary, except in cases where the signification is a deviation from the plain literal sense, a particular application of the term; or in a case, where the sense of the word may be doubtful, and of questionable authority. Numerous citations serve to swell the size of a Dictionary, without any adequate advantage. But this is not the only objection to Johnson's exemplifications. Many of the passages are taken from authors now little read, or not at all; whose style is now antiquated, and by no means furnishing proper models for students of the present age.

In the execution of this work, I have pursued a course somewhat different; not however without fortifying my own opinion with that of other gentlemen, in whose judgment I have confidence. In many cases, where the sense of a word is plain and indisputable, I have omitted to cite any authority. I have done the same in many instances, where the sense of a word is wholly obsolete, and the definition useful only to the antiquary. In some instances, definitions are given without authority, merely because I had neglected to note the author, or had lost the reference. In such cases, I must stand responsible for the correctness of the definition. In all such cases, however, I have endeavored to be faithful to the duty of a lexicographer; and if in any instance, a mistake has escaped me, I shall be happy to have it suggested, that it may be corrected.

In general, I have illustrated the significations of words, and proved them to be legitimate, by a short passage from some respectable author, often abridged from the whole passage cited by Johnson. In many cases, I have given brief sentences of my

own; using the phrases or sentences in which the word most frequently occurs, and often presenting some important maxim or sentiment in religion, morality, law or civil policy. Under words which occur in the scriptures, I have often cited passages from our common version, not only to illustrate the scriptural or theological sense, but even the ordinary significations of the words. These passages are short, plain, appropriate, and familiar to most readers. In a few cases, where the sense of a word is disputed, I have departed from the general plan, and cited a number of authorities.

In the admission of words of recent origin, into a Dictionary, a lexicographer has to encounter many difficulties; as it is not easy, in all cases, to determine whether a word is so far authorized as to be considered legitimate. Some writers indulge a licentiousness in coining words, which good sense would wish to repress. At the same time, it would not be judicious to reject all new terms; as these are often necessary to express new ideas; and the progress of improvement in arts and science would be retarded, by denying a place in dictionaries, to terms given to things newly discovered. But the lexicographer is not answerable for the bad use of the privilege of coining new words. It seems to be his duty to insert and explain all words which are used by respectable writers or speakers, whether the words are destined to be received into general and permanent use or not. The future use must depend on public taste or the utitlity of the words; circumstances which are not within the lexicographer's control.

Lexicographers are sometimes censured for inserting in their vocabularies, vulgar words, and terms of art known only to particular artisans. That this practice may be carried too far, is admitted; but it is to be remarked that, in general, vulgar words are the oldest and best authorized words in language; and their use is as necessary to the classes of people who use them, as elegant words are to the statesman and the poet. It may be added that such words are often particularly useful to the lexicographer, in furnishing him with the primary sense, which is no where to be found, but in *popular use.* In this work, I have not gone quite so far as Johnson and Todd have done, in admitting vulgar words. Some of them are too low to deserve notice.

The catalogue of *obsolete* words in Johnson has been considerably augmented by Mason and Todd. I have, though, somewhat reluctantly, inserted nearly the whole catalogue, which, I presume, amounts to seven or eight, and perhaps, to ten thousand words. Most of these may be useful to the antiquary; but to the great mass of readers, they are useless....

In the Preface to the *American Dictionary,* Webster explained the patriotic motives that influenced him in his choice of quotations. Again, it was from Johnson that he started:

"The chief glory of a nation," says Dr. Johnson, "arises from its authors." With this opinion deeply impressed on my mind, I have the same ambition which actuated that great man when he expressed a wish to give celebrity to Bacon, to Hooker, to Milton and to Boyle.

I do not indeed expect to add celebrity to the names of *Franklin, Washington, Adams, Jay, Madison, Marshall, Ramsay, Dwight, Smith, Trumbull, Hamilton, Belknap, Ames, Mason, Kent, Hare, Silliman, Cleaveland, Walsh, Irving,* and many other Americans distinguished by their writings or by their science; but it is with pride and satisfaction, that I can place them as authorities, on the same page with those of *Boyle, Hooker, Milton, Dryden, Addison, Ray, Milner, Cowper, Davy, Thomson* and *Jameson....*

It is true, that many of our writers have neglected to cultivate taste, and the embellishments of style; but even these have written the language in its genuine *idiom*. In this respect, Franklin and Washington, whose language is their hereditary mother tongue, unsophisticated by modern grammar, present as pure models of genuine English, as Addison or Swift. But I may go farther, and affirm, with truth, that our country has produced some of the best models of composition. The style of President Smith; of the authors of the Federalist; of Mr. Ames; of Dr. Mason; of Mr. Harper; of Chancellor Kent; [the prose] of Mr. Barlow; of the legal decisions of the Supreme Court of the United States; of the reports of legal decisions in some of the particular states; and many other writings; in purity, in elegance and technical precision, is equaled only by that of the best British authors, and surpassed by that of no English compositions of a similar kind.

Webster, being an ardent patriot engaged in compiling an American dictionary, and not having literary tastes, might have set out methodically to replace Johnson's quotations with quotations from American authors. Happily he did not do so. The *American Dictionary* contains fewer quotations than Johnson, but many of those it does contain are taken from Johnson, and Webster often retained the names of Johnson's authors even when he had taken out the quotations. Occasionally he put in the names of American writers, and now and then an American quotation, but there are less of those than the Preface might lead one to expect. For the most part, the praise in the Preface for the style of American writers can be dismissed as harmless patriotic puff, but the dig at Barlow is rather unpleasant. Barlow's literary reputation was as a poet, and Webster was delivering a calculated insult by limiting his approval to Barlow's prose. He was quite right, of course. The *Columbiad*

is dreadful poetry, and it is also a sore trial to a lexicographer, because Barlow used nouns and adjectives as verbs with tasteless abandon. Webster, however, should have spared Barlow, in memory of their former friendship, and in acknowledgment of a more tangible debt; without Barlow's encouragement and financial support the *Grammatical Institute* might never have been published, and without the money from the spelling book Webster would certainly not have been able to compile the dictionary. Barlow himself was out of reach of Webster's ingratitude, however. He died in 1812.

Webster had often expressed his intention of cutting down Johnson's quotations. For example, in the subscription-paper of August 1807, he said that, "as Johnson's Quarto Dictionary is so large and expensive as to prevent its general use in this country, one great object, in the present work, will be to retrench or modify his exemplifications of definitions, in such a manner as to reduce it to about one half the size and cost of that work." He did indeed retrench Johnson's exemplifications, but he added so much elsewhere that the *American Dictionary* ended up being larger and more expensive than Johnson, even without the *Synopsis*. There is an advertisement (dated November 28, 1828) that is always included in the first English edition of the quarto dictionary, and is sometimes bound in at the beginning of Volume I of the 1828 American printing;[4] in it, Webster listed his additions to Johnson's vocabulary in five categories:

1. Words of common use, many of which are as important as any in the language. Of these, the following may be mentioned as examples. *Nouns*— grandjury, grandjuror, eulogist, consignee, consigner, mammoth, maltreatment, iceberg, parachute, malpractice, fracas, entailment, perfectibility, glacier, firewarden, safety-valve, savings-bank. *Adjectives*— gaseous, lithographic, peninsular, repealable, retaliatory, dyspeptic, missionary, nervine, meteoric, mineralogical, reimbursable. *Verbs*— to quarantine, revolutionize, retort (v.i.) electioneer, re-organize, oxydize, magnetize. Many hundred words of this kind, have been added.

2. Participles of verbs. Most of these have been omitted in the English dictionaries; and it is owing probably to this omission, that many participles have been mis-spelled by doubling the final consonant of the verb, in cases where the established rules of the language forbid such a change. In addition to this, words of this class, in numerous instances, lost all

reference to action and time, and express the *quali-ties* of objects. Being, in such cases, merely *adjectives* of a participial form, they often need a new defini-tion to explain their meaning.

3. Terms of frequent occurrence in historical works; especially those derived from proper names. Such are Shemitic, Punic, Augean, Augustan, Arun-delian (marbles,) Gregorian (year,) Parian (chroni-cle.) In defining such terms, the object or opinions in question are not merely referred to the person from which they derived their names, but are briefly described, in order the spare the general reader a ref-erence to Encyclopedias or other works, for the true meaning of such words.

4. Legal terms. A considerable number of these were inserted by Johnson in his dictionary. Others are here added, which appeared of equal or greater importance. In numerous instances, Johnson has mistaken the precise sense of legal terms, confound-ing house-breaking, for example, with burglary, theft with robbery, murder with the simple killing of a man unlawfully. In the present work, legal terms are defined, it is believed, with technical precision.

5. Terms in the Arts and Sciences. Of these, some thousands have been added to our language within the last fifty years, of which a small number only have as yet found their way into any work of this kind. An accurate definition of these terms, in ac-cordance with the advanced state of science at the present day, is now rendered important to all classes of readers, by the popular character given of late to the sciences, and the frequent occurrence of scientific terms and allusions in literary works. The exact number of these terms, now introduced for the first time into a work of this nature, is not known. It can-not, however, be much short of four thousand. Among them are some of the most common words in the language, such as oxyd, muriate, sulphate, sul-phuric, nitric, azote, phosphoresce, phosphorescent, planetarium, polarize, polarization, &c. Since the time of Johnson, a complete revolution has taken place in almost every branch of physical science. New departments have been created, new principles de-veloped, new modes of classification and description adopted. It is not surprising, therefore, that a great part of his definitions of terms in the Arts and Sci-ences are, at the present day, erroneous or defective. These definitions (as indeed almost every error in the work) stand without correction in the late edi-tion of his dictionary by Mr. Todd; who seems to have confined his labors to the insertion of new words, and the addition of etymologies from Horne Tooke. Hence we find that in that edition, the defini-tion of coral, as "a *plant* of a stony nature," of water, as "a very fluid *salt*," of fermentation, as "a motion which subtilizes the soft and *sulphureous* particles," of gas, as "spirit not capable of being coagulated," with hundreds of others founded on views of sci-ence long since exploded, are still retained in their original shape, without comment or correction....

Webster's Working Method

With the *Synopsis*, a substantial amount of the manuscript is available, and by studying it one can work out Webster's research technique. When we come to the dictionary, only small portions of manuscript survive, but we have the advantage of the printed work, which must be near enough identical to the final draft of the manuscript. The only bits of manuscript that I have examined are those in the Pierpont Morgan Library in New York. They are entirely in Webster's handwriting, in booklets like those of the *Synopsis*, each made from usually be-tween five and ten sheets of paper, folded in half and stitched. The Morgan Library has most of five of those booklets. The first, alphabeti-cally, is marked on the front "5 — Ad to Ad-monitory," but the last two half-sheets are miss-ing, and the last entry it contains is "Admission." The next one, marked "6 — Admortization to Affect," is also incomplete, missing the page be-tween "Advowson" and "Affability." The other booklets are marked as having originally con-tained "Bale to Bankruptcy," "Barter to Bavin," and "Broach to Brush." One can see that Web-ster always started composing (or transcribing) onto the inside right hand pages, leaving space for later additions or alterations on the facing left hand pages. The definitions are generally pretty close to those that appear in the dictio-nary, but these booklets are definitely not parts of the final version of the manuscript, since the corresponding sections of the *American Dictio-nary* contain additional details and meanings, and sometimes entire entries, that are not in this manuscript. We saw in the previous chap-ter that, "after writing through two letters of the alphabet," Webster laid aside his manu-scripts to concentrate on etymology. The Mor-gan Library booklets are, I think, parts of that first draft of A and B that was written before the *Synopsis*. They contain no references to the class-structure of the *Synopsis*, and they display a good deal of uncertainty about etymology. A superficial examination suggests that they could not pre-date the *Synopsis*, because they contain material that was added to Johnson's dictionary by Todd, and Todd's Johnson was not pub-lished until after Webster had finished work on the *Synopsis*. Sometimes Webster thought of Todd's words independently and defined them

himself, but more often he copied or adapted Todd's definition, and sometimes he also cited an authority given by Todd. In all those cases, however, one can see by a close inspection that the words taken from Todd are later additions to the manuscript, either squeezed between earlier entries on the right-hand pages, or put on the left. These manuscript booklets were written by Webster before he had access to Todd, and he added to them afterwards.

The definitions and their composition would seem to have given him little difficulty. We shall unravel his technique in a moment. Where he had serious problems (as his own account made clear) was in tracing the origins of words. He would put down a list of kindred words in various languages, with some speculation on roots and primary meanings. Later, he often changed his mind, crossed it all out, and wrote another chunk of speculative etymology on the blank left hand page. If he later changed his mind again, he would cross out what was on the left hand page, and stick a strip of paper over the crossed-out entry on the right, to provide space for another guess. I wanted to unstick those strips to see what was underneath, but did not feel able to do so under the watchful eye of Pierpont Morgan's librarian. In the booklet "Barter to Bavin," there is one section of right hand page which is three layers thick, with two strips of afterthought stuck over the original entry. This allowed for four attempts at an etymology for the word *bask* (three on the right, and one on the facing left hand page). The two visible guesses are completely different, and even the last of those was finally discarded. The only bit not crossed out says, "The origin of this word is not obvious." Ten years work on the *Synopsis* shed no further light on the etymology of *bask*, and the same statement appears in the dictionary. From a study of those bits of manuscript, it is at once plain why Webster had to leave the dictionary and embark on methodical research into the origin of words; the non-methodical approach took up too much time, and too much space in the manuscript. It is possible that it also took up too much space on the table. To gather definitions, Webster would read through a variety of reference books (mostly in English). To study etymology, he had to look up the same or similar words in dictionaries of twenty different languages. The table

probably did not have enough room for both sets of reference books. In theory, an understanding of the primary meanings of roots was supposed to throw light on the correct usage of English words in nineteenth century America, but in practice that seldom happened. Speculative etymology and definition turned out to be largely separate operations. It made sense for Webster to deal with them separately, and I am doing the same thing. Etymology was in the previous chapter; in this one, we are concerned with definitions and examples.

The pre-*Synopsis* part of the manuscript was written in New Haven, before Webster moved his family to Amherst, and it was no doubt written at the same circular table that he afterwards used for the *Synopsis*—"the large circular table which he had used for some years at New Haven." For writing definitions, the first book on the table would initially have been his 1799 Johnson, or at least the first of its two fat quarto volumes. At the end of the second volume, Mason's *Supplement* is bound in: *A Supplement to Johnson's English Dictionary*, "of which the palpable errors are attempted to be rectified and its material omissions supplied," by George Mason (1801) but the binder has clipped the edges of some of Webster's marginal notes, which shows the binding to be of later date.

Next to Johnson would have been the first volume (since Webster was starting at the beginning of the alphabet) of Dobson's Philadelphia reprint of the 3rd edition of the *Encyclopædia Britannica*. After those, I am not certain of the order of the books, but they included Bailey's and Ash's dictionaries, Thomas Martyn's *The Language of Botany*, William Nicholson's *Dictionary of Practical and Theoretical Chemistry*, Quincy's *Lexicon Physico-Medicum* and Kirwan's *Elements of Mineralogy*. References to all those books are to be found in the Morgan manuscript material.

Johnson provided the framework on which Webster built, both as to word-list and definitions. A few of Johnson's words are left out (not very many), but his definitions are often improved. Johnson's definitions tend to be rather skimpy, because he assumed that he had a literate readership, and because he relied on quotations to make meanings clear. Webster wanted to cut out most of the quotations, and he therefore

had to enlarge many of the definitions. He also added words to Johnson's list. Some of these were words suggested by Johnson's words (including, as he said in his classification, the participles of verbs), some came from other reference books, and some were words that Webster himself decided to add, without prompting from anyone. Johnson defined *adroit* as "Dexterous; active; skilful" and added a quotation from "*Jerv.Don Quix.*" Webster left out the quotation, but enlarged the definition: "Dextrous; skilful; active in the use of the hands, and *figuratively*, in the exercise of the mental faculties; ingenious; ready in invention and execution." Johnson's next word is *adroitness*; Webster would later slip *adroitly* in between (citing Chesterfield), but that word and the citation were from Todd. *Additionally* was a word he thought of for himself. Similarly, between *adulatory* and *adult*, Webster added *adulatress*—"A female that flatters with servility."

Johnson generally gave single names to identify his authorities, but those names were of two quite different types. Some were the authority for definitions that had been copied from other reference books, such as Harris (the *Lexicon Technicum*), Cowell (a law dictionary), Miller (gardening) or Quincy (medical). The abbreviation *Dict* generally meant Bailey.The other names were authorities for usage, being the authors of his quotations. There is no difficulty in knowing which are which, because the names identifying the sources of definitions follow the definitions, and the names of authors follow the quotations. Where Webster cut out Johnson's quotations, he nevertheless often kept in the names of Johnson's authorities, as well as furnishing authorities of his own. In Webster, therefore, a definition with no quotation is often followed by a name (sometimes by more than one), which may indicate any one of four different things. Many of them are easily identified, but there is nothing in the location to indicate whether such a name indicates (a) a reference book that provided Johnson's definition; (b) the source of Webster's definition; (c) the author of a quotation in Johnson, which Webster had taken out; or (d) the author of a passage that Webster knew, but did not put in.

Webster's next major source was the *Encyclopædia*, indicated by the contraction *Encyc*.

Here the problem was not lengthening, as with many of Johnson's definitions, but shortening. He had to distill a definition from a relatively long encyclopedia article. He would later become adept at extracting something useful from the first sentence or two, but at the beginning (at least with shorter articles) he was prepared to read the whole thing. Here is the *Encyclopedia* article on *adamites* (a word not in Johnson):[5]

ADAMITES, in ecclesiastical history, the name of a sect of ancient heretics, supposed to have been a branch of the Basilidians and Carpocratians.

Epiphranius tells us, that they were called Adamites from their pretending to be re-established in the state of innocence, and to be such as Adam was at the moment of his creation, whence they ought to imitate him in his nakedness. They detested marriage; maintaining that the conjugal union would never have taken place upon earth had sin been unknown.

This obscure and ridiculous sect did not at first last long; but it was revived with additional absurdities in the twelfth century, by one Tandamus, since known by the name of *Tanchelin*, who propagated his errors at Antwerp in the reign of the Emperor Henry V. He maintained that there ought to be no distinction between priests and laymen, and that fornication and adultery were meritorious actions. Tanchelin had a great number of followers, and was constantly attended by 3000 of these profligates in arms. His sect did not, however, continue long after his death: but another appeared under the name of *Turlupins*, in Savoy and Dauphiny, where they committed the most brutal actions in open day.

About the beginning of the fifteenth century, one Picard, a native of Flanders, spread these errors in Germany and Bohemia, particularly in the army of the famous Zisca, notwithstanding the severe discipline he maintained. Picard pretended that he was sent into the world as a new Adam, to re-establish the law of nature; and which, according to him, consisted in exposing every part of the body, and having all the women in common. This sect also found some partizans in Poland, Holland, and England: they assembled in the night; and it is asserted, that one of the fundamental maxims of their society was contained in the following verse:

> *Jura, perjura, secretum, prodere noli.*

Webster's manuscript has the following précis of that article:

Adamites, in ~~Eccles~~ Church history, a sect ~~who~~ of visionaries who pretended to establish a state of innocence, & like Adam ~~go~~ went naked. They abhorred marriage, holding it to be the effect of sin. Several attempts have been made to revive this sect — one as late as the 15th Century. *Encyc.*

Let us next dissect a manuscript entry that cites two authorities. Again, it is a word not included in Johnson:

Adstric'tion. *n.* [L. *adstrictio, asstrictio,* of *ad* & *stringo,* ~~*stringere,*~~ to strain or bind fast. ~~Eng. strong~~ See *Strict*] A binding fast; among physicians the rigidity of a part of the body, occasioning a retention of natural evacuations; costiveness; the styptic ~~quality~~ effects of medicines.

Encyc. Quincy

I have tried to lay out the entry more or less as it appears in the manuscript, save that the suggestion "See *Strict*" is actually written above, not after, the crossed out words "~~Eng. strong.~~" It is tempting to suggest that the word crossed out was *string* (which does come from the same root as the Latin *stringere,* to tighten), but I am pretty sure it was *strong.* The words "strain or" were added later, probably after the compilation of the *Synopsis;* a remarkable number of Webster's primary meanings in the *Synopsis* have to do with straining.

That definition can be broken down into three parts. The first, "A binding fast," is simply a translation of the Latin. The next part, "among physicians the rigidity of a part of the body," comes directly from the *Encyclopædia,* in which the entry is *"adstriction,* among physicians, a term used to denote the rigidity of any part." The remainder comes from Quincy, neatly blended with the *Encyclopædia* material in such a way as to eliminate the words "respective emissaries," which the reader might not have understood. This is Quincy's definition:

Adstrictio. Costiveness. It either expresses the styptic quality of medicines, or the retention of the natural evacuations by the rigidity of the respective emissaries.[6]

If we compare the manuscript entry with what appeared in the dictionary, we see only slight differences. Those differences, however, neatly demonstrate both that this was *not* the final manuscript, and that it *was* the basis of the later manuscript. The dictionary says this:

ADSTRIC'TION *n.* [L. *adstrictio, astrictio,* of *ad* and *stringo,* to *strain* or bind fast. See *Strict.*]
A binding fast. Among *physicians,* the rigidity of a part of the body, occasioning a retention of usual evacuations; costiveness; a closeness of the emunctories; also the styptic effects of medicines.

Encyc. Quincy.

The words "a closeness of the emunctories" came from Rees' *Cyclopædia,* which Webster usually acknowledged as *Cyc.* The fact that they were added later shows that the Morgan Library manuscript could not have been the final one.[7] An indication that this manuscript was used as the basis for the later one is the change of Quincy's words "the natural evacuations" into "usual evacuations," which was done by mistake. In the Morgan manuscript, the word *natural* is divided, with *nat-* at the end of one line, and *ural* at the beginning of the next. The word *usual* in the dictionary is a misreading of *ural,* which could only have happened in reading from a manuscript in which the word *natural* was so divided. The alteration made no significant difference to the sense, and the word *usual* remained in the dictionary until *adstriction* was redefined in the edition of 1864.

During the years that he worked on the dictionary, Webster acquired many more reference books, so that the range of citations in the dictionary is much wider than that in the Morgan manuscript. Sometimes, his later reading caused him to add to a definition that he had already written; an example we have just seen is the addition of "a closeness of the emunctories" to the definition of *adstriction.* Occasionally, the later book did not agree with the earlier, and Webster would find himself putting in two contradictory definitions of the same word. This happened in the definition of *aerometry.* The first definition would have been in the manuscript booklet "Admortization to Affect," but it was in the missing page, so we must reconstruct it.

Webster would have started from the Encyclopedia entry:

AEROMETRY, the science of measuring the air. It comprehends not only the doctrine of the air itself, considered as a fluid body; but also its pressure, elasticity, rarefaction, and condensation. But the term is at present not much in use, this branch of natural philosophy being more frequently called Pneumatics. See PNEUMATICS.

That would have given him a definition for the missing page of the Morgan manuscript:

Aerom'etry, *n.* The science of measuring the air, including the doctrine of its pressure, elasticity, rarefaction, and condensation. *Encyc.*

That is an example of standard Webster contraction — an editorial technique that requires

scarcely any knowledge or understanding of the subject-matter and that reduces a short paragraph into a single coherent sentence. It is done almost entirely by leaving words out, with the minimum amount of creative writing. In that example, Webster himself contributed only one word, "including" — a neat substitute for "It comprehends not only." In the *Encyclopædia*, the word *doctrine* referred to "the air," not to "pressure, elasticity etc.," but since the word is more or less meaningless in this context, the change made no difference.

Long after that was written, Webster added Andrew Ure's *Chemical Dictionary* to his table. This was definitely post-*Synopsis*, since Ure's book was not published until late in 1820. In it, Webster found the following entry:

AEROMETER. The name given by Dr. M.Hall to an ingenious instrument of his invention for making the necessary corrections in pneumatic experiments, to ascertain the mean bulk of the gases. It consists of a bulb of glass 4½ cubic inches capacity....

Ure went on to describe Dr. Hall's apparatus, and the way it worked. He cited as his authority an article in the *Journal of Science*. This gave Webster a new entry for the dictionary. Characteristically, he cited the *Journal of Science*, which he had not read, rather than Ure, which he had:

AEROM'ETER, *n*. ... An instrument for weighing air, or for ascertaining the mean bulk of gases.
Journ. of Science.

Again, the first part, "weighing air," is a translation, and the rest is a Webster contraction. That is straightforward enough, but Ure's information suggested to Webster that his original definition of *aerometry* was wrong. Rather than rewrite it, he added a correcting post-script:

AEROM'ETRY, *n*. [*as above*] The science of measuring the air, including the doctrine of its pressure, elasticity, rarefaction, and condensation.   *Encyc.*
    Rather, aerometry is the art or science of ascertaining the mean bulk of the gases.
Encyc. Ure.

Ure's *Chemical Dictionary* was only one of many reference books that Webster added to his table after the period of the Morgan manuscript. Most of them were specialist works, but one general encyclopedia joined Dobson's Britannica, Samuel Bradford's Philadelphia reprint

of Abraham Rees' *Cyclopædia* (1802–1820). Webster cited it as *Cyc*. Similarly, *Mar. Dict*. indicated either an edition of William Falconer's *Universal Dictionary of the Marine* or another marine dictionary closely based on Falconer. *Dict. of Nat. Hist* was (not surprisingly) *A Dictionary of Natural History*, from which Webster took many definitions with very little alteration.

Since the pre-*Synopsis* manuscript only got as far as *B*, we have to look at a later part of the *American Dictionary* to see how Webster's technique matured. A representative part will be found toward the middle of the alphabet. In the compilation of a long book, there is often manifest a variation in pace, somewhat like that in a long-distance running race. Early on, the compiler proceeds slowly and carefully, determined to be thorough and accurate. He soon realizes that at the rate he is going, his book will be far too long if it ever gets finished at all. He polishes up his technique and adopts a longer stride. Later, with the end of the race in sight and perhaps a deadline in mind, he may be seen to hurry. To be sure of finding Webster loping through the lexicon at a typically even pace, we must look at him at work on the letter *L*.

The letter L was chosen for study by two earlier wanderers in the Webster wilderness. The first was Joseph W. Reed, Jr., whose article "Noah Webster's Debt to Samuel Johnson" appeared in *American Speech* in 1962.[8] Reed counted 2,024 words and 4,505 meanings in *L*, out of approximately 70,000 words and perhaps 150,000 meanings in the whole of the *American Dictionary*. Of those 4,505 meanings, he found that the definitions of 1,481, or about one third, had their origin in Johnson. He classified derivation from Johnson in three degrees, which he called "transfer" (i.e., direct copying), "revision," and "influence." This is the passage which summed up his conclusions:

Webster copied 333 of Johnson's definitions word for word ... Of these, Johnson is cited as source for the definition in only sixteen instances. Webster made very slight alterations (no more than three words changed, transposed, omitted or added) in 987 definitions. These I noted as revisions. The narrowest interpretation of this category (in eighty six instances) involved only one word:
    Lace, n.3 *J*. A plaited string with which women
            fasten their clothes.
        W. A plaited string with which females
        fasten their clothes.

Webster used *female* for Johnson's *women* almost universally. The altered word makes no substantive change in definition, but must be considered a revision. Slightly more substantive revisions follow:

   *Lousy, adj.*1 J. Swarming with lice; overrun with
      lice.
      W. Swarming with lice; infested with
      lice.
   Lacerable, adj. J. Such as may be torn.
      W. That may be torn.

Of 987 revisions, Webster credits Johnson with the definition of eighteen.

I recorded 161 influenced definitions, a category difficult to delimit. Webster clearly used Johnson's definition as a starting point for such meanings, but added or qualified to such an extent that they cannot be considered revisions. Still, he retained words or phrases with a distinctly Johnsonian ring, such as:

   Lake, n.2 J. A middle colour, between ultrama-
        rine and vermilion, yet it is rather
        sweet than harsh. It is made of
        cochineal.
      W. A middle colour, between ultrama-
        rine and vermilion, made of
        cochineal.

Webster unquestionably wrote the definition with his Johnson at his elbow, but omitted so much that an exact degree of debt is difficult to establish.

I do not agree with Reed that the degree of Webster's debt to Johnson in that last definition is at all hard to establish. It is another standard Webster contraction. Indeed, it is a particularly nice example, since every word came directly from Johnson, with no words changed, added, or rearranged. All that Webster did to get his definition from Johnson's was to cross out a few words in the middle:

A middle colour, between ultramarine and vermil-ion, ~~yet it is rather sweet than harsh. It is~~ made of cochineal.

One of Johnson's most commonly quoted fits of classical whimsy is his definition of *net-work*: "Any thing reticulated or decussated, at equal distances, with interstices between the intersections." It was supported by quotations from Spenser, Addison, and Blackmore. Webster left out the quotations and rewrote the definition, though not without traces of the original, producing a much clearer description of something like a fishing net. What he lost in the process was the indication (provided in Johnson by Blackmore's quotation referring to "this curious and wonderful *net-work* of veins")

that the word may be used figuratively. This is Webster's definition:

NETWORK, *n.* A complication of threads, twine or cords united at certain distances, forming meshes, interstices or open spaces between the knots or intersections; reticulated or decussated work.
                             Addison.

Reed identifies only one of Webster's other reference books:

Webster's dependence on the phrasing of technical sources seems to have been at least as faithful as his dependence on Johnson. I have traced only one of these: *The Mariner's Dictionary* (cited by Webster as *Mar.Dict.*). In the *L*'s there are thirty-four new technical terms and twenty new technical meanings from the vocabulary of seamanship, most of which can be traced to *The Mariner's Dictionary; or, American Seaman's Vocabulary of Technical Terms, and Sea Phrases....*[9] The few omitted were for the most part specialized senses of other words having a more significant general meaning (e.g. *labor*). Quite a few of Webster's definitions (e.g. *leech-line*) are direct transfers from this source, and many more depend heavily on its phrasing as, for example:

Mar. Dict.   *Lateen sail,* a triangular sail, frequently used by xebecs, polacres, settees, and other vessels navigated in the Mediterranean Sea.
           Lateen yard, a long yard, used to extend the preceding sail upon it, slung about one-quarter from the lower end, which is brought down as [sic] the tack, while the upper end is raised in the air, in an angle of about 45 degrees.

Webster   *Lateen,* adj., A *lateen* sail is a triangular sail, extended by a *lateen* yard, which is slung about one quarter the distance from the lower end, which is brought down at the tack, while the other end is elevated at an angle of about 45 degrees; used in xebecs, polacres and setees, in the Mediterranean.
                             Mar. Dict.

Before I saw Reed's article I had supposed that Webster's *Mar. Dict.* was an edition of *An Universal Dictionary of the Marine* by William Falconer, author of *The Shipwreck, A Poem.* Many of Falconer's definitions appear virtually unaltered in the *American Dictionary.* Furthermore, Falconer's definition of *lateen-sail* includes the words "extended by a lateen yard," which appear in Webster's definition, but not in the above quotation from the *American*

Seaman's Vocabulary. The difference, however, is not material, and I rather like the idea that Moore copied from Falconer, the *American Seaman's Vocabulary* copied from Moore, and Webster copied from the *American Seaman's Vocabulary*.

For additions to Johnson's word-list of a general sort (rather than those to be found in specialist technical dictionaries and encyclopedias) two obvious sources come to mind. One is Mason's *Supplement*, which Webster certainly had, as it is now bound in at the back of his copy of Johnson. The other is Todd's edition of Johnson. Was Todd also on Webster's table? Todd's contribution to Johnson is easy to identify, because Todd put an asterisk by every word that he added. Webster was not impressed by Todd's additions. In December 1823 he wrote to Samuel Latham Mitchill in New York, reporting his progess (he had reached the letter *R*) and hoping for a contribution towards the expenses of his planned trip to England. "I sincerely wish that some persons of wealth would put about $2000 at hazard on this undertaking," he wrote; "If I succeed in selling the copy[right] I will repay the money...." This is what he said about Todd:

Todd's Edition of Johnson has supplied many words, but I am surprised to find that nine tenths of them are antiquated words of old writers now scarcely read at all — the improvements in definition are very few, while almost all the words introduced by the modern improvements in botany, geology, mineralogy & chemistry, are omitted.[10]

We have already seen how Todd's words were added to the Morgan manuscript, and we have seen the paragraph in the Introduction to the *American Dictionary* in which Webster admitted having "inserted nearly the whole catalogue" of words added by Mason and Todd, even though he thought most of them were useless. We have also seen Webster's complaint in the Advertisement that Johnson's definitions in the arts and sciences "stand without correction in the late edition of his dictionary by Mr. Todd; who seems to have confined his labors to the insertion of new words, and the addition of etymologies from Horne Tooke." That is not the only mention of Todd in the Advertisement:

The dictionary of Walker has been found by actual

enumeration, to contain, in round numbers, *thirty-eight* thousand words. Those of Johnson, Sheridan, Jones, and Perry, have not far from the same number. The American edition of Todd's Johnson contains *fifty-eight* thousand. In the work now submitted to the public, the number has been increased to *seventy* thousand.

All those references to Todd were in Webster's own words. Is it possible that when he wrote them, he had never so much as opened Todd's Johnson? That is what he later claimed. After the publication of the *American Dictionary*, he must have been accused of copying from Todd — which would have been a sensitive subject — and he denied it absolutely. Among the manuscript fragments in the New York Public Library, there is this signed statement in Webster's handwriting:

If it should be supposed that in compiling my American Dictionary, I borrowed from Todd's Johnson, let it be known that I have never seen that work, except on a bookseller's shelf & have never opened the volumes. I made some use of Chalmers' Abridgment, & have sometimes given credit for words to Todd instead of Chalmers....

July 1833   N.Webster

Here we have Webster in a position of some difficulty. If he had used Todd, his denial was simply untrue. If he had not used it, his implying that he had was dishonest. Furthermore, the denial was pointless. If it was wrong to copy from Todd's Johnson, it would have been equally wrong to copy from Chalmers' abridgment of Todd — and Webster could not deny that he had taken several thousand of Todd's words, since the dictionary itself said that he had done so.

One sentence in the Introduction to the *American Dictionary*, under "Orthography", might be taken to indicate that Webster had made a close examination of Todd. He says: "With like inconsistency Walker and Todd write *daub* with *u* and *bedawb* with *w*, deviating in this instance from Johnson...." In fact, this proves nothing except that Webster was using the 1799 edition of Johnson. Johnson himself had defined *bedawb* as "To dawb over ...," and then, in the letter *D*, used the spelling *daub*. Walker and Todd both copied the inconsistency from Johnson, and Chalmers copied it from Todd. The only dictionary in the whole series in which the mistake was corrected, the

word *bedaub* being defined as "to daub over," was the eighth edition of Johnson, the one that Webster used. Webster supposed that this was the authentic text of Johnson, and that Walker and Todd had changed it. This does not prove that he had looked at Todd, because he might have assumed (correctly) that Todd's spelling was the same as that in Chalmers.

There is one more piece of evidence. In Webster's public letter to John Pickering, he wrote, "You also frequently mention the insertion of words in the new edition of Johnson by the Reverend Mr. Todd. Of this edition I have seen but one number, and from that I judge that the editor will improve the vocabulary...."[11] That was written in December 1816. By then, the first seven parts of Todd's Johnson had been published in London, but they may not all have arrived in America. Webster had examined the first section, which goes as far as *blood-consuming*. He could not have formed his view of Todd from an examination of Chalmers' abridgment, because Chalmers was not published until 1820. So Webster's saying of Todd, "I have never seen that work, except on a bookseller's shelf & have never opened the volumes," was untrue, or was at best a careful truth—what he had seen was not the *whole* of Todd's Johnson, nor was it in the form of a *volume*, but some of it he had seen.

Nevertheless, a close examination of Webster's entries for the words in *L* that Todd had added to Johnson shows that probably Webster was *not* using Todd. He did include about 275 of Todd's words (though some of Webster's definitions came from elsewhere) but all that he took from Todd is to be found in Chalmers' abridgment. Furthermore, he did not often (at least in *L*) "give credit for words to Todd instead of Chalmers," even though he had no objection in principle to using the names of second-hand authorities. I only spotted one such reference to Todd, after the word *lum*.

Surprisingly, Webster gives Johnson as the authority for the word *lurdan*,[12] which is another of Todd's additions and is not in Johnson. That small mistake has rather startling implications. Let us consider how it could have happened. How can you tell, if your are using Chalmers, which words were added to Johnson by Todd? Chalmers does not mark them. If you have a copy of Todd's Johnson, you can look to

see whether a word is marked with an asterisk, but Webster did not have Todd's Johnson. Webster, therefore, could identify a word as being one of Todd's only by looking in Johnson, and finding that the word was not there. Webster's citing the authority of Johnson for his definition of *lurdan*, a word that is not in Johnson's Dictionary, shows that Webster took the word from Chalmers *without looking in Johnson*. This in turn suggests that, by the time he reached the letter *L*, he may have been using Chalmers as his primary source, rather than Johnson. That is by no means impossible. If Chalmers supplied all that Webster needed for *Todd's* words, the same was true of *Johnson's*. Indeed, Chalmers (or Johnson doing his own earlier abridgment) did much of Webster's weeding for him, taking out the quotations, but leaving in the names of the authors. Chalmers' abridgment, in fact, contained just the bits of Todd's Johnson that Webster wanted.

Since Webster certainly had Johnson's Dictionary available to him, it is generally not possible to determine whether he took Johnson's material directly from it or via Chalmers. At the beginning he would have had to use Johnson, but there are signs that he later transferred to Chalmers. A small example is in the entry for the verb *languish*, which Johnson illustrated with a quotation from Hosea: "The land shall mourn, and every one that dwelleth therein, shall *languish*... *Hosea*." Those are not exactly the words of the authorised version, but Todd copied them, adding chapter and verse, "*Hosea*, iv.3." Chalmers left out the quotation, but included the reference, in the form "*Hosea*, iv." Webster used Chalmers' form of the reference, but he got the quotation right: "Therefore shall the land mourn, and every one that dwelleth therein shall *languish*. Hosea iv." It looks as though he took the reference from Chalmers, and then looked up the verse in the Bible, rather than in Johnson's Dictionary.

Like Ure's *Chemical Dictionary*, Chalmers was not available at the time of the pre-*Synopsis* manuscript. It was published in 1820; between then and 1823 when Webster wrote to Mitchill, Chalmers must have joined the other books on the lexicographer's table, and been used to update the Morgan manuscript. Thereafter Webster would seem to have used it, to some degree, in place of Johnson. He cannot

have abandoned Johnson entirely (or he would not have known that *lum* was one of Todd's words) but Chalmers' handy octavo would have been more convenient to use as his primary reference work than the two quarto volumes of Johnson, and in most cases it would have given him as much of Johnson as he needed.

Webster did not include all of Todd's additions. Those that he rejected are mostly not only obsolete and obscure, but regional as well, and Webster's judgment in excluding them was sound. A few, however, seem perfectly respectable. It is not easy to see why he disapproved of *lapel* (which Todd called "a modern word"), *lissom*, or *Londoner*.[13]

The other study of the letter *L* in the *American Dictionary* is in chapter II of *The Development of American Lexicography, 1798–1864*, by Joseph H.Friend. Friend compared the entries from *la* to *laird*, finding that Webster had 141 entries to Johnson's 84, and that Webster omitted only two of Johnson's words, *labra* and *laced mutton*. He did not explain the meaning of either word, merely saying that the latter was "low" (which would have been Webster's reason for leaving it out). Johnson was less of a prude than either Webster or Friend, and he included those words in his dictionary because both were used by Shakespeare—*labra* in *The Merry Wives of Windsor* ("Spanish, A lip. Not used") and *laced mutton* in *Two Gentlemen of Verona* ("An old word for a whore"). Friend adds nothing to what we have already observed of Webster's dependence on Johnson, but we can usefully look for ourselves at one of his examples, the word *label*. A careful examination provides further evidence that Webster was here using Chalmers' Octavo rather than Johnson's Quarto. This is Johnson's entry:

1. A small slip or scrip of writing.[14]
       When wak'd, I found
    This *label* on my bosom; whose containing
    Is so from sense in hardness, that I can
    Make no collection of it.
                    Shakspeare's Cymbeline.
2. Any thing appendant to a larger writing.
       On the *label* of lead, the heads of St.Peter
    and St.Paul are impressed from the papal seal.
                    Aycliffe's Parergon.
3. [In law.] A narrow slip of paper or parchment affixed to a deed or writing, in order to hold the appending seal. So also any paper, annexed by way of

addition or explication to any will or testament, is called a *label* or codicil.   *Harris.*
       God joined my heart to Romeo's; thou our hands;
    And ere this hand, by thee to Romeo seal'd,
    Shall be the *label* to another deed,
    Or my true heart with treacherous revolt
    Turn to another, this shall slay them both.
                    Shaksp.

The name *Harris* identifies the source of the third of those definitions, the legal one, as John Harris' *Lexicon Technicum*. It is not in Harris' first edition (1704), but Johnson was probably using the fifth edition (1736), and it is certainly there. Harris also gave another meaning of *label*, but Johnson left it out because it was not sufficiently literary. It is the "labe" part of an astrolabe.

To a twentieth century reader, "a small slip or scrip of writing," is a very inadequate definition of *label*. In its current sense, it means a piece of paper, card or other material attached to (or detached from, or intended to be attached to) some article, to convey information relating to that article—such as (for example) a description of the contents of a container, instructions for taking a medicine, the name of the maker of a shirt, or the intended destination of a parcel. Johnson's definition would include an index card, which we would not consider to be a label, but it would exclude a luggage label when it had not yet been written on. Perhaps in Johnson's day that sense of *label* was not well established. Todd should have included it, but he was more interested in old meanings than new ones. Indeed, the meaning of *label* that he added was older than Johnson's, and he therefore put it first:

1. The earliest sense seems to be that of a small slip of silk, or other materials; a kind of tassel; as, "a *label* hanging on each side of a mitre; *labels* hanging down on garlands or crowns; also jesses hanging at hawks' legs." Barret's Alveary, 1580.

He then repeated Johnson's meanings 1, 2 and 3, renumbered 2, 3 and 4. In the *Encyclopædia*, there are three entries:

LABEL a long, thin, brass rule, with a small sight at one end, and a centre-hole at the other; commonly used with a tangent-line on the edge of a circumferentor, to take altitudes, &c.
LABEL, in law, is a narrow slip of paper, or parchment, affixed to a deed or writing, in order to hold

the appending seal.— Any paper annexed by way of addition or explication, to any will or testament, is also called a label or codicil.

LABEL, in heraldry, a fillet usually placed in the middle along the chief of the coat, without touching its extremities. Its breadth ought to be a ninth part of the chief. It is adorned with pendants; and when there are above three of these, the number must be specified in the blazoning.

It is used on the arms of eldest sons while the father is alive, to distinguish them from the younger; and is esteemed the most honourable of all differences. See HERALDRY.

The first of those definitions is taken from the *Lexicon Technicum*, and is the one that Johnson did not use — part of an astrolabe. The second, also from the *Lexicon Technicum,* is the one that Johnson did use.

Now for Webster. These are his definitions:

1. A narrow slip of silk, paper or parchment, containing a name or title, and affixed to any thing, denoting its contents. Such are the *labels* affixed to the vessels of an apothecary. *Labels* also are affixed to deeds or writings to hold the appended seal.
Harris.
2. Any paper annexed to a will by way of addition; as a codicil.   *Encyc.*
3. In *heraldry*, a fillet usually placed in the middle, along the chief of the coat, without touching its extremities. It is adorned with pendants, and used on the arms of the eldest son, to distinguish him from the younger sons, while the father is living.
Encyc.
4. A long thin brass rule, with a small sight at one end, and a center-hole at the other, commonly used with a tangent line on the edge of a circumferentor, to take altitudes, &c.   *Encyc.*

That entry cuts Harris' legal definition of *label* in half. Part of it appears (attributed to *Harris*) as the last sentence of sense 1, while the other half provides sense 2, attributed to *Encyc.* In Johnson, Todd, and the Encyclopedia, Harris' definition is all in one piece. The oddity is immediately explained when one looks at Chalmers. He left out all the quotations of course, but he also left out the numbers which separate the different senses of the words, and (following Johnson's own octavo abridgment) he left out the latter part of Harris' legal definition. This is Chalmers' entry:

A small slip of silk, or other materials; a kind of tassel. A small slip or scrip of writing. *Shakspeare.* Any thing appendant to a larger writing. *Aycliffe.* In law: A narrow slip of paper or parchment affixed to a

deed or writing, in order to hold the appending seal. *Harris.*

Webster would have written his first definition using no other source than Chalmers. It summarised Chalmers' entry, with the addition of an explanation of the modern meaning of *label.* He then put Chalmers aside and took up the *Encyclopædia.* His other three definitions came directly from the three definitions in the *Encyclopædia,* but he did not want to repeat the part of the legal definition that he had already taken from Chalmers. That is how Harris' definition came to be split in half. It is a clear sign that at this stage in the work Webster was using Chalmers' abridgement for Johnson's words, not just for words added by Todd.

After considering their respective definitions of *label* as a noun, Friend gave Webster credit for including the verb *to label,* which Johnson had omitted. It is true that the verb is not in Johnson, but Webster does not deserve the credit for including it. The verb and the definition were among Todd's additions, and Webster copied them from Chalmers.

The "astrolabe" definition of *label* as "a long thin brass rule …etc." provides an attractive example of one of the problems of lexicography. If you are not familiar with a subject, how do you know whether a definition is true or not? The answer is, you have to use sources that you trust. If you trust John Harris (D.D. and F.R.S.), you take his word for it. In fact, you take all his words for it. You reproduce his definition, word for word. That definition was in the first edition of the *Lexicon Technicum,* published in 1704. The *Encyclopædia* copied it from Harris (changing "ruler" to "rule"). Webster, placing his trust in the *Encyclopædia,* copied the definition into the *American Dictionary.* That same definition reappeared in successive Websters, and it is to be found in a *Webster's New Twentieth Century Dictionary* dated 1979.[15] It is there categorized as *Obs.,* but the wording is Harris' wording, virtually unaltered after 275 years!

To point the contrast in attitude between Johnson and Webster, let us look at one more entry in *L,* the word *lion.* Johnson's definition demonstrates the essentially *literary* character of his dictionary: "The fiercest and most magnanimous of fourfooted beasts." That may be

said to fail as a definition because (as Reed observed) if it were one's only guide, one could not identify the lion in a room filled with four-footed beasts. Indeed, it may not even be true. Is a real live lion more fierce and more magnanimous than any other quadruped? It is a pointless question, or a rather it is a question that misses the point, because Johnson's lion is not to be found in the hot and dusty African plains, but between the covers of a book. It is the lion of myth and metaphor. Johnson is not seeking to explain what a lion is (his readers may be supposed to know that already), but what the word *lion* means.

Webster discarded that definition entirely. He replaced it with something much more useful to the ignorant explorer, which he concocted out of the article *Felis* in the *Encyclopædia*. That article spends about five pages on the lion, from which these are extracts:

FELIS, in zoology, a genus of quadrupeds.... The largest lions are from eight to nine feet in length.... His head is very thick, and his face is beset on all sides with long bushy yellowish hair....The lions nourished under the scorching sun of Africa or the Indies, are the most strong, fierce and terrible.... The aspect of the lion corresponds with the noble and generous qualities of his mind. His ... gait is stately and his voice tremendous.

A bit of rearrangement gave Webster his definition:

LION ... A quadruped of the genus Felis, very strong, fierce and rapacious. The largest lions are eight or nine feet in length. The male has a thick head, beset with long bushy hair of a yellowish color. The lion is a native of Africa and the warm climates of Asia. His aspect is noble, his gait stately, and his roar tremendous.

Murray said that Webster was "a great man, a born definer of words",[16] but I am not sure how closely he had examined Webster's work. Webster was certainly a more careful definer of words than Johnson, and when he found Johnson's definitions of ordinary words inadequate, the ones that he wrote himself were usually an improvement. For the most part, however, the definitions in the *American Dictionary* were not Webster's original work: They were borrowed or adapted from other sources, and the accumulation of definitions was a largely mechanical operation. Round and round in the circular table, extracting words from his collection of

reference books. The result was a significant advance in lexicography, not because Webster defined so well, but because he defined so widely. His major contribution to the development of the dictionary was the inclusion of thousands of "Terms in the Arts and Sciences" which had previously been available only in specialist dictionaries.

It might be supposed, from that description of Webster's working method, that the *American Dictionary* is impersonal, giving no more clues to the character of its compiler than does a telephone directory. No such thing! Johnson has been criticised, even by Boswell,[17] for allowing traces of humor or prejudice to show in his dictionary, but the *American Dictionary* is a far more personal work than Johnson's Dictionary, giving evidence of Webster's character, experiences, and beliefs. I have selected some examples, loosely divided into categories.

RELIGION AND MORALITY

This category comes first because for the twenty years before the dictionary was published, Webster's religion was fundamental to his life, and so it became fundamental to the dictionary as well. Indeed, the *American Dictionary* contains so much of Webster's religion that a facsimile was issued in 1967 by the Foundation for American Christian Education. The Preface to that edition says that "Noah Webster's 1828 *American Dictionary* remains today the pure repository of three essential ingredients of *America's Christian History*. It reflects our Christian philosophy of life, our Christian philosophy of government, and our Christian philosophy of education. Unmistakably it reveals the degree to which the Bible was America's basic textbook and how it was related to all fields. Noah Webster as a Christian scholar laid his foundation of etymology upon the Scriptures and his research into the origin of language stems from this premise. One cannot read his definitions nor study his discussion of the grammatical construction of our language without encountering at every point a Scriptural Christian philosophy of life."

Christianity is to be found in the dictionary in meanings and definitions, in quotations from the Bible and in Webster's own sentences illustrating the use of words. To illustrate Webster's scriptural attitude to definitions, let me quote

Reed's description of Webster's definition of *light*:

A kind of fragmentation popular with Webster is the separate citation of theological meaning or scriptural connotation. For example, *light*, n., carries thirteen meanings (n.15 through n.26 and *light of the countenance*) dependent upon Biblical interpretation. The meanings listed under these headings are either not valid in any other context (e.g., 'joy,' 'Christ,' 'saving knowledge,' 'prosperity, happiness,' 'support,' 'Gospel,' 'gifts and graces of Christians,' 'a true Christian,' 'a good king'), or else they have already been expressed in an earlier nontheological definition (e.g., 'understanding').

Of Webster's religious and moral sentiments, a short sample must suffice: "The *love* of God is the first duty of man, and this springs from just views of his attributes or excellencies of character, which afford the highest delight to the sanctified heart. Our disobedience to God's commands admits of no *justification*. We cannot *justify* disobedience or ingratitude to our Maker. Let youth *keep company with* the wise and good."

PERSONAL OBSERVATIONS AND
RECOLLECTIONS

There are said to be three mentions of Johnson's native Staffordshire in his dictionary, but the identification of his birthplace is not obtrusive: "LICH, A dead carcase .... *Lichfield,* the field of the dead, a city in Staffordshire, so named from martyred christians. *Salve magna parens.*" Webster's dictionary, by contrast, provides all sorts of information for his biographer. In 1824–25, he travelled to Europe with William to complete the work. It was the only time he ever went abroad. After their return he must have carried out a final revision of the manuscript, and his foreign trip, still fresh in his mind, furnished useful examples: "We *arrived* at Havre de Grace, July 10, 1824. We *staid* at the Hotel Montmorenci. In the Royal Library at Paris, I saw a bathing-tub of porphyry, of beautiful form and exquisite workmanship. In France, *windows* are shut with frames or sashes that open and shut vertically, like the leaves of a folding door. We *left* Cowes on our return to the United States, May 10, 1825." There are also echoes of a more distant past: "The revolution in America was within the author's *memory*." "The comet of 1769 [which I saw] when it rose

in the morning, presented a luminous train that extended nearly from the horizon to the meridian." The Aurora Borealis, "in America, in March 1782, ... overspread the whole hemisphere." *Star-shoot* is "that which is emitted from a star," but "the writer once saw the same kind of substance from a brilliant meteor, at Amherst in Massachusetts." For an example of the verb *to witness*, Webster recalled the summer, nearly forty years before, when he had marched in ceremonial procession with the Philological Society: "I *witnessed* the ceremonies in New York, with which the ratification of the constitution was celebrated, in 1788." Pride in his home town prompted the example "The asylum at Hartford in Connecticut was the first institution in American for teaching the deaf and *dumb* to read and write." A heartfelt sentiment, though not a recollection, furnished an example of *expend*: "I hope the time, labor and money *expended* on this book will not be wholly misemployed." In another example he said that "to make dictionaries is *dull* work" but this cannot safely be taken to represent his own view, since it was copied from Johnson.[18]

Webster also makes personal appearances in the dictionary as etymologist and definer. On these occasions, he is often engaged in a dialogue with Johnson:

BASALT ... Lunier refers it to the Ethiopic *basal*, iron, a word I cannot find....

BLOW ... I have not found it in the cognate dialects....

BOLDNESS ... I cannot, with Johnson, interpret this word by *fortitude*, or *magnanimity*. Boldness does not, I think, imply the *firmness* of mind, which constitutes fortitude, nor the *elevation* and *generosity* of magnanimity.

CLOUD ... I have not found this word in any other language....

CUT ... I have not found the word in any of the Gothic or Teutonic languages....

DEMON ... The origin and primary sense of this word I have not been able to ascertain.

EXPIATE ... The primary sense is probably to *appease*, ... which is the usual sense of *atone* in most languages that I have examined....

MOTHER ... We observe that in some other languages, as well as English, the same word signifies a female parent, and the thick slime formed in vinegar; and in all the languages of Europe here cited, the orthography is nearly the same as that of *mud* and *matter*..... The word *matter* is evidently from the Ar.[19] *madda*, to secrete, eject or discharge a purulent substance; and I think cannot have any direct

connection with *mud*.... If this word had its origin in the name of the earth used for the forms of castings, it would not be a singular fact; for our word *mold*, in this sense, I suppose to be so named from *mold*, fine earth. The question remains *sub judice*.

OPEN ... Johnson interprets *open*, in this passage, by not cloudy, not gloomy. I think the definition wrong....

PYRITE ... I have anglicized this word, according to Darwin and the French mineralogists; making *pyrites* a regular plural.

SOLEMN .... I doubt the correctness of this definition of Johnson ...

WEASEL/WEESEL ...I know not the meaning of this name. In G. *wiese* is a meadow.

Webster's Little Lectures

From time to time the teacher in Webster gained ascendancy over the lexicographer, and switched off the mechanism that generated standard Webster contractions. The resulting entries are not definitions so much as little lectures. One is on the subject of preserving fish:

DUNNING, The operation of curing codfish, in such a manner as to give it a particular color and quality. Fish for dunning are caught early in spring, and often in February. At the Isles of Shoals, off Portsmouth, in New Hampshire, the cod are taken in deep water, split and slack-salted; then laid in a pile for two or three months, in a dark store, covered, for the greatest part of the time, with salt-hay or eel-grass, and pressed with some weight. In April or May, they are opened and piled again as close as possible in the same dark store, till July or August, when they are fit for use.

Even more information is provided about sugar:

A well known substance manufactured chiefly from the sugar cane, *arundo saccharifera*; but in the United States, great quantities of this article are made from the sugar maple; and in France, a few years since, it was extensively manufactured from the beet. The saccharine liquor is concentrated by boiling, which expels the water; lime is added to neutralize the acid that is usually present; the grosser impurities rise to the surface, and are separated in the form of scum; and finally as the liquor cools, the sugar separates from the melasses in grains. The sirup or melasses is drained off, leaving the sugar in the state known in commerce by the name of *raw* or *muscovado* sugar. This is farther purified by means of clay, or more extensively by bullocks' blood, which forming a coagulum, envelops the impurities. Thus clarified, it takes the names of *lump, loaf, refined,* &c. according to the different degrees of purification. Sugar is a proximate element of the vegetable kingdom, and is found in most ripe fruits, and many farinacious

roots. By fermentation, sugar is converted into alcohol, and hence forms the basis of those substances which are used for making intoxicating liquors, as melasses, grapes, apples, malt, &c.

The *ultimate* elements of sugar are oxygen, carbon and hydrogen. Of all vegetable principles, it is considered by Dr. Rush as the most wholesome and nutritious.

One of the most remarkable of these harangues is about perpetual copyright. Webster thought it very unfair that the man who made barrels, say, created something that became his own property indefinitely, whereas Webster, who made spelling books, had to remake them every few years because his copyright ran out. The groundwork for a little lecture is laid in sense 4 of the word *property*:

4. The exclusive right of possessing, enjoying and disposing of a thing; ownership. In the beginning of the world, the Creator gave to man dominion over the earth, over the fish of the sea and the fowls of the air, and over every living thing. This is the foundation of man's *property* in the earth and in all its productions. Prior occupancy of land and of wild animals gives to the possessor the *property* of them. The labor of inventing, making or producing any thing constitutes one of the highest and most indefensible titles to *property*....

The lecture follows, by which Webster hoped to persuade his readers that a writer was morally entitled to a perpetual property in what he had created:

Literary property, the exclusive right of printing, publishing and making profit by one's own writings. No right or title to a thing can be so perfect as that which is created by a man's own labor and invention. The exclusive right of a man to his literary productions, and to the use of them for his own profit, is entire and perfect, as the faculties employed and labor bestowed are entirely and perfectly his own. On what principle then can a legislature or a court determine that an author can enjoy only a *temporary property* in his own productions? If a man's right to his own *productions in writing* is as perfect as to the *productions* of his farm or his shop, how can the former be abridged or limited, while the latter are held without limitation? Why do the *productions* of *manual labor* rank higher in the scale of rights or *property* than the *productions* of the *intellect*?

Lesser Lectures and Eccentric Spellings

Another manifestation of Webster the teacher appears in the form of rather bad-tempered

didactic interpolations, not long enough to be classed as little lectures, with which he defended positions that he knew to be controversial. They are often to be found when he was recommending unconventional spellings of particular words. These are not the same as unconventional spellings of classes of words, which are considered below. Here are some examples:

BRIDEGOOM ... a compound of *bride* and *gum, guma,* a man, which, by our ancestors, was pronounced *goom.* This word, by a mispronouncing of the last syllable, has been corrupted into *bridegroom,* which signifies a *bride's hostler; groom* being a Persian word, signifying a man who has the care of horses. Such a gross corruption or blunder ought not to remain a reproach to philology.

CHIMISTRY ... The orthography of this word has undergone changes through a mere ignorance of its origin, than which nothing can be more obvious. It is the Arabic kimia,[20] the occult art or science, from kamai, to conceal. This was originally the art or science now called alchimy. ... If lexicographers and writers had been contented to take the orthography of the nations in the south of Europe, where the origin of the word was doubtless understood, and through whom the word was introduced into England, the orthography would have been settled, uniform, and corresponding exactly with the pronunciation.

COMPTROLL ... If this word were of genuine origin, both the verb and its derivative, *comptroller,* as applied to a public officer, would not be sense. But there is no such legitimate word in English, nor in any other known language.

IELAND ... This is the genuine English word, always used in discourse, but for which is used *island,* an absurd compound of Fr. *isle* and land, which signifies *land in water-land,* or rather *ieland-land.*

ISLAND ... This is an absurd compound of *isle* and *land,* that is, *land-in-water land,* or *ieland-land.* There is no such legitimate word in English, and it is found only in books. The genuine word always used in discourse is our native word, Sax. *ealond,* D.G. *eiland.*

LESSER ... This word is a corruption; but too well established to be discarded.

MORTGAGER ... *Mortgagor* is an orthography that should have no countenance.

RHYME/RIME ... The deduction of this word from the Greek [by Johnson] is a palpable error. The true orthography is *rime* or *ryme*; but as *rime* is hoar frost, and *rhyme* gives the true pronunciation, it may be convenient to continue the present orthography.

RIBIN ... This word has no connection with *band,* and the common orthography is grossly erroneous.

In the *Compendious Dictionary*, Webster had derived many eccentric spellings from his study of Anglo-Saxon. His work on the *Synopsis* gave

him etymological reasons for objecting to the conventional spelling of many other words. He was particularly proud of having traced to its origin the word used by hog-callers in Connecticut, as explained in the definition of the word, *chuk*:

A word used in calling swine. It is the original name of that animal, which our ancestors brought with them from Persia, where it is still in use, Pers. *chuk,* Zend. *chuk,* a hog; Sans. *sugara.* Our ancestors, while in England, adopted the Welsh *hwc,* hog, but *chuck* is retained in our popular name of *woodchuck,* that is, wood hog. This is a remarkable proof of the original seat of the Teutonic nations. I have taken *chuk* from Adelung. The French *cochon* may be the same word.

To reflect that derivation, Webster used the spelling *woodchuk* for "the popular name in New England of a species of the Marmot tribe of animals, the *Arctomys monax.*" His knowledge of French enabled him to spot the mistake in the mess of *pottage* that Jacob gave Esau — *potage* is "the more correct orthography." Similarly, the word *passager* "is usually corrruptly written *passenger.*" Anglo Saxon led him to the correct spelling *parsnep,* because "the last syllable of this word is the Sax. *næpe,* L. *napus,* which occurs also in *turnep.*" In his lectures, Webster liked to point out that a *nightmare* ("usually the effect of indigestion or of a loaded stomach") has no connection with horses and should be spelled *nightmar.* In the dictionary, that corrected spelling appears without any comment, as does *porpess* for *porpoise. Jail* is "sometimes written very improperly *gaol.*" For *juice,* "the regular orthography is *juse.*" *Mould* is "an incorrect orthography." For *neighbor,* "the true orthography, as this word is now pronounced, is *nehboor.*" Under *negro,* Webster observes: "It is remarkable that our common people retain the exact Latin pronunciation of this word, *neger,*" and he accordingly included a separate entry under that spelling. *Pincers* is "an erroneous orthography of *pinchers,* which see." For *proceed,* "the more correct orthography is *procede.*" *Prophecy* "ought to be written *prophesy.*" There are many such eccentric spellings of individual words, of which these are just examples. Some of them we shall meet again.

SPELLING OF CLASSES OF WORDS

Working from Johnson (or Chalmers) Webster had to change the spelling in various classes

of words, and he usually changed it to what is now (and often was then) the conventional American form. One class where modern British spelling also differs from that of Johnson, is words such as *publick* and *musick*. Here, Webster was more conservative than many of his contemporaries, preserving or restoring the *k* in the verbs *frolick*, *mimick* and *traffick*. An explanation is given in the entry for the letter *K*:

Formerly, *k* was added to *c*, in certain words of Latin origin, as in *musick*, *publick*, *republick*. But in modern practice, *k* is very properly omitted, being entirely superfluous, and the more properly, as it is never written in the derivatives, *musical*, *publication*, *republican*. It is retained in *traffick*, as in monosyllables, on account of the pronunciation of the derivatives, *trafficked*, *trafficking*.

There is a peculiar inconsistency here, since the spelling *mimick* is used for the verb only, the noun and adjective both being spelled *mimic*, whereas *traffick* and *frolick* have the *k* in all senses. Where the same words had appeared in the *Compendious*, the spellings had been the same (the *Compendious* did not include *mimick* or *frolick* as verbs). The spellings *almanack* and *havock* also survived from the *Compendious*. Two more unexpected *k*'s appear in *picknick*, "An assembly where each person contributes to the entertainment." The spelling and definition both came from Chalmers, though Webster attributed them to Todd.

The termination -*er* in such words as *center* was continued, of course, from the *Compendious*, as was the mistake of entering *luster* after *lustrate* and *lustration*

In most of the words where modern British spelling differs from American, the *American Dictionary* has the American forms. Was Webster, then, the father of American spelling? No. For two reasons he was not. First, many of the American forms were gaining acceptance anyway, often before Webster had acquired any influence at all. Secondly (and this is to some degree proof that Webster had little effect) he continued to use and to recommend many other reformed spellings that were never accepted. Oliver Wendell Holmes' old gentleman in his study might give a misleading indication by pulling the strings on his weathervane, but he could not change the direction even of the lightest breeze. The wind of change that swept away Johnson's spelling, and Chaucer's too, was

something much more powerful than any of Webster's huffing and puffing.

In the 1820s, and for many years thereafter, there was a lively argument between those Americans who favoured the spelling of Johnson and Walker, and those who did not. Somewhat similar is an argument today between supporters of British and American spellings. Not quite the same, because Britain did not entirely stick to Johnson's principles. It is an argument that I refuse to enter, taking the peaceful view that in these matters there is no right or wrong, only what is conventional and what is not. For the great majority of words, there is no difference between British and American spelling, or between Johnson's and Webster's, and where there is a difference, each is "correct" if and where it is generally accepted. The *American Dictionary* appeared in a time of change, when the exact position of the borderline of convention was uncertain; but looking back after nearly two hundred years, we get a clearer view, and can see that the spelling of the dictionary is more or less what has turned out to be conventional American spelling, overlaid with Webster's personal eccentricities.

The number of eccentricities is less than it was in the *Compendious*— most notably the silent *e* has been restored to such words as *examine* and *imagine*, (though not *maiz*; and some words, such as *jasmin/jasmine* and *vultur/vulture* are given both ways).

One class that Webster had not previously considered was words ending in -*iff*. They would sound the same with one *f*, and Webster, still keen to expunge silent letters, decided that the other should go. The decision was taken when he was some way into the dictionary, and he did not go back over what he had already written, with the curious result that the entry *bailiff* contains the words "...an officer appointed by the sheriff," but in *sherif* ("*Sherif* is the true orthography....,") the spelling *bailif* is used. The moment of decision can be located precisely, since in the definition of one meaning of PIPE, there are two *f*'s in "accounts of sheriffs &c.," but *plaintif* and *pontif* have only one. Single syllable words such as *skiff*, *stiff*, *tiff* and *whiff* all have two, and one might suppose that this was intended to be the general rule, except that in a list of "corrections" at the very end of the dictionary Webster suggests

clif, as well as correcting *bailif, caitif, dandruf* and *mastif*.

Under *thumb/thum*, both spellings are given, but with the instruction "The common orthography is corrupt. The real word is *thum*." Webster accordingly uses *thum* (though *thumbed/ thummed* is defined as "Having thumbs"). The word *plumb* has its *b*, but under *plum* (the fruit) there is a note: "Dr. Johnson remarks that this word is often written improperly *plumb*. This is true, not only of this word, but of all words in which *b* follows *m*, as in *thumb, dumb*, &c." In the etymology of *dumb* (class Dm. No. 3) Webster says that "In this word, *b* is improperly added," but he does not remove it. He puts no *b* in *redout*, however, since "the usual orthography, *redoubt*, is egregiously erroneous."

Another familiar reform to a class of words is the omission of *a* from words such as *feather* and *leather*. Each of those entries has a note, "The most correct orthography is *fether/lether*." Webster generally uses that spelling, but it was a half-hearted attempt at reform. In the main definitions he gave the alternative spellings *feather/fether* and *leather/lether* bracketed together — this is referred to as "doubling" — those entries being in the places dictated by the conventional spelling. There were no separate entries under *fether* or *lether*. So if you looked up *portmanteau*, you would find it to be "A bag usually made of lether …," but to find out what *lether* was, you had to know the conventional spelling. In the definition of *boot*, the spelling *leather* is used (more than once) suggesting that the decision to leave out the *a* may have been taken when the dictionary was already under way. Most of the derivatives of *lether* are doubled as well, though *leather-coat, leather-dresser, leather-jacket* and *leather-mouthed* are not, even though *nerfling* is defined as "A fresh water fish of Germany, of the lether-mouthed kind…." In the *Compendious*, the spelling *wether* had been given as an alternative to *weather*, but not used. In the *American Dictionary*, *weather* has only the conventional spelling.

RUDE WORDS

In his progress report to Judge Dawes in July 1809, Webster explained that one of his reasons for compiling a dictionary was "to omit some vulgar and obscene words, which the English compilers have injudiciously inserted." Web-ster was particularly sensitive to rude words, and when he had finished work on the dictionary he set about expurgating the Bible. "Some Scattered Reminiscences of my Grandfather," by Emily Fowler,[21] confirm that this was his motive:

It was a personal aversion to the occasional coarse phrasing of the Bible which largely influenced him to retranslate it, for with his high and pure ideal of moral life, this source of it was at war; he thought that the expressions of the earlier translators did not do justice to the spirit of holiness inculcated. Free conversation and jokes with *sous-entendres* were very obnoxious to him, and if one was made in his presence, he rose and left the room; if the offender were one of his own family, the rebuke was sharp and instantaneous.

Probably in early life his temper was quick, but it very rarely showed itself in domestic intercourse, When he was angry, it was against sin, and not as a personal offence against himself. Once when something coarse or impertinent was said in his presence he rebuked the culprit so severely that one of his little girls, who sat by said: 'Papa makes me siver (shiver) like a top.' In my many months of residence with him I never saw him roused to anger but once, and that was when a dubious and rather indelicate word was mentioned before him.

In the *American Dictionary*, his attitude to rude words was the same as it had been in the *Compendious* — he left them out. Thus *fart* and *turd* are still excluded. However, *bum* is in — "The buttocks; the part on which we sit" — and so is *arse*: "The buttocks or hind part of an animal." The wording of both definitions is Johnson's, and Webster cited Johnson as his authority for the first of them, in case he should be criticised for including it. He also included the expression *To hang an arse*, defined as "to lag behind; to be sluggish, or tardy." Johnson had described that as "a vulgar phrase," but presumably Webster did not think so, or he would have left it out. Indeed, I have to revise my earlier assertion that he excluded *arse* and *bum* from the *Compendious*. It seems more likely that they were omitted only because the *Compendious* was based on an edition of Entick in which they did not appear.

When Webster positively asserts that a word is *not* vulgar, it is safe to assume that he used the word, and Johnson condemned it. Thus, of *wabble*, Webster writes "Its place cannot be supplied by any other word in the language. It is neither low nor barbarous." And why? Because

Johnson had described *wabble* as "a low bar-barous word."

POLITICS

The men who drafted the American consti-tution had studied political theory, and under-stood the difference between a democracy and a republic. In a democracy, all voting citizens assemble to make decisions; in a republic, the voters elect representatives who make decisions for them. What they did not understand so well was political practice. In particular, they did not anticipate the emergence of opposing po-litical parties. This was manifest in the arrangements they prescibed for presidential elections. Each elector voted for two candi-dates. The candidate who received the greatest number of votes would be president, and the person with the second largest number, vice-president. The problem was that the electors had no way of specifying which candidate they wanted to be president and which vice-presi-dent. If the parties were not well defined, the re-sult was likely to be a president and vice-pres-ident with differing political views. With better party organisation, there would be a dead-heat between two men from the same party. This happened in 1801 when Jefferson (who was a deist) and Burr (who was a scoundrel) defeated the Federalist candidate, John Adams. There could be no doubt that the electors had in-tended Jefferson to be president, but Burr had the same number of votes, and refused to step aside. After that spot of bother, the constitution was amended.

Webster, too, had studied political theory. He understood that America was a republic, in which the voters elect representatives, not a democracy. But who should be entitled to vote? One cause of the War of Independence was the colonists' objection to being taxed by an En-glish Parliament in which they had no voice. If you pay taxes, you should have a say in how your money is spent. Conversely, if you do not pay taxes, you should not have a say in how the taxpayers' money is spent. On one side of the taxpayer's dollar, "No Taxation without Rep-resentation"; on the other, "No Representation without Taxation." Webster was a property-owner and a tax-payer, and he opposed any ex-tension of the suffrage to those who did not pay taxes. The state of Connecticut was of the same

mind: Its new constitution, adopted in 1818, limited suffrage to "white males of twenty-one years of age and upwards, who are resident cit-izens for six months, and have a freehold of seven dollars yearly value, or who shall have performed military duty for one year, or paid a tax, provided they sustain a good moral char-acter." For Webster, Democrats were not of good moral character, and democracy, Jacobin Jeffersonian democracy, was a dangerous thing. It carried a threat of mob-rule and French-rev-olutionary disorder. His political creed can be found in the *American Dictionary* by fitting sev-eral definitions together:

CITIZEN, … In the *U. States*, a person, native or naturalized, who has the privilege of exercising the elective franchise, or the qualifications which enable him to vote for rulers, and to purchase and hold real estate.

DEMOCRACY, … Government by the people; a form of government, in which the supreme power is lodged in the hands of the people collectively, or in which the people exercise the powers of legislation. Such was the government of Athens.

DEMOCRAT, *n*. One who adheres to a govern-ment by the people, or favors the extension of the right of suffrage to all classes of men.

FEDERALIST, … An appellation in America, given to the friends of the constitution of the United States, at its formation and adoption, and to the po-litical party which favored the administration of President Washington.

JACOBIN, … the member of a club, or other per-son, who opposes government in a secret and un-lawful manner or by violent means; a turbulent dem-agogue.

JACOBINICAL, … turbulent; discontented with government; holding democratic principles.

REPUBLIC, … a state in which the exercise of the sovereign power is lodged in representatives elected by the people. In modern usage, it differs from a democracy or democratic state, in which the people exercise the powers of sovereignty in person. …

STATESMAN, *n*. A man versed in the arts of gov-ernment; usually, one eminent for political abilities.

STATESWOMAN, *n*. A woman who meddles in public affairs; in *contempt*.

PREPOSTEROUS, … Perverted; wrong; absurd; contrary to nature or reason; not adapted to the end; as, a republican government in the hands of females, is *preposterous*.

FROM MANUSCRIPT TO PRINT

Webster finished the manuscript of the *American Dictionary* in Cambridge, England, in January 1825, at which time he still hoped to

issue the dictionary and the *Synopsis* together as a set. No American printer would have had the types needed to print them, but he was confident that the London book trade would recognise the value of his work, and be keen to publish it. He told Ellsworth to sell five shares of bank stock to keep him in funds, and on January 27, he wrote to Rebecca: "I have written to Mr. Ellsworth to send me the amount of $500 in a bill of Exchange, & if I can finish the publication, by mid-summer, that will be as much as I shall want." He had earlier written to Daniel Webster from Cambridge, on October 16, 1824,[22] asking him to put a petition before Congress to allow the book to be imported into America free of duty:

Your petitioner has been many years engaged in researches into the origin, history & affinities of languages, & in writing a Dictionary of the English language, which work is now almost completed; together with an Appendix, containing a Synopsis or Comparative View of the principal elementary words in more than twenty different languages. This work is intended to embrace many improvements in lexicography; but cannot at present be printed in the United States, as no printing office has all the necessary types. Your petitioner therefore, for the purpose of completing this work in the best manner, & printing it with the proper characters, has been under the necessity of resorting to an English press. But as the work is American & intended for the use of his fellow citizens, your petitioner prays your Honourable Body to grant your petitioner, his heirs & assigns, the privilege of importing copies of the said *Dictionary of the English Language* & of *the said Synopsis of Languages,* into the United States, free of duty, for the term of five years.

Daniel Webster and Congress obligingly did as they were asked, but Webster never took advantage of his import licence, because he was unable to find a London publisher interested in his work. He submitted one of his manuscript booklets (Callat to Canvass) to Byron's publisher, John Murray, for evaluation. Murray kept it for some weeks but then declined publishing. The problem was that two large dictionaries were already in the offing. A second edition of Todd's Johnson was being prepared (which came out in 1827) and Charles Richardson's *New English Dictionary* was to be published in due course, most of it having already appeared in the *Encyclopædia Metropolitana.* Webster suspected a conspiracy. When he got

his manuscript back, he noticed pencil marks by some of the words, which had not been there before. He recorded his suspicions in the *Memoir*, and in two separate notes, now in the New York Public Library. In the words of one of them, "The MS was probably put into the hands of Mr. Richardson .... But perhaps into the hands of Mr. Todd, editor of Johnson's Dictionary." I have looked at those parts of the letter *C* in the second edition of Todd's Johnson, and I can see no sign of borrowing from Webster. Richardson's Dictionary contains slightly more in the way of definitions (and even more quotations) than the corresponding part of the encyclopedia, but with so small a sample it is not possible to say whether any of the additional material came from Webster's manuscript. The difference in style is so great that Richardson could have derived no more than ideas for words to be included.

Disappointed in London, Webster returned home, sailing for New York from Cowes on May 10, 1825. The problem in America, in addition to the absence of the necessary types, was that he was unlikely to find a publishing house able or willing to finance so large an undertaking as the printing of his great work. Even in London, Johnson's Dictionary had been commissioned by a consortium. On the other hand, the publication of an American dictionary to rival Johnson's was a patriotic undertaking, and Webster was well-known in America from the widespread use of his spelling book. Also, the earlier objection to his attempted subscription (that he could not say when, or even if, the dictionary would be finished) no longer applied. He found a publisher, Sherman Converse, who was at least prepared to test the water. Converse printed four sample pages from the manuscript, between *A* and *G*, described as "a Specimen of the lexicography of Webster's Dictionary; but not of the type, paper and printing — the type and paper not being yet procured. The type will be new, and the oriental words printed in their proper characters. The references of Class and Number to the Synopsis stand as in the original; but no specimen of the Synopsis can be given without suitable type, nor without printing two or three entire sheets."

On February 6, 1826, Converse sent a copy of his Specimen to Jefferson, with a hand-written Prospectus, and a covering letter:

Sir, Permit me to enclose for your inspection a copy of Mr. Webster's Prospectus to his large Dictionary and a few printed extracts from the work. Mr. W. has bestowed upon this work simply, almost 30 years of industrious labour, and in the opinion of Judge Trumbull (McFingal) who has examined nearly all of the letter *a*—in ms—has compiled a work which comprises more philological research than all the English Lexicons hitherto published, and which if published will do great credit to Mr. Webster and to our country. Should the other gentlemen whom I propose to address on the subject, accord in opinion with Judge Trumbull, and think the work of sufficient importance to give me a letter of recommendation, I may obtain sufficient patronage to lay it before the public.

The Dictionary will be comprised either in three large Octavo volumes, or one very large quarto (in Bds at $20) I have sent to Leipsic for founts of Oriental type and should sufficient patronage be obtained to warrant its publication, no care or expense will be spared to make it a superior specimen of typography. It cannot be published with safety without one thousand subscribers—and though the business of obtaining subscribers to books, has become odious from imposition, I feel a confidence that the claims which Mr. Webster has upon his country will secure to his work a cheerful and liberal patronage. If I mistake not, the honour of his Country is implicated in the result of the contemplated effort.

The copy of the prospectus which I enclose does not comprise the part relating to what he calls his synopsis—which is a learned exhibit of about 20 different languages giving a comparative view of radical words and will be of use only to the scholar. I doubt whether it can be published without an unwarrantable sacrifice. From the very few extracts which I send you, an adequate opinion, not to say a crititcal one, can scarcely be formed of the work; yet with the help of the prospectus, a distinct idea may be formed of the plan and the examples may give an imperfect one of the execution—If, Sir, on examination, you shall think the work of sufficient importance to merit your attention, and shall feel authorised to give me a short communication which may be of service in the publication of the Prospectus, it will afford particular encouragement in the effort which I propose to make.

Jefferson's reply is dated February 20, 1826:

Sir, I have duly reciev^d [sic] your favor of the 6th asking my examination and opinion of the plan of Mr. Webster's dictionary. of which you inclosed me a sample. but worn down with age, infirmity and pain, my mind is no longer in a tone for such services. I can only therefore express my respect and best wishes for its success.

Jefferson was using the polygraph, an ingenious machine of his own invention that waved a second pen in parallel with the writer's hand, making a copy of what he wrote. The polygraph copy of his letter to Converse is in very small and shaky writing that confirms, in so far as it was not due to the imperfections of the machine, that he was in truth "worn down with age, infirmity and pain" when he wrote it. Indeed, his right wrist had been a source of discomfort for many years, ever since he had broken it falling over in France, and his generally poor state of health was such that he died only a few months after writing to Converse.[23]

Converse had better luck with other dignitaries, so that when he published the Prospectus in the *Connecticut Herald* on May 2, 1826, it was supported by 14 recommendations from prominent men. The proposed subscription at $20 a copy was not a success, but the faithful and generous John Jay, now 81 years old, came good yet again. This time, the letter came from his son William:

Sir, My father sometime since desired Mr. Converse of New Haven to place his name on the list of subscribers to your Dictionary, for six copies. It has since occurred to him that the expense which this great work has already cost you, & that which must still attend its publication might perhaps render it convenient to you to receive the amount of his subscription in advance. He therefore desires me to inform you that you are at liberty, should you think proper, to draw on my Brother P.A.Jay, 398 B^d:way New York, for $120; but it w^ld. afford my Father more pleasure, could he have an opportunity of paying you this sum in person. He likewise desires me to assure you of his best wishes for the success of your book, & for your own health and prosperity.

Despite the poor response to his pleas for support, Converse decided to go ahead with the publication of the dictionary, though not of the *Synopsis*. He arranged for the work to be printed by Hezekiah Howe of New Haven. This was not going to be entirely straightforward, however, since there were parts of Webster's manuscript that the compositors were unable to read. I refer to it as "Webster's manuscript" but what the compositors were trying to read was not all in Webster's handwriting, as most writers on Webster say or imply. They contrast Webster's situation with that of Johnson, who had a number of amanuenses (mostly Scottish) beavering away in his attic, writing out the passages that he had marked in other books for inclusion in

his dictionary. The source of the error is, no doubt, the fact that the only surviving parts of the manuscript *are* in Webster's handwriting, but they were not the pages submitted to the printer. Let us start with a footnote from Mrs. Ford's *Notes on the Life of Noah Webster*:

It is interesting to know that Webster himself performed the great manual as well as mental labor; for the entire work — with all the authorities, quotations, and passages cited to illustrate the meaning of words — was written out in his own hand. Such also was the fact with the *Synopsis of Words in Twenty Languages*, and indeed with the whole series of his productions from the earliest years of his life. He never had the aid of an amanuensis in any of his literary labors, except in the proof-reading of his *Dictionary*— and later in its revision when his sight began to fail him, at the age of eighty.[24]

What Mrs. Ford writes about the *Synopsis* is manifestly wrong; Webster wrote out the first version, but much of what survives is William's fair copy. Nevertheless, later biographers have accepted her statement about the manuscript of the dictionary without question. Warfel says that "the entire manuscript is in Webster's own handwriting."[25] Leavitt writes, "With negligible assistance, he not only compiled but wrote out in his own hand the entire manuscript of a dictionary comprising 70,000 listings, a Preface of textbook proportions and much supplementary material."[26] Both Warfel and Leavitt reproduce manuscript pages in Webster's handwriting, but they are from a pre-*Synopsis* booklet containing part of the letter *B*. It is not one of those in the Morgan Library, but is of the same period. Rollins does not show any of Webster's manuscript, but he too refers to "70,000 entries, all written out by his own hand."[27] In fact, the manuscript of the dictionary went through the same process as that of the *Synopsis*. Webster wrote the first drafts, and then made William transcribe it. This was anticipated in Webster's letter to Dr. Mitchill in December 1823:

In order to give my work all the completeness of which it is susceptible, I purpose to go to England the next summer, if life & health permit; & there finish & publish it.... I must be in England, with my son as transcriber, twelve or eighteen months, before the work can be completed....

William later said that he had been employed six or eight hours a day transcribing,

when he was with his father in England,[28] and confirmation of this is to be found in Webster's letters to Rebecca from Cambridge. On October 16, 1824, he wrote, "William reads French well.... His eyes are better, I think, & he devotes most of his time to copying for me." On December 26, "William is gone to the Chapel for evening service. His eyes have been weaker these three weeks past, owing to straining them by writing at night. But they are gaining strength."

It seems likely, therefore, that much of the final manuscript of the *American Dictionary* was a fair copy in William's handwriting. If it was, it should have been largely free from crossings out, additions or corrections, though, as with the *Synopsis*, Webster would have had to insert any words written in Arabic, Hebrew, and other exotic characters. Even with a fair copy, however, errors of transcription were to be expected in turning the manuscript into printed sheets, particularly of words or names unknown to the typesetter. Technical and scientific terms were going to be one problem area. Even more difficulty would result from oriental characters. Converse therefore decided to hire a proofreader to compare the first proof sheets of the dictionary with the manuscript. He needed someone with scientific training, and with a knowledge of foreign languages. We have now to meet Rev. William Chauncey Fowler, who had courted Webster's widowed daughter, Harriet Cobb, while Webster was in Europe. Webster had given his consent to their marriage by letter from England, and the wedding took place on July 26, 1825, about six weeks after Webster and William returned from Europe.[29]

Fowler knew the very man for the proofreading job — James Gates Percival, who was known as a poet, but who was also a doctor, surgeon, geologist, and student of linguistics. When Fowler went to Yale as a freshman in 1813, Percival was there as a sophomore, and Fowler became his friend. Almost his only friend, because Percival was melancholy and somewhat reclusive. He went on to study botany and medicine, taking his M.D. in 1820. In 1823, Fowler used his influence to secure for Percival the post of professor of chemistry at West Point, a ludicrously inappropriate situation, since Percival was the least military and

most insubordinate character imaginable. He resigned from West Point the following year, and became for a time a surgeon in Boston. When Converse was looking for a suitable proofreader for the dictionary, Percival was again unemployed, and Fowler proposed him for what must have appeared a more suitable job than the one at West Point. Fowler may also have wanted to fill the job so that he, Fowler, could not be coerced into doing it himself. A contract was drawn up between Converse and Percival in January 1827:

This Indenture witnesseth, That, whereas Sherman Converse proposes to publish an American Dictionary of the English Language by Noah Webster, LL.D., and whereas said Converse has contracted with Hezekiah Howe, of New Haven, to superintend the printing of the same, it is mutually understood and agreed by and between said Converse and James G.Percival as follows, viz.: The said Howe is to read the first proof of said work, of each sheet as it comes from the press and by copy, to correct the same, and to furnish a clean proof; which clean proof the said Percival agrees to compare with the proof read by the said Howe, to see whether the errors marked by the said Howe are corrected by the printer, and to mark such as are not; after which he is to read said proof with Mr. Webster by copy, which when read is to be corrected by the printer, and a clean proof taken for said Percival, and one for Mr. Webster; which clean proof said Percival is to compare with the one already corrected, and mark any errors previously marked, and not corrected by the printer. Said Percival is then to read the said proof, and Mr. Webster will also read his; which two proofs are to be corrected, and two clean proofs taken; which clean proofs said Percival is to compare with those already corrected, one of which Mr. Howe's printer is to read, and said Percival the other, and to revise both after they are corrected, by a clean proof, to stand by the form as it is going to press, to see that every error mark is corrected. Said Percival is to see that the last proof read is taken from the form after is is placed on the press for printing, in order to avoid errors by transferring it from the imposing-stone. All the above readings and revisions the said Percival is to give the said proofs promptly and faithfully, and at the time the said work requires, so as to facilitate as far as possible the progress of the work; and in no case is he to suffer any other engagement to interfere with a faithful execution of this contract. And if, in the judgment of said Percival, any additional reading or readings of any proof or proofs of said work shall be necessary, said Percival shall give it them. And the said Percival agrees to attend to the fulfilment of this contract, without interruption, from the commencement of the printing of said work

to its completion, except prevented by sickness. And the said Converse agrees, on his part, to pay the said Percival eight hundred dollars for his said services, to be rendered as above, provided it takes not exceeding ten months to complete the work; and it is understood that one sheet of said work per day is to be executed. If it exceeds ten months to complete the work, then said Converse is to pay said Percival in proportion as for the ten months. Said Converse further agrees to pay said Percival one hundred dollars at the completion of each half volume, and the remainder at the completion of the entire work.

In witness whereof we have hereunto set our hands this eleventh day of January, 1827, in New York.

S.CONVERSE.

JAMES G. PERCIVAL.[30]

On May 3, Percival wrote to a friend that the printing had not started because the special paper and types had not yet come, though they were hourly expected. On July 1, he wrote, "The Dictionary is under way, but progresses slowly. At its present rate of progression, it will be almost a life-interest with me. It obliges me to close and lengthy application, but on the whole it is not an uninteresting or uninstructive employment."

Percival's contract had anticipated that the printers would be able to produce the first proof from the manuscript without assistance, but this proved to be impossible, and the contract was modified on July 4, 1827, to require Percival to read the manuscript:

Whereas it has become necessary for James G.Percival to read the manuscript of Webster's Dictionary, preparatory to its being put in the hands of the compositors, and whereas the said Percival has agreed to read and correct the same, which will be an extra labor not recognized in the above contract, I hereby agree to pay, or cause the said Percival to be paid, for such extra service, the sum of two hundred and fifty dollars. This extra service is to consist in a general inspection of the whole manuscript, and a particular inspection of all the scientific words, and a careful correction of errors which he may discover in or under such words, and a careful attention to the alphabetical arrangement of the whole vocabulary.

S.CONVERSE.

The contract was again modified, August 29, 1827:

It is now ascertained that the proof-readers can examine only three sheets per week. This circumstance is not to affect the compensation to the said J.G.Percival, as agreed upon in the above contract.

On December 4, 1827, Percival wrote to his friend George Hayward expressing his dissatisfaction with the way things were going:

I must give up my engagement with the Dictionary, or it must be essentially modified. I cannot any longer endure the labor I have gone through. I will give my occupation for two days in getting out one sheet. I begin (say Monday morning) at seven o'-clock a.m., with reading the first proof from the manuscript, and get it ready for the printer by five o'clock p.m. I cannot do it in less time. Then as soon as I can set about it, I take up the manuscript for the next sheet, about which I am often occupied till nine or ten o'clock. This depends on the amount of revision. I am then quite exhausted enough to go to bed. I take the manuscript next morning early to the author and make revisions on his authorities, and settle with him the corrections. This occupies till ten o'-clock, sometimes eleven or more. I immediately sit down then to the second proof which I complete by three o'clock at least; after that I have to make two revisions, — one at the press, — so that it is often seven o'clock before all is finished. I have then an evening's leisure. This has been my employment for most of six months, and I am now done with it. I cannot, and will not, go through twenty months at least of such incessant labor; for it will take fully that time to finish. The world may cry out what they choose; but when I find myself bound by Gordian knots, I will cut them. Some arrangement must be made to lighten my task, or I shall resign it entirely. It is not necessary that I should do all this; but my assistance, or that of some one as competent, is absolutely necessary…. My situation is one of disgust and toil…. I regret that I have ever engaged in the thing. It will be one of the miseries of my life to think of it; and I pray that I may find a safe deliverance. As I find it, I appear to be obliged to correct the blunders of ignorance, I feel like the living tied to the dead….

Dr. Hayward replied:

I hope you will not break off with the Dictionary before you write to me; and I think if you are dealing with gentlemen, the task might be made much lighter to you….

Indeed a new arrangement was made, December 24, 1827, and recorded on the contract:

I have this day made a new arrangement with Dr. Percival as to his services, but his compensation is to remain the same.

Percival wrote to Hayward January 9, 1828:

I have made some more favorable arrangement with the Dictionary, by which I am relieved from most of the mechanical part of my task, and I now hope to

respire from my excessive labors. I need it in body and spirit. The Dictionary is still an odious task to me….

He kept it up, however, until the autumn. Altogether, Percival worked for Converse for about sixteen months, from May 1827 until September 1828, which was about two months before the printing was completed. He received, "when fully employed on the Dictionary, $95 per month." As Ward's *Life* says, "It had been to him a severely laborious work; and though he separated from it before it was entirely finished, owing to some misunderstanding between himself and Dr. Webster, it was a welcome release."

Ward writes that the relations between Webster and Percival

were not always the pleasantest. They both had a good degree of independence and firmness; and it was Percival's peculiarity that when he thought he was right, nothing could change him. He was a much more thorough scholar in etymologies and the scientific bearings of words than Dr. Webster; and this can be truly said without disparagement. Hence he held on to his opinions with great tenacity, and was unwilling that any words should pass through his hands, unless they were correctly defined and set forth in every particular. Dr. Webster did not regard such accuracy as absolutely necessary, and his time was too valuable to be wasted in controversies. It is not strange, therefore, that Percival and Dr. Webster often parted, at the Doctor's study, both thoroughly vexed at each other, nor that finally these disputes over literary inaccuracies, through Percival's honest zeal and Dr. Webster's honest pride of position, should ultimately, as they did, lead Percival to discontinue his labors.[31]

It was indeed a problem that both men were conspicuously obstinate, and it could not have made matters easier that Percival was in some respects rather better qualified than Webster. He had a scientific degree, he is said to have read ten languages with fluency, and he had sufficient knowledge of recent German advances in philology to be critical of Webster's etymology. When he said that he was "obliged to correct the blunders of ignorance," and that he felt "like the living tied to the dead," this was the reaction of an intelligent man who knew something of the new linguistics, to the antediluvian etymology of Webster's *Synopsis*. Criticism of that sort could not have been welcome to Webster, who had spent ten years laboriously comparing words in different languages, and

who knew that his conclusions were sound. He did not need to study what others had done in the field, because if they agreed with him they were right, and if they did not, they must be wrong. Also, he felt that he literally did not have time to listen to argument from Percival. His time was "too valuable to be wasted in controversies" not because he was very busy, but because he was very old. At the end of the Advertisement, Webster wrote that in his labours on the dictionary, "a long life has passed insensibly away," and he would soon be "beyond the reach of censure or applause." He was nearly 70 years old, more than twice Percival's age, and he wanted to get his book printed and published without further delay.

Webster's only acknowledgment that Percival made any contribution to the dictionary is also in the Advertisement. In the paragraph dealing with "Terms in the Arts and Sciences," he says: "In this department of the present work, the latest and most approved writers have been taken as guides; the several articles have been submitted to the revision of Professor Olmsted of Yale College, and Dr. James G. Percival; and assistance has been occasionally afforded by Professor Silliman of Yale College, and other gentlemen distinguished for scientific attainments."

The printed text of the *American Dictionary* was now complete, but something was still lacking. Webster's 1799 Johnson had an engraved portrait frontispiece of the great man, "from a painting by Sir Joshua Reynolds." Webster's dictionary, too, must have a portrait. Luckily, there was a suitable image ready to hand. One of Webster's oldest friends and collaborators was Jedidiah Morse, "the father of American Geography." He was a neighbour in New Haven, and his children were friends of Webster's children. His son Finley Morse,[32] in particular, was a friend of Harriet's — and Finley Morse was a portrait painter. Before Webster's trip to Europe, Morse had been back in New Haven and rather short of money, and Harriet, with the family habit of finding jobs for their friends, engaged him to paint her father's portrait. He painted Percival at the same time. The picture of Webster used in the *American Dictionary* is an engraving of Morse's portrait.

According to Warfel, "as soon as the Dictionary was completed, Webster, despite the raw late November winds, rode in his carriage to Jay's home in Westchester, New York, and there presented to the aged Justice the first two completed sets." If he did, it was no more than Jay deserved, and was less than he had subscribed for, but I doubt the truth of the tale. It is the sort of story one would expect to find in Mrs. Ford's book of family folklore, but it is not there, and I do not know where Warfel got it from. Sadly, by the time Jay received the books (for which he had made the first payment in 1813) he was nearly 84, and he was too old and infirm to read them. Once again, it was his son William who wrote:

Bedford 31st: Decr: 1828

Sir,

I received by Mr. Cook, your letter of the 15th: inst: & the copies of your dictionary for which my Father subscribed. My Father desires me to thank you for the two additional copies, mentioned in your letter, & to assure you, that he accepts them as a mark of the continuance of those friendly feelings which you have so long manifested towards him. His state of health deprives him of the pleasure of examining the dictionary, but he both hopes and believes, that it will be productive of reputation and emolument to its author.

The partial inspection I have yet been able to give this great work, convinces me that it is a very valuable acquisition to our literature, & that it affords a proud proof of American talent & learning.

14. Two More Dictionaries and Another Spelling Book, 1829

Webster had invested a great deal of time, effort, and money in the preparation of his quarto dictionary, and there was no possibility that the sales of the book would provide anything like a reasonable return. Apart from anything else, at least ten years had been spent on the *Synopsis,* which had no commercial value at all. Also, Webster regarded the *American Dictionary* as an important work, and thought that its importance should be reflected in its price. To most prospective purchasers, however, $20 was more than they expected to pay for any dictionary.

None of this mattered much if money was to be made out of abridgments. A large dictionary may not make money on its own, but its reputation will help to sell smaller versions. The smaller ones can be extracted from the larger with very little effort, and should therefore provide a very satisfactory return. The commercial success of the quarto cannot be judged in isolation; it is a father whose children go out into the world to work for him, and the profitability of the enterprise is determined by the combined income of the whole family.

Johnson made an octavo abridgment of his big dictionary—"Abstracted from the Folio Edition by the Author"; Chalmers similarly abridged Todd's Johnson, and Webster must always have intended to do the same to his own quarto. Entick had abridged the abridgment, and Webster would do one that size as well. Johnson's literary aims were not the same as Webster's, but the claims he made for himself and for his "Abstract" dictionary in its Preface, might have been spoken by Webster with very little amendment:

THE PREFACE

Having been long employed in the study and cultivation of the English language, I lately published a Dictionary like those compiled by the academies of Italy and France, for the use of such as aspire to exactness of criticism, or elegance of style.

But it has been since considered that works of that kind are by no means necessary to the greater number of readers, who, seldom intending to write or presuming to judge, turn over books only to amuse their leisure, and to gain degrees of knowledge suitable to lower characters, or necessary to the common business of life: these know not any other use of a dictionary than that of adjusting orthography, and explaining terms of science or words of infrequent occurrence, or remote derivation.

For these purposes many dictionaries have been written by different authors, and with different degrees of skill; but none of them have yet fallen into my hands by which even the lowest expectations could be satisfied. Some of their authors wanted industry, and others literature: some knew their own defects, and others were too idle to supply them.

For this reason a small dictionary appeared yet to be wanting to common readers; and, as I may without arrogance claim to myself a longer acquaintance with the lexicography of our language than any other writer has had, I shall hope to be considered as having more experience at least than most of my predecessors, and as more likely to accommodate the nation with a vocabulary of daily use. I therefore offer to the Publick an Abstract or Epitome of my former Work.

In comparing this with other dictionaries of the same kind, it will be found to have several advantages.

I. It contains many words not to be found in any other.

II. Many barbarous terms and phrases by which other dictionaries may vitiate the style, are rejected from this.

III. The words are more correctly spelled, partly by attention to their etymology, and partly by observation of the practice of the best authors.

IV. The etymologies and derivations, whether from foreign languages, or from native roots, are more diligently traced, and more distinctly noted.

V. The senses of each word are more copiously enumerated, and more clearly explained.

VI. Many words occurring in the elder authors, such as Spenser, Shakespeare, and Milton, which had been hitherto omitted, are here carefully inserted; so that this book may serve as a glossary or expository index to the poetical writers.

VII. To the words, and to the different senses of each word, are subjoined from the large dictionary the names of those writers by whom they have been used; so that the reader who knows the different periods of the language, and the time of its authors, may judge of the elegance or prevalence of any word, or meaning of a word; and without recurring to other books, may know what are antiquated, what are unusual, and what are recommended by the best authority.

The words in this Dictionary, as opposed to others, are more diligently collected, more accurately spelled, more faithfully explained, and more authentically ascertained. Of an abstract it is not necessary to say more: and I hope it will not be found that truth requires me to say less.

To produce just such an "abstract edition" was Webster's intention. When the time came, however, he did not feel up to the job. He had been twenty years in labour before giving birth to the great *American Dictionary*, and he was tired. He was not in very good health, and he was, after all, 70 years old. He deserved a rest. But was there any need for him to do the work himself? All that was required was to go through the quarto dictionary with a blue pencil, striking out most of the quotations, comments and etymology, and shortening some of the definitions. The Introduction and Grammar would go, and the octavo abridgment would be ready for the press. Any reasonably literary and painstaking fellow could do the job, given a set of simple instructions. Did his publisher, Converse, by any chance, know a suitable person?

As it happened, Converse knew the very man: Joseph Emerson Worcester, a Yale graduate, living in Cambridge, Massachusetts. Not long before, he had been employed to edit another octavo dictionary, putting Walker's pronunciation into Chalmers' abridgment of Todd's Johnson. He was particularly interested in pronunciation, and had prepared a *Synopsis of Words Differently Pronounced by Different Orthoepists*.

Converse wrote to Worcester, asking if he would undertake the abridgment of Webster's *American Dictionary*. No, replied Worcester, he would not. He was at work on a small dictionary of his own, and he wanted to get on with it. Converse wrote again, and a second time Worcester refused.

Now Converse knew, at least as well as Webster and probably better, that the octavo abridgment was financially vital to the success of the whole enterprise. He had no other candidate than Worcester in mind, and he was therefore determined that Worcester should do the job. He went in person to Massachusetts, and finally persuaded Worcester to agree, by offering to pay him $2,000. It was a decision that Worcester would come to regret. He was a peaceful, scholarly type, whose academic tranquillity was to be disturbed by vicious personal attacks, first by the pugnacious Webster, and then by Webster's publishers, over a period of twenty-five years. These were the first skirmishes in what became known as "the War of the Dictionaries."

None of this could have been foreseen in 1829, when Webster authorized Converse to entrust to Worcester the work of abridging the two volume quarto dictionary into a single octavo volume. The most obvious problem then was that Worcester had to be paid, and Webster did not have any money. Converse, however, was confident that the abridgment would sell, and he was willing to accept the risk of abridging and sterotyping the octavo dictionary at his own expense. Webster was to pay five hundred dollars towards Worcester's fee, but that would come out of his share of the profits on the sale of the dictionary.

As it turned out, Worcester was prepared to do much more for his money than just the blue-pencil job outlined above. He did that, indeed, but he also added to the octavo many words that were not in the quarto dictionary. Webster suggested a few of them, but most were supplied by Worcester. Some, like *lapel* and *Londoner*, came from Chalmers' Todd's Johnson with which, of course, Worcester was very familiar. Worcester also contributed his *Synopsis of Words Differently Pronounced by Different Orthoepists* as introductory matter, on the understanding that he would be free to use it again when his own dictionary came out.

If these had been the only influences on Webster's octavo dictionary, Worcester might have lived his life in scholarly peace, and perhaps the name of Webster would never have become a household word. Worcester's torment, and the ultimate success of Webster's dictionaries, came about because Webster's son-in-law, the Rev. Professor Chauncey Allen Goodrich, took a hand in the business.

Goodrich was married to Webster's second daughter, Julia. They lived in New Haven, because Goodrich was professor of rhetoric and oratory at Yale. One reason for the Websters' move from Amherst to New Haven in 1822 was to be near the Goodriches, who would give any necessary help to Rebecca, and keep an eye on Webster's business interests, while Webster and William were away in Europe. Goodrich had always been somewhat in awe of the stern Webster, who had been a friend of his grandfather, his father, and his uncle, long before Goodrich was born, and who had frightened him since he was a child. At the same time, in Webster's old age Goodrich came to have a certain ascendancy over him. This was partly because Webster depended on him as the only man in the family who was within reach when Webster or Rebecca needed help — and it may have been partly for religious reasons. Goodrich was also, as we shall see, a cunning fellow and commercially very astute.

When the matter of the abridgment was under discussion, Goodrich understood, just as Converse did, that it was the octavo that would make their fortunes, not the quarto. He also remembered the fierce opposition that Webster had encountered whenever, in the past, he had proposed the adoption of his eccentric spellings. The *Compendious Dictionary* had been full of them, and had been ridiculed as a result. There were not so many in the *American Dictionary*, but still quite enough for Webster's critics to make jokes about. Without doubt, those orthographical oddities were, and would continue to be, an obstacle to the commercial success of the dictionary. The trouble was, Webster believed in them, and he had an obstinate attachment to his beliefs, particularly when everybody else disagreed with him. Goodrich did not much care whether Webster's spellings were right or wrong; if they interfered with sales of the dictionary, they were a bad idea. But what could he do about it?

His solution was beautifully simple and efficient. Because Webster was not feeling well enough to involve himself in the abridgment of the big dictionary, Goodrich volunteered to act as his representative, supervising the work on his behalf. This is explained in the opening words of the octavo's Preface:

The author of the American Dictionary of the English Language has been prevented, by the state of his health, from attending, in person, to its abridgment into the octavo form. The work has, therefore, been committed, for this purpose, to Mr. J.E.WORCESTER, of Cambridge, Massachusetts, who has strictly adhered to the general principles laid down for his direction by the author. Cases of doubt, arising in the application of these principles, and such changes and modifications as seemed desirable, in a work of this kind, intended for general use, have been referred, for decision, to PROF.GOODRICH, of *Yale College,* who was requested by the author to act, on these subjects, as his representative.

The sting is in that last sentence. Goodrich gave himself permission to introduce "such changes and modifications as seemed desirable, in a work of this kind," *whether Webster would have approved of them or not.* That is to say, the changes he introduced were the ones that Goodrich, not Webster, considered "desirable"; and what Goodrich desired was a dictionary that would sell, not one that was linguistically correct. Webster was not consulted, and he had no direct dealings with Worcester.

It would not have done to clear out the eccentric spellings completely, for that would have made Webster look even more ridiculous than he did already. What Goodrich did was to reduce their impact. The abridged dictionary was constructed in such a way that, though many of the eccentric spellings remained, they might never be noticed by the average reader. The reader would look up a word in its normal spelling, would find it in its expected place in the word list, and would find no eccentric spellings in the definition. Goodrich called this "doubling," which meant giving both the conventional and the abnormal spellings bracketed together. Where Webster advocated and used an eccentric spelling, such as *drouth, lether, nightmar* or *porpess,* Goodrich (or Worcester, at Goodrich's direction) left it in, but always put the normal spelling first. The dictionary entry was always alphabetically in the place of the

Portrait of J.E. Worcester from his *Dictionary of the English Language* (1859).

conventional spelling, and the conventional spelling was used in definitions. Thus, Webster's entry for *ieland* disappeared completely. Under *island*, The octavo gave the alternative spellings *island* and *iland*, but used only the former. An *islander* was "An inhabitant of an island," and an *islet* was "A little island." In the quarto, Webster had used the spelling *ieland* in both of those definitions. To have done otherwise would have been inconsistent with his statement that *island* was "an absurd compound of Fr. *isle* and land, which signifies *land in water-land*, or rather *ieland-land*."

Sometimes, Webster had himself used doubling, so that in the quarto the alternative spellings *feather* and *fether* appeared bracketed together. Webster, however, doubled all the derivatives as well (from *fether-bed* to *fethery*) and used *fether* in the definitions. The octavo only gave the conventional spelling for the derivatives, and always used *feather* in its definitions — a *feather-bed* was "A bed filled with *feathers*."

For the words *pontiff* and *sheriff*, where Webster lopped off the second "F," the octavo again gave both spellings, but used the conventional one.

Webster's least acceptable "correction," *bridegoom*, received little sympathy in the octavo.

The entry is under *bridegroom* only, without doubling, and Webster's comment that this "gross corruption or blunder ought not to remain a reproach to philology" is diluted into a quiet note in parentheses: "Originally and properly, bridegoom."

Also with a view to public acceptability and commercial success, Goodrich had Worcester eliminate some of Webster's oddities of pronunciation. His comment in the quarto that *angel* is "Usually pronounced *āngel*, but most anomalously" appears in the octavo, but the indicated pronunciation is Ā N'GEL.

In this form, satisfactory to Goodrich and to Converse, the octavo abridgment was printed and published. When Webster discovered what they had done, he was very upset. The changes introduced into the octavo had made him appear to be inconsistent with himself. He did not even like Worcester's *Synopsis of Words Differently Pronounced*, because his own authority as the arbiter of correct pronunciation was weakened by his being held up to a comparison with others. He so disliked the octavo that he wanted to dissociate himself from it entirely, and he made it known in the family that he was considering selling the copyright. This was discussed between the two sons-in-law who were involved with the dictionaries, Goodrich, and Harriet's husband William Fowler. They agreed that a sale should be prevented at all costs. Goodrich put a high value on the copyright of the octavo, and he had a very low opinion of Webster's bargaining skill and commercial acumen. Soon after their discussion, Fowler had to go back to Middlebury, Vermont, where he was professor of mineralogy and chemistry, and he left the matter in Goodrich's hands, Goodrich assuring him that he would "endeavor to prevent all bargains." About two weeks later, however, Webster did sell the copyright in the octavo, and he sold it for very much less than Goodrich had said he thought it was worth. Goodrich did not mind. He was the one who bought it.

The octavo dictionary was, as anticipated, much more profitable than the quarto, and it was reprinted by Converse several times. Unhappily, Converse then went bankrupt (for

reasons unconnected with Webster's dictionaries) and Goodrich had to look around for someone else to publish the octavo. The stereotype plates were offered to George and Charles Merriam, printers and booksellers of Springfield, Massachusetts, but they turned them down. They had started in business together only two or three years previously, and had not the confidence or the resources to take on the publication of the dictionary. They were the nephews of Ebenezer Merriam of Brookfield, who had published an edition of Perry's *Royal Standard English Dictionary*, and they would continue the family tradition of dictionary-publishing after Webster's death — but that was still some years ahead.

Goodrich was now faced with a problem that he had not anticipated: people that he approached about publishing the octavo were worried about competition from the quarto. This had not troubled Converse, because he published both, but to a possible publisher of the octavo alone there was a risk that Webster might decide to bring out a cut-price stereotyped edition of the *American Dictionary*. It would sell for much less than $20, and might seriously interfere with sales of the octavo. This time, Goodrich could not find a solution by going behind Webster's back. He approached the old man directly, and convinced him that it would not be fair to him, if Webster were to publish a smaller and cheaper edition of the existing quarto, because it would substantially reduce the value of the rights in the octavo that he had sold to Goodrich. Webster was persuaded to add a stipulation to their earlier contract, in these terms:[1]

Whereas I have transferred to Chauncey A Goodrich all my right & title to the premium for copy-right of my Octavo dictionary, stipulated to be paid to me by Sherman Converse; now if said Chauncey A Goodrich should purchase in whole or in part the stereotype plates of said dictionary, & I should hereafter prepare a copy of my Quarto Dictionary for publication in the octavo size, I promise that I will not publish or permit to be published such an edition in octavo on stereotype plates, without some agreement with said Goodrich that I shall secure him and any persons who may be associated with him from any injury that may result from such publication, by reduction of the price of the larger work, & supplanting the Octavo in the market.

New Haven May 7. 1833   N.Webster

Once he had that assurance, Goodrich was able to strike a deal with N.& J.White of New York for them to publish the octavo. As Merriams later expressed it, "The work became in their hands, and those of their successors, a very valuable publication." It was into a fifteenth edition by 1836.

Goodrich's low opinion of his father-in-law's worldly wisdom was abundantly justified. Webster had not only sold the most profitable part of his lexicographical enterprise for a fraction of what it was worth; he had also tied his hands so that the *American Dictionary*, the flagship of the fleet, was unlikely ever to make a profit.

In Fowler's pamphlet describing these events, *Printed but not Published,* he recounts conversations that he later had with White and with Goodrich, "in reference to purchasing the right to stereotype the large work." This suggests that Fowler did not know the details of Webster's promise of May 1833, and that he believed Webster had undertaken not to publish *any* stereotyped edition of the *American Dictionary.* In fact, Webster's promise only fettered his right to publish a stereotyped octavo edition of the work; a stereotyped quarto would not have been prohibited. After Webster's death, Ellsworth, his executor, seems to have been under the same misapprehension. Goodrich, of course, could have explained the true position, but it was not in his interests to do so; any restriction on the publication of a cheap edition of the *American Dictionary* could only help the sales of the octavo abridgment.

Webster never forgot that the royalties on the octavo had given Goodrich more than his fair share of the communal cake. In his will, he made provision for all his children except Julia Goodrich, to whom he left absolutely nothing. The reason was explained in the will itself; She and her husband received "the sum of thirty seven cents on every copy of my Octavo dictionary which shall be printed & sold, during twenty eight years from its first publication, which will probably include a full share or more than an equal share of my property, when divided among my children."

Webster's next dictionary was a square octavo,[2] a little larger than Entick, called *A Dictionary of the English Language: Abridged from the American Dictionary, for the use of Primary*

Schools and the Counting House. Reading the Preface, one can sense the bitterness he felt at the way he had been made to betray his own principles in the octavo. He explained why the orthography of the *Primary School Dictionary* was not the same as that of either of the larger dictionaries:

> While I was engaged in writing the Quarto Dictionary and in the supervision of the press, I was so much occupied with the more difficult departments of the work, the etymologies and definitions, that some errors in orthography escaped observation, which an exclusive attention to that subject would have prevented. These I have corrected; and a further consideration of some points, has induced me to make a few alterations. Hence some discrepancies will be found between that work and this. Other discrepancies will appear between this work and the octavo edition, some of which I should have prevented, if I had been able to superintend the preparation of the copy for the press. But the number of these I am not able to ascertain; as it is not probable that I shall ever again read the whole of that or of the quarto edition. My intense and long continued labors render repose essential to my health and comfort, during the short period of life which remains.

> But the reader is informed that wherever discrepancies appear between this work and the larger ones, this duodecimo volume, my last work, all written and corrected by myself, is to be considered as containing the pointing, orthography, and pronunciation which I most approve.

That was written in December 1829, when Webster's spirits were low. As it turned out, he had several more years of active life left. Time to prepare his version of the Bible, and a revised edition of the *American Dictionary*. Neither of those made him any money, of course, but the little *Primary School Dictionary* sold rather well. My copy is dated 1833, just four years after its first publication, and it is the thirteenth edition.

The other book that appeared in 1829 was the *Elementary Spelling Book*. The second term of copyright in the *American Spelling Book* was not due to expire until March 1832, but Webster did not want to wait until then to introduce its replacement. In 1826, after his return from Europe with the completed manuscript of the *American Dictionary*, he had written to the *American Journal of Education* announcing not only that his great dictionary was finished, but also that his spelling book would "be adjusted to a uniformity with the dictionary in pronun-

ciation." In July 1827, he wrote to Hudson & Co. telling them that he planned a new edition of the spelling book. As might be expected, they were not too pleased with this news. They had paid Webster a lot of money for rights in the 1804 *American Spelling Book*, and those rights still had nearly five years to run. Hudsons' licensees were paying them for selling the book, and their continued income depended on those licensees continuing to sell it. They said they would only agree to Webster's plan on three conditions: if they were given all the rights in the new speller; if there were to be an orderly transition from the old book to the new one; and if their licensees consented. They said that Webster would be in breach of his contract with them if he introduced the new speller in competition with the old.

Did they have a case? It is certainly true that they would not have agreed to make the stipulated payments, if they had supposed that Webster might at any time diminish the value of what he was selling them, by preparing and promoting a competing work. This, however, was not prohibited by the terms of the agreement they had signed. Webster argued that all he had sold to Hudsons were rights in the *American Spelling Book* for fourteen years, and they still had the exclusive right to print and sell that book.

Because he was busy working on the *Primary School Dictionary*, Webster wanted someone else to compile the new spelling book for him. His first candidate for the job was Daniel Barnes, the principal of the high school in New York, but Barnes was killed in an accident when he had completed only part of the work. Then on December 15, 1828, Webster made an agreement with another New York schoolmaster, Aaron Ely:

> that the said Ely shall take the materials for a spelling book prepared by said Webster, & with these & such materials as the said Ely has prepared, & may hereafter prepare, shall as soon as may be compile a spelling book for said Webster, submitting the same to the revision of said Webster, for which labor & services the said Webster ... shall be held to pay to the said Ely ... in the month of March which shall be in the year 1832, one thousand dollars.

The fact that Ely's payment was to be withheld until March 1832, the same month that the copyright in the *American Spelling Book* was to

expire, suggests that Webster may in 1828 have contemplated delaying publication of the new spelling book until then. If so, he changed his mind. Despite Hudson's protests, it was published in New York in 1829. The title of the new book was deposited in the Connecticut District Court on May 22, 1829, the same day as the title of the *Primary School Dictionary*.

To compete with his own earlier speller, Webster had to emphasise that the new version was better — that is to say, he had to attack his own *American Spelling Book*, which Hudson & Co. and their licensees were still selling. This message was contained in the very title that he deposited for the new book; it was called *The Elementary Spelling Book; being an improvement on the American Spelling Book. By Noah Webster, LL.D.*

The frontispiece of the *Elementary Spelling Book* is an allegorical picture representing a virtuous youth being led by Wisdom (the goddess Minerva) to the Temple of Fame, which is to be entered through the portico marked "Knowledge." The picture had previously been used as a frontispiece to some editions of the *American Spelling Book*, where it appeared over a verse that was not used in the *Elementary*:

> KNOWLEDGE and FAME are gain'd
>   not by surprise;
> He that would win, must LABOR
>   for the prize:
> 'Tis thus the youth, from lisping A.B.C.
> Attains, at length, a Master's high degree.

I do not know whether that verse was original or not. The last two lines were later used beneath the frontispiece of Sanders' spelling book of 1845, but he may have copied them from Webster. The picture Webster used was certainly not original; it was copied from Volume I of Dodsley's *Preceptor*, where it was one of a pair. The matching plate in Dodsley's Volume II shows an incautious youth being lured away from the path of Virtue by Pleasure (represented by a topless temptress), little realising that he will in consequence suffer Want, Care, Disease, and keen Remorse. The two pictures, in fact, tell the story of Tommy and Harry.

In the *Elementary*, the last number in the table "Of numbers is 1829, MDCCCXXIX, but all the other Roman numerals are the same as in the *American Spelling Book*. Indeed, throughout the *Elementary*, there is much that is familiar, but also much that is new. In the *American*, one had to wade through twelve lessons of meaningless syllables before coming to any words; even then, the words were only the tedious rows and columns of *bag, fag, cag, gag, hag, rag* &c.; now, most of the meaningless syllables have disappeared, and words appear even before the syllables — alongside the letters of the alphabet there are examples of their use, from *ape* to *zest*. An improvement copied from Marshall's spelling book is the introduction of sentences at the earliest possible moment, starting with Marshall's own sentences, *go on, go in, go up*, immediately after the first table, *ba be bi bo bu by*. The *Elementary* also copies Marshall in dividing up the long lists of words into more digestible helpings. In the *Elementary* there are, for example, only ninety words in the first list of "Words of two syllables, accented on the first," where in the American Spelling Book there were three hundred. Many of these lists are followed by sentences, using some of the words in the preceding list in such a way as to explain their meaning or character. Thus the first word in that list is *Ba ker* in both books, but only in the *Elementary* is one told that "Bakers bake bread and cakes."

Apart from a little dip into Marshall, it appears this material was not copied from any other work, but that very fact restricted the compiler to the limited resources of his own mind. The result is often repetitive. Within a span of eighteen pages, the reader learns that "A cat can eat a rat"; "Cats devour rats and mice"; "A cat will kill and eat rats and mice"; "A cat can catch rats and mice"; and "The cat and mouse live in the house." As an example of the use of the word *brass*, one is told that "Brass is made of zink and copper"; later, following a table of "Words of two syllables, accented on the first," "Brass is a compound of copper and zink." The latter sentence illustrates another problem which results from having shorter tables — neither *compound* nor *copper* is included in the table that precedes the sentence.

Sometimes, one gets the impression that the repetitiveness is a deliberate attempt to implant an improving message. There are the usual religious and moral precepts, of course, and there

Frontispieces from volumes I and II of Dodsley's *Preceptor* **and from Webster's** *Elementary.*

have come from Marshall's "Clean your teeth. Wash your mouths. Then your breath will be sweet." Marshall also had a table giving "Five reasons for not using Spirituous Liquors," but that is as nothing compared to the sustained attack on alcohol maintained throughout the *Elementary Spelling Book*:

He must not drink a dram. No man can make a good plea for a dram. The man who drinks rum will soon want a loaf of bread. Strong drink leads to the debasement of the mind and body. We look with amazement on the evils of strong drink. We pity the slavish drinkers of rum. The drunkard's face will publish his vice and his disgrace. There is a near intimacy between drunkenness, poverty, and ruin. It is customary for tipplers to visit taverns. Rum, gin, brandy and whisky, are destructive enemies to mankind. They destroy more lives than wars, famine and pestilence. The drunkard's course is progressive; he begins by drinking a little, and shortens his life by drinking to excess. Many persons spend too much time in taverns. Intemperance is the grievous sin of our country. Liquors that intoxicate are to be avoided as poison. Drunkards are worthless fellows, and despised. Strong liquors inflame the blood, and produce diseases. Intemperate people are exposed to inflammatory diseases. Ardent spirits stimulate the system for a time, but leave it more languid. The love of whisky has brought many a stout fellow to the whipping-post.

is a good deal of information about political theory and the American system. A novelty, for Webster, is encouragement of dental hygiene: "Keep your mouth clean, and save your teeth. A tooth brush is good to brush your teeth." The idea for that lesson, though not the words, may

The preoccupation with drink must have been Ely's, for it has no parallel elsewhere in Webster's writings.

A feature of the *Elementary* that is certainly Webster's rather than Ely's is the method of indicating pronunciation, using what are described in the "Key" as "Points and marks to designate sounds." Previously, little numbers had been used to distinguish the different sounds of the vowels; now, this is done by dots and accents above or below the letters, or, in the case of the *yu* sound of *u* (as in *union*) a little tail on the letter. Similarly, the sounds of consonants other than their primary sounds are indicated by the addition of accents or marks. Webster then borrows another idea from Marshall, printing a row of common words across the top of each pair of pages, to show the points and marks in use. If in doubt as to how to pronounce the word *äsp*, for example, one looks at the top of the facing page, and finds that the vowel sound *ä* is that in the word *bär*: the word is to be pronounced *ahsp*. The *Primary School Dictionary*, published at the same time as the *Elementary*, uses the same system, and has the same words printed across the top of each pair of pages.

The publication of *The Elementary Spelling Book*, describing itself as "an Improvement on the American Spelling Book," may have led Nathan Guilford of Cincinnati to assume (only a year or so prematurely) that the *American* was out of copyright. He thought that if Noah Webster could improve on the *American*, so could Nathan Guilford. In 1831, he published a spelling book with a title cunningly contrived to suggest that Webster had written it. It was called *The Western Spelling Book; being an Improvement of the American Spelling Book, by Noah Webster*. Like Marshall, he used Walker's pronunciation system, and he printed Walker's pronunciation reminders across the top of each pair of pages, but he had the good sense not to use Walker's spelling. He copied the titles of most of Webster's tables changing their content somewhat, and adopted a feature of the *Elementary* in numbering the tables in Arabic as well as Roman numerals. Since his book was avowedly based on the *American*, it is surprising how much he changed, but he copied Webster's table *Of Numbers* so exactly that he ended with MDCCCIV, the year the *American Spelling*

Book was published, rather than the appropriate year for his own book, MDCCCXXXI. Another part of what he copied was very personal to Webster — it was roughly half the section in which Webster's children appeared. Harriet and Mary once again recite most of their poems. William's interrogation has been rewritten to cover distances and weights and measures, as well as coinage. When Guildford's book was published, William, the youngest of those three children, was nearly 30 years old. Such a Peter Pan prolongation of his childhood would be rather comical, save that it prompts the sad reflection that Webster's favourite daughter, Mary, was already dead.

Hudson's letters to Webster touched upon Guilford's infringement of copyright, as well as Hudson's attempts to hold Webster to their agreement:

Hartford 18 Aug 1831

Sir,

Mr. Ellsworth has recently called on me for the documents relating to the copyright of the spelling book — It occurred to me that if Guilford was trespassing upon the American Sp. book I was the only person that could prosecute a claim upon him — if I am correct in this, it is important that I retain the papers in my hands, especially for the present, as I am expecting to see my Agent at Cincinnati soon here.

As the contracts with the present publishers will soon expire, & as it is important that the publication of one of the books should be kept up without intermission, would it not facilitate that object as well as remove all hesitation & doubt and save the trouble of much correspondence by sending me a sort of general letter that may be communicated to all the publishers, that they are to pay me for all copies of both books, printed previous to 15 March next? If I have no evidence of this sort *to exhibit to them*, they may not recognise my claim & if none is made by you they may perhaps feel satisfied to continue their labours & not account till I can prove my title.

I have understood that some persons other than the old publishers had been authorised by you to publish the new book; will you be so good as to inform me who they are & what number they were authorised to print?

* * * * *

Hartford 27 Aug 1831

Sir,

I am favoured with yours of 20 ins. As the object is to stop the publication of Guilfords book by an *injunction* I have no objection to the application being made in your name alone. If the suit were for

damages I should consider myself entitled to what might be recovered. As he has infringed your right to the new book will you have occasion for any other documents than those that shew your title to that? if any relating to the old book, will it be any other than the newspapers in which the entry was published?

I am sorry that you have given liberty to Terham & Letson to print 9000 copies after the expiration of Sept^r.; as I have already paid them $100 & have engaged to pay them $100 more, when their last note becomes due, in consideration of the damage they suffered from the publication of the new book; & this I explicitly stated to you in our last personal interview, to which you replied, it ought not to be done for you knew that their complaint was utterly groundless. And I submit whether this & the permission given to other publishers to make up their deficiencies *after* Septr. will not have the effect to diminish their efforts to work off their full complement during the life of their contract & thus prevent the necessity for printing an additional number during the coming six months on which they would have to pay me the copyright — no one has asked *me* for an extension of time but they have asked & have permission to print till March by paying me for the same — it appears to me that the permission you have so given operates directly against my interests notwithstanding I am to be paid for all printed previous to 15 March.

P.S. In justice to myself I shall write to Terham & Letson that I shall require payment for all they print after expiration of their contract till March.

* * * * *

Hartford 12 Sep. 1831

Sir,

Agreeably to your request I send herewith by Mr. Ellsworth the newspapers in which the record of the American Sp. book was published. The attested copy of the Clerks record I ought not to part with as it is the most imporant evidence of my title to the copyright.

I am this day informed by one of the publishers under my right that he is not to answer to me but to White Gallaher & White for the Elementary Sp. book that may be published after the 14 Septr. and that the American Sp. book cannot be printed after 14 Septr. and that on the authority of a letter from you. As I have never consented to any such interference I must express my surprise at it, as well as my intention to counteract its effects upon my interests as far as practicable.

* * * * *

Hartford 22 Sept.1831

Sir,

I was duly favoured with yours of 14 ins^t. and altho not requiring a reply, I notice it as I am not accu-

somed to rest satisfied under an imputation of departure from an agreement. It was *our* agreement that the Elementary Sp. book might be published *with* the old one & substituted for it as the present publishers thought proper, but it was never agreed that the old one should in any other way be suspended till my right had expired — have I departed from this agreement either in letter or spirit? it was also *our* agreement that I should have the sole disposal of the right to print the new work for which I was to have a commission — did I not at once do what could then be done to commend the work to the goodwill of the present publishers? and notwithstanding there was an injurious departure from this agreement on the other side have I ever done any thing to impede the success of the work?

Can the dismissal of the old book from one half or two thirds of the schools in New England be imputed to me at the same time that I am charged with requiring the publishers to print annually a much larger number than the market requires? A year or two will show which mode will be best for the work & for the author — to require the publisher to take a specific interest in the work, share the responsibilities & thus ensure his exertions, — or, to let him publish an many as he pleases & when he pleases & thus occasionally to have a deficiency & then a surplus for an overstocked market, with no powerful inducement to resist the introduction of other works, but ready at all times to take hold of any thing more attractive. The former mode I have no doubt if adopted two years ago would have placed at this time in the hands of the author fifteen to twenty thousand dollars with a certainty of increase — that, in hand, would have been sure. The latter mode may give more in aggregate but I doubt it; and the trouble attending it will be much increased.

I have not complained of any "attempt to injure" me, but I have sufficient grounds for complaining that the effect of the measures adopted have been injurious to my interest. And I am sorry that a respectful intimation of that fact should make it appear necessary to refer me to the law for redress.

* * * * *

Hartford 27 Oct 1831

Sir,

I was duly favoured with yours of 28th ult^o.... I write now only to relieve myself from an imputation of having advanced a groundless claim. I do not think the *inference* correct, that my agency was suspended, because there was no reply to my claim for travelling expenses; had that been the fact as you supposed. But we are not left to inferences — your reply to my letter of 29 Oct^o 1828, was by the *next mail* — no objection was made to my terms, but you agreed "in general" to what I wrote. *After this*, the *circular* was drawn up, printed & distributed, & my best exertions to introduce the new book were in

requisition, as will appear by your letters of 8 & 15 Nov., till 19 March when our *agreement* was *nullified*, by which I mean, that, that which was properly to be done by two parties was done by one.

P.S. I have the satisfaction to state that the house who complained to you that they should lose the sale of 20,000 copies a year by my proceedings, have to their own surprise printed all they were entitled to, & are still printing — the same house compelled me to pay them $200 for injury received from the introduction of the *new book!*

* * * * *

Hartford 21 Dec 1832

Sir,

Will you do me the favor to send me a copy of the returns that have been made to you of the Elementary Sp. book published from Sep. 1831 to March last? A number of the publishers have made no returns to me & some who have claimed that the copyright is to be paid to you — if any such has been already paid to which I am entitled by our agreement I shall be glad to receive the amo.

* * * * *

In one respect, Webster failed to learn by his earlier experience. The first editions of the *Elementary* contained no fables or pictures. This made made some people prefer the old *American Spelling Book*, and Webster contemplated reintroducing it. His licensees in Cincinnati, Corey & Fairbank, wrote advising against this course:

Cincinnati, May 27, 1833

Dear Sir,

We have this day been informed by Mr. Peck, of the firm of Durrie & Peck, that you contemplate *re*-publishing your *old* Spelling Book. Being engaged in publishing the *new* one, we cannot, of course, but feel some interest in your decision, as the re-introduction of the *old* will greatly embarrass the introduction of the *new* one, which we have succeeded, in a good measure, in accomplishing in this region. It is not, however, a matter of *mere* personal interest that induces us to address you. We believe that this contemplated change is not called for, at least, in this region. The old book has now gone out of use, and the new one has generally taken its place, & is decidedly *preferred* wherever it has been introduced. It has not only taken the place of the old one, but in several places where the old one had been discarded, it has been introduced. In this very city, the old one had been superseded by *Guilford's* — so soon as we had published the "Elementary" book, the Visitors and Trustees of the Common Schools here, excluded Guilfords & introduced it, and the teachers are all

well satisfied with it. Whenever orders have been sent for the old ones we have filled them with the *new*, and so have all the Booksellers here; and we do not learn that any dissatisfaction has resulted from this course. We have published, since last fall, between 30 and 40,000 of the new ones, & have made arrangts. to complete at the rate of about 100,000 per year....

In their next letter, (July 23, 1833) Corey & Fairbank suggested some alterations to the *Elementary Spelling Book* that would overcome objections that had been made to it, "viz: the want of a *due proportion* of *reading lessons*, and of some *pictures.*" This would render the republication of the *American* unnecessary. They suggested leaving out ten pages or so, "and substituting in their place, the reading lessons, pictures, fables etc. — the tables on the pages above alluded to are seldom used, and we think might well be dispensed with...." Webster followed this advice, and restored four of the fables from the *American Spelling Book*: Fenning's story "Of the Boy that stole Apples," and, from Dodsley, "The Country Maid and her Milk pail," "The Two Dogs," and "The partial Judge." There were also pictures (taken from Bewick) illustrating short paragraphs about three animals: the dog ("this dog is the mastif ..."), the stag, and the squirrel.

The spelling *mastif* is one of many unconventional spellings in the *Elementary Spelling Book.* The *Elementary,* unlike the *American,* was largely a new book, and it therefore used the spelling that Webster approved at the time when it was compiled. In the Preface, he said that he had corrected "the few errors in orthography" that occurred in the *American Spelling Book* but those "corrections" were less often putting right misprints or mistakes than reflections of Webster's changing view of what spelling was correct. His view in 1829 was not represented by the quarto dictionary, for his opinions on spelling had changed during the years that he had worked on that, and its beginning was not consistent with its end; nor by the octavo, in which Worcester, under Goodrich's guidance, had concealed Webster's eccentricities of spelling. In 1829, the only authoritative guide to Webster's spelling was the little *Primary School Dictionary,* which, he wrote, "is to be considered as containing the pointing, orthography, and pronunciation which I most approve."

The spelling of the *Primary School Dictionary* is largely that of the latter part of the *American Dictionary*, but the trend toward innovation has stopped, and there has been a perceptible movement the other way. The single-F spelling is used in *bailif, caitif, dandruf, mastif* &c., but not in *cliff. Gazel* is so spelled in the definition of *antelope* as well as in its own entry. *Maiz* also is established, but *grouse* has its *e* (except in the definition of *quail*). Of Webster's pet peculiarities, *bridegoom, nightmar* and *tung* are in, but in the entry *island*, Webster used the conventional spelling, where he had used *ieland* in the *American Dictionary*. Similarly, *feather/fether* and *leather/lether* are given as alternatives in both dictionaries, but in the *American* Webster used the phonetic spellings in the definitions; now he uses the conventional spellings.

15. Webster in Washington, 1830-31

When he was in England, Webster learned that the copyright position there had changed. The American Copyright Act of 1790, which was still in force in the United States, had been based on the Statute of Queen Anne, the Copyright Act 1709. That act had been amended in 1814,[1] and authors in England now enjoyed 28 years protection in the first instance, which was then continued for life if the author had not died during the first 28 years. From Webster's point of view in 1825, this was much better than the American Act, which gave protection in the first instance for only 14 years. When he had published his first spelling book, he was 25, and he was single. He could look forward to 28 years' protection, which would have seemed to stretch ahead forever. When he finished the dictionary, however, he was nearly 70, and he had a large family. It was unlikely that he would survive another 14 years, and if he did not, the copyright in his major works would lapse after that period, leaving his family without his support. As Webster knew, this had happened to the family of Timothy Dwight (who had succeeded Stiles as president of Yale in 1795), after Dwight's death in 1817. It seemed to Webster that two alterations were needed to the American law to meet the needs of elderly authors: the first term of copyright should be longer; and when the author died during the first term, it should be possible for his widow and surviving children to secure the benefit of the second term.

Webster also knew of various cases in England in which it had been argued in the courts that an author had the right *at common law*, to stop others from printing his books without his permission; that is, it was argued that this right existed whether or not there was a copyright act giving statutory protection, and that it con-

tinued to exist even after a statutory period of copyright protection had come to an end; it existed *in perpetuity*. This seemed to Webster to be a very good idea indeed. The argument had finally failed both in Scotland and in England, but he would see whether a different outcome could not be achieved in America.

When he was back home, Webster wrote another letter to Daniel Webster:

New Haven, September 30th, 1826

Sir,

Having, since my return from Europe, had no opportunity of seeing you, I take this occasion to express to you my acknowledgments for complying with my request and procuring an Act of Congress enabling me to import copies of my dictionary and synopsis into the United States free of the duties imposed by the tariff. When I wrote to you from Cambridge in England, I had not offered my manuscripts to the book sellers; and I supposed that I should find no difficulty in procuring them to be published, but after I went to London, I soon found that the principal publishers were engaged in a new edition of Johnson and in a new work of a like kind; and they would not bring to market a work that might come in competition with those in which they were engaged. The smaller booksellers and publishers could not undertake so heavy a publication. I am, therefore, obliged to wait for types to execute the work in this country; and this has caused a great delay. But this delay, I find, will be very useful to the work; and on the whole I have reason to be very well satisfied with the result, both of my voyage and of my application to the English booksellers.

There is another subject, Sir, to which I take the liberty to invite your attention.

Since the celebrated decision respecting copyright by the highest British tribunal, it seems to have been generally admitted that an author has not a permanent and exclusive right to the publication of his original works at common law, and that he must depend wholly on statutes for his enjoyment of that right. As I firmly believe this decision to be contrary

to all our best established principles of *right* and *property*, and as I have reason to think such a decision would not now be sanctioned by the authorities in this country, I sincerely desire that, while you are a member of the House of Representatives in Congress, your talents may be exercised in placing this species of property on the same footing as all other property as to exclusive right and permanence of possession.

Among all modes of acquiring property or exclusive ownership, the act or operation of *creating* or *making* seems to have the first claim. If anything can justly give a man an exclusive right to the occupancy and enjoyment of a thing, it must be the fact that he has *made* it. The right of a farmer and mechanic to the exclusive enjoyment and right of disposal of what they *make* or *produce* is never questioned.

What, then, can make a difference between the produce of *muscular* strength and the produce of the *intellect*? If it should be said that the purchaser of a bushel of wheat has obtained not only the exclusive right to the use of it for food but the right to sow it and make increase and profit by it, let it be replied, this is true; but if he sows the wheat, he must sow it on his own ground or soil. The case is different with respect to the copy of a book which a purchaser has obtained, for the copy-right is the *author's soil*, which the purchaser cannot legally occupy.

Upon what principle, let me ask, can my fellow citizens declare that the productions of the farmer and the artisan shall be protected by common law or the principles of natural and social right without a special statute and without paying a premium for the enjoyment of their property, while they declare that I have only a temporary right to the fruits of my labor, and even this can not be enjoyed without giving a premium? Are such principles as these consistent with the established doctrines of property and of moral right and wrong among an enlightened people? Are such principles consistent with the high and honorable notions of justice and equal privilege which our citizens claim to entertain and to cherish as characteristic of modern improvements in civil society? How can the *recent origin* of a particular species of property vary the principles of ownership? I say nothing of the inexpedience of such a policy as it regards the discouragement of literary exertions. Indeed, I can probably say nothing on this subject that you have not said or thought; at least, I presume you have often contemplated this subject in all its bearings.

The British Parliament about ten or twelve years ago passed a new act on this subject, giving to authors and proprietors of new works an absolute right to the exclusive use of the copy-right for twenty-eight years, with some other provisions which I do not recollect, but the act makes or continues the condition that the author or proprietor shall deposit *eleven copies* of the work in Stationer's Hall for the benefit of certain public libraries. This premium will often amount to *fifty pounds sterling* or more. An effort was made by publishers to obtain a repeal of this provision; but it was opposed by the institutions which were to receive the benefit, and the attempt failed.

I have a great interest in this question, and I think the interests of science and literature in this question are by no means inconsiderable.

I sincerely wish our legislature would come at once to the line of right and justice on this subject, and pass a new act, the preamble to which shall admit the principle that an author has, by common law or natural justice, the sole and *permanent* right to make profit by his own labor, and that his heirs and assigns shall enjoy the right, unclogged with conditions. The Act thus admitting the right would prescribe only the mode by which it shall be ascertained, secured, and enjoyed, and violations of the right punished; and perhaps make some provisions for the case of attempts to elude the statute by slight alterations of books by mutilations and transpositions.

Excuse me, Sir, for the trouble I give you, and believe me, with much respect,

Your obedient Servant,
N. Webster

Webster had been troubled by compilers of rival spelling books who had attempted to elude the statute by making "slight alterations, ... mutilations and transpositions" to his own speller.

In an earlier chapter, we looked at the part of Webster's paper "Origin of the Copy-right Laws in the United States" covering the period in the 1780's, when he had been lobbying for copyright protection in the separate states for the benefit of the *Grammatical Institute*. The paper takes up the story again with Webster's second copyright campaign. This time he wanted to secure improved protection, for the benefit of the *American Dictionary*. Most of the above letter to Daniel Webster is quoted, introduced in this way:

When I was in England, in 1825, I learned that the British parliament had, a few years before, enacted a new law on copy-rights, by which the rights of authors were much extended. This led me to attempt to procure a new law in the United States, giving a like extension to the rights of authors. My first attempt appears in the following letter.

That is rather misleading. In his letter, Webster was not trying to obtain for American authors protection similar to that afforded by the British statute of 1814; what he wanted was an acknowledgment from Congress that, in America

at least, authors were entitled to perpetual copyright at common law, and that no legislative act was necessary to create such a right. It might be suggested that Webster never really believed this, and that his letter was intended only to establish a bargaining position, but the little lecture in the *American Dictionary* under *property* shows that after his visit to England, Webster firmly believed that any curtailment of copyright was tantamount to depriving an author of property that was legitimately his by act of creation.

Daniel Webster was not persuaded. He replied to Webster's letter:

Boston, October 14, 1826

Dear Sir,

I have received yours of the 30th of September, and shall with your permission, lay it before the committee of the judiciary next session, as that committee has in contemplation some important changes in the law respecting copy-right. Your opinion, in the abstract, is certainly right and uncontrovertible. Authorship is, in its nature, ground of property. Most people, I think, are as well satisfied (or better) with the reasoning of Mr. Justice Yates, as with that of Lord Mansfield, in the great case of Miller and Taylor. But after all, property, in the social state, must be the creature of law; and it is a question of expediency, high and general, not particular expediency, how and how far, the rights of authorship should be protected. I confess frannkly, that I see, or think I see, objections to make it perpetual. At the same time I am willing to extend it further than at present, and am fully pursuaded that it ought to be relieved from all charges, such as depositing copies, &c.

As the case which disposed of the matter in the House of Lords had been decided in 1774, it might be thought that Webster, in suggesting, more than fifty years later, that there might still be perpetual copyright in the United States, was flogging a horse that had been dead for rather a long time. In fact the horse had at least one race left in it; it didn't win, but it only lost by a majority decision. The case was *Wheaton v. Peters*, decided in the U.S. Supreme Court in the January Term of 1834. The plaintiff, Henry Wheaton, had been the Supreme Court reporter between 1816 and 1827, and had published reports of the decisions of the Court during those years— *Wheaton's Reports*. The defendant, Richard Peters, published *Condensed Reports of Casis in the Supreme Court of the United States*,

covering all the decisions of the Court from its inception up to the January term of 1827 — including, therefore, reprints of much that was in *Wheaton's Reports*. Wheaton claimed that this was an infringement of his copyright, but he was unable to furnish any conclusive proof that a copy of his work had been deposited with the secretary of state, as required by the 1790 Act. His case was: (i) a copy probably had been deposited; (ii) even if it had not, this did not prevent his having copyright under the statute; (iii) if it did, so that he had no statutory copyright, he nevertheless had copyright at common law. The defendant argued (i) that the deposit of a copy was requisite for copyright to be enjoyed under the statute; (ii) that there was no copyright at common law; and (iii) that nobody could claim copyright in decisions of the Supreme Court anyway. The case has a somewhat incestuous quality to it because Peters had succeeded Wheaton as Supreme Court reporter, and he therefore found himself reporting, at very great length, on a case in which he was himself the defendant. Peters won convincingly, which may be why his account of the case occupies more than one hundred pages of Volume VIII of *Peters' Reports*. When asserting that the deposit of a copy with the secretary of state was a precondition for the subsistence of copyright, the defendant's counsel drew the Court's attention to Section 1 of the supplementary Copyright Act of 1802, which described it as one of "the requisites enjoined in the third and fourth sections of said act." What did the word "requisite" mean? Even in 1834, one looked it up in Webster. Counsel submitted that

Requisite is aptly defined by the American lexicographer, Noah Webster, to be "so needful that it cannot be dispensed with; something indispensable"[2]

In the end, neither the courts nor Congress recognized the existence of perpetual copyright at common law, and Webster did not pursue it any further; but for more than four years, following his exchange of letters with Daniel Webster, he was an active and persistent lobbyist for improved statutory protection. He did not encounter opposition, so much as apathy. He was eventually responsible both for the form of the resulting legislation (which was rather odd) and for its being enacted as soon as it was, in the face

of congressional disinterest, but he was not the only one, or the first, to have seen that the American law was due for revision; as Daniel Webster told him, the judiciary committee already "had in contemplation some important changes."

One thing Webster wanted to change was the way the date had to be expressed in the copyright notice in every book. Under the 1790 act, the required form was "On the   day of   in the   year of the independence of the United States of America." This had caused Webster some inconvenience in January 1804, when he renewed the copyright in the old spelling book, and he now had another reason for objecting to it. Since his religious awakening, he had come to regard it as unchristian. He wrote to Daniel Webster:

New Haven Jany 29, 1827

Dear Sir,

It would gratify me to know that the Judiciary Committee have in contemplation a new Copyright law. Some new provisions are much wanted, and the date required in the present law is a singularity that exposes the government to the ridicule of the most candid men abroad. I sincerely hope I may never be obliged to insert such an *atheistical* date [to use a word borrowed from a foreign journal] in any publication of mine. The Session of Congress, I suppose, will be short, but I hope this subject will not be omitted.

Webster's hope was disappointed. Congress did not get to the subject of copyright in that session, and the title of the *American Dictionary* was therefore deposited "on the fourteenth day of April, in the fifty-second year of the Independence of the United States of America." Webster was obliged to insert an atheistical date in its first two abridgments as well, and in the *Elementary Spelling Book*, all of which were published before the new copyright act came into force. When it did, the "atheistical date" was abolished, which may have been due to Webster's suggestion, since the first drafts of a proposed new copyright bill (in February 1828) had not changed the way in which the date was to be expressed. On the other hand, the supplementary act of 1802 had already introduced the new form for the notice to be impressed on the face of maps, charts, etchings and engravings: "Entered according to act of Congress, the day of   18.."

In 1827 and 1828, Webster hoped to achieve his aim of extending copyright protection with the help of Ralph Ingersoll, a representative from Connecticut; but, despite "a petition signed by many respectable literary men [which] was, about this time, presented to Congress, praying for the same object," no bill was passed. Then in 1829, his son-in-law, William Ellsworth, (Emily's husband,) was elected to Congress and appointed to the Judiciary Committee; Webster hoped that Ellsworth might do the trick. In Webster's words, "before [he] left home, I applied to him to make efforts to procure the enactment of a new copyright law; and sent a petition to Congress, *praying for the renewal of the copyright of one of my books.* This petition, being referred to the judiciary committee, brought the subject distinctly into consideration." The words that I have put into italics show that Webster was, once again, concerned as much with the protection of his own works as with improving the lot of authors in general.

The petition that Ellsworth took to Washington sought an extension of the term of copyright for the *American Spelling Book*. Since the *American* was already being replaced by the *Elementary*, and since Webster did not at that time intend to reissue it, he must have wanted the copyright extended so that he could prevent its continued publication by others. That is just what he had done in 1804, when the new *American Spelling Book* replaced the Philadelphia revision. Ellsworth's first response was not encouraging:

Your petition for a renewal of the spelling book, I presented, yesterday, to Congress, it was referred to the Committee of the Judiciary and this morning was taken up in the Committee. The members of the Committee said such applications had often been made but they had uniformly reported against the applicant.

In February 1830, Ellsworth wrote that there was some hope for a bill enlarging the term of copyright generally, but virtually no hope for Webster's petition:

Nothing has yet been done with the copyright law. there is so much business before us and we so dilatory

that it is impossible to say when the bill will come to its turn. I shall watch it. The Judiciary Committee would have reported against your petition had they reported atal [sic]. As they agreed to the gen relief or bill reported by me, I thought it not best to urge your petition at this time. There is much more chance for the *bill* than for your petition.

Ellsworth, however, could not find any means to bring the copyright bill before the House. Webster's paper (which nowhere mentions that Ellsworth was his son-in-law) describes these events:

Mr. Ellsworth formed a report, stating the terms of time for which copy-rights are secured to authors in Great Britain, France, Russia, Sweden, Denmark, and certain states in Germany. He also formed a bill for a law intended to embrace all the material provisions of the old laws, with those of the bill reported by the former judiciary committee..... But such was the pressure of business, and so little interest was felt in the bill, that no efforts of Mr. Ellsworth could bring it before the House in that session. Finding the efforts of the friends of the bill in Congress to be unavailing to obtain a hearing, I determined in the winter of 1830-31 to visit Washington myself, and endeavor to accomplish the object.

Webster went to Washington in December 1830. On his way there, he came down with 'flu. It was a bad attack, and he was quite ill during his first ten days in the capital. After that, he rather enjoyed himself. Many members of Congress had learned to read in the blue-backed speller, and were disposed to treat him kindly — as the book had been first published nearly fifty years before, they may have been surprised to discover that he was still alive. He dined at the White House, and he delivered a lecture. A picture of the visit builds up in the letters that he wrote to his wife and family. Rebecca was in New Haven, near Julia Goodrich and her husband, the professor. Emily was in Washington because Ellsworth was in Congress, and Harriet was in Middlebury with William Fowler. Goodrich, as proprietor of the octavo dictionary, had a particular interest in the extension of the term of copyright; he sent the publisher, Sherman Converse, to Washington to lobby on his behalf — a move that was not popular with Webster — as Mrs. Ford says, "between [Converse] and Webster there was already much animus on account of the abridged edition, 1829."[3]

The letters start immediately after Webster's arrival in Washington:

Dec.14. 1830

Dear Becca,

I arrived here last evening, & have taken a small room at Mr. Fletcher's, next to Emily's. This is very pleasant.

My cold has proved pretty severe. The influenza has affected my head, & my lungs have been oppressec. I remained two days at Baltimore, & find myself somehat relieved My cold is digesting & my appetite is good. I hope therefore to experience no serious inconvenience from this visitation.

...As to William, it is probable he will come & see me, & he must have a pair of pantaloons. It rains, as it has done half the time since I left home. I have seen none of our friends here & shall not go abroad till the weather is better.

...Mr. E is preparing a new Copy-right bill & a report on the subject, which I hope will be laid before Congress early in the session. I hope you will all remain in health and safety....

* * * * *

Decr 17 1830

Dear Becca,

My cold is gradually abating. My lungs are much relieved; but the catarrh in my head makes it feel like a cook'g turnip. Yesterday & today I have taken a short walk, but I shall make no calls, till I feel better. Judge Cranch has called on me, as have Eliott & his wife & your brother James....[4]

...I have a snug room with a fire, & pass most of my time alone & not able to read much on account of my eyes which are affected by the influenza. Emily is now abroad making calls & delivering cards. This is no small business. She says she has some cold, but is pretty well. It is pretty cold; the last night made considerable ice.... I shall say little about my stay here. If I can effect the object, or contribute to it, for which I am striving, the absence of a few weeks is a thing of no moment. Mr. Grundy has doubts about passing a general law for securing literary property, as long as the bill proposes, but he says he will grant me almost anything, 40 years perhaps, for my great labors. But most of the members of Congress seem not to have considered the subject, & we shall know more of their opinions when the report is made & published....

In fact, Ellsworth's report and bill were presented to the House on the very day of that last letter, December 17, 1830. The first form of the bill that had been put before the House in 1828 had merely proposed to substitute a single term

of 28 years for the 14 and 14 of the 1790 act—
an improvement for elderly authors, but no
very great alteration. An amendment was considered at that time to add a renewal term of
fourteen years for authors still living at the end
of twenty eight years. This was the state of
affairs when Ellsworth came into the picture.
Ellsworth's bill was based on the amended bill
of 1828, but it incorporated an important alteration that Webster had suggested. Webster's
handwritten note on his copy of the 1828
Amendment says: "The last section does not
give the privilege of renewal to the widows and
children of deceased authors. This defect was
supplied by Mr. Ellsworth, at my request, which
had special reference to the case of the widow
& heirs of Dr. Dwight." Ellsworth's researches
into foreign copyright provisions had shown
that, before 1826, the French law had given a
life interest to an author and his wife, followed
by 26 years for their children. This may have
been what gave Webster the idea of a statute
that would make provision for children. The
sight of Dwight's family unprotected would
certainly have put into his mind the thought
that his own dependants might before long find
themselves in a similar situation.

The sections of Ellsworth's report explaining the injustice of the old law, and the justification for extending the term of copyright
and giving rights to dependants, were therefore
almost certainly written with Webster in mind,
and may even have been written by Webster
himself; he says in his paper that when Ellsworth prepared the report and bill, he "obtained from his friends some suggestions which
enabled him to correct some errors and supply
defects." Here is part of Ellsworth's report, the
second paragraph of which is clearly a restatement of Webster's thoughts in his definition
of "literary property" in the *American Dictionary*:

by the existing laws, a copy-right is secured to the
author, in the first instance, for fourteen years; and
if, at the end of that period, he be living, then for
fourteen years more; but, if he be not then living, the
copy-right is determined, although, by the very
event of the death of the author, his family stand in
more need of the only means of subsistence ordi-
narily left to them....

Upon the first principles of proprietorship in
property, an author has an exclusive and perpetual
right, in preference to any other, to the fruits of his
labor. Though the nature of literary property is peculiar, it is not the less real and valuable. If labor and
effort in producing what before was not possessed or
known, will give title, then the literary man has title,
perfect and absolute, and should have his reward: he
writes and he labors as assiduously as does the mechanic or husbandman. The scholar, who secludes
himself, and wastes his life, and often his property,
to enlighten the world, has the best right to the
profits of those labors.... It cannot be for the interest or honor of our country that intellectual labor
should be depreciated, and a life devoted to research
and study terminate in disappointment and poverty......

This bill secures to the author a copy-right for
twenty-eight years, in the first instance, with a right
of renewal for fourteen more, if, at the end of the first
period, the author be living, or shall leave a family.
It is believed that the provisions of the bill are not too
liberal, and that Congress ought not to do less than
is proposed.....

* * * * *

December 29, 1830

My Dear Harriet W,

I have been here more than a fortnight promoting
the passage of a law extending the rights of authors.
I was confined for ten days with a violent cold or
influenza, but am now in good health.....

Yesterday I called on the President, introduced by
Mr. Grundy of Tennessee, who is a lodger with us.[5]
The President asked me to dine with him, and I
could not well avoid it. We sat down at 6 o'clock and
rose at 8. The President was very sociable and placed
me, as a stranger, at his right hand. The party, mostly
members of the two houses, consisted of about
thirty. The table was garnished with artificial flowers
placed in gilt urns, supported by female figures, on
gilt waiters. "We had a great variety of dishes, French
and Italian cooking. I do not know the names of one
of them. I wonder at our great men who introduce
foreign customs, to the great annoyance of American
guests. To avoid annoyance as much as possible, the
practice is to dine at home, and go to the President's
to see and be seen, to talk and to nibble fruit, and to
drink very good wines. As to dining at the President's table in the true sense of the word, there is no
such thing." (The foregoing paragraph in [inverted]
commas might well appear in the prints, but the
writer must not be known.)...

* * * * *

On the evening of January 3, Webster delivered a lecture with remarkable effect, as described in his paper:

[I] read a lecture in the Hall of the Representatives, which was well attended, and as my friends informed me, had no little effect in promoting the object of obtaining a law for securing copy-rights. The difficulties which had prevented the bill from being brought forward now disappeared.

Emily Ellsworth was there too, and wrote at greater length:

It was an interesting lecture to all who heard it. Some complained it was too short. He spoke nearly an hour. The darkness and humidity of the weather prevented some from attending. I think, however, enough were there to get the bill through. All I believe who heard him were convinced. He said nothing by way of self-praise — perfectly indirect. He urged no claims. He said, should the bill for extending the copyright law be carried successfully, he should rejoice for himself, for his family, for his country. I think it will succeed.

* * * * *

Jany 7. 1831

Dear Becca,

Emily & I have just returned from the Capitol, & we were in the gallery when the House of Rep^vs passed the Copyright bill, without a division. It is believed the bill will meet no obstacles in the Senate. By this bill, authors &c have an absolute exclusive right in their works for 28 years, with the right of renewal to them, their widows & children for 14 more. I have reason to think my presence has been very useful in this affair; & I rejoice very much in the result. If the bill should pass the Senate, it will add very much to the value of my property.

I begin to be invited to parties, but shall avoid them as much as possible, except those that are given by N.England people. We go today, I believe, to Dr. Sewall's. I am invited to Mr. Ingham's next week, & as the house is opposite my lodgings, I shall go with our family, but it is all disagreeable to me; & as I wish to avoid parties I have called on none of the heads of departments, & foreign ministers....

* * * * *

Jany 26. 1831

My Dear Becca,

I had hoped before this to have communicated the news of the passage of the Copyright bill; but I am disappointed. There are yet five or six bill[s] before it on the calendar; & it may not come to its turn for several days. But I rest more contented on account of the weather, which renders it unsafe for me to travel....

I keep myself much at home, by a good fire in my

bed room. I dined at the Presidents, & had an invitation to an evening party of six or seven hundred at Mr. Ingham's....

Mr. Goodrich writes that Mr. Converse came here at his suggestion to aid the Copy-right bill. Fortunately the bill had passed the House of Representatives before he arrived A more unpopular man could not be selected; & if any opposer of the bill had stated to the house how Mr. C. has used or abused his monopoly (as it is called) of my dictionary, he probably would have defeated the bill. I hope no knowledge of it will reach the Senate. Two days ago, a Gentleman from Boston asked me where he could get a copy of my Quarto. He said he could not get it at the booksellers and knew not where to find it. I will not trouble myself to write what I know, nor express my feelings on this subject; & I hope Mr. Goodrich will not write to me on the subject any more. The truth is not one fifth part of the United States are supplied with the books....

Mr. E. has a letter from Mr. G. for Converse; but whether he is yet in the city or not I do not know. I have not seen him & hope I shall not....

* * * * *

[To William Chauncey Fowler, Harriet's husband]

January 29, 1831

Reverend and Dear Sir,

It is with pleasure I inform you that the bill for extending copyrights has passed both Houses of Congress and now waits only for the President's signature. This will secure copyrights to authors and proprietors for 28 years in the first instance, and the right of renewal to their widows and children for 14 more. This law will add much to the value of my property, and I cannot but hope I may now make dispositions of copyright which will make me comfortable during the remainder of my life, and secure to Mrs. Webster, if she should survive me, a decent independence.

My presence here has, I believe, been very useful and perhaps necessary to the accomplishment of the object. Few members of Congress feel much interest in such a law, and it was necessary that something extra should occur to awaken thheir attention to the subject. When I came here I found the members of both houses coming to me and saying, they had learned in my books, they were glad to see me, and ready to do me any kindness in their power. They all seemed to think, also, that my great labors deserve some uncommon reward. Indeed, I know of nothing that has given me more pleasure in my journeys, the last summer and this winter, than the respect and kindness manifested towards me in consequence of the use of my books. It convinces me that my fellow citizens consider me as their benefactor and the benefactor of my country.

The friendly attitude shown to him by members of Congress offered Webster an opportunity of which he took full advantage: He passed around the following testimonial to his works, and persuaded 31 Senators and 73 members of the House of Representatives to sign it:

The subscribers highly appreciate Dr. Webster's purpose and attempt to improve the English Language, by rendering its orthography more simple, regular, and uniform, and by removing difficulties arising from its anomalies. It is very desirable that one standard dictionary should be used by the numerous millions of people who are to inhabit the vast extent of territory belonging to the United States; as the use of such a standard may prevent the formation of dialects in states remote from each other, and impress upon the language uniformity and stability. It is desirable also, that the acquisition of the language should be rendered easy, not only to our own citizens, but to foreigners who wish to gain access to the rich stores of science which it contains. We rejoice that the *American Dictionary*, bids fair to become such a standard, and we sincerely hope that the author's elementary books for primary schools and academies will commend themselves to the general use of our fellow citizens.

The testimonial was reprinted in the *Elementary Spelling Book*, and (with the names of all the signatories) in the *Primary School Dictionary*, and it was widely used in advertisements.

* * * * *

Feby 3 1831

My Dear Becca,

The bill for enlarging copy-right has been enrolled, & is I suppose with the President. When published, I will send a copy to Mr. Goodrich....

* * * * *

Feby 7 1831

My Dear Becca,

I have enclosed a newspaper to Mr. Goodrich containing the Copy-right law. My great object is now accomplished, & as soon as the weather moderates a little, I shall leave Washington....

* * * * *

The development of the 1831 Copyright Act exactly mirrored Webster's changing requirements. Section 1 of the act extended the first term of copyright from 14 years to 28, and Section 2 gave the right of renewal, for a further 14 years, to a surviving author and to any surviving widow or child of a deceased author. Those were the provisions that Webster had wanted before the publication of the *American Dictionary*. By 1830, however, he needed more. Not only the quarto dictionary, but two abridged versions of it, and the new *Elementary Spelling Book*, had been published. Sections 1 and 2 of the new act applied to new works, but not to books that had been published before the act was passed. To cover these, Ellsworth's bill, as originally drafted, contained a section at the end, Section 16, which provided that "any author or authors ... who have heretofore obtained the copyright thereof, according to law, should be entitled to the benefit of the act ... with the same privilege to himself, or themselves, his or their widow, child or children, of renewing the copyright at the expiration thereof."

The idea of a statute that would make provision for children may have been suggested to Webster by the pre-1826 French copyright law. The idea of two-term copyrights, of course, was old. To Webster, who did not expect to live into the second term, it must have seemed sensible to combine the two ideas, by giving dependants the right to the second term. The result, however, was an extraordinary hybrid. It had no parallel anywhere in the world, and it caused unexpected problems for Webster's family and, during more than a hundred years, for many others. Imagine an author who died during the first term of copyright; he would own his copyright for the first 28 years, and could sell it, license it, or leave it in his will to anyone he liked; the renewal term, however, was not his to dispose of — it would go to his surviving widow or children, *whether he liked it or not*. He might have made a will leaving all his American copyrights to a foundation set up to promote his own literary reputation, and leaving nothing to his children — either because they were well provided for already, or because he disliked them. Nevertheless, when the copyrights came up for renewal, the interests would go to the children, not to the foundation. This process became known as "will-bumping" — the provisions of the author's will were "bumped" by the Copyright Act.

That problem was already inherent in Ellsworth's bill when he presented it to the House on December 17, 1830. Then something happened

to persuade him to put forward a last minute amendment to Section 16 — an amendment that introduced another problem altogether. From the nature of the amendment, it is easy to guess what that "something" was: It was Webster's attack of 'flu during his first week in Washington. Add to this that Webster was over 70, and that they still did not know just when the copyright bill might pass into law. If past experience was any guide, it might be some time. It occurred to them that Webster might die, and they suddenly realised that Section 16 as drafted did not mention the copyright in the published works of an author who had died before the bill became law. Ellsworth hurriedly redrafted Section 16 to put in references to the "heirs, executors and administrators" of an author who "shall not be living at the passage of this act," and he presented the new form to the House on January 6, 1831. Despite some opposition, the House voted in favor. By this time, Webster was sufficiently recovered to have given a lecture in Congress three days before, but the amendment must have been devised during his illness, and it was certainly put forward with him in mind. This is clearly shown by the fact that Ellsworth enlisted the support of J. W. Huntington, another member from Connecticut, who "strenuously supported the measure," and said that he "would cite a single case by way of illustration. *Webster's Dictionary*,… that unrivaled work, that monument of the learning, industry and genius of its author."[6]

The amended form of Section 16 was thought to give Webster and his family all the protection that he required, whether or not he lived to see it pass into law:

Sec.16. … If such author be living at the passage of this act, then such author shall continue to have the same exclusive right to his book for such additional period of time as will make up the term of twenty-eight years, with the same right to his widow, child or children to renew the copy-right, at the expiration thereof, as is above provided in relation to copy-rights originally secured under this act. And if such author shall not be living at the passage of this act, then, his heirs, executors and administrators, shall be entitled to the like exclusive enjoyment with the like privilege of renewal to the widow, child or children.[7]

When Webster wrote to Fowler telling him of the new law, he said that it secured copyrights "to authors and proprietors for 28 years in the first instance, and the right of renewal to their widows and children for 14 more." There is a significant mistake in that description: Section 2 of the Act did not just give a right of renewal to widows and children, but also to any author who survived the first 28 years. Webster failed to mention the possibility of renewal by the author himself. It is not surprising that he should have made such a mistake, because it was his children's right to renew, not his own, that he had been anxious to secure. It was very unlikely that he would have the opportunity to renew his own recent copyrights, as he was already 72. When the *American Dictionary* entered its second term he would be nearly a hundred. What is rather remarkable is that Section 16 of the 1831 Copyright Act, because it had been drafted with Webster's personal requirements in mind, contained the same mistake. For works covered by a copyright obtained before the passage of the act, it gave a right of renewal after 28 years to the author's widow, child or children if he were dead, *but not to the author himself, if he were still alive.* The mistake was not in Ellsworth's original Section 16; it was introduced in the drafting of the last minute amendment.

Because the section only applied to works published before the act came into force, it could have no effect after 28 years. The mistake, therefore, was only troublesome for that period, and Congress did not bother to correct it.

Webster was not immediately aware of the mistake. Not long after the new act came into force, the copyright in the *American Spelling Book* of 1804 approached its twenty-eighth birthday. The last six months of its copyright began on September 14, 1831, and onSeptember 26 he deposited the title to secure a renewal of the copyright, in the District Clerk's Office in the District of Connecticut.[8] Soon afterwards he discovered that because he was still alive, there was no right of renewal, and the copyright lapsed. This was not a commercial disaster, because under the old law the copyright would have come to an end at that time anyway, which was in part why the *Elementary Spelling Book* had been introduced. It did mean, however, that everything in the *American* passed into the public domain in 1832, and after that date Webster had no legal right to complain if

any of it was copied. We know that he wanted the copyright in the *American Spelling Book* extended, both because he applied for renewal and because the petition that Ellsworth took with him to Washington when he was first elected to Congress sought an extension of that same copyright.

The other unexpected results of the new act were the effects of will-bumping, which interfered with Webster's testamentary intentions. By his will, Webster divided his residual estate between five people. Four were his children, Emily, Harriet, William and Eliza; the fifth was his grand-daughter, Mary Southgate, whom he had taken into his family and treated as his own child, after the death of her mother.[9] The two children who did not get a share were Julia Goodrich, because she enjoyed the benefit of the money her husband made from the octavo dictionary, and Louisa, the unmarried daughter, who was mentally retarded. Louisa and Webster's wife Rebecca were given an annuity. Those arrangements governed the distribution of profits from Webster's works during the first term of copyright, but thereafter Webster's will was "bumped," and it was the Copyright Act that determined who should get a share of the literary loot. Rebecca died in 1847, so that in 1856, twenty-eight years after the publication of the *American Dictionary*, the 14-year renewal term was vested in the surviving children —*all* the surviving children. Thus Julia and Louisa were included, but the grand-daughter Mary, for whom Webster had wished to make provision, was excluded. A year later, Goodrich's rights in the octavo came to an end, and all the surviving children, not just the Goodriches, gained the benefit of the renewal of that copyright. Again, Mary was excluded, but Louisa got a share. She also shared in the renewal term of the *Elementary Spelling Book*. Those benefits were given her by the Copyright Act, and did not affect her right to receive her annuity under Webster's will.

In all the Webster archives, the most touching documents, perhaps the only touching documents, are Lousia's letters to William. Louisa was devoted to her only brother, and was upset if he did not write to her often. What made correspondence more difficult was the fact that Louisa could neither read nor write: Julia Goodrich read William's letters to her, and, in

careful copperplate, wrote Louisa's replies. In 1857-58, various members of the family suffered losses through the failure of railroads and other businesses in which they had invested, and they wrote to tell William how hard up they were. At the same time, Louisa was enjoying the unexpected and unintended benefits of will-bumping, and wrote to William that she had no money worries at all. This letter is dated January 16, 1858:

Dear Honey,

I am very well off myself for my bills are settled & Mr. White [the executor] has sent me my dividend, so I shall buy some fresh candy soon when the weather clears up. My candy box is audacious full now though I give some every Sunday to Webster [Louisa's and William's nephew] who goes to church with me in the morning....

Miss McIntyre is going to be married soon to Capt.Townley.... I do believe my turn will come next, & I am all ready to absqualidate, for Sister has just furnished a complete sett of cotton shimmediddles & nightgowns and skirts. Why should not I go off as well as another. I have a good judgement & think I will accept the next offer & come out west. I'll telegraph beforehand so that the fatted turkey may be stuffed and pudding baking.

But I can't collect any more ideas they are so promulged and evidenced. Don't forget my love & remember that Dr. Bacon 'proves very much in his preaching — it is skilful & corrupt but not tangible. The singing is curmendous & the organ plays distinctively about all the notes flying in antics.[10]

Louisa was nearly 50 years old then, but her mind had remained that of a child.

The original copyright in the octavo abridgment had been in the joint names of Webster and Worcester. When the 1831 Copyright Act came into force, Worcester was thought to be a confirmed bachelor, and it would have seemed unlikely, therefore, that he might leave any widow or child to claim a share in the renewal term in 1857. In 1841, however, at the age of 57, Worcester married the daughter of a Harvard professor. Ellsworth, as Webster's executor, addressed the question of defeating any claim that Worcester might make to an interest in the renewal. On January 17, 1845, he wrote to William:

Can you inform me if Mr. Worcester, when he made the 8vo abridgement, did not give your father a bond or some writing that he would make no claim on the dictionary & if so where it is. Mr. Fowler says there is such a writing. I dont know that Worcester thinks

of claiming anything, but as that book was taken out in his name in part I ought to have the paper in my hands. Perhaps brother G has it, & if so, I should like a copy at least.

Ellsworth was not thinking clearly. Even if he had found such a "writing," it would have been completely useless to him. If Worcester proved to be still alive in 1857, the mistake in the drafting of section 16 of the Act would prevent his applying for a renewal. If he had died leaving a widow or surviving child, any promise he had made in his lifetime to surrender his rights in the dictionary would not have affected the rights of his dependants in any way. He could not have "disinherited" them by contract, any more than Webster, by his will, had been able to prevent Julia and Louisa enjoying a share in the posthumous renewals of his copyrights. As it happened, Worcester was still alive in 1857 and therefore had no right to a renewal. In any case, he was too honest a man even to think of making a claim.

Warfel sums up Webster's relationship with Ellsworth in this way:

William W. Ellsworth, Emily's husband, rose steadily in Connecticut politics until he reached the governorship. Early he had shaken off the patriarchal rule; never did he assist Webster in his plans, the copyright legislation excepted. Webster respected the achievements of Ellsworth, but often lamented his son-in-law's unwillingness to aid financially in bringing out the 1840 Dictionary.[11]

I take a less charitable view. Ellsworth never helped Webster at all. He took advantage of his position in Congress to secure the passage of a new copyright act, which he drafted in such a way as to ensure that Webster's children would continue to derive an income from Webster's works, for many years after Webster's death. That was, indeed, what Webster wanted, but Ellsworth did it for the benefit of the family, not for Webster's benefit. He was married to Webster's eldest daughter, and the rights secured to them by the new act proved to be worth a lot of money.

16. Cobb v. Webster; Webster v. Worcester, 1829–1835

Webster lived nearly fifteen years after the publication of the *American Dictionary*. They were years punctuated by bad-tempered attacks, some made by Webster against others, and some made against Webster. The enemy was usually the compiler of a competing dictionary or spelling book, the most persistent being Lyman Cobb, who produced both. Nevertheless, Appleton's *Cyclopædia of American Biography* does not paint a picture of a scoundrel:

COBB, Lyman, author, b. in Massachusetts about 1800: d. in Potter co., Pa., 26 Oct., 1864. He was one of the greatest educators of his time, and was also active in charitable enterprises, being a member of numerous benevolent societies. He was the author of "Evil Tendency of Corporal Punishment" (New York, 1847) and numerous text books, including "Just Standard for Pronouncing the English Language" (New York, 1825); "Spelling Book" (1826) with "Introduction" (1831), and "Expositor" (1835); several readers (1831–'44); "Miniature Lexicon of the English Language" (1835–'54); "Arithmetical Rules and Tables" (1835); a new series of spelling books (1843); and "New Pronouncing School Dictionary" (1843).

Webster had a very different opinion. By producing both spelling books and dictionaries, Cobb was operating in an area that Webster considered to be his own, and Webster disliked him even more because he was a disciple of Walker, both in spelling and pronunciation. His 1835 dictionary was advertised as "Cobb's Abridgment of J.Walker's CRITICAL PRONOUNCING DICTIONARY," and boasted that "Mr. Walker's principles of orthography and pronunciation are strictly followed." Cobb spelled *honour* and *labour* with a *u*, *publick* with a *k*, and *traveller* with a double *l*. Furthermore,

he had the effrontery to say that he was right and Webster was wrong. Webster's view of Cobb can be found in an article, *The Age of Spelling Books*, written some years later:[1]

When Walker's dictionary appeared in the US, a number of Spelling Books were compiled with a view to introduce his pronunciation. It is not worth while to mention Marshall, Crandal, & the compilers of that poorest of all Spelling Books, Sears; but some notice may be taken of Lyman Cobb, who figures as a book-maker. This man was from Lenox in Massachusetts; a poor boy, afterward a kitchen boy in Albany. Illiterate as he was, he had recourse to school-keeping in western New York, studied Walker's dictionary & made a Spelling Book. His booksellers, to introduce this book into schools, in some instances exchanged it for Webster's, & *burnt the latter*. Cobb or his booksellers sent agents from one end of the US to the other to introduce his book, but in general without success. Cobb failed, & is now a baker in New York. But his booksellers laid one third of the towns in New York under bondage for many years. Last winter the teachers in one County revolted, & determined not to use Cobb's old orthography any longer. In consequence of this, the papers inform us that Cobb is making a new Spelling Book, with Webster's orthography.

Cobb's first attack on Webster was made before the publication of the *American Dictionary*. It took the form of a series of 13 articles signed "Examinator," which appeared in the Albany *Argus* between July 1827 and March 1828. The whole series was then reprinted in Cobb's first anti-Webster pamphlet, *A Critical Review of Noah Webster's Spelling-Book*. The spelling book in question was the *American*, which "Examinator" had examined in minute detail. He criticized it under the headings Contents, Classification, Arrangement, Orthography, and "Pronunciation," and added insult to injury by referring to

"Mr. Webster" throughout, disregarding Webster's honorary LL.D., conferred by Yale in 1823. Cobb compared the spelling of the *American Spelling Book* with that of the 1806 *Compendious Dictionary* and of the 1817 *School Dictionary* (which had replaced the *School Dictionary* of 1807). He found very many inconsistencies. Webster made only one response to this attack, in a letter that he sent to the editor of the Albany *Argus* midway through the series. It did not contain a very vigorous defence probably because Webster knew by this time that the *American Spelling Book* would soon have to be replaced by a new one, consistent with the *American Dictionary*. He knew also that his earlier views on spelling could not all be defended, but he would not allow Cobb to suggest that there was anything wrong with his pronunciation:

The *American Spelling Book*, as it was originally published, was compiled in the year 1782, before the close of the War of the Revolution. At that time, the subject of English philology was little attended to in this country, and had but recently begun to engage the attention of the English. To compile an elementary book at that time, which should be tolerably perfect, was no easy task; and notwithstanding all the faults of my book, the scheme, arrangement, and execution of it may be considered as a great advance in the means of elementary instruction. Neither in orthography nor in pronunciation had I, in many cases, any settled principles or authoritites to follow, but it so happens that my pronunciation is generally correct; and that book has done more, I presume, than all other causes, to correct the vulgar errors that formerly prevailed. Since my return from England, I have examined the work; and I find that, excepting words of unsettled pronunciation, the pronunciation of my book accords nearly with that of all well-bred people in England.
  That there are some errors, defects, and inconsistencies in the work is not to be wondered at....

Webster's publications in 1828 and 1829 — the *American Dictionary*, the octavo abridgment, the *Primary School Dictionary*, and the *Elementary Spelling Book* — provided Cobb with a vast amount of additional material. He reviewed each in turn, and again combined his attacks into a pamphlet. By this time, he was concentrating on the inconsistency of Webster's spelling, and his second pamphlet was called:

A
CRITICAL REVIEW
OF THE
ORTHOGRAPHY
OF
DR. WEBSTER'S SERIES OF BOOKS
FOR
SYSTEMATICK INSTRUCTION
IN THE
ENGLISH LANGUAGE:
INCLUDING
HIS FORMER SPELLING BOOK,
AND THE
**ELEMENTARY SPELLING-BOOK,
COMPILED BY AARON ELY,**
AND PUBLISHED UNDER THE NAME OF
NOAH WEBSTER, LL.D.

As that title shows, one of Cobb's accusations was that Webster had not written the *Elementary Spelling Book* at all; he had paid Ely to write it, and then published it under his own name. Webster's reply to the second pamphlet was a printed letter "TO THE PUBLIC," dated November 15, 1831,[2] which first refused to answer that charge, and then both denied it and admitted it:

His unfounded conjectures and one palpable falsehood respecting the authorship of my *Elementary Spelling Book*, I will not particularly notice, as no candid and intelligent man will believe them....
  My School Dictionary and *Elementary Spelling Book* are compilations entirely my own. I employed a person to write for me: but every part of these works was corrected, arranged, and the words marked for pronunciation by my own hand....

Finding inconsistencies in Webster's orthography is not difficult, but to find all of them is tedious work. Webster called it "the drudgery of *letter-hunting* through a series of volumes," and Cobb made a thorough job of it. There are inconsistencies in the *American Dictionary* because it had taken twenty years to compile, and Webster's ideas had changed during that period: Cobb hunted them out. Then he pointed out in minute detail where the octavo did not agree with the *American Dictionary* — the result, as we have seen, of Goodrich's influence on Worcester. The *Primary School Dictionary*, of course, did not agree with either of them because Webster was trying to put things right. In

his letter "TO THE PUBLIC," he again disclaimed responsibility for the octavo:

Being oppressed with labor during the publication of my quarto and in danger of sinking under it, the superintendence of the octavo was committed to a learned friend: and it is stated in the Preface, that I am not responsible for any modifications of the orthography.

Cobb claimed that it was his attack in the Albany *Argus* that persuaded Webster to abandon the *American Spelling Book* and replace it with the *Elementary*. Had not Webster boasted, he asked, not long before, that the tables in the *American Spelling Book*, especially those of irregular words, were so constructed and so nearly complete that they could not be improved? At that time, the new edition was said to be intended only to "adjust" the pronunciation to uniformity with that of the dictionary, but the differences between the *American* and the *Elementary* could not be described as merely a matter of "adjustment." Cobb was probably mistaken. The 1804 copyright was due to expire in 1832, and Webster would always have intended to have a replacement spelling book ready by then. It would not have been worthwhile to carry out any significant "adjustment" to a book that was anyway going to be replaced in a year or two. It is possible, however, that Cobb's attack on the *American* prompted Webster to release the *Elementary* earlier than he would otherwise have done. Whether or not that was so, I believe that Cobb may have had another and more significant influence on Webster's conduct. I think it likely that his laborious listing of all the differences in spelling between the octavo and the other dictionaries was what made Webster dislike the octavo so much that he sold his interest to Goodrich.

Cobb, or the agents seeking to sell his books, kept up the attack on Webster for another ten years or so, particularly in the Western states. In the end, he made little impression on Webster's sales, not because his criticisms of Webster were unfounded, but because he himself had nothing better to offer.

In the battle between Webster and Cobb, it was Cobb who was the aggressor throughout. Such blows as Webster struck at Cobb can be justified as self-defense. In the next battle, Webster went on the attack, making a totally unprovoked assault on the unfortunate Worcester. While Webster was in Washington agitating for improved copyright protection, Worcester, having finished work on the octavo abridgment of Webster's quarto, completed his own little dictionary. It was published in Boston, by Hillard, Gray, Little and Wilkins, late in 1830. The New York Public Library has a copy printed in Burlington, Vermont, the next year, which at first sight looks surprising: the publisher named on the title page is Chauncey Goodrich! That, however, was not Webster's son-in-law Chauncey Allen Goodrich or his uncle, but a cousin who was a bookseller in Burlington.[3]

Worcester's *Comprehensive Pronouncing and Explanatory Dictionary of the English Language* was not in competition with either of Webster's larger dictionaries; in size and scope it is more nearly comparable with the *Compendious Dictionary* of 1806, having very small type, short definitions, and words tightly packed on the page. Like the *Compendious*, it has no etymology, or quotations or authorities supporting definitions, and it merely indicates parts of speech by one or two letters. It is most sophisticated in relation to Worcester's particular interest, pronunciation. The pronunciation of each word is indicated by diacritical marks and accents, and in addition, where earlier orthoepists had disagreed on the pronunciation of a word, Worcester gave their different recommendations in the entry for that word. This was not his original plan; he had intended to include in the dictionary the *Synopsis of Words Differently Pronounced* that he had contributed to Webster's octavo, but then he decided that it would be more convenient to the user if all the information about a word were in one place.

Perhaps because he was busy in Washington on the copyright question, Webster took no great interest in Worcester's dictionary at the time that it was published. When he got home, he wrote to Worcester, on March 22, 1831, asking whether he had borrowed many words and definitions from Webster's books; Worcester replied on March 25: "No, not many." That answer might be taken either as an admission by Worcester that he had taken *some* words from Webster, or as a polite response to an impertinent question. The fact that Webster asked the question at all shows an incipient jealousy.

Webster was next occupied with replying to Cobb's attacks on his inconsistent orthography, with the English reprint of his quarto, and with the preparation of his expurgated and corrected version of the King James Bible, published in 1833. Only after that did his smouldering resentment with Worcester burst into flame. The underlying motive was financial; Webster was always worried about money, and in his mind Worcester was to blame, at this time, in more ways than one. Worcester had made the alterations to the octavo which provided Cobb with bullets to shoot at Webster. It was Worcester's fault that Webster had felt compelled to sell that valuable property. And now Worcester's little dictionary was interfering with the sale of Webster's *Primary School Dictionary*, the rights to which he had retained.

The first attack on Worcester was in an anonymous article which appeared on Wednesday, November 26, 1834, in the *Palladium*, a weekly newspaper published in Worcester, Massachusetts:[4]

WEBSTER'S DICTIONARY. A gross plagiarism has been committed by Mr. J.E.Worcester on the literary property of Noah Webster Esq. It is well known that Mr. Webster has spent a life, which is now somewhat advanced, in writing a dictionary of the English language, which he published in 1828, in two quarto volumes. Three abridgments have since been made; one in an octavo form — and two still smaller, for families and primary schools. To aid in the drudgery of producing these abridgments, Mr. Webster employed Mr. Worcester who, after becoming acquainted with Mr. Webster's plan, immediately set about appropriating to his own benefit the valuable labors, acquisitions, and productions of Mr. Webster. He has since published a dictionary, which is a very close imitation of Webster's; and which, we regret to learn, has been introduced into many of the primary schools of the country. We regret this, because the public, inadvertently, do an act of great injustice to a man who has rendered the country an invaluable service, and ought to recieve the full benefit of his labors. If we had a statute which could fix its grasp on those who pilfer the products of the mind, as readily as our laws embrace the common thief, Mr. Worcester would hardly escape with a light mulct. At all events, before people buy his wares, they would do well to inquire how he came by them.

It was not our intention, when we commenced this article, to write a critique on Webster's works; but in connexion with the above it may be well to state what, in our opinion, constitute some of the claims which he has to the patronage of Americans. His works have been produced only by immense labor, expense, and personal sacrifice; indefatigable application to all the means which Europe, as well as America, could furnish for a perfect dictionary of our language. In a judicious use of those means, he has been remarkably successful; and should literary pilferers rob him of his pecuniary rights, they cannot rob him of his well-earned fame.

Walker's dictionary, which is the one most commonly used, contains 38,000 words; Johnson's 58,000; while Webster's contains 70,000....

That was about half the article. The remainder extolled the virtues of Webster's Dictionary. Worcester replied to this in the *Palladium* forDecember 10, 1834:

SIR, — A friend has recently called my attention to a notice of Dr. Webster's Dictionary in your paper, which has the appearance of being editorial, and which begins with the following extraordinary statement: — " A gross plagiarism has been committed by Mr. J.E.Worcester on the literary property of Noah Webster Esq.... Mr. Webster employed Mr. Worcester who, after becoming acquainted with Mr. Webster's plan, immediately set about appropriating to his own benefit the valuable labors, acquisitions, and productions of Mr. Webster."

As you, Mr. Editor, are unknown to me, I am bound to believe that you were not aware that you were publishing a statement that is grossly false, but that you were informed that it was true, and that you supposed that you should promote the cause of justice by giving it publicity. I, however, know it and declare it to be utterly false, and I have ample means of proving it to be so, before any impartial tribunal. If what I say is true, you must feel that you have done me, (I am willing to believe unintentionally) a serious injury. I know not on whose evidence you have relied, but I do know that whoever has made you believe the truth of the statement has grossly imposed upon you; and I appeal to your candor and sense of justice, whether, upon reflection, you can think you have done right, or acted in accordance with the rule which requires one to do by others has he would be done by, in publishing such a charge without having satisfactory evidence of its truth.

As no proof of the accusation is given by you, I had thought of leaving the subject for the present, with my explicit denial of its truth, feeling an assurance that those who best know me would believe the correctness of my assertion, at least, till some evidence was produced against it. I beg leave, however, in justice to myself and from respect for the public, to make the following statement.— The design of my "Comprehensive, Pronouncing, and Explanatory Dictionary," was formed in 1827, while editing "Johnson's Dictionary as improved by Todd, and abridged by Chalmers, with Walker's Pronouncing Dictionary combined,," and before the appearance of Dr. Webster's quarto Dictionary. But before my

dictionary was prepared for the press, the publisher of Dr. Webster's Dictionary made repeated applications to me by letter, to form for him an abridgment of it, which I promptly declined. He then made a journey expressly for the purpose of engaging me to undertake the work. I mentioned to him that one objection in my mind to doing it was that I was preparing a small dictionary of my own; but at his urgent solicitation I was induced to undertake it, and to suspend the preparation of my own, until it was completed. I also consented to insert the "Synopsis of words differently pronounced," which I was preparing for my own use, with an express stipulation, in the contract, that I should have a right to make such use of the Synopsis as I pleased, in my own Dictionary. This subject is mentioned, as you may see, at the beginning of the Preface to my Dictionary.

After having finished the abridgment, I proceeded in the preparation of my own work; but so far from appropriating the labors of Dr. Webster to my own use, I challenge any one to enumerate a dozen words in my Dictionary for which I cannot readily give other authorities than Dr. Webster, or to show that with respect to the rise, orthography, or pronunciation of a dozen words, I have been governed solely or chiefly by his authority. I have the most extensive collection of works on English Lexicography that I know of in the possession of any individual, or in any single library; and I have been for a good while attentive to this sort of literature. This I say, not from ostentation, but to show that in preparing such a work as I have published, I have little occasion to be indebted to Dr. Webster.

My Dictionary is far from being "a close imitation" of Dr. Webster's. It differs widely in its plan, in the selection of words, and in the orthography of a considerable number of words; the notation is entirely different; and the pronunciation is treated of in a very different manner. The Dictionaries of Dr. Webster with which mine may be supposed to come in competition, are "two smaller forms, for families and primary schools," neither of which I had seen until after mine was prepared for the press, and the smallest one I never saw at all, so far as I remember, except once or twice in a bookstore. I say nothing in praise of mine or in dispraise of his; but cheerfully leave the decision of their comparative merits to the public; with the assurance that I have ample means of showing that I came as lawfully by my materials as Dr. Webster did by his.

It is unpleasant, Mr. Editor, to be thus called upon to publicly defend ones self against such a calumny; but it would be far more unpleasant were not the case easily and perfectly defensible.

J.E.WORCESTER

Cambridge, Dec.2, 1834.

I have previously mentioned only one of the "smaller forms" of Webster's Dictionary, the 1829 abridgment "for the use of Primary Schools and the Counting House." A thinner duodecimo primary school dictionary was published in 1833. Since Worcester's dictionary had come out in 1830, he could not possibly have copied anything from that one.

A letter from Webster himself appeared a week later, in the *Palladium* for December 17, 1834:

SIR—I see in your paper some remarks made on the plagiarisms committed on my Dictionary by J.E.Worcester, and Mr. Worcester's denial of the fact. I wrote to Mr. Worcester, March 22, 1831, inquiring whether he had borrowed many words and definitions from my books. He replied, by letter dated March 25, and wrote:—"*No, not many.*" That he borrowed *some* words and definitions, I suppose to be proved by the fact that they are found in no British Dictionary; at least in none that I have seen. How many he took, I know not, and shall not take the trouble to examine. Had he taken more, his works would have been less defective, and more correct. Of his plagiarisms of another kind, you will hear more hereafter.

Respectfully Yours,

N.WEBSTER.

To spoil poor Worcester's Christmas, there was a further editorial in the *Palladium* for December 24, 1834:

WEBSTER'S AND WORCESTER'S DICTIONARIES—Our controversy on this subject is with Mr. Worcester himself, and not with any volunteer, however learned, who may feel himself called upon to denounce as barbarians all who have not been within the charmed circle of Harvard College.

We have leisure only for a cursory review of Worcester's book; but in addition to the circumstances that Mr. Worcester published his dictionary shortly after he had completed an abridgment of Webster's, and his subsequent acknowledgment that he had made some use of Webster's in the compilation of his own, the following words are a confirmation of our charge. They are found in none of the English dictionaries in common use, and were undoubtedly taken from Webster's: *abatable, deliquesce, dutiable, farrow, effloresce, emphasize, irredeemable, lockage, notarial, outlay, phospohorescent, philosophism, prayerful, prayerless, promissee, magnetize, safety-valve, semi annual, manifest (an invoice,) land-office, lengthy.* The word *lengthy* is improperly condemned by Mr. Worcester. It has been used by our best writers for half a century. If Mr. Worcester reads the London Quarterly Review, he will find it used occasionally in that journal.

In many instances, Mr. Worcester has undoubtedly appropriated to his own use Webster's definitions

with slight modifications; as in *clearance, debenture, levee, clergyable, clothier, &c....*

There follow further attacks on Worcester, not related to the alleged copying from Webster. Among other things, Worcester is criticized for the incompleteness of his dictionary — because he left out many words that are in Webster. When he includes words that are in Webster, he is guilty of plagiarism, but if he omits some of them, his dictionary is defective! The article concludes:

Webster's dictionary is now used, to a great extent, as a standard work. It has opposers, but the current of public opinion is in its favor. In a few particulars his system is not adopted. A great proportion of the members of Congress (not always the best judges, to be sure,) have recommended it, and in a certificate have expressed a wish that it may become a standard work. In the adoption of the one or the other we have not a particle of personal interest. But we regret that the products of the mind, which have been garnered up with unwearied and long-continued toil, should be pillaged and appropriated to their own use by "eleventh-hour" laborers.

Up to this point, the exchanges had been little more than small-arms fire. Webster, however, had been preparing to deliver what he hoped would be a damaging broadside. He uncoverd his heavy weapons in a letter that appeared in the *Palladium* on January 28, 1835. His previous letter had been addressed to the editor; this one was to Worcester in person:

New Haven January 25 1835.
Mr. J.E. Worcester.

SIR — Before I saw in the Worcester Palladium a charge against you of committing plagiarism on my dictionary, I had not given much attention to your dictionary. Nor have I now read & compared with mine one tenth part of the work. But in running over it, in a cursory manner I have collected the following words, which *prima facie* would seem to have been taken from my dictionary:

Abatable	Assignor	Augean	Bateau
Cartrut	Caucus	Chowder	Congregationalist
Congressional	Clapboard	Dell	Dutiable
Deliquesce	Digraph	Emphasize	Effloresce
Educational	Effervescent	Electioneer	Farrow
Fructescence	Fracas	Glazing	Governmental
Grandjury	Graphite	Griddle	Hydrant
Irredeemable	Instanter	Isothermal	Johannes
Judiciary (noun.)	Kumiss	Land-office	Lapstone
Landslip	Leach	Leachtub	Magnetize
Mazology	Mishna	Moccason	Monitorial

Muscovado	Muskrat *or*	Musquash	Notarial
Neap (of a cart &c.)	Neptunian	Outlay	Obsidian
Obstetrics	Ochlocracy	Olivaceous	Ophiologist
Ophiology	Philosophism	Phosphoresce	Phosphorescence
Phosphorescent	Prayerful	Prayerless	Promisee
Pappoose	Pistareen	Pledgee	Postfix
Postnote	Raca	Ramadan	Razee
Redemptioner	Rhabdology	Rock-crystal	Roil, roily
Repealable	Safety-valve	Semiannual	Sectional
Sabianism	Saltrheum	Savings-bank	Scorify
Scow	Sheepshead	Spry	Squirm
Spinning-jenny	Spinning-wheel	Seraskier	Siderography
Siderographical	Slump	Succotash	Selectman
Sparse	Sou	Souvenir	Suffix n.& v.
Tirade	Tenderloin	Teraphim	Test v.
Thammuz	Tetaug	Tomato	Tuffoon
Uranology	Varioloid	Vapor-bath	Vermivorous
Vishna	Voltaism	Volcanist	Waffle
Whiffletree	Wilt	Winter-kill	Zumology

I will thank you, sir, to state in what other dictionary except mine, you found the foregoing words, and how many or which you borrowed from mine. Your compliance with this request will oblige

Your humble Servt
N. WEBSTER.

Worcester's reply appeared in the *Palladium* for February 11:

Cambridge, February 6, 1835
DR. NOAH WEBSTER: —

SIR, — On Friday last I received a copy of the Worcester Palladium, in which was found a letter addressed by you to me, containing a list of one hundred and twenty-one words from my Dictionary, "which," you say, "*prima facie*, would seem to have been taken from your Dictionary"; and you add that you "will thank me to state in what other Dictionary, except yours, I found the words, and how many or which I borrowed from yours."

As a lawyer, Sir, you are aware, that, when an accusation is made, the burden of the proof lies not with the accused, but with the accuser. It might not, therefore, perhaps be improper for me to take the ground that your request is an unreasonable one, and for that reason to decline to comply with it. I will not, however, avail myself of this right. I think I may truly say that in my transactions with you, it has been my intention to act uprightly and faithfully, nor do I know that an individual of those who are most acquainted with the facts (yourself excepted) has a different impression. In answer to the charges which have appeared against me in the Worcester Palladium, I have already made some statements of facts, none of which, so far as I know, have been, or can be, disproved. You now call for something further, and it shall be cheerfully granted. I feel indeed gratified by the manner in which you have been pleased to make the request; for though I have no love of

contention, yet if I must be dragged into a newspaper controversy in defence of myself in this matter, I should prefer that, of all men in the world, it should be with yourself, writing under your own name.

You evidently supposed, Sir, that none of the words in your list were to be found in any Dictionary that was published before the appearance of your own work; but I confess I am somewhat surprised at this fact, inasmuch as, from your reputation as a lexicographer, it might naturally be supposed that you were extensively acquainted with works of this sort, and especially with the works which are so well known to all persons who have any just pretensions to much knowledge of this kind of literature, as are the several publications which I shall name. I shall not go out of my own library, or mention any work that I was not in the habit of consulting in preparing my Dictionary.

Of the *one hundred and twenty-one* words in your list, *eighteen* are found in an edition of Bailey's Dictionary, published more than a century ago, and *twenty-one* in a later edition; *thirty-five*, in Ash's Dictionary, published in 1775; *thirty-seven*, in Todd's Johnson's Dictionary combined with Walker's, edited by J.E.Worcester, and published before the appearance of yours; *twenty-one*, in Mr. Pickering's Vocabulary, published in 1816; not less than *thirty* in the Encyclopaedia Americana, and nearly as many in Brewster's New Edinburgh Encyclopaedia; — and in these several works, upwards of *ninety* of the words are found, and many of them several times repeated. I have, in addition to the works above mentioned, about fifty English Dictionaries and Glossaries, in a majority of which I have ascertained that more or less of the words in question are to be found, but I have not leisure, at present, to go through a minute examination of them.

Of your hundred and twenty-one words, six or seven are not to be found, so far as I can discover, in your Quarto Dictionary, and one of them is one of those three thousand words which are contained in Todd's Johnson's Dictionary, but are not to be found in your great work, and which were inserted by me in the octavo abridgment of your Dictionary. Whether any of the others are among the words which were inserted in the abridgment at my suggestion, I cannot say with certainty.

From the preceding statement, you may perceive, Sir, that your *prima facie* evidence is sufficiently disposed of, as it respects the most of the words in question. You inquire "in what other *Dictionary*" the words are to be found; and in your former communication to the Worcester Palladium, you were so candid as to say, "that I borrowed some words from you, you suppose to be *proved* by the fact that they are in no British Dictionary; at least in none that you have seen." Now, Sir, it appears to me that it would be quite as sound logic to infer from the above statements, that you have not seen, or at least have not carefully examined, many British Dictionaries, as it

would to infer, with respect to a list of words, that because yout do not know of their existence in British Dictionaries, they must, therefore, have been taken from yours; for it appears sufficiently evident that there may be words in British Dictionaries that you are not aware of. You seem also to have overlooked the circumstance that there are, besides Dictionaries, other sources for obtaining words, which are open to me, as well as to you; and if my success in finding words *out of* Dictionaries should bear as good a comparison with yours, as it seem to bear in finding the words in question *in* them, (I only put the case hypothetically), it would not appear very wonderful, if I were able to find the few remaining words without any assistance from your labors. Of the hundred and twenty-one words, you have given authorities, in your Dictionary, for only thirty-nine; but I can, without going out of my own library, furnish authorities, in all cases different from yours, for upwards of a hundred of them.

With respect to your inquiry, how many or which words I borrowed from you, I have already said that I did not know that a single one was inserted on your sole authority. I do not affirm this to have been the fact, for I am aware that oversights of this sort may happen; but if any have been so inserted, I sincerely regret the circumstance, and will engage to erase from my Dictionary every word that you will prove to have been thus inserted. But if I saw in your Dictionary a word with which I was familiar, or which I knew was in established use, or found in respectable authors, I regarded it as a word belonging, not exclusively to any individual, but to all who write and speak the language, to be used by them on all proper occasions, even though it was not to be found in any Dictionary but yours. Take, for example, the very common compound word *semi-annual*, one in your list, which is not to be found in any of the English Dictionaries that I have examined, and you are entitled to the merit, so far as I know, of having been the first to insert this word in a Dictionary; yet you cannot doubt that I was familiar with this word before your Dictionary was published; and as I have had occasion to use it repeatedly in my other publications, I thought myself authorized to insert it also in my Dictionary. All the words in your own Dictionary were surely to be found in Dictionaries previously published, or had been previously used by other persons, except such as you coined or stamped anew, in order to enrich or embellish the language; and with regared to all words which owed their origin or new form to you, such as *ammony, bridegoom, canail, ieland, naivty, nightmar, prosopopy*, &c., it has been my intention scrupulously to avoid them, as being your own property, and I have not even inserted them in my Vocabulary of Words of Various Orthography, being willing that you should for ever have the entire and exclusive use of them. There is a considerable number of words in my Dictionary which are not to be found in yours; yet they have all,

I believe, had the sanction of respectable usage: I can therefore claim no exclusive property in them; and you are perfectly welcome, as I have before intimated to you, to have them all inserted in your Dictionary.

Should you be disposed, Sir, to pursue the examination of my Dictionary further, and honor me with any more of your inquiries, I will attend to them as promptly as my engagements may render it convenient.

Having paid such attention to your request as my engagements have permitted, and answered your inquiry, in some measure, I trust, to your satisfaction, I would now, Sir, respectfully make a request of you, which is, *that you would be so good as to inform me whether the charges against me in the Worcester Palladium were occasioned by any statements made by you, or whether you had ever made, or are now prepared to make, any such statements.*

Your compliance with this request will oblige

Your humble servant,

J.E.WORCESTER

Webster's next sally appeared in the February 18 *Palladium*:

New Haven Feb.13, 1835

MR.J.E.WORCESTER

SIR — I thank you for the information given to me in your letter of the 6th Inst. — I could add to the list of words in my last if necessary.

You mention certain words which "owed their origin or new form" to me. I have indeed anglicized some words of foreign origin. These stand as candidates for reception; it being my desire to reduce the number of anomalies and give to foreign words generally used with us, an English form. But in regard to two or three of the words named, you give me credit for what I have not done. I have corrected the spelling of *night-mare*, the common orthography being wrong & even ludicrous. The last syllable is from the Saxon, but it has nothing to do with mare. So far is *ieland* from being *mine,* that it is as old as our language, and uniformly so written in the Bishop's Bible, except that *y* is sometimes used for *i*.

But, Sir, you have added my definitions to some words found in other dictionaries, & have used my terms. You have borrowed several of my rules of orthography, found, I believe, in no other book. You have stated that my dictionary is among the principal authorities you have cited; and you have cited it perhaps in every page of your own; and often more than once in a page.

Now, Sir, observe the consequence. In my *first* edition, I had to decide on the pronunciation of thousands of words for which I had no guide but my own judgment and no assistance whatever. It was to be expected that on revision I should make some alterations in the accentuation. Cases may occur, in which my ultimate decision may be different from

your notation; in which case your present notation will be contradicted. This must doubtless be the fact, and this shows how improper it was for you to meddle with my books. My quarto Dictionary cost me about *twenty years labor and twenty thousand* dollars. For this labor and such an expense I could never receive remuneration, had the market been left open. — How unkind then was it for you, who had been intrusted with the task of making an abridgment, and been well rewarded for it, to sit down and introduce some of my improvements into a book of your own compilation, and to put in operation several sets of stereotype plates; for such I am informed is the fact. Now, Sir, rather than treat you in this manner, I would beg my bread.

One or two remarks only shall close this correspondence. The scheme you have adopted of citing several authorities for the pronunciation of words, is in opposition to my views of *encouraging uniformity*, and to the views of the best scholars that I have consulted. In many cases it tends to *unsettle* the pronunciation, which, in this country, has long been undisputed. I have adopted a different method, that of deciding different modes of pronunciation by analogy. Thus instead of giving English authorities, perhaps forty years old, for the accent of *detinue*, I resort to other words of like formation, *avernue, retinue, revernue*, and by the customary practice in these, I decide the accent of *detinue*. The same rule has been pursued in other classes of words. In many cases, this rule would soon put an end to any doubts on the subject.

In a few cases, I have altered the customary spelling of words. These instances are few, and in words whose orthography has been corrupted by mere mistake or rather by egregious blunder. Such words are *comptroller, country-dance, furlough, redoubt, zinc* and a few others. I have thought and I still think it the duty of the lexicographer [to] correct such palpable mistakes, and not to follow implicitly the English books. Whether the corrections shall be received or not I shall be satisfied that I have done my duty.

If, in regard to the use you have made of my books, in your compilation, your mind is quite at ease, long may you enjoy it.

N.WEBSTER.

NOTE — … As Dr. Webster has not seen fit to reply to Mr. Worcester's query, *whether the charge of plagiarism against himself made in the Palladium, was occasioned by any statement of his*, WE will give him the desired information, by the declaration that no communication of any character or description, ever passed between Dr. Webster and the editor of the Palladium until after Mr. Worcester's original reply.

Worcester's answer appeared on March 11:

To DR.N.WEBSTER

Sir — I beg leave to say a very few words in reply to your letter which appeared in the Worcester

Palladium of the 18th inst. At the commencement of this controversy I stated that I had little fear of being injured by having the matter thoroughly investigated; and the result, I think, has thus far verified the truth of my remark. I have not met with an individual who has intimated an opinion that any thing wrong has been proved against me. And if it is indeed so, there must be something far from right elsewhere, which it becomes those who are concerned to reflect on. It is better to suffer wrong than to do wrong.

In your last letter, you make the three following charges, viz: — that I have added your definitions to words found in other Dictionaries; that I have borrowed several of your rules of orthography; that I have cited your Dictionary in perhaps every page of mine.

With respect to the first two of these charges, they are assertions without proof; and any attempt to establish the truth of them, I can forewarn you, will be found as ineffectual as have been similar attempts which have been made. Whoever will look over my Preface to Johnson and Walker's Dictionary, and the Introduction to Walker's Rhyming Dictionary, may see without going further, that I had little occasion to be indebted to you for the rules of orthography which I adopted. Subsequently to my finishing the edition of Johnson and Walker's Dictionary, I went over further and an extensive examination of the disputed points of English orthography, and the number of cases in which my decision (whether right or wrong) differs from yours, with respect both to the orthography and pronunciation of doubtful words, is sufficient to show that I decided independently of your authority.

With respect to the third charge, it is true that in relation to words of doubtful or disputed pronunciation, I cited your authority [not in every page surely, but in a great part of the pages] in connection with the most eminent English orthoepists, as Sheridan, Walker, Perry, Jones, &c. I thought it was treating you with respect to do so, and never dreamed it would displease you. If I had known that you would rather be entirely omitted, I should have been inclined to act accordingly.

In my last letter, after complying with your request, I took the liberty, Sir, to make the following request of you, viz; *that you would be so good as to inform me whether the charges against me in the Worcester Palladium were occasioned by any statements made by you, or whether you had ever made, or are now prepared to make, any such statements.* This request it seemed to me was very reasonable; but you have seen fit "to dodge the question," and yet make an appeal to the public sympathy under the pretence of having been injured.

The fact which has already been stated, should be remembered, that the design of my Dictionary was formed, before the publication of your large work, and before I had any knowledge that you intended to publish a smaller form. My object was to supply a want which seemed to me to exist; but I had no intention or thought of interfering with your interest. I undertook the task of making the octavo abridgment of your large Dictionary, after having begun my own work, with much reluctance, upon urgent application, and after having twice declined to do it. Were the case to occur again, I should be likely to adhere to my first decison.

J.E.WORCESTER

Cambridge, Feb.28, 1835

NOTE — the first part of the question above propounded, was explicitly and definitely answered in the Palladium of Feb.18th.

Webster's last shot appeared in the *Palladium* for March 25, 1835

New Haven, March 14,1835

To J.E. Worcester

SIR — In the Palladium of the 11th, you write that my assertions respecting your taking my definitions and rules of orthography, are without proof. Now, sir, when I see such an example as the following, I judge by inference that you copied from my book: —

Clapboard, (English definition,) a board cut ready to make casks. According to *Webster*, 4to, a thin narrow board for covering houses. *Webster*, 12 mo, a narrow board for covering houses. *Worcester*, a thin narrow board for covering houses.

In this case, I do not attempt to prove that you copied from my book. I leave the public to judge of the fact. I find many such examples in your book. That you took your rules of orthography (Preface, page XVII,) from Johnson, Walker, or other English works cannot, I believe, be true; for no such rules are found in those books; and none such are followed in any English work that I have ever seen. I formed the rules myself. With these remarks, I close the correspondence.

N.WEBSTER.

That was, indeed, the close of the correspondence. Webster never answered Worcester's question "whether the charges against me in the Worcester Palladium were occasioned by any statements made by you, or whether you had ever made, or are now prepared to make, any such statements?" Worcester accused him of dodging the question, but that is surely not right. To *dodge*, as the *American Dictionary* defines it, is

to evade by a sudden shift of place; to escape by starting aside; as to *dodge* a blow aimed; to *dodge* a cannon-ball. [*This is a common word, very expressive and useful, but not admissable in solemn discourse or elegant composition.*]

Webster did not dodge the question; he ignored it. The editor's response, purporting to give "the desired information" is much more dodgy: He set out only part of the question, and made a "declaration" that failed to answer even that part:

As Dr. Webster has not seen fit to reply to Mr. Worcester's query, *whether the charge of plagiarism against himself made in the Palladium, was occasioned by any statement of his*, WE will give him the desired information, by the declaration that no communication of any character or description, ever passed between Dr. Webster and the editor of the Palladium until after Mr. Worcester's original reply.

That has the whiff of careful truth about it. It may well be that no communication had passed *directly* between Webster and the editor of the *Palladium* before Webster's first letter; it does not at all follow that the original editorial was not "occasioned by" some statement made by Webster. I have no doubt that the information did come from Webster, either directly or indirectly. The statements made in praise of Webster and his dictionary, and the nature of the accusation against Worcester, are all pure Webster. What was really upsetting him was competition, not plagiarism. The great selling points for his dictionaries were the improvements that he had made over Johnson: he had improved many of the definitions; he had put in many words that were not in Johnson at all (particularly technical and scientific terms); and he had updated Johnson's old-fashioned spelling. If nobody else did the same things, Webster would have the market to himself, and might recoup some part of his investment. That was why he regarded it as trespassing on his territory for Worcester to include words that he regarded as his, and "American" spelling. This can be seen in Webster's letter of February 13, 1835:

My quarto Dictionary cost me about *twenty years labor and twenty thousand dollars*. For this labor and such an expense I could never receive remuneration, had the market been left open. How unkind then was it for you, who had been intrusted with the task of making an abridgment, and been well rewarded for it, to sit down and introduce some of my improvements into a book of your own compilation, and to put in operation several sets of stereotype plates....

Nobody but Webster would have regarded the incorporation into a dictionary of some of the same words, and some of the same "improvements" that he had put into his, as being "a gross plagiarism ... on the literary property of Noah Webster Esq.." This is why I feel certain that Webster himself instigated the *Palladium* attack, and (perhaps indirectly) furnished the material. The editorial was then written by someone who had probably never seen Worcester's dictionary. It is hard to believe that anyone who had seen it could describe it as being "a very close imitation of Webster's"—it looks nothing like any of the Webster dictionaries referred to.

What is remarkable about the *Palladium* correspondence is that each side could have put forward a case that would have been much more damaging to the other, but failed to do so. Webster's basic argument, that Worcester must have taken words from Webster's dictionary, because they were not in any other English dictionary, was fundamentally flawed. A lexicographer is not in the business of inventing words, and putting a word into his dictionary, even if he is the first to do so, does not give him any exclusive right to it. Then, in support of that unsound argument, Webster produced a list of words most of which were in several other dictionaries; that was simply careless. It was even more careless to include words that were not in his own quarto. Those were bad points badly made, and Worcester dealt with them effectively. An even worse point was Webster's complaining that his dictionary was "among the principal authorities you have cited; and you have cited it perhaps in every page of your own." That was in relation to pronunciation, where Worcester listed the recommendations of several authorities, where they disagreed. Webster, cited as *Wb*, was one of those authorities, but not necessarily the one that Worcester himself agreed with. In these cases, he did not *copy* Webster's pronunciation; he merely *quoted* it. Webster's further point that Worcester should not have quoted him, because he (Webster) might later change his mind as to the correct pronunciation, was not carefully considered: If Webster's views were so changeable, no user of Webster's own dictionary could safely rely on it. Indeed, the fact that Webster kept changing his views on orthography was an argument used against him by critics of his recommended spellings.

The only substantial point made by Webster in the correspondence was that Worcester had copied his definition of the word *clapboard*. In answer to Webster's challenge to find the word in any earlier dictionary, Worcester could reply that it was in Pickering's *Vocabulary* of 1816 (though Pickering quoted Webster's *Compendious* as his authority). That, however, would not have explained why Worcester's definition was identical, word for word, to that in Webster's Quarto. That never was explained, because Webster only drew attention to the definition in his last letter. If Webster had wanted to show that he had a genuine grievance against Worcester, he should have given more examples of that sort, where his text had been copied. Taking items from his word list was not wrongful.

If Worcester had written his own definition of *clapboard*, it is unlikely that he would have used exactly the same words as Webster; it is probable, therefore, that unless Webster himself copied the definition from someone else, Worcester did copy his wording from Webster. Before the question of plagiarism arose, Worcester acknowledged in his Preface that he had made some use of Webster's "work of vast learning and research":

In preparing this work, much use was made of Jameson's Dictionary; but the two works which may properly be considered as forming the basis of it, are the dictionaries of Johnson and Walker, of which Jameson's professes to be chiefly a combination. It contains, however, several thousand words not found in Johnson or Walker. Mr. Todd added to his edition of Johnson's Dictionary about 12,000 words, and of these Mr. Jameson retained all that he deemed important, and in addition to them, inserted a considerable number of technical terms. The words which Jameson selected from Todd, and the others which he added, are here retained, together with many more derived from Crabb's "Technological Dictionary," Maunder's "New and Enlarged Dictionary," Dr. Webster's Dictionary, and other miscellaneous sources.

If Worcester did indeed copy several definitions from Webster, a detailed exposure might have caused him some embarrassment, particularly if he could be said earlier to have denied that he had done so. Consider the word *squirm* from Webster's list as an example. To challenge Worcester to find it in any other dictionary was a foolish thing to do; it is in Bailey's octavo ("to move very nimbly about, spoken of an Eel") with the abbreviation "*S.C.*," which means "South Country." It is not in Johnson, but Ash, in 1775, took it from Bailey (misprinted as "Squirn"). Pickering included it in his *Vocabulary* in 1816, citing both Bailey and Ash. It is not in Webster's *Compendious Dictionary* of 1806, nor in his quarto or the octavo abridgment, though the quarto says that the word *swarm*, "by the common people in New England, is pronounced *squirm* or *squuurm*." Barker picked this up and put a separate entry in the English edition of the quarto under *squirm*, "to move as a *worm*." Webster's view that *squirm* and *swarm* (as in "to swarm up a tree") are the same word is reflected in the *Primary School Dictionary* definition "to wind, twist and struggle, to climb by embracing and scrambling. [Eng. swarm.]." Worcester's definition, "to wind or twist about: *a word used in America, and provincial in England*," used two of the same words, *wind* and *twist*, as Webster, but if he took them from Webster, he was nevertheless expressing his own view of the meaning of the word, rejecting the suggested connection with *swarm*. The words "*provincial in England*" show that he was using Bailey, so that he would have included *squirm* in his word list whether Webster had it or not. There is not enough evidence here to convict Worcester of copying from Webster, since, as Johnson said in No. 143 of *The Rambler*, "All definitions of the same thing must be nearly the same." But if the words did come from Webster, it could only have been from the *Primary School Dictionary*, and Worcester denied having seen either of Webster's smaller dictionaries until after his was prepared for the press. It would have been more telling for Webster to ask Worcester where his definition came from, rather than asking him in what earlier dictionaries the word had appeared.

This points towards the more damaging strategy that was available to Webster — quoting a large number of definitions to prove that Worcester had copied from one or another of Webster's dictionaries. There would have been a risk attached to pursuing such a strategy, but it was a risk that Webster was never able to see, arising as it did from the fact that the Webster pot was blacker than the Worcester kettle. Worcester, with the finest collection of dictionaries and encyclopedias in America,

would have had no difficulty in showing that a large proportion of Webster's *American Dictionary*, and therefore of all the abridgments, was made up of definitions that Webster had himself copied from others. I think Worcester knew that he had this powerful weapon in his armory, and that he was giving Webster a delicate warning of it when he wrote at the end of his first letter to the *Palladium*: "I have ample means of showing that I came as lawfully by my materials as Dr. Webster did by his." If that was a threat, it was one that he never carried out. Worcester was a gentle man, and apart from a little dig at Webster's eccentric spellings, he defended himself without attacking Webster.

17. William Goes West, 1835–1839

In November 1834, Webster received another letter from the firm of Corey & Fairbank, in Cincinnati:

Hon. Sir

The object of this communication is to inquire whether you will be willing to furnish us with a set of stereotype plates for your smallest School Dictionary and also for your History of the United States on the same terms as you furnish other publishers, or we paying you so much for the use of them per copy on all we might print. If you should be willing to do this we have no doubt but that we can introduce them in the West to a much greater extent & consequently sell a vastly greater quantity of each, than can be sold provided they are published at the East only. We should then be able to bring them into more succcessful competition with Hales History, Goodrich's D[itt]o. Walker & Worcester's Dictionaries all of which are published here. There is no common school book published in the East only that can be introduced extensively here provided a similar work is published by an enterprising publisher in the West....

That enquiry seemed to offer not only the possibility of greatly increased sales of Webster's works, but also the opportunity of a place for William. If William offered Corey & Fairbank the rights in the works they wanted to publish as his contribution to the capital of the enterprise, would they take him into partnership? It turned out that they wanted some money as well, but Webster was prepared to lend that. William set out from New Haven in May 1835. In July, he reached Cincinnati, and the firm of Corey & Fairbank became Corey, Fairbank & Webster. He was full of confidence in the business, but it was doomed from the start. Corey & Fairbank demanded payment from the new firm of $15,150, which was alleged to be the

value of the copyrights and other property that they transferred into it. That money had to be borrowed from the bank. Then Fairbank, who was already too ill to work, died within a month of William's arrival. Corey & Webster went on selling books, but the more books they sold, the worse their financial position became. The problem was that they were selling on credit, and not all their customers paid for the books they bought. In order to print books to sell, the firm borrowed more money. The more books they printed, the more they had to borrow, and the greater the interest charges became. Within a year of William's joining the partnership, even he could see that bankruptcy was inevitable. The $1,000 that Webster had lent him in September 1835 had been nothing like enough to stave off disaster.

Webster's letters show his concern at the failure of William's business, only partly motivated by the fear that the sale of his books might be interrupted. He was also increasingly anxious to arrange for publication of a second edition of the *American Dictionary*. The first edition had numerous inconsistencies, as Cobb had enjoyed pointing out, and it needed to be replaced anyway, because stocks were running low. Another concern was the continued unauthorised printing of the *American Spelling Book*. Here are some excerpts from letters. Unless otherwise indicated, they are all from Webster to William:

[July 14, 1835] ... The ill health of Mr. Fairbank may bring additional labor on you — do what you can bear & no more....

[Aug. 29, 1835] ... I regret to hear that one of the partners is dead. I hope this event will not disturb the operations of the house....

Opposite: Booklist of Corey, Fairbank & Webster, 1835.

THE subscribers have formed a Partnership under the firm of COREY, FAIRBANK & WEBSTER, and intend carrying on the business of bookselling and publishing in its various branches, at the old stand occupied by Corey & Fairbank, 186, Main street.

A. W. COREY,
D. W. FAIRBANK,
WM. G. WEBSTER.

Cincinnati, July 1st, 1835.

LIST OF BOOKS,

PUBLISHED BY

COREY, FAIRBANK & WEBSTER,

CINCINNATI, OHIO.

Webster's Elementary Spelling Book,	per doz.	$ 1 00
The Western Primer; designed as an Introduction to Webster's Spelling Book; containing 70 Cuts,	per. gr.	4 50
The Primary Reader, to succeed Webster's Spelling Book,	per doz.	1 50
The Elementary Reader; designed as the first book after Webster's Spelling Book, with 120 Cuts,	do.	2 00
Hall's Western Reader; designed to succeed the Elementary Reader,	do.	2 50
Webster's School Dictionary,	do.	4 50
Webster's History of the United States,	do.	4 00
Webster's Improved Grammar,	do.	3 75
Murray's Grammar, improved. By Enoch Pond, A. M.	do.	1 12¼
Miss Beecher's Geography for Children, on an improved plan, with eleven colored Maps and numerous Engravings,	do.	3 00
The Pocket Testament, plain sheep,	each	0 31
Do. Do. running colors,	do.	0 35
Do. Do. flaps gilt, with fine Engravings,	do.	0 56
Do. Do. folded and collated,	per 100	25 00
Webster's Edition of the Bible,	per copy	2 50
Watts' and New Select Hymns, 32mo. This work embraces all the Psalms and Hymns of Dr. Watts, entire and unaltered, together with an addition of between two and three hundred Hymns. By Rev. James Gallaher,	per doz.	4 50
Do. Do. Do. 18mo.	do.	7 50
Do. Do. Do. 32mo. tucks, gilt edges,	do.	9 00
New Select Hymns, 18mo.	do.	3 50
Do. Do. 32mo.	do.	2 50
Watts' Psalms and Hymns, 32mo. sheep,	do.	3 50
Do. Do. 18mo. sheep,	do.	6 00
Lectures on Scepticism. By Lyman Beecher, D. D. These lectures embrace the following subjects: 1. The causes and remedy of Scepticism; 2. The falsehood, folly, and anti-republican tendencies of Political Atheism; 3. The God of the Bible,	do.	5 00
Introduction to the Criticism and Interpretation of the Bible, for General Use. By C. E. Stowe, Professor of Biblical Literature in Lane Seminary,	do.	
The Christian Lyre. The Music printed in patent notes. By Joshua Leavitt,	do.	5 00
Mitchell's Chemistry, on the basis of Reid; with Plates and Diagrams. ☞ This book has already been adopted as the text-book in most of the colleges of the west,	per copy	2 80
Eberle on Children,	do.	2 75
Eberle's Notes of his Practice, 2d edition,	do.	1 25
Young Ladies' Assistant in Drawing and Painting. By Maria Turner,	do.	0 42
Irving's Life of Columbus, for schools,	per doz.	4 50
Life of Black Hawk, dictated by himself,	do.	3 00
Hints on the connection of Labor with Study, as a Preventive of Diseases peculiar to Students. By Thomas D. Mitchell, M. D., 18mo.	per copy	0 20
Munsell's Map of Kentucky; large, three feet by four,	do.	6 00
Do. Pocket Do.	per doz.	4 50
The Statutes of Ohio, in three volumes, superroyal 8vo.	per vol.	6 00
Hammond's Reports of Cases decided in the Supreme Court of Ohio, 6 vols. 8vo.	do.	4 00

[Sept. 3, 1835] ... for $1,000 send me your note payable in 3 years, with annual interest....[1]

[Sept. 22, 1835] ... your note is defective — not having the words *value received* — & of course good for nothing. You may send me another correctly worded, but leaving out *interest*, though you may pay interest, if you can. Leave that at present....

[Oct. 8, 1835] ... I have directed the piratical printers of my old books in Concord to be prosecuted.

I would suggest whether it would not be advisable to publish in Kentucky, or at least in Tennessee, a short note like this — "The public are cautioned against buying Webster's American Spelling Book — the editions now in market are pirated, badly printed & incorrect. The author expressly disclaims them."

[Nov. 9, 1835] ... I want now to publish my Quarto in octavo — & my Synopsis. I would also publish my miscellaneous writings, if I was able or could find a publisher. Durrie & Peck would publish the Quarto, if they could get sufficient aid.

Mr. Smith tells me that Lyman Cobb is delivering lectures on school keeping &c in Pennsylvania. He will probably continue to do so as long as he lives — & he will have adherents among the common people. His books are nearly banished from New England.

Your Western people begin to think that they must make their own school books. This is well enough; but one exception should be urged in every part of the country: this is, that books for teaching to spell & pronounce English words ought *not to be multiplied*. It is important that all the people of this country should follow one dictionary & Spelling book, that all may speak & write alike. This is a matter of national importance. And as my books take the lead, & no other can, for a long time, be substituted, it should be, I think, a point with all who direct the schools, to inculcate these opinions & discourage the use of various books. Let us, as far as possible, be in this respect, one people.

Wherever your agents go, let them give notice that the editions of my American Sp. Book now in market are all pirated editions & incorrect.

Any such accusation of piracy would have been completely groundless. A reprint of the *American Spelling Book* in 1835 might have been badly printed, and Webster would certainly not have authorized it, but it could not have been a pirated edition because the copyright in the *American* had expired in 1832.

In November 1836, Webster issued another of his printed circulars, "*To Messrs.* A.PICKET *and* J.W.PICKET," attacking some other compilers of spelling books. Like Worcester, they were criticized when they were supposed to

have copied from Webster's books, and then criticized again (for not agreeing with him) when they did not copy from his books:

In the year 1783, before the close of the revolutionary war, I compiled a published an elementary book for the instruction of the youth of this country. In this I introduced a new division of syllables, a new classification of words, and a new and simple key for exhibiting the pronunciation. It has been agreed by all subsequent writers on the subject, that these were important improvements on the schemes of preceding compilers; and the fact is proved by the circumstance that every later compiler has adopted my general plan.... This work has, during nearly forty years, been the chief means of my support, and has been the only source from which supplies for my family were drawn while I was compiling my large dictionary. It is now the principal means of my subsistence in old age.

Under these circumstances, while I cannot object to any attempts to improve elementary books, I feel that my younger competitors ought to respect my rights. Justice, honor, and morality demand that no person shall pillage my book, nor any part of it, for the improvement of his own, and thus make *my own labor* the means of depriving me of subsistence.

Let me ask, then, was not the "Alphabet of Numbers," in your former edition, page 11, taken chiefly from mine, in the 163d page of the Elementary Spelling Book?

In your New Juvenile Spelling Book, your scheme of the vowels contains *seven points* which are the same as in my key, or plan of notation, used in my spelling book and smaller dictionaries. It cannot be supposed that this coincidence was *casual*. A great part of eight pages, from p. 97 to 104, consists of tables of difficult or irregular words classed in the same manner as mine, differing only in details; and your division of syllables is the same. .....

Permit me now to ask, on what principle of morality do you justify this license? Is not my scheme as much my property as my house or my books? Have you any more right to take part of it for your profit than you have to take a book from my library, or a bushel of corn from my field? You may say that others have committed a like trespass on my property. True; all compilers of similar books have been gulty of the same thing to a greater or less extent; and I shall leave them as I leave you, to answer for their conduct at a higher tribunal than earth can furnish....

Walker and other English writers make three syllables of *bravery, slavery, knavery*, and you follow them. But *brave* is one syllable, and *ry* is one; and I know of no arithmetic that makes *one* and *one* to be *three*. This error has proceeded from an inattention to the effect of the letter *r*, which is always preceded by a slight sound of *e* in words of this sort. Thus *more, mire*, are pronounced *moer, mier*. This has led

authors into the mistake. But *bravery* is no more a word of three syllables than *safety* or *sagely*. So the English make two syllables of *nicely, niceness*, but three syllables of *nicety* — a strange inconsistency!

No doubt because Webster brought it to his attention, Professor Goodrich also found himself looking at Picket's spelling book. As a serious academic, he may initially have thought such matters beneath his notice, but he would soon have realised that this was a mistake. Financially, the spelling book was more important to Webster (and therefore to his family) than all his other books put together. Goodrich was not a warm supporter of Webster's peculiarities of spelling and pronunciation — particularly when they interfered with sales — and since those peculiarities were the feature of the *Elementary Spelling Book* on which Webster's critics concentrated their attacks, Goodrich tried to persuade Webster to remove them from the book. He wrote a long letter in which one can see a very real concern for Webster's financial interests (and those of his family). He had three arguments:

1. Webster's peculiar spellings were wrong;
2. Even if they were not wrong, it was impossible to persuade people that they were right;
3. To strengthen the spelling book against his critics, and therefore sell more copies, Webster would not need to change his views on spelling — he would only need to change some of the words used in the spelling book, leaving out the words of disputed orthography.

Because Goodrich was a subtle fellow, he concealed the sharpness of his first point beneath a layer of unctuous flattery, and by reversing the order of the three points. He then went on to criticize Webster's peculiarities of pronunciation — either they were wrong, or they represented old-fashioned New England speech. Whichever it was, they were objectionable to people who lived in other parts of the United States. This is how his letter began:

My dear Sir,

In reading Picket's Spelling Book the thought struck me, that I had never examined your *own* in the *revised edition*, and I immediately devoted all my leisure time for three days to this employment. It afforded me a high gratification. I never before was so sensible of the excellence of your general plan, or of the extent to which valuable improvements have been introduced in the new work. In the hands of a

faithful and judicious teacher, every page may be made the means of impressing the most important distinctions on the minds of children as to the meaning and use of the words which occur in the spelling lessons. It is not so *amusing* as the old one, but it is far more instructive.

In reading over the lists of words, I marked a number of errors in ~~orthography~~ printing, which ought to be corrected. Of these, I inclose a schedule to be made use of for that purpose.

Anxious as I am to promote the circulation of your works, both from the deepest affection for yourself and from a full persuasion of their high excellence, I have been led, while going through the Spelling book, to consider objections which are made to them by your opponents. On this subject, I would beg leave to offer a few suggestions, the result of extended inquiry and observation during the last six years.

Almost all these objections have turned on two points — some peculiarities of spelling and of pronunciation which are laid hold of by interested men; and urged on the public to prevent the circulation of your elementary works. On this subject permit me to offer the following remarks.

I consider it certain, that the *general principles* of your orthography will prevail, I mean those enumerated in the communication which you showed me about a month since. On the first publication of your dictionary, I feared exceedingly, that some of them would be thought too decided innovations, particularly those in words like *traveler, center*, & *pretense*. But I have seen with very high gratification that in this country, at least, the indications are decisively of a change in your favor. It must of necessity be slow. A generation must pass away before it can be fully accomplished, but it *will* take place, and you will do for large classes of words in the English language, what Voltaire, with all his popularity, could never accomplish for the French as to a single diphthong (oi) — you will have given order and regularity to our orthography. To accomplish this, however, you have labored, and must still labor, under the imputation of a love of novelty and innovation, from men who have not time or capacity to understand your principles. This prejudice has been used against you by Cobb and other interested men; and I fear will be so used still more hereafter, to the great injury of your property.

Under these circumstances, I have asked myself very seriously the question "How far ought Dr. Webster to go in his sacrifices for the improvement of our orthography." As to the *classes* of words alluded to above, I have no doubt. But there are some thirty or forty isolated words, which now create almost all the difficulty; and as to those I do begin to feel, that you ought not to be loaded with the responsibility of carrying through the change in respect to them, that they embarrass your operation very materially as to the larger and more important *classes*, and that your property and peace of mind must be injured

throughout the remainder of your life, if the whole of the burden is thrown upon you. Is it not more than any single man could have hoped to accomplish, to give order and regularity to the *classes* of words alluded to above?

What, then, is the suggestion which I have to make on this subject? It is, the inquiry whether you might not be justified to leave, in future, any attempt at improvement, beyond the general classes above mentioned; and in your Spelling book, at least, cancel a few words which are most objected to, substituting for them others of uncontested orthography? The great instrument of attack upon you, out of New England, is to send forth agents with your own book marked in certain places, where words occur which are deemed objectionable. It is not to be disputed, that the spelling and pronunciation of these words are different from those which generally prevail in our country, especially out of New England. Now these words strike a multitude of men to whom the books are shown, very unpleasantly. They look like *vulgarisms*, or *useless innovations*, and there is not a people on earth who dread the imputation of either of [those] things, so much as educated men of the middle, western, and southern states. It is a feeling against which you cannot reason; nor will certificates from what will be called "Yankee Colleges" avail. Fashion has almost omnipotent force in these matters, and I do fear that your spelling book will be more and more the object of attack, while this system can be carried on.

To explain my views fully, I will mention all the words of this class which occur in the spelling book. They are but few, but they lay the foundation for incessant attack.

p. 43. *Maiz.* I believe there is not another word in our language which ends with a single z when the preceding vowel sound is long. Such words always take the *e* final to indicate the fact. Why write *baize* and yet *maiz*? Is not this an inadvertence respecting the true analogy, like that of writing *wo* without the final *e* in your dictionary, which you have since corrected?

58. Sleezy for sleazy. As there are nearly 200 words in which *ea* has the sound of ē, why should this single word be altered?

58.60. Melasses. This word is constantly occurring in commerce, and is always spelt with an o. Careful speakers always sound the o, as they do in *opinion*. Negligent speakers give the first syllable an obscure sound approaching to that of short *e*, as they do in *all* unaccented syllables in o; but I am not aware that any one *designedly* pronounces the first syllable with the sound of *e*. Is mere derivation a sufficient reason for this change? We do not write *Ingland*, though the word is derived from *Ingvones*, and is pronounced with the sound of *I*.

64. Ribin for ribon. If my observations and inquiries do not wholly deceive me, the present generation of educated men universally pronounce this

ribon. The other spelling is very strongly objected to as calculated to sanction what is (right or wrong) felt to be a vulgarism.

65. Gimblet. As the *b* is silent, is it not better to omit it in this word?

64. Porpess Would not porpus be better?

72. Steril) Ermin) Are there not multitudes of words which may as well be altered as these? e.g. agile, fragile, examine, determine.

84. Highth) Drouth) All my observations and inquiries for many years have led me to the conclusion that the sound of *th* in these words is dropped by the present generation of educated men. Drouth is still heard among the commonalty of New England, but for this very reason is regarded in the middle, southern and western states, as a vulgarism. I have painful reason to know, that the spelling and pronunciation of these words and of ribin, have acted very powerfully against your works.

87. Nightmar. The *a* in the last syllable of this word is always, I believe, pronounced long. Is not the final e necessary to make it so?? As this word stands in the spelling book, it ought to be pronounced nightmar (rhyming with *car*). Can this pronunciation ever prevail?

104. Pinchers for pincers. The latter is accordant with etymology (pincer.) The present generation of well-educated persons conform their pronunciation, I believe, to this orthography. There certainly are very strong objections to "*pinchers*" among the warmest friends of Dr. Webster, while his enemies make use of this word with great effect, to injure his works.

87. Hainous for heinous. This is very strongly objected to, and used as a powerful instrument of attack. Is a derivation which not one out a thousand can understand, a sufficient reason for a change, which strikes the public eye as the blunder of an illiterate writer? In the case of this word, "pinchers," "drouth," "highth," "ribin," and a few more, we have, as I suppose, the key to an objection of the Editor of the Indianapolis paper, that Dr. Webster suffers the errors of an ignorant man (Ely) to pass under his name. I should have looked on this orthography in just the same light.

Chimistry and) derivatives) For some years, I have been warmly interested in the attempt to introduce this orthography; but I begin to be hopeless of success. All the teachers of this science are resolute in adhering to the old orthography. They admit the etymological reasons, but consider change is too great an evil to be encountered. We have also "Chemical Bank" with their notes in circulation, so that legislation must be altered before the change can be effected. In the meantime the pronunciation of the young is rapidly conforming itself to the prevalent orthography.

Envelop) Develop) I am not aware that this has ever been followed by those who adopt your general principles. Whenever I meet with the word it has the *e* final. Still I do not consider it important.

These are all the words of this class which I remember in the spelling book. There are some others which you have dwelt upon at the close of the Remarks prepared for the "Knickerbocker," to which similar observations will apply — Suvran is an example. While *eign* is retained in *foreign* and *o* in *son* and many other words, why should they be changed in this word? This question is constantly asked.

Goodrich then devoted several pages to attacking Webster's pronunciation, questioning some of his dearest beliefs. He did not agree, for example, that *slave-ry* and *brave-ry* were words of two syllables. "Would you," he asked, "say groce-ry?"

Goodrich's personal views, and his underlying concern for the welfare of Webster's dependants, can be seen in the closing pages of his letter:

The suggestion which I have made respecting these words goes no farther necessarily than this, that other words should be *substituted* for these, thus taking away the ground of objection without abandoning the orthography and pronunciation in question. Still, if you feel as to any of these words or all of them, as you have done respecting *fether* for feather, *wo* for woe, *ile* for isle (now in the spelling book) that they had better be surrendered, I think it most desirable to do so. You proposed these changes for the consideration of the public; you may very properly withdraw them in a spelling book and school dictionary which are designed to teach youth the *actual* orthography of our language.

In this connection I would beg leave to suggest that many cavils would be obviated if you were to draw out briefly on a single page, your *leading* principles of orthography, with the reasons and authorities, and have this pasted in as an *avant courier*, to any spelling book published. This would show instructors and school committees why you write duelist, offense &c., and remove much prejudice. If to this you were to add, that you had formerly proposed changes in some other (individual) words, but had withdrawn them from a work designed to exhibit the actual orthography (though without surrendering your judgment on the subject) nearly every objection would be removed.

I am aware that some trouble and expense must arise from these alterations. There are some however, which *must* be made. I mean the correction of very obvious misprints. When this is doing, it will be but little additional expense to make the changes proposed. I cannot doubt that every publisher would find his interest in thus removing the principal ground of attack on the work.

When I look at the vast extent to which our language must reach within a single century, I feel a strong desire to see it kept uniform and consistent, by the instrumentality of *one set* of school books which shall fix its laws. I do believe that nothing but the objections now mentioned will prevent your works from doing this noble service; and I do exceedingly fear, that while these objections remain they will be a fatal barrier in the way of this their high office.

When I see that your support in the decline of life, the support of a beloved family at the west [i.e. William's], and the means of providing for the subsistence of those whom you may leave helpless behind you, are all dependent on the yearly income of your works, I do feel no ordinary solicitude to see the great instrument of attack on your elementary works, wrested from the hands of your opponents. I do fear for the result if this is not done; but I must leave the decision with yourself, certain that you will appreciate, as I could wish, the sentiments of veneration and love with [which] I have ventured to write thus freely.

C.A.Goodrich

There is no date on the letter, but it must have been written towards the end of 1835, since it refers to the draft of an article Webster had written, which appeared in *The Knickerbocker, or New York Monthly Magazine* in March 1836, entitled "Philology." Also, Webster mentioned Goodrich's letter in one he wrote to William on January 1, 1836:

Mr. Goodrich has lately examined it [the *Elementary*] critically; he thinks it less *amusing* but more *instructive* than the American. We think of making some further corrections & slight alterations in it, to remove some objections. These I will send you ere long.

Durrie & Peck still hesitate about publishing the 4to, partly on the account of the fear of war.

Webster did not share Goodrich's views on what spellings were correct. When the revised *American Dictionary* was issued as a royal octavo in 1841, only one of Goodrich's words had a different spelling to that given in the quarto — *gimlet* replaced *gimblet*. Only one other change of spelling was made in the *Elementary Spelling Book* in response to Goodrich's letter: *sleezy* was altered to *sleazy*. Those had been given as alternative spellings in the 1828 dictionary, and would be again in 1841. Webster was not prepared to change his spelling of *chimistry* or its derivatives, nor, despite what he said in his letter to William, was he very keen on removing such disputed words from the spelling book as a way of avoiding criticism. The removals he did make were far from thorough. In one table,

"*Words in which* c *before* h *has the sound of* k," the word *chimical* was taken out, along with *alchimy* and *chimistry*, but *chimist* was left in. The spelling *chimistry* was unchanged in the sentence "Lectures on chimistry are delivered in our colleges," and *alchimic* and *alchimistic* were untouched. *Chimical* also survived in the sentence "A matrass is a chimical vessel; but a matress [sic] is a quilted bed." In a list of words that "*usually or always end in* al," *chimical* was replaced by *comical*. The word *ribin* was changed in a word list to *savin* (defined in the *Primary School Dictionary* as "a tree or shrub of the juniper kind"); but *ribin* remained in the sentence "Some worship a gay and splendid dress, consisting of silks and muslins, gauze and ribins." The word *opake*, which was in Goodrich's list of misprints but was a Webster spelling, was replaced by *rebate*, but that was balanced by changing *turquois* (which had inadvertently been spelled in the French manner before 1836) to *turkois*.

In fact, Goodrich's list was far from complete. There were other eccentric spellings in the *Elementary* that silently vanished away after Webster's death. Here are some of them; each pair consists of a word as it appeared in the 1841 edition, coupled with the corresponding word from an *Elementary* of 1880. In most cases, the spelling has been corrected, but sometimes a different word has been substituted for Webster's word, in the table or sentence where it appeared:

zink-zinc; maiz-corn; respit-spinal; turnep-turnip; potatoe-potato; melasses-molasses; porpess-mystic; parsnep-parsley; ratan-rattan; steril-sterile; ermin-ermine; jasmin-jasmine; highth-thief; nightmar-monster; turkois-turkey; hainous-surfeit; subtil-subtile; barbacue-barbecue; flagelet-floweret; cimiter-cimeter; cutlas-cutlass; chimical-chemical; matress-mattress; chimistry-chemistry; sythe-scythe; anchoret-anchorite; orchester-orchestra; chimist-chemist; mastich-distich; alchimic-alchemic; alchimistic-alchemistic; ribins-ribbons; mastif-mastiff;

There are other words whose spelling was changed between 1841 and 1880 (such as *paltroon/poltroon* and *tortion/torsion*), but the first of those forms do not appear in any Webster dictionary, and they may have been misprints. The list above, includes only those words whose authenticity is shown by the fact that (save for one) the first word in each pair is so spelled in the *Primary School Dictionary* or in the quarto. The exception is *barbacue*, which is the spelling given in the *Compendious Dictionary*.

It is impossible to tell how many more copies of the *Elementary* might have been sold if Webster's eccentricities had never been included, or how many fewer if they had been left unaltered, but even with such eccentricities as it contained, it sold remarkably well. In his letter of November 9, 1835, when it had been on the market for six years, Webster wrote to William:

I think you err in stating the annual sales of the Elementary at *half a million*. According to the returns, the last year, the number is short of that, tho' it rises above 400,000. But is it advisable to boast so much?... Will it not expose me to heavy assessments in taxation, on the popular supposition that I have a very large income?

As it turned out, William had not erred at all. In the letter of January 1, 1836, Webster told him that "from the returns of licensees for printing the Elementary, ... the sales annually cannot be less than half a million." Monaghan calculates licensed sales to have been 506,700 in 1835, but this would seem to have led to overstocking, since sales slumped the following year. Between 1832 and 1842, annual sales fluctuated from a low of 12,000 copies in 1836, to over 820,000 in 1839; total sales for those ten years amounted to about 3.4 million copies. In the 1850s, sales were said to exceed 1.5 million a year; and the *Elementary* of 1880, fifty years after the book was published, bears the boast on the cover: "More than **1,000,000** Copies of this Work are sold Annually."

The continuing sale of unauthorised editions of the *American Spelling Book* must have convinced Webster that some people preferred the old book to the new one, which made him think that he might himself republish it. On January 4, 1836, he wrote to E.W. & C. Skinner, who were the publishers of the *Elementary* in Albany:

I visited Concord last summer, but I found that the *American* is printed by men of no responsibility; the real owners of the plates & publishers not being easily discovered. I have had thoughts of prosecuting the men — but the difficulty of finding the real trespassers, & of getting evidence, together with the distance & the expenses & delay of law-suits & the uncertainty of the issue, have deterred me from the attempt.

I believe the better way for me & for all the publishers of the *Elementary* would be this — the *American* is very incorrect, & I have so informed the public in Concord through the prints, & have disclaimed the book in its present state. The best method to be taken, in my view, is for me to correct the work, & make some valuable improvements in it, & let all the publishers of the *Elementary* print & publish the American, the genuine copy. In this copy, I would insert an advertisement that all the copies not thus designated are *pirated* and *very incorrect* & caution the public against buying the pirated editions. This would soon supersede the old editions. The books being alike & correct, it would be a matter of indifference to me which is used....

I should like to know your opinion on this plan.

P.S. Query. If the public prefer the American, is it not my duty to let them have it, I mean, a correct copy?

Webster's later letters to William continue to mention his plans for the *American Dictionary*, as well as his hopes that something may be saved from the wreck of William's business:

[Jan. 5, 1836] ... If Durrie & Peck should undertake an edition of the 4to in 8vo, it is possible that Corey & Webster may be concerned with them to advantage. I will suggest it to them.

[Jan. 23, 1836] ... Nothing is yet done respecting the large Dictionary, & Durrie & Peck will probably wait for some decisive measures in our government....

[Feb. 15, 1836] ... I hear nothing further about the printing of the 4to....

[April 6, 1836] ... Mr. Goodrich is on his way & will be in Cincinnati in three or four days.

I know the importance of the West to me & my agents & probably to my heirs. Whatever I can do shall be done.

I should suppose a few wealthy friends in Cincinnati might be found to contribute & make some advances to carry on the publications, taking such security from the firm as may be satisfactory — & continue the business, till some person can be found to undertake it.

In whatever arrangements the house may make, with creditors, I hope you will, by some means, reserve a right to my best publications hereafter, when circumstances will permit....

I feel distressed for you & Mr. Corey & his family — but sympathy is all I can give at present for relief.

[William to Webster, April 17, 1836] ... Is it not expedient to *announce* the intended republication of the large Dicty — in a less expensive form, & with complete improvements &c., &c.?

We continue to have calls for the 4to....

[William to Webster, April 19, 1836] ... Do you not think that, by some exertion, N.& J.White, perhaps with some other influential House, could be induced to undertake the republication of the 4to Dictionary?

[May 3, 1836] We are all distressed by your last letters. I still hope some means may be devised to enable you to continue your business. It is vastly important that it should be continued not only to yourself & me, but to others concerned in the property of my books. Upon a fair exhibition of your debts & credits, if the credits exceed the debts, I should hope that some man of property would step in & sustain you. If not, then secure me & Mr. G. as well as you can. Furniture to be secure must be delivered to my lawful agent, & he must take possession of it & lock it up. ....

[July 7, 1836] ... Mr. Fowler has determined to quit his profession & wishes to engage in bookselling. Had I heard of your disappointment in the failure of Mr. Burgess to comply with his engagements, I should have conversed with him on removing to Cincinnati. As it is I shall write to him & to Mr. Burgess & see if a plan of a book-establishment cannot be effected. Possibly it can be. My fear is, that there can be no delay in your affairs & that the disposal of your copy-rights &c will take place, before a plan can be matured. I wish you could go forward in the publication of the Elementary at least, untill we can devise & execute a plan to keep an establishment of bookselling in Cincinnati. Mr. Fowler, though not bred to bookselling, is a man of such judgment & prudence, that I would trust him with the management of such a concern; & if he should undertake it, he would give his whole attention to it. He is now treasurer of the College, & conducts the business to great acceptance.

I am determined that the business shall be carried on either by you or by a new firm. I will see what can be done, as soon as possible. I hope no proceedings of your house will operate to prejudice my designs. But this frustration of the plan is sudden & unexpected — & a new plan cannot be formed in a moment.

As to your prejudice against Mr. Fowler, I care not a cent for it. You & the family have no better friend than Mr. Fowler, & he is deeply impressed with the importance of sustaining my publications — & no man can do more to effect in this business. If Mr. Burgess & Mr. Fowler can be united, they would accomplish the object, & make the necessary advances. Whether the climate of the West will suit your sister or not cannot be known, without a trial; but certainly, it would be more favorable than that of Vermont.[2]

[July 26, 1836] By your letters to me & to Mr. Goodrich, I find [you] to rely too much on the certainty that Mr. Fowler will engage in the bookselling business in Cincinnati. He is a cautious man & will not change his business without a full knowledge of all the circumstances which can affect him. I have written to him, recommending that he should, early

in autumn, visit Cincinnati, with Harriett. She is mending, & possibly the climate of that city may be sufficiently mild for her health. Should he decide on this, he might be at least some weeks in Cincinnati, & bring his mind to a conclusion, respecting changing his business & residence. I shall probably hear from him within 8 or 10 days....

[Sept.13, 1836] ... In consequence of a letter from England, I have written to Black, Young & Young, [3] to send to my care three hundred copies of the English reprint of my dictionary, on certain conditions favorable to my own interest. If they comply, I shall postpone the printing of the work for the present. The work will come, if at all, at a less price than the American Edition. I hope to hear from them in due season.

An advertisement in the New Haven *Daily Herald* on September 19, 1836, announced that the first edition of the *American Dictionary* was sold out and that demand would in future be filled with copies of the English edition. There could be no doubt that a new American edition would soon be required — and this did not at all please Webster's elder daughters. He was nearly 80 years old, and they did not want to see their hoped-for inheritance disappearing into yet another of their father's unprofitable publishing ventures. Webster asked both Ellsworth and Goodrich for financial support, and both refused. From Harriet's husband, William Fowler, he thought that he might get editorial help as well as financial, and he offered him a partnership. Fowler's pamphlet tells the story:

A few years after the publication of his great work, [Dr. Webster] told me he was meditating a new edition of it, and proposed to me to be associated with him as joint editor in preparing it for publication. In the years 1837-8 he repeatedly proposed to me to become editor with him in publishing that work, to be so mentioned on the title page, urging me to remove my family to New Haven, to his house, saying that he would mortgage his house to raise his half of the funds; that I might have one half of the profits, as I should own one half of the copyright and one half of the capital; that if I preferred it, on account of my wife's health, he would sell or rent his house, and remove with me either to Philadelphia or Cincinnati; telling me, in conversation and by letter, that "if I expected to have an unbroken family I must leave Middlebury;" traveling with my wife the greater part of one summer, and interesting her in this plan of a literary and pecuniary partnership in the Dictionary. He visited Middlebury twice that summer, chiefly on that business....

I entertained the proposal of Dr. Webster, to enter into a partnership, so far as to say to him, that if I could ascertain the value of the lien which Mr. Goodrich had on the large work, which would prevent its being published in a form that would injure the sale of the abridged octavo, then owned by Mr. Goodrich and Mr. White, and if I could buy off Mr. Goodrich and Mr. White, at a fair price, so that the large work could be published in any form in which we should choose to publish it, and also could obtain a publisher on favorable terms, I would undertake to unite with him in its publication, as joint editor and owner.

Accordingly, at the request of Dr. Webster, I went to New York and laid the subject before the Harpers. They readily declared that if they could publish the contemplated edition of the work, unincumbered by the check which Mr. Goodrich held upon it, they would pay for the copyright a very "pretty fortune" to Dr. Webster.

I then applied to Mr. White for information which would enable me to judge what I ought to pay to Mr. Goodrich and Mr. White, for liberty to publish the work in a cheap form, and he refused to give me any statement on the subject; but said that Mr. Goodrich, being a brother, undoubtedly would give the desired information.

The next day I returned to New Haven and told Dr. Webster what I had done, and also told him I should, with his approbation, apply to Mr. Goodrich for the information which I wanted, as a preliminary to a partnership. Accordingly, after tea one evening, I went to Mr. Goodrich's and asked him some questions as to the amount of the sales, which he refused to answer. He was greatly agitated; said that Mr. White was unwilling to have him disclose the amount of the sales and profits; said, in allusion to his sharp bargain with Dr. Webster for the abridged octavo, that immediately after he had made the bargain with Dr. Webster, "on his knees he made a vow to consecrate all the profits of the work to holy purposes." I told him, that "the use which he made of it did not alter the nature of the transaction," by which he obtained the property; that, if it did alter it, any case, even of fraud, might be justified, by devoting to "holy purposes" what had been obtained by the fraud; that he knew that the Dictionary was worth more than he paid for it, when he bought it of Dr. Webster, as he had often told me it was. And I told him that it was *especially* unfair and ungenerous to Dr. Webster and his family, to go to him some time after the contract was made, and persuade him, by appeals to his generosity, to tie up his own hands, by entering into *additional* stipulations not to stereotype the large work in a form that would lessen the price to the purchaser and make it profitable to Dr. Webster. And when he admitted that he had found the octavo profitable, I told him that he ought therefore to release Dr. Webster from the stipulation just mentioned. He said in reply, that he had parted with the power to others, to release Dr. Webster from that stipulation. To this I said, that having obtained the

work at a low price — much lower than he told me it was worth — he could afford to make some sacrifice of a portion of his profits, and that if he would use the same shrewdness and skill in negotiation with the other joint owner or partner, which he had used with Dr. Webster, in getting the work out of his hands, he might restore to Dr. Webster the right to publish it in the most advantageous form. But *he evidently did not wish to restore that right to Dr. Webster, to increase the sale of a Dictionary that would, in market, be a rival of his own.*

He entered into no defense for violating his promises to me, and for obtaining the work at a much less price than he had a different times told me it was worth, but endeavored to excuse himself, by appealing to the "holy purposes" to which he had devoted some of the money, and the good he had done with it. In reply, I told him that Dr. Webster and his family might prefer doing good with the money in their own way, without making him the almoner of their bounty. The interview was altogether an unpleasant one to us both. I obtained no evidence that Mr. Goodrich *wished to release Dr. Webster* from the unfortunate stipulation which he had persuaded Dr. Webster generously to annex to the original contract, some considerable time after that contract was made. Thus Dr. Webster was unable to stereotype the American Dictionary and publish it in a cheap and popular form; while the abridged octavo still continued to yield large profits to Mr. Goodrich, or its owners and publishers.

In this interview I found I could not enter into this partnership with Dr. Webster, who was deeply dissatisfied with Mr. Goodrich, without involving myself also in a quarrel with the latter. Accordingly, for this and some other reasons, I declined the offer of Dr. Webster, and accepted a professorship in Amherst College.

Fowler's view of Goodrich may have been biased, and Fowler himself was not the most conciliatory of men. Goodrich had the reputation of being a godly fellow, and if he swore that he would apply the profits of the octavo abridgment to "holy purposes," he probably did so. In 1828, he bought a holy magazine, the *Christian Spectator,* which he continued to publish thereafter. The purchase of the magazine could not have been financed by profits from the dictionary because the octavo was not published until the following year, but some of the profits may have kept the magazine running. Another holy purpose can be identified with greater certainty. In 1838, Goodrich proposed the establishment at Yale of a professorship in pastoral theology, and he gave $5,000 towards the cost. The person appointed to the post must have been well

qualified, since he remained in office until his death in 1860. It was Goodrich himself.

Meanwhile, things were going no better for William in Cincinnati:

[Emily Ellsworth to Webster, Oct. 31, 1836] ... I had not heard of William's defeated plans until Mr. Jones returned from N[ew].H[aven]. He was certainly born under an unlucky planet.

'Tis pity he ever left N.H. where he lived so sweetly....

[Dec. 4, 1836] ... I will do whatever I can, to place you in a way to obtain a living. I have addressed a letter to Mr. Ellsworth on the subject. I regret that you cannot continue in bookselling in Cincinnati — but if it is not practicable, we must submit.

In the mean time, if you are distressed for money, you may take any money for your use, which my books there will bring, or sell any of the furniture. You may also take the premium on the History due from Burgess & Morgan, if necessary.

I should be willing to part with all the premium on the Sp. Books, arising from copies published in your city, & apply it to raise a capital in bookselling for you, if you could be resinstated in the business. But I see no way at present by which this can be done.

I have a letter from London by which I learn that Black & Armstrong have purchased the stock of Black, Young & Young, & have my dictionary. They will sell copies to me very low, & if I can find a bookseller to undertake the importation, I shall do it; but this is uncertain....

We live in hope of something more favorable for you & the country. But we are wicked as a people & we are punished with a wretched administration.

[Jan. 5, 1837] ... As to an office under govt, I do not think you can obtain one, at least, it is against probability; & if you could, nothing but dire necessity should induce you to accept it. There is no security for *holding* an office under such a capricious government. It is better, if possible, to rely on your own exertions for subsistence....

I have not yet succeeded in finding a person to import copies of my Dictionary from England. I will try to effect it, or to procure it to be printed in this country.

[Jan. 7, 1837] ... In reflecting on some mode of business for your subsistence, the following plan has occurred to me.... join with Mr. Cranch in publishing a Daily paper, on the following plan. Let the paper be *impartial*; that is a reporter of facts of public interest, in politics, literature, morals & religion, *without comment by the Editor.* Take no part with any man or party. State facts with candor & caution, & leave readers to make their own comments. This would attach to the paper men of all parties, & the Editor would escape controversy & censure. This is the plan on which every paper ought to be conducted.

Another material part of the plan would be, not to obtain subscribers at all, but to sell the paper daily, as is done in London. Honest boys & poor men may take a number of papers daily, & go about selling them, say at three cents each, which would amount to less than ten dollars a year, & the price being small, more persons would take the paper at three cents a day, than at ten dollars a year. The carriers may have the papers at 2 cents or 2½ each & thus get a dollar or half dollar a day....

If Mr. Cranch & you on consultation *privately* should concur with me in opinion, I would aid in establishing the paper....

[Jan. 23, 1837] ... I wrote to you two or three weeks ago suggesting the project of a newspaper to be edited by our friend Cranch on a plan different from any others. To this I have no answer.

I wish to know whether the stocks of the company of Corey & Webster will pay the debts. If not, I suppose you must return what you received, & of course you will be left entirely destitute. If you cannot be discharged from all your responsibilities, you cannot enter upon any business, as you would be liable to be continually harrassed with the old debts. If you could get a clerkship, you might earn something. We do not here find any business for you at present. But if nothing presents to you for support, you must dispose of your heavy furniture, & bring your family to New Haven. We shall cheerfully provide for you, till you can find business. ...

[Feb. 3, 1837] ... It seems to be an opinion here among your friends that you can at present have no business equal to the support of your family — & that the better way for you is to let Rosalie & the children come over the mountains, & live with us, till you can get business that will support you.

We are contriving schemes to aid you — but I do not know how our contrivances will terminate. Mr. Goodrich is trying to find you a place in La Fayette in a new institution formed by Ellsworth & Curtis — but this cannot be brought to a conclusion till Spring. ...

[Harriet Fowler to Webster, Feb. 13, 1837] ... We have understood that a plan is thought of to set William up again in business — but after all his past ill success I wonder very much at such a plan. Whoever advances money for William must do it with the expectation of sacrifice unless he can negotiate the business with another partner in some way to secure himself from loss.

William has already had quite too much of anothers[4] patrimony and in saying this I speak the opinion of each of my sisters, and when I look about and see how other young men labor to support themselves independently of their friends, I confess I feel ashamed of the selfishness of my brother, who is *willing* that continual sums should be advanced for him by his father who has already advanced so much.— He ought to go and find employment — try & try again — and Rosalie & her children will find a home with us. ... When brother Jones failed & all his household goods were attached he did not look to his parents or friends for help — and if we should be in like circumstances tomorrow neither should we think of doing it. Not that I feel my dear parents, that as your children we have not an equal claim with William upon your purse — but I trust we feel grateful for husbands who are willing to work and economise, who rise early & sit up late to earn support for their families.... You may think I feel but little for William and his family — I do *feel*, and in every proper way will do my part to assist them. I think that you & dear mother gave quite too much after all you have done for him, and I do verily believe had William been left to his own resources some years since he might now have been earning a competence in some situation, for his family....

[P.S. by Fowler] ... In a letter to Mrs. Goodrich I stated very simply what I thought would be best for W. Were I in his circumstances I should not be willing to receive any more from my father but should prefer being put upon my own efforts. As to putting him in business, it would I believe be *more* expensive to support him this *indirect* way that to do it directly. William's habits of mind do not adapt him to mercantile business. ...

[Mar. 1, 1837] ... I think the plan proposed is most eligible, if you can get a place in the new establishment at La Fayette, I hope you will. As Rosalie & the children are going to Virginia, you can dispose of many articles of furniture, & I will authorize Mr. Cranch to release them. But I think you will do well to keep the more essential articles, & such as pack into a small compass; store them, till you want to use them. It is difficult to replace many things in new settlements. If you should fail to get the place proposed, other clerkships or agencies may be offered, perhaps. New establishments are continually springing up in the West. You must seize upon any thing that offers that will bring you compensation. You may grow upon small beginnings.

[Apr. 8, 1837] ... With my consent, N & J White are to transfer their privilege of publishing my school dictionaries to Francis J Huntington, who is removing to New York, and they have agreed to release to me the right of licensing publishers of the Elementary on the West of the Allegany mountains. I have requested this, for the purpose of granting to you this power of licensing in the West; & I suppose the contracts here will be completed in a week or ten days, when I will send to you a power of attorney authorizing you to grant licenses. I think it important in this crisis to strengthen my interest by extending the privilege of publishing that book to at least *one* person, perhaps to *two*, in Indiana & Illinois, and perhaps to one in Detroit & one in St.Louis.... If you can sell licenses to the amount of 100,000 copies a year, the commission, 2 mills out of 7, or 200 dollars will be a good item for you.

William left Cincinnati and moved to Lafayette, Indiana, where he took a job in a bank.
Rosalie and their two boys joined him there in
May 1838. While they were in Cincinnati, they
had had a third child, Rebecca, who had been
persistently unwell, and she had died during
Rosalie's visit to Virginia. Things might have
been much worse, however, since the steamer
on which Rosalie and the boys had been travelling to rejoin William, the *Moselle*, blew up
shortly after they had disembarked.

In Lafayette, William found himself for the
first time in his life doing rather well. He was
promoted in the bank, which gave him more
pay, he was earning some money as a notary
public, and he received commission from those
who took licenses to print the *Elementary
Spelling Book*. He planned to build a house and
settle down. Webster had other ideas. Having
failed to get Fowler to help in producing a new
edition of the *American Dictionary*, he thought
that William's help would be better than nothing, and called him back to Connecticut:

New Haven, May 1, 1839

Dear William,

I have yours of the 19th ult. in which Rosalie mentions that you have some thoughts of buying a lot &
building. I hope you will not. I intend that you shall
return to Connecticut. Since I last wrote, Mr. White

has consented to resign the agency of the Speller, &
the commission I now pay on his agency & yours
would support your family. I shall close the agreement with him soon.

I wrote you respecting the affairs of Corey & Webster. It is most likely, if you have property, you will
be troubled for the deficit, & you had better return
here, & if necessary get an act of insolvency at once.

I am resolved, by some means, to put the large
dictionary to press, & I have one or two other books
that must be pushed into the market. I want your
aid, & if my Speller should continue in use, I can
maintain your family, till you can find business. I
am becoming old & infirm & I want your aid. I hope
you will not buy, till you hear further from your
affectionate father,

N Webster

Rosalie was reluctant, but William was a dutiful son and brought his family back to Connecticut so that he could help his father with the
dictionary. The agreement between them was
very much what Webster had offered Fowler,
since William was able to make available to his
father the money that had been intended to pay
for the house in Lafayette, Indiana — "four hundred and fifty doll's of Rosalie's funds ... & ...
several hundred doll's of my own Western sav-
ings, which I put into the Dict^y without expectation of reimbursement, while Emily & others
were harrassing him by their unnatural opposition to his dearest plans."[5]

18. Webster's Last Years, 1839–1843

After the dustup with Worcester, Webster, looking for signs of "borrowing," carefully examined new dictionaries that came his way. The Morgan Library has several manuscript pages of notes made during these examinations. One is headed "Words in Cobb's Maunder, borrowed from Webster's Dicty." On the other side it has "Words in Cobb's Dictionary not spelled right." Most are words such as *cancelled*, where Cobb used a double *l*. Another list is headed "Words omitted in Richardson's Dictionary," but Webster gave up after covering three pages of notes, because he had only reached *appointee*. A list of all the words that Richardson omitted would have filled a book. On the fourth page, Webster totted up the words and gave a concise summary:

Here is a list of *four hundred and seventy words* which Richardson has omitted in the first *eighty pages* of his dictionary. The words derived from these & not specified above would swell the number to seven or eight hundred, or more. It is remarkable also that some words have no definition; of which *admiral* is an example.

Webster and Richardson approached both lexicography and etymology from such fundamentally different positions that each saw only the weaknesses in the other's work and could not appreciate its virtues. Richardson had written of Webster that he

disarmed and stripped himself for the field and advanced unaided and unskilled, to the combat. He abjured the assistance of Skinner and Vossius and the learned elders of lexicography; and of Tooke he quaintly says, 'I have made no use of his writings.' There is a display of oriental reading in his preliminary essays which, as introductory to a Dictionary of the English Language, seems as appropriate and as

useful as a reference to the code of Gentoo laws to decide a question of English inheritance. Dr. Webster was entirely unacquainted with our old authors....

Webster replied with a scathing attack on Richardson's dictionary, and on his scholarship. Since their two dictionaries were so different that neither man could derive any benefit from the work of the other, this is an argument that need not concern us.

A dictionary from which Webster did derive some assistance is the subject of another manuscript page in the Morgan Library, headed "On Knowles' Dict$^{ry.}$" In it, Webster noted inconsistencies, and what he considered to be mistakes in spelling or pronunciation, in James Knowles' *Pronouncing and Explanatory Dictionary of the English Language*. A separate narrow strip of manuscript contains "Words in Knowles' Dictionary from Webster."

Knowles' Dictionary was published in London in 1835, having earlier been issued in seven parts. Its most remarkable feature is the the word *lithotriptist*, which appears in the word list as a separate entry between *P* and *Q*. The first edition of the dictionary had a slip of paper tipped in before the title page, drawing attention to it:

Look for a New Word, after the last word
in P., and a farther explanation in an added Page
at the end of the Volume.

This is the definition of the word:

LITHOTRIPTIST ... A professor and operator, in the recently discovered art of Lithotripsy; which consists in breaking, triturating, and pulverizing the stone in the bladder, and removing all the particles of it. This term is not to be found in any Dictionary

extant, and should have immediately followed the word Lithontriptic, in the preceding Part IV. of this Dictionary, published on the first of April. It is here, with thanks to God, a sense of duty to the public, and a deep feeling of gratitude to the Professor Baron Heurteloup, associated with his name; he having, on Saturday, the fourth of April, in presence of several surgeons, and physicians, in about five minutes, operated on the author, whose age is seventy-three, without giving him much uneasiness; and by his consummate skill, not only relieved him from a state of suffering, which he had endured for twelve months, but preserved his life, which, in all human probability, he must have lost under the operation of lithotomy.

The extra page at the end of the dictionary described Knowles' operation, or rather a sequence of five operations, and then called upon His Most Gracious Majesty William the Fourth, "beloved as he is by the mass of the people for the sailorlike openness of his character, the goodness of his heart, and the uprightness of his intentions," to support the funding of an Institution in which Baron Heurteloup might triturate the stones in the bladders of the nation's poor, free of charge.

After Knowles' death in 1840, his dictionary was published by Henry Bohn, who, as we shall see, published Webster's quarto at the same time. The page describing Knowles' lithotripsy was no longer included, but the definition of *lithotriptist* still appeared between *P* and *Q*.

One result of Webster's examination of Knowles' dictionary was a short paragraph in a New Haven newspaper in February 1840:

English Plagiarisms. — KNOWLES, an Englishman, has published a dictionary, for the purpose of correcting the errors of Walker, whose dictionary has done extensive mischief in corrupting the pronunciation of our language in this country. This book of Knowles' is not a defining dictionary; in regard to definitions, the work is little better than our pocket dictionaries. But the author has copied into his book *nearly every word* which WEBSTER has added to the list of words in former dictionaries, amounting to some thousands, without giving credit to the author; the more important original definitions of Webster are copied word for word.

Webster had to read Knowles very thoroughly to discover what words he had copied, and in the course of that reading he found a good many words in Knowles that were not in the *American Dictionary*. Surely Webster would not add them to his list "without giving credit to the author," or copy Knowles' definitions "word for word"? He was at the time working on the revision of the quarto, and he must have finished work on the letter *A* when he got hold of Knowles' Dictionary, since Knowles' words beginning with *A* went into the Addenda at the end of Volume II. The first page of addenda contains 96 definitions, from *abaca* to *agalaxy*, of which ten are attributed to Knowles. In each case, Webster's definition came entirely from Knowles' Dictionary, which casts some doubt on the sincerity of the assertion that, in regard to definitions, Knowles' was "little better than our pocket dictionaries." So far as plagiarism is concerned, it might be said in Webster's defense that he did not criticize Knowles merely for copying his definitions but for doing so "without giving credit to the author"; that is true, though it would have looked odd if Knowles had acknowledged Webster in a dictionary that did not identify any of its sources. Be that as it may, it is certainly more objectionable to "borrow" another man's work if you do not give him credit for it. If we take a closer look at the first page of Webster's Addenda, however, we find that, in addition to the ten words credited to Knowles, there are another 45 (including *abaca* and *agalaxy*) that Webster took from Knowles without acknowledgment. On that page, more than half the Addenda came from Knowles. For letters after *A*, Webster must have been still working on the manuscript when he examined Knowles' Dictionary, since words and definitions from Knowles went into the body of the dictionary, also without acknowledgment.

When the draft of the revised dictionary was complete, Webster saw a way of getting around the undertaking that he had given to Goodrich. The idea came from the spelling book, where his policy had been to prolong the copyright by making some alterations in the book from time to time, and giving it a new title. A spelling book with a sufficient number of alterations was a different book, and entitled to a new copyright. Could he not do the same thing with the dictionary? His promise to Goodrich had been not to publish a stereotyped octavo edition of the original quarto, the *American Dictionary*; but he had made so many alterations and additions in preparing the new edition he would be justified in saying that it was no longer

the same book. He could change its title, and it would not be caught by the undertaking.

Goodrich got wind of this, and asked Fowler to persuade Webster not to change the title. Fowler would not have been eager to help Goodrich, but he did discuss the matter with Webster, and found him resolute. Webster said to Fowler that…

though he [Goodrich] studiously conceals from me what the amount of his profits are, I nevertheless know that it will be doing him no injury to stereotype my work, inasmuch as he has been fully rewarded. I shall therefore alter the title-page, and take out a new copyright. I have added so many thousand words to this edition, and have expended so much labor upon it, that I am justified in giving it a new title and taking out a copyright for it as a new book, as I have done in the case of the Spelling-book.

In due course, proof sheets of a new title page were printed, calling the book *A Comprehensive Dictionary of the English Language*. When Goodrich saw the altered title-page at the printers, he knew that Fowler had failed him and that he would have to rely on his own powers of persuasion:

He went to Dr. Webster and appealed to his affection and his pride of authorship. "Would Sir Isaac Newton," said he, "after having enlightened the world and gained a great reputation by his 'Principia' have been willing to change the title of a second edition? and are you willing to change the title of your great work?" Dr. Webster was thus overpersuaded to lay aside the new title-page, which was already printed and corrected. By doing this, he changed the time during which his heirs would own the copyright of his great work, and also kept himself still in the power of Mr. Goodrich and Mr. White. Still, he never changed his views, as to the right and wrong of the whole transaction of Mr. Goodrich. About a month before his death, he expressed himself with emphasis and great strength of feeling, in the most distinct terms, in reprobation of the conduct of Mr. Goodrich in this matter. The conversation took place in his front room, and was the last conversation I had with him, so that it seems to me like his dying words. In that conversation, as at other times, he said to me, "He never shall again have the power to alter my Dictionary." I did not then understand what was the import of this declaration. But when, in his will, he cut him off from an inheritance, I could understand its import; by that act of disinheriting him, he intended to debar him from all power over his works.

If Fowler was right that Webster intended by the terms of his will to keep Goodrich from interfering with his works in future, the attempt

was a complete failure. Goodrich had already contrived to dilute Webster's eccentricities in the octavo abridgment during Webster's lifetime, and as a result it had been the most profitable of the Webster dictionaries. After Webster's death, Goodrich would do the same thing to all the other Webster dictionaries, from the smallest school duodecimo to the *American Dictionary* itself. In the war that followed between Webster's dictionaries and Worcester's, an important factor in Webster's ultimate success was Goodrich's having removed much that was most characteristic of Webster, from the dictionaries that bore his name.

The copyright notice in the second edition of the *American Dictionary* is dated September 1840, but the book was issued in 1841, in two volumes, royal octavo, at $15 a set, "Published by the Author." The title page describes it as "First Edition in Octavo, containing the whole Vocabulary of the Quarto, with corrections, improvements, and several thousand additional words." The page size was reduced from quarto to royal octavo to reduce the cost (since Webster was paying for the publication), but it is convenient to think of it as the second edition of the quarto, so that the Worcester abridgment can be referred to as the octavo without confusion. Future editions of the big dictionary would all be in quarto, and for the avoidance of doubt came to be referred to as "The Unabridged."

Even as late as October 1840, while the dictionary was in the press, Webster thought of trying to raise money by attracting subscribers. Subscription papers were printed, offering the book "handsomely bound in Calf and gilt" at $14, or in sheep at $13, but the attempt does not seem to have been pursued and many of Webster's later manuscript notes are written on unused subscription papers. He used them in November 1840 for an article, "Remarks on Spelling Books," in which he told the story of his own spelling book during nearly sixty years. Notice that he does not distinguish between the different versions of the book, and complains of others copying his ideas, even though his 1790 copyright had long since expired, and though the ideas themselves were never protected by copyright anyway:[1]

In the year 1782, while the American army was lying in Newburgh, I crossed the Hudson, established a school in Goshen, & compiled an elementary book,

which was published in 1783, under the title *The First Part of the Institute*; a title recommended by the late President Stiles, as preferable to that of *Spelling Book.* On a revision of the book the title was changed.

In this book, I introduced alterations to the usual mode of constructing such books in England, which I deemed to be, & which have proved to be, valuable improvements.

1. A division of syllables according to the pronunciation,. Thus *ha-bit, ta-lent*, the English mode, was rejected, & *hab-it, tal-ent* substituted.

2. A Key to the pronunciation of the vowels, & such an arrangement of words, that a single figure indicated the proper sound of the vowels of accented syllables in whole columns.

3. A new classification of words. To accomplish this, I examined the whole language from the beginning to the end of the vocabulary.

4. The reduction of the letters *tion* & *sion* to one syllable, instead of the English mode; that is, *mo-tion, de-lu-sion*, instead of *mo-ti-on, de-lu-si-on.*

These were deemed to be valuable improvements, & they have since been introduced into every book of the kind since compiled.

These improvements were *my property.* No law then existed to secure this property. I set myself to obtain laws for the purpose in several of the states, journeyed to South Carolina, & made personal application to several legislatures, from some of which I obtained the law. This was before Congress had powers to enact a similar law.

When I appeared at Hartford to publish the Spelling Book in 1783, I could find no man who encouraged me tht I should succeed, except the late Judge Trumbull & Joel Barlow. But the book was published & has succeeded. More persons have been instructed in that book, than there are now inhabitants in the United States.

Soon after this book began to be had in reputation, Mr. Alexander made a like book, copying my plan. But Mr. Caleb Bingham of Boston told him, that his book was so similar to mine that is was of no use to introduce it into schools. The book was a failure.

In a few years, my book became popular, & Matthew Carey applied to me for the copy-right. Not agreeing to my price, he determined to compile a similar book himself. He made his book & printed it. But he told me afterward that his examination had convinced him that I had so well done my work that no great room for improvement remained. His book proved a failure; but it was then, as it is now, an easy task to make a Spelling Book.

After Walker's dictionary appeared in this country, with the reputation of being the standard of orthoepy in England, several men undertook to compile Spelling Books on his plan of orthography & pronunciation, & made strenuous exertions to supplant my book. Among these were E H Marshall of Rochester, New York. This man had the audacity to publish a Spelling Book, a great part of which was my

book *unaltered*, but he made some additions, & gave the orthography & pronunciation of Walker. Marshall procured commendations of his book, which filled a sheet. that was posted up in public houses. It gained a pretty extensive circulation, in the Northern States, & is still used to a limited extent. But in one town in New Hampshire, the number of *sixty thousand* copies which had been annually printed, is now reduced to *five thousand.*

Lyman Cobb also, ~~an illiterate man~~, compiled a Spelling Book on Walker's principles. He tells his readers, in his Preface, "that Webster's method of defining the various sounds of the vowels, & representing the accented syllables is so simple & so judicious as perhaps to require no alteration, or admit of essential improvement." Accordingly, he adopted my plan of syllabication, & took my Key with no alteration other than the transposition of two figures. He changed the order of words in most of his tables; but copied *ten* or *twelve* of my tables, with a few alterations. Great expense & labor were applied to the spread of this book; agents were sent from Michigan to Georgia; & the man *has failed.* His booksellers, however keep the book in circulation; and great numbers of children are still instructed in the obsolete orthography of Walker & in a pronunciation which, in England, is now denounced as *intolerable* & absolute *absurdity* & *vulgarity.*

Several other compilers constructed Spelling Books on my general plan, making similar plagiarisms from my book, all with a view to introduce either Walker's orthography or prounciation, or both .... More recently have appeared Worcester's & Leonard's Spelling Books in New England, & Sander's & Town's in New York, & a new one of Bentley, on somewhat different principles.... All three have adopted my general plan of dividing syllables; and most of them have plagiarized some of my tables, with little alteration.

In the West, Picket has published a Spelling Book on my plan of syllabication; as has President McGuffey....

Of these compilers, seven or eight have violated my rights, by incorporating in their works, my classes of words, which are under the protection of the Copy-right Law; I could undoubtedly obtain injunctions to restrain the publication of their books. But I leave them to be disposed of by public opinion. The sales of my Spelling Book have been gradually increasing ever since the first publication, & now exceed the sales of all other books of the kind. Doubtless, had my books continued without competition, the sales would have been much larger, but the small premium for copy right which I have received has supported my family during twenty years in which I was occupied in preparing my Quarto dictionary, & this, with some additions from other books, has enabled me to put to the press a new edition. Had my opposers succeeded in supplanting my Spelling Book, my large dictionary could not have

been compiled. Whether the want of it would be an evil, my fellow citizens must judge.

I would state further that the ~~diminution of~~ want of income will probably prevent the publication of A Synopsis of Principal Words in twenty languages, which was prepared by the labor & researches of ten years. The full benefit of my improvements would have prevented this deficiency....

One remark ought here to be made, that Americans have very much over-rated English authorities in philology: I did so myself till I had arrived to the middle age of man. Researches of far greater extent than any pursued by British authors have undeceived me. There is no such thing as profound & accurate scholarship in English philology, either in the universities of England or in the colleges in this country. I am now but a tyro myself in this vast department of literature; but probably I have made advances which will lead to valuable improvements, when my body shall repose in the grave.

In 1841 another competing spelling book *The English Spelling Book*, appeared, written by the Rev. A. B. Chapin, editor of *The Practical Christian and Church Chronicle*. It was promptly attacked in the *New Haven Daily Herald* by someone calling himself "Americanus." A tedious exchange of correspondence followed in which Americanus was so obviously fighting Webster's corner that he was suspected to be Webster himself, even though Webster contributed to the correspondence in his own name. As it turned out, Americanus was William. The original cause for discontent was that Chapin was thought to have taken advantage of his position as chairman of the school committee of New Haven to persuade the committee to sanction the introduction of his book into the Lancasterian school. This was considered to be cheating, particularly as a close inspection of the book showed it to be full of mistakes. Webster wrote a letter to Chapin which he did not send, but William made it the basis of the first of Americanus' letters to the *Daily Herald*. Chapin hit back by pointing to errors and inconsistencies in Webster's *Elementary Spelling Book*. The correspondence continued until January 1842, by which time the *Daily Herald* was fed up with it and would have no more. Both sides published pamphlets, William's addressed *To the friends of American Education*. Chapin's, like Cobb's earlier pamphlets, was a review of Webster's orthography. Webster's answer to Cobb had been that his inconsistency in spelling was merely a sign of the development of his ideas

over a period of years; Chapin cut away that ground by comparing the *Elementary Spelling Book* ("copy right secured May 22, 1829"), the *Primary School Dictionary* ("copy right secured same day"), and the octavo dictionary ("copy right secured July 10, 1829"). Poor old Webster was again being made to suffer for Goodrich's interference with his spelling in the octavo. Since the *Daily Herald* had closed its columns to the correspondence, the final exchange of letters took place in Chapin's *Church Chronicle*. William explained that his father wanted it to stop, "not because he fears a candid examination of his principles, but because the discussion is as uninteresting to the public, as it is profitless to the parties." He was quite right on both heads.

One letter which appeared in the *New Haven Daily Herald* in the course of the Chapin-Americanus correspondence, on January 4, 1842, was nothing to do with the argument, but was full of extravagant praise for Webster:

It is sad to see that veteran in letters, the venerable Dr. Webster, compelled, on the wintry verge of the autumn of life, to turn literary constable and endeavor, almost single handed, to drive the multitudinous herd of poachers from his ancient and rightful province in literature. And it is sad, too, that he who is truly and greatly a benefactor to his race, must leave it for posterity to adjust his reputation to this character, and award to his name, when he no longer remains to enjoy it, that honor which is due to his merit, and which is so covetously withheld from him while living. Of the millions who have been indebted to Noah Webster for the best means of rudimentary education in the English language, ever enjoyed by human beings, scarcely a thousand, perhaps, have had any more consciousness of that indebtedness, than they have had of their indebtedness to God for the air they breathe; and scarcely ten, if, indeed five, have duly appreciated the merits of their benefactor. In truth, few are competent to form a just estimate of the value of such labors as Dr. Webster's; for few have any conception of what these labors have been, and what has been their effect in this country. But the truth is, that no man has done better service for the English language than Noah Webster.

Dr. Johnson was, in his day, a literary mammoth, and perhaps had a richer fancy and more varied accomplishments as a literary man than Dr. Webster, but as a philologist and lexicographer, he was less erudite and less accurate. And in our times, Dr. Webster stands alone....

But Dr. Webster has probably done less for the English language in our country by his dictionary than

by his spelling book. But for the all-prevailing presence of this book throughout our wide extended country, nothing could have saved us from as great a diversity of dialects as there is in England. We have now some few phrases peculiar to different sections of our country, yet as a general fact, the whole land has but one tongue — one dialect. And this is principally owing to the fact that nearly every one who has learned to read, has acquired his rudiments from Webster's Spelling Book, or some other spelling book compiled from Webster's, and only so far excellent as it was a compilation from his. For it is a truth not to be denied or concealed, that, of the numerous books of this kind, which, during the last quarter of a century, have been introduced into our schools as improvements on Webster's, if all that they owe to the labors of Webster were taken from them, scarcely one of them would have merit enough to render it worthy of being preserved from the flames. Besides, it is probably true that Dr. Webster is the only man in our country, who ever made a spelling book *with the paramount purpose of benefitting the language and the people.* Most, if not all others, who make books of this kind, make them not from an honest and intelligent conviction that public good demands them, but because they hope to make them the means of pecuniary emolument. Actuated by a spirit of this kind, multitudes of literary loafers and bookmaker's hacks have been employed to manufacture 'school books' very greatly to the injury of the cause of education. I do not mean to imply that Dr. Webster has labored for fifty years without any regard to a pecuniary recompense; but I mean to say that the paramount motive which has led him through half a century of literary toil, has been of a far higher motive and nobler and more philanthropic character. And he may rest assured that though poachers and pirates may infest the borders of his empire and enrich themselves with the spoils which he can spare without impoverishment, yet it will be long ere the sceptre of his dominion will depart from him.

The letter appeared in the *New Haven Daily Herald* with no signature, but it had earlier been printed in the *Hampshire Gazette*, on December 28, 1841, over the signature S. What makes the letter remarkable is that S was here establishing his unquestionable pro-Webster credentials, in order to build a base from which to accuse Webster of plagiarism. On January 24, 1842, S wrote to Webster from Northampton:

Sir,

Having endeavoured to do justice to you in public, I feel that it is a duty which I owe to you as well as to another, to call upon you either publicly or privately for a public avowal of your reason for not acknowledging, nor giving any intimation of your indebtedness to the Rev. Dr. William Allen, formerly

President of Bowdoin College, and now a resident in this place, for six or seven thousand new words added to the last edition of your Dictionary — some of which are inserted in the body of your dictionary, but most of them placed in the Apendix [sic]. These words with their definitions and authorities were with much care and labor collected and arranged by Dr. Allen in the course of his literary pursuits extending over more than thirty years, and generously forwarded to you to be inserted in the last edition of your Dictionary. That you should have entirely omitted to acknowledge your indebtedness to Dr. Allen is a mystery to your friends who know that you are too rich in well-earned reputation, to grudge any man his pittance of honour, and too honest to withhold any man's dues. The fact is as it is, however, and *must* be explained by somebody, sooner or later, and if not done while you live, will as surely be attempted when you no longer remain to correct any wrong view which may be taken of the matter. I therefore now call your attention to the subject, and I do it in this private manner, that any public explanation which you may give may seem to be entirely spontaneous and therefore the more honorable. Permit me thus respectfully to suggest the propriety of making a communication to the Hampshire Gazette on the subject in question, and leave nothing of this kind to be settled after your death. For it must be obvious to you, Sir, that, if this becomes a matter of public accusation instead of acknowledgment, it will be delicious food for your enemies, and possibly an inexplicable ground of painful doubt to your friends....

Without access to Dr. Allen's list of words, we cannot judge whether Webster had made use of it or not. S seems to have been in no doubt, however, and it would certainly not have been out of character for Webster to have used it without acknowledgment. He made no response to S's letter, and when the matter was raised again after Webster's death, William told the Merriams that Webster had received the list, but had not used it. Disappointed with Webster, Allen sent the list to Worcester, who did use it, and acknowledged that he had done so in the Preface to his 1846 *Universal Critical Dictionary of the English Language*: "The Rev. Dr. William Allen, late President of Bowdoin College, having collected several thousand words not found in any dictionary, favored the Compiler with the use of his manuscript, which afforded between fourteen and fifteen hundred additions."

Back in 1784, the first attack against Webster's works was launched by Dilworth's Ghost.

Nearly sixty years later, Dilworth struck again. It was the last newspaper exchange in Webster's lifetime. This letter to the editor appeared in the *New York Tribune,* in March 1843:

My Dear Sir: Why will you persist in disfiguring everything passing through your press by spelling '*hight*' and '*trave-ler*'? Why select two or three words in which Webster has departed from a standard established by the lapse of two hundred years, and not follow him in all his nonsense? If in your own writings only you manifested this affectation, there would be less cause for complaint; but the orthography of your correspondents is made to suffer, and even books published and republished by you are not exempt from your violence in this particular. Farnham's Travels are to be emasculated and made to conform to this modern jargon. To plain, old-fashioned readers, this is annoying to a degree you would not deem possible. I like your paper, 'The Tribune;' I like many of your publications; I take the one daily, and buy some of the others — and what is better, *pay promptly.* Can you not consent to go back to the mode of spelling you were taught at school? — and in doing so, adhere to the established usage of nine hundred and ninety-nine thousandths of all who write the language. No one follows your lead; you must remain alone in this singularity. Do oblige me; and by way of showing my gratitude, I promise to present to any charitable Society you may designate the sum of *ten dollars* under the signature (not over) of

OLD DILWORTH.

If this friendly overture be denied, may I beg you to make your spelling *fish* or *flesh* — Webster or Walker? No half way compromise: go the whole — *hight. trave-ler,* (reducing the word to the eye of a learner to two syllables,) *defense, offense,* &c.&c.

The editor replied in some "Remarks" printed below Old Dilworth's letter. He pointed out that Webster's spelling was more consistent than Walker's since, for example, it left the *k* off *critic,* because there was no *k* in *critical*; in the same way, *defense* and *offense* match *defensive* and *offensive.* The editor concluded: " 'Old Dilworth' shows little consideration in asking us to spell our Editorials one way and Communications another — to follow Webster in our paper and Walker in our books. We shall not do it. We would like to oblige him, but not at the expense of justice and the English Language. He may pocket his $10."

Webster, now 84 years old, could not resist the reappearance of an old adversary, and he wrote to the editor on March 22, 1843:

Your correspondent, 'Old Dilworth', seems not well to understand his subject. He objects to your spelling, but spells *trave-ler* in two syllables, as though he wanted another *l* to make out the word. Now if he would divide the syllables properly, *trav-el-er,* he would see that another *l* is not wanted.

You have answered his objections very correctly and with judgement.

'Old Dilworth' should learn not to write about what he does not fully comprehend. The rule for spelling *traveler* with one *l,* a rule that extends to a great many words, was laid down by Bishop Lowth, seventy or eighty years ago, and was approved by Walker, whose authority seems to have some weight with your correspondent, though I esteem it of little value. But Lowth and Walker did not follow their own rule: I have not only adopted the rule as correct, but have followed it throughout my books.

One thing I claim as my right, that men who undertake to censure what I have done, should *read my rules before they condemn my practice....*

Webster was there obscuring the fact that for very many years he himself had not accepted Lowth's recommendation that *traveler* should have only one *l.* Even among the reformed spellings of the *Compendious Dictionary* he put two *l*'s in *traveller.* Had he remembered this, he might have spotted a cleverly baited trap, but he did not spot it, and walked straight in. The trap was sprung in Old Dilworth's reply, dated March 24:

To NOAH WEBSTER, ESQ. — Your advice that "old Dilworth" "should learn not to write about what he does not fully comprehend," is received by him in all meekness and humility; — he will endeavor to profit by it. You will permit him, however, to urge in extenuation of his ignorance, that his early education (such as it was) was acquired in a mud-walled school house, in a remote district of country, and that his mode of spelling was *derived entirely* from a book called "WEBSTER'S *Spelling Book.*" Perhaps you may have heard of such a work. He was a diligent scholar, and soon mastered that book thoroughly. Blessed with a most retentive memory, he has never forgotten that "Noah Webster, Junior" directed his learners to spell "height" and "traveller." 'Old Dilworth' is, and was, quite aware that "trave-ler" may be divided into syllables thus 'trav-el-er,' but he is also aware that it is not usual to divide words into syllables in books, other than Spelling Books and Dictionaries, and that therefore an adult learner (and we have thousands of them annually from Europe) meeting with the word 'traveler' would be very likely to consider it a word of two syllables. "Old Dilworth" is unable to perceive what literary benefit is to accrue from these innovations. To him it seems but the affectation of learning, applied to the smallest

possible object, and leading to no beneficial result. He is therefore unwilling to unlearn what was acquired with so much painstaking, and occasional applications of the ferule, the more especially as he is supported in his "*old jargon*" by an authority so unquestionable as "NOAH WEBSTER, JUNIOR."

OLD DILWORTH.

After helping his father with the royal octavo edition of the *American Dictionary*, William had found something to do as Americanus in the correspondence with Chapin. This kept him occupied during the winter of 1841-42, but what was he to do next? To entice him back from Indiana, Webster had promised to give him the rights in the spelling book that White had agreed to relinquish, and it was suggested that he might be established in the bookselling business in New York. This was strenuously opposed by his sisters. The spelling book was the goose that laid most of the family's golden eggs, and they were certain that if it was entrusted to William he would either kill it or run off with it. On October 14, 1842, Ellsworth wrote to Webster:

Will you suffer me to suggest what all your daughters & their husbands are united in, that aside from the perils of business peculiar to this period, we do not believe you will promote your own interest or comfort, or the interest of William, by establishing him in business with another capital. We are anxious to have you relieved from all care and anxiety, & should rejoice if you would find it agreeable to place your books in the hands of some active, energetic and able bookseller, to sell for you and pay you the avails. In this we may be mistaken, but it has often been expressed as our conviction....

To his credit, Webster was not dissuaded from giving William what he had promised — exclusive rights in the *Elementary Spelling Book*. This was not free, of course; indeed the amount Webster wanted for himself actually went up. When William had been granting licences in the West, his power of attorney from Webster provided that licensees should pay a premium of "seven mills for each copy which by said licensees shall be permitted to be printed; neither more nor less, of which premium, two sevenths, or two mills for each copy licensed to be printed, shall be the commission to be taken by said William for his agency, & five mills for each copy licensed to be printed shall be paid to me...." Now, Webster wanted 6 mills a copy, or

0.6 cents, so that to maintain his premium at 0.2 cents, William had to find licensees willing to pay a royalty of 0.8 cents per copy. The second power of attorney, dated April 8, 1843, covered all the books over which Webster had control, but the *Elementary Spelling Book* was financially the most important:

Whereas my son William G Webster has formed a partnership with Lucius E Clark, for the purpose of carrying on the business of publishing & selling books in the city of New York under the firm of Webster & Clark — Now be it known that I Noah Webster of New Haven in Connecticut do by this instrument make, constitute & appoint the said Webster & Clark my lawful attorneys & agents to manage the concerns of my several publications herein specified. I do authorize the said Webster & Clark to print, publish & vend my Elementary Spelling Book in the city of New York, & to have & enjoy the exclusive right of printing the same in said city. And I further authorize them to grant licenses to persons in other parts of the United States to print & publish the said Elementary Spelling Book, & to enjoy the exclusive right of granting such licenses in the United States, so long as this power of attorney shall remain unrevoked. ..... the said Webster & Clark shall at the end of every six months render to me, my executors, administrators or assigns a true account of all the copies of said Spelling Book which they shall have printed & licensed to be printed in the United States, during the preceding six months, & shall then pay to me, my executors, administrators or assigns, the sum of six mills for every copy of said Spelling Book....

I further grant to the said Webster & Clark the right of printing & publishing my edition of the Bible & Testament, and of my Improved Grammar, & of my History of the United States, & of my Manual of Useful Studies,...

I further grant to the said Webster & Clark the exclusive right to print any edition or editions of my American Dictionary that may be hereafter wanted to supply the market, if they *can & choose* to print & publish the same; on the condition of their paying to me or to my executors, administrators or assigns one dollar for each copy, as the premium for copy-right. But if they can not or choose not to print & publish the said dictionary, then this grant shall be void, & the publication of the same may be intrusted to other persons.

I shall intrust to the said Webster & Clark any other works which I may have for sale, as also all copies of my large Dictionary.

The following month, another book was added to the list of Webster & Clark, *A Collection of Papers on Political, Literary, and Moral Subjects*. It was the book which contained his paper "On the Origin of Copy-right Laws in

LIST OF BOOKS

PUBLISHED AND OFFERED TO THE TRADE

BY

WEBSTER & CLARK,

No. 130 Fulton Street,

NEW YORK.

THE AMOUNT OF SALES OF BOOKS SENT US WITHOUT ORDERS WILL BE CONSIDERED PAYABLE IN OUR PUBLICATIONS.

THE AMERICAN DICTIONARY OF THE ENGLISH LANGUAGE, by NOAH WEBSTER, LL. D. *Trade Price.*
A new Edition, containing Eighty-Five Thousand words, with Portrait of the Author, 2 vols. royal 8vo., sheep, 13.50
  Do.   Do.   Do.   Do.   folded, 12.00
  This work is acknowledged by the most eminent scholars, both in England and in the United States, to be
  the best English Dictionary ever published.   Many valuable additions have been made to this Edition.

THE ELEMENTARY SPELLING BOOK, by DR. WEBSTER, a new and improved Edition, printed and
• bound in superior style, - - - - - - - - - - - - - - - - per doz.   1.25
  This Spelling Book is now used in the United States more extensively than *all* others.

HISTORY OF THE UNITED STATES, for Schools, by DR. WEBSTER, - - - - - - - - - 37½

MANUAL OF USEFUL STUDIES, by DR. WEBSTER, a reading and study book for the higher classes
in Academies and Schools.   Highly recommended. - - - - - - - - - sheep,   45

AN IMPROVED GRAMMAR OF THE ENGLISH LANGUAGE, by DR. WEBSTER, - - -   34

PEARL POCKET BIBLE, with corrections of the language by DR. WEBSTER, - - - - - sheep, E. R. 1.00

  Do.   Do.   Do.   Do.   - - - - tucks, gilt, 1.25

  Do.   TESTAMENT,   Do.   Do.   - - - - sheep, E. R. 31

  Do.   Do.   Do.   Do.   - - - - tucks, gilt, 50

THE NEW TESTAMENT, for Schools, 12mo. Do.   Do.   - - - - sheep,   25
  An excellent School Testament.

The following work is published for the author, and is offered on cash account only :
A COLLECTION OF PAPERS ON POLITICAL, LITERARY, AND MORAL SUBJECTS, by
  NOAH WEBSTER, LL. D. - - - - - - - - - - - - - - muslin, stamped, 1.37½
  MAY, 1843.

Book List of Webster & Clark, from a copy in the New York Public Library.

the United States," and it was his last published work. On May 11, 1843, he wrote to a Mr. Parker, in Ithaca, instructing him to send some books to Webster & Clark at 130 Fulton Street, New York. His letter concluded:

I have published a small volume of papers containing my own writings, & accounts of transactions in which I had an agency. The last article contains a brief account of the errors in our language & in school books. And here I close my literary labors.

New York was near enough to New Haven for Webster to be able to take a close interest in William's business. On May 18, Webster wrote to him:

I should like to know whether you are able to make an agreement with Mr. Cooledge for the printing of the Speller. If he will continue to print the book, & give you eight mills copy-right, it may be for your convenience that he should continue to print the book, as the outlay for such large numbers will at

present be difficult for you to meet, & the two mills premium may be better for you than to incur large debts. This arrangement may continue, for some time, to his satisfaction, as well as for your convenience.

I should like to know whether you made any agreement with Griswold.

I intend get a good review of the Collection of papers here. A few copies have been sold, & good judges speak well of it. ...

On May 22, Webster wrote again:

With regard to Sanford of Cleveland, I should say, all proper measures must be taken to detect his trespasses, & put a stop to them. I wish you to ascertain from Mr. Cooledge whether he ever sold any of the Spellers in sheets — if not, then, if Sanford has had books with Cooledge's imprint bound in Cleveland, they must have been forged. This is an important fact. If the trespass can be clearly proved, Sanford shall be prosecuted, poor as he is....

On the back, William wrote, "The last letter ever written by my father, the day he was seized with pleurisy." Sixty years earlier, when Webster planned to compile a spelling book, he set out to secure copyright protection for it. It turned out to be "the most widely published work written by one person (two, if you wish to give Aaron Ely his due) that the world has ever known."[2] For a large part of those sixty years the spelling book was (thanks to that copyright) his major source of income. It is appropriate that the last letter he wrote should have been about infringement of the copyright in the spelling book.

19. Executors, Heirs, and Renewers

Webster died on May 28, 1843. His will (dated October 10, 1839) first directed the payment of his funeral charges and just debts, and then provided for his widow and for their unmarried daughter Louisa:

I give to my beloved wife, Rebecca, all the household furniture which she shall choose to take for her accommodation, & all such books from my library, as she shall desire & select. I give to her also the annual sum of seven hundred & twenty dollars for her maintenance during her widowhood, & for the maintenance of my daughter Louisa, And if Louisa shall survive her mother, I will that she shall have three hundred dollars annually for her support during her life.

And I give to my wife the use of my dwelling house during her widowhood, if she shall desire it.

He left $1,000 each to Emily, Harriet and Eliza, and two hundred dollars to the maid, Lucy Griffin, "for her faithful services." There were certain specific bequests of books and manuscripts, and the residue of the estate was to be divided equally between four of his children, Emily, Harriet, William and Eliza, and his grand-daughter, Mary Trowbridge (daughter of Webster's fourth child, Mary Southgate). Julia Goodrich, Webster's second daughter, was left nothing because she was deemed to be receiving her share from the royalties on the octavo abridgment. To prevent any possible unfairness to Julia, a saving clause was included in the will:

If in the course of events, it shall appear that my daughter Julia & her husband, Chauncey A Goodrich, shall not receive from the copy right of my dictionary as stated above, an equal share of my property, my will is that her share shall be made equal from my other property.

After the will was read, Goodrich wrote a letter to the family, seeking to show that he had reason to be dissatisfied. His argument may have been that the profits from the octavo dictionary should not have been a ground for denying to himself and Julia a share in Webster's estate, because he had dedicated them to "holy purposes." The other members of the family no doubt felt that what he had done with Julia's share was his affair; the fact that he had given it away (if indeed he had) did not entitle him to part of their share. In any event, he did not get it.

The will named five executors, "my beloved consort, Rebecca, William W Ellsworth, Roger S Baldwin, Henry White & my son William G Webster." It was characteristic of Webster's attitude to William that he should have named him last. Anyway, William's appointment was revoked by a codicil made May 3, 1843 — less than four weeks before Webster's death — because William had "removed his family and taken his residence in New York."

The Probate records of New Haven contain two entries relating to Webster's estate:

7th June 1843

Rebecca Webster and Roger S. Baldwin declined acting as Executors of said Will and refused to give bonds and William W. Ellsworth and Henry White Esq., two of the executors appointed by said Will appeared in Court, accepted said trust, and gave bonds with sufficient surety in the sum each of fifty thousand dollars.

4th August 1843

Inventory:

Real Estate	$7,375
Personal Estate	34,881.56
Credits etc. considered good	6,904.32
	$49,160.88

Almost $50,000 was a tidy sum in 1843, but very little of it was in a form that would provide ready cash. The house could not be sold because Rebecca and Louisa continued to live in it, and a large part of the personal estate was made up of 1,420 unsold copies of the 1841 royal octavo dictionary in unbound sheets, and Webster's copyrights. The dictionaries would prove to have been overvalued, but with careful management (which Ellsworth would do his best to provide) the copyrights would eventually be very valuable.

At that time, a married woman was treated more or less as a piece of property belonging to her husband, and her property was treated as if it were his. All the decisions about Webster's residuary estate were taken by the men. No doubt each man consulted his wife, and the sisters may have consulted each other, but it was the men who wrote to each other, held family meetings, and decided what to do. Though the will left the property to William, three of his sisters and his niece, the sisters' husbands spoke of themselves as "heirs." In the maneuvering that followed, the active participants were Ellsworth, Fowler, Goodrich, and William.

Ellsworth was in the dominant position. He was socially dominant, having been state governor the year before, and he alone was both an executor and an heir. He saw it as his duty to take over the management of Webster's estate to provide the maximum possible return for the benefit of the other heirs. To his own enrichment he was, as he told the others from time to time, quite indifferent. He was prepared to make business decisions, but he had no time for philological or lexicographical disputes. If a book had to be written or abridged, one paid somebody to do it; it did not much matter who, provided he came cheap and got on with the job.

Fowler saw himself as Webster's literary heir. He had been Webster's confidant, and he believed that the exclusion of Goodrich from Webster's will was intended, in part, to protect the *American Dictionary* from being interfered with in the way that Goodrich had interfered with the octavo. Fowler felt that he had a better right than Goodrich because he was an heir and Goodrich was not. He would defend Webster's principles against Goodrich. At least, he would try. As it turned out, he was no match at all for the ingenious Goodrich.

William was hardly a match for anyone. It had always been a great disadvantage to him that he was Webster's only son. The daughters were not to be involved in business, and their husbands could not be ordered about. William could. As soon as he left Yale, Webster had dragged him off on the trip to Europe. He was very seasick on the way, and when he got there he had to transcribe bits of the *American Dictionary* for six or eight hours a day. For some months after their return, he had been made to copy out the *Synopsis*. After that, Webster kept setting him up in bookselling businesses (mainly to sell Webster's books, of course) and the businesses went bust, partly because Wiliam, though he inherited his mother's cheerful disposition, was just as bad a businessman as his father.

In the month immediately after Webster's death, Ellsworth was busy in court. He returned to Hartford on July 1, 1843, and entered with enthusiasm into his duties as executor. He had opposed Webster's granting rights to William's firm of Webster & Clark, believing that it was not a sound business decision. His first task, therefore, was to persuade William that the firm had no rights at all. What they had, said Ellsworth, was a license which had been terminated by Webster's death. On July 4, 1843, Ellsworth wrote a letter to the firm, signed by himself and Henry White, the other executor:

Messrs. Webster & Clark

Gentlemen,

The executors of Dr. Webster, find that there is a wide difference between themselves and yourselves, as to the character & effect of the writing of the date of the eight of April last, signed by Dr. Webster and yourselves. Before we can properly decide what ought to be done, in the premises, the right construction of the writing must be settled. We propose therefore that this be done, at once, by two professional gentlemen. The executors by no means admit, that the contract is, in any part of it, a bargain and sale, but they claim that the power to publish, is a mere power, which has been put an end to by the death of Dr. Webster....

This was followed by a letter to William personally, two days later:

My dear Sir,

I went to New Haven, on Monday, & from there Mr. White & myself sent a letter to your [business] house which I presume you received & will answer as soon as you well can.

You will excuse me for writing you individually to make a suggestion, which you will consider, as made from the best feelings, & you will give it, its proper weight, if it be entitled to any.

Is there not a radical difficulty in your establishment in NY, which *must* disappoint your hopes & perhaps greatly injure the interests of the family? How can your two families live on your business, besides the expences of the business, suppose you should have the powers continued. From the spelling book you cannot realise more than $500 clear, and from your book capital even should you continue a book store (which I think you told me you should not) can you certainly expect to make much if anything?

The spelling book *must* be *managed* by some *active bookseller*; it cannot be made a mere occasional and incidental business by some one engaged in other business. This we could not consent to, & if we did, it would soon run the book down. Aside from a book store, your father never contemplated your managing the spelling book, and Mr. Goodrich & myself are fully agreed in this, that there is not the least reason to suppose your *two* families can live on the business. In a short time your capital will be consumed & you will not be able to do justice to the powers and trusts you now claim. We do feel that your respected father did not judge wisely for you & the rest of us, in calling in Mr. Clark and establishing your house in NY (if he had anything to do with it) upon any expectations which he could justly entertain. The business could not possibly support more than one family — a valuable part of it you have obviously been obliged to give to another house, and it appears clear to me, that you cannot go on long with any part of the business....

I deeply regret that neither you nor our father were willing to consult some of us before an establishment was got up in NY; we might perhaps have done you a service, as well as saved the executors of your father from the unhappy dilemma in which they are placed. I wish to do you full justice — I never did expect anything from the estate, & for myself would cheerfully abandon it now, but I feel quite certain that if much be saved for anybody, the trusts must be committed to an efficient, strong, & well established house, to men active in the *publishing business*. The spelling book should not have been taken from White.

Yours truly, WWEllsworth

Ellsworth was no doubt right to suppose that entrusting the management of Webster's literary property to William was (from the point of view of the other heirs, at least) not a very sensible or satisfactory arrangement. But, the assertion that Webster & Clark did not have the rights Webster had given them was nonsense. In the New York Public Library one can see not only the original contract, in Webster's handwriting, but also counsel's opinion taken by William and his partner from Mr. E. W. Chester of 64 John Street. Counsel advised that since the contract provided for payments to be made to Webster, *or to his executors, administrators or assigns*, it was clearly anticipated that it would remain in effect after Webster's death. Indeed, since Webster was already 84 years old when he drew up the contract, no other intention would have made sense.

When Ellsworth wrote to William "a valuable part of [the business] you have obviously been obliged to give to another house," he was referring to the fact that Webster & Clark had sold the copyright in the spelling book to the New York firm of George F. Cooledge & Brother, for the remainder of the first term. If the agreement between Webster and William's firm had continued to operate, Webster & Clark would have received royalties from Cooledge at the rate of 8 cents for every ten books. From this, they would have had to pay Ellsworth and White, as executors, the sum provided for in their agreement with Webster, "six mills for every copy of said Spelling Book," or six cents for ten copies; but William, as one of the heirs, would have received a fifth of that back from the executors. This would have left William substantially better off than the other heirs. If William and his partner split the net royalty equally, 100 copies of the *Elementary* would yield 80 cents, of which Clark would have ended up with 10 cents, the other heirs with 12 cents each, and William, entitled to a partner's share and an heir's share, with 22 cents. Since the sales of the *Elementary* were then over half a million copies a year, that would have given William much more than his sisters. One can see why Ellsworth wanted all the heirs to have an equal share of Cooledge's royalties. His argument, however, that the agreement must come to an end so that the spelling book could be "managed by some active bookseller," was also nonsense. Cooledge already had the rights in the spelling book, and bringing the agreement to an end would make no difference at all to the way that the spelling book was "managed"— it would only affect who got the money.

Mr. Chester advised William that Webster himself could not have terminated the agreement unless Webster & Clark consented or were

in breach of their obligations, and his executors had no more right to terminate than he would have had. William, however, did not want to get into a fight with Ellsworth, and the partners agreed to surrender their rights to the executors in exchange for a lump sum payment.

In a letter dated August 7, 1843, Ellsworth responded to William's surrender with a characteristically warm and generous gesture:

Dear Brother,

It occurred to me, after leaving you, that you might have been subjected to some expenses touching the business lately transacted in NY. I therefore send you $5 which will cover the same, unless they be more than I know of.

With kind sentiments
Your's
Wm W Ellsworth

Despite this peace offering, William must have felt that he had been singled out for attack, since three months later Ellsworth wrote to him (Nov. 29, 1843):

I am sure you have no reason to feel that I shall persecute you or your family. As ex[or], I shall try to see what is correct & will not knowingly depart from it....

Nevertheless, the attacks continued. There was a feeling in the family that Webster had been too soft on William. Each time he set him on his feet, he would say ,"Never again !" but he would do it again. William's sisters greatly overestimated the amount that Webster had spent rescuing William; as a result, they thought that William did not deserve an equal share in Webster's estate. On January 13, 1844, Ellsworth wrote a seven page letter, not to William but to his wife Rosalie, expressing their resentment:

Let me say, first of all, that not one of them wishes to withhold what their respected and beloved parent has given his son, nor to allude even (except for the present purpose) to what Dr. Webster was pleased in his life time, to do for his son; although you are aware, that before your marriage Dr. Webster did feel & declare (as I have been told) that he should do no more for his son. However this may be, they suppose that their brother received from Dr. Webster, before his death, not less than $15,000, for which, however, some services were rendered which should be taken into account. This sum is equal to one half of all the estate left by Dr. Webster, in which estate, brother W has his share, & no one regrets it....

For myself, let me add, that so far as I can judge, brother committed a vital error in returning from Indiana to Conn[t]. There, he was, and felt that he was, a man, independent, beloved, confided in and useful....

William's reply to Ellsworth, dated January 27, clearly shows the tensions that existed between William and his elder sisters:

When your wife took occasion to evidence her jealousy of my father's kindness to me, & before that idolized parent was cold in his grave, to rebuke his memory for having "lavished his thousands" on his son, I felt that his fears respecting two members of his family were about to be realised, & that I might be a victim to their mercenary suspicions. For three years before his death, we had frequent conversations respecting the state of family feeling, & more than once he told me that the *jealousy, irritability*, & *incessant, unfilial* opposition to his every purpose of *one* individual, gave him more anxiety that all his other troubles....

Before I left Ind[ian]a, I had the most pressing appeals from my father to return to N.Haven. He needed my aid in his labors, & he wanted the presence of his son to comfort his old age—a comfort which some heartless members of his family would have denied him. To persuade me, he offered many inducements....

I *do feel*, and feel most keenly the conduct of my family toward me, from the hour they attempted to deprive me, without indemnity, of rights and provisions solemnly guaranteed me by my sainted father, an attempt which, thank God, public opinion & most righteous law measurably defeated....[1]

Ellsworth refused to show that letter to his wife, so William wrote an even longer one, a circular, which he sent to Emily, Harriet and Eliza. It was dated March 16, 1844:

In a communication adressed by brother Ellsworth to my wife, some weeks ago, I saw with astonishment & grief that you have been laboring under the impression that before my father's death I had received not less than $15,000 ! This estimate is so extraordinary, so unfounded, that I sat down at once to repel the insinuation as based on idle jealousy & calculated to do great injustice. As was natural with a thousand painful recollections, awakened by this assertion, I wrote with feeling, and my letter, from a mistaken sense of "justice to Emily & myself" was withheld from her.

As I am preparing to leave forever, a family who with one or two exceptions have manifested but little love for me or mine, and am about to cast my lot among the friends of my wife, I am not willing to go away with that strange suspicion haunting your thoughts that my beloved father had during his life

given me so much as to render any bequest at his death injustice to his daughters, & that consequently, as intimated by brother Ellsworth, they deserve the praise of munificent generosity in not "wishing to withhold from me my share of the estate."

After that, he gave his whole financial and commercial history, showing how little he had cost his father, and how much work he had done in exchange. He did not then leave his family "forever," but he did take Rosalie to visit her relations in Virginia while tempers cooled.

Soon after his return, William was attacked again. Ellsworth had discovered that George F. Cooledge & Brother of New York, to whom Webster & Clark had sold the copyright in the *Elementary Spelling Book*, were publishing a little dictionary that William had compiled. It was called *A Sequel to Webster's Elementary Spelling-Book, or, A Speller and Definer*. On October 11, 1844, Ellsworth wrote to William:

My Dear Sir,

There was handed to me, two days since, a new dictionary published by the Messrs.Cooledge, "compiled" by yourself. I do not know what sum you received for the compilation, but it ought to be a large one to make such a thing politic, for one interested in the estate of Dr. Webster. For if this compilation can be sustained, I should consider any abridgment of the A[merican] Dictionary of little value. Yours is taken chiefly out of the last edition, with less variation from it than in the small dictionary sold by Huntington. I have carefully examined the "compilation" and compared it. There is scarce a definition in the "compilation" which, so far as it goes, is not taken verbatim from the A Dictionary (the last edition) and even where there is a difference, it is evident you had the large dictionary before you, and made a verbal evasion only. Nearly the whole thought of the "compilation" belongs to Dr. Webster's labors.

This book is so directly and obviously made from the large dictionary, that I must, in justice to the estate, and as a matter of pure necessity, take measures to suppress it, or the estate must suffer immensely.

I have always thought litterary [sic] property insecure, and if this compilation can stand, shall give up all hope of securing much to the estate.

Respectfully yours,

WWEllsworth.

This time, William was not going to give up without a fight. He denied having copied anything from Webster:

New York, Oct.14.1844

Hon.W.W.Ellsworth,

Dear Sir,

Last summer, the Messrs.Cooledge bro't me a copy of Ely's School Dictionary intended as a Supplement to Webster's Sp. Book, which they thought of purchasing for publication if I would revise it and correct the errors which were in it. This little work was founded on my father's labors, and as such was commended by him & by Mr. Goodrich & their certificates are published. My father had no fears that his larger works would suffer by the circulation of Ely's.

On examining Ely's dictionary, I told the Messrs Cooledge I shd prefer to compile a new one, & as they were determined to have a *Sequel to the Speller*, a book of definitions, they desired me to undertake the task.

Accordingly, I procured copies of *Ash, Bailey, Maunder, Walker*, & particularly *Jameson*, & from these, selected such words & definitions, as I thought would make a book of the size of the Speller. I undertook the work with a full appreciation of the rights of authors, & of the penalties of their violation, & consequently never opened the American Dictionary or the abridgment (except two or three times to resolve my doubts respecting the *transitive* or *intransitive* nature of a verb.) *Every word and every definition* in my book, you will find in some of the works from which my father copied, all of which preceded his. This will account for your belief in my compilation being founded in the American Dictionary.

In examining the proof sheets, I had occasion only a few times to refer to the large work, & this was to ascertain how a particular word was *divided*. And I never dreampt of your taking my little work as an infringment on the rights of others. On the other hand, I feel that it would be used, if at all, only in *primary schools*, among a class of pupils, who must use a very cheap book of definitions, *or none at all*, & that its circulation, if any where, would be in the South or West, where father's dictionaries are known but slightly, & that the consequences of its notoriety, should it receive any, would be to give new interest to the reputation of the larger works & tend to enhance the popularity of their author. And this I believe will be the effect, & your fears respecting a diminution of the sales of the school dictionary be groundless.

The public are calling for a larger school dictionary. rather than a smaller, & mine contains less than a third as many words as the smallest of Webster's.

In conclusion, I do not perceive why I have not the same right to compile a book that Ely, Grimshaw, Hazen, Cobb, Gallaudet & a dozen other men have exercised, several of them with Webster's orthography, and without one question of their right.

I shall be in N.Haven the rest of the Week, &

should you be there, I will show you the works from which I composed mine.

Truly yrs,

W.G.Webster.

Ellsworth did not want to get into an argument with William over the origin of his definitions. It would do none of them any good to show that Webster himself had just copied definitions from earlier dictionaries. Nor, indeed, would it do the "heirs" any good to suppress Cooledge's *Speller and Definer*. What Ellsworth wanted was for the family to get something out of it. With this in mind, he wrote to George F.Cooledge & Brother on November 4, 1844:

Gentlemen,

Not until this time have I had time to fully examine the minor dictionary published by you. Had we known that you wanted such a book, we could doubtless have provided you with one. The pages containing the key & directions are nearly verbatim with the same in the Elementary Spelling Book, which cannot properly be published & issued, except as part of, & with the whole spelling book. The whole book is apparently put forth by Mr. Webster as out of the labors of his father, & the definitions are in some cases alike in both dictionaries & but little varying, as far as they go, in ... any of them.

I should be sorry to do you any injustice, or Mr. Webster. Will you inform me what the expense has been to you & say if this is paid you by me, it will be acceptable to you to discontinue the publication of the dictionary, unless I should make some new arrangement with you for its publication, as under & from the estate of Dr. Webster. There is a contract between Huntington & the Estate forbidding Dr. Webster from making *any* school dictionary. I might satisfy him that *this* dictionary will not *hurt* him, & then satisfy Mr. Wm.Webster, & as to the book as it is, making some satisfactory contract with you, in which case you could go on with it. My solicitude is not so much about *this* dictionary, as it is the mode or manner in which the book is got up & published, & the inducement it presents to more serious incroachments upon the rights of Dr. Webster.....

Cooledge took the attitude that this was something for William to sort out with "the Governor." Since William was anyway having to deal with Cooledge's complaint that his word list was not suitable for an elementary dictionary, he prepared a revised edition of the little dictionary in 1845, with a modified pronunciation key. It sold a great many copies, and Ellsworth did not object again.

At the same time as addressing that problem, Ellsworth set about organizing the other Webster dictionaries. The largest one, the *American Dictionary*, had been published in royal octavo by Webster himself, but his attempt to obtain subscribers had failed, and he was left with many copies on his hands, in the form of unbound sheets. As Webster's executor, Ellsworth had to find a buyer for them, and a publisher for a future edition. He was not at that time concerned with the octavo, which was being published by White for Goodrich, but White also published the larger of the primary school dictionaries. The smaller one was published by the firm of Huntington & Savage. Ellsworth had therefore to deal with several publishers, and with his fellow heirs, and with Goodrich. His output of letters was prodigious. To William alone he often wrote two or three times a week, and sometimes twice in one day. It was not just the existing dictionaries he had to deal with — new ones were wanted as well. "It is our policy," he wrote to William, "to fill every place."[2] Webster had planned a "Pocket Edition" with Huntington. William should compile it. A new abridgment was needed, larger than the school dictionaries but smaller than the octavo, which would be called the "University" edition. It would be edited by Fowler.

Ellsworth's job was made more difficult by bitter jealousies and competing interests, of which he seems to have been totally unaware. Fowler wanted to control revisions of the dictionaries in order to maintain the integrity of Webster's system. Goodrich wanted to control revisions for just the opposite reason. He had toned down Webster's peculiarities in the octavo, and he wanted to do the same thing in the other dictionaries as well. William wanted to prepare new editions because he would be paid for doing it. Ellsworth's letters to William show the executor becoming increasingly exasperated with Huntington's commercial deviousness, and Fowler's academic jealousy:

[April 18, 1846] ... Mr. H is a very difficult man to do business with. He is wanting in every quality which I should desire in our publisher, except energy, & that only for himself exclusively. He is tricky & impudent without measure, & then still more impudent in his professions of fairness &c.—I know him to the very bottom.

[Feb. 8, 1847] ... As yet, tho' several letters have

passed between us, Mr. Fowler has refused to consent to a new dictionary. His real objection is, I believe, that you and not he may be called on to make it.

[Feb. 25, 1847] … After some 6 letters between Mr. Fowler & myself, I utterly despair of all cordial intercourse or friendly cooperation on his part, for the future, however clear may be, even his *interest* in such cooperation. He is the most extraordinary man I ever met with

[Mar. 7, 1847] … With all my heart I would write to Mr. Fowler, if I knew *exactly* what I wanted him to assent to, & had the least hope he would give his assent. Brother William, he will not assent to *anything*; tis his very principle of action. His late letters to me have been little better than an insult.

[Apr. 15, 1847] … Mr. H is not a man of truth, honesty or honor, in the matter of the dictionaries, & any man who deals with him will come to that conclusion.

[Apr. 20, 1847] … With Fowler on one side & Huntington on the other I am worn out & quite discouraged.

Of all the threads that passed through Ellsworth's fingers, I want to follow just two. One leads to the *University* dictionary, of which Fowler was to be the editor and Huntington the publisher. It first appeared in 1845, with a revised edition in 1850. The other would lead to the first Merriam-Webster, a revision of the *American Dictionary*, edited by Goodrich. It is dated 1847, but was first issued in 1848.

Ellsworth's first concern was to find a buyer for the unsold copies of Webster's 1841 edition. On November 14, 1843, he wrote to William:

As to the dictionaries on hand, six dollars down is what I have expected, which is less than the price in the inventory. I have supposed that about $6 would only cover the original cost. I have never supposed, that in the end, there would be found to be any profit in the entire edition, tho I think your father's ideas were otherwise….

He found a buyer two weeks later, though he did not get the "six dollars down" that he had hoped for. J. S. & C. Adams, of Amherst, Massachusetts, agreed to a price of $5.50 a set for the unbound sheets, payable at nine and twelve months. They were, said Ellsworth, "three of the *very best* names in Amherst," and their notes were "as safe as if issued by the bank." So that they would have a clear field to sell what they had bought, Ellsworth gave an undertaking not to publish another edition of the big dictionary within three years. On December 5, 1843, he passed on their instructions

for the first 200 sets. William was to send them to.

"Charles B Clark, Bookbinder Andover Mass, by the Norwich SteamBoat & Rail Road to Boston, then by Rail Road to Andover — Keep Dry." This is the exact direction — will you see it *exactly* complied with…

Having given the Adams three years to sell the remainder of the 1841 dictionary, Ellsworth then had to find a publisher interested in bringing out a new edition at the end of that three year period. He was offering the balance of the first term of copyright in the dictionary, expiring in 1856. No one was interested. The obstacle was the undertaking that Webster had given to Goodrich, prohibiting the publication of a stereotyped edition. As Fowler had earlier discovered, no publisher was willing to pay for a white elephant that would be incapable of earning its keep.

The solution to this apparently insoluble problem was provided by the partnership of George and Charles Merriam, of Springfield, Massachusetts. This was not the same firm as the "good old-fashioned booksellers," Merriams of Brookfield, that Webster had first threatened to sue and then licensed, but it was the same family. The Brookfield firm was set up in 1797 by two brothers, Ebenezer and Daniel Merriam, with a press that (like most early American presses) had once belonged to Franklin. Daniel later went back to farming, but his sons stayed in the printing business. Two of them, George and Charles, set up their own business in Springfield in 1831, and they were later joined by their younger brother, Homer. They had earlier turned down the opportunity to print the octavo after Converse's bankruptcy, but they became interested in the *American Dictionary* when J. S. & C. Adams offered them the balance of the 1841 edition, which they had been unable to sell. The Merriams were not particularly tempted by that on its own, but it would give them the opportunity to distribute what was still the only large American dictionary, and they were excited by the idea of a "Merriam" edition later on. To achieve this, they had to fashion a three-way deal. They bought the remainder of the old edition from J. S. & C. Adams, they bought a copyright licence from Webster's executors, and they hired Goodrich to prepare the new edition.

On December 10, 1844, Ellsworth reported to William:

I have licenced the publication of the royal 8° until 1856, which is the expiration of 28 years from the date of the large quarto. When I sold the dictionaries to the Messrs.Adams last year, I bound myself not to publish another edition under three years, so that the licence now sold to the Merriams is for about nine or ten years. This I sold for $2800 paid down. I should have been happy, in the sale, to have availed myself of your advice had you not been in Virginia, & I did not consult Mr. G. because he had no interest in the sale & as Mr. Fowler, Mr. White [the other executor] & I agreed, I did not hesitate to embrace what I am confident is an excellent sum for the estate. Indeed, tho' I had applied to some fourteen publishers, I could never *get an offer* for this copyright, because of the restriction given to Mr. Goodrich & Mr. White [the publisher]. This restriction well nigh ruins the large dictionary. I recollect your letters to me, wishing every thing to be sold at once, if I could do it, & I was fully satisfied that the estate would never find it wise to publish another edition, & indeed the exors. *could* not have done it. Besides, the Merriams have bought all the present edition, & I suppose intend to put it off cheap, & thus the country, to our advantage, will be filled with *Webster*, to the exclusion of Worcester's new *large* dictionary, now advertised.[3]

For myself, I do think, the licence given for $2800 is about so much entirely saved, as I could see no prospect of doing anything, in any other way.... I am confident that I could not do as well were I to go over the ground again.... I think the future income of the estate, which is now clear (except the annuities to our mother and sister to be deducted) will be for some years at least $3000, & who of the children will have the copyrights when renewed & what they may be worth, I cannot guess....

I hope no unnecessary legal questions touching literary property will be raised, & if not, we have a comfortable little income, in the whole, from the labors of your respected father.

Yours truly, WWEllsworth.

What is particularly interesting in that letter is Ellsworth's saying that nobody would offer for the copyright in the *American Dictionary* because of the "restriction given to Mr. Goodrich & Mr. White," which "well nigh ruins the large dictionary." The edition of the *American Dictionary* that the Merriams later brought out under Goodrich's editorship was a stereotyped quarto, which would not have been prohibited by the "restriction." In relation to a book of that size, Goodrich actually had no bargaining strength at all, except what was given him by the

other parties' ignorance of his weakness. He must also have realised that since his exclusive rights in the octavo abridgment lasted only until the end of the first term of copyright, even his perceived bargaining position was weakening year by year. To balance this, he would (through Julia) get a share in the copyright of the *American Dictionary* in 1856, and it would then be to his advantage to promote the sales of the book, which previously he had considered to be a competitor to the octavo. By accepting the editorship of the *American Dictionary*, Goodrich was putting himself in the ideal position to promote its sale by toning down Webster's eccentricities, just as he had done (through Worcester) in the octavo. He probably did not anticipate how much oppposition he would have to overcome from Harriet's husband, William Fowler.

The executors had entrusted to Fowler the task of preparing the abridgment of the *American Dictionary* known as the *University* edition. This is his later account of these events:

The first question I put to Mr. Ellsworth was: "How can it be settled *what changes are necessary?*" "Why, in the book which you are preparing, you can make the alterations." I told him it would be a delicate business to make alterations, and some of the family may be opposed. He replied: "I do not think there will be any difficulty. You can go on and make the alterations." Thus he gave me full authority, as an executor, to make alterations in the University abridgment of the Dictionary which I was preparing.

In this conversation, there was a basic misunderstanding between Fowler and Ellsworth. Fowler regarded Webster's literary legacy as a sacred trust, and was afraid that the family, sharing this view, would object to his making any changes to Webster's work. Ellsworth, quite rightly, thought that the other "heirs" did not much care one way or the other. They would not be likely to object to any alterations that Fowler would want to make, so he told Fowler to go ahead. Ellsworth did not realise that Goodrich, given half a chance, would want to make many more changes than would be acceptable to Fowler. Fowler did not think Goodrich had any rights in the matter, because he was not an heir, and interpreted Ellsworth's permission as putting him in sole charge of the orthography of Webster's works. Ellsworth had not intended anything of the sort, but that was what Fowler believed:

Mr. Ellsworth, as executor, and heir in common with me, committed the whole subject to me, and authorized me to act according to my best judgment in the case, and to say that all "necessary changes" in the orthography would be made, and that I should be judge of what was necessary. Having been for a long time engaged in the study of the English language, in the preparation of my own work, which has since been published — having enjoyed the full confidence of Dr. Webster, and the best opportunities for knowing what were his views — having the good-will of my fellow-heirs, and authorized, by repeated declarations of Mr. Ellsworth, to act for the family in the premises, I determined that nothing should be wanting on my part to promote the perfection and popularity and accuracy of Dr. Webster's works....

Thus having full power to make "necessary alterations," so far as an executor and heir could give it, I went on to prepare a few changes on the basis of Dr. Webster's system, and in close conformity with it, looking through the whole vocabulary, carefully reading whatever Dr. Webster had written, and recalling his conversations with me on the same points. Having prepared a list of words as candidates for change, I wrote to New Haven to consult Mr. Goodrich, as I had previously told Mr. Ellsworth I should....

After spending most of the forenoon with him at his room, but without expressing my views or showing him my list of words, he told me, as the result of "his mature reflections on the subject," that he was of the opinion that *no alterations ought to be made in the orthography and pronunciation, but that more words should be doubled!* Was this unexpected decision the result of his own unhappy experience in making alterations in the abridged Octavo, or was it owing to an unwillingness to have any one but himself make alterations in Dr. Webster's works?...

Or was it, perhaps, that Goodrich wanted the *University* edition (in which he would have no share) to be a less effective competitor to his own octavo?

When the idea of licensing Merriams to produce a new edition of the *American Dictionary* was being discussed, Fowler immediately insisted that the orthography of that edition must be the same as that of his *University* edition. Everyone agreed; but what was that orthography to be? Fowler had meant that the big dictionary should incorporate those changes, and only those changes, that he wanted to make in the *University* edition. Goodrich of course had other plans, as Fowler soon discovered:

While I thus had the whole subject of alterations committed to me without reserve, I received a letter from Mr. Goodrich, stating that he was about to edit the large work for the Merriams, and *requesting me to authorise him, without consulting any one, to make alterations!* I regarded this as a very cool piece of arrogance from one who had told me that no alterations ought to be made, who had dissatisfied Dr. Webster and myself and others by making alterations [to the Octavo]. I regarded this as a cool piece of arrogance towards me, who was acting as an editor of the University edition, with full power to make alterations.

Fowler complained to Ellsworth, who replied that any changes Fowler and Goodrich agreed on would be fine with the executors. This shows that he had still not understood the nature of the problem — that Fowler and Goodrich were never going to agree. Ellsworth's mind was anyway occupied with a different problem: He wanted to ensure that the Merriams should not be able to claim a fresh copyright in their new edition, to the exclusion of Webster's family. He wrote to Fowler on January 9, 1845:

When I sold the Merriams the Dictionary, I stipulated, or, rather, they did, in the instrument, that no *change* should be made without my consent; I, however, remarked to them, and so stated in a subsequent letter, that such alterations as you and Mr. Goodrich should approve of, would doubtless meet the assent of the executors.

The alterations *cannot*, and should not, be the property of others, and secured by copyright, as brother William sayd Mr. Goodrich *suggests*. The Merriams told me that any alterations would be made at their expense, and I have informed William that the executors will by no means consent to have *other* owners in this Dictionary. I referred the Merriams to you and Mr. Goodrich. The alterations are not original matter, *capable* of a copyright.

Fowler replied, January 11, 1845:

I do not feel inclined to give general liberty of alteration to any one. Besides other reasons, this is decisive. The large work ought to correspond with the work which I have in hand to prepare for the press, and which will contain all the disputed or doubtful words. I should very *strongly insist* that no alterations should be made in the large work that were not previously made in the duodecimo which I am preparing. I feel that I ought to have a voice and agency in them.

As to the matter to be added, I am, with you, fully of the opinion that neither brother Goodrich nor the Merriams ought to be allowed to have any lien upon it. Mr. Merriam, as I thought, and now think, had the work low enough, and brother Goodrich has had profit enough from the Dictionaries, without asking for more. I have no doubt that *you will keep the*

matter in such a shape that all the alterations and additions shall belong to the family, without any foreign claim upon them, to be used by them and no one else, as soon as the Merriams' term has expired.

Ellsworth either failed to see, or chose to ignore, that Fowler was claiming the sole right to decide on alterations. In any case, the claims of Fowler and Goodrich were clearly incompatible; each claimed to be entitled to decide what changes should be made, and neither would accept the authority of the other. Ellsworth proposed a middle course: The only changes made should be those that they *both* agreed upon; where they disagreed, no change should be made. He suggested this in a letter to Goodrich on January 14, 1845:

I have concluded that the executors are safe, and acting wisely in leaving the extent and character of alterations to be made, to you, Mr. Fowler, and, I should have added, brother William, had he not been absent, and I had no knowledge that he intended to return. I think his opinion should certainly be taken.

As Mr. Fowler has already prepared the School Dictionary, in which he may have to make further alterations, in view of alterations to be made in the large Dictionary, I have requested him to immediately let you know what principles he has adopted, and he will confer with you. If you differ as to the propriety of certain alterations, that would induce the proprietors to omit them, and retain which you both advise to be proper, and I trust you will be able to concur throughout.

Of course the Merriams will pay, as they told me they would, for the improvements in their own work. The omissions and correcitons in spelling and pronunciation cannot be the subject of copyright, nor would it be proper for any third person to tack a distinct interest on to this Dictionary or its abridgment.

At an acrimonious meeting in Ellsworth's office, Goodrich finally accepted the proposed arrangement. Thereafter, he and Fowler had a number of meetings, going through the letter *A* in the dictionary, and agreeing on the alterations to be made. Believing that the problem was solved, Ellsworth wrote to William, January 17, 1845:

Our brothers Goodrich & Fowler have come to a perfect and pleasant agreement & the school dictionary is now underway in the hands of the printer....

Later on, however, Fowler found Goodrich increasingly reluctant to cooperate. Finally, he wrote out the following agreement for both of them to sign:

The subject of any alterations deemed necessary in Webster's Dictionary, an edition of which Messrs. Merriams, of Springfield, are intending to publish, having been referred to us for decision, we hereby agree to accept the reference, and perform the duty in accordance with a letter dated January 14, 1845, from W.W.Ellsworth to Chauncey A.Goodrich.
Feb.6, 1845.

Goodrich refused to sign. This put Fowler in a difficult position. He had promised his publisher, Huntington, that the orthography of the *University* edition would be the same as that of the future edition of the big dictionary, which was obviously desirable from the publisher's point of view. This could only be achieved, however, either by the two editors reaching agreement (which seemed to be impossible) or by Fowler agreeing to accept any changes Goodrich might propose — which Fowler was not willing to do. Fowler appealed to Ellsworth once again, and Ellsworth persuaded Goodrich to accept a modified form of the earlier arrangement: In case of disagreement between Fowler and Goodrich, instead of there being no changes made, Ellsworth himself would act as "umpire." This seemed to work. Fowler takes up the story again:

Under this new arrangement, we went on harmoniously, so far as I have ever known — I, consenting to some changes, which I was not inclined to, and he, I suppose, giving up some preferences. I never knew of more than three or four words which he wished to change that were not changed, and then he acquiesced cheerfully. There was not a word that Mr. William Webster wished to have changed that was not changed.

And, in order to have the corrections as perfect as possible, I wrote to Mr. Goodrich, after he had had every opportunity, in the course of publication of the work, to suggest alterations, he having received from me all the proof sheets. I wrote to him, moreover, about the time that the plates were to receive the final corrections, giving him an opportunity of proposing other *alterations still*. The *University edition*, of which I was the editor, was to be printed *first*, and I considered it very important that all those alterations should be made judiciously, because they would first come out to the public, and the large book was to be conformed to this.

The final corrections were made, The Preface and Memoir and Rules, prefixed to the work, were printed. A thousand copies were struck off. I rejoiced that I had completed my severe labors in getting out the edition, and I rejoiced to believe that Mr. Goodrich was entirely satisfied.

This was the state of affairs when, in October, Fowler was surprised to receive a note from Ellsworth enclosing a letter from William. The letter proposed a meeting of all the family of Dr. Webster, and of the publishers, Merriams and Huntington. Fowler replied that he could not see the need for such a meeting, but that if one were held, he would attend. When the meeting took place, Goodrich stated what alterations he was proposing to make in the big dictionary, and Huntington, who wanted the *University* edition to conform to the quarto, agreed to make the same alterations. Fowler said nothing. Nobody had told him the meeting was taking place, so he was not there. When he found out about it, he was not pleased:

Without my knowledge or consent, he [Goodrich] contrived to get into his hands my book, that is, a book which I had edited, namely: the University edition of the Dictionary; a book for which I was responsible before the community. Where was faith — where was honor? Yes, in violation of faith, in violation of honor, he broke his agreement with me. In violation of honor, in violation of truth, he foisted into a book, edited by me and owned by me in part, his alterations of Dr. Webster's system, and called them my alterations.

In the Preface of the University edition of Webster's Dictionary, is the following sentence: "The changes in orthography and pronunciation have been made under the direction of Rev. CHAUNCEY GOODRICH, formerly professor of Rhetoric and Oratory in Yale College, Rev. WILLIAM C.FOWLER, lately professor of Rhetoric and Oratory in Amherst College, and WILLIAM G.WEBSTER, Esq., member of the family of Dr. Webster, who was acquainted with his views and his principles." Thus was he guilty of a literary forgery, as another is guilty of forgery by altering the body of a record, or deed, or bank note, while the signature remains. The changes in orthography and pronunciation were not "made under the direction of Rev. William C.Fowler," but in violation of his rights and wishes, and intruded without his knowledge on the book edited by him.

Ellsworth clearly did not understand what had happened. When Huntington sent the executors a bill for $290 "for extra work in printing the dictionary ... for *undoing* and doing over the 2 time what had been approved & ordered by Mr. Fowler," Ellsworth thought that Fowler ought to pay it !⁴

Despite what had gone before, Fowler had some hope that he would be consulted about the changes to be made to the big dictionary. Of course, he wasn't:

Instead of giving me notice that the work was ready for examination, as to the alterations, and thus giving me, as one of the referees, an opportunity to form a judgment concerning them, he gets Mr. Ellsworth to write to me that there would be a family meeting, on a certain day, "for final action." I do not *know* that he was aware that I was in New York at the time. At any rate, I never knew of the meeting until the day was past. I immediately went from Amherst down to New Haven to examine the work, according to my agreement with Mr. Goodrich and Mr. Ellsworth, for deciding upon the alterations, when Mr. Goodrich told me it was too late for me to have a voice in the matter, according to the agreement. I concluded that the family meeting at that time was a sham, in order to get rid of me. How could the "family," during the short time they were together, decide understandingly upon the alterations in 600 pages? Why was it necessary to substitute a "family meeting" in place of the other arrangement?

Fowler wrote a letter of protest to Goodrich, who took no notice.

Fowler's friend Percival now comes into the story again. When we last met him, he was uncomfortably in harness with Webster, working on the first edition of the *American Dictionary*. Now he would work briefly with Goodrich on the revision of the same work. In between, he had been engaged in geology, and in this capacity he came into contact with Ellsworth. Their extraordinary meeting shows in Percival the same rigid adherence to principle that had brought his collaboration with Webster to an end in 1828, and would later make it impossible for Goodrich to continue to employ him on the 1847 revision.

Back in 1835, Percival had been persuaded by the then governor of Connecticut, Henry Edwards, to undertake a geological survey of the state. To do the job thoroughly, Percival proposed to travel on foot, but the governor thought that would be too slow and told him to use a horse. Edwards was right, for even on horseback it took Percival five years to ride round the entire state gathering geological information. During that time he was receiving payments from the state, though they scarcely covered his expenses. Meanwhile, in 1838, Ellsworth had succeeded Edwards as governor, and by 1840 he was becoming impatient. The State of Connecticut had been paying Percival for five years; Percival was said to have accumulated a great deal of information, but he had not produced the survey for which the state was

paying him. Ellsworth described him, very unfairly, as "a literary loafer," and set a deadline: Percival had to produce his report, ready for the press, by April 1841. He could not have his final payment until he had produced the report, and had it approved by the governor.

Nearly a year after the deadline, Percival finally brought the report to Ellsworth for approval, and on March 22, 1842, Ellsworth wrote to William, describing their meeting:

As to Dr. Percival, I hardly dare trust myself to express even to you, my real sentiments. He is certainly the most singular man I ever met with. His last interview with me is a true sample of what has preceded, and I am most happy that at our last meeting he brought with him his friend Henry Barnard Esq., who knows exactly what was said and done. They came into my office together. He had on a cloak apparently covering a round package which was in a coarse strawpaper, the extreme end of which I could just see. He said he had come to deposit with me his report & get my certificate, as the law required, that the report was *"complete for publication."* I requested him to hand it to me, that I might see and certify, if it was complete, as I presumed, of course, it was. He said no—he should not leave it with me (tho the law expressly requires it) nor let me see it unless I would *first promise* him to give the certificate. I expressed my surprise at such a request, and answered him it was not right for me to do such a thing. I did not doubt his word, but so long as he kept the report I could not certify. I told him if he doubted my word he might leave the report with Mr. Barnard & I would look at it in *his* house, or if he would get the certificate of Prof.Silliman or Prof.Olmsted, that would satisfy me. Mr. Barnard then joined with me in the above request & told Dr. Percival that my objection to certify what I had not seen and could not see, was most reasonable; this request was oft repeated by us, but the Doctor would not do anything, or *say anything*, and finally went away with the *thing* under his cloak. Some ten days after a report was sent me through the kindness of Prof.Silliman with a certificate that the report was complete. Prof.Jackson & myself examined & thought it complete as a *report*, tho not for publication exactly, but I thought the law had been complied with substantially & I sent notice by the next mail to Dr. Percival that I had passed to the controller the certificate.[manuscript torn].... for the $1000.

Ellsworth's position here is very easy to understand: He was not prepared to certify his approval of a report that he had not been allowed to look at. Any person of reasonable intelligence could have foreseen that he would adopt that position. Why, then, did Percival take the

report to him and then refuse to let him see it? It does not at first seem to make sense. Either you take your report to the governor and show it to him, or you do not bother to take it at all. In fact, Percival's conduct, though bizarre, was entirely logical. The clue lies in his offering to leave the report if Ellsworth would first promise to give the required certificate. The basis of Percival's unspoken argument was the fact that Ellsworth did not know the first thing about geology. How, then, could he judge whether or not the document Percival produced was what it was supposed to be? How could anyone, who had not spent five years riding round every corner of Connecticut? To be fair to Ellsworth, he admitted that he was not competent to judge Percival's work, but he was required by law to go through the motions. To Percival, it was a matter of trust. If Ellsworth was not qualified to criticize the report, he would have to take it on trust that it really did contain a true and accurate geological survey of the state; but if he was prepared to give Percival that much trust, why would he not promise his certificate before he saw the report? Ellsworth's refusal to promise was a sign of distrust, and was therefore a personal slight. The impasse was unbreakable, and Percival left with his report, and without Ellsworth's certificate. This was the more remarkable because he was desperately in need of the money, which he could not get without the Governor's certificate.

Percival was saved by the intervention of a friend (perhaps Henry Barnard) who sneaked off with the report and gave it to professor Silliman at Yale without Percival's knowledge or consent. Silliman told Ellsworth that it was satisfactory. Strictly speaking, Percival had failed to comply with the terms required by the legislature and was not entitled to his pay; but, as Ellsworth said afterwards to Fowler, "We huddled it up, we huddled it up." The report, when published, made an octavo volume of 495 pages, accompanied by a geological map of Connecticut. It was described by a critic in words that would have been equally appropriate to Webster's *Synopsis*: "a work distinguished for its great learning and research, but which was defective in method and in distinctness of practical application."

Since then, Percival had gone from bad to

worse, and he was now living the life of an insanitary hermit in rented rooms in the New Haven hospital:

He had three rooms. His library and minerals were in one, his study in another, his bedroom in another. His bed was simply a cot, with mattress above. There were no sheets, and a block of wood placed under the mattress served for a pillow. There were two woollen blankets on the bed, very dirty. Places at the foot showed that he had laid down with his shoes on, and it was evident that he had often slept in his clothes. The rooms were very untidy, and probably never swept. There were perhaps two inches of rolling lint upon the floor. There was a beaten path from his bed to his stove, to his writing table, to his library, and to the door. .... His living was exceedingly plain and simple. He used to go to the stores in the evening to buy crackers, herrings, dried-beef, fruit, and other food which could be easily prepared; and as his health was often miserable, it was no unusual thing for him to go whole days without food. In this way, his personal expenses were reduced to a minimum; and as he had his rooms for a nominal sum, he could live almost upon nothing. This explains why he could subsist so many years with no other visible means of support than the chance jobs of scientific or literary work which came to him.[5]

Because he was abnormally sensitive, Percival always refused gifts of money, even when he was in the greatest need. His friends therefore did their best to find literary odd jobs that he could do. For Professor E. A. Andrews, he translated letters *A* and *B* of *Freund's Latin Lexicon*.[6] In 1843 he assisted William in compiling addenda to the *American Dictionary*.[7] Then Goodrich offered him employment on his revision of the "unabridged," but once again, he only managed *A* and *B*. This is recorded in Goodrich's Preface:

The editor at first made an arrangement with Dr. James G.Percival, who had rendered important assistance to Dr. Webster in the edition of 1828, to take the entire charge of revising the scientific articles embraced in this work. This revision, however, owing to causes beyond the control of either party, was extended to little more than two letters of the alphabet; and the editor then obtained the assistance of his associates in office, and of other gentlemen in various professional employments.

One of Percival's coworkers was the Rev. Samuel W. Barnum, who was helping Goodrich with the revision of the octavo dictionary that was going on at the same time as the revision of the quarto. Barnum wrote some reminis-

cences in a letter to the New Haven *Palladium*, Thursday, February 21, 1884:

My personal knowledge of Dr. Percival and of Webster's dictionary extends back to March, 1845, when I came to New Haven to assist Professor Goodrich in the revision of the octavo edition of Webster's dictionary, and Dr. Percival had been for several months working on the revision of the "unabridged" or larger dictionary, both of which were published in 1847, the former by Harper & Brothers, the latter by George and Charles Merriam. For two years and a half I occupied the same room with Professor Goodrich, No. 138 (now 186,) in the third story of the (now old) college chapel. In that room the main part of both revisions was carried on and completed. For several months after I began to occupy that room, Dr. Percival came frequently — usually, I think, about once a week — from his own room at the state hospital to consult Professor Goodrich in regard to the work which he in the meantime had been doing by himself. I know that Dr. Percival insisted on reading to Professor Goodrich every important change which he made and obtaining his approval. This consultation took place either in the room where I was, or in the little room adjoining, which then contained the library of Professor Goodrich's kinsman, Rev. George Cotton....

Goodrich said in the Preface that Percival's continued work on the dictionary was prevented by "causes beyond the control of either party," which is sometimes taken to be a polite way of saying that Percival had gone off his head. That would not be inconsistent with Barnum's account, where he said that one of the reasons for Percival's discontinuing the work was that

excessive application, which has been already noticed in speaking of his work on the first edition, made him sick. At any rate, we missed him for several weeks in the summer of 1845, and then he became pale and haggard, and said that he must give up, and that somebody else could probably do the work more satisfactorily. The contract between him and Professor Goodrich was accordingly canceled....

According to a writer in *Putnam's Monthly* for December 1856, however, Percival's arrangement with Goodrich was broken off because "he could only work in his own time and way. Nothing could be passed over until thoroughly finished; and the consequence was, that he would sometimes spend days upon some single insignificant word, whose history, if attainable, was of no importance." If so, it was the same quest for perfection that had so enraged Webster in 1828.

By the various stratagems described above, Goodrich contrived between 1829 and 1845 to get virtual ownership of the octavo abridgment for 28 years and editorial control of both the *American Dictionary* and the *University* edition. He was thus able to tone down or eliminate, in all the Webster dictionaries, any of Webster's oddities that he disapproved of. Because the oddities had been an obstacle to the sale of the dictionaries, Goodrich was happy to emphasize that they had gone. In a letter to the *Morning Courier and New-York Enquirer*, February 21, 1849, he went so far as to say that the orthography of the 1847 *Webster's Dictionary* was not Webster's orthography at all.[8]

The subject of the correspondence was an edition of Macaulay's *History of England* that had been reprinted in America. The publishers, Harper & Brothers, were also the publishers of Goodrich's octavo Webster dictionary, and they used its spelling in all their works. In accordance with this practice they changed Macaulay's spelling, using what opponents referred to as "the orthography of Webster." Since Webster had recommended much odder spelling than was now to be found in the dictionaries, Goodrich denied that the orthography was Webster's and explained the difference:

The Messrs. Harpers, in common with great numbers of our editors and publishers, together with a large and increasing portion of our community, have taken for their standard the revised edition of Dr. Webster's dictionary. In this edition, the most offensive peculiarities of his former system are laid aside; and there is really nothing left which can with any propriety be called *his*.

A similar statement appeared in the revised *University* dictionary published the following year, on which, not surprisingly, Fowler's name did not appear. It contained an advertisement in these terms:

SINCE the first publication of this edition, in 1845, the *American Dictionary* has been carefully revised, under the general superintendence of that accomplished scholar, Professor Goodrich, of Yale College, and numerous and important changes have been made in the vocabulary of that work. This has made it necessary to revise all the abridgments of Dr. Webster's original work, so as to bring the entire series into uniformity in *Orthography* and *Pronunciation*. The whole of it has been examined in special reference to the peculiarities which had been objected to, all of which, it is believed, are now removed, and the

work better fitted to hold the place it was designed to occupy in public estimation.
NEW HAVEN, *April*, 1850.

New Haven, where the advertisement was written, was the place of residence of the "accomplished scholar" himself, Professor Goodrich.

Later on, we shall see that the Merriams, too, had occasion to emphasise that the orthography of the 1847 Webster quarto was not Webster's orthography. When the copyright in that edition expired, it was photographically reprinted by a company in Chicago that claimed to be "preserving intact the monument of Noah Webster's genius and industry." The Merriams' response was that the Goodrich-Webster

does not "preserve intact" Dr. Webster's work. On the contrary, the motive of the revision was partly *to rid the work of some of Dr. Webster's dearest peculiarities as a lexicographer.*

Fowler reported the comments of other scholars who criticized Goodrich's alterations as a departure from "Webster's system":

Others also know that Mr. Goodrich, in the Merriam Dictionary, substituted, to a large extent, his own system for Dr. Webster's. Messrs. SOULE and WHEELER who, in 1861, published a very valuable Manual on English Pronunciation and Spelling, refer to Dr. Webster's edition of 1841 for his system; but to the Merriam Edition for Mr. Goodrich's system.

KLIPSTEIN, an Anglo-Saxon scholar, in a note to his Preface to his *Analecta Anglo-Saxonica*, speaks of the "debt of gratitude which the American people owe to their eminent lexicographer, Noah Webster, for his labors in the improvement of English orthography." .... But he adds: "Since the foregoing paragraph was penned, we perceive that the heirs of Dr. Webster, in republishing his works, have deviated considerably from his principles. They might have added to his system, or even placed the new and the old in juxtaposition with each other, but it is questionable whether they had the *moral right* to alter anything."

Now, I could assure Dr. Klipstein that the "heirs" of Dr. Webster had very little to do with the alterations of Dr. Webster's system, contained in the Dictionary published by the Merriams, and edited by Mr. Goodrich. Mr. Goodrich was not an heir. The heirs were not guilty of the moral wrong of making the alteration.

As we have seen, Webster had contrived to keep making money out of his spelling book by revising it whenever the copyright was due to expire. In discussions with Fowler, Webster

said that his heirs should pursue the same policy with the dictionaries:

Dr. Webster always spoke with the greatest confidence of the final success of his works, and of the great pecuniary advantages his family would derive from them. When inquired of, as to the effect of the copyright law upon the different members of his family, he said that the same course could be taken with the Dictionaries, that he had taken with his Spelling-book, to keep it in possession of his heirs. As his heirs had the whole right, they could bring out a new edition, with additions, improvements, and in that way keep the work as their own for a long term of years. This, he declared, is the course which he should advise, and the course they naturally would take without his advice.... He repeatedly said to me: "You will, after I am gone, naturally take the same course with the Dictionaries, in the successive editions, which I have taken with my Spelling-book; my family will receive the benefit of my labors for a long time to come. By making improvements in the successive editions, and taking out a copyright for them, they will continue to be the owners of the work."

Ellsworth's insistence that the Merriams should not be permitted to acquire any copyright in Goodrich's revision was prompted by a wish to follow this advice. For the same reason, William was allowed no rights in the pocket dictionary published by Huntington, beyond what he was entitled to by reason of his share in Webster's estate. The *University* edition was registered for copyright "by Wm. W. Ellsworth and Henry White, Executors of Noah Webster, deceased." Ellsworth soon realized, however, that Webster's policy was impossible to implement, due to the peculiar provisions of the 1831 Copyright Act and the lack of harmony among the members of Webster's family. The executors represented Webster's *heirs*, and if they commissioned a new edition and obtained a fresh copyright on behalf of the estate, that would belong to the heirs. The new copyright, however, would cover only the material added to the earlier edition. The rights in the earlier edition, after the first term of copyright, would vest in an overlapping but different set of people — not the heirs but the *surviving children*.

In 1856 and 1857 the *American Dictionary* and the octavo abridgment entered their second terms of copyright. The letters between the family members no longer referred to their rights as "heirs," but to their rights as "renew-

ers." This was doubly bitter for Fowler. He had been able to feel superior to Goodrich because he, through Harriet, had been an heir, and Goodrich was not. Harriet, however, died in 1844, long before the end of the first copyright term, and Fowler therefore gained nothing from the renewals of copyright. Julia Goodrich, on the other hand, was still alive and therefore became a "renewer." Through her Goodrich gained the benefit of the share which had been denied him by Webster's will. When the various copyrights were renewed, the application was in the names of Emily Ellsworth, Julia Goodrich, William Webster, Eliza Jones, and Louisa Webster. The granddaughter, Mary Trowbridge, was so upset at being deprived of the share that Webster undoubtedly meant her to have, that she, or her husband on her behalf, brought an action against the executors. Since the renewal term was a gift from the legislature to the surviving children, it did not form part of Webster's estate, and her action could not succeed.

The royal octavo, according to its copyright notice, was "entered according to the Act of Congress, in the year 1840, by Noah Webster, LL.D. In the Clerk's Office in the District Court of Connecticut." As this was a new edition of an earlier work, that registration protected only the material that Webster had added to the *American Dictionary* of 1828. In the same way, the Goodrich- Webster was "Entered according to Act of Congress, in the year 1847, by George and Charles Merriam, In the Clerk's Office in the District Court of the District of Massachusetts." Ellsworth may have believed that the matter added by Goodrich was not entitled to copyright protection, but there was no way in which he could stop the Merriams applying. After the publication of the Goodrich-Webster, the surviving children or their spouses patched up their differences sufficiently to agree to divide the benefit of the copyright renewals equally, so that each would get a share, whether or not they survived until the renewal dates. The Merriams then negotiated with Ellsworth, Goodrich, Henry Jones (husband of Webster's daughter Eliza), William, and the executor White (representing the interests of Louisa), for the right to publish the big dictionary during the "renewal term." An agreement was reached. William's copy of the contract is in the New York Public Library, and it shows that he

was originally to be paid 60 cents per book, but later agreed to accept $950 a year instead. The Merriams also acquired the renewal term in the *Elementary Spelling Book,* which made Cooledge very cross.

The copyright notice in a Goodrich-Webster quarto printed during the renewal term (after 1856) lists three separate registrations, which between them record the development of the book. The third one covers the bulk of the work: It is the registration by the "renewers" in 1856, which secured the continuation of Webster's original 1828 copyright. Then there is the registration by Webster of the royal octavo in 1840; and, covering the latest amendments by Goodrich, the Merriams' registration in 1847. During the renewal period from 1856 to 1870, the Merriams paid royalties only to the renewers, but the inclusion of the 1840 registration acknowledges that they were using the material that Webster had added to the *American Dictionary* in the royal octavo. The first term of copyright in that material did not end until 1868, and those rights still belonged to Webster's heirs or their successors, not to the renewers. Fowler, in other words, was entitled to some payment through most of the renewal term. The Merriams knew this, but decided to ignore it. They thought that he was unlikely to sue, and that if he did he would not be able to prove much damage. Mary Trowbridge was in the same situation. She would have done better if she had sued the Merriams rather than her grandfather's executors.

20. Ogilvie's *Imperial Dictionary*, 1850

The publication of Webster's *American Dictionary* in America, in 1828, was followed by a slightly modified English reprint, edited by E. H. Barker, in 1831-32. The print run in England, 3,000, was actually higher than the 2,500 of the first American edition. Barker removed the word *American* from the title, but Webster's eccentricities and Americanism remained, despite which the book sold fairly well in England. This was because it filled a need. Johnson's dictionary had been a conservative work when it was issued seventy-five years earlier, and it had not been significantly updated since. Todd's contribution was to add older words rather than newer ones, and he did not introduce any sort of technical vocabulary. Most other post-Johnson dictionaries were derived from Johnson's in one way or another, with compilers adding their own varieties of pronunciation or spelling. Walker, as we have seen, wrote in his Preface that he had "scrupulously followed Dr. Johnson," whose dictionary had been "deemed lawful plunder by every subsequent lexicographer." Perry's 1805 *Synonymous, Etymological, and Pronouncing English Dictionary* said on its title page that it was "Extracted from the Labours of the late Dr. Samuel Johnson." Richardson, of course, owed no debt to Johnson, but his was not really a useful dictionary at all, and it certainly did not provide a serious British competitor to Webster.[1] To some, however, it was a source of shame that the leading dictionary of the English languge was the work of an American, and the need was felt for a British work. There was a gap in the market, and into that gap hopped the one-legged lexicographer, John Ogilvie.

In considering the influence of Webster's *American Dictionary* outside the United States, Leavitt says that Webster was "increasingly the arbiter of definitions in British life," until the appearance of Ogilvie's *Imperial Dictionary* in 1850, "itself largely indebted to the American source."[2] The extent of Ogilvie's debt to Webster is something we shall shortly discover. For lovers of lexicographical lore, and Webster-watchers in particular, the *Imperial Dictionary* is a source of rare delights.

In 1838, John Ogilvie was employed by the Scottish publishers Blackie & Son to prepare an abridgment of Webster for the British market. After working on this for some months, Ogilvie devised a more ambitious plan: He persuaded the publishers to let him expand Webster's dictionary instead of contracting it. The result was the *Imperial Dictionary*, which began to come out in parts in 1847 and first appeared as a complete work in 1850. A supplement followed in 1855.

A more energetic publishers' first concern would have been to incorporate the content of the supplement into the dictionary itself, in any subsequent edition. That is what the Merriams would have done, but Blackie & Son took no such trouble. The supplement continued to appear separately, half at the end of each volume, in the reprint of 1859 and again in 1874. The 1874 edition is particularly good value because it contains all the material of the earlier editions (save that a forbidding portrait of Ogilvie has replaced the previous allegorical frontispiece), together with some splendid plates, and there is a biographical notice as well — an obituary notice, in fact, Ogilvie having died in 1867. The author of this memoir claims that it "cannot fail to be interesting," even though it is "devoid of striking events." Here it is:

JOHN OGILVIE was a son of William Ogilvie, who occupied, as tenant, a small farm, called Knowhead, on the estate of Crombie, in the parish of Marnoch, and county of Banff. His mother was Anne Leslie, a daughter of a farmer in an adjoining parish; and he was born on 17th April, 1797. He was the third of a family of six children, who were taught reading at home, and there also received careful moral and religious training, while made useful in farm labours as soon as their strength permitted. The subject of our memoir, after receiving additional instruction for two quarters at a parish school, went out as a farm-servant, at the age of twenty-one, in the exercise of his employment, he received a kick from a horse on his right knee, the effects of which forced him, after much severe suffering, to submit to the amputation of the leg, above the knee. Unfitted now for farm labour, he supported himself, for a few years, by teaching a subcription-school in a rural district ... often expressing to a friend his regret that he had not got a classical education. Encouraged by this friend, ... he began the study of Latin in June, 1823; and the result showed how disaster or deprivation, instead of damping the ardour of a brave heart, will stimulate its efforts, and accelerate its progress. He continued his school, however, for twelve months longer, getting a weekly lesson from a neighbouring schoolmaster, under whom, resigning his school, he gave his undivided attention to Latin for the next four months. In those sixteen months, under so great disadvantages during three-fourths of them, he made such progress that, in October, 1824, he gained a high bursary at Marischal College, Aberdeen.... It was enough, aided by a little private teaching, to clear off his college and other expenses, and carry him through the usual curriculum of four sessions, until he took the degree of A.M., on the 4th April, 1828, after the statutory examinations. He continued as a private teacher in Aberdeen, till the 13th May, 1831, when he was appointed teacher of mathematics at Gordon's Hospital, in that city, as the result of a comparative trial with several other candidates, whose qualifications were above the common standard. The lame peasant lad having thus fought his way to a comfortable position in society, could employ his leisure hours in those occupations to which his bias directed him, and in which he could win emolument as well as literary distinction....

In the year 1836, while Messrs.Blackie & Son were publishing an improved and annotated edition of Stackhouse's History of the Bible, some contributions were sent by Mr. Ogilvie, which were of such a suggestive and satisfactory character, that he was requested to continue his communications; and when the work was completed, in the year 1838, the publishers entered into an arrangement with him to prepare an English dictionary for popular use. This publication was to be mainly an abridgment of Webster's dictionary; but after many months had been expended in the task, it became evident both to editor and publishers, that a more ample work than any abridgment could produce was required. The great and acknowledged desideratum of the day was a complete English and technological dictionary, and nothing less would have proved satisfactory. In consequence of this conviction, the work already done was laid aside, and Mr. Ogilvie commenced anew upon a greatly enlarged and more comprehensive plan. The result of ten years' unremitting labour and research was the "Imperial Dictionary, English, Technological, and Scientific." In recognition of the great merits of the Imperial Dictionary the Senatus Academicus of Marischal College, Aberdeen, conferred upon Mr. Ogilvie the degree of LL.D., on the 15th January, 1848. The success of this work, and the direction it had given to his studies, was naturally followed by other cognate productions, in which he was employed during the rest of his life, comprising the long period of thirty years. During the earlier part of it he spent as much time upon these philological occupations as was consistent with his duties in Gordon's Hospital; and after his retirement from that institution, his whole time, with that of several assistants, was devoted to the work in question....

He remained in office in Gordon's Hospital till the month of July, 1859, when he got a retiring allowance of £60 a year. In his situation of teacher, he acquitted himself so satisfactorily, that, a few months after his retirement, he was presented, by a number of those who had been his pupils, with a substantial token of their gratitude. During his long tenure of office, not only his zeal as a teacher, but his quaint sayings and caustic jokes, had won upon their esteem. On the 15th of November, 1842, he married Miss Susan Smart, daughter of a farmer and grain merchant near Stonehaven. By her death, on the 20th May, 1853, he was left with two daughters and a son, who still survive. He was a man of very retiring manners, yet he was distinguished by his social qualities in company, though sometimes thought misanthropical by those who did not know him, or were unable to appreciate his dry humour. With his life of intellectual toil is also to be taken into account his health, which had never been vigorous after the accident already referred to, and the fact that for many years before his death he was almost blind. In recognition of the boon he had conferred on the nation at large by the eminently useful character of his literary labours, an application was made by his friends to obtain for him a pension on the civil list; but although the application was made by leading men of all sects and parties, it did not meet with the response which might well have been expected. After his death, a similar application, similarly supported, and with the same disappointing result, was made in favour of his daughters, who were left with a very defective provision for their support. He was seized with typhoid fever in the midst of his literary labours, and after two months of suffering died at

A portrait of John Ogilvie from Volume I of Ogilvie's *Imperial Dictionary*.

Strawberry Bank, Aberdeen, on the 21st of November, 1867, aged seventy years.

There, then, is John Ogilvie. The loss of his leg rendered him unfit for farming, and he turned to teaching as an alternative source of support. In leaving the farm for the schoolroom, he was following the path that Webster himself had trodden some forty years earlier. Webster, too, would not have hesitated to bring himself to the attention of a publisher by sending unsolicited contributions "of a suggestive and satisfactory character" when he had something to say on the subject of someone else's book. Unlike Webster, Ogilvie remained a teacher until his retirement at the age of 62, which was some years after the publication of the *Imperial Dictionary* and its supplement. Throughout the material time, therefore, he was working on the dictionary only in his spare time. Another, and a more important difference is that Ogilvie had absolutely no training, experience or preparation to equip him with the skills of the lexicographer. The *Imperial Dictionary* was his first book of any kind. Apart from his suggestive contributions to Stack-

house's *History of the Bible*, his only earlier writing was some poetry, such as *Imitations of Horace in the Scottish Garb*, and even his biographer described him as "a fourth-rate poet." One must suppose that the biographical notice was intended to show him in the most favourable light possible, but the author's honesty compelled him to concede that Ogilvie was "sometimes thought misanthropical by those … who could not appreciate his dry humour." His picture, facing the title page of the dictionary, shows him as he might have looked when a student arrived late during one of his lectures.

From the moment that Ogilvie stopped working on just another Webster abridgment and decided to produce "a complete English and technological dictionary," his aim was to offer the market something clearly bigger and better than Webster. This is the message conveyed by the title. Webster's was still, at that stage, *An American Dictionary*— Ogilvie's was to be *The Imperial Dictionary*. Nothing parochial here — this was the dictionary for the empire on which the sun never set. The Merriams came gradually to the same idea; their first Webster, the 1847 Goodrich revision, still had "American" in its title (except in England, of course), and so did the Webster-Mahn of 1864. In 1890, Webster became for the first time "International." When Ogilvie began his task, the current Webster was still the first edition, published in America in 1828 and in London in 1831. The original plan was to prepare an abridgment of that one, corresponding, perhaps, to the abridgment carried out by Worcester in America. Webster's own second edition of the main work, the royal octavo, came out in 1841, and that was the one that Ogilvie mainly used. Goodrich's revision, the first published by the Merriams, was issued in 1848, too late to influence the main *Imperial Dictionary* but in time to be useful for the supplement. Ogilvie's aim, as expressed in the 1860 Preface, was "to keep the field against American Dictionaries which are introducing into this country vitiated forms of orthography, and many undesirable novelties of speech." The "American Dictionaries" he was referring to were Webster's. Webster himself would have denied that his tinkering with the language was either

undesirable or novel, but he would have been delighted with the acknowledgment that his dictionary was making an impact in England.

For a number of years previous to 1839, Ogilvie tells us, "a great revolution had been taking place in the English language." Old words had gone out of use or had acquired new meanings, and new words had been introduced. A new English dictionary was required. With admirable frankness, he describes the method by which he simplified the task of providing one:

In order to carry into effect the great object above specified, in the most eligible manner, and to avoid the immense labour and long delay which an entirely new compilation would necessarily involve, it appeared advisable to select some appropriate existing Dictionary as a *basis*, without, of course, interfering with copyright. Fortunately, on this point no difficulty was experienced. The American Dictionary of Dr. Webster presented itself as being by far the most suitable for the purpose. In its etymologies, its copious vocabulary of English words, and its clear and accurate definitions, it stood unrivalled. Its high claims were universally recognized throughout the United States; and in this country too, where it had obtained a pretty wide circulation, it was acknowledged to be superior to all other English dictionaries.

Let us pause for a moment to reflect that, as a starting point for the practice of Ogilvie's labour-saving lexicography, Webster's dictionary was the only candidate. Ogilvie had to use an American dictionary, because only in America could he find a suitable dictionary of the English language that was not protected by copyright in England. In 1839, Webster's was the only large-scale American dictionary; Worcester's *Universal and Critical Dictionary* was not published until 1846. Ogilvie's pious claim that "of course" he would wish to avoid "interfering with copyright" is so much sanctimonious humbug. What he wanted to avoid was copyright interfering with him. "Fortunately, on this point no difficulty was experienced" because Webster's work, first published in America, did not enjoy copyright protection in England.

Having thus far praised the good qualities of Webster's dictionary, Ogilive now has to expose its shortcomings:

But notwithstanding the recognized excellence of Webster's Dictionary, it fell short in several important respects of the standard aimed at in the IMPE-

RIAL DICTIONARY. Having been produced expressly for the people of the United States, it contained many words, terms, significations, modes of speech and of spelling, and allusions to customs peculiar to the United States, and not recognized in this country. It also contained not a few English words, which though current in the States, had become obsolete in the mother country. Its grand defect, however, lay in the technological and scientific departments, and in the entire want of illustrative engravings. Many thousand technological and scientific terms were awanting, while in those given, the explanations in many cases were either inaccurate or too meagre.

The editor's great task, therefore, in preparing the IMPERIAL DICTIONARY, was to subject Webster's Dictionary to a thorough revision; to alter, emend, modify, curtail, or add, wherever it was found necessary; to correct objectionable orthographies; and to free it from Americanisms, or at least to distinguish such. More especially his labour consisted in superadding to Webster all the principal technological and scientific terms which he had omitted, or which had been introduced since his time, collecting them from the best and newest sources, and by explaining them as clearly as possible, and calling in the aid of diagrams and engravings, to bring them within the grasp of the non-scientific reader. On the whole, the new matter thus superadded to Webster's Dictionary amounts to nearly one-fourth of his entire work. To Webster's addition of 12,000 words to Todd's Johnson, a further addition has been made of at least 15,000 words, terms and phrases; and this number has been still further augmented by 20,000 in the SUPPLEMENT, thus rendering the IMPERIAL DICTIONARY far more extensive in its vocabulary than any of its predecessors.

Generally speaking, the IMPERIAL DICTIONARY aims at containing all purely English words, and all words not English which are in ordinary use, together with the principal technical and scientific terms in present use, and such as are to be met with in works not purely scientific. More particularly, this Dictionary has for its object—

1. To comprehend all the words contained in Johnson's Dictionary, with the additions of Todd and Webster, and words selected from the other standard Dictionaries and Encyclopedias, together with many thousand words and terms in modern use, not included in any former English dictionary.

2. To exhibit the etymologies of English words, deduced from an examination and comparison of words of corresponding elements in the principal languages of Europe and Asia....

Surely that last bit seems familiar? "An examination and comparison of words of corresponding elements in the principal languages of Europe and Asia" sounds very much like

Webster's great trek through the dictionaries of all the languages of the world that he had been able to teach himself to read. His magical mystery tour through the history of language, from God and Adam chatting in the Garden of Eden, by way of the earlier Noah and his linguistically significant sons, spreading westward across the world through Europe to England, and from England to America. And there it is, in Ogilvie's *Imperial Dictionary*— practically the whole of Webster's weird and wonderful Introduction. Ogilvie even included Webster's paragraphs on orthography, despite the fact that he was going to remove Webster's un-English spelling from the dictionary. It would not have been so bad if Ogilvie had reprinted the Introduction, unaltered, as Webster's Introduction, in Ogilvie's edition of Webster's Dictionary, but he did nothing of the sort. In the earlier editions of the *Imperial Dictionary*, Ogilvie was said to be the "Editor," but later this description disappeared and the book became *Ogilvie's Imperial Dictionary*— and in neither form was it acknowledged to be an edition of Webster. Furthermore, Webster's Introduction, which was by far the most personal part of his book, the part he had created entirely himself, and the part which he believed to contain his major contribution to philological learning, was not reprinted without alteration. Throughout, Ogilvie changed Webster's "I" to "we," and "my" to "our." By this simple device, he laid claim to all of Webster's research. Here is a sample. First, Webster:

In the course of my investigations, I very early began to suspect that b,f,p,c,g and k, before l and r, are either casual letters, introduced by peculiar modes of pronunciation, or the remains of prepositions; most probably the latter. I had advanced far in the Dictionary, with increasing evidence of the truth of this conjecture, before I had received Owen's Dictionary of the Welsh language. An examination of this work has confirmed my suspicions, or rather changed them into certainty.

Change "my" into "our", and the passage will be found to refer to Ogilvie's Dictionary, and to Ogilvie's nonexistent team of researchers. This is how Ogilvie printed it:

In the course of our investigations, we very early began to suspect that b,f,p,c,g and k, before l and r, are either casual letters, introduced by peculiar modes of pronunciation, or the remains of preposi-

tions; most probably the latter. We had advanced far in the Dictionary, with increasing evidence of the truth of this conjecture, before we had received Owen's Dictionary of the Welsh language. An examination of this work has confirmed our suspicions, or rather changed them into certainty.

That is thoroughly dishonest. There is no reason to believe that Ogilvie had ever seen Owen's Welsh dictionary, and it is unlikely that he was even able to read the Arabic, Syriac, Ethiopic, Chaldee and Hebrew characters that Webster mastered with so much labour, and sprinkled with such enthusiasm through his Introduction. The one language we know Ogilvie to have studied is Latin, yet he copied Webster's obvious misprint when he wrote "thus *ad* in Latin becomes *f* in affero." In the 1847 Webster, "*f*" was corrected to "*af*," but Ogilvie had copied the Introduction from the 1841 edition, and he did not correct the mistake even when it was put right in Webster.

According to the biographical notice, the *Imperial Dictionary* was published in parts, beginning in 1847. It was not completed until 1850. Those dates are interesting, when one considers that Ogilvie's honorary LL.D. "in recognition of the great merits of the Imperial Dictionary," was conferred on him by Marischal College in January 1848. The decision to award the degree must have been taken some time before that, when only a small proportion of the work had been published. Why did he get the degree? Surely not as a reward for a few pages of definitions. If the first part of the *Imperial Dictionary* to be published was the Introduction, Ogilvie was given a doctorate because he republished Webster's research as if it had been his own.

In the remainder of the *Imperial Dictionary* Ogilvie did, as he promised, add a lot of technical stuff to Webster, but aside from leaving out many of the quotations, he took scarcely anything away. He usually changed Webster's spelling into standard English, but did not always remember to make consequential alterations. *Dulbrained*, for example, he changed to *dullbrained*, but he did not move it — it stayed in the alphabetical list before *dulcet* and *dulcimer*. Some American references were translated also, so that in Webster's example of *eastward*: "New Haven lies eastward from New York," Ogilvie substituted "Edinburgh" and

"Glasgow." Otherwise, Webster's definitions and etymologies were largely unchanged. Because Webster said that the fruit of the avocado pear was insipid, Ogilvie thought so too. Webster found custard to be "an agreeable kind of food," and Ogilvie agreed with him. He also repeated the description of the comet of 1769, which Webster was rather proud of having seen (at the age of 10), only changing Webster's spelling of *opake, vapor* and *center* in the definition and leaving out the words "which I saw." Ogilvie was not born until 1797.

Of *cut*, both Webster and Ogilvie write "I have not found the word in any of the Gothic or Teutonic languages"; this statement was true in each case, no doubt, but one must question whether Ogilvie had conducted much of a search for it. Similarly, both say of *cloud*, "I have not found this word in any other language." I could multiply such examples by the hundred, but it is not necessary to do so; it must already be manifest that Ogilvie's experiencing no difficulty in the matter of "interfering with copyright" does not indicate any unwillingness on his part to plagiarize, but that he prudently copied a work that was unprotected by copyright in the market in which his book was to be sold.

In 1850, when the *Imperial Dictionary* was first published as a complete work, it was in competition with the Goodrich-Webster of 1847. At the end of the Webster were a number of more or less useless tables, exhibiting the correct pronunciation of Scriptural, Classical and Modern Geographical Names. To help with the Modern Geographical, there were also Rules for the Pronunciation of the Principal European Languages. These were prepared under the direction of Professor Noah Porter of Yale and were his first contribution to the Webster dictionaries.[3] None of those tables had been in the earlier Webster dictionaries that Ogilvie had ransacked, and not having them placed the *Imperial* at a disadvantage. Blackie & Son received letters suggesting that they should provide similar addenda. What were they to do?

None of Ogilvie's criticisms of Webster's Dictionary applied to those tables: They contained no objectionable orthography, they needed no illustrative engravings, and they had no technical or scientific omissions, having no technical or scientific content at all. Blackies

popped them into their Supplement without having to alter them in any way.

Before we leave Ogilvie, we must look at his pictures.

The ILLUSTRATIVE ENGRAVINGS form a peculiar and important feature of this Dictionary — a feature in which it stands altogether unrivalled. In selecting the illustrative figures, the greatest care has been taken to secure perfect accuracy — a work of no small difficulty, when the number of authorities consulted and the variety of the subjects are taken into account, and when it is remembered that different authorities, expecially writers on the natural sciences, often describe the same thing under different names. The Engravings, scattered over the pages of the Dictionary and Supplement, are above TWO THOUSAND FIVE HUNDRED in number.

There are, indeed, a great many engravings "scattered over the pages" of the *Imperial Dictionary*. Some of them are useful to clarify definitions; others are quite unnecessary for that purpose; all are crisp, clear and attractive. The 1874 edition also has, towards the beginning of each volume, a number of full page plates which are really rather handsome. They are curiously and satisfactorily varied. In Volume I we find Anatomy in two plates — a skeleton, and a gentleman with all his muscles exposed. There are separate pages of Archaeology, Birds, and Fish. There is a Fortress, with instructions on siege warfare, and a variety of Guns. There are Insects, and a Lighthouse in section and in plan, with illustrations of lighting apparatus. The magneto-electric light was thought likely to supersede all other methods of lighting, but the French were still burning olive oil. In Volume II, the plates include Mollusca, Palaeontology, Reptilia and Amphibia, and a Ship, first showing its spars and standing rigging, then in full sail. There is an Iron Ship also, and a magnificent sectional drawing of "Her Majesty's Screw Steam Ship of War, Duke of Wellington, 131 guns." Finally, there are Steam-Engines, Stationary and Locomotive. I would unhesitatingly agree with Ogilvie that "The ILLUSTRATIVE ENGRAVINGS form a peculiar and important feature of this Dictionary."

We have seen Ogilvie's technique in the verbal part of lexicography; it would be interesting to know whether he had an equally efficient way of gathering illustrations. The idea for the 1874 pictorial section (and even some of the

plates) may have come from later Webster dictionaries, and I would not be surprised to find that he made wholesale raids on illustrated textbooks of one sort or another, but I am not sufficiently familiar with the field to be able to identify them. The only source I can immediately recognize is Bewick's *Quadrupeds.*

If Webster had lived to see the *Imperial Dictionary*, he would no doubt have been very upset. In reality, however, Ogilvie only did to Webster, rather more blatantly, what Webster had done to Johnson. The basic principle of Ogilvie's labour-saving lexicography was expressed by Webster himself, in the Introduction to the *American Dictionary*. He was writing about Johnson's dictionary, and Johnson's name is the only word in this passage that I have changed:

A considerable part of [Webster's] Dictionary is however well executed; and when his definitions are correct and his arrangement judicious, it seems to be expedient to follow him. It would be mere affectation or folly to alter what cannot be improved.

This sort of lexicographical "following" is something we have met many times before. Ogilvie followed Webster rather more closely than Webster had followed Johnson, but the reason for the following was the same in each case, and each was as justifiable as the other.

After Ogilvie's death, the *Imperial Dictionary* was revised, and considerably enlarged, under the editorship of Charles Annandale. The result was a fine general purpose English dictionary, in four volumes. When the Century Publishing Co. of New York decided to publish its own dictionary, it wanted to use Annandale's Ogilvie as a basis, and obtained permission from the publishers to do so. This had the curious result that some of Ogilvie's borrowings from Webster's royal octavo recrossed the Atlantic, and became part of the *Century Dictionary*. Knowing the history of the *Imperial Dictionary*, the Century Company asked the Merriams for permission to use this material, which the Merriams granted. This is recorded in a little notice in the *Century Dictionary* that only makes sense to those who know the story of Ogilvie:

By permission of Messrs. Blackie & Son, publishers of The Imperial Dictionary by Dr. Ogilvie and Dr. Annandale, material from that English copyright work has been freely used in the preparation of THE CENTURY DICTIONARY, and certain owners of American copyrights having claimed that undue use of matter so protected has been made in the compilation of the Imperial Dictionary, notice is hereby given that arrangement has also been made with the proprietors of such copyright matter for its use in the preparation of THE CENTURY DICTIONARY.

The secretary of the Century Company at that time, and later its president, was Webster's great-grandson, William Webster Ellsworth, who refers to these matters in his literary reminiscences, *A Golden Age of Authors*. [4] He says that the company's original intention was that "the plates of the Imperial should be Americanized," but later they changed their plans, and finally made no use of it at all.

In asking the Merriams' permission to use their material, the Century Company was just being polite. The Merriams would have had no right to complain if the Century Company had chosen to copy the whole of Ogilvie's Dictionary, because the Webster dictionary that Ogilvie had plundered was by then out of copyright. In any case, why should the Merriams mind? Their current edition was then *Webster's International Dictionary* of 1890, from which practically all traces of Webster's work had been removed. They had nothing to fear from anything in the *American Dictionary* of 1841.

21. *A Gross Literary Fraud Exposed*, 1853-54

Worcester published his second dictionary, *A Universal Critical Dictionary of the English Language,* in 1846. It was substantially larger than his first one. Indeed, his Boston publishers contrived to issue it as a quarto, by providing unusually wide margins around the printed text. With more conventional margins, it was a large octavo, matching very closely the size and weight of the Webster octavo abridgment that Worcester himself had prepared.

Any lexicographer other than Worcester would have felt free to make use of any and all earlier dictionaries in compiling his own. Worcester, however, had been deeply wounded by the attacks on him and on his first dictionary in the Worcester *Palladium* in 1834 and 1835, and he did not want to risk the same thing happening again. In the Preface to his 1846 dictionary, he made clear exactly what use he had made of Webster this time:

A considerable number of words have been taken from several English dictionaries, particularly those of Ash, Richardson, and Smart. With respect to Webster's Dictionary, which the Compiler several years since abridged, he is not aware of having taken a single word, or the definition of a word, from that work, in the preparation of this; but in relation to words of various or disputed pronunciation, Webster's authority is often cited in connection with that of the English orthoepists....

The Merriams would seem to have inherited Webster's distrust of Worcester, and in September 1846 they sent a copy of his dictionary to William, with a letter inviting him to examine it:

You will notice Worcester's remark that he is not conscious of having drawn a word or definition from Webster. Incredible as this might appear, if on examination there is apparent ground for believing it

true, it will indicate at once the propriety of our respecting his rights, which we should certainly wish to do.

William's examination supported Worcester. His reply to the Merriams is dated September 15, 1846:

I have for some days been collating Worcester.... In the examination of his work, I am astonished at the extent and character of his omissions — & am gratified that the diffference will be so much in our favor. This fact alone seems to indicate that he can not have borrowed very largely from us — And when in addition to this, we consider the meagerness of his definitions, it does not strike me that we have much to fear from him....[1]

In subsequent discussion in the press of the relative merits of the Webster and Worcester dictionaries, it was never suggested that Worcester had borrowed from Webster. In any case, Worcester himself took very little notice of the press comment at that time, because he was unable to read it. As he later wrote:

There has been, as I have understood, considerable controversy relating to the Dictionaries in the newspapers and literary journals, particularly in the city of New York; but it took place when I had little use of my eyesight, and I have seen little of it. While my Dictionary was passing through the press, one of my eyes became blind by a cataract, and not a great while after, the sight of the other eye was lost in the same way; and though my eyesight has been in some measure restored, yet for a great portion of the time since its failure, I have been able to do little or nothing as a student....

Worcester's publishers at this time were the Boston firm of Wilkins, Carter & Co. Not long after the 1846 dictionary came out, they received an inquiry from a London publisher, Henry

Bohn, who said that he would like to publish it in England. A friend of theirs, a Mr. James Brown, was going to Europe early in 1847, so they authorised him to negotiate with Bohn (or with any other London publisher who might be interested) for a reprint of the book. Brown returned with a letter from Bohn containing proposals that Wilkins & Carter accepted, and they accordingly sent a set of the stereotype plates for Worcester's dictionary to London. The plates would be delivered to Bohn as soon as he made the first payment.

After shipping the plates, they waited to hear further from Bohn, but nothing came. By the next year, they were somewhat impatient and wrote to him urging him to complete their agreement. Bohn wrote back saying that he was sorry the plates had been sent. Wilkins & Carter heard a rumour that might explain Bohn's reluctance to proceed with the publication of Worcester: It was said that he had become interested in the sale of Webster's Dictionary. Several more letters passed, but with no result.

In the autumn of 1849, more than two years after the plates had been sent, Mr. Carter himself went to Europe for his health. He hoped also to see Bohn and come to some arrangement with him, but he was not well enough to manage this. Then in the summer or autumn of 1850, Bohn wrote to Boston again, asking at what price Wilkins & Carter would sell him the plates. Wilkins named a figure, Bohn paid, and finally he took delivery of the plates. Carter was then in Italy, but he must have passed through London on his way home, for when he arrived back in Boston in the summer of 1851, he had with him a copy of Bohn's reprint of Worcester's dictionary. For the most part, it was the same as the Boston edition, having been printed from an identical set of plates. In the title page and the Preface, however, significant alterations had been made. The title page described it as "A UNIVERSAL CRITICAL AND PRONOUNCING DICTIONARY OF THE ENGLISH LANGUAGE: INCLUDING SCIENTIFIC TERMS, COMPILED FROM THE MATERIALS OF NOAH WEBSTER, LL.D. BY JOSEPH E.WORCESTER." Webster's name was written bigger, bolder and blacker than Worcester's. The Preface had suffered a number of minor changes and one major one. The minor changes were of an editorial sort, such as

altering the spelling of *labor* to *labour* (except for one that was missed) and shortening it a bit by pruning odd words here and there. Also the date of the Preface was changed from "July 1846" to "July 1849." The major change was the omission of the whole of the passage quoted above, in which Worcester denied having taken any words or definitions from Webster.

Wilkins and Carter could be in no doubt that if he saw this dictionary Worcester would be very distressed. It had been bad enough when Webster had accused him of using Webster's materials in his first dictionary. This was much worse, for the title page of his own book contained an admission of the same wrongdoing, substituted for his denial in the Preface. Then Wilkins and Carter asked themselves, what would be gained by showing it to Worcester? Nothing could now be done to stop its distribution. Worcester did not even know that his dictionary had been reprinted in London, so he was not going to ask to see a copy. Would it not be kinder to keep it from him? That was certainly the easiest thing to do, and it is what they did. They put their copy in a drawer and hoped that nobody else in America would discover what Bohn had done.

It was a forlorn hope. In 1852, one of the Merriams was on a book-selling tour of Britain. In a bookshop in Alnick, Northumberland, he asked the proprietor, "What dictionary do you sell?" "Webster's," the man replied — but what he produced was a copy of Bohn's Worcester. It was labeled on the spine "Webster's and Worcester's Dictionary." In London, the book was widely advertised as "Webster's Dictionary ... enlarged and revised by Joseph E.Worcester."

When Worcester was able to read again, one of the first things that caught his eye was an advertisement in an English journal by which he was considerably puzzled. It was, he said, "an advertisement of a Dictionary published in London, in the title of which my name was connected with that of Dr. Noah Webster, in a way that I did not understand, and could not account for." Then, not long afterwards, he saw a letter from G. & C. Merriam in the *Boston Daily Advertiser* of August 5, 1853, that made the meaning of the advertisement all too clear. It included these paragraphs:

Mr. Worcester having been employed by Dr. Webster or his family, to abridge the American Dictionary of the English Language, some years afterwards, and

subsequently to Dr. Webster's death, in presenting to the public a Dictionary of his own, of the same size as the Abridgment prepared by him of Webster, says in his Preface, that he 'is not aware of having taken a single word, or the definition of a word' from Webster in the preparation of his work.

Now mark this fact. An edition of Worcester's Dictionary has recently been published in London, and sought to be pushed there, in which the paragraph we have cited is carefully suppressed, and is advertised as 'Webster's Critical and Pronouncing Dictionary, &c.,' enlarged and revised by Worcester.' On the title-page Webster is placed first, in large type, and Worcester follows in another line in smaller type; and the book is lettered on the back, 'Webster's and Worcester's Dictionary'!

"This," said Worcester, rather mildly, "was new and surprising to me; for I did not know that my dictionary had been published in London." He went to John Wilkins' office in Boston, seeking more information. Mr. Wilkins was not available. Three or four times Worcester called. Eventually Wilkins had to see him, and admitted that he not only knew about the Bohn edition, but for two years had had a copy of it. Clearly he did not want to be present when Worcester examined it, since he did not take it out of the drawer and give it to him, but said that he would send it round to Worcester's address. Worcester saw the book for the first time on August 23, 1853. The following day he wrote to Wilkins, setting out the facts in so far as he knew them. His letter concluded:

I would now ask, what is to be done in this matter? You will not suppose that I ought to feel satisfied to have it remain uncontradicted; yet I am very averse to appear before the public in any controversy relating to a publication of my own. You are aware, as well as other persons who have been concerned in publishing works which I have prepared for the press, that my habit has been to leave my books to the management of the publishers, without defending them from any attack, or doing any thing to injure any works that may come in competition with them; nor do I wish to deviate from this course.

As I have no pecuniary interest in the London edition of the Dictionary, I think I am entitled to be protected from being injured in this manner; and as you have made the contract, if there has been one made, with the London publisher, I must call your attention to the subject and I do so in full confidence that you will wish to have the matter set right, and have no wrong done to any one.

Truly yours,
J.E.WORCESTER

Wilkins replied a week later, giving an account of his late firm's dealings with Bohn (which I have described above) and explaining his reasons for not having told Worcester about it before:

You may well think it strange that I did not at the time call your attention to the subject of this literary imposition; but as I did not see any means of remedying the evil, and knowing that the condition of your eyes was such that you could make but little if any use of them, I did not feel in haste to trouble you with a knowledge of it. I have, however, never seen any notice of this spurious publication in this country, until you called my attention to one. Had any such notice met my eye, I should certainly have deemed it my duty to call your attention to the volume brought home by Mr. Carter.

Had I leisure to narrate the details of our business transaction with Mr. Bohn, I think it would appear to be, on his part, as commercially dishonorable, as this literary enterprise is fraudulent and disgraceful.

Your obedient servant,
JOHN H.WILKINS.

Worcester had written to Wilkins "in the full confidence" that he would "wish to have the matter set right." Wilkins, however, suggested no means of doing this, nor is it easy to see what he could have done. There were, in reality, two separate matters causing Worcester concern; one in Britain, the other in America. The first, and underlying one, was the publication of his dictionary in London with its title page and Preface "remodelled." Nothing was ever done about that. The "fraud" Worcester went on being printed in London for another ten years. I have a Scottish copy, identical to the Bohn imprint, save that it does not have the word "Universal" in the title, and it is labelled *Webster's Dictionary* on the spine, with no mention of Worcester at all. It was published in Glasgow by "William Collins, Publisher & Queen's Printer," in 1862.

The other matter, which was of more direct and personal concern to Worcester, was, in his words, the fact that "the publishers of Webster's Dictionary are endeavoring to make use of this dishonest proceeding of the London publisher to my injury...." There was something he could do about that—which was to make sure that everyone he could reach should know the true facts. He wrote a pamphlet, *Literary Fraud Exposed*, which was distributed by his new

publishers, Jenks, Hickling & Swan. It set out all the history given above, with a copy of Worcester's letter to Wilkins, and of Wilkins' reply. In addition, Worcester corrected certain factual inaccuracies which had been both in the Merriams' letter to the *Boston Daily Advertiser* and in some of their advertising circulars. For example, he was not, he said, "employed by Dr. Webster or his family to abridge the American Dictionary"; he was employed by the publisher, Sherman Converse. He also retold in an appendix the events of 1834-35, reprinting all the letters that had been exchanged in the Worcester *Palladium*, in order to make it clear why he had deliberately refrained from using any of Webster's materials in his later dictionary.

This initiated a barrage of pamphlets involving, on the one side the Merriams (*A Gross Literary Fraud Exposed*), and on the other, Worcester's publishers, supported by Sherman Converse, with poor old Worcester as pig-in-the-middle. Worcester's publishers described Webster as "a vain, weak, plodding Yankee, ambitious to be an American Johnson, without one substantial qualification for the undertaking." The Merriams replied that Webster's reputation was so high that Worcester's dictionary could only be sold in England by attaching Webster's name to it. Jenks, Hickling & Swan countered that nobody in England had heard of Webster and that Webster's name had been attached to Worcester's excellent dictionary in England as a way of creating a reputation for Webster. On the contrary, said the Merriams: Webster's dictionary was so highly regarded in England that Ogilvie's *Imperial Dictionary* had been based upon it.

Sherman Converse came into the controversy to support Worcester against the Merriams. It must be admitted that he was prejudiced and bitter, watching others reaping a rich harvest that he had sown. He had invested a lot of money printing the 1828 quarto, but it could not be profitable because Webster insisted on selling it for $20 and had undertaken not to stereotype it. Now the Merriams were doing very nicely selling a stereotype edition for $6. Converse had paid Worcester $2,000 to prepare the octavo abridgment, but he no longer had the right to print that one either, and it was making a tidy profit for Goodrich and for N. & J. White. Those profits should have been his.

Converse said that it was he, not Webster or Webster's family, who had employed Worcester to abridge the *American Dictionary*. He said that he had undertaken the abridgment entirely at his own risk. The Merriams replied that he had been acting as Webster's agent, and that Webster had agreed to contribute $500 towards Worcester's fee out of his royalties on the octavo.

The Merriams claimed that Worcester had been influenced by Webster toward Webster's manner of spelling; the dictionary that Worcester edited in Philadelphia had used Johnson's orthography, but after he worked on the Webster octavo he had adopted some of Webster's reforms. Worcester replied that he had used Johnson's spelling on the publisher's instructions (he was, after all, preparing an edition of Johnson's dictionary), and that when working on Webster's octavo he had actually taken out some of Webster's reforms. If anything, the spelling in Webster's dictionaries was gradually getting closer to that favoured by Worcester.

The Merriams denied that they had ever suggested that Worcester was a party to "the London Fraud"; Worcester denied that he had said that they had suggested it. The Merriams said that he had said it, or at least implied it.

There were other charges and counter charges that need not be further ventilated. For a year, in 1853-54, the pamphlets whizzed to and fro, mostly missing the point, if there was one. Nobody ever believed that Worcester himself was in any way a party to the "London Fraud," nor was that what worried him. What really upset him was the suggestion that perhaps it wasn't a fraud at all. The Merriams' initial letter contrasted the denial in Worcester's Boston Preface of any borrowing from Webster, with the admission in the London title page that his dictionary was "compiled from the materials of Noah Webster." They implied that the London title page cast doubt on the truth of Worcester's denial. They continued to suggest that Worcester had something to explain in this area. "Errors in definitions, and in other respects," they said, "into which Dr. Webster was inadvertently led in his first, but corrected in subsequent editions, are found faithfully embodied in Worcester." Since Worcester continued to deny having taken anything from Webster, the Merriams were prepared to concede

that he might have copied the errors from some other dictionary, such as Knowles', that had copied them from Webster, but that explanation, they said, "would show that [Worcester] transcribed blindly, not relying on his own judgment."

If it is true that Worcester's dictionary contained some errors that were in Webster's first edition but which had been corrected in his second, this would seem to be conclusive proof that Worcester was *not* copying from Webster, for he would surely have used the later edition. Such errors might have been taken by Worcester from Webster indirectly — Worcester copying from someone who had copied from Webster — but it is much more likely that Worcester had taken the definitions from the same sources that Webster himself had used. The Merriams would not have wished to suggest that, however, because it implies that Webster, too, had "transcribed blindly, not relying on his own judgment," as indeed he had.

One feels sorry for Worcester, caught up in this unpleasantness, but it is not easy to feel sympathy for either publisher. Their pamphlets are tedious, repetitive, humorless and unattractive, and are increasingly burdened with advertisements and testimonials for their respective dictionaries. The testimonials are from presidents of colleges, statesmen, distinguished scholars and writers, and are either commendatory circulars that such people have been persuaded to sign, or excerpts from letters written in response to being sent a free dictionary.

There is nothing more to be said about the American end of the "gross literary fraud," but the English end warrants more investigation. First, why did Bohn agree terms with Wilkins & Carter for a reprint of Worcester's dictionary, and then apparently change his mind? This may have been because there was at that time a period of antagonism in England toward all American dictionaries, due in part to Harpers' use of the spelling of Goodrich's Webster in their American reprint of Macaulay's *History of England*. A correspondent in England wrote to the Merriams:

I find there is a great prejudice against all American dictionaries here now, & it has been increased very much by the notices of the alterations of Macaulay in the U.S. in the American periodicals — you have no idea how strong the English feeling is on this subject since it has been awakened.

Then, when Bohn decided to print Worcester after all, why did he do it in the form of the "London fraud"? It is not easy to believe (as the Merriams suggested) that Worcester's dictionary could only have been sold in England if it had Webster's name on it. If that were the reason, why use Worcester's name at all? The countersuggestion, that Bohn's title page was contrived by the Merriams to manufacture a reputation for Webster in England, is not convincing either. Webster's quarto was already well known in England. On the other hand, there is something very suspicious in the Merriams' behavior. The rumor that Bohn "had become interested in the sale of Webster's Dictionary" was perfectly true; in fact he was interested in Webster long before he approached Worcester's publishers. E. H. Barker, the editor of the London edition of Webster's *American Dictionary* (described by the D.N.B. as "a classical scholar of greater industry than judgment") had engaged in a series of expensive lawsuits. In the first, which was ten years in preparation, he succeeded in establishing his father's legitimacy. He then failed in an action claiming certain valuable family estates and was ruined. His library was sold, and he was imprisoned for debt. According to the Webster bibliography, Bohn bought the unsold sheets of the dictionary in 1835, and in 1840 he reissued it with his own name as publisher, at the bargain price of £2-12-6d.[2] That was before Webster's second edition, the royal octavo, and long before the Merriams came into the picture at all. Then in 1848 the Goodrich-Webster quarto was issued by the Merriams in America, and Bohn published it in London the same year. This could not have been a pirate edition. It was printed on a genuine set of stereotype plates, and the the Merriams must have supplied either the printed pages, or (more probably) the plates. Furthermore, when Bohn's questionable conduct over Worcester was exposed, it is inconceivable that the Merriams would not have mentioned it if Bohn had issued an unlicensed edition of their dictionary. Bohn, in fact, was the Merriams' licensee in London. In the pamphlet exchanges over the "London fraud," the Merriams never admitted to having had any dealings with him at all, and they never mentioned his issue of the Goodrich-Webster. Somewhere in there,

one smells a rat. It is unlikely that the Merriams would have instigated the fraud, but there was no reason for them to be much upset by it. It gave them some excellent ammunition to use against Worcester in America, and commercially it did them no harm, because when it came out they had no interest in the Webster octavo dictionary. In 1864, Bohn sold the stock, copyrights and stereotypes of his "Bohn's Libraries" business to Bell & Daldy (later George Bell & Sons) and they also became Merriams' distributors for Great Britain and the British Empire.

My own surmise is that, because he was publishing editions of Webster's quarto, Bohn wanted to publish the octavo abridgment of Webster's Dictionary as well, but he could not get it. The copyrights in the quarto and the octavo were still in separate ownership, and Goodrich had his own London publisher for the octavo: Ingram, Cooke, & Co. of 227, Strand. Unable to get the real Webster octavo, Bohn created a convincing facsimile. From the outside, my Scottish "fraud" Worcester looks just like my Webster octavo, save that one is bound in black, and the other in brown. They are otherwise virtually identical in size and appearance, and each has *Webster's Dctionary* in gold letters on its spine. If I am not mistaken, Bohn described his dictionary as "compiled from the materials of Noah Webster LL.D. by Joseph E.Worcester" because he was passing it off, not just as a dictionary by Webster, but as a *particular* Webster dictionary — as the octavo abridgment of 1829, which really had been "compiled from the materials of Noah Webster LL.D. by Joseph E.Worcester."

From an American viewpoint, Bohn might appear to have been little better than a crook. In fact, he was rather a distinguished character. He was one of the most successful London publishers of his time, and a well-known public figure. When he first approached Wilkins & Carter about publishing Worcester's Dictionary, he respected the rights of American authors, but soon afterwards his attitude changed. He gave the reasons for this in a pamphlet describing a public meeting (at which he had spoken) on *The Question of Unreciprocated Foreign Copyright in Great Britain*. The Preface explained the background, and his personal situation:

It is well known that for many years past, all our best books have been systematically reprinted abroad, sometimes in France or Germany, but oftener in America, without consent of the English proprietor, and always at a price which defies competition from those who incur the cost of Copyright. We perhaps should have no right to complain of this, as it is according to the laws of the country where it is practised, and every State must be presumed to know what is best for its own subjects; but it has been assumed, on the other hand, that foreigners, by first or even simultaneously publishing their works in Great Britain, whether resident in it or non-resident, are entitled to the benefit of our statutes, and may therefore claim for themselves, and their assigns, an exclusive Copyright in this country although we are denied one in their own....

In this state of things one or two spirited publishers in the music trade felt justified in printing certain portions of the works of foreign composers which had been published as English Copyright. They sustained several actions successfully, and the judgments and strong opinions pronounced on these occasions by the soundest lawyers, taken in conjunction with the manifest intention of the International Copyright Act, pointed out to others the course open to them to pursue.

At and about this period several of my most popular Copyright books had been reprinted in America to my serious loss, and on the other hand, an American book, Emerson's *Representative Men*, of which I had arranged for the so-called Copyright in this country, was reprinted against me by a London publisher. As the rival printer of Emerson had previously begun reprinting Washington Irving's works, I at once determined on the double retaliation of printing Irving against him, and reprinting American literature generally...

POSTSCRIPT

HENRY G.BOHN, as the Editor of these pages, and largely concerned in the question at issue, thinks it right to assure his American brethren, with whom he is happy to be in constant intercourse, that he is actuated by no other motive than his desire to protect himself against severe and unnatural losses arising from a condition of the law which ought not to exist....

Whenever an International Copyright between the two great countries shall be finally established, he will be found as ready as any one to encourage the literary productions of America by purchasing at its fair value the right of publishing in England.

August 18th, 1851.

Washington Irving, whose works Bohn decided to reprint, had himself spoken in support of international copyright for authors at a dinner given to Charles Dickens at the City Hotel,

New York, on February 19, 1842. Irving summed up the case: "It is but fair that those who have laurels for their brows should be permitted to browse on their laurels."

Not long after the date of Bohn's pamphlet, on November 13, 1851, Robert Lytton Bulwer wrote to his father:

It would be hopeless to get a bill through Congress about International Copyright, unless indeed the authors in England were willing to subscribe among themselves for a certain amount — perhaps ten or twelve thousand pounds, for a sum to buy *the American Congress....*"[3]

While passing off necessarily involves deception of the purchasing public, it is unlikely that this was Bohn's primary intention. He being the sort of man that he was, it is more probable that the publication of the "fraud" Worcester was part of an ongoing battle, either with American publishers generally, or with the publishers of the Webster octavo.

Ingram, Cooke & Co. sought to counter the threat by issuing a warning to the trade, a copy of which appears at the back of their 1853 edition of Webster's octavo:

CAUTION TO BOOKSELLERS AND THE PUBLIC

The publishers of WEBSTER'S DICTIONARY, Royal 8vo, feel once more the necessity of calling attention to the undermentioned NOTICE, as another inferior English Dictionary is being advertised as WEBSTER IMPROVED.

NOTICE. — Webster's Dictionary of the English Language. Royal 8vo.

The Trade is respectfully informed the "WEBSTER'S DICTIONARY OF THE ENGLISH LANGUAGE," Royal 8vo, can only be obtained from the present Proprietors, Messrs. Ingram, Cooke, and Co., no other English House having any interest whatever in this Property.

It becomes necessary to state this fact, as an erroneous opinion is prevalent that "Worcester's Dictionary," which is avowedly a mere compilation from the materials of Webster (see Title of Worcester) is the book announced as published at 227, Strand.

---

22. Thomas Heber Orr and the Process of Primitive Wordgrowth

Ogilvie's *Imperial Dictionary* pretended to be a new dictionary "on the basis of Webster's," when it was really no more than an enlarged and illustrated edition of Webster's *American Dictionary*. Bohn's "London Fraud" pretended to be a Webster, when in fact it was a Worcester. The next one I want to show you is a fake too, but of a rather more subtle sort: It claimed to be a new edition of Webster, "Corrected, Improved and Enlarged," when it was in truth a reprint of Webster with hardly any alterations, *and it was not enlarged at all.* I stress the nonenlargement, because it is the neatest trick in the production of this extraordinary book. It was issued in 1858 by another Scottish publisher, William Mackenzie. Like Ogilvie's publisher, he was free to take advantage of an American Webster because of the absence of copyright protection. The editor of this one was Thomas Heber Orr, who described himself as "Discoverer of the Process of Primitive Wordgrowth," and who was surely the ultimate practitioner of cost-cutting and labour-saving lexicography.

From the outside, this Webster looks really quite handsome. It is in two volumes, fractionally smaller than quarto size, with florid gold decoration on the spines. Volume I has two title pages, which show it (truthfully) to be *Webster's Dictionary of the English Language, Revised and Enlarged by Professor C.A.Goodrich.* That external appearance is only the first of several deceptions, but it is certainly the most fundamental. This looks like a Webster quarto, and from the title page you would suppose it to be the Goodrich revision—the first Merriam-Webster—dated 1847 but still the current edition ten years later. It is not that one at all. At the same time that Goodrich was editing the

quarto for Merriams, he was revising the Worcester octavo abridgment on his own account. This one is a reprint of the abridgment. It is the octavo Webster, swollen by the addition of "An Introductory Essay on the Philosophy of Language and General Grammar," and "A Sketch of the Origin and Progress of the Art of Language," and got up to look like the quarto. If the *American Dictionary* may be said to have fathered the octavo abridgment, so that the Bohn fraud was a Worcester trying to look like the octavo's twin brother, here we have the son, with some padding to make him fatter, dressed up in his father's familiar two-piece suit.

Next, let us examine the claim that it was "Corrected, Improved, and Enlarged," by Thomas Heber Orr. First, consider *enlargement.* I am here concerned only with the dictionary itself, not with the "added matter." The important thing you need to know to understand Mr. Orr's motivation is that he had a set of stereotype plates for printing the Goodrich-Webster octavo dictionary. The cheapest way of printing it was to use those plates whenever possible, and he wanted to save money.

Imagine that he had a plate which would print page 170 of the dictionary, containing all the words from *chirp* ("To make the noise of certain small birds") to *choke-cherry* ("The popular name of a species of wild cherry, remarkable for its astringent qualities"). The word *chloroform* would go on that page. It was not in the 1847 Webster, because chloroform was first used as an anaesthetic in Edinburgh in that very year. As a Scot, Orr would have been proud of that Scottish achievement, and would have been keen to add *chloroform* to the dictionary. But if he did so, the plate for page 170

would have to be remade, which would be a breach of Orr's Cost-Cutting Rule Number One: *The fewer words you add, the more money you save.*

But you may ask whether the addition of *chloroform* to page 170 would not push *choke-cherry* onto page 171, which would push the last word on page 171 onto page 172, and so on. Would not Orr have to remake all the plates from page 170 onwards? Quite right! Indeed, the length of the entry for *chloroform* is such that it would displace not just *choke-cherry*, but the two prededing entries as well — the verb *choke* ("To have the windpipe stopped") and the noun ("The filamentous or capillary part of the artichoke").

Only now is Thomas Heber Orr's true greatness revealed. He did add the word *chloroform* to the dictionary, but his page 170 still starts with *chirp* and it still ends with *choke-cherry*! He achieved this conjuring trick by shortening "Composed" to "Comp" in one definition on the same page (which gained a whole line) and by removing altogether the entries for *chlorophæite*, *choanite*, and *choir-service*, none of which would be missed. This provided just the amount of space needed for the definition of *chloroform*. Cost-Cutting Rule Number Two: Whenever anything is added to a page, exactly the same amount of text must be removed from somewhere else on the same page, so that the layout of the succeeding pages will not be disturbed.

By applying this brilliant but simple rule, Orr maintained the precise pagination of the Webster dictionary. Every page of Orr's Webster starts with the same word, and ends with the same word, as the Goodrich octavo. The defining part of Orr's Webster has, of course, exactly the same number of pages as Goodrich's, because with very few exceptions it was printed from identical plates. Orr's claim to have "enlarged" Webster is particularly cheeky, therefore, because his own ingenious method of saving costs made it impossible for him to enlarge it at all.

What of "corrected and improved?" We can see what corrections and improvements he thought necessary, by looking at the Preface. In it, he complains of several faults in Webster's dictionary.

The high standing in public estimation of WEBSTER'S ENGLISH DICTIONARY induced the present publisher to prepare this edition of that valuable work. With that object in view, he deemed it advisable to adopt the best American edition, and make on it whatever improvements might be requisite.

In the improvements made by us, it has been our study, at the same time to preserve as authentic as possible the edition of Goodrich's Webster, and to give it as correct and mature as our opportunites and position enabled us to do, — in fact to make no alteration that was not decidedly called for; and, on the other hand, to fill up or correct any defect or deficiency that Professor Goodrich, in our position, would have done.

We have taken special care that all the references to etymology should be given with accuracy, all the quotations in Hebrew, Greek, and the other languages having been revised.

That last paragraph is high-grade Orr. He had not revised anything at all in Hebrew, Greek, or any other languages, but who was going to check? This is a particular application of Cost-Cutting Rule Number Three, which is further exemplified in the following paragraph:

Several new terms have been inserted. In the present career of the civilized world, a very few years ushers into our language a number of new words, — the result of the progress of science, the advancement of art, the extension of travel, and the enlargement of commerce. For instance, a *brougham, chloroform, gutta percha*, and *telegram*, are words unknown to Goodrich's Webster, and yet with us they have become household words, and demand insertion in a dictionary.

Orr did indeed clear out some words to make space for *brougham, chloroform*, and *gutta percha*, but, despite its demand to be inserted, *telegram* did not get in. Cost-Cutting Rule Number Three says: It is cheaper to make promises in the Preface than changes in the text.

The next section of the Preface provides further examples of the application of this rule:

Every dictionary leaves some definitions defective, and the defects are seldom appreciated till some person, unacquainted with the usages of the language, and trusting entirely to the dictionary for the value of the terms so defined, are found to fall into error. We may give an instance or two of inaccuracy of this sort, in things well known, and easily understood. The word Macademize is thus defined in Webster:-

"Mac-ad'am-ize, v.t., to cover, as a road-way or path, with small broken stones, so as to form a smooth hard surface."

Now long before Macadam, the road-maker, was ushered into being, road-ways and paths were thus covered, and though often complained of, generally acquired for a time the requisite surface. But what

Macadam advocated, as an important improvement in road-making, was the laying of roads with a sufficient depth of the broken stones, or road-metal, as it is called, the lowest stratum being made of larger and, it might be, softer stone, so as to admit of a percolation or filtration between the stones, for securing the dryness of the road, lessening the necessity of repairs, and also yielding a smooth hard surface.

In the same way, in the third sense of the word Pick, it is stated to be -

"3. Among printers, foul matter which collects on printing types."

But this, by any printer, would be called dirt or foulness; but a pick is a particle of extraneous matter on any printing surface, whether type, stereotype, rule, or woodcut.

Being now familiar with Orr's economical approach, you will not be surprised to learn that, even though he believed those definitions to be wrong, he did not upset his printing plates by changing them. He reprinted the Goodrich-Webster definitions of *macademize* and *pick,* exactly as they appear above. Similarly, later in the Preface he objected to Webster's explanation of the meaning of *porridge* in America, and to the suggestions that *porpoise* and *bridegroom* should be spelled *porpess* and *bridegoom,* but he reprinted all the things he objected to, without any alteration.

That is as far as we need go in pursuit of Thomas Heber Orr as cost-cutting lexicographer. We have not finished with him, however. His most remarkable manifestation is yet to come — as "The Discoverer of the Process of Primitive Wordgrowth." This is a theory so utterly ludicrous that I really suspect that it may have been published as a practical joke, or as a satirical comment on the absurdity of other etymological theories. The Preface explains that it is offered as a substitute for Webster's Introduction:

There was nothing, perhaps, that recommended the American Dictionary to the learned of this country, so much as the fullness of its etymology, and the excellence of its Introduction, where the nature of the derivations of our words, and their relation to the diction of other languages, was handled and illustrated.... In the present edition the Introduction might have been given in full, but for its length and its abstruseness to the mass of perusers, and it might have appeared in an abridged form, but that its desultory nature rendered it extremely difficult of satisfactory abridgment. In these circumstances, it appeared desirable to the present publisher to take a middle course, and adopt as a substitute a bird's eye view of a theory of the primitive structure of language furnished by the editor, and hereto subjoined....

THE PRIMITIVE STRUCTURE OF LANGUAGE

A NEW THEORY OF ETYMOLOGY

In the construction of language certain rules have been followed, the investigation of which has more or less exercised the ingenuity of after ages. Language, like every other structure for human use, is continually during that use undergoing a process of mutilation, or dilapidation, by the hand of time, and as continually subjected to a process of repair by the hand of man. And the rules by which this repair is now effected appear to be simple, and natural, and easy;... if the original plan of construction, or the primitive rules by which it was carried out, could be discovered, a certain and satisfactory means of analysing and tracing the derivation of the roots and main branches of word-growth would be arrived at, — an instrument furnished, whereby not only much in the dead languages would be rendered more strikingly clear, but the meaning of many ancient names, and the working of several antique usages brought to light, whence many a lost or obliterated point of ancient history might be recovered.

By "looking narrowly to the grammar of the dead languages — the Gothic, the Sanscrit, the Hebrew, the Greek, the Latin — and observing the way in which their chief parts are built up," Orr claims to have discovered the primitive rules by which one word is formed from another. The essence of the system is that you start with a given word, and, by making some small addition or alteration to it, you create another word which is its opposite, or is in some other way related to it. Orr's first examples are these:

The derivative connection is shown in the form of the word, by an expression of negation added to the word whence it is formed, as: —

King,	Baron,	With,
ex-king.	baron-*ess.*	with-*out.*

One does not need to be a student of Sanscrit to spot that the two words in each of those pairs are related, though they are not precisely opposites.

Some of Orr's connections are a lot more obscure. His next rule tells that "in the earliest times," you got from one word to its opposite by adding a consonant on the beginning:

The derivative negation was made in the earliest times by prefixing one consonantal letter, such as n,m,s,v, or t. Thus:-

AY, yes.   HE, the high sex,
NAY, *not yes.*   SHE, *not he,* the *lower* sex
ITER, eater salt, — common salt used to food.
NITER, *not iter,* not eating salt

To make it easier to change one word into its opposite by prefixing a consonant, it is permitted to respell either or both of the words. By this means it can be shown that *cider*, a type of drink, is the opposite of and is derived from *eider*, a type of duck. You might suppose that it was the first letter that had been changed, but no; the "derivative negation" was made by prefixing an *s*. This is how it happened:

IDER, or EIDER, eater, fine for eating, delicate as food, especially applied to a species of duck.

SIDER, or CIDER, *not ider,* or an eatable thing, but *drink*, good for drinking.

Next, Orr tells us that, instead of putting the added consonant at the beginning of a word, you can put it on the end. With a little more creative misspelling (but not the same misspelling as last time), this enables him to derive *citron* from *cider* (and therefore, at one remove, from *eider*):

CIDER, or CITER, *not an eater* (eating) apple, but a *drinker* one.

CITERN, or CITERON, or CITRON, *not a cider apple,* but still a *drink* one.

Since it is also permitted to change one word into its opposite by adding a consonant in the middle, or by changing a vowel, the system is wonderfully flexible. *Fee,* meaning "bound" or "engaged," is the opposite of *Free*. If you misspell *feast* ("*a social eating*") as *fist*, it is at once obvious that *fast* ("*not a social eating, a re-*

fraining from eating") is its opposite and was derived from it.

Here are some of Orr's more playful fancies:

BATTER, *flour beat up with water.*
BUTTER, *not batter,* but yet a *stuff beat up.*

BATCHER, *a baker, one that manages a batch.*
BUTCHER, *not a baker,* but *one that supplies material for bake-meat.*

BATCHER, *one that manages a batch.*
BOTCHER, *one that does not manage a batch.*

Orr assures his readers that these ridiculous rules "form the basis of the new etymology, are applicable to all languages, so far as has been seen, and promise to elevate derivational philology into a science. The theory of derivation by a contrast in the meaning of words arising from the change of a single letter, is a very remarkable phenomenon. Though it has been under our attention for several years, it is only of late that we have found out some of its richest workings and rarest capabilities."

The last rule that Orr explains is said to be "of very general use." It enables you to create both nouns and verbs by adapting one of the words in a phrase. First, nouns:

The *gait* distemper, The *gait* animal, The *park* animal,
     gout   goat   pork

His final series of transformations does the same thing for verbs. It is the end of his essay, and I believe he meant it to be read as a message:

I *think* you kind,
I *thank* you.

I *winder* from my path,
I *wander.*

I *wander* in amazement,
I *wonder.*

I have *maist* (old word for most) needs to go
I ..... *must* .... go.

23. Webster's *Pictorial Edition* and Worcester's *Dictionary of the English Language*, 1859-60

During the 1850s, it became increasingly obvious that the etymological basis of Webster's *Synopsis*, and therefore of Webster's Dictionary, was unsound. Webster had scorned the theories of the German scholars, Bopp and the brothers Grimm and Schlegel, but their work had proved to be more solid than his, and the Merriams came to realise that a dictionary built on the sand of the *Synopsis* could not withstand the waves of progress. If their slogan "Get the Best" was to remain credible, Webster's etymology would have to be removed from Webster's Dictionary. Who could they employ to do the job? Since they themselves wanted to get the best, and since all the best English etymologists seemed to be Germans, they hired a German. He was Dr. C. A. F. Mahn of Berlin, and in 1854 the Merriams arranged for him to undertake the entire revision of the etymology, for their new edition of the *American Dictionary*.

When this was announced, it was taken by Webster's critics as yet another sign that there would soon be little that was actually Webster's work left in Webster's Dictionary. This point was made most clearly in correspondence in 1859 in *The Home Journal*, a New York magazine edited by George P. Morris (known as "General" Morris from his rank in the militia) and N. Parker Willis.

Morris was not thought to be sympathetic to Webster's system.[1] Knowing this, his friend John Cotton Smith had some years earlier sent him a copy of a little story that had been written by Smith's great-uncle, "Governor" Smith, on the flyleaf of one of his Webster dictionaries. It was a story designed to display a variety of Webster's peculiar spellings. Governor Smith is someone we have met before — he was Juliana's brother Jack. It is curious to think that the letter to Morris was written from the Smiths' house in Sharon, where, 74 years before, Webster had conducted his school. Webster was then not long out of Yale, had not even started to compile his spelling book, and was teaching his pupils to spell after the fashion of Johnson's Dictionary. This is the letter that Morris received:

Sharon House, June 10th./55

My Dear Gen[1]

I send you "the Bible by Noah Webster" — which I found in our Library — Also the specimen of Webster's orthography which I copy from the fly Leaf of his folio Dictionary, where it is in Governor Smith's hand writing — and is entitled

"A specimen of Webster's orthography (in part) selected from his various dictionaries, five in number, and no two alike —

A *groop* of *Neger wimmen* black as *sut* were told to *soe* and hold their *tungs*; but *insted* of *soing* they left their *thred*, regardless of *threts*, and went to the *theater* — where they saw as *grotesk* an exhibition as you can *imagin*, to wit, a *Porpess*, a *Zeber*, and a *Lepard* from an eastern *iland*; also a *ranedeer*, a *woodchuk*, a *racoon*, a *weesel* and a *Shammy*. Likewise a *gillotin*, a *chimist* with specimens of *granit*, and a *hucster* with his *cags* and *fassets*, and above all a *Specter* rising from a *sepulcher*, a most *redoutable fantom* full seven feet in *highth*, his *color* of *ocher*, a *hagard* face, eyes without *luster*, a *lether* cap *crouded* with *ribins* and *fethers*, a *somber cloke*, an *opake scepter* in one hand, a *marvelous saber* or *cimetar* in the other; and with these *accouterments* he *vanted* his *valor* and *thretened* to *massacer* every *hypocrit* and *libertin* present. Whereat the *neger-wimmen* were frightened and ran home — But for this *hainous misbehavior* their *steddy superior*

290

being at no loss to *determin* on the proper *disciplin*, in his *suveran* pleasure tied them up by the *thums*, and with the *vigor requisit* to punish such *maneuvers* denied them their *Maiz* and *Melasses!*" ...

Mrs. Ford says that this letter shows "that old friends and classmates may in later life grow as wide apart in sympathy as the Poles," [2] but the fact that Jack Smith satirized Webster's spelling eccentricities in private shows nothing of the sort. If there was a divergence of views, the movement was on Webster's side, for it was he, not Smith, who changed his way of spelling. Smith (who was not Webster's classmate) must nevertheless have taken a continuing interest in his old friend's publications, or he would not have had five different Webster dictionaries and a copy of his Bible. The "various dictionaries," are likely to have been the *Compendious* of 1806, the quarto *American Dictionary* (1828), the octavo and *Primary School* abridgments (both 1829), and the 1841 royal octavo. The qualification "no two alike" is true of these, but it suggests a greater randomness than is actually apparent. The greatest number of eccentric spellings is to be found in the 1806 dictionary (some given as alternatives), and Webster discarded many of them progressively as the years went by. The only emphasized words that are not in the *Compendious* in Smith's spellings are *woodchuck, raccoon, chemist, haggard, ribbon, massacre* and *sovereign*, which have those conventional spellings. *Shammy* appears in *shammy-lether*, but the animal itself is spelled *chamois* or *shamois*. The *American Dictionary* of 1828 has all the eccentric forms that are not in the *Compendious* (sometimes as alternatives), but by then some of the 1806 eccentricities had disappeared. In particular, by 1828 the silent *e* had been restored to such words as *imagine, libertine, determine*, and *requisite*. Goodrich, of course, by his instructions to Worcester, had reduced the impact of the oddities in the octavo abridgment.

When it was announced that Mahn was going to remove Webster's etymologies from the dictionary, an article appeared in *The Home Journal* for March 1859, suggesting that such of Webster's eccentric spellings as remained should go too:

WEBSTER'S DICTIONARY

The very title of this dictionary, ("An American Dictionary of the English Language,") is provocative of controversy. It is an assumption of originality and of superiority on the part of the author, which could not escape dispute on either side of the Atlantic. And, indeed, a warfare has followed the publication of the work, exceeding, both in intensity and duration, almost any strife in the annals of bibliography.

We are not about to take part in the strife, however, for sundry good reasons. In the first place, all has been said that need be said. The arguments have substantially exhausted the subject; and we are free to confess that the points taken against Webster's peculiarities have been forcibly presented, and have not been answered. Certainly, then, there is no occasion for us to interfere.

Our present purpose is to *state the case* in a manner somewhat different from anything we have hitherto seen, and leave our readers to judge for themselves of its merits....

Webster's etymologies were not quite so genuine as the author and his friends claimed them to be. They were numerous enough; but they were deficient both in precision and authenticity. The "London Quarterly Review," about the year 1836, effectually disposed of Webster's claims to authority in the matter of etymology. And now, we learn, not confidentially, but as an item of literary news, that a learned German professor has been for years at work entirely remodelling Webster's etymologies, and that the conclusion of his labors will soon be realized in a new edition of the dictionary, with all these changes incorporated into its pages.

This fact is an interesting one; and it encourages us to propose to the enterprising publishers of Webster's book, *one more change*, infinitely less in laboriousness and expensiveness, but not less required by the exigencies of the language. We refer to the orthography.

Webster's orthography has been the stumbling-block of the dictionary through its whole history. That is the feature of the work that has provoked the greatest hostility against it; that is the feature which has rendered the work really and permanently mischievous; and that is the feature for which no adequate excuse can be put forward. That peculiarity has impeded the sale of the work by thousands on thousands of copies; and yet that peculiarity is so insignificant in actual dimensions, that it bears about the same proportion to the whole work as a mosquito bears to the bulk of a man he is tormenting. To exhibit the real magnitude of this *petite misère* before the eyes of our readers, so that they can weigh and measure it for themselves, we will now spread the entire monster in our columns—hands, feet, head, organs and dimensions; and we can imagine their exclamation:—"What! is that all? *That! Has that* made so much uproar in the literary world?"

I.—MISCELLANEOUS

Correct orthography.	Webster's orthography
Axe	Ax
Comptroller	Controller
Contemporary	Cotemporary

Correct orthography.	Webster's orthography
Defence	Defense
Offence	Offense
Pretence	Pretense
Ambassador	Embassador
Gauntlet	Gantlet
Drought	Drouth
Height	Hight
Manoeuvre	Maneuver
Molasses	Melasses
Mould, ing, ed, er etc.	Mold, etc.
Moult, ing, ed	Molt, etc.
Plough, ing, ed	Plow, etc.
Practise, (*verb*,)	Practice
Staunch	Stanch
Ton	Tun
Wo	Woe

Class II contained 28 "WORDS PROPERLY SPELLED WITH TWO L'S, ETC., WHICH WEBSTER SPELLS WITH ONE," from *bevelling* to *worshipping*.

Class III, from *control* to *wilful*, was a list of 10 "WORDS PROPERLY SPELLED WITH ONE L, WHICH WEBSTER SPELLS WITH TWO." Finally, in Class IV, there were 13 "WORDS PROPERLY TERMINATING IN RE, WHICH WEBSTER SPELLS ER." The article then summed up:

This list contains *seventy-two* words, which, with their derivatives, chiefly in Class II., (as *travelling, travelled, traveller*,) may amount to one hundred and forty, in all. Some words may have been omitted; but one hundred and sixty would include every item of Webster's innovation.

We omit such words as *public, music, physic*, etc., formerly spelled with a final *k*; and *honor, favor*, etc., formerly spelled with a *u*, because those two classes of changes have been gradually adopted by good writers in America without any reference to Webster. Webster's friends, indeed, claim these changes as Webster's, but every educated man knows the claim is without the slightest foundation.

The sum of the matter is, that for the sake of doing "some new thing," with one hundred and sixty words, in a dictionary containing *eighty thousand* words, Webster has managed to perplex and confuse the orthography of our vernacular for, (past, present and future,) perhaps, three generations. That is the actual evil he has done. The good he has done, in this behalf, is best expressed by "a figure 9 with the tail cut off."

We have, therefore, a word of advice to the publishers of Webster's Dictionary: while you are about the work of reformation in etymology, which is voluminous, reform your orthography, which is no work at all, for we have here done it to your hand,

without charge. Your book will then deserve the patronage you have so long claimed for it; and we shall be able conscientiously to do what we never yet have done — recommend it to our friends.

That article has the appearance of an editorial, though *The New York Century* of March 26 remarked that it, and many similar articles, "though anonymously published, are known to have proceeded from the pen of Mr. EDWARD S. GOULD." If it was written or provoked by one of the editors of *The Home Journal*, there can be no doubt that Morris was responsible, rather than his co-editor N. P. Willis, but it was to Willis that William wrote to complain. He said that the editorial was

disingenuous. It is so in this respect — that very many of the words enumerated in the list given are not so spelled in any of our books which have for years been offered to the public — for example, *Gantlet, Groop, Melasses, Stanch, tun, Crystalize* &c. &c. and to most of the others both forms of spelling are given. These are not "innovations" of my father, for they were recommended by British scholars long before his earliest publication. Our Boston enemies grossly misrepresent us in a precisely similar way, and these misrepresentations, 'though answered a hundred times, are constantly reiterated — indeed our friends feel that every objection urged in the article today *has* been satisfactorily met again & again.[3]

The "Boston enemies" to whom William referred were the publishers and supporters of the rival Worcester dictionaries. William was there putting forward the standard response to criticism of Webster's spelling, that the obviously unacceptable eccentricities had only been suggested by his father in an experimental way, many years earlier, and that they had long since disappeared from Webster's works. That was not entirely true. Four of William's six examples, *gantlet, melasses, stanch,* and *tun,* were still to be found in the current Webster quarto.

William wrote to the Merriams also, who replied on March 22, saying that they believed it to be Morris, not Willis, who was opposed to Webster. Their letter did not refer to the fact, but they had a printed recommendation of Webster's dictionary from N. P. Willis, on their writing paper:

"Webster's Dictionary" has been my sole authority so long, that to be asked my opinion of it seems like being questioned as to my preference for my own country to any other.

It is one of the Washington-sized glories of our

country, that such a life work as that Dictionary should have been done among us. It has gathered the broken columns of other philologistic temples of our language, and built them into an American Parthenon. We should nationally be proud of it — as, indeed, there is no denying that we are, I believe — and our colleges, literary institutions, and schools, should, with grateful unanimity, avow their honor for it, adopt and cherish it.[4]

A few days later, William saw General Morris in person, who must have given him either a copy of Governor Smith's little story or a list of the italicized words in it, for on April 4, William wrote to Morris:

I will try to answer your queries respecting the list of abominable looking words which you gave me on Sat[y]. There are, I think, *seventy* in all italicized of which only *twelve* are in accordance with our present orthography & three or four of these, as *vigor, color,* &c in accordance with yours. *Forty two* of them are spelled in a manner I never saw before, as *wimmen, neger, sut, soe, lepard, massacer,* &c &c. and if my father ever thus spelled them, it must have been before your day or mine, but I have his edition of 1806 by me to verify my belief that this is pure scandal. Of the twelve first alluded to, the words *Plow/Plough* (the first in the Bible spelling), *Theatre/Theater, Sceptre/Scepter, Centre/Center, Maneuvre/ Maneuver* and others, are given in both forms of spelling. As to *ax* without the *e,* it is thus spelled to perfect the analogy in that entire class of nouns, as *tax, box, fox* &c. As to *melasses,* tho my father preferred this spelling on a/c of its etymology, as well as on the authority of Edwards West Indies, our revised editions for the last 14 years have not so given it, altho Smart the highest, and Clark the latest, British authority so spell the word & give its definition....[5]

The inaccuracies in that letter cannot be explained as mere carelessness. The statement "I have his edition of 1806 by me to verify my belief," clearly implies that William had looked into the *Compendious Dictionary* and failed to find the peculiar spellings in it. If he had not looked there, it was dishonest to imply that he had; if he had looked, it was dishonest to say that those spellings were not there. And *melasses,* as I have said, still appeared in the current quarto.

Meanwhile, the original article had provoked correspondence in *The Home Journal.* The first contributor signed himself "Jonathan":

Gentlemen — I have read with great interest and satisfaction your comments on Webster's Dictionary. The remodelling of Webster's etymologies is "a consummation devoutly to be wished;" yet, the refor-

mation you propose is of far greater importance to the public interest generally. It is much more essential to the people that a correct standard of spelling should be before them, than that the remote etymologies of words should be accurately recorded, in a dictionary. Spelling is a matter of every-day use, while the roots of words are quite beyond, or below, the people's necessities. Therefore, I say, your proposed reformation is altogether the more important of the two.

I was equally astonished and gratified at your list of Webster's peculiarities: astonished that so small a matter, in extent, should have made so much disturbance; and gratified, that the disease could be cured with so little trouble. You are quite right in saying that these peculiarities have seriously impeded the success of Webster's Dictionary. I have no doubt that the copies which would *otherwise* have been sold, might be numbered by tens of thousands; while, on the other hand, those who have bought the book *by reason* of its orthography, may, as you happily express it, be described "by the figure 9 with the tail cut off." The "profit and loss," therefore, of the Webster experiment is all on one side.

One difficulty presents itself in view of these changes; namely, the proper title of the dictionary after the changes have been made. The book, so altered, could hardly be called "Webster's Dictionary:" but that is a matter for the publishers to consider. I hope the two reforms may be speedily and thoroughly carried out; and if the publishers in so doing, find it necessary to "pocket their pride," they will have the substantial consolation of pocketing something else much more available for this world's purposes: to wit, the profit on a largely increased sale of their book.

There is another reason why Webster's publishers should bestir themselves in this matter. WORCESTER'S Dictionary, revised and enlarged, having correct orthography throughout, and being in every other respect the equal of Webster's, and in some respects greatly its superior, is just on the eve of publication; and this work will be a terrible rival to Webster's, if the reforms in the latter are not speedily carried out.

JONATHAN.

William now joined the *Home Journal* correspondence, pointing out that Webster's "peculiarities" could not greatly have impeded the sale of his works, since those works were selling at the rate of 1.5 million copies a year. In any case, said William, the words of disputed orthography amounted to only 42 out of 90,000, and most of those were given both ways. The 1.5 million copies were, of course, mostly spelling books not dictionaries, and the spelling books did not contain Webster's more peculiar

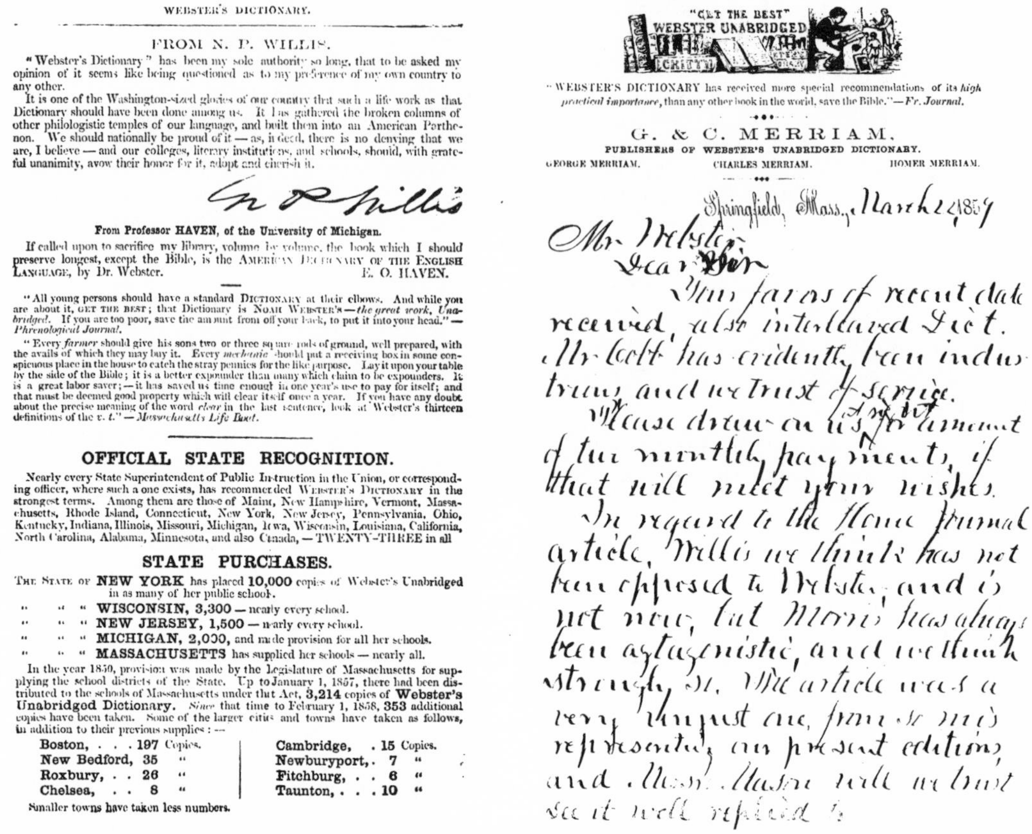

WEBSTER'S DICTIONARY.

FROM N. P. WILLIS.

"Webster's Dictionary" has been my sole authority so long, that to be asked my opinion of it seems like being questioned as to my preference of my own country to any other.

It is one of the Washington-sized glories of our country that such a life work as that Dictionary should have been done among us. It has gathered the broken columns of other philologistic temples of our language, and built them into an American Parthenon. We should nationally be proud of it — as, indeed, there is no denying that we are, I believe — and our colleges, literary institutions, and schools, should, with grateful unanimity, avow their honor for it, adopt and cherish it.

N. P. Willis

From Professor HAVEN, of the University of Michigan.

If called upon to sacrifice my library, volume by volume, the book which I should preserve longest, except the Bible, is the AMERICAN DICTIONARY OF THE ENGLISH LANGUAGE, by Dr. Webster.   E. O. HAVEN.

"All young persons should have a standard DICTIONARY at their elbows. And while you are about it, GET THE BEST; that Dictionary is NOAH WEBSTER'S — *the great work, Unabridged.* If you are too poor, save the amount from off your back, to put it into your head." — *Phrenological Journal.*

"Every farmer should give his sons two or three square rods of ground, well prepared, with the avails of which they may buy it. Every mechanic should put a receiving box in some conspicuous place in the house to catch the stray pennies for the like purpose. Lay it upon your table by the side of the Bible; it is a better expounder than many which claim to be expounders. It is a great labor saver; — it has saved us time enough in one year's use to pay for itself; and that must be deemed good property which will clear itself once a year. If you have any doubt about the precise meaning of the word *clear* in the last sentence, look at Webster's thirteen definitions of the v. t." — *Massachusetts Life Boat.*

OFFICIAL STATE RECOGNITION.

Nearly every State Superintendent of Public Instruction in the Union, or corresponding officer, where such a one exists, has recommended WEBSTER'S DICTIONARY in the strongest terms. Among them are those of Maine, New Hampshire, Vermont, Massachusetts, Rhode Island, Connecticut, New York, New Jersey, Pennsylvania, Ohio, Kentucky, Indiana, Illinois, Missouri, Michigan, Iowa, Wisconsin, Louisiana, California, North Carolina, Alabama, Minnesota, and also Canada, — TWENTY-THREE in all

STATE PURCHASES.

THE STATE OF NEW YORK has placed 10,000 copies of Webster's Unabridged in as many of her public schools.

"   "   "   WISCONSIN, 3,300 — nearly every school.
"   "   "   NEW JERSEY, 1,500 — nearly every school.
"   "   "   MICHIGAN, 2,030, and made provision for all her schools.
"   "   "   MASSACHUSETTS has supplied her schools — nearly all.

In the year 1850, provision was made by the Legislature of Massachusetts for supplying the school districts of the State. Up to January 1, 1857, there had been distributed to the schools of Massachusetts under that Act, 3,214 copies of **Webster's Unabridged Dictionary.** Since that time to February 1, 1858, 353 additional copies have been taken. Some of the larger cities and towns have taken as follows, in addition to their previous supplies : —

Boston, . . .	197 Copies.	Cambridge, .	15 Copies.
New Bedford,	35 "	Newburyport,.	7 "
Roxbury, . .	26 "	Fitchburg, . .	6 "
Chelsea, . .	8 "	Taunton, . . .	10 "

Smaller towns have taken less numbers.

"GET THE BEST" WEBSTER UNABRIDGED

"WEBSTER'S DICTIONARY has received more special recommendations of its *high practical importance*, than any other book in the world, save the Bible." — *Fr. Journal.*

G. & C. MERRIAM,
PUBLISHERS OF WEBSTER'S UNABRIDGED DICTIONARY.
GEORGE MERRIAM.   CHARLES MERRIAM.   HOMER MERRIAM.

Springfield, Mass., March 22, 1859

[handwritten letter:]

Mr. Webster
Dear Sir

Your favor of recent date received, also interleaved Dict. Mr. Cobb has evidently been industrious and we trust of service.

Please draw on us for amount of the monthly payments, if that will meet your wishes.

In regard to the Home Journal article, Willis we think has not been opposed to Webster, and is not now, but Morris has always been antagonistic, and we think strongly so. The article was a very unjust one, from so much represented, our present editions, and Messrs. Mason will we trust see it well replied to —

The Merriams' March 22, 1859, letter to William. Webster Family Papers, Manuscripts and Archives, Yale University Library.

---

spellings. For the more widely accepted variants, however, such as -*er* rather than -*re* in words like *theater*, and having only one *l* in *traveler*, the spelling book was very important. Conservatives might be offended, but those who had become familiar with Webster's spellings when they were children would *expect* to find them in a dictionary.

The next contributor to the correspondence was "Vindex," who summed up Webster's long-term philological achievement:

The short of the case seems to be, that whereas the admirers and supporters of Webster have for many years glorified the American lexicographer for his immortal labors in reforming the English language; and whereas those labors consist mainly in etymologies more numerous than the world ever before saw, in definitions more perfect than the world ever before saw, and in the spelling of "forty-two words" in a style that the world never before saw — it now appears that this herculean lexicographical achievement is mainly discredited by its former trumpeters, and has dwindled down to the aforesaid spelling of

"forty-two words in a dictionary containing *ninety thousand* words;" and that even that spelling is presented, alternatively, in the right way and the wrong way, so that any man may take his choice between them!! *Sic transit gloria Websteri!*

William replied to this, pointing out once again (and again inaccurately) that the spellings complained of were not those of the current series of "Webster" books. Vindex answered that the spellings certainly had been recommended by Webster when he was alive, and if they were now discredited, this merely emphasised how much of Webster's work had been removed. "If, after all this retraction and repudiation, there is anything left of Webster in the dictionary," Vindex asked, "what is it?"

The next person to write to *The Home Journal* was a librarian called Poole, who sent a long article that he called "The Orthographical Hobgoblin," defending the "incorrect" spellings that the *Home Journal* had attacked. He signed himself "Philorthos." *The Home Journal,*

however, had had enough of the subject and rejected the article. Poole then sent it to the *New York Daily Tribune*, where it was published on June 21, 1859, and it was reprinted by Merriams as a pamphlet, which they distributed for advertising purposes.

To assess Webster's responsibility for the way that Americans spell today, we must first discount those changes to the spelling of Johnson that would have happened anyway. As the *Home Journal* article said, "We omit such words as *public, music, physic*, etc., formerly spelled with a final *k*; and *honor, favor*, etc., formerly spelled with a *u*, because those two classes of changes have been gradually adopted by good writers in America without any reference to Webster." That is certainly right. The final *k* has disappeared in England also, which cannot be attributed to Webster. It has even disappeared from the words *frolick, mimick* and *traffick*, where Webster retained it even in the 1841 royal octavo. The *u* was disappearing in America before Webster recommended that it go, and even in England it has gone from some words in which Johnson had it, such as *errour* and *superiour*. I think it likely that England would have gone further in this direction had it not been seen as an American way of spelling and therefore inherently less cultured than the English way. Webster's etymological and phonetic spellings, *bridegoom, nightmar, porpess, iland, highth, drouth, fether, lether, dum, thum, embassador, chymistry, melasses* and the rest, have all been rejected, save that *plow* and *ax* are acceptable alternative spellings (perhaps preferred in America to *plough* and *axe*). The other survivors of Webster's orthography are the *s* in words such as *defense* and *offense*, the omission of *u* from *molt* and *mold*, and the large class of words that may be represented by the single *l* in *traveler*. As Webster himself emphasized, he did not originate any of these, but they were unquestionably part of his system, and without his support they might not have become part of American spelling, or not as soon as they did. They only survived in Webster's works, however, because Goodrich allowed them to do so. As Fowler observed, the 1847 Merriam-Webster contained Goodrich's system of spelling, not Webster's. In Goodrich's own words, "The most offensive peculiarities of [Dr. Webster's] system are laid aside; and there is nothing left which can with any propriety be called *his*."

A significant piece of information contained in Jonathan's letter to *The Home Journal* was the fact that a new, revised and enlarged edition of Worcester's Dictionary was about to be published. The book referred to is Worcester's quarto *Dictionary of the English Language*; it has a copyright notice dated 1859, but the book was not issued until early in 1860. *Appleton's Cyclopædia of American Biography* credits Joseph Worcester with having produced the first illustrated English dictionary, but this is clearly a mistake, since Worcester's quarto appeared ten years after the completion of Ogilvie's *Imperial Dictionary*, and Ogilvie's was by no means the first illustrated dictionary in England. Bailey's Volume II had some illustrations in the text, mainly of a heraldic sort, and the Bailey folios had rather more, as well as some full pages containing multiple cuts. Barlow's dictionary had a number of plates amongst the pages of text, and Barclay had both plates and maps.

Worcester does have a nearer claim to having issued the first American illustrated dictionary. That was certainly what he meant to do. During 1859, his publishers placed advertisements in the press announcing this intention. They included reproductions of pages of the forthcoming work, showing one or two rather dismal little pictures. Sample pages were distributed, and advance subscriptions were taken. The Merriams saw this as a challenge. Webster had fired the first shots at Worcester, the opening salvo in the War of the Dictionaries, twenty-five years earlier. After his death, G. & C. Merriam had become the champions of his cause in the business of the "gross literary fraud." They were quite happy to conduct another campaign. If Worcester was going to produce an illustrated dictionary of the English language, they would produce one too. Furthermore, if they could possibly manage it, the first illustrated American dictionary would be a Webster, not a Worcester. But how could this be achieved?

In 1859, the current Webster was still the Goodrich revision of 1847. Since then, many new words had been collected — words like *brougham, chloroform, gutta percha* and *telegram* — that demanded to be included in the next edition. That edition, the one for which Mahn was revising the etymology, was not

ready, however, because it was not due. The
gathering of words, which was by now contin-
uous, was not just to keep the dictionary up to
date; it was to ensure that a new and revised edition would always be ready by the time the copyright in the old one ran out. There was certainly
no question of preparing the new edition (eventually issued in 1864), providing it with illustrations, and getting it to market, before the publication of the advertised Worcester dictionary.

In fact, there was not time to produce a new
dictionary at all. The most that they could do in
the time was to reprint the 1847 quarto from the
existing stereotype plates, with the collected new
words added as a supplement. Further padding
could be provided by the inclusion of a "Table of
Synonyms" that Goodrich was working on. But
what about the illustrations? Worcester's pages
had them amongst the text; each illustration was
where you would expect to find it — by the entry
for the corresponding word. The Merriams did
not have time to do that, because it would have
meant remaking the whole dictionary, and they
would not have been able to use their existing
printing plates. The best that could be done was
to print the pictures all together in a section of
81 pages, headed "PICTORIAL ILLUSTRATIONS
FOR WEBSTER'S UNABRIDGED DICTIO-
NARY." In an Introduction to the Illustrations,
the reader was told the advantages of this arrangement, without being told the true reason for it:

Another distinguishing peculiarity (and, it is believed, excellence) here introduced, is that the Illustrations in a given department are grouped and presented by themselves. Thus will be found together,
in alphabetical arrangement, the cuts illustrative of
Architecture, Botany, Carpentry, Coats of Arms, En-
tomology, Geology, Geometry, Ichthyology.... The
advantages of this arrangement are obvious, as are
those of having the Illustrations together; since, besides admitting of better mechanical execution, the
consulter has thus placed before him, at one view, the
diagrams or engravings illustrative of an entire department. There is, at the same time, usually appended to the engravings the number of the page
where the verbal definition can be found, under the
appropriate word in the vocabulary; and also in the
body of the work, a star, *, to the words in the vocabulary which are illustrated in the Pictorial department, and even to the particular definition so illustrated, where there are more than one. Thus the
consulter will find little if any inconvenience from
this grouping of the cuts, which has in every other
respect very important advantages.

Goodrich and the Merriams had for some
time been keeping a watchful eye on the
progress of Worcester's dictionary, and their es-
timates of its likely publication date were much
more accurate than those of Worcester's publishers. On January 1, 1858, Goodrich wrote to
William: "From all I can learn, it is not probable that Worcester's Quarto will be out under
two years"— and he was right to within a week.
Towards the end of that year, on December 17,
Goodrich wrote again, explaining in detail the
Merriams' commercial strategy for dealing with
the Worcester threat:

It is wholly uncertain when Worcester's book will be
out. The publishers speak of next May, but in all
probability an allowance must be made of five or six
months. It cannot be sold under about $7.50 at re-
tail. The distribution of the cuts throughout the volume will somewhat increase the expense by requiring the paper to be of a superior order. The plan of
Messrs.G.& C.Merriam, to meet the exigency at the
time of Worcester's appearance, is an able and far-
reaching one. They have employed Sobieski to frame
a pronouncing vocabulary of great names throughout the world. It contains 8,000 articles, and fills
forty or fifty pages. They have had 1500 cuts engraved, classifying the subjects to some extent. These
will occupy nearly one hundred pages of the appendix, and can be printed in a superior style by the use
of appropriate paper. These cuts have references to
the words in the vocabulary to which they belong;
and a mark of reference will be cut into the existing
plates pointing to the fact that the word thus noted
has an engraving to illustrate it. The appendix on
which I have been employed for the last fifteen
months, will probably contain eight thousand articles. It has been much enriched by contributions
from Prof.Dana. My impression is that it will occupy
nearly eighty pages of the Quarto, crowded as com-
pactly as possible, for we shall be much pressed for
room. The printing of the appendix will be soon
commenced. Messrs.Merriams are also very urgent,
that I should enlarge the discriminations of synonyms, as given in the New University, and have this
inserted in this appendix....
    It is the plan of Messrs.Merriams to have all these
things stereotyped by May or June. Then they will let
their editions on hand run down as low as possible,
and issue a new edition of the Quarto with all this
additional matter making a volume of about 1750
pages. They will throw it into market from Maine to
California a month or two *in advance* of Worcester,
with a view to "take out the wind from his sails." I
presume they will sell it at two dollars a copy lower
than his, certainly one dollar or one fifty. They think
that the plates being all together, may be on the
whole an advantage. They will certainly make a

greater show; and the classification of all terms together, say in Botany, Heraldry, Natural History &c. will enable the reader to *compare* the objects more easily. They have undoubtedly gone to great expense in these preparations, and seem determined to fight the battle to the utmost of their strength. The work as here described is expected to be kept before the public only two or three years, and they hope by means of it to continue their hold on the market. In the meantime they wish the revision to be going on, and to commence the printing say within a year or fourteen months after the appearance of the appendix described above.

I have thought you might be interested to learn these details. They may have been mentioned already by Messrs.Merriams; but the whole matter is kept as much as possible a secret. It would be desirable therefore that *nothing of what has here been stated should be mentioned to anyone....*

This was the origin of the *American Dictionary of the English Language,* Pictorial Edition, of 1859. In all subsequent editions, the Merriams put the illustrations beside the definitions to which they belonged, in the conventional manner. The public, however, had found the pages of pictures in the 1859 Pictorial to be the most entertaining part of the book. The "Pictorial department" proved so popular, in fact, that it was retained, in addition to the illustrations in the text, in every American Merriam-Webster unabridged, until 1934.

The Merriams easily won the race. Worcester's quarto dictionary was not delivered to subscribers until early January, 1860.

In matters of disputed pronunciation, Worcester again cited Webster as one of his authorities, as he had done in his first dictionary in 1830, and again in 1846 — after all, Webster's fatuous argument that he should not be cited because he might later change his mind, could no longer be even a possible objection. Remembering all the previous unpleasantness, Worcester was careful to explain in his Preface exactly what use he had made of Webster's works:

In the preparation of this Dictionary, assistance has been derived not only from that of Johnson, but from various other Dictionaries and Glossaries. Several Pronouncing Dictionaries have been used with respect only to pronunciation. In relation to many of the words of various or disputed pronunciation, Dr. Webster's authority is often cited in connection with that of the English orthoepists; and the edition of his dictionary made use of is that of 1841, the latest that was published during the life of the author. With respect to a very few words of doubtful origin, Dr. Webster's etymology is noted in connection with that of other etymologists; but in no case, so far as is known, without giving him credit. In other respects, the rule adopted and adhered to, as to Dr. Webster's Dictionary, has been to take no word, no definition of a word, no citation, no name as an authority, from that work.

As in 1846, the Merriams were not prepared to take that statement on trust, and again they invited William to look into it. The paper on which they wrote to him already incorporated a large advertisement for their "RECENTLY ISSUED" Pictorial Edition:

January 16 1860

Dear Sir

Worcester has made its appearance, and is being delivered to the 6,000 subscribers obtained previous to its issue. The common edition is not yet ready. The vol makes quite a respectable appearance, and we must anticipate it will have a considerable sale. Yet, neither in its literary or material aspect, would it ever have seen the light but for Webster, doubtless — yet probably there may be no open violation of copyright.

On February 4, 1860, they wrote again, promising to send William a copy of the Worcester dictionary. Their letter shows a clear awareness of the extent of Webster's debt to Johnson's Dictionary and other sources, and acknowledges that Worcester was equally entitled to make use of them:

Worcester has made its appearance, and is a large pretentious volume. It exhibits all Mr. Worcester's characteristics — an industrious collection of words and materials — "other men labored, and he entered into their labors." But as a *definer,* he does not, and cannot, come within bow-shot of Webster -

We will endeavor within a day or two to send you a copy by Express within a day or two [sic], that you may see what it is.

Please notice and mark any cases where he seems to have drawn from us, either by literal transcription, or colorable alteration.

We have much, of course, drawn from Johnson and others, to which Worcester has the same right, but *not* the *moral* right, certainly, to absorb, largely, our labors. It will be a matter of curiosity to notice what he has done, although no very practical results may follow. Have you the means of verifying what he actually *has* taken from Webster — and not obtained elsewhere?

The next Merriam-Webster Unabridged, the Webster-Mahn of 1864, contained a definition

of the word *jew,* as a verb, "To cheat or defraud; to swindle." Early in 1872, a Mr. A. S. Solomons complained, and the Merriams replied, "We have ordered the objectionable word to which you refer stricken out entirely, and another word and definition substituted." In a letter to the *Chicago Tribune,* March 13· 1872, the Merriams excuse was that their definition "must have been drawn from Worcester"—a remarkable reversal of Webster's attitude. Notice the word "drawn," meaning taken or copied, both in the letter to William and in the letter to the *Chicago Tribune.* "*To jew*" is indeed in Worcester, defined as "to cheat," and Solomons complained to those publishers also. It disappeared from Webster's Unabridged in 1872 and 1873, but reappeared in 1874 because the Merriams had two sets of printing plates, and had only corrected one of them. The alert Mr. Solomons spotted it, and complained again. The same page of the Unabridged defined *Jesuit* as "A crafty person; an intriguer," which also provoked complaints, but the Merriams resolutely refused to change it.

When the Webster Pictorial Edition appeared, Worcester's publishers must have been vexed that theirs was not to be the first American illustrated dictionary—and what made it worse was that they had brought it upon themselves. If they had only kept quiet about their intentions a little longer, the Merriams would not have been able to beat them to it. At the time, however, there seemed to be no risk. They would have realized that the Merriams would eventually copy the idea, but it would not have seemed possible for the Merriams to get there first. Even if it had occurred to them that the Goodrich-Webster plates could be used if the pictures were put in a separate section, how could the Merriams, in no time at all, find 1,500 pictures suitable to illustrate Webster's Dictionary? Actually, that was the easiest part, because Ogilvie had already done it. Apart from the coats of arms of the American states, practically all the pictures in the Pictorial Edition came from the *Imperial Dictionary.*

The 1864 Webster-Mahn boasted that "an entirely new selection of illustrations has been made for this edition." About half of those came from the *Imperial Dictionary* as well.

So, in the end, we can leave old Ogilvie's soul to rest in peace. He took Webster's words, and the Merriams took his pictures. Quite a fair exchange, really.

24. The Right to Use the Name "Webster"

If one considers Walker to be the leading authority on pronunciation, and Chalmers' abridgment of Todd's Johnson to be the best octavo dictionary for definitions, it makes sense to combine the two. That is what Worcester had been employed to do in Philadelphia in 1828. Webster, however, scorned Walker's pronunciations such as "*egg-yarden*" and "*bensh*." He thought that he was himself the highest authority on orthoepy, and in America his reputation was bolstered by the widespread use of his spelling book. In England he did not enjoy that status. He was regarded as a good man for definitions, but, even in the second half of the nineteenth century, Walker's was still the name to drop in matters of pronunciation. In England also, Webster's works were in the public domain, so any publisher who wanted to put Walker's pronunciation into Webster's Dictionary was free to do so. The man who subjected Webster to this posthumous indignity was the London publisher William Tegg, who in 1866 put out *Walker and Webster Combined*. It was an octavo abridgment of Webster's dictionary, in which "the Definitions of Webster and the Pronunciation of Walker are United." It even had Walker's name first on the title page. If Webster saw it from beyond the grave, his only consolation would have been that Tegg did exactly the same thing to Worcester.

In America, where copyright was maintained in Webster's works, the publication of the Webster-Mahn dictionary in 1864 marked the beginning of a period of peace and prosperity for the Merriams. Some American conservatives continued to prefer Worcester's spelling, and those who bothered to read the indicated pronunciations did not like to be told

(by a German) that the noun *rise* sounds like *rice* (to distinguish it from the verb, pronounced *rize*) or that *squalor* is pronounced *squaylor*, but in all other respects the 1864 Webster was generally considered to be the best English dictionary available. Furthermore, Worcester died in 1865, and the 1860 version of his dictionary was reprinted virtually unchanged for over twenty years. The 1864 Webster Unabridged, by contrast, was a new dictionary when first published, and the Merriams added progressively larger supplements to it, in 1879 and 1884. The latter was timed so that the Webster would not appear out of date when compared with Funk & Wagnall's *Standard Dictionary*, which appeared in 1883-84. Then, in 1890, the Webster-Mahn was replaced by another new edition, *Webster's International Dictionary*, meeting the challenge presented by the *Century Dictionary* of 1889–91.

By this time, the Merriams were in sole and undisputed possession of all the subsisting American rights in the Webster dictionaries. The rights of Webster's children, arising from the renewal in 1856 of the 1828 *American Dictionary* copyright, had come to an end in 1870. The copyright in the original octavo abridgement expired the following year. From the 1847 registration of the Goodrich-Webster onwards, all later rights belonged to the Merriams.

The quarto was the largest in a family of "Webster" dictionaries. Other members of the family were the school dictionaries sold through the American Book Company — *Webster's Collegiate Dictionary*, *Webster's Academic Dictionary*, *Webster's High School Dictionary*, *Webster's Common School Dictionary* and *Webster's Primary School Dictionary*. All were owned

and controlled by the Merriams. They also had the rights in the *Elementary Spelling Book*, selling 1.5 million copies a year. It was published by the American Book Company, but its successive revisions were registered for copyright by G. & C. Merriam, in 1857, 1866, and 1880.

Such comfort and security were too good to last. In 1890, the hissing of an entrepreneurial snake could be heard in the the Springfield grass, disturbing the tranquillity of the Merriams' peaceful paradise, and the name of the snake was Ogilvie.

The earlier Ogilvie, in Scotland, had taken advantage of the fact that Webster's *American Dictionary* was not protected by copyright in Great Britain. This one, George W. Ogilvie of Chicago, noticed that the American copyright in the 1847 Goodrich-Webster expired in 1889. What Ogilvie then published (or supplied to other publishers) appeared under various titles, such as *Webster's Unabridged Dictionary* and *Webster's Encyclopedic Dictionary*, but in all cases the main part of the work was a photolithographic reproduction of the whole of the defining part of the 1847 Goodrich-Webster.

One of Ogilvie's customers was the publisher of a New York-based magazine called *Texas Siftings* which offered a copy of Ogilvie's Webster to anyone who would take out a year's subscription to the magazine, at an extra cost of just one dollar. "HOW IS THIS?" asked their advertisement in a New York paper, and went on to explain how it was:

Recognizing the fact that, from the high character of your paper, its readers must necessarily be of the class that appreciate good literature, we are desirous of having the following offer made to them, and would be pleased if you would publish it in your next issue.

"Texas Siftings" is a national paper, published weekly in New York, contains 16 pages of high class humorous and literary matter, illustrated weekly with 25 to 30 engravings by some of the best artists and cartoonists in the United States. It is too well known to require further description.

Is there a man, woman or student in the United States who can do without Webster's Dictionary?

The annexed cut shows a facsimile of the size of the page of this dictionary. It is bound in leather, printed in the most excellent manner, and beautifully illustrated.

It contains over 1,600 pages, weighs over 9 pounds, has 1,500 illustrations, 15,000 synonyms, and an Appendix of 10,000 new words.

One hundred thousand copies of Webster's Dictionary have been printed for the Texas Siftings Publishing Company, and are now ready for delivery. These books contain every word that the great Noah Webster, LL.D., ever defined, and, in addition to that, they contain tens of thousands of new words that have been invented since Webster produced his Dictionary.

Webster's Dictionary has heretofore been sold for no less a sum than $10 per copy, but, owing to the extraordinary cheapening of paper and wonderful economy in labor connected with the improvements in machinery, that enables publishers to print ten sheets in the same time and at the same cost that they used to print one, we can offer this great and valuable Dictionary at a very much smaller price than it has ever been offered before.

The price of "Texas Siftings" is $4 a year. "Siftings" and this Dictionary, which in itself is worth $10, will be delivered at the residence of any person who sends to us the sum of $5.

To the ordinary reader of this advertisement it may seem rather peculiar that we can afford to do this. Well, that is our business. We think that there are over two hundred thousand people in the United States who would be glad to get Webster's Dictionary, such as we advertise, for $5. We want to catch them, and every one of them will, before they can get a Dictionary, have to subscribe for "Texas Siftings" for one year. They cannot get Webster's Dictionary in any other way. Do you see the point? We may lose a lot of money to get this large number of subscribers, but when we get them we will hold them, or if we don't, the loss will be ours.

Send $5 to "Texas Siftings" Publishing Company, New York, and you will get "Texas Siftings" one year, and also will have delivered at your home, either by mail or express, a copy of Webster's Dictionary.

The text was in a narrow column beside a reproduction of the title page of the $1 dictionary. Most of the title page was an exact copy of that of the Goodrich-Webster, but where the Merriam dictionary might have had at the bottom of the title page:

SPRINGFIELD, MASS.
PUBLISHED BY GEORGE AND
CHARLES MERRIAM,
CORNER OF MAIN AND STATE STREETS

1854.[1]

This one was said to be

PUBLISHED FOR TEXAS SIFTINGS
PUBLISHING COMPANY,
47 JOHN STREET, NEW YORK

1890.

That was all thoroughly, and deliberately, misleading. The *Webster's Dictionary* that had been sold for $10 was not the 1847 Goodrich-Webster at all, which cost only $6. The publication date of 1890 suggested, and was intended to suggest, that what was on offer was the new *Webster*, the *Webster International.* The *Texas Siftings* offer was especially irritating for the Merriams, and even more likely to mislead the public, because it was based on a marketing scheme of their own, and one of which they were particularly proud. In November 1877, Horace Greeley's *Weekly Tribune* had offered a copy of *Webster's Unabridged* absolutely free, to anyone who took out a three-year subscription, at a cost of $10. Since the dictionary alone then sold for $12, this was something of a bargain, and greatly increased the distribution of Webster's quarto dictionaries.

The Merriams had earlier conducted the War of the Dictionaries against Worcester's publishers, by exchange of pamphlets, with vim and vigour. They now turned the same publicity machine with equal enthusiasm against Ogilvie, his customers, and his companies. This time, however, there was an added ingredient: They embarked on a series of lawsuits, spread over more than twenty-five years.

Their cause of action was not copyright, though this fact is sometimes obscured by references to "the copyright in the title *Webster's Dictionary.*" What we are now concerned with is another tort altogether. In American jurisprudence, it is called *unfair competition*; in England it is *passing off.* G. & C. Merriam said that they had for many years been the only publishers of "Webster" dictionaries, having published a great many of them and in many different forms. As a result, the name "Webster" had come to be associated exclusively with their goods and their business: It had acquired a secondary meaning, so that members of the public, seeing a dictionary with the name "Webster" in its title, would assume that it was one of theirs.

The difficulty with that argument was that the words "Webster's Dictionary" were descriptive. They were not, strictly speaking, the title of any book, but the books were known as *Webster's Dictionary*, and those were the words on the spine, even if it said *An American Dictionary of the English Language* on the title page.

The copyright in the book had expired, and the Merriams had therefore to accept that Ogilvie, or anybody else, was free to reprint it. But if the work was in the public domain, that must include the name by which it was known. It was nonsensical to suggest that Ogilvie was allowed to publish the book because it was out of copyright, but had to call it by a different name because "Webster" had become associated with a particular publisher while the copyright was in force.

The Merriams were persistent chaps, but their claim to a monopoly in the "Webster" name was clearly and firmly rejected by judges up and down the United States, over and over again. The first was Justice Miller, in Missouri, on September 26, 1890:

I want to say, however, with reference to the main issue in the case, that it occurs to me that this proceeding is an attempt to establish the doctrine that a party who has has the copyright of a book until it has expired may continue that monopoly indefinitely, under the pretense that it is protected by a trade-mark, or something of that sort. I do not believe in any such doctrine, nor do my associates. When a man takes out a copyright for any of his writings or works he impliedly agrees that, at the expiration of that copyright, such writings or works shall go to the public and become public property.... The grant of a monopoly implies that, after the monopoly has expired, the public shall be entitled ever afterwards to the unrestricted use of the book.... The contention that the complainants have any special property in "Webster's Dictionary" is all nonsense, since the copyright has expired. What do they mean by "their book," when they speak of Webster's Dictionary? It may be their book if they have bought it, as a copy of Webster's Dictionary is my book if I have bought it. But in no other sense than this last indicated can the complainant say of Webster's Dictionary that it is their book. [2]

Thayer J. in the same court, a year later:

I have no doubt that defendant is entitled to use the words "Webster's Dictionary" to describe the work that it is engaged in publishing and selling. Those words were used to describe Webster's Dictionary of the edition of 1847, and, as the copyright on that edition has expired, it has now become public property. Any one may reprint that edition of the work, and entitle the reprint "Webster's Dictionary." [3]

The Merriams' action against *Texas Siftings* came before District Judge Shipman in New York, in March 1892. He followed the earlier decisions which established that "the plaintiffs

are not entitled to an exclusive use of the name 'Webster's Dictionary' upon copies of editions the copyrights of which have expired, for the name is not a trade-mark." [4]

The plaintiffs' attempt to secure monopoly rights in the name "Webster" was described by Justice Miller as "the main issue in the case," but it was not the only issue. The Merriams made various other complaints, with mixed success. They objected to the fact that Ogilvie's "Webster" was of similar size and general appearance to their own, but these features were held to be commonplace. They objected to the use of a picture of an open book as an advertising device, but that was held to be commonplace too. In one important respect, however, the Merriams succeeded. The courts were satisfied that the Ogilvie "Webster" had been got up and advertised in such a way that many customers would be misled. They would buy it believing that it was a new edition, not realizing that it was a reprint of the 1847 dictionary. The court decided that Ogilive and his customers such as *Texas Siftings* were entitled to use the name "Webster" but must take positive steps to distinguish their publications from the Merriams'. This requirement was eventually distilled into a simple disclaimer, which had to appear on the title page of any non-Merriam "Webster" dictionaries, and in advertisements, circulars, notices and announcements referring to them: "This dictionary is not published by the original publishers of Webster's Dictionary or by their successors."

With that as the outcome, both sides could claim to have won. The Merriams had succeeded in establishing that the various defendants had been guilty of unfair competition and were liable to pay damages. The defendants had succeeded also, for they could go on using the name "Webster."

For a time, things went quiet in the law courts, and the Merriams concentrated on publicity. They published advertisements headlined "WEBSTER ANCIENT AND MODERN. DON'T BE DUPED," and a pamphlet, *WEBSTER'S ENCYCLOPEDIC DICTIONARY (SO CALLED). WHAT IT IS, AND WHAT IT IS NOT.* To emphasise the superiority of the current Merriam publication, they were quite rude about the Goodrich-Webster that Ogilvie was reprinting. Goodrich had concealed Webster's personal ec-

centricities of spelling, but the Introduction, embodying Webster's Bible-based linguistic theory, was untouched, and the 1847 etymology was still that of Webster's *Synopsis*. "The etymologies are utterly misleading," said the Merriams' advertisement, quoting the *American Bookseller*. And in the pamphlet they said that "the etymology of the 1847 edition of Webster's Dictionary is not revised, and, of course, is utterly untrustworthy in the light of present knowledge." They also disputed a claim that Ogilvie had made in his Preface, to be "preserving intact the monument of Noah Webster's marvellous genius and industry." The 1847 edition, the Merriams averred, was by no means the work that Noah Webster had left. It was "a revision edited by Dr. Chauncey A. Goodrich, who began the work after Dr. Webster's death. It does not 'preserve intact' Dr. Webster's work. On the contrary, the motive of the revision was partly to rid the work of some of Dr. Webster's dearest peculiarities as a lexicographer."

The lull in the litigation was brought to an end by Ogilivie's publishing, in 1904, a revised version of his dictionary. He called it *Webster's Imperial Dictionary* or *Webster's Universal Dictionary*, and he issued circulars and advertisements that conveyed the impression, by the use of such phrases as "The latest complete authentic Webster's Dictionary," that it was the successor to *Webster's International Dictionary*. The Merriams reacted by sending threatening letters and circulars around the trade saying (untruthfully) that they had the exclusive right to the name "Webster" in the title of dictionaries. This time, two lawsuits resulted. Ogilvie sued the Merriams, and was granted an injunction to restrain them from sending out their circulars. They sued him for unfair competition. Once again, they failed in their attempt to stop him from using the name "Webster," but he was ordered to stop issuing misleading advertisements, and the disclaimer that he was required to put on the dictionaries was revised, the approved form being that quoted above.

In 1905 a new American Trade Marks Act came into force, under which the registration of proper names was permitted. The Merriams registered eight new trade marks and tried yet again to claim a monopoly in the Webster

name. Once again, they failed. In the words of Mr. Justice Day:

The registration of the trade-marks relied upon, having the name "Webster" as applied to dictionaries of the English language as their chief characteristic, was made long after the expiration of the copyright securing to the publishers the exclusive right to publish the Webster dictionaries. After the expiration of a copyright of that character, it is well-settled that the further use of the name, by which the publication was known and sold under the copyright, cannot be acquired by registration as a trade-mark. [5]

Publishing dictionaries in which the copyright had expired avoided infringement, but it had the disadvantage, from a marketing point of view, that the dictionaries one was trying to sell had to be at least forty-two years old. What Ogilvie wanted was a way of copying more up to date books, which would not involve him in copyright problems. The answer that he came up with was exactly what had occurred to John Ogilvie in Scotland, some sixty years before: He would borrow something from the other side of the Atlantic.

In June 1904, Ogilvie formed an Illinois corporation, the United Dictionary Company, with a capital stock of $1500. In January 1905, he sent for a copy of a dictionary published in London by George Bell & Sons, under the title *Webster's Brief International Dictionary*. He had it photographically reproduced, and the United Dictionary Company announced in the *Publishers' Weekly* that it intended to sell the work in the United States. This was particularly cheeky, because George Bell & Sons were the Merriams' London agents, and *Webster's Brief International Dictionary* was for the most part identical to the *Webster's High School Dictionary* that was sold (and protected by copyright) in America. The Merriams immediately sued the United Dictionary Company, claiming that the intended publication would infringe their copyright. Ogilvie's reply was that the book published in England did not have the copyright notice required by United States copyright law; it was therefore unprotected by copyright in the United States. Not surprisingly, this argument did not appeal to an American court which held that the United States law did not have any extra-territorial effect and could not require the inclusion of a copyright notice in books published abroad. The proper notice appeared in copies of *Webster's High School Dictionary* published in the United States, so copyright subsisted in that work, and it would be infringed by the publication by the United Dictionary Company of what was substantially an identical work.

Ogilvie now disappears for a while from the legal record, because in May 1908 his business was ostensibly taken over by one Arthur J. Saalfield, or the Saalfield Publishing Company. It may be that this was an attempt to avoid the injunctions that had been granted against Ogilvie himself and his company, but if so it failed: The court held that as Saalfield was doing exactly the same things as Ogilvie, he should be subject to the same injunctions. The transfer to Saalfield would appear to have been a sham anyway, since it later came out that "the firm of Weed, Miller and Nason, of Cleveland, and George F. Bean, of Boston, Massachusetts, who had appeared respectively as solicitors and counsel for defendant Saalfield in the defense of the suit, were in fact retained and employed by Ogilvie for that purpose and paid by him and acted under his instructions and directions." [6] I shall therefore ignore Saalfield, assuming that Ogilvie continued to be the moving spirit behind the business.

His next choice for transatlantic borrowing was not a copy of a Merriam-Webster. It was the English *Twentieth Century Dictionary* which he put on the market in America in 1907 under the title *Webster's Intercollegiate Dictionary*. The Saalfield Publishing Company also used the titles *Webster's Adequate* and *Webster's Sterling Dictionary* for the same book. In respect of the first of those titles, the Merriams had an additional ground of complaint — it was confusingly similar to their own *Webster's Collegiate Dictionary*. That complaint was upheld by the court, and the Saalfield Publishing Company was therefore subjected not only to the former injunction requiring a disclaimer, but also to a complete prohibition of the use of the name *Webster's Intercollegiate*. [7]

In the same case, the Merriams' lawyers thought up a new line of attack. They had previously failed to prevent the use of the name *Webster's Dictionary* because it was descriptive of the book that the defendant was publishing. It now occurred to them that the defendant could be said to be using the name "Webster"

improperly, because a reprint of the *Twentieth Century Dictionary* was not a Webster dictionary at all. Unfortunately, by the time they thought of that argument, the case against Saalfield had been going on for over four years, and the Court would not allow them to "reshape the litigation" during the hearing of an appeal. They therefore deployed the same argument against Ogilvie's next borrowing, a dictionary published in England under the title the *British Empire Dictionary*. Ogilvie's company, now called the Syndicate Publishing Company, proposed to sell it in America under the title *Webster's Crown Dictionary*.

The resulting judgment is the most interesting in the whole series of cases on the right to use the name, because it examines just what it means to the public when they see "Webster's" on a dictionary. It could not be a matter of content, because *Webster's International Dictionary* was like George Washington's axe [8] — successive revisions over the years had replaced nearly the whole of the original work. The name "Webster" was justified only because the book could trace its ancestry back, through those revisions, to the *American Dictionary* of 1828.

The Merriams, of course, continued to assert that "Webster" meant them and nobody else, but the trial judge, District Judge Hand, was not persuaded:

The complainant brings this suit upon the theory that the book published is in fact not based upon Webster's dictionary at all; that is has no right to be called Webster's Dictionary in any sense; and that it is a fraud to call it such. Indeed, they do not concede that any one has any right but themselves to use the word "Webster's" upon a dictionary, unless it be one of the original dictionaries published by Webster himself, and even in that case they insist that it must be distinguished by the statement that it is one of the original Webster's dictionaries, a fact which would probably destroy any possibility of its sale anyway. Their pretension extends even to the point of forbidding the sale of any dictionary honestly compiled upon Webster's original sources, since they assert that the name "Webster," when applied to any such compilation or abridgment, necessarily implies their own responsible supervision and authorship. I have not, however, the least doubt at the outset in overruling so extreme an assertion as this. It is quite clear that any honest compilation or abridgment at the present time of Webster's work is entitled to describe itself as such, and that the most which the complainant's supposed right could in any case do would be adequately to indicate that a work so described

was not a compilation or abridgment by the original publishers of Webster's Dictionary or their successors. Indeed, it is a preposterous assertion to say that the name "Webster's," as at present used by the complainants themselves, does not indicate to the public mind that their work has some connection with Webster's original work other than that they choose to publish it, or that it need not be the result of a legitimate literary descent from his original. In other words, even though the word indicates prima facie that the book is the complainant's compilation, it also still indicates that it is a compilation with Webster as its original source, and it is in this sense that Judge Coxe spoke when he said that the word had two meanings, a proprietary and a descriptive. Nor is there any inconsistency in such a dual meaning; the word may mean "Merriam's Compilation from Webster" quite as well as "Merriam's Compilation." If it does, it must as well answer to one part of its definition as to another; in short, it must be a compilation from Webster or it is a fraud. I pay not the least attention to those witnesses who say that it means only "Merriam's Compilation." If the name "Webster" has this descriptive significance, it is quite clear that it will also honestly describe any actual compilation from any one of Webster's dictionaries, provided that some suffix be added to distinguish the compilation from Merriam's. The word need not by any means be confined to the original work of Webster himself. Indeed, the only authority which has ever independently given the complainant any trade rights in the name "Webster" itself refused absolutely to forbid the defendant from using the name upon what was in every sense a compilation.

In Merriam v. Ogilive,... Judge Colt says that Ogilvie's work was an enlarged and revised edition of the Webster of 1847. Now the edition of 1847 was not by any means a simon-pure Webster.... it had been revised and enlarged by Chauncey A. Goodrich.... The work which the Circuit Court of Appeals of the First Circuit permitted to bear the name "Webster" had passed through two revisions of one sort or another, and this may be enough to dispose of the assertion that the only work which may be called "Webster" is some book just as it left the hands of Noah Webster....

What is it that they [the public] do mean, either by a Webster's dictionary or a dictionary based upon Webster's? It seems to me that they mean the way the book has been made up more than its present contents, its history rather than its present identity with its source. The word at least denotes what I should call literary descent from Webster's original books (that is, that each book in the series, of which this is the last, was made up by its author with its predecessor before him, only changing the spelling, definition, vocabulary, and the rest as his opinions and learning indicated to him that changes were required to adapt the book to the present); and that this succession goes back without break to some

work by Webster himself. Nor is it indeed possible for the complainants to take any other position than this without putting themselves in the position of foisting upon the public a spurious work. Their own last edition (that of 1909) is a book of almost totally different literary contents from any book with which Noah Webster had anything to do. They have the alternative of accepting the definition of "Webster" as indicating this kind of descent or of maintaining that "Webster" means any work of theirs and has no descriptive significance whatever.... Of course, a "Webster" dictionary must own Webster as its father originally; and in the case at bar, although the heredity of the complainants' 1909 Webster is all that gives it its character as a Webster, yet it still has that character, remote now as the content may be. The complainant is in no position to deny a purely descriptive use of the word to any other dictionary which is as legitimate as its own. The constant iteration that all such are "bogus" or not "genuine" is merely a childish extravagance.[9]

The right of Ogilvie's company to use the name "Webster" thus depended upon its being able to show that the *Crown Dictionary* was descended from a genuine "Webster." Most immediately, it was derived from the *British Empire Dictionary*. Could the *British Empire Dictionary* trace its ancestry back to Webster's work? As it turned out, it could. The immediate parent of the *British Empire Dictionary* was Charles Annandale's 1883 revision of (John) Ogilvie's *Imperial Dictionary,* and the *Imperial Dictionary,* as we have seen, incorporated virtually the whole of Webster's *American Dictionary,* admitting on its title page that it had been constructed "On the Basis of Webster's English Dictionary." By this curious chain of borrowing, John Ogilvie (who died in 1867) came to the rescue of George in 1913, and the Merriams' action against the Syndicate Publishing Company failed.

That decision taught Ogilvie an important lesson: If a dictionary could trace its ancestry back to Noah Webster, it could use the name "Webster's," so long as it displayed the disclaimer "This dictionary is not published by the original publishers of Webster's Dictionary or by their successors." There was no need for him to stick with an out-of-date reprint of the 1847 Goodrich-Webster — he could get his own people to update it. The result was *Webster's Universal Dictionary.* I have an example before me, dated 1936. It has the required disclaimer printed on the front cover of each volume, and

on the spine, and on the title page, so we know that it is not a Merriam-Webster. Its claim to the name "Webster," however, arises from its pedigree, as to which there can be no doubt, since the title page describes it as "The Unabridged Dictionary by Noah Webster LL.D., Edited under the supervision of Thomas H. Russell, LL.D.; A.C.Bean, M.E., LL.B.; and a staff of eminent scholars, educators, and specialists." Some indication of the literary and linguistic skills of this high-powered team is provided by the information on the title page that the book contains "A Comprehensive Addenda of Newest Words." Facing the title page is a truly hideous representation of Webster himself. In the Preface, there is a passage headed "Origin of the Work" which gives a refreshingly honest account of Ogilvie's methods and motives:

The idea which has found embodiment and expession in this new Dictionary was conceived by Mr. George W.Ogilvie ten years ago. By way of practical equipment for the task, he had many years' experience as a publisher of works of reference, the names of several of which are household words in America. Recognizing the opportunity for literary and commercial enterprise in a field wholly unoccupied, and at the same time realizing the vastness and importance of the project, he made arrangements with a view to the completion of the editorial work within as brief a space of time as was consistent with the requisite care and accuracy, the object being to secure uniformity throughout the entire work and to obviate a difficulty often experienced by lexicographers — that of finding the early portions of their work practically out of date before the end was ready for the printer. Thus the final literary labors of preparing this work for the press were compressed into a period of three years, during which comparatively brief time, however, its extensive corps of editors were compelled to strive without ceasing and with the expenditure of much midnight oil.

In the preliminary matter, there is a "Partial List of Reference Works and other Publications Consulted or Used in the Preparation of this Dictionary." It is a very impressive list, extending to almost three pages of small print, with three columns on each page. Let us notice just two of the entries:

Webster's International Dictionary..........................
　　　　　　　　　　　　　　G.& C. Merriam Co.
Webster's Unabridged Dictionary, The Original.....
　　　　　　　　　　　　　　Geo. W.Ogilvie & Co.

What Ogilvie began was merely a reprinting and marketing exercise, and of the most dubious morality. The courts, however, confirmed his right to use the name "Webster," and with that encouragement the business developed into genuine, if undistinguished, lexicography. In the family tree of dictionary descent, the Ogilvie-Webster branch continued to multiply and thrive in parallel, and in competition, with the Merriam-Websters. To the Merriams, the Ogilvie dictionaries bear the taint of illegitimacy, but their descent from Webster, on whichever side of the blanket, cannot be disputed. Indeed, because they have been less thoroughly revised than the Merriam-Webster dictionaries, they have more of Webster in them. The 1979 *Webster's New Twentieth Century Dictionary* in which the "astro-label" definition from the *Lexicon Technicum* of 1704 appears is a direct descendant in the Ogilive line, published by Simon and Schuster. [10]

Before Simon & Schuster, the Ogilvie-Webster dictionaries were published by The World Publishing Company. An examination of their 1957 *Webster's New World Dictionary of the American Language, College Edition* shows how much the Merriam's position had been eroded by the 1950s. It is no longer essential for a dictionary to be able to to show descent from Noah, to justify the use of the name "Webster," on the contrary, this one claims to be "neither an abridgment nor a revision of some earlier work. It is a new dictionary in which every definition has been written afresh...." Its only connection with Webster is that it "derives from the best traditions in British and American lexicography and is based especially on the broad foundations laid down for American dictionaries by Noah Webster."[11] If we go on to read the account of the development of the English Dictionary in the preliminary matter, however, we discover that the "broad foundations for American dictionaries" were not laid down by Webster at all, but by Worcester:

The first American dictionaries were unpretentious little schoolbooks based chiefly on Johnson's *Dictionary* of 1755 by way of various English abridgments of that work.... The most famous work of this class, Noah Webster's *Compendious Dictionary of the English Language* (1806) was an enlargement of Entick's *Spelling Dictionary* (London, 1764), distinguished from its predecessors chiefly by a few encyclopedic

supplements and emphasis upon its (supposed) Americanism. The book was never popular and contributed little either to Webster's own reputation or to the development of the American dictionary in general....

The first important date in American lexicography is 1828. The work that makes it important is Noah Webster's *American Dictionary of the English Language* in two volumes. Webster's book has many deficiencies — etymologies quite untouched by the linguistic science of the time, a rudimentary pronunciation system actually inferior to that used by Walker in 1791, etc. — but in its insistence upon American spellings, in definitions keyed to the American scene, and in its illustrative quotations from the Founding Fathers of the Republic, it provided the country with the first *native* dictionary comparable in scope with that of Dr. Johnson. It was not, as is often claimed, the real parent of the modern American dictionary; it was merely the foster-parent. Because of its two-volume format and its relatively high price it never achieved any great degree of popular acceptance in Webster's own lifetime. Probably its greatest contribution to succeeding American dictionaries was the style of definition writing — writing of a clarity and pithiness never approached before its day....

The first American lexicographer to hit upon the particular pattern that distinguishes the American dictionary was Webster's lifelong rival, Joseph E.Worcester. His *Comprehensive, Pronouncing, and Explanatory Dictionary of the English Language* (1830), actually a thoroughly revised abridgment of Webster's two-volume work of 1828, was characterized by the addition of new words, a more conservative spelling, brief, well-phrased definitions, full indication of pronunciation by means of diacritics, use of stress marks to divide syllables, and lists of synonyms. Because it was compact and low-priced, it immediately became popular — far more popular, in fact, than any of Webster's own dictionaries in his own lifetime.... The first Webster dictionary to embody the typical American dictionary pattern was that of 1847, edited by Noah Webster's son-in-law, Chauncey A.Goodrich, and published by the Merriams.

It is curious to see the old rumor that Worcester's 1830 dictionary was copied from Webster repeated after such a long time. Later in this account, Ogilvie is remembered. He is not generally considered to be a significant figure in the development of the American dictionary, but the larger dictionaries in his own family usually mention him. Here, he comes into the story after the *Century Dictionary,* which was "considered by many authorities to be basically the finest ever issued by a commercial publisher,"

but which had lost much of its popularity because of inadequate subsequent revision:

> The only other new unabridged dictionaries that have appeared in the period are Webster's *Imperial Dictionary of the English Language* (1904), and Funk and Wagnalls *New Standard Dictionary* (1893). The first of these, the only unabridged dictionary ever published west of the Appalachians, was issued in Chicago by George W.Ogilvie, a publisher who carried on his own private guerrilla "war of the dictionaries" against the Merriam Company between 1904 and circa 1917. At the moment, the most important advances in lexicography are taking place in the field of the abridged collegiate-type dictionaries.

That last sentence uses "collegiate-type" as a descriptive expression, showing yet further erosion of what the Merriams had formerly regarded as their own exclusive territory. *Webster's New World Dictionary of the American Language* is of the size and weight of the Merriam-Webster *Collegiate*, but uses the words *College Edition* with impunity, because these have come to be descriptive and commonplace. It does not even have to carry the disclaimer, because there are by now so many non-Merriam Webster dictionaries on the market in America that it can no longer be said that, without a disclaimer, people will assume any "Webster" dictionary to be a Merriam. In fact, things have gone so far the other way that it is the Merriam dictionaries that now bear a disclaimer of any connection with the other "Webster" dictionaries. Here is one from a 1989 paperback, *The New Merriam-Webster Dictionary*:

A GENUINE MERRIAM-WEBSTER

The name *Webster* alone is no guarantee of excellence. It is used by a number of publishers and may serve mainly to mislead an unwary buyer.

A Merriam-Webster® is the registered trademark you should look for when you consider the purchase of dictionaries or other fine reference books. It carries the reputation of a company that has been publishing since 1831 and is your assurance of quality and authority.

The smallest Webster dictionary of all is neither a Merriam-Webster nor an Ogilvie. It is *The Little Webster*, published by the German company Langenscheidt. To a student of the early history of English dictionaries, it is particularly appealing. Inside, it is called the *Lilliput Webster,* and it really is small — no more than 5cm. high. Since the type is not unreadably fine, there is room for no more than a dozen entries on each page. Thus constrained by shortage of space, the editors found themselves forced to return to the seventeenth-century tradition, and publish a "hard words" dictionary:

> It occurred to us that most dictionaries contain a large number of words which are known to the reader and which he rarely needs to look up. In order to gain as much space as possible for words which we felt the reader might really need to look up, we decided to leave out as many words of this simple kind as we could…. The result has been that the "Lilliput Webster" has room to explain an unusually large number of relatively rare and difficult words (more than 7,000).

In 1990, the publishers Random House decided that "Webster's" in the title of an English dictionary was entirely descriptive, and that any English dictionary that did not call itself "Webster's" was at a disadvantage in the marketplace. They retitled their "collegiate-type" dictionary *Webster's College Dictionary*, and in it the word "Webster's" was defined as meaning "a dictionary of the English Language." The Merriams sued, complaining of the combination of "Webster" and "College," and also of the use of a red and white cover, which they said was confusingly similar to the cover of the Merriam-Webster *Collegiate Dictionary*. A jury found in their favor, but the verdict, and the award of $2 million damages, was overturned on appeal in September 1994.

Thus the name "Webster" no longer implies a connection with the Merriam company of Springfield, Massachusetts, nor does it nowadays imply any descent from, or any connection whatsoever with, the works of Noah Webster. The book sold by the American booksellers Barnes & Noble as *My First Webster Dictionary* is their reprint of a book sold in England under the title *My First Oxford Dictionary*. The Barnes & Noble *Webster's New Universal and Unabridged Dictionary* began life as *The Random House Dictionary of the English Language*. I have even seen one "Webster" dictionary in which the name "Webster" only appeared on the dust jacket. "Webster" has lost all distinctiveness and is therefore valueless as a trade mark. But if "Webster" in the title of a dictionary is not an indication of trade source, or of quality, or of content, why do publishers attach the name to

more and more dictionaries? For the same reason, of course, that publishers make all their decisions — because it sells books. The American public *trust* the name Webster, and are more willing to buy a dictionary that has the name on it than one without. No other name or trade mark has achieved that sort of status. It may not be logical, but it is a rather remarkable memorial. In fact, I can think of only two other men who have stood on the soil of the New World who have achieved comparable fame — Columbus, its discoverer, and Washington, its savior. "Webster" is, and will be, the name on its Dictionaries. These three make a Trinity of Fame.

Notes

Preface

1. Boswell's *Life of Johnson,* 5 April 1776.
2. Ibid., late 1748 : "The necessary expense of preparing a work of such magnitude for the press must have been a considerable deduction from the price stipulated to be paid for the copyright. I understand that nothing was allowed by the booksellers on that account."
3. Taken from the 5th edition, 1696. It first appeared in the 4th edition, 1678.
4. The 4th edition.
5. "The Fourth Edition [1703] Improved from the several Works of *Stephens, Cooper, Holyoke,* and a Large MS. in three Volumes, of Mr. John Milton, &c...."
6. From *Memoir of the Author,* in Webster's *American Dictionary,* 1847 "Goodrich" edition.
7. Ford's children were also literary, but it was not a happy family. One son, Paul Leicester Ford, novelist and bibliographer, was a hunchback. In 1902, at the age of 37, he was shot and killed by his brother Malcolm Webster Ford, a magazine writer, who then killed himself.
8. Hereafter cited as Ford.
9. See Ford II, pp. 315, 354.
10. New York, 1953. Hereafter cited as *Letters.*
11. New York, 1975. Hereafter cited as Morgan.
12. 1980. Hereafter cited as *Journey.*
13. op. cit. p. 47.
14. op. cit. p. 34.
15. 1983. Hereafter cited as Monaghan.
16. Hereafter cited as *Noah's Ark.*

Introduction

1. Preface, p. xix.
2. *Freeman's Journal,* 25 April 1787.
3. Ford, vol. I, p.272.

Chapter 2

1. *Lempriere's Universal Biography,* London, 1808.

2. Feb. 21, 1785.
3. This is exactly contemporary with Bailey's definition of Kidnapper as "a Person who makes it his Business to decoy Children or young Persons, to send them to the English Plantations in America."

Chapter 3

1. "Fuliginous ... Pertaining to soot; sooty; dark; dusky." Webster's *American Dictionary.*
2. Reproduced from Starnes and Noyes' *The English Dictionary from Cawdrey to Johnson, 1604– 1755.*
3. In the Preface to *General French and English Dictionary* by A. Spiers, Ph.D.
4. From The Preface to Buchanan's *Essay towards Establishing ... an Elegant and Uniform Pronunciation of the English Language,* 1766.
5. *Grammatical Institute,* Part I, Introduction, p. 6.

Chapter 4

1. From *Origin of the Copy-right Laws of the United States,* in *A Collection of Papers on Political, Literary and Moral Subjects,* by Noah Webster, New York, 1843, pp. 173–174.
2. *Origin of the Copy-right Laws in the United States,* p. 174; emphasis added.
3. Heading added later.
4. *The Art of Reading,* Lecture I.
5. *Lectures on Elocution* &c, p. 258.
6. *Sheridan's Dictionary,* p. 64.
7. *Lectures on Elocution* &c, p. 258.
8. *National Gazette,* Aug. 11, 1792. The pronunciation grawt was usual before what is known as the Great Vowel Shift, but at that time boat,and moat would have been pronounced bawt, and mawt. All those vowels should have shifted together, and it is curious to find grawt surviving.
9. *New York Journal*; Letters, pp. 11-19.
10. From the Preface to *Sheridan's Dictionary.*
11. *Lectures on Elocution,* p. 244.

12. Sheridan follows Johnson's spelling in the dictionary itself, but does not always remember to do so in the Preface. In the very next sentence, he uses the spelling "public," and elsewhere in the Preface and Grammar, one finds "center" (last page of Preface), "Ach and its derivatives, as headach," (p. 21), and "fantastic" (p. 64).

Chapter 5

1. *Travels in North America in the Years 1841–42*, N.Y., 1852, p. 53.
2. Letters p. 355.
3. New York, 1843. Facsimile edition, Burt Franklin Research and Source Works Series #249, New York, 1968.
4. Warfel, p. 58.
5. Avis, p. 22.
6. The "literary gentlemen" were concerned to restrain piracy of Trumbull's *M'Fingal*—see *The Memorial History of Hartford County* by J.Hammond Trumbull (1886) Vol I, p. 157n.
7. Memoir, No. 13.
8. Ford, I, p. 94.
9. Letters, pp. 39–40.
10. This letter is in the manuscript collection of the Library of Congress.
11. 1709, 8 Ann.c.21 in the list of Statutes, but in some catalogues numbered c.19.
12. The provision allowing copyright to a resident who was not a citizen of the United States was not generously interpreted by the American courts. When the English author Captain Marryatt had been living in America for more than a year, he registered the title of a book he had written, to secure copyright. Later, he sued an infringer but lost. The court said that one year of residency was not enough — he needed six years' uninterrupted residence — and he would have to take an oath of allegiance. The captain was unwilling to take such an oath, because he was an officer in the Royal Navy, and feared that it would subject him to the disagreeable consequence of being strung up from the yard-arm of his own vessel.

Chapter 6

1. Ford II, p. 447.
2. Webster's papers in the *Connecticut Courant* signed "Honorius" had been directed against the Middletown Convention.
3. Ford II, p. 447.

Chapter 7

1. In May 1831, Webster's son William married David Stuart's daughter, Rosalie.
2. Ford I, pp. 92–94.

3. Ford I, pp. 96–97.
4. Ford I, p. 110.
5. Ford I p. 110–111.
6. Ford I, p. 101.
7. Ford I p. 102–4.
8. Ford II, pp. 455–458.
9. Ford II pp. 405–406.
10. Letter in my possession.

Chapter 8

1. For his writings on the subject of Commutation of veterans' pay.
2. Letters, pp. 59–62.
3. Monaghan p. 52.
4. Memoir No. 18.

Chapter 9

1. This is quite a common mistake — see for example Journey, p. 48.
2. *American Magazine*, p. 565.
3. Jansen's *Stranger in America* described a planter's family in which negro wenches waited at table in a state of perfect nudity. Quoted in the *Quarterly Review* for Jan. 1814, Vol.XX p. 513, which mentioned a number of strange American habits, including kidnapping Scotsmen, Welshmen and Hollanders to sell them into slavery.
4. *American Magazine*, p. 347.
5. *Collections of the Massachusetts Historical Society*, 5th series, III (1877), 59; quoted in Ford I, p. 185.
6. pp. 309–403.
7. *History of the Arts of Design*, Vol. I, p. 316.
8. Quoted in Warfel, p. 187.

Chapter 10

1. Dissertations, pp. 352–3.
2. This letter is in the Pierpont Morgan Library.
3. Ford I, p. 269.
4. Warfel, p. 216.
5. Ford II, pp. 426–7.
6. Ford I, pp. 365–6.
7. Ford I, pp. 412–3.
8. Ford I, p. 376.
9. Ford I, p. 276.

Chapter 11

1. Letter to Benjamin Rush, Feb.27, 1799.
2. *A Brief History of Epidemic and Pestilential Diseases*, Vol I, p. 338. Charles Holt's letter is quoted in Ford Vol.I, p. 461-2n. The original is in the Webster papers in the New York Public Library.
3. Vol. XLVI, p. 914. "Scotch books," he wrote,

"like their countrymen, are not much in repute in any part of North America."

4. Isaiah Thomas also reprinted Perry's spelling book, *The Only Sure Guide to the English Tongue.*

5. Different editions of Entick used different spellings. In 1767 it had *-our*; in 1787 (a new edition, revised, corrected and enlarged throughout, with William Crakelt's table of homophones) it was mostly *-or*; the 1805 edition gave both.

6. *The Development of American Lexicography, 1798–1864,* p. 12.

7. *American Review and Literary Journal,* I (April–June 1801), p. 214.

8. *American Speech,* Vol. 9 (1934), p. 264.

9. Ph.D.Diss, George Peabody College for Teachers (1936).

10. George Philip Krapp, *The English Language in America,* Vol.I, p. 358.

11. In Boston, the title was deposited on October 7, 1790 by the Boston firm of Thomas & Andrews, as "proprietors" of the copyright, because in 1789, Webster had sold them the copyright in the Institute in Rhode Island, Massachusetts and New Hampshire.

12. p. 37.

13. Noah's Ark, p. 42.

14. This letter is in the manuscript collection of the Library of Congress.

15. Letter dated January 12, 1842, to Mr. Harris. Pierpont Morgan Library.

16. Webster had changed *learn* to *teach,* in response to the criticism of Dilworth's Ghost.

17. Compendious Dictionary. Preface, p. xix.

18. American Speech, Vol. 21, p. 3.

19. Charlton Laird later served as a special editor on *Webster's New World Dictionary of the American Languge.* He returned to Webster several times. In *The Miracle of Language* (1953), Laird wrote, "Few men have been able to commit and print so many errors in solemn places as he did. Yet Noah Webster, in spite of his bad temper and his occasional bad judgment, was a very great man." In *Language in America* (1970), he said that Webster was "...the preeminent cracker-barrel lexicographer ... more a hack of all intellectual trades than a scholar.... he had neither wit nor profundity, and he probably never felt the lack of either quality."

20. Original letter in the manuscript collection of the Library of Congress.

21. Letter to NW, August 1, 1809, quoted in Ford II, pp. 71-72.

22. Letter to David Ramsay, October, 1807. Letters, p. 287.

23. *Columbiad,* Book X, Lines 599–610 (pp. 380–381).

24. *Edinburgh Review,* Vol 15 (Oct.1809) p. 39.

Chapter 12

1. The review of his *Dissertations* and *Essays and Fugitiv Writings* in the *Critical Review,* concluded that

he was "imperfectly acquainted with the subject which he pretends to discuss," and called him "the incompetent grammarian." *Critical Review,* October 1797, pp. 175–177.

2. *Something,* pp. 332–333.

3. *American Dictionary,* Preface

4. *On the Origin and Progress of Language* Vol.I, pp. 187–188.

5. *The Annals of the World Deduced from the Origin of Time ...* by James Ussher, London 1658, p. 1.

6. Letter to Dr. Thomas Miner, Nov. 21st, 1836.

7. *Dissertations* &c. p. 316.

8. Letters, pp. 318–324.

9. Letter to Dawes, December 20, 1808.

10. Memoir, No. 51.

11. Ford II, p. 116. Mrs. Ford does not make it clear, but I think it most probable that the description was part of the Reminiscences of Mrs. E.S.W.Jones (Webster's daughter Eliza).

12. Warfel, p. 349.

13. Morgan, p. 175.

14. Monaghan, p. 104.

15. *A Collection of Essays and Fugitiv Writings,* p. 392.

16. Warfel, p. 43.

17. Journey, p. 21.

18. Warfel, p. 348.

19. Letters p. 410.

20. *The Works of Sir William Jones,* 1799, Vol. I, p. 26.

21. Jones wrote with equal fluency in English, Latin, Greeek, French and Arabic. Louis XVI met him, and is said to have exclaimed, "He is a most extraordinay man! He understands the language of my people better than I do myself!"

22. *The Works of Sir William Jones,* 1799, Vol. I, p. 139.

23. In the Dictionary, Webster gives the spellings *villany* and *villainy*; he uses *villany.*

24. Warfel, p. 347.

25. Mencken, 4th ed. p. 9.

26. *The Evolution of English Lexicography,* pp. 43–44.

27. *The Development of American Lexicography 1798–1864,* pp. 77–78.

Chapter 13

1. *Richardson's Dictionary,* Preface, p. 5.

2. *The Evolution of English Lexicography* by James A.H. Murray, p. 44.

3. Taken from Letters, p. 367.

4. It takes up three pages in the English edition, but only one and a half in the American. In this chapter I shall refer to it as "the Advertisement."

5. I have used the original (Edinburgh) 3rd edition of *Britannica,* because I do not have a copy of Dobson's edition. Dobson's additions resulted in some differences in pagination, but the content of

purely historical articles such as this one would not have been altered.

6. From *The American Medical Lexicon,* published by T and J Swords, New York, 1811.

7. A clearer sign, if one is needed follows in the dictionary: the word adularia ("A mineral deemed the most perfect variety of felspar....") is not in the manuscript at all.

8. pp. 95–105.

9. [Reed's footnote:] "Washington City D.C., 1805. This was an American pirated edition of J.J.Moore, *The British Mariner's Vocabulary; or Universal Dictionary of Technical Terms and Sea Phrases ... London, 1801.*"

10. The original letter is in the Library of Congress. Webster used the conventional spelling "chemistry," forgetting that he recommended "chimistry."

11. Letters, p. 392.

12. Defined by Todd as "Blockish; stupid; lazy; sluggish." Webster just has "Blockish."

13. He included all three in the 1841 edition of the *American Dictionary,* but only after Worcester had put them into the 1829 abridgment.

14. Friend, or his printer, "corrected" scrip to scrap, but mistakenly. Johnson defines scrip as "a schedule; a small writing."

15. Second Edition, published by Simon & Schuster.

16. *The Evolution of English Lexicography*, p. 43.

17. "His introducing his own opinions, and even prejudices, under general definitions of words, while at the same time the original meaning of the words is not explained, as his Tory, Whig, Pension, Oats, Excise, and a few more, cannot be fully defended, and must be placed to the account of capricious and humorous indulgence."

18. cf. H.C.Wyld's 1932 *Universal Dictionary,* which has the example "Damn this dictionary!"

19. Arabic characters omitted.

20. Arabic characters omitted.

21. Ford II, pp. 378–9.

22. Mrs. Ford refers to Daniel Webster as "a very distant kinsman" (Ford II, p. 297), and Rollins calls him Webster's "more famous distant cousin" (Journey, p. 124), but I know of no evidence that they were related. Warfel says that Noah Webster's name "has coalesced with that of the famous orator and statesman who was not even his kinsman." (Warfel, pp. 1-2).

23. As every American child knows, the second and third Presidents of the United States, John Adams and Thomas Jefferson, both died on the 50 anniversary of American Independence, July 4, 1826.

24. Ford, p. 293.

25. Warfel, p. 359; but he also says, on p. 441, that what is in the Pierpont Morgan Library is "the main portion of the manuscript of the Dictionary," which it certainly is not.

26. Noah's Ark, p. 21.

27. Journey, p. 123.

28. Letter dated March 16, 1844, from William to Emily, Harriett and Eliza. William G. Webster Papers, NYPL.

29. The next daughter, Eliza Steele Webster, married Henry Jones six weeks after that, September 5, 1825.

30. That contract, and extracts from Percival's correspondence, are to be found in *The Life and Letters of James Gates Percival*, by Julius H.Ward, Boston, 1866.

31. p. 285.

32. Samuel Finley Breese Morse, generally known as Samuel, but close friends called him Finley. He later became famous as the designer of an electric telegraph and devised the Morse Code. In March 1843, Congress voted an appropriation of $30,000 for the construction of Morse's telegraph. Governor Ellsworth's twin brother Henry, who was Commissioner of Patents, sent his young daughter Annie to Morse's hotel with the good news, and her reward was to choose the first message that was sent on the new telegraph. She chose words from the Bible suggested by her mother (Chauncey Allen Goodrich's sister Nancy,) "What hath God wrought!" (Numbers 23,23).

Chapter 14

1. The original document is in the Sterling Memorial Library, Yale.

2. It is often referred to as a duodecimo. I shall call it the *Primary School Dictionary.*

Chapter 15

1. 54 Geo.III, c. 156.

2. An earlier occasion when Webster's Dictionary was used in court was in October 1833, in the case of The State of Connecticut v. Prudence Crandall. Miss Crandall was a schoolteacher who was prosecuted for breach of a Connecticut statute that made it illegal to "establish in this State any school ... for the instruction or education of colored persons, who are not inhabitants of this State." The pupils in question were the children of free parents in Pennsylvania, New York and Rhode Island, who had come to Connecticut to attend Miss Crandall's school. Her counsel argued that the law was unconstitutional. Chief Justice Daggett "charged the jury that the law was constitutional; blacks not being citizens of the United States within the meaning of the Constitution." In part, this conclusion was based upon Webster's definition of the word "citizen." On appeal, in July 1834, the conviction was quashed on a technicality. One of the Defendant's counsel was Webster's son-in-law, William Ellsworth.

3. Ford II, p. 323 n.

4. Mrs. Eliot was the daughter of Rebecca's sister Nancy and her husband William Cranch;

they, and James Greenleaf, were all living in Washington.

5. The President was Andrew Jackson; Felix Grundy was a Senator.

6. Gales & and Seaton's *Register of Debates in Congress*, Vol.7, pp. 422–423

7. I have simplified the wording a bit, taking out references to joint authors, works other than books, and so forth.

8. These particulars are written inside the front cover of a copy of the book in the Library of Congress.

9. Mary Webster Southgate died in February 1819 at the age of twenty, when her daughter was three weeks old. The daughter was taken into Webster's household two years later, because her father, Horatio Southgate, had formed a liaison with his housekeeper. His house was thought to be no longer a safe place for a girl to live.

10. Letter in the Sterling Memorial Library, Yale.

11. Warfel p. 418.

Chapter 16

1. The Bibliography says that this article was published anonymously "signed by "Teacher," ... in the Hampshire Gazette, November 30, 1841, [and] reprinted in part in the *Boston Courier*, December 3, and the *New Haven Daily Herald*, December 14. The compiler believes that this was written by Webster...." The compiler is certainly right; I used Webster's manuscript, which is in the New York Public Library.

2. Included in Letters, pp. 428–431, but Warfel omitted the words "of the octavo" in the following quote.

3. The Bibliography p. 91, mistakenly identifies the publisher as Chauncey Allen Goodrich.

4. I have corrected some misprints and irregular spellings in the *Palladium* material.

Chapter 17

1. Letter in the Morgan Library.

2. Harriet had been unwell. She would seem to have suffered from tuberculosis.

3. Publishers of Barker's edition of the Quarto dictionary.

4. This word is unclear in the manuscript. Monaghan transcribes it as "Fathers."

5. Letter from William to Ellsworth, dated January 27, 1844; Sterling Memorial Library, Yale.

Chapter 18

1. This is transcribed from a manuscript in the New York Public Library. Some of the paragraphs

that I have transcribed were later crossed out in the manuscript and rewritten, but I give the original draft, as representing Webster's first uncensored thoughts. A later manuscript version of the same article, under the title *A Brief History of Spelling Books*, is in the Pierpont Morgan Library.

2. Monaghan, p. 208.

Chapter 19

1. Letter in Sterling Memorial Library, Yale.

2. April 13, 1846.

3. Worcester's *Universal Critical Dictionary of the English Language*, which was published in 1846.

4. Letter, Ellsworth to William, October 30, 1845.

5. Ward, p. 463–4.

6. Ward, p. 474.

7. Bibliography, p. 235.

8. The letter as printed is signed with the initials "A.C.G.," but Fowler says it was written by Chauncey Allen Goodrich.

Chapter 20

1. The London firm of Bell and Daldy later published, at the same time, both the London edition of the 1864 Webster-Mahn, and an 1867 reprint of Richardson's *New Dictionary of the English Language*.

2. Noah's Ark, p. 35.

3. He later took over as editor of the 1864 Webster-Mahn, after Goodrich's death in 1860, and he was in sole charge of the Webster International of 1890.

4. Houghton Mifflin Co. 1919, pp. 203–4.

Chapter 21

1. Letter in the Sterling Memorial Library, Yale.

2. There is scope for some confusion here, because more than one Bohn was selling the book at the same time, and their businesses were unconnected. Item 8025 in the *Catalogue of Ancient and Modern Books in all Languages on sale by James Bohn, No. 12 King William Street, Strand* (London, 1840) is "WEBSTER'S (Dr.) English Dictionary, enlarged and improved by Ed.H.Barker; 2 vols. 4to. (published at 5l.5s.) bds. 2l.12.6d."; our man is Henry George Bohn, who reissued Barker's edition with a title page saying: "LONDON: PUBLISHED BY HENRY G. BOHN, YORK STREET, COVENT GARDEN. MDCCCXL."

3. Quoted in Barnes *Authors, Publishers and Politicians*, p. 184.

Chapter 23

1. Though on April 2, 1831, as editor of his earlier magazine the *New York Mirror*, he had written

to Webster, "We have just resolved to adopt your Dictionary and given the requisite orders to the printer."

2. Ford II, p. 446, where the letter is printed.

3. Letter in the Sterling Memorial Library, Yale.

4. The same letter refers to an interleaved copy of Webster's dictionary that Lyman Cobb had given them, in which he had written words to be added to the new edition. "Mr. Cobb has evidently been industrious and we trust of service." He cannot have been as illiterate, or such a villain, as Webster thought.

5. Letter in the Sterling Memorial Library, Yale.

Chapter 24

1. The year that appeared on the title page was the year of printing, not the year in which the edition was registered for copyright.

2. Merriam et.al. v. Holloway Pub.Co. *Federal Reporter*, Vol. 43, p. 450 at 451, 452.

3. Merriam et.al. v. Famous Shoe & Clothing Co. *Federal Reporter*, Vol. 47 p. 411 at 413.

4. Merriam et.al. v. Texas Siftings Pub.Co. *Federal Reporter*, Vol. 49 p. 944 at 947–948.

5. G.& C Merriam Company v. Syndicate Publishing Company, 237 U.S. 618 at p. 622.

6. G.& C..Merriam Company v. Saalfield, 241 U.S.22 at p. 25.

7. Saalfield Pub.Co. v. G.& C.Merriam Co. 238 *Federal Reporter* p. 1 at p. 14.

8. It is said that the little axe with which George Washington chopped down Parson Weems' fictional cherry tree was carefully preserved in the family of one of Washington's admirers. They also used it, however, and the handle had to be replaced from time to time. The head was also renewed, when the old one was worn down by repeated sharpening.

9. G.& C. Merriam Co. v. Syndicate Pub.Co. 207 *Federal Reporter*, p. 515 at pp. 515–517.

10. See p. xxx.

11. Foreword, p. vii.

Appendix

Reproduced in the following pages are various items of interest, including title pages, sample pages — some of which include marginalia — of definitions and illustrations, copyright notices, and the Advertisement from the royal octavo Webster's. American editions are identified by the year of copyright deposit, though the first edition may have been issued the following year and the copy reproduced may have been printed later.

E N T I C K'S

New Spelling Dictionary,

TEACHING

To WRITE and PRONOUNCE the *ENGLISH* Tongue
with Ease and Propriety:

In which each Word is accented according to its just and natural Pronunciation; the Part of Speech is properly distinguished, and

THE VARIOUS SIGNIFICATIONS ARE RANGED IN ONE LINE;

WITH

A LIST of PROPER NAMES of MEN and WOMEN.

THE WHOLE

Compiled and digested in a Manner entirely new, to make it a

COMPLETE POCKET COMPANION

FOR THOSE

Who read MILTON, POPE, ADDISON, SHAKESPEARE, TILLOTSON, and LOCKE, or other *English* Authors of Repute in *Prose* or *Verse*: And in particular to assist *young* People, *Adventurers, Tradesmen* and *Foreigners*, desirous of understanding what they speak, read and write.

To which is prefixed,

A GRAMMATICAL INTRODUCTION to the *English* Tongue.

NEW EDITION. REVISED, CORRECTED, and ENLARGED throughout,

TO WHICH IS NOW ADDED,

A Catalogue of Words of *similar* Sounds, but of different *Spellings* and *Significations.*

By WILLIAM CRAKELT, M.A.

Rector of Nursted and Ifield in Kent.

L O N D O N:

PRINTED FOR CHARLES DILLY, IN THE POULTRY, 1787.

Lan'guishment, Lan'guish, f. a softness of mien
Lan'guor, f. a faintness, a heaviness of spirits
Lan'iate, v. a. to tear in pieces, rend, kill, butcher, [fond-
Lanif'erous, Lanif'erous, a. bearing wool [slay
Lan'ifice, f. a woollen manufacture, spinning, &c.
Lank, a. not filled, languid, faint, slender, thin
Lank'ness, f. a want of flesh, thinness, slenderness
Lan'quenet, f. a game at cards, a common soldier
Lan'tern, Lan'thorn, f. a case for a candle; a thin
Lap, f. a seat on the thighs, a fold or plait, drink
Lap, v. a. to wrap round, fold over, bind, lick up
Lap'dog, f. a little dog for the lap, dog, favorite
Lap'ful, f. as much as the lap can hold or bear
Lap'idary, a. engraved upon stone, monumental
Lap'idary or Lap'idist, f. one who deals in gems
Lap'idate, v. a. to stone, to kill in or by stoning
Lapid'eous, a. stony, resembling stone, rough, hard
Lapides'cence, f. a stony concretion or hardness
Lapidif'ic or Lapidif'ical, a. forming into stones
Lapidification, f. the act of forming into stones
Lap'per, f. one who laps, one who wraps up, &c.
Lap'pet, f. a loose part of a woman's headdress
Lapse, v. to lose the proper time, fall, glide, slip
Lapse, f. a fall, slow fall, slip, small error, change
Lap'sed, part. fallen, gone, forfeited, descended
Lap'wing, f. a bird, the name of a swift noisy bird
Lap'work, f. one thing wrapped, &c. over another
Lar'board, f. the left-hand side of a ship or boat
Lar'ceny, f. theft, petty theft, low petty robbery
Lard, f. grease of swine; v. a. to stuff with bacon
Larder, f. a place where meat is kept, a house
Large, a. big, bulky, wide, full, copious, plentiful
Large'ly, ad. abundantly, extensively, liberally
Large'ness, f. greatness, bulk, wideness, extent
Lar'gess, f. a gift, present, dole, bounty at harvest
Lark, f. a bird, the name of a small singing bird
Lar'um, f. an alarm, a machine that strikes loud
Lasciv'ious, a. lewd, lustful, wanton, fond, soft

Lasciv'iously, ad. wantonly, lewdly, loosely, softly
Lasciv'iousness, f. wantonness, looseness, fond- [ness
Lash, f. part of a whip, a stroke, a snare [fasten
Lash, v. a. to scourge, strike, satirize, tie,
Lass, f. a girl, young maid, very young woman
Las'situde, f. fatigue, weariness, languor, weak-
Lass'lorn, a. forsaken or left by a mistress [ness
Last, a. latest, hindmost, following the rest, next
Last, v. a. to continue; f. a mould, a lead, the end
Last, Last'ly, ad. in the last time or last place
Las'cage, f. a custom paid for freightage, ballast
Last'ing, part. a. continuing, very durable, strong
Latch, f. a catch for a door; v. a. to fasten with
Latch'et, f. a shoestring, a fastening [a latch
Late, a. slow, out of due time, advanced, deceased
Late, ad. far in the day or night, unseasonably
Lated, a. late, benighted, overtaken by the night
Lately, Lat'erly, ad. not very long ago, just now
Lateness, f. a being late, time now far advanced
Latent, a. secret, private, hidden, concealed, deep
Lat'eral, a. placed upon the side, passing sideways
Laterality, f. the quality of having distinct sides
Lat'erally, ad. sidewise, on one side, by the side
Lat'eran, f. one of the Pope's palaces at Rome
Lath, v. a. to fit up, form or fasten, with laths
Lath, f. a thin piece of wood to support tiles, &c.
Lathe, f. a turner's tool, a division of a county
Lath'er, v. to cover with ladder, to form a froth
Lath'er, f. the froth of soap and water, a sweat
Lath'ing, f. a fitting up with laths, an invitation
Lat'in, a. a tongue, the ancient Roman language
Latinism, f. an idiom of or in the Latin tongue
Lat'inist, f. a person who is skilled, &c. in Latin
Lat'inize, v. n. to make Latin, to turn into Latin
Lation, f. a motion or removal in a right line
Latish, a. somewhat late, growing late [beak
Latiros'tres, a. broad-beaked, having a broad
Lat'itancy, f. the state of lurking or lying hid
Lat'itant,
L

ABOVE, LEFT: Title page of Entick's *New Spelling Dictionary*, 1787, and (*RIGHT*) a typical page of definitions. Entick's Dictionary was the basis of Webster's 1806 *Compendious Dictionary. OPPOSITE, LEFT:* Title page of Webster's first dictionary, the 1806 *Compendious Dictionary,* and (*RIGHT*) a typical page of definitions.

LAN [—172—] LAT

Lampoon', n. abuse, personal slander
Lampoon', v. t. to abuse personally, libel, ridicule
Lampoon'er, n. a writer of personal satire
Lam'prel, Lam'prey, Lamp'ron, n. a kind of eel
Lana'rious, a. relating to or bearing wool
Lan'ate, a. covered with a wooly hair
Lance, n. a long spear; v. t. to pierce, cut, lay open
Lan'ced, pa. opened or cut with a lance, pierced
Lance'ly, a. suitable to or becoming a lance ob.
Lan'ceolate, a. shaped like a lance
Lan'cet, n. a surgical instrument to let blood
Lanch, v. t. to cast as a lance, throw, dart, let off
Lanch, n. the sliding of a ship into the water
Land, n. a country, region, earth, ground, urine
Land, v. to let, put or come on shore, to arrive
Land'dam, v. t. to stop urine, stop, kill, destroy
Land'ed, a. having an estate in land, set on shore
Land'fall, n. land first seen as vessels approach
Land'flood, n. a great flood, inundation, overflow
Land'forces, n. pl. soldiers that serve on land
Lan'grave, n. a title, German title, count, earl
Land'gravate, n. the territory of a landgrave
Land'holder, n. a person who is possessed of land
Land'ing, n. a place to land at, the top of stairs
Land'jobber, n. one who speculates in land
Land'lady, n. the mistress of land, an inn, &c.
Land'less, a. destitute of property or fortune, poor
Land'locked, a. shut in or inclosed by land
Land'lord, n. an owner of land or houses, a master
Land'mark, n. a mark of boundaries or direction
Land'office, n. an office for the disposal of lands
Land'scape, n. a prospect of a country, a picture
Land'slip, n. a detached portion of a hill which slides down

Land'tax, n. a tax put upon land and houses
Land'waiter, n. one who watches the landing of
Land'ward, ad. towards or near the land (goods
Lane, n. a narrow street, a close passage or road
Lar'grage or Lan'grel, n. pieces of old iron for shooting from cannon
Lan'guage, n. all human speech, a tongue, a style
Lan'guaged, a. knowing various languages
Lan'guagemaster, n. one who teaches languages
Lan'guet, n. a leaden tongue used by weavers
Lan'guid, a. faint, weak, feeble, heartless, dull
Lan'guidness, n. faintness, weakness, feebleness
Lan'guish, v. t. to melt, pine, droop, lose strength
Lan'guishingly, ad. meltingly, feebly, tediously
Lan'guishment, Lan'guish, n. a softness of mien
Lan'guor, n. faintness, lowness, heaviness (ings
Lan'iard, n. a short piece of rope or line for fasten-
Lan'iate, v. t. to tear in pieces, rend, kill, butcher
Lania'tion, n. the act of tearing or butchering
Lani'ferous, Lani'gerous, a. bearing wool, ob.
Lan'ifice, n. a woollen manufacture, spinning, ob.
Lank, a. not filled, thin, slender, languid, faint
Lank'ness, n. a want of flesh, thinness, slenderness
Lan'net, n. a bird of the long-winged hawk kind

Lant'ern, Lant'horn, n. a case for a candle; a thin
Laodice'an, n. a native of Laodicea in Asia
Lap, n. a feat on the thighs, fold, plait, drink
Lap, v. t. to wrap round, fold over, bind, lick up
Lap'dog, n. a little dog for the lap, a favorite
Lap'ful, n. as much as the lap can hold or bear
Lapida'rious, a. stony, consisting of stones
Lap'idary, a. engraved upon stone, monumental
Lap'idary, Lap'idist, n. one who deals in gems
Lap'idate, v. t. to stone, to kill by stoning
Lapid'eous, a. stony, like stone, hard, rough
Lapides'cence, n. a stony concretion or hardness
Lapides'cent, a. turning to stone, petrifying
Lapidif'ic, Lapidif'ical, a. forming into stones
Lapidification, n. the act of forming into stones
Lapid'ify, v. to form or turn to stone
Lap'lander, n. a native of Lapland in Europe
Lap'per, n. one who laps, one who wraps up
Lap'pet, n. a loose part of a woman's headdress
Lap'ping, n. a licking up with the tongue
Lapse, v. i. to slip, glide, fall, descend, go
Lapse, n. a slip, error, oversight, fall, course
Lap'sided, a. having one side heavier than the
Lap'wing, n. the name of a swift noisy bird (other
Lap'work, n. one thing wrapped over another
Lar'board, n. the left-hand side of a ship or boat
Lar'ceny, n. theft, petty theft, petty robbery
Larch, n. a tree, a species of pine
Lard, n. grease of swine; v. t. to stuff with bacon
Lard'er, n. a place where meat is kept, a house
Large, a. big, bulky, wide, full, copious, plentiful
Large'ly, ad. abundantly, liberally, extensively
Large'ness, n. greatness, bulk, wideness, extent
Large'ss, n. a gift, present, dole, bounty at harvest

Lark, n. the name of a small singing bird
Lark'spur, n. a genus of plants of several species
Larmier, n. a flat jutting part of a cornish
Laryngot'omy, n. a cutting open of the windpipe
Lar'ynx, n. a cavity in the throat by which the voice is regulated, the windpipe
Lar'um, n. an alarm, a machine that strikes loud
Lar'va, n. the caterpillar state of insects
Las'car, n. a seaman in the East Indies
Lasciv'ious, a. wanton, lewd, lustful, fond, soft
Lasciv'iously, ad. wantonly, lewdly, loosely, loftly
Lasciv'iousness, n. wantonness, lustfulness
Lash, n. a part of a whip, stroke, snare, gin
Lash, v. t. to scourge, strike, satirize, tie, fasten
Lash'ing, n. a piece of rope for occasional fastening
Lass, n. a girl, young maid, young woman
Las'situde, n. fatigue, weariness, languor, weakness
Las'lorn, a. forsaken or left by a mistress
Last, a. latest, hindmost, following the rest, next
Last, v. i. to continue; n. a mold, load, end
Last, Last'ly, ad. in the last time or place
Last'age, n. a custom paid for freightage, ballast
Last'ing, pa. a. continuing, durable, strong
Latch, n. a catch for a door; v. t. to fasten with a
Latch'et, n. a fastening, a shoestring (catch

A
Compendious Dictionary

OF THE

English Language.

In which FIVE THOUSAND Words are added
to the number found in the BEST ENGLISH COMPENDS;

The ORTHOGRAPHY is, in some instances, corrected;

The PRONUNCIATION marked by an Accent or other suitable Direction;

And the DEFINITIONS of many Words amended and improved.

TO WHICH ARE ADDED FOR THE BENEFIT OF THE

MERCHANT, the STUDENT and the TRAVELLER,

I.—TABLES of the MONEYS of most of the commercial Nations in the world, with the value expressed in Sterling and Cents.

II.—TABLES of WEIGHTS and MEASURES, ancient and modern, with the proportion between the several weights used in the principal cities of Europe.

III.—The DIVISIONS of TIME among the Jews, Greeks and Romans, with a Table exhibiting the Roman manner of dating.

IV.—An official List of the POST-OFFICES in the UNITED STATES, with the States and Counties in which they are respectively situated and the distance of each from the seat of Government.

V.—The NUMBER of INHABITANTS in the United States, with the amount of EXPORTS.

IV.—New and interesting CHRONOLOGICAL TABLES of remarkable Events and Discoveries.

By NOAH WEBSTER, Esq.

From Sidney's Press.

FOR HUDSON & GOODWIN, BOOK-SELLERS, HARTFORD, AND INCREASE COOKE & CO.
BOOK-SELLERS, NEW-HAVEN,

1806.

A

DICTIONARY

OF THE

ENGLISH LANGUAGE:

IN WHICH

THE WORDS ARE DEDUCED FROM THEIR ORIGINALS,

AND

ILLUSTRATED IN THEIR DIFFERENT SIGNIFICATIONS BY EXAMPLES FROM THE BEST WRITERS.

TO WHICH ARE PREFIXED

A HISTORY OF THE LANGUAGE,

AND

AN ENGLISH GRAMMAR.

BY SAMUEL JOHNSON, LL. D.

IN TWO VOLUMES.

VOL. I.

THE EIGHTH EDITION; CORRECTED AND REVISED.

Cum tabulis animum cenforis fumet honefti :
Audebit quæcunque parùm fplendoris habebunt,
Et fine pondere erunt, et honore indigna ferentur,
Verba movere loco ; quamvis invita recedant,
Et verfentur adhuc intra penetralia Veftæ :
Obfcurata diu populo bonus eruet, atque
Proferet in lucem fpeciofa vocabula rerum,
Quæ prifcis memorata Catonibus atque Cethegis
Nunc fitus informis premit et deferta vetuftas.   HOR.

LONDON:
PRINTED FOR J. JOHNSON, C. DILLY, G. G. AND J. ROBINSON, W. J. AND J. RICHARDSON, D. OGILVY AND SON,
R. BALDWIN, ELMSLEY AND BREMNER, F. AND C. RIVINGTON, R. FAULDER, J. CUTHELL, J. WALKER, W. LOWNDES,
J. MATTHEWS, LACKINGTON AND CO. J. SCATCHERD, G. WILKIE, T. EGERTON, T. PAYNE, R. LEA, VERNOR AND
HOOD, T. N. LONGMAN, CADELL AND DAVIES, J. AND A. ARCH, MURRAY AND HIGHLEY, S. BAGSTER, LEE AND
HURST, J. HARDING, AND I. NEWBERY.

1799.

Title page of Johnson's *Dictionary of the English Language*, Eighth Edition, 1799, in two volumes quarto. This was the edition that formed the basis of Webster's *American Dictionary* and his view of what a proper dictionary should look like.

[Manuscript notes at top:] Tompion. n. tompon
Tombac. tomentose
Tomato. Eng. solanum.
tomahawk n & verb
Tone. verb. Columb. 172·233·283
Iuis. don - tone or thon

TOL

the people came about him, pitying him: Plato passing by, and knowing he did it to be seen, said, If you pity him indeed, let him alone to himself.
Bacon.

There wants nothing but consideration of our own eternal weal, a *tolerance* or endurance of being made happy here, and blessed eternally. *Hammond.*

To TO'LERATE. *v. a.* [*tolero*, Latin; *tolerer*, French.] To allow so as not to hinder; to suffer; to pass uncensured.

Inasmuch as they did resolve to remove only such things of that kind as the church might best spare, retaining the residue; their whole counsel is, in this point, utterly condemned, as having either proceeded from the blindness of those times, or from negligence, or from desire of honour and glory, or from an erroneous opinion that such things might be *tolerated* for a while. *Hooker.*

We shall *tolerate* flying horses, harpies, and satyrs; for these are poetical fancies, whose shaded moralities requite their substantial falsities. *Brown.*

Men should not *tolerate* themselves one minute in any known sin. *Decay of Piety.*

Crying should not be *tolerated* in children. *Locke.*

We are fully convinced that we shall always *tolerate* them, but not that they will *tolerate* us. *Swift.*

TOLERA'TION. *n. s.* [*tolero*, Lat.] Allowance given to that which is not approved.

I shall not speak against the indulgence and *toleration* granted to these men. *South.*

[Manuscript: Sax·Ch 1000 ... Gr TEΛOS ...]

TOLL. *n. s.* [This word seems derived from *tollo*, Latin; toll, Saxon; *tol*, Dut. *told*, Danish; *toll*, Welsh; *taillie*, Fr.] An excise of goods; a seizure of some part for permission of the rest.

Toll, in law, has two significations: first, a liberty to buy and sell within the precincts of a manor, which seems to import as much as a fair or market; secondly, a tribute or custom paid for passage. *Cowell.*

Empson and Dudley the people esteemed as his horse-leeches, bold men, that took *toll* of their master's grist. *Bacon.*

The same Prusias joined with the Rhodians against the Byzantines, and stopped them from levying the *toll* upon their trade into the Euxine. *Arbuthnot.*

To TOLL. *v. n.* [from the noun.]
1. To pay toll or tallage.
I will buy a son-in-law in a fair, and *toll* for him: for this, I'll none of him. *Shakspeare.*
Where, when, by whom, and what y' were told for,
And in the open market *toll'd* for? *Hudibras.*

2. To take toll or tallage.
The meale the more yeeldeth, if servant be true,
And miller that *tolleth* takes none but his due. *Tusser.*

3. [I know not whence derived.] To sound as a single bell.
Hath but a losing office, and his tongue
Sounds ever after as a sullen bell,
Remember'd *tolling* a departed friend. *Shakspeare.*
Our going to church at the *tolling* of a bell, only tells us the time when we ought to go and worship God. *Stillingfleet.*

Toll, toll,
Gentle bell, for the soul
Of the pure ones. *Denham.*

You love to hear of some prodigious tale,
The bell that *toll'd* alone, or Irish whale. *Dryden.*

They give their bodies due repose at night:
When hollow murmurs of their ev'ning bells
Dismiss the sleepy swains, and *toll* them to their cells. *Dryden.*

With horns and trumpets now to madness swell,
Now sink in sorrows with a *tolling* bell. *Pope.*

To TOLL. *v. a.* [*tollo*, Latin.]
1. To ring a bell.
When any one dies, then by *tolling* or ringing of a bell the same is known to the searchers. *Graunt.*

2. To take away; to vacate; to annul.
A term only used in the civil law: in this sense the *o* is short, in the former long. *tollo* 4

[Manuscript bottom left:] Tolmen. Faber. 2. 413.

TON

An appeal from sentence of excommunication does not suspend it, but then devolves it to a superior judge, and *tells* the presumption in favour of a sentence. *Ayliffe.*

3. To take away, or perhaps to invite. Obsolete.
The adventitious moisture which hangeth loose in a body, betrayeth and *tolleth* forth the innate and radical moisture along with it. *Bacon.*

TO'LLBOOTH. *n. s.* [toll and booth.] A prison. *Ainsworth.*

To TO'LLBOOTH. *v. a.* To imprison in a tollbooth.
To these what did he give? why a hen,
That they might *tollbooth* Oxford men. *Bp. Corbet.*

TOLLGA'THERER. *n. s.* [toll and gather.] The officer that takes toll.

TO'LSEY. *n. s.* The same with *tollbooth.* *Dict.*

TOLUTA'TION. *n. s.* [*toluto*, Latin.] The act of pacing or ambling.
They move *per latera*, that is, two legs of one side together, which is *tolutation* or ambling. *Brown.*

They rode; but authors having not
Determin'd whether pace or trot,
That is to say, whether *tolu ation*,
As they do term 't, or succussation,
We leave it. *Hudibras.*

TOMB. *n. s.* [*tombe*, *tombeau*, Fr. *tumba*, low Latin.] A monument in which the dead are enclosed. *[Manuscript: Whiter 98.218]*
Methinks, I see thee, now thou art below,
As one dead in the bottom of a tomb. *Shakspeare.*
Time is drawn upon *tombs* an old man bald, winged, with a sithe and an hour-glass. *Peacham.*
Poor heart! she slumbers in her silent *tomb*:
Let her possess in peace that narrow room. *Dryden.*
The secret wound with which I bleed
Shall lie wrapt up, ev'n in my herse;
But on my *tomb*—stone thou shalt read
My answer to thy dubious verse. *Prior.*

To TOMB. *v. a.* [from the noun.] To bury; to entomb.
Souls of boys were there,
And youths that *tomb'd* before their parents were. *May.*

TO'MBLESS. *adj.* [from tomb.] Wanting a tomb; wanting a sepulchral monument.
Lay these bones in an unworthy urn,
Tombless, with no remembrance over them. *Shakspeare.*

TO'MBOY. *n. s.* [Tom, a diminutive of Thomas, and boy.] A mean fellow; sometimes a wild coarse girl.
A lady
Fasten'd to an empery, to be partner'd
With tomboys, hir'd with that self-exhibition
Which your own coffers yield! *Shakspeare.*

TOME. *n. s.* [French; τομος, *Arab*]
1. One volume of many.
2. A book. *Busb. 834/395*
All those venerable books of scripture, all those sacred *tomes* and volumes of holy writ, are with such absolute perfections framed. *Hooker.*

TOMTI'T. *n. s.* [See TITMOUSE.] A titmouse; a small bird.
You would fancy him a giant when you looked upon him, and a *tomtit* when you shut your eyes. *Spectator.*

TON. *n. s.* [*tonne*, French. See TUN.] A measure or weight.
Spain was very weak at home, or very slow to move, when they suffered a small fleet of English to fire, sink, and carry away, ten thousand *ton* of their great shipping. *Bacon.*

TON, TUN, in the names of places, are derived from the Saxon *tun*, a hedge or wall; and this seems to be from *bun*, a hill, the towns being anciently built

TON

on hills, for the sake of defence and protection in times of war. *Gibson's Camden.*

TONE. *n. s.* [ton, French; *tonus*, Latin.]
1. Note; sound. *[Manuscript: Whiter 242]*
Sounds called *tones* are ever equal. *Bacon.*
The strength of a voice or sound makes a difference in the loudness or softness, but not in the *tone.* *Bacon.*
In their motions harmony divine
So smooths her charmed *tones*, that God's own ear
Listens delighted. *Milton.*

2. Accent; sound of the voice.
Palamon replies,
Eager his *tone*, and ardent were his eyes. *Dryden.*
Each has a little soul he calls his own,
And each enunciates with a human *tone.* *Harte.*

3. A whine; a mournful cry.
Made children, with your *tones*, to run for 't,
As bad as bloody-bones, or Lunsford. *Hudibras.*

4. A particular or affected sound in speaking.

5. Elasticity; power of extension and contraction. *an· Cot· P· 189*
Drinking too great quantities of this decoction, may weaken the *tone* of the stomach. *Arbuthnot.*

TONG. *n. s.* [See TONGS.] The catch of a buckle. This word is usually written *tongue*; but, as its office is to hold, it has probably the same original with *tongs*, and should therefore have the same orthography.
Their hilts were burnish'd gold, and handle strong,
Of mother pearl, and buckled with a golden *tong.* *Spenser.*

[Manuscript: Goth. tuggo]

TONGS. *n. s.* [tang, Saxon; *tang*, Dut.] An instrument by which hold is taken of any thing; as of coals in the fire.
Another did the dying brands repair
With iron *tongs*, and sprinkled oft the same
With liquid waves. *Spenser.*
They turn the glowing mass with crooked *tongs*;
The fiery work proceeds. *Dryden.*
Get a pair of *tongs* like a smith's *tongs*, stronger, and toothed. *Mortimer.*

TONGUE. *n. s.* [tung, Saxon; tongue, Dutch.]
1. The instrument of speech in human beings.
My conscience hath a thousand several *tongues*,
And ev'ry *tongue* brings in a sev'ral tale,
And ev'ry tale condemns me for a villain. *Shaksp.*
Who with the *tongue* of angels can relate? *Milton.*
They are *tongue*-valiant and as bold as Hercules where there's no danger. *L'Estrange.*
My ears still ring with noise; I'm vext to death,
Tongue-kill'd, and have not yet recover'd breath. *Dryden.*
Tongue-valiant hero, vaunter of thy might,
In threats the foremost; but the lag in fight. *Dryd.*
These have been female Pythagoreans, notwithstanding that philosophy consisted in keeping a secret, and the disciple was to hold her *tongue* five years together. *Addison.*
Though they have those sounds ready at their *tongue's* end, yet there are no determined ideas. *Locke.*
I should make but a poor pretence to true learning, if I had not clear ideas under the words my *tongue* could pronounce. *Watts.*

2. The organ by which animals lick.
They hiss for his return'd, with forked *tongue*
To forked tongue. *Milton.*

3. Speech; fluency of words.
He said; and silence all their *tongues* contain'd. *Chapman.*
Much *tongue* and much judgment seldom go together; for talking and thinking are two quite different faculties. *L'Estrange.*
First in the council hall to steer the state,
And ever foremost in a *tongue* debate. *Dryden.*

4. Power of articulate utterance.
Parrots, imitating human range,
And singing-birds in silver cages hung. *Dryden.*

[Manuscript bottom right:] Ame Sat. tingua - W. Jawod
Ir. teanga } Scot. teanhra
or ting - } Arm. Teaut

A page from Webster's copy of Johnson's Dictionary, with Webster's manuscript notes. These show that he had been reading, among other things, Whiter's *Etymologicon Magnum* and Barlow's *Columbiad*. Rare Books Division, New York Public Library, Astor, Lenox and Tilden Foundations.

A

NEW DICTIONARY

OF THE

ENGLISH LANGUAGE;

BY

CHARLES RICHARDSON.

VOL. I.

LONDON:

WILLIAM PICKERING, CHANCERY LANE.

WILLIAM JACKSON, CEDAR STREET, NEW YORK.

1837

The 1837 title page of Richardson's *New Dictionary of the English Language,* in two volumes quarto. There is an earlier (1836) title page, which does not mention a New York publisher.

If, as Peter Nonius will have it, the aire be so *angust*, what proportion is there betwixt the other three elements and it? To what use serves it?—*Burton. Anat. of Mel.* p.250.

ANHA'NG, *v.* To hang. See HANG.

And right anon, the ministers of the toun
Han hent the carter, and so sore him pined,
And eke the hosteler so sore engined,
That they beknew hir wickednesse anon,
And were *anhanged* by the necke bon.
Chaucer. The Nonnes Preestes Tale, v. 15,068.

"Do, way!" said Guy, "therof speak nought!
By him that all this world hath wrought,
I had liever thou were *an-hong!*
Ellis. Romances, vol. ii. *Guy of Warwick.*

ANI'ENT, *v.* } Fr. *Anéantir*, to annihilate,
ANIE'NTISE. } from *Neant*, nothing. And *Neant*, It. *Niente*, is thus traced by Menage, in his Dict. Etymologique. Nihil, nihilare, nihilans, nihilantis, nihilante, nihante, *niente*. In his Origini della Lingua Italiana, he offers other conjectures. In the Mid. Latin, *Nihilare*, and various derivatives, were in common use. See them in Du Cange. Mr. Tyrwhitt says—

Reduced to nothing.

That wikkidliche. and wilfulliche. wolde mercy *anyente*.
Piers Plouhman, p. 335.

And eke ye han erred, for ye han brought with you to youre conseil ire, coveitise, and hastifnesse, the which three thinges ben contrary to every conseil honest and profitable: the which three thinges ye ne han not *anientissed* or destroyed, neither in yourself ne in youre conseillours, as you ought.—*Chaucer. The Tale of Melibeus.*

ANI'GHT. On night. In the night.

As Edmond sat myd ys ost *anygt* in such solas,
As folc mygte, that ver wounded & sor & wery was.
R. Gloucester, p. 305.

This Dido hath suspection of this
And thought well that it was all amiss
For in his bed he lyeth *a night* and siketh.
Chaucer. Legend of Dido, p. 203.

He mot one of two thynges chese,
Where he woll haue hir suche *on night*
Or els vpon daies light.
For he shall not haue both two.—*Gower. Con. A.* b. i.

Cæs. Let me haue men about me, that are fat,
Sleeke-headed men, and such as sleepe *a-nights.*
Shakespeare. Julius Cæsar, Act i.

How doth Janivere thy husband, my little perriwinckle: is he troubled with the cough of the lungs still? Does he hawk *a-nights* still?—*Marston. Malcontent*, Act ii. sc. 2.

A'NILE, *adj.* } It. *Anile;* Lat. *Anilis*, from
ANI'LITY, *n.* } *Anus*, an old person. Dicta ab *annorum* multitudine, (Festus.)

Agedness; the imbecility or decrepitude of old age.

Thoresby, who amidst his puerile or *anile* ideas, could not avoid the superstition of dreams, related to my author, that Lodge being on a fishing party at Mr. Boulter's, at Stank near Harwood, dreamed that he should be buried in Harwood church.—*Walpole. A Catalogue of Engravers.*

Since the day in which this reformation was begun, by how many strange and critical turns has it been perfected and handed down, if not "entirely without spot or wrinkle," —at least, without great blotches or marks of *anility!*
Sterne, Ser. 21.

ANIMADVE'RT, *v.* } Fr. *Animadversion;*
ANIMADVE'RSAL. } It. *Animavversiòne;* Sp.
ANIMADVE'RSION. } *Animadvercion;* Lat.
ANIMADVE'RSIVE. } *Animadvertere*, (*Animus,*
ANIMADVE'RTOR. } *Ad-vertere*,) to turn the mind to. See ADVERT.

To turn the mind, thoughts, or attention, to; to perceive, to consider, to judge, to censure, to remark, to observe.

Sir Moth, has brought his politic bias with him,
A man of a most *animadverting* humour;
Who, to endear himself unto his lord,
Will tell him, you and I, or any of us,
That here are met, are all pernicious spirits,
And men of pestilent purpose, meanly affected
Unto the state we live in.—*B. Jonson. Mag. Lady*, Act ii.

That lively inward *animadversal:* it is the soul itself; for I cannot conceive the body doth *animadvert*, when as objects, plainly exposed to the sight, are not discovered, till the soul takes notice of them.
More. Song of the Soul, p. 422. Notes.

In the *animadversions*, saith he [the confuter], I find the mention of old cloaks, false beards, night-walkers, and salt lotion therfore the *animadverter* haunts playhouses and bordelloes; for if he did not, how could he speak of such gear?—*Milton. Apology for Smectymnuus.*

There may be a simple internal energy or vital autokiensie, which is without that duplication, that is included in the nature of συναισθησις, con-sense, and consciousness, which makes a being to be present with itself, attentive to its own actions, or *animadversive* of them, to perceive itself to do or suffer, and to have a fruition or enjoyment of itself.
Cudworth. Intellectual System, p. 159.

Let the soul that actuates one of the said eyes, be indued with an higher faculty of *animadversion* (I mean with a greater degree of the *animadversive* ability) than the soul hath, that actuates the other.
Glanvill. The Vanity of Dogmatizing, Pref.

Now it is acknowledged by this learned *animadverter*, that some, yea, a pretty many, of the ancients understand this place, John xiv. 28. of Christ's divine nature, and insist upon it, that he is inferior to the Father, because he is his Son.—*Bp. Bull. Life by Nelson.*

If the stage becomes a nursery for folly and impertinence, I shall not be afraid to *animadvert* upon it.
Spectator, No. 34.

They were wise enough to consider what a sanction it would give their performances, to fall under the *animadversion* of such a pen.—*Examiner*, No. 26.

If the two houses of parliament, or either of them, had avowedly a right to *animadvert* on the king, or each other, or if the king had a right to *animadvert* on either of the houses, that branch of the legislature, so subject to *animadversion*, would instantly cease to be part of the supreme power.—*Blackstone. Commentaries*, b. i. c. 7.

A'NIMATE, *v.* } Fr. *Animer;* It. *Animare;*
A'NIMATE, *adj.* } Sp. *Animar;* Lat. *Animus;*
A'NIMAL, *n.* } Gr. *Ανεμος*, breath, spirit.
A'NIMAL, *adj.* } To give life, breath, spirit,
A'NIMALISH. } literally and met.
ANIMA'LITY. } To inspirit, to enliven, to
A'NIMALIZE. } encourage, to invigorate, to
A'NIMANT. } quicken.
A'NIMATED. } *Animant* and *Animalish* are
ANIMA'TION. } not infrequent in Cudworth.
A'NIMATOR. }

And as Job setteth the resurreccion ayenste the sorrows and pains of death, so dothe Daniel here for our consolacion sette it ayenste our persecucion which did so *animate* the faithfull in tymes paste that thei refused the delyuerance from death of bodye for that lyfe and resurreccion to come.
Joye. Expos. of Daniel, c. 12.

Kynge Edwarde beeyng nothyng abasshed of thys small chaunce, sente good woordes to the Earl of Penbroke, *animatynge* and byddynge hym to bee of a good courage.
Hall. Edward IV. an. 8.

——— And other suns perhaps
With their attendant moons, thou wilt descry,
Communicating male and female light;
Which two great sexes *animate* the world,
Stored in each orb perhaps with some that live.
Milton. Paradise Lost, b. viii.

Man hath his daily work of body or mind
Appointed, which declares his dignity,
And the regard of heaven on all his ways;
While other *animals* inactive range,
And of their doings God takes no account.—*Id. Ib.* b. iv.

No man can perish for being an *animal* man, that is, for not having any supernatural revelations, but for not consenting to them when he hath, that is, for being carnal as well as *animal;* and that he is carnal is wholly his own choice. In the state of *animality* he cannot go to heaven; but neither will that alone bear him to hell.
Bp. Taylor. Of Repentance, c. 6. s. 2.

The body is one, not only by the continuity of all the parts held together with the same natural ligaments, and covered with one and the same skin: but much more by the *animation* of the same soul quickening the whole frame.
Bp. Hall. Christ Mystical.

But no Atheist ever acknowledged conscious *animality* to be a first principle in the universe: nor that the whole was governed by any *animalist*, sentient, and understanding nature, presiding over it as the head of it.
Cudworth. Intell. System, p. 198.

The third [of the Platonick Trinity] is sometimes said to be Παντα ψυχικως, all things *animally*, that is, self-movably, actively, and productively.—*Id. Ib.* p. 582.

Balbus, in Cicero, declares, that to be a Theist is to assert that the world was generated or produced at first from *animal* principles, and that it is also still governed by such a nature.—*Id. Ib.* p. 198.

For these effluctions penetrate all bodies, and like the species of visible objects are ever ready in the medium, and lay hold on all bodies proportionate or capable of their action: those bodies likewise being of a congenerous nature, do readily receive the impressions of their motor; and if not fettered by their gravity, conform themselves to situations, wherein they best unite unto their *animator*.
Brown. Vulgar Errours, b. ii. c. 2.

Here fabled chiefs in darker ages born,
Or worthies old whom arms or arts adorn,
Who cities rais'd, or tam'd a monstrous race,
The walls in venerable order grace:
Heroes in *animated* marble frown,
And legislators seem to think in stone.
Pope. Temple of Fame.

Animate bodies are either such as are endued with a vegetative soul, as plants; or a sensitive soul, as the bodies of *animals*, birds, beasts, fishes, and insects; or a rational soul, as the body of man, and the vehicles of angels, if any such there be.—*Ray. On the Creation.*

How near of kin soever they may seem to be, and how certain soever it is, that man is an *animal*, or rational, or white, yet every one at first hearing perceives the falshood of these propositions; humanity is *animality*, or rationality, or whiteness.—*Locke. On Hum. Underst.* b. iii. c. 8.

Would the polite Egyptian priests, who first *animalized* the asterisms, do, like Tom Otter in the comedy, bring their bulls and bears to court? would they exalt them into heaven, before they had made any considerable figure upon earth? the fact is indeed just otherwise.
Warburton. The Divine Legation, b. iv. s. 4.

Wherever we are formed by nature to any active purpose, the passion which *animates* us to it, is attended with delight, or a pleasure of some kind.
Burke. On the Sublime and Beautiful.

The love of God ought continually to predominate in the mind, and give to every act of duty grace and *animation.*
Beattie. Elements of Moral Science, pt. ii. c. 2.

ANIMO'SITY. Fr. *Animosité;* It. *Animosità;* Sp. *Animosidad;* Lat. *Animosus*, from *Anima*, met. spirit. See ANIMAL.

Fulness, warmth of spirit; vehemence of passion. Applied where the passion is malevolent.

How apt nature is, even in those who profess an eminence in holiness, to raise and maintain *animosities* against those, whose calling or person they pretend to find cause to dislike.
Bp. Hall. Letter of Apology.

You shall hear them pretending to bewail the *animosities* kept up between the Church of England and Dissenters, where the differences in opinion are so few and inconsiderable; yet these very sons of moderation were pleased to excommunicate every man, who disagreed with them in the smallest article of their political creed.—*Examiner*, No. 19.

What can be imagined more trivial than the difference between one colour of livery and another in horse-races? Yet this difference begat two most inveterate factions in the Greek empire, the PRASINI and VENETI, who never suspended their *animosities* till they ruined that unhappy government.—*Hume*, pt. i. Ess. 8.

A'NKLE, *n.* } A. S. *Ancleow;* D. *Enckel;*
A'NKLED. } Ger. *Enckel*, which Wachter
A'NKLE-BONE. } thinks is the diminutive of *Anke;* the bone at the bottom of the leg, by which it rests upon the foot. As *Haunch* is the part by which the lower limbs are *hankyd* or *hanged* (from *Hangan*, A. S.) upon the body or trunk, so *Ancle-bone* may be—

The bone by which the foot is *hankyd* or *hanged* to the leg.

In the name of Jesus Chryst of Nazareth, ryse vp and walke. And he toke hym by the ryght hande, & lyfte hym vp. And immediatly his fete and *ancle-bones* receaued strẽgth.—*Bible*, 1539. *Actes*, c. 3.

This said, a work not worthy him, he set to: of both feete,
He bor'd the nerves through, from the heele, to th' *ankle*, and then knit
Both to his chariot, with a thong of whit leather, his head
Trailing the centre.—*Chapman. Homer. Iliad*, b. xxii.

Then his fell soul a thought of vengeance bred,
(Unworthy of himself and of the dead;)
The nervous *ancles* bor'd, his feet he bound
With thongs inserted through the double wound.
Pope. Id. Ib.

Niece. ——— A tolerable man,
Now I distinctly read him.
Well *ankled*, two good confident calves.
Beaum. & Fletch. Wit at several Weapons

The next circumstance which I shall mention, under this head of muscular arrangement, is so decisive a mark of intention, that it always appeared to me, to supersede, in some measure, the necessity of seeking for any other observation upon the subject: and that circumstance is, the tendons, which pass from the leg to the foot, being bound down by a ligament at the *ancle*.—*Paley. Nat. Theol.* c. 9.

A'NNALIZE, *v.* } Fr. *Annales;* It. *An-*
A'NNALIST. } *nali;* Sp. *Annales;* Lat.
A'NNAL. } *Annalis*, from *Annus*, a
A'NNARY. } year; Gr. Ετος.

A page from Richardson's dictionary, showing the characteristic bracketing of groups of words, rudimentary definitions, and wealth of quotations.

AN

AMERICAN DICTIONARY

OF THE

ENGLISH LANGUAGE:

INTENDED TO EXHIBIT,

I. The origin, affinities and primary signification of English words, as far as they have been ascertained.
II. The genuine orthography and pronunciation of words, according to general usage, or to just principles of analogy.
III. Accurate and discriminating definitions, with numerous authorities and illustrations.

TO WHICH ARE PREFIXED,

AN INTRODUCTORY DISSERTATION

ON THE

ORIGIN, HISTORY AND CONNECTION OF THE

LANGUAGES OF WESTERN ASIA AND OF EUROPE,

AND A CONCISE GRAMMAR

OF THE

ENGLISH LANGUAGE.

BY NOAH WEBSTER, LL. D.

IN TWO VOLUMES.

VOL. I.

He that wishes to be counted among the benefactors of posterity, must add, by his own toil, to the acquisitions of his ancestors.—*Rambler.*

NEW YORK:
PUBLISHED BY S. CONVERSE.

PRINTED BY HEZEKIAH HOWE—NEW HAVEN.

1828.

TOP: Title page of Webster's *American Dictionary of the English Language*, 1828, in two volumes quarto. Aspiring to be an American Johnson, Webster based his dictionary on Johnson's quarto, and his title is Johnson's title preceded by the word *American*, even to the colon after *Language*. BOTTOM: The copyright notice in the *American Dictionary*, with "atheistical" date of deposit.

SEC

SE'ATED, *pp.* Placed in a chair or on a bench, &c.; set; fixed; settled; established; furnished with a seat.

SE'ATING, *ppr.* Placing on a seat; setting; settling; furnishing with a seat; having its seats assigned to individuals, as a church.

SEAVES, *n. plu.* [Sw. *säf*; Dan. *siv*; Heb. סוף suf.] Rushes. [*Local.*]

SE'AVY, *a.* Overgrown with rushes. [*Local.*]

SEBA'CEOUS, *a.* [Low L. *sebaceus*, from *sebum*, *sevum*, tallow, W. *saim*. Qu. Eth. *sebach*, fat.] Made of tallow or fat; pertaining to fat.

Sebaceous humor, a suet-like or glutinous matter secreted by the sebaceous glands, which serves to defend the skin and keep it soft. *Core. Parr.*

Sebaceous glands, small glands seated in the cellular membrane under the skin, which secrete the sebaceous humor. *Parr.*

SEBA'CIC, *a.* [supra.] In *chimistry*, pertaining to fat; obtained from fat; as the *sebacic* acid. *Lavoisier.*

SE'BATE, *n.* [supra.] In *chimistry*, a salt formed by the sebacic acid and a base. *Hooper. Lavoisier.*

SEBES'TEN, *n.* The Assyrian plum, a plant of the genus Cordia, a species of jujube. *Lee. Core.*

SE'CANT, *a.* [L. *secans*, *seco*, to cut or cut off, coinciding with Eng. *saw*.] Cutting; dividing into two parts.

SE'CANT, *n.* [It. Fr. Sp. *secante*, supra.]
1. In *geometry*, a line that cuts another, or divides it into parts. The secant of a circle is a line drawn from the circumference on one side, to a point without the circumference on the other. In *trigonometry*, a secant is a right line drawn from the center of a circle, which, cutting the circumference, proceeds till it meets with a tangent to the same circle. *Encyc.*
2. In *trigonometry*, the secant of an arc is a right line drawn from the center through one end of the arc, and terminated by a tangent drawn through the other end.

SECE'DE, *v. i.* [L. *secedo*; *se*, from, and *cedo*, to move. *Se* is an inseparable preposition or prefix in Latin, but denoting departure or separation.]
To withdraw from fellowship, communion or association; to separate one's self; as, certain ministers *seceded* from the church of Scotland about the year 1733.

SECE'DER, *n.* One who secedes. In Scotland, the *seceders* are a numerous body of presbyterians who seceded from the communion of the established church, about the year 1733.

SECE'DING, *ppr.* Withdrawing from fellowship or communion.

SECERN', *v. t.* [L. *secerno*; *se* and *cerno*, to separate.] In *the animal economy*, to secrete.

The mucus *secerned* in the nose—is a laudable humor. *Arbuthnot.*

SECERN'ED, *pp.* Separated; secreted.

SECERN'ENT, *n.* That which promotes secretion; that which increases the irritative motions, which constitute secretion. *Darwin.*

SECERN'ING, *ppr.* Separating; secreting; as *secerning* vessels.

SEC

SECES'SION, *n.* [L. *secessio*. See *Secede*.]
1. The act of withdrawing, particularly from fellowship and communion. *Encyc.*
2. The act of departing; departure. *Brown.*

SE'CLE, *n.* [Fr. *siècle*; L. *seculum*.] A century. [*Not in use.*] *Hammond.*

SECLU'DE, *v. t.* [L. *secludo*; *se* and *claudo*, *cludo*, to shut.]
1. To separate, as from company or society, and usually to keep apart for some length of time, or to confine in a separate state; as, persons in low spirits *seclude* themselves from society.

Let eastern tyrants from the light of heav'n *Seclude* their bosom slaves. *Thomson.*
2. To shut out; to prevent from entering; to preclude.

Inclose your tender plants in your conservatory, *secluding* all entrance of cold. *Evelyn.*

SECLU'DED, *pp.* Separated from others; living in retirement; shut out.

SECLU'DING, *ppr.* Separating from others; confining in solitude or in a separate state; preventing entrance.

SECLU'SION, *n. s* as *z.* The act of separating from society or connection; the state of being separate or apart; separation; a shutting out; as, to live in *seclusion.*

SECLU'SIVE, *a.* That secludes or sequesters; that keeps separate or in retirement.

SEC'OND, *a.* [Fr. from L. *secundus*; It. *secondo*; Sp. Port. *segundo*; from L. *sequor*, to follow. See *Seek.*]
1. That immediately follows the first; the next following the first in order of place or time; the ordinal of two. Take the *second* book from the shelf. Enter the *second* house.

And he slept and dreamed the *second* time. Gen. xli.
2. Next in value, power, excellence, dignity or rank; inferior. The silks of China are *second* to none in quality. Lord Chatham was *second* to none in eloquence. Dr. Johnson was *second* to none in intellectual powers, but *second* to many in research and erudition.

Second terms, in *algebra*, those where the unknown quantity has a degree of power less than it has in the term where it is raised to the highest. *Encyc.*

At second-hand, in the second place of order; not in the first place, or by or from the first; by transmission; not primarily; not originally; as a report received *at second-hand.*

In imitation of preachers *at second-hand*, I shall transcribe from Bruyere a piece of raillery. *Tatler.*

SEC'OND, *n.* One who attends another in a duel, to aid him, mark out the ground or distance, and see that all proceedings between the parties are fair. *Watts. Addison.*
2. One that supports or maintains another; that which supports.

Being sure enough of *seconds* after the first onset. *Wotton.*
3. The sixtieth part of a minute of time or of a degree, that is, the *second* minute or small division next to the hour. Sound moves above 1140 English feet in a *second.*
4. In *music*, an interval of a conjoint degree,

SEC

being the difference between any sound and the next nearest sound above or below it. *Busby. Encyc.*

SEC'OND, *v. t.* [L. *secundo*; Fr. *seconder*; It. *secondare*.]
1. To follow in the next place.

Sin is *seconded* with sin. [*Little used.*] *South.*
2. To support; to lend aid to the attempt of another; to assist; to forward; to promote; to encourage; to act as the maintainer.

We have *supplies* to second our attempt. *Shak.*

The attempts of Austria to circumscribe the conquests of Buonaparte, were *seconded* by Russia. *Anon.*

In God's, one single can its ends produce, Yet serves to *second* too some other use. *Pope.*
3. In *legislation*, to support, as a motion or the mover. We say, to *second* a motion or proposition, or to *second* the mover.

SEC'ONDARILY, *adv.* [from *secondary*.] In the second degree or second order; not primarily or originally; not in the first intention. Duties on imports serve primarily to raise a revenue, and *secondarily* to encourage domestic manufactures and industry.

SEC'ONDARINESS, *n.* The state of being secondary. *Norris.*

SEC'ONDARY, *a.* [L. *secundarius*, from *secundus.*]
1. Succeeding next in order to the first; subordinate.

Where there is moral right on the one hand, not *secondary* right can discharge it. *L'Estrange.*
2. Not primary; not of the first intention.

Two are the radical differences; the *secondary* differences are as four. *Bacon.*
3. Not of the first order or rate; revolving about a primary planet. Primary planets revolve about the sun; *secondary* planets revolve about the primary
4. Acting by deputation or delegated authority; as the work of *secondary* hands. *Milton.*
5. Acting in subordination, or as second to another; as a *secondary* officer. *Encyc.*

Secondary rocks, in *geology*, are those which were formed after the primary. They are always situated over or above the primitive and transition rocks; they abound with organic remains or petrifactions, and are supposed to be mechanical deposits from water. *Cleaveland.*

A secondary fever, is that which arises after a crisis, or the discharge of some morbid matter, as after the declension of the small pox or measles. *Quincy.*

Secondary circles, or *secondaries*, in *astronomy*, circles passing through the poles of any of the great circles of the sphere, perpendicular to the planes of those circles.

Secondary qualities, are the qualities of bodies which are not inseparable from them, but which proceed from casual circumstances, such as color, taste, odor, &c.

Secondary formations, in *geology*, formations of substances, subsequent to the primitive.

SEC'ONDARY, *n.* A delegate or deputy; one who acts in subordination to another; as the *secondaries* of the court of king's bench and of common pleas. *Encyc.*

Liberality

A page from Lyman Cobb's copy of the *American Dictionary*. Cobb's marginal notes are mostly on Webster's spelling, but here he comments on Webster's sentence showing the use of the word *second*: "Dr. Johnson was *second* to none in intellectual powers, but *second* to many in research and erudition."

A

DICTIONARY

OF

THE ENGLISH LANGUAGE:

INTENDED TO EXHIBIT

I. THE ORIGIN AND THE AFFINITIES OF EVERY ENGLISH WORD, AS FAR AS THEY HAVE BEEN ASCERTAINED, WITH ITS PRIMARY SIGNIFICATION, AS NOW GENERALLY ESTABLISHED;—

II. THE ORTHOGRAPHY AND THE PRONUNCIATION OF WORDS, AS SANCTIONED BY REPUTABLE USAGE, AND WHERE THIS USAGE IS DIVIDED, AS DETERMINABLE BY A REFERENCE TO THE PRINCIPLE OF ANALOGY;—

III. ACCURATE AND DISCRIMINATING DEFINITIONS OF TECHNICAL AND SCIENTIFIC TERMS, WITH NUMEROUS AUTHORITIES AND ILLUSTRATIONS.

TO WHICH ARE PREFIXED

AN INTRODUCTORY DISSERTATION

ON

THE ORIGIN, HISTORY, AND CONNECTION OF THE

LANGUAGES OF WESTERN ASIA AND OF EUROPE;

AND

A CONCISE GRAMMAR, PHILOSOPHICAL AND PRACTICAL, OF THE ENGLISH LANGUAGE.

By NOAH WEBSTER, LL.D.

NEW YORK, 1828.

IN TWO VOLUMES.

" He that wishes to be counted among the benefactors of posterity, must add, by his own toil, to the acquisitions of his ancestors."—*Rambler*.

REPRINTED BY E. H. BARKER, Esq. *of Thetford, Norfolk,*

FROM A COPY COMMUNICATED BY THE AUTHOR, AND CONTAINING MANY MANUSCRIPT CORRECTIONS AND ADDITIONS:

WITH AN APPENDIX BY THE EDITOR.

VOL. I.

LONDON:

PUBLISHED BY BLACK, YOUNG, AND YOUNG,

FOREIGN BOOKSELLERS TO THE KING,

2 TAVISTOCK STREET, COVENT GARDEN.

MDCCCXXXI.

Comparatively rare 1831 title page of Barker's London edition of the *American Dictionary of the English Language.* The word *American* does not appear on the title page. The promised "Appendix by the editor" was never published, and it is not referred to in the more common 1832 title page.

A

DICTIONARY

OF

THE ENGLISH LANGUAGE:

INTENDED TO EXHIBIT

I. THE ORIGIN AND THE AFFINITIES OF EVERY ENGLISH WORD, AS FAR AS THEY HAVE BEEN ASCERTAINED,
WITH ITS PRIMARY SIGNIFICATION, AS NOW GENERALLY ESTABLISHED;—

II. THE ORTHOGRAPHY AND THE PRONUNCIATION OF WORDS, AS SANCTIONED BY REPUTABLE USAGE, AND WHERE
THIS USAGE IS DIVIDED, AS DETERMINABLE BY A REFERENCE TO THE PRINCIPLE OF ANALOGY;—

III. ACCURATE AND DISCRIMINATING DEFINITIONS OF TECHNICAL AND SCIENTIFIC TERMS, WITH NUMEROUS
AUTHORITIES AND ILLUSTRATIONS.

TO WHICH ARE PREFIXED

AN INTRODUCTORY DISSERTATION

ON

THE ORIGIN, HISTORY, AND CONNECTION OF THE

LANGUAGES OF WESTERN ASIA AND OF EUROPE;

AND

A CONCISE GRAMMAR, PHILOSOPHICAL AND PRACTICAL, OF THE ENGLISH LANGUAGE.

By NOAH WEBSTER, LL.D.

NEW YORK, 1828.

IN TWO VOLUMES.

" He that wishes to be counted among the benefactors of posterity, must add, by his own toil, to the acquisitions of his ancestors."—*Rambler.*

REPRINTED BY E. H. BARKER, ESQ., *of Thetford, Norfolk,*
FROM A COPY COMMUNICATED BY THE AUTHOR, AND CONTAINING MANY MANUSCRIPT CORRECTIONS AND ADDITIONS.

VOL. I.

LONDON:

PUBLISHED BY HENRY G. BOHN,

YORK STREET, COVENT GARDEN.

MDCCCXL.

Title page of Henry G. Bohn's 1840 reissue of Barker's edition of the dictionary. The pages of the dictionary are Barker's pages, and this title page is exactly the same as an 1832 Barker title page except for the change of date and having Bohn's name and address in place of those of Black, Young, and Young.

[Handwritten at top: No·a·chi·an a Relating to the time of Noah, the patriarch. Phillips. Geol.]

NITRIFICA'TION, n. The process of forming or converting into niter.

NI'TRIFY, v. t. [niter, and L. facio.] To convert into niter.

NI'TRITE, n. A salt formed by the combination of the nitrous acid with a base.

NI'TROGEN, n. [Gr. νιτρον, niter, and γινναι, to produce.]

[struck-through line] [See Azote.]

NITROG'ENOUS, a. Pertaining to nitrogen producing nitrogen.

NITROLEU'CIC, a. Designating an acid obtained from leucine acted on by *Braconnot.*

NITROM'ETER, n. [Gr. νιτρον and μετρεω, to measure.]
An instrument for ascertaining the quality or value of niter. *Ure.*

NITRO-MURIAT'IC, a. *[struck-through]* The nitro-muriatic acid is a *[struck-through]* mixture of nitric and muriatic acid.

NI'TROUS, a. Pertaining to niter; partaking of the qualities of niter, or resembling it. *Nitrous* acid is one of the compounds formed of nitrogen and oxygen, in which the oxygen is in a lower proportion than that in which the same elements form *nitric* acid.

NI'TRY, a. Nitrous; pertaining to niter; producing niter. *Gay.*

NIT'TER, n. [from nit.] The horse bee that deposits nits on horses. *Med. Repos.*

NIT'TILY, adv. [from nitty] Lousily. [Not used.] *Hayward.*

NIT'TY, a. [from nit.] Full of nits; abounding with nits. *Johnson.*

NI'VAL, a. [L. nivalis, from nix, nivis, snow.]
Abounding with snow; snowy. [Not used.] *Dict.*

NIV'EOUS, a. [L. niveus.] Snowy; resembling snow; partaking of the qualities of snow. *Brown.*

NO. an abbreviation of number, Fr. nombre; as, No. 8, No. 10.

NO, adv. [Sax. na or ne; W. na; Russ. ne; Says. na; Pers. Zend, id.]
1. A word of denial or refusal, expressing a negative, and equivalent to nay and not. When it expresses a negative answer, it is opposed to yes or yea. Will you go? No.
It is frequently used in denying propositions, and opposed to affirmation or concession. "That I may prove them, whether they will walk in my law, or no." Exod. xvi. No, in this use, is deemed less elegant than not, but the use is very general.
2. After another negative, it repeats the negation with great emphasis.
There is none righteous, no, not one. Rom. iii. 1 Cor. v.
Sometimes it follows an affirmative proposition in like manner, but still it denies with emphasis and gives force to the following negative.
To whom we gave place by subjection, no, not for an hour. Gal. ii.
Sometimes it begins a sentence with a like emphatical signification, strengthening the following negative.

[Handwritten circled note at bottom: or more probably a compound of Nitrogen, Oxygen, & Chlorine]

No, not the bow which so adorns the skies, So glorious is, or boasts so many dyes. *Waller.*
3. Not in any degree; as, no longer; no shorter; no more; no less.
4. When no is repeated, it expresses negation or refusal with emphasis; as, no, no.

NO, a. Not any; none.
Let there be no strife between thee and me. Gen. xiii.
2. Not any; not one.
Thou shalt worship no other God. Ex. xxxiv.
3. When it precedes where, as in no where, it may be considered as adverbial, though originally an adjective.

NOBIL'IARY, n. [See Noble.] A history of noble families. *Encyc.*

NOBIL'ITATE, v. t. [L. nobilito. See Noble.] To make noble; to ennoble.

NOBILITA'TION, n. The act of making noble. *More.*

NOBIL'ITY, n. [L. nobilitas.] Dignity of mind; greatness; grandeur; that elevation of soul which comprehends bravery, generosity, magnanimity, intrepidity, and contempt of every thing that dishonors character.
Though she hated Amphialus, yet the nobility of her courage prevailed over it. *Sidney.*
They thought it great their sovereign to control,
And named their pride, nobility of soul. *Dryden.*
2. Antiquity of family; descent from noble ancestors; distinction by blood, usually joined with riches.
When I took up Boccace unawares, I fell on the same argument of preferring virtue to nobility of blood and titles, in the story of Sigismunda. *Dryden.*
3. The qualities which constitute distinction of rank in civil society, according to the customs or laws of the country; that eminence or dignity which a man derives from birth or title conferred, and which places him in an order above common men. In Great Britain, nobility is extended to five ranks, those of duke, marquis, earl, viscount and baron.
4. The persons collectively who enjoy rank above commoners; the peerage; as, the English nobility; French, German, Russian nobility.

NO'BLE, a. [Fr. & Sp. noble; Port. nobre; It. nobile; L. nobilis, from nosco, novi, to know.]
1. Great; elevated; dignified; being above every thing that can dishonor reputation; as, a noble mind; a noble courage; noble deeds of valor. *Milton.*
2. Exalted; elevated; sublime.
Statues, with winding ivy crown'd, belong
To nobler poets for a nobler song. *Dryden.*
3. Magnificent; stately; splendid; as, a noble parade; a noble edifice.
4. Of an ancient and splendid family; as, noble by descent.
5. Distinguished from commoners by rank and title; as, a noble personage.
6. Free; generous; liberal; as, a noble heart.
7. Principal; capital; as, the noble parts of the body. *Johnson.*
8. Ingenuous; candid; of an excellent disposition; ready to receive truth. Acts, xvii.
9. Of the best kind; choice; excellent; as, a noble vine. Jer. ii.

NO'BLE, n. A person of rank above a commoner; a nobleman; a peer; as, a duke, marquis, earl, viscount or baron.
2. In Scripture, a person of honorable family or distinguished by station. Exod. xxiv. Neh. vi.
3. Originally, a gold coin, but now a money of account, value 6s. 8d. sterling, or $1 48 cts. *Camden.*

NO'BLEMAN, n. A noble; a peer; one who enjoys rank above a commoner, either by virtue of birth, by office or patent. *Dryden.*

NO'BLEWOMAN, n. A female of noble rank. *Cavendish.*

NO'BLENESS, n. Greatness; dignity; ingenuousness; magnanimity; elevation of mind or of condition, particularly of the mind.
His purposes are full of honesty, nobleness and integrity. *Taylor.*
Greatness of mind and nobleness their seat
Build in her loveliest. *Milton.*
The nobleness of life is to do this— *Shak.*
2. Distinction by birth; honor derived from a noble ancestry.

NOBLESS', n. [Fr. noblesse, from Sp. nobleza.]
1. The nobility; persons of noble rank collectively; including males and females. *Dryden.*
2. Dignity; greatness; noble birth or condition. [In these senses, not now used.] *Spenser. B. Jonson.*

NO'BLY, adv. Of noble extraction; descended from a family of rank; as, nobly born or descended. *Dryden.*
2. With greatness of soul; heroically; with magnanimity; as, a deed nobly done. He nobly preferred death to disgrace.
3. Splendidly; magnificently. He was nobly entertained.
Where could an emperor's ashes have been so nobly lodged as in the midst of his metropolis and on the top of so exalted a monument? *Addison.*

NO'BODY, n. [no and body.] No person; no one. *Swift.*

NO'CENT, a. [L. nocens, from noceo, to hurt, from striking. See Annoy.]
1. Hurtful; mischievous; injurious; doing hurt; as, nocent qualities. *Watts.*

NO'CIVE, a. [L. nocivus.] Hurtful; injurious. *Hooker.*

NOCK, n. A notch. [Obs.] [See Notch.]

NOCK, v. t. To place in the notch. [Obs.] *Chapman.*

NOCTAMBULA'TION, n. [L. nox, night, and ambulo, to walk.]
A rising from bed and walking in sleep. *Beddoes.*

NOCTAM'BULIST, n. One who rises from bed and walks in his sleep. Arbuthnot uses noctambulo in the same sense; but it is a less analogical word.

NOCTID'IAL, a. [L. nox, night, and dies, day.]
Comprising a night and a day. [Little used.] *Holder.*

NOCTIF'EROUS, a. [L. nox, night, and fero, to bring.] Bringing night. [Not used.] *Dict.*

NOCTIL'UCA, n. [L. nox, night, and luceo, to shine.]
A species of phosphorus which shines in

A N

AMERICAN DICTIONARY

OF THE

ENGLISH LANGUAGE;

FIRST EDITION IN OCTAVO,

CONTAINING

THE WHOLE VOCABULARY OF THE QUARTO, WITH CORRECTIONS, IMPROVEMENTS
AND SEVERAL THOUSAND ADDITIONAL WORDS:

TO WHICH IS PREFIXED

AN INTRODUCTORY DISSERTATION

ON THE

ORIGIN, HISTORY AND CONNECTION OF THE LANGUAGES OF WESTERN ASIA AND EUROPE,

WITH AN EXPLANATION

OF THE PRINCIPLES ON WHICH LANGUAGES ARE FORMED.

BY NOAH WEBSTER, LL. D.

MEMBER OF THE AMERICAN PHILOSOPHICAL SOCIETY IN PHILADELPHIA; FELLOW OF THE AMERICAN ACADEMY OF ARTS
AND SCIENCES IN MASSACHUSETTS; MEMBER OF THE CONNECTICUT ACADEMY OF ARTS AND SCIENCES; FELLOW OF
THE ROYAL SOCIETY OF NORTHERN ANTIQUARIES IN COPENHAGEN; MEMBER OF THE CONNECTICUT HISTORICAL
SOCIETY; CORRESPONDING MEMBER OF THE HISTORICAL SOCIETIES IN MASSACHUSETTS, NEW YORK AND
GEORGIA; OF THE ACADEMY OF MEDICINE IN PHILADELPHIA, AND OF THE COLUMBIAN INSTITUTE
IN WASHINGTON; AND HONORARY MEMBER OF THE MICHIGAN HISTORICAL SOCIETY.

GENERAL SUBJECTS OF THIS WORK.

1. ETYMOLOGIES OF ENGLISH WORDS, DEDUCED FROM AN EXAMINATION AND COMPARISON OF WORDS OF CORRESPOND-
ING ELEMENTS IN TWENTY LANGUAGES OF ASIA AND EUROPE.
2. THE TRUE ORTHOGRAPHY OF WORDS, AS CORRECTED BY THEIR ETYMOLOGIES.
3. PRONUNCIATION EXHIBITED AND MADE OBVIOUS BY THE DIVISION OF WORDS INTO SYLLABLES, BY ACCENTUATION,
BY MARKING THE SOUNDS OF THE ACCENTED VOWELS, WHEN NECESSARY, OR BY GENERAL RULES.
4. ACCURATE AND DISCRIMINATING DEFINITIONS, ILLUSTRATED, WHEN DOUBTFUL OR OBSCURE, BY EXAMPLES OF THEIR
USE, SELECTED FROM RESPECTABLE AUTHORS, OR BY FAMILIAR PHRASES OF UNDISPUTED AUTHORITY.

IN TWO VOLUMES.

VOL. I.

NEW HAVEN:

PUBLISHED BY THE AUTHOR.

Sold by CROCKER & BREWSTER, *Boston;* F. J. HUNTINGTON & Co., *New York;* THOMAS, COWPERTHWAIT & Co.,
Philadelphia; CUSHING & BROTHER, *Baltimore;* and E. MORGAN & Co., *Cincinnati.*

PRINTED BY B. L. HAMLEN.
1841.

ABOVE: Title page of Webster's 1840 royal octavo (deposited to secure copyright in September 1840, but first issued 1841).

OPPOSITE, TOP: A page from Barker's edition of the Dictionary with manuscript notes for additions and alterations to be made in the 1840 Royal Octavo. The notes at the top of the page adding the adjective "Noachian" are in Webster's handwriting. Those at the left hand side and at the bottom of the page are in the handwriting of Professor William Tully. *OPPOSITE, BOTTOM:* Advertisement from the 1840 Royal Octavo, crediting Professor Tully with "the correction of definitions in several of the sciences."

AN AMERICAN DICTIONARY

OF THE

ENGLISH LANGUAGE;

CONTAINING

THE WHOLE VOCABULARY OF THE FIRST EDITION IN TWO VOLUMES QUARTO; THE ENTIRE CORRECTIONS AND IMPROVEMENTS OF THE SECOND EDITION IN TWO VOLUMES ROYAL OCTAVO;

TO WHICH IS PREFIXED

AN INTRODUCTORY DISSERTATION

ON THE

ORIGIN, HISTORY, AND CONNECTION, OF THE LANGUAGES OF WESTERN ASIA AND EUROPE,

WITH AN EXPLANATION

OF THE PRINCIPLES ON WHICH LANGUAGES ARE FORMED.

BY NOAH WEBSTER, LL. D.,

Member of the American Philosophical Society in Philadelphia; Fellow of the American Academy of Arts and Sciences in Massachusetts Member of the Connecticut Academy of Arts and Sciences; Fellow of the Royal Society of Northern Antiquaries in Copenhagen; Member of the Connecticut Historical Society; Corresponding Member of the Historical Societies in Massachusetts, New York, and Georgia; of the Academy of Medicine in Philadelphia, and of the Columbian Institute in Washington; and Honorary Member of the Michigan Historical Society.

GENERAL SUBJECTS OF THIS WORK.

I.—ETYMOLOGIES OF ENGLISH WORDS, DEDUCED FROM AN EXAMINATION AND COMPARISON OF WORDS OF CORRESPONDING ELEMENTS IN TWENTY LANGUAGES OF ASIA AND EUROPE.

II.—THE TRUE ORTHOGRAPHY OF WORDS, AS CORRECTED BY THEIR ETYMOLOGIES.

III.—PRONUNCIATION EXHIBITED AND MADE OBVIOUS BY THE DIVISION OF WORDS INTO SYLLABLES, BY ACCENTUATION, BY MARKING THE SOUNDS OF THE ACCENTED VOWELS, WHEN NECESSARY, OR BY GENERAL RULES.

IV.—ACCURATE AND DISCRIMINATING DEFINITIONS, ILLUSTRATED, WHEN DOUBTFUL OR OBSCURE, BY EXAMPLES OF THEIR USE, SELECTED FROM RESPECTABLE AUTHORS, OR BY FAMILIAR PHRASES OF UNDISPUTED AUTHORITY.

REVISED AND ENLARGED,

BY CHAUNCEY A. GOODRICH,

PROFESSOR IN YALE COLLEGE.

WITH PRONOUNCING VOCABULARIES OF SCRIPTURE, CLASSICAL, AND GEOGRAPHICAL NAMES.

SPRINGFIELD, MASS.

PUBLISHED BY GEORGE AND CHARLES MERRIAM,

CORNER OF MAIN AND STATE STREETS.

1854.

Title page of the 1847 Goodrich-Webster, the first new edition published by G. & C. Merriam. (Taken from a copy printed in 1854.)

A

DICTIONARY

OF THE

ENGLISH LANGUAGE;

CONTAINING

THE WHOLE VOCABULARY OF THE FIRST EDITION IN TWO VOLUMES QUARTO; THE ENTIRE CORRECTIONS
AND IMPROVEMENTS OF THE SECOND EDITION IN TWO VOLUMES ROYAL OCTAVO;

TO WHICH IS PREFIXED

AN INTRODUCTORY DISSERTATION

ON THE

ORIGIN, HISTORY, AND CONNEXION OF THE LANGUAGES OF WESTERN ASIA AND EUROPE,

WITH AN EXPLANATION

OF THE PRINCIPLES ON WHICH LANGUAGES ARE FORMED.

BY NOAH WEBSTER, LL.D.

*Member of the American Philosophical Society in Philadelphia; Fellow of the American Academy of Arts and Sciences in Massachusetts;
Member of the Connecticut Academy of Arts and Sciences; Fellow of the Royal Society of Northern Antiquaries in
Copenhagen; Member of the Connecticut Historical Society; Corresponding Member of the Historical Societies
in Massachusetts, New York, and Georgia; of the Academy of Medicine in Philadelphia,
and of the Columbian Institute in Washington; and Honorary
Member of the Michigan Historical Society.*

GENERAL SUBJECTS OF THIS WORK.

I.—ETYMOLOGIES OF ENGLISH WORDS, DEDUCED FROM AN EXAMINATION AND COMPARISON OF WORDS OF CORRESPONDING
ELEMENTS IN TWENTY LANGUAGES OF ASIA AND EUROPE.

II.—THE TRUE ORTHOGRAPHY OF WORDS, AS CORRECTED BY THEIR ETYMOLOGIES.

III.—PRONUNCIATION EXHIBITED AND MADE OBVIOUS BY THE DIVISION OF WORDS INTO SYLLABLES, BY ACCENTUATION, BY
MARKING THE SOUNDS OF THE ACCENTED VOWELS, WHEN NECESSARY, OR BY GENERAL RULES.

IV.—ACCURATE AND DISCRIMINATING DEFINITIONS, ILLUSTRATED, WHEN DOUBTFUL OR OBSCURE, BY EXAMPLES OF THEIR USE,
SELECTED FROM RESPECTABLE AUTHORS, OR BY FAMILIAR PHRASES OF UNDISPUTED AUTHORITY.

REVISED AND ENLARGED,

By CHAUNCEY A. GOODRICH,

PROFESSOR IN YALE COLLEGE.

WITH PRONOUNCING VOCABULARIES OF SCRIPTURE, CLASSICAL, AND GEOGRAPHICAL NAMES.

LONDON:

HENRY G. BOHN, YORK STREET, COVENT GARDEN.

MDCCCXLVIII.

Title page of the 1848 London issue of the Goodrich-Webster by Henry G. Bohn. The only differences from the Merriam printing are the name and address of the publisher and the omission of the word *American* from the title.

PICTORIAL EDITION.

AN
AMERICAN DICTIONARY
OF THE
ENGLISH LANGUAGE;

CONTAINING

THE WHOLE VOCABULARY OF THE FIRST EDITION IN TWO VOLUMES QUARTO; THE ENTIRE CORRECTIONS
AND IMPROVEMENTS OF THE SECOND EDITION IN TWO VOLUMES ROYAL OCTAVO;

TO WHICH IS PREFIXED

AN INTRODUCTORY DISSERTATION

ON THE ORIGIN, HISTORY, AND CONNECTION, OF THE LANGUAGES OF WESTERN ASIA AND EUROPE, WITH
AN EXPLANATION OF THE PRINCIPLES ON WHICH LANGUAGES ARE FORMED.

BY NOAH WEBSTER, LL.D.,

Member of the American Philosophical Society in Philadelphia; Fellow of the American Academy of Arts and Sciences in Massachusetts;
Member of the Connecticut Academy of Arts and Sciences; Fellow of the Royal Society of Northern Antiquaries in Copenhagen;
Member of the Connecticut Historical Society; Corresponding Member of the Historical Societies in Massachusetts,
New York, and Georgia; of the Academy of Medicine in Philadelphia, and of the Columbian Institute
in Washington; and Honorary Member of the Michigan Historical Society.

GENERAL SUBJECTS OF THIS WORK.

I.—ETYMOLOGIES OF ENGLISH WORDS, DEDUCED FROM AN EXAMINATION AND COMPARISON OF WORDS OF CORRESPONDING ELE-
MENTS IN TWENTY LANGUAGES OF ASIA AND EUROPE.
II.—THE TRUE ORTHOGRAPHY OF WORDS, AS CORRECTED BY THEIR ETYMOLOGIES
III.—PRONUNCIATION EXHIBITED AND MADE OBVIOUS BY THE DIVISION OF WORDS INTO SYLLABLES, BY ACCENTUATION, BY
MARKING THE SOUNDS OF THE ACCENTED VOWELS, WHEN NECESSARY, OR BY GENERAL RULES.
IV.—ACCURATE AND DISCRIMINATING DEFINITIONS, ILLUSTRATED, WHEN DOUBTFUL OR OBSCURE, BY EXAMPLES OF THEIR USE,
SELECTED FROM RESPECTABLE AUTHORS, OR BY FAMILIAR PHRASES OF UNDISPUTED AUTHORITY.

REVISED AND ENLARGED,

BY CHAUNCEY A. GOODRICH,

PROFESSOR IN YALE COLLEGE.

WITH PRONOUNCING VOCABULARIES OF SCRIPTURE, CLASSICAL, AND GEOGRAPHICAL NAMES.

TO WHICH ARE NOW ADDED

PICTORIAL ILLUSTRATIONS,

TABLE OF SYNONYMS, PECULIAR USE OF WORDS AND TERMS IN THE BIBLE, APPENDIX OF NEW WORDS,
PRONOUNCING TABLE OF NAMES OF DISTINGUISHED PERSONS, ABBREVIATIONS, LATIN,
FRENCH, ITALIAN, AND SPANISH PHRASES, ETC.

SPRINGFIELD, MASS.
PUBLISHED BY GEORGE AND CHARLES MERRIAM,
CORNER OF MAIN AND STATE STREETS.

1859.

ABOVE: The four copyright notices in the Pictorial Edition:
(i)   the 1840 royal octavo (Webster);
(ii)   the 1847 Goodrich-Webster (G. & C. Merriam);
(iii)   the renewal in 1856 of Webster's 1828 copyright (Webster's surviving children);
(iv)   the 1859 Pictorial Edition (G. & C. Merriam).

OPPOSITE: Title page of the Webster Pictorial Edition of 1859, in which the definition pages are reprints of the 1847 Goodrich-Webster, with references added by the footnote "*See Pictorial Illustrations.*"

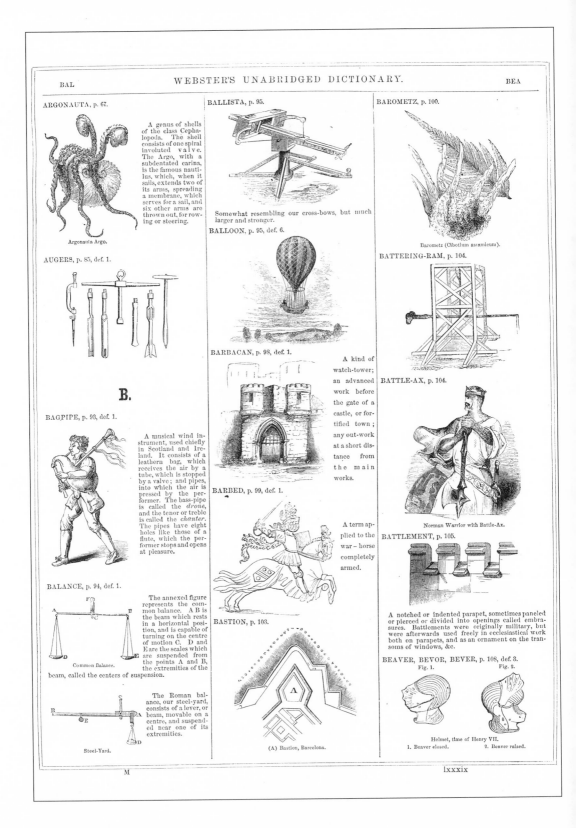

ARGONAUTA, p. 67.

A genus of shells of the class Cephalopoda. The shell consists of one spiral involuted valve. The Argo, with a subdentated carina, is the famous nautilus, which, when it sails, extends two of its arms, spreading a membrane, which serves for a sail, and six other arms are thrown out, for rowing or steering.

Argonauta Argo.

AUGERS, p. 85, def. 1.

B.

BAGPIPE, p. 93, def. 1.

A musical wind instrument, used chiefly in Scotland and Ireland. It consists of a leathern bag, which receives the air by a tube, which is stopped by a valve; and pipes, into which the air is pressed by the performer. The bass-pipe is called the *drone*, and the tenor or treble is called the *chanter*. The pipes have eight holes like those of a flute, which the performer stops and opens at pleasure.

BALANCE, p. 94, def. 1.

The annexed figure represents the common balance. A B is the beam which rests in a horizontal position, and is capable of turning on the centre of motion C. D and E are the scales which are suspended from the points A and B, the extremities of the beam, called the centers of suspension.

Common Balance.

The Roman balance, our steel-yard, consists of a lever, or beam, movable on a centre, and suspended near one of its extremities.

Steel-Yard.

BALLISTA, p. 95.

Somewhat resembling our cross-bows, but much larger and stronger.

BALLOON, p. 95, def. 6.

BARBACAN, p. 98, def. 1.

A kind of watch-tower; an advanced work before the gate of a castle, or fortified town; any out-work at a short distance from the main works.

BARBED, p. 99, def. 1.

A term applied to the war – horse completely armed.

BASTION, p. 103.

(A) Bastion, Barcelona.

BAROMETZ, p. 100.

Barometz (Cibotium assamicum).

BATTERING-RAM, p. 104.

BATTLE-AX, p. 104.

Norman Warrior with Battle-Ax.

BATTLEMENT, p. 105.

A notched or indented parapet, sometimes paneled or pierced or divided into openings called embrasures. Battlements were originally military, but were afterwards used freely in ecclesiastical work both on parapets, and as an ornament on the transoms of windows, &c.

BEAVER, BEVOR, BEVER, p. 108, def. 3.

Fig. 1.   Fig. 2.

Helmet, time of Henry VII.
1. Beaver closed.   2. Beaver raised.

A typical page from the Pictorial Illustrations section of the 1859 Pictorial Edition. All the illustrations on this page are from Ogilvie's *Imperial Dictionary*.

THE

IMPERIAL DICTIONARY,

ENGLISH, TECHNOLOGICAL, AND SCIENTIFIC,

ON THE

BASIS OF WEBSTER'S ENGLISH DICTIONARY, WITH THE ADDITION OF MANY THOUSAND WORDS AND
PHRASES, INCLUDING THE MOST GENERALLY USED TECHNICAL AND SCIENTIFIC TERMS,
WITH THEIR ETYMOLOGY AND THEIR PRONUNCIATION.

ALSO,

A SUPPLEMENT,

CONTAINING AN EXTENSIVE COLLECTION OF WORDS, TERMS, AND PHRASES IN THE VARIOUS DEPARTMENTS
OF LITERATURE, SCIENCE, AND ART, TOGETHER WITH NUMEROUS OBSOLETE, OBSOLESCENT,
AND SCOTTISH WORDS,
NOT INCLUDED IN PREVIOUS ENGLISH DICTIONARIES.

BY JOHN OGILVIE, LL.D.

ILLUSTRATED BY ABOVE 2500 ENGRAVINGS ON WOOD.

VOLUME I.

LONDON:
BLACKIE & SON, PATERNOSTER BUILDINGS, E.C.;
GLASGOW AND EDINBURGH.
1874.

Title page of Ogilvie's *Imperial Dictionary*, 1874 reprint. In the previous edition, the words "ON THE BASIS OF WEBSTER'S ENGLISH DICTIONARY" were much larger, and Ogilvie was named only as Editor.

BATTERY   BATTLE   BATTORY

half thick. The battens of commerce are seven inches broad and two and a half inches thick. In *marine lan.*, thin pieces of oak or fir, nailed to the mast head, and to the midship post of the yard.—*Battens of the hatches*, scantlings of wood, or straightened hoops of casks, applied to confine the edges of the tarpaulings close down to the sides of the hatchways, to prevent the entrance of water in a storm.—*Tracing battens*, pieces of wood about three inches thick, nailed to the beams of the ship, instead of cleats, to sling the seamen's hammocks to.

BAT'TEN, *v. t.* To form with battens.

BAT'TENED, *pp.* Formed with battens.—2. Become fat.

BAT'TENING, *n.* In *arch.*, narrow battens fixed to a wall, to which the laths for the plastering are nailed.

BAT'TER, *v. t.* [Fr. *battre;* It. *battere;* L. *batuo*, to beat. See BEAT.] 1. To beat with successive blows; to beat with violence, so as to bruise, shake, or demolish; as, to *batter* a wall.—2. To wear or impair with beating; as, a *battered* pavement; a *battered* jade.—3.To attack with a battering ram.—4. To attack with heavy artillery, for the purpose of making a breach in a wall or rampart. In *Scotland*, to paste, or cause one body to adhere to another, by means of a viscous substance.

BAT'TER, *v. i.* To incline from the perpendicular. Thus a wall is said to batter when its face recedes as it rises.

BAT'TER, *n.* [from *beat* or *batter.*] A mixture of several ingredients, as flour, eggs, salt, &c., beaten together with some liquor, used in cookery. In *Scotland*, a glutinous substance used for producing adhesion; paste.

BAT'TERED, *pp.* Beaten; bruised; broken; impaired by beating or wearing.

BAT'TERER, *n.* One who batters or beats.

BAT'TERING, *ppr.* Beating; dashing against; bruising or demolishing by beating.—2. In *milit. affairs*, the firing with heavy artillery on some fortification or strong post of the enemy.—*Battering pieces*, large pieces of cannon used in battering a fortified town or post.

BAT'TERING-RAM, *n.* In *antiq.*, a military engine used to beat down the walls of besieged places. It was a large beam, with a head of iron somewhat resembling the head of a ram, whence its name. It was suspended by ropes in the middle to a beam which was supported by posts, and balanced so as to swing backward and forward, and was impelled by men against the wall. It was sometimes mounted on wheels.

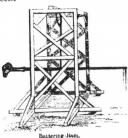

Battering-Ram.

BAT'TERY, *n.* [Fr. *batterie;* Sp. *bat-*

eria; It. *batteria.* See BEAT.] 1. The act of battering or beating.—2. The instrument of battering.—3. In the *milit. art*, a parapet thrown up to cover the gunners and others employed about them, from the enemy's shot, with the guns employed. Thus, *to erect a battery*, is to form the parapet and mount the guns. The term is applied also to a number of guns ranged in order for battering, and to mortars used for a like purpose.—*Cross batteries* are two batteries which play athwart each other, forming an angle upon the object battered.—*Battery d'enfilade*, is one which scours or sweeps the whole line or length.—*Battery en echarpe*, is that which plays obliquely.—*Battery de revers*, is that which plays upon the enemy's back.—*Camerade battery*, is when, several guns play at the same time upon one place.—*Floating batteries*, batteries erected either on simple rafts, or on the hulls of ships, for the defence of the coast, or for the bombardment of the enemy's ports.—4. In *law*, the unlawful beating of another. The least violence or the touching of another in anger is a battery.—5. In *electrical apparatus and experiments*, a number of coated jars placed in such a manner, that they may be charged at the same time, and discharged in the same manner. This is called an *electrical battery.*—6. *Galvanic battery*, a pile or series of plates of copper and zinc, or of any substances susceptible of galvanic action.

BAT'TING, *n.* The management of a bat at play.—2. Cotton or wool in masses prepared for quilts or bed-covers.

BAT'TISH, *a.* [from *bat*, an animal.] Resembling a bat; as, a *battish* humour.

BAT'TLE, *n.* [Fr. *bataille;* W. *batel*, a drawing of the bow, a battle; Sp. *batalla;* It. *battaglia*, from *beating.* [See BEAT.] Owen supposes the Welsh *batel*, to be from *tel*, tight, stretched, compact, and the word primarily to have expressed the drawing of the bow. This is probably an error. The first battles of men were with clubs, and some weapons used in *beating*, striking. Hence the club of Hercules. And although the moderns use different weapons, still a battle is some mode of beating or striking.] 1. A fight, or encounter between enemies, or opposing armies; an engagement. It is usually applied to armies or large bodies of men; but in popular language, the word is applied to an encounter between small bodies, between individuals, or inferior animals. It is also more generally applied to the encounters of land forces than of ships, the encounters of the latter being called *engagements.* But *battle* is applicable to any combat of enemies.—2.† A body of forces, or division of an army. The main body, as distinct from the van and rear.—*To give battle*, is to attack an enemy; *to join battle*, is properly to meet the attack; but perhaps this distinction is not always observed.—*A pitched battle*, is one in which the armies are previously drawn up in form, with a regular disposition of the forces. —*To turn the battle to the gate*, is to fight valiantly, and drive the enemy, who hath entered the city, back to the gate; Is. xxviii.

BAT'TLE, *v. i.* [Fr. *batailler;* Sp. *batallar.*] To join in battle; to contend in fight; sometimes with *it;* as, to *battle* it.

167

BAT'TLE, *v. t.* To cover with armed force.

BAT'TLE-ARRAY, *n.* [*battle* and *array.*] Array or order of battle; the disposition of forces preparatory to a battle.

BAT'TLE-AXE, *n.* An axe anciently used as a weapon of war. It has been used till of late years by the highlanders in Scotland.

Norman Warrior with Battle Axe.

BAT'TLED, BAT'TELED, or EMBAT'TLED, *a.* Terms used in *her.*, when the chief, cheveron, fesse, &c., is (on one side only,) borne in the form of the battlements of a castle or fortification.

BAT'TLE-DOOR or BAT'TLE-DORE, *n.* (bat'tl-dore.) An instrument of play, with a handle and a flat board or palm, used to strike a ball or shuttle-cock; a racket.—2.† A child's horn-book.

BAT'TLEMENT, *n.* [This is said to have been *bastillement*, from *bastille*, a fortification, from Fr. *bâtir*, *bastir*, to build. Qu.] A wall raised on a building with openings, or embrasures, or the embrasure itself. A notched or

Battlements.

indented parapet, sometimes panelled or pierced, or divided into openings called embrasures. Battlements were originally military, but were afterwards used freely in ecclesiastical work both on parapets, and as an ornament on the transoms of windows, &c.

BAT'TLEMENTED, *a.* Secured by battlements.

BAT'TLE-PIECES, *n.* In *paint.*, pictures descriptive of fights or battles.

BAT'TLING, *n.* Conflict.

BATTOL'OGIST, *n.* [See BATTOLOGY.] One that repeats the same thing in speaking or writing. [*Lit. us.*]

BATTOL'OGIZE, *v. t.* To repeat needlessly the same thing. [*Lit. us.*]

BATTOL'OGY, *n.* [Gr. βαττολογια, from βαττος, a garrulous person, and λογος, discourse.] A needless repetition of words in speaking.

BAT'TON or BATTEN, *n.* [from *bat.*] In *com.*, pieces of wood or deal for flooring, or other purposes. [See BATTEN.]

BAT'TORY, *n.* Among the *Hanse towns*, a factory or magazine which the merchants have in foreign countries.

AN

AMERICAN DICTIONARY

OF THE

ENGLISH LANGUAGE;

EXHIBITING THE

ORIGIN, ORTHOGRAPHY, PRONUNCIATION, AND
DEFINITIONS OF WORDS·

BY NOAH WEBSTER, LL. D.

ABRIDGED FROM THE QUARTO EDITION OF THE AUTHOR;

TO WHICH ARE ADDED, A

SYNOPSIS OF WORDS

DIFFERENTLY PRONOUNCED BY DIFFERENT ORTHOEPISTS;

AND

WALKER'S KEY

TO THE

CLASSICAL PRONUNCIATION OF GREEK, LATIN, AND
SCRIPTURE PROPER NAMES.

———

FIFTEENTH EDITION.

———

NEW YORK:
PUBLISHED BY N. AND J. WHITE,
63 WALL STREET.
———
1836.
E. Sanderson, Printer.

ABOVE: Title page of the 1829 octavo Webster, abridged by Worcester from the *American Dictionary*, 1836.

OPPOSITE: A typical page from Ogilvie's *Imperial Dictionary*. The three illustrations all appear in the page from Webster's Pictorial edition.

A

CRITICAL AND PRONOUNCING

DICTIONARY

OF

The English Language:

INCLUDING SCIENTIFIC TERMS, COMPILED FROM THE MATERIALS

OF

NOAH WEBSTER, LL.D.,

BY

JOSEPH E. WORCESTER.

NEW EDITION, TO WHICH ARE ADDED WALKER'S KEY TO THE
PRONUNCIATION OF CLASSICAL AND SCRIPTURE PROPER NAMES, ENLARGED
AND IMPROVED; A PRONOUNCING VOCABULARY OF MODERN
GEOGRAPHICAL NAMES; AND AN ENGLISH GRAMMAR.

GLASGOW:

WILLIAM COLLINS, PUBLISHER & QUEEN'S PRINTER.

MDCCCLXII.

Title page of the "Fraud" dictionary that purported to have been "Compiled from the Materials of Noah Webster" but was actually a reprint of Worcester's dictionary (1862 Glasgow printing).

Title Page

A

DICTIONARY

OF THE

ENGLISH LANGUAGE:

ABRIDGED FROM THE

AMERICAN DICTIONARY,

FOR THE USE OF

PRIMARY SCHOOLS AND THE COUNTING HOUSE.

BY NOAH WEBSTER, L.L.D.

Thirteenth Edition.

NEW-YORK:

PUBLISHED BY N. & J. WHITE, 108 PEARL STREET.

SOLD ALSO BY WEBSTER AND SKINNER, ALBANY; RICHARDSON, LORD, AND HOLBROOK,
BOSTON; KIMBER AND SHARPLESS, AND TOWER AND HOGAN, PHILADELPHIA;
CUSHING AND SONS, BALTIMORE; D. F. ROBINSON AND CO. HARTFORD;
O. STEELE, ALBANY; STEELE AND FAXON, BUFFALO; HOGAN
AND CO. PITTSBURG; J. N. WHITING, COLUMBUS, O.

STEREOTYPED AT E. WHITE'S TYPE AND STEREOTYPE FOUNDERY

1833.

Dictionary Page 243

L A M   book, dōve, fṳll, use, can, châise, ģem, as, thin, thou.   **L A M**   **L A N**

Lack′-ey, *v. t.* or *i.* to attend as a footman.
La-con′-ic, } *a.* very short, or brief, pithy, ex-
La-con′-ic-al, } pressive.
La-con′-ic-al-ly, *ad.* with pithy brevity.
La′-con-ism, } *n.* a brief sententious phrase or
La′-con-icism, } expression.
Lac′-tant, *a.* suckling, feeding with the breast.
Lac′-ta-ry, *a.* milky, soft; *n.* a dairy house.
Lac′-te-al, *a.* pertaining to milk or chyle.
Lac′-te-ous, *a.* milky, like milk. [chyle.
Lac′-tes′-cent, *a.* producing milk or white juice.
Lac-tif′-er-ous, *a.* conveying milk.
Lad, *n.* a boy, a young man.
Lad′-der, *n.* a frame with rounds for steps.
Lade, *v. t. p.* laded; *pp.* laded, laden; to load,
   freight, throw with a dipper.
La′-den, *p.* of *Lade*, [lādn.]
La′-ding, *ppr.* putting on or in, loading.
La′-ding, *n.* load, cargo, that which a ship carries.
La′-dle, *n.* a dipper with a handle, receptacle of
   a mill wheel.
La′-dy, *n.* a well-bred woman, a title of respect.
La′-dy-day, *n.* the annunciation, March 25.
La′-dy-like, *a.* genteel; well-bred, delicate.
La′-dy-ship, *n.* the title of a lady.
Lag, *a.* coming after, slow, sluggish.
Lag, *v. i.* to loiter, delay, move slowly.
Lag′-ged,* *p.* of *Lag*.
Lag′-ging, *ppr.* loitering, moving slowly.
La-ġoon′, *n.* a fen, marsh, or shallow pond.
La′-ic, La′-ic-al, *a.* pertaining to people not of
   the clergy.
Laid, *p.* and *pp.* of *Lay*; placed, deposited.
Lain, *p.* of *Lie*.
Lair, *n.* the bed of a wild beast.
Laird, *n.* in Scotland, a lord, owner of a manor.
La′-i-ty, *n.* the people as distinct from the clergy.
Lake, *n.* a large collection of water surrounded
   by land, a red color. [tars.
La′-ma, *n.* the pontif or doity of the Asiatic Tar-
Lam′-an-tin, *n.* the sea cow. a species of walrus.
Lamb, *n.* a young sheep, a title of Christ.
Lamb, *v. t.* or *i.* to bring forth young, as a sheep.
Lamb′-ent, *a.* playing o'er the surface, licking.
Lamb′-kin, *n.* a young or small lamb.
Lamb′-like, *a.* gentle, meek, humble.

Lame, *a.* unsound in a limb, imperfect.
Lame, *v. t.* to make lame, to disable or cripple.
La′-med,* *p.* made lame, disabled.
Lam′-el, *n.* a very thin plate or scale.
Lam′-el-lar, } *a.* formed or, disposed in thin
Lam′-el-late, } plates or scales.
Lam′-el-li-form, *a.* having the form of a plate.
Lame-ly, *ad.* in a halting manner, imperfectly.
Lame-ness, *n.* impaired state, imperfection.
La-ment′, *v. t.* or *i.* to weep, mourn, bewail.
Lam′-ent-a-ble, *a.* mournful, grievous.
Lam′-ent-a-bly, *ad.* with sorrow, grievously.
Lam-ent-a′-tion, *n.* expression of sorrow, cries
   of grief.
Lam′-in, *n.* a thin plate, a coat lying over another
Lam′-in-ar, *a.* consisting of thin plates.
Lam′-in-a-ted, *a.* plated, lying in plates.
Lam′-mas, *n.* the first day of August.
Lamp, *n.* a vessel with oil for light, a light.
Lamp′-black, *n.* a fine soot collected from the
   smoke of burning resinous substances.
Lamp′-as, *n.* a lump of flesh in the roof of a
   horse's mouth.
Lam-poon′, *n.* a personal satire or abuse.
Lam-poon′, *v. t.* to abuse with written satire.
Lam-poon′-ed,* *p.* abused in writing.
Lam-poon′-er, *n.* one who writes personal satire
Lam′-prey, *n.* a fish resembling the eel.
La′-nate, *a.* woolly, having hairs like wool.
Lănce, *n.* a spear, a weapon of war to be thrown.
Lănce, *v. t.* to pierce, to open with a lancet.
Lăn-ced,* *p.* pierced, cut open.
Lan′-ce-o-lar, *a.* tapering towards the end.
Lan′-ce-o-late, *a.* shaped like a lance, tapering
Lăn-cer, *n.* one who carries a lance in war.
Lăn-cet, *n.* a surgical instrument to let blood.
Lănch, *v. t.* to cast, to dart, to cause to slide
   into water.
Lănch, *n.* the sliding of a ship into the water.
Land, *n.* ground, country, region, a strip un-
   plowed.
Land, *v. t.* or *i.* to come, set, or put on shore.
Lăn′-dau, *n.* a four-wheeled carriage, whose top
   may be thrown back.
Land′-ed,* *p.* disembarked, set on shore.
Land′-ed, *a.* having land, consisting in land
Land′-fȧll, *n.* land first seen as a vessel approaches.

LEFT: Title page of Webster's 1829 *Primary School Dictionary* and a typical page of definitions.

Lăg'gēr, n. a loiterer; an idler. [ple.
La-gōōn', n. a large pond or lake.
Lā'ic, Lā'i-cal, a. belonging to the laity or peo-
Lā'ic, n. a layman, opposed to clergyman.
Laid, (lād) imp. t. & pp. from Lay.
Lain, (lān) pp. from Lie.
Lair, (lâr) n. the couch of a boar or wild beast.
Laird, (lârd) n. the lord of a manor. Scottish.
Lā'i-ty, n. the people, distinct from the clergy.
Lake, n. a large extent of inland water; a color.
Lā'ky, a. belonging to a lake.
Lā'ma, n. the sovereign pontiff of the Tartars, and head of the Shaman religion; a quadru-
Lămb, (lăm) n. the young of a sheep. [ped.
Lămb, (lăm) v. a. to yean; to bring forth lambs.
Lăm'ba-tive, a. taken by licking.
Lăm'ba-tive, n. a medicine taken by licking.
Lăm'bent, a. playing about; gliding lightly over.
Lămb'kin, (lăm'kin) n. a little lamb.
Lămb'like, (lăm'lik) a. mild; innocent.
Lămbs'-wool, (lămz'-wûl) n. ale mixed with sugar, &c. [letter A.
Lăm-dōīd'al, a. having the form of the Greek
Lame, a. crippled; disabled; imperfect.
Lame, v. a. to make lame; to cripple.
Lăm'el-lar, or Lăm'el-ar, a. composed of thin scales or flakes. [films or plates.
Lăm'el-lat-ed, or Lăm'el-at-ed, a. covered with
Lāme'ly, ad. like a cripple; imperfectly.
Lāme'ness, n. the state of a cripple; weakness.
La-mént', v. n. to mourn; to wail; to grieve.
La-mént', v. a. to bewail; to mourn; to bemoan.
La-mént', n. lamentation; expression of sorrow.
Lăm'ent-a-ble, a. to be lamented; mournful.
Lăm'ent-a-bly, ad. mournfully; pitifully.
Lăm-en-tā'tion, n. an expression of sorrow.
La-mént'er, n. one who mourns or laments.
Lā'mi-a, n. a fish call: I; a sea-cow. [witch.
Lā'mi-a, n. [L.] a kind of demon; a hag; a
Lămi-na, n. [L. lami-næ;] [L.] a thin plate; one coat or layer laid over another.
Lăm'i-na-ry, a. plated; consisting of plates
Lăm'i-nat-ed, or layers.
Lăm'mas, n. the first day of August.
Lămp, n. a light made with oil and a wick.
Lăm'pass, n. a lump of flesh in a horse's mouth.
Lămp'black, n. a fine soot from burning pitch.
Lăm-pōōn', n. a personal satire; ridicule; abuse.
Lăm-pōōn', v. a. to abuse with personal satire.
Lăm-pōōn'er, n. a scribbler of personal satire.
Lăm'prey, (lăm'prē) n. a fish like the eel.
Lance, n. a long spear; a weapon of war.
Lance, v. a. to pierce; to cut; to open, as a surgeon; to cut in order to a cure.
Lance'o-late, a. shaped like a lance.
Lance-pe-sade', n. the officer under the corporal.
Lance'er, n. one that carries a lance; one armed with a lance.
Lăn'cet, n. a small pointed instrument.
Lănch, v. a. to dart; to throw. See Launch.
Lăn'ci-nāte, v. a. to tear; to rend; to lacerate.
Lăn-ci-nā'tion, n. tearing; laceration.
Lănd, n. a country; a region; earth; ground.
Lănd, v. a. to set on shore.
Lănd, v. n. to come to shore.
Lănd-dāy', [lăn-dâw', W. P. J. Ja.; lăn'dâw, Wb.] n. a coach or pleasure carriage.
Lănd'ed, a. consisting of or having land.
Lănd'fall, n. sudden translation of real estate.
Lănd'flood, (lănd'flŭd) n. an inundation.
Lănd-fōr-cęs, n. pl. troops that serve on land.
Lănd'grave, n. a German title of dominion.
Lănd-grā'vi-āte, n. the territory of a landgrave.

Lănd'hōld'ęr, n. one who holds lands.
Lănd'ing, n. a place to land at; the stair-top.
Lănd'jŏb-bęr, n. one who buys and sells land.
Lănd'lā-dy, n. a mistress of an inn; a hostess.
Lănd'less, a. destitute of land.
Lănd'lŏcked, (lănd'lŏkt) a. enclosed with land.
Lănd'lōp-ęr, n. a landman.
Lănd'lōrd, n. the master of an inn; a host.
Lănd'man, n. one who lives or serves on land.
Lănd'mark, n. a mark of boundaries.
Lănd'-ŏf-fice, n. an office for the sale of land.
Lănd'scape, n. the prospect of a country.
Lănd'slide, n. a portion of a hill or mountain
Lănd'slip, that slides or slips down.
Lănd'-tăx, n. tax laid upon land and houses.
Lănd'-wait'ęr, n. an officer of the customs.
Lănd'ward, ad. towards the land.
Lāne, n. a narrow street; an alley; a passage.
Lăn'gręl-shŏt, or Lăn'grāģe, n. a kind of chain-shot.
Lăn'guāģe, (lăng'gwāj) n. human speech; style.
Lăn'guid, (lăng'gwid) a. faint; weak; feeble.
Lăn'guid-ly, (lăng'gwid-le) ad. weakly; feebly.
Lăn'guid-ness, n. weakness; feebleness.
Lăn'guish, (lăng'gwish) v. n. to grow feeble.
Lăn'guish-ęr, n. one who pines or languishes.
Lăn'guish-mĕnt, n. a state of pining; softness.
Lăn'guor, (lăng'gwŭr) n. faintness; weakness.
Lā'ni-āte, v. a. to tear in pieces; to lacerate.
Lă'ni-fice, n. woollen manufacture.
La-nīģ'ęr-oŭs, a. bearing wool.
Lănk, a. loose; lax; not fat; slender; faint.
Lănk, v. n. to become lank; to fall away.
Lănk'ly, ad. loosely; thinly.
Lănk'ness, n. want of plumpness.
Lănk'y, a. lank; thin and tall: vulgar.
Lăn'nęr, n. a species of hawk.
Lăn'nę-rĕt, n. a little hawk.
Lăn'sque-nĕt, (lăn'ske-nĕt) n. a common foot soldier; a game at cards.
Lăn'tęrn, n. a case for a candle.—a. thin. [hair.
La-nū'ģi-noŭs, a. downy; covered with soft
Lăn'yārd, n. pl. small ropes, or pieces of cord.
Lăp, n. that part of a person sitting which reaches from the waist to the knees.
Lăp, v. a. to wrap or twist round; to involve.
Lăp, v. n. to be spread or turned over any thing.
Lăp, v. a. & n. to lick up.
Lăp'dŏg, n. a little dog, fondled by ladies.
La-pĕl', n. a part of a coat; the facing.
Lăp'fŭl, n. as much as the lap can contain.
Lăp'i-dā-ry, n. one who deals in stones or gems.
Lăp'i-dā-ry, a. monumental; inscribed on stone.
Lăp'i-dāte, v. a. to stone; to kill by stoning.
Lăp-i-dā'tion, n. a stoning.
La-pĭd'e-oŭs, a. stony.
Lăp-i-dĕs'çençe, n. stony concretion.
Lăp-i-dĕs'çent, a. growing or turning to stone.
Lăp-i-dĭf'ic, a. forming stones.
La-pĭd-i-fi-cā'tion, n. the act of forming stones.
La-pĭd'i-fŷ, v. a. & n. to turn into stone.
Lăp'i-dist, n. a dealer in stones or gems.
Lā'pis, n. [L.] a stone.
Lā'pis lăz'u-li, n. the azure stone, from which ultramarine is prepared.
Lăp'pęr, n. one who wraps up; one who laps.
Lăp'pĕt, n. a part of a dress that hangs loose.
Lăpse, n. flow; fall; glide; petty error; mistake.
Lăpse, v. n. to glide; to slip; to fall from right.
Lăpsed, (lăpst) p. a. fallen. [maker.
Lăp'stōne, n. a stone used by a cobbler or shoe-
Lăp'sus līn'guæ, [L.] a slip of the tongue.
Lăp'wing, n. a noisy bird with long wings.

mien, sïr; mōve, nōr, sŏn; bŭll, bür, rûle.—C, G, ç, ğ, soft; C, G, ç, ğ, hard; ş as z; x̌ as gz;—this.

COMPREHENSIVE

PRONOUNCING AND EXPLANATORY

DICTIONARY

OF THE

ENGLISH LANGUAGE,

WITH

PRONOUNCING VOCABULARIES

OF

CLASSICAL AND SCRIPTURE PROPER NAMES.

By J. E. WORCESTER,

BOSTON:

HILLIARD, GRAY, LITTLE, AND WILKINS.

BOSTON TYPE AND STEREOTYPE FOUNDERY.

1830

A

DICTIONARY

OF THE

ENGLISH LANGUAGE.

BY

JOSEPH E. WORCESTER, LL. D.

MULTA RENASCENTUR QUÆ JAM CECIDĒRE, CADENTQUE
QUÆ NUNC SUNT IN HONORE VOCABULA, SI VOLET USUS:
QUEM PENES ARBITRIUM EST, ET JUS, ET NORMA LOQUENDI.

HORACE.

LONDON:

SAMPSON LOW, SON & CO., 14 LUDGATE HILL.

EDINBURGH: JOHN MENZIES. DUBLIN: McGLASHAN AND GILL.
PARIS: STASSIN AND XAVIER. ROTTERDAM: KRAMERS.
BOSTON, U. S. A.: BREWER AND TILESTON.

ABOVE: Worcester's 1859 *Dictionary of the English Language*—first issued January 1860, and *almost* the first American illustrated dictionary.

OPPOSITE: Worcester's *Comprehensive Pronouncing and Explanatory Dictionary*, 1830, described in the *Palladium* as "a very close imitation of Webster's."

STRU-MŌSE', } *a.* [L *strumosus.*] (*Med.*) Having
STRU'MOUS, } swellings in the glands; scrofulous. *Dunglison.*

STRU'MOUS-NĔSS, *n.* The quality of being strumous. *Clarke.*

STRŬM'PET, *n.* [Gael *strumpaid, striopach.* — Dut. *strontpot*, a chamber-pot *Skinner.*] A harlot; a prostitute; a bawd; a punk. *Shak.*

STRŬM'PET, *a.* Like a strumpet · false; inconstinent; unchaste. *Shak.*

† **STRŬM'PET**, *v. a.* To debauch, to whore. *Shak.*

STRŬM'STRŬM, *n.* A noisy musical instrument; — so called from its sound. *Dampier.*

STRŬNG, *i. & p.* from *string*. See STRING. *Gay.*

STRŬN'TAIN, *n.* A tape made of coarse worsted, less than an inch broad. [Scot.] *Jamieson.*

STRŬSE, *n.* A long craft used for transport on the inland waters of Russia. *Simmonds.*

STRŬT, *v n.* [Ger *strotzen.* — "Perhaps from *straught*, past part of *stretch.*" *Richardson.*] [*i.* STRUTTED; *pp* STRUTTING, STRUTTED.]
1. To walk with affected dignity; to stride pompously; to swell with stateliness.
Does he not hold up his head, and *strut* in his gait? *Shak.*
2. To swell; to protuberate.
As thy *strutting* bags with money rise,
The love of gain is of equal size. *Dryden.*

STRŬT, *n.* 1. An affectation of stateliness or dignity in walking; a pompous stride.
Certain gentlemen, by smirking countenances and an ungainly *strut* in their walk, have got preferment. *Swift.*
2. (*Arch.*) A piece of timber placed obliquely in the framed part of a building, serving to keep a main beam in its proper situation; — called also *brace*, and *stretching-piece.* *Britton.*

STRU-THI-Ō'NĒS, *n pl.* [Gr. στρουθός, a bird; ὁ μέγας στρουθός, the great bird, the ostrich.] (*Ornith.*) An order of birds incapable of flight, with very short wings, and long, strong legs, including the family *Struthionidæ.* *Gray.*

STRU-THI-ŎN'I-DÆ, *n. pl.* [See STRUTHIONES.] (*Ornith.*) A family of birds, including the sub-families *Struthioninæ, Apteryginæ*, and *Otidinæ*; ostriches. *Gray.*

STRU-THI-O-NI'NÆ, *n. pl.* [See STRUTHIONES.] (*Ornith.*) A subfamily of birds of the order *Struthiones* and family *Struthionidæ*; ostriches.

Struthus camelus.

STRU'THI-OŬS, *a.* [Gr. στρούθειος; στρουθός, a bird; L. *strutheus.*] Relating to, or resembling, the ostrich. *Brande.*

STRŬT'TER, *n.* One who struts *Todd.*

STRŬT'TING, *n.* The act of one that struts. *Cook.*

STRŬT'TING-LY, *ad.* With a strut, vauntingly.

STRU'VITE, *n.* (*Min*) A crystalline mineral found in guano from Saldanha Bay, coast of Africa, and composed chiefly of phosphoric acid, magnesia, oxide of ammonium, and water. *Dana.*

STRY̆CH'NI-A, *n.* (*Chem.*) A solid, crystalline, inodorous, bitter, and very poisonous alkaloid, obtained from several species of plants of the genus *Strychnos*, and principally from the seeds of *Strychnos nux vomica*; — called also *strychnine.* *Dunglison.*

STRY̆CH'NĪNE, *n.* Strychnia. — See STRYCHNIA.

STŬB, *n.* [A. S. *styb, stybb*; Frs. *stobbe*; Dan. *stub*; Sw. *stubbe*; Icel. *stubbr, stubbi.*]
1. A thick, short stock, left when the rest is cut off; the stump of a tree
Upon cutting down an old timber tree, the *stub* hath put out sometimes a tree of another kind. *Bacon.*
2. A log; a block "Stocks and *stubs*" *Milton.*

STŬB, *v a* [*i.* STUBBED; *pp.* STUBBING, STUBBED.]
1. To force up, to extirpate, to eradicate; to grub up; — frequently with *up*
He *stubs up* edible roots out of the ground. *Grew.*
2 To strike, as the toes, against some object in walking or running. [U. S] *Bartlett.*

STŬB'BED, *a.* 1. Truncated; short and thick.
Against a *stubbed* tree he reels. *Drayton.*
2. † Hardy; stout. "The hardness of *stubbed*, vulgar constitutions." *Bp. Berkeley.*

STŬB'BED-NĔSS, *n.* State of being stubbed. *Bai.*

STŬB'BI-NĔSS, *n.* State of being stubby. *Clarke.*

STŬB'BLE (stŭb'bl), *n.* [Dim. of *stub. Richardson.* — From L. *stipula*, a stalk, a stem. *Menage.*] The root ends of the stalks of wheat, rye, oats, and other grains or grasses, left in the field standing as they grew, after having been reaped by the sickle or scythe. *Brande.*

STŬB'BLED (stŭb'bld), *a.* 1. † Stubbed. *Skelton.*
2. Covered with stubble. *Gay*

STŬB'BLE-GOOSE (stŭb'bl-gôs), *n.* A goose fed among stubble. *Chaucer.*

STŬB'BLE-RĀKE (stŭb'bl-rāk), *n.* A rake for gathering stubble. *Wright.*

STŬB'BORN, *a.* [*Minsheu* derives this word from *stout-born*; *Junius* from the Gr. στιβαρός, thick, stout, sturdy; and *Lye*, from the preceding *stub*; the last appears the more probable — *stubb, stubber, stubberen, stubbern, stubborn. Richardson.*]
1. Hard to be moved; obstinate; inflexible; unyielding; wilful; headstrong; contumacious.
He believed he had so humbled the garrison, that they would be no longer so *stubborn.* *Clarendon.*
2. Persisting; persevering; steady.
All this is to be had only from the epistles themselves with *stubborn* attention and more than common application. *Locke.*
3. Stiff; not pliable; not easily bent; firm.
Take a plant of *stubborn* oak. *Dryden.*
4. Harsh; rough; rugged.
We will not oppose any thing that is hard and *stubborn*, but by a soft answer deaden their force. *Burnet.*
Syn. — See OBSTINACY.

STŬB'BORN-LY, *ad.* In a stubborn manner; obstinately; inflexibly; wilfully. *Locke.*

STŬB'BORN-NĔSS, *n.* The quality of being stubborn; obstinacy; contumacy; inflexibility.
He chose a course least subject to envy, between stiff *stubbornness* and filthy flattery. *Hayward.*
Syn. — See CONTUMACY, OBSTINACY.

STŬB'BY, *a.* Full of stubs; stubbed. *Grew.*

STŬB'-MŌR-TISE, *n.* A mortise that does not pass through the timber mortised. *Loudon.*

STŬB'-NAIL, *n.* A nail broken off; a short, thick nail. *Simmonds.*

STŬC'CŌ, *n.* [It. *stucco*; Sp. *estuco*; Fr. *stuc.* — From its being a composition *stuck* or fixed upon walls. *Tooke.*] A fine plaster for covering walls, and for interior decorations, usually made of pulverized marble and gypsum. *Weale.*

STŬC'CŌ, *v. a.* [It. *stuccare*] [*i.* STUCCOED; *pp.* STUCCOING, STUCCOED.] To overlay or cover with stucco; to plaster with stucco.
The apartment at the end is very warmly *stuccoed* with moss and hay. *Goldsmith.*

STŬC'CŌED (stŭk'kōd), *p. a.* Covered or overlaid with stucco. "*Stuccoed* walls." *Cowper.*

STŬC'CŌ-ER, *n.* One who stuccoes. *Wright.*

STŬCK, *i. & p.* from *stick*. See STICK. *Addison.*

† **STŬCK**, *n.* A thrust. *Shak.*
It is a corruption of *stock*, itself abbreviated from *stockado.* *Nares.*

STŬC'KLE (stŭk'kl), *n.* A stook. *Ainsworth.*

STŬD, *n.* [A. S. *studu*; Dut. *stut*; Ger. *stütze*; Dan. *stötte*; Sw. *stötta*; Icel. *stytta.* — Ir. *stid.*]
1. A piece of timber inserted in a sill to support a beam; a post or prop. *Weale.*
2. A nail with a large head driven in work chiefly for ornament, an ornamental knob.
A belt of straw and ivy buds,
With coral clasps and amber *studs.* *Raleigh.*
3. An ornamental button, link, or catch for a shirt bosom. *Simmonds.*

STŬD, *n.* [A. S. *stod*; Old Ger. *stout*; Ger. *stute*, a mare; Dan. *stodhest*, stallion; Sw. *sto*, a mare; Icel. *stedda*, a mare. — Gael. *steud*, a steed.] A collection of breeding horses and mares; — also the place where they are kept. *Davies.*
In the *studs* of Ireland, where care is taken, we see horses bred of excellent shape, vigor, and size. *Temple.*

STŬD, *v. a.* [*i.* STUDDED; *pp.* STUDDING, STUDDED.] To adorn with studs or knobs.
Their harness *studded* all with gold and pearl. *Shak.*

† **STŬD'DER-Y**, *n* A place where a stud of ho[rses] is kept. *Holin[shed.]*

STŬD'DING-SĀIL, *n.* (*Naut.*) A light sail outside of a square sail, on a boom rigged from the yard. *D[ana.]*

STU'DENT, *n.* [L. *studeo, studens*, to be zeal[ous,] to apply one's self to learning. — See STUD[Y.]
1. One who studies or examines, — part[icu]larly one given to books; a bookish man.
Keep a gamester from dice, and a good *student* fro[m his] book.
2. One engaged in study in a literary inst[itu]tion; a scholar; as, "A *student* of a colleg[e."]
Syn. — See SCHOLAR.

STU'DENT-SHIP, *n.* State of a student. *A. [...]*

STŬD'-HORSE, *n* [A. S. *stod-hors.*] A br[eed]ing horse; a stallion. *Kno[wles.]*

STŬD'IED (stŭd'id), *p. a.* 1. Closely or caref[ully] examined; carefully read, — premeditated.
2. Versed in any study or branch of learni[ng;] qualified by study; learned.
Some man reasonably *studied* in the law. *B[acon.]*
3. † Having any particular inclination.
A prince should not be so loosely *studied* as to remem[ber] so weak a composition. *S[hak.]*

STŬD'IED-LY, *ad.* In a studied manner. *T[...]*

STŬD'I-ER, *n.* One who studies; a student.
Lipsius was a great *studier* of the stoical philosophy. *Till[otson.]*

STU'DI-Ō, *n.*; pl. ***STU'DI-ŌS.*** [It.] A st[udy] — the office or work-shop of an artist.
Studios for painters are erected [in Rome] on the t[op of] houses, the lower rooms of which are let to sculptors. *B[...]*

‖ **STU'DI-OŬS** [stū'de-ŭs, *P. J. F. Ja. Sm.* [...] stū'jus, *S.*; stū'dyus, *E. K.*; stū'de-ŭs *or* stū'j[us,] *W.*], *a.* [L. *studiosus*; It. *studioso*; Sp. *es[tudi]oso*; Fr. *studieux.*]
1. Zealous; assiduous; diligent; eager.
Studious to find new friends and new allies. *T[...]*
2. Devoted to study, books, or learn[ing;] given to contemplation; contemplative; [medi]tative; thoughtful; reflective.
The *studious* and contemplative part of mankind.
3. Attentive; careful; zealous; — with [*of.*]
Studious of pious and venerable antiquity.
4. Suitable for study or contemplation.
To walk the *studious* cloisters pale. *[Milton.]*

‖ **STU'DI-OŬS-LY**, *ad.* In a studious man[ner;] diligently; zealously; eagerly; attentively.
All of them *studiously* cherished the memory of thei[r hon]orable extraction. *Att[erbury.]*

‖ **STU'DI-OŬS-NĔSS**, *n.* Quality of being stud[ious.]

STŬD'-WORK (-wŭrk), *n.* (*Masonry.*) A [wall] built between studs or quarters. *C[...]*

STŬD'Y, *n.* [L. *studium*; *studeo*, to be eag[er,] zealous; It. *studio*; Sp. *estudio*; Old Fr. *es[tude*;] Fr. *étude.*]
1. Application of the mind to a subject; [con]tinued attention; meditation; investigation; search; — in a restrictive sense, applicati[on of] the mind to books and learning.
Just men they seemed, and all their *study* bent
To worship God aright and know his works.
Without *study* this art is not attained. *H[...]*
During the whole time of his abode in the univ[ersity] Hammond generally spent thirteen hours of the [day in] *study.*
2. A studious mood; absorption of the [mind] in meditation; deep cogitation; perplexity.
The King of Castile, a little confused and in a *study*
That can I not do with my honor.
3. The pursuit or acquisition of knowl[edge,] literature, or learning; learning.
Studies serve for delight, for ornament, and ability. [Their] chief use for delight is in privateness and retiring; for [orna]ment, is in discourse; and for ability, is in the judgme[nt and] disposition of business. . . . Crafty men contemn *studie[s, sim]ple* men admire them; and wise men use them, for the[y teach not] their own use.
It would have been well if Bacon had added som[ething] as to the mode of *study.* *H[...]*
Beholding the bright countenance of truth in th[e quiet] and still air of delightful *studies.*
4. Subject of study or attention.
The Holy Scriptures . . . are her daily *study.*
5. An apartment appropriated to study.
Let all *studies* and libraries be towards the east. *[...]*
6. (*Fine Arts.*) A finished sketch from na[ture,] generally intended to aid in the compositi[on of] a larger and more important work, or as [a me]morial of some particular object for future [use,] or to facilitate drawing or composition.

ABOVE: First title page of *Webster's Improved Dictionary.* There is no date on it, but the editor's Preface (by Thomas Heber Orr) is dated December 15, 1857, and the book was probably issued in 1858.

OPPOSITE: A typical page from Worcester's 1859 dictionary.

A DICTIONARY

OF THE

ENGLISH LANGUAGE;

EXHIBITING THE

ORIGIN, ORTHOGRAPHY, PRONUNCIATION, AND DEFINITIONS OF WORDS.

BY

NOAH WEBSTER, LL.D.

TO WHICH ARE ADDED,

A SYNOPSIS OF WORDS DIFFERENTLY PRONOUNCED BY DIFFERENT ORTHOËPISTS,
AND WALKER'S KEY TO THE CLASSICAL PRONUNCIATION OF GREEK, LATIN,
AND SCRIPTURE PROPER NAMES.

REVISED AND ENLARGED BY PROFESSOR C. A. GOODRICH.

WITH THE ADDITION OF

AN ORTHOËPIC VOCABULARY OF MODERN GEOGRAPHICAL NAMES.

A NEW EDITION, CORRECTED, IMPROVED, AND ENLARGED,
BY THOMAS HEBER ORR,
Discoverer of the Process of Primitive Wordgrowth.

WITH AN

INTRODUCTORY ESSAY ON THE PHILOSOPHY OF LANGUAGE AND GENERAL GRAMMAR,
BY SIR JOHN STODDART, KNT., LL.D.

AND A SKETCH OF THE ORIGIN AND PROGRESS OF THE ART OF WRITING,
BY HENRY NOEL HUMPHREYS,
Author of "The Illuminated Books of the Middle Ages."

VOLUME I.

WILLIAM MACKENZIE,

45 & 47 HOWARD STREET, GLASGOW;   39 SOUTH BRIDGE, EDINBURGH;
22 PATERNOSTER ROW, LONDON.

Second title page of *Webster's Improved Dictionary*, claiming that the book was "Corrected, Improved and Enlarged, by Thomas Heber Orr, Discoverer of the Process of Primitive Wordgrowth."

CHIRP (churp), v. i. [Ger. zirpen.] To make the noise of certain small birds, or of certain insects.

CHIRP, v. t. To make cheerful.—*Pope.*

CHIRP, n. A particular voice of certain birds or insects.

CHIRP'ER, n. One that chirps, or is cheerful.

CHIRP'ING, ppr. or a. Making the noise of certain small birds.

CHIRP'ING (churp'ing), n. The noise of certain small birds and insects.

CHIRP'ING-LY, adv. In a chirping manner.

CHIRRE, v. i. [Sax. ceorian.] To coo, as a pigeon.

CHIR'RUP, v. t. To cheer up; to incite or animate; to quicken; as, to chirrup one's horse. 2. v. i. to chirp.

CHI-RUR'GEON, n. [Gr. χειρουργος.] A surgeon; one whose profession is to heal diseases by manual operations, instruments, or external applications.

† CHI-RUR'GE-RY, n. [Gr. χειρουργια.] Surgery.

† CHI-RUR'GIC, } a. Pertaining to surgery; surgical.
† CHI-RUR'GIC-AL, }

CHIS'EL, n. [Fr. ciseau.] An instrument of iron or steel, used either for paring wood or stone.

CHIS'EL, v. t. To cut, gouge, or engrave with a chisel.

CHIS'EL-ED, pp. or a. Cut or engraved with a chisel.

CHIS'EL-ING, ppr. Cutting with a chisel.

CHIS'LEU, n. [Heb. כסלו.] The ninth month of the Jewish year, answering to a part of November and a part of December, in the modern division of the year.

CHIT, n. [Sax. cith.] 1. A shoot or sprout. 2. A lively child, in familiar language. 3. A freckle, i. e., a push.

CHIT, v. i. To shoot; to sprout, as a seed or plant.

CHIT–CHAT, n. [See CHAT, CHATTER.] Prattle; familiar or trifling talk.

‡ CHITTER, v. i. [Dutch citteren.] To shiver.

CHITTER-LING, n. The frill to the breast of a shirt.

CHITTER-LINGS, n. pl. [G. kuttel.] The smaller intestines of swine, &c., fried for food.

CHITTY, a. 1. Childish; like a babe. 2. Full of chits or sprouts.

* CHIV'AL-RIC (shiv-), a. Partaking of the character of chivalry.

* CHIV'AL-ROUS (shiv'al-rus), a. Pertaining to chivalry, or knight-errantry; warlike; bold; gallant.

* CHIV'AL-ROUS-LY, adv. In a chivalrous spirit.

* CHIV'AL-RY (shiv'al-re), n. [Fr. chevalerie.] 1. Knighthood; a military dignity, founded on the service of soldiers on horseback, called knights: a service formerly deemed more honorable than service in infantry. 2. The qualifications of a knight, as valor and dexterity in arms. 3. The system of knighthood; the privileges, characteristics, or manners of knights; the practice of knight-errantry, or the heroic defense of life and honor. 4. An adventure or exploit, as of a knight. 5. The body or order of knights. —6. In English law, a tenure of lands by knight's service.

CHIVE, n. See CIVE.

CHIVES, n. pl. In botany, slender threads or filaments in the blossoms of plants.

CHLAMY-PHORE, } n. [Gr. χλαμυς and φερω.] A small
CHLA-MYPH'O-RUS, } South American quadruped, allied to the armadillo, and covered with a scaly shell like a cloak.—Harlan.

CHLA'MYS, n. [L. and Gr.] A tunic or loose coat worn by the ancients over the vest or doublet.—Elmes.

CHLO-RA-CET'IC AC'ID, n An acid formed by the action of chlorine on acetic acid.—Dana.

CHLO'RAL, n. A liquid composed of chlorine, carbon, and oxygen, obtained by the action of chlorine upon alcohol.

CHLO'RATE, n. A compound of chloric acid with a salifiable base.

CHLO'RIC, a. Pertaining to chlorine, or obtained from it. —Chloric acid, that acid of chlorine and oxygen which contains the greatest proportion of oxygen.

CHLO'RID, n. A term applied to combinations of chlorine, corresponding to the oxyds; a non-acid combination of chlorine with another element.

CHLO-RID'IC, a. Pertaining to a chlorid.—Ure.

CHLO'RINE, } n. [Gr. χλωρος.] A greenish yellow gas, ob-
CHLO'RIN, } tained from common salt. It is a powerful agent in disinfecting, and also in bleaching.

CHLO-RI'O-DINE, } n. A compound of chlorine and
CHLO-RI-OD'IC AC'ID, } iodine.

CHLO'RIS, n. [Gr. χλωρος.] The greenfinch, a small bird.

CHLO'RITE, n. [Gr. χλωρος.] A soft, olive-green mineral, consisting of minute scales, and somewhat soapy to the touch. It is allied to talc, but contains also silica, magnesia, and alumina.—Dana.

CHLO'RITE, n. A salt formed of chloric acid and a base.

CHLO-RIT'IC, a. Pertaining to or containing chlorite; as, chloritic sand.—Lyell.

CHLO'RO-CAR-BON'IC, } a. Terms applied to a com-
CHLO'RO-CAR-BON-OUS, } pound of chlorine and carbonic oxyd.

CHLO-RO'PAL, n. A greenish, earthy mineral, consisting of silica and oxyd of iron.—Dana.

CHLO-RO-CY-AN'IC, a. Comp. of chlorine and cyanogen

CHLO'RO-FORM, n. [Chlorid and formyle.] A terchlorid of formyle, a light, volatile, colorless, fragrant, and inflammable fluid, which has supplanted ether, among the medical profession, as an agent in procuring temporary insensibility. It was first used for this purpose by Dr. Simpson of Edinburgh in 1847, and has since met with universal adoption. It is obtained by gentle distillation from a mixture of alcohol, chlorid of lime, and water.

CHLO-ROM'E-TER, n. [Gr. χλωρος and μετρον.] An instrument for testing the decoloring or bleaching powers of chlorid of lime.

CHLO-ROM'E-TRY, n. The process for testing the bleaching power of any combination of chlorine.

CHLO'RO-PHANE, n. [Gr. χλωρος and φαινω.] A variety of fluor spar, from Siberia.

CHLO'RO-PHYL, n. [Gr. χλωρος and φυλλον.] The green matter of the leaves of vegetables.

CHLO-RO'SIS, n. [Gr. χλωρος.] 1. The green sickness; a disease of females, giving them a pale hue. 2. A disease in plants, giving them a pale hue.

CHLO-ROT'IC, a. 1. Pertaining to chlorosis. 2. Affected by chlorosis.

CHLO'ROUS, a. Chlorous acid, that acid of chlorine and oxygen which contains the smallest proportion of oxygen.

CHLO-ROX-AL'IC, a. Chloroxalic ether, an oxalic ether containing chlorine instead of hydrogen.—Chloroxalic acid, a name formerly used for chloracetic acid.

CHLO'RU-RET, n. The old name of a chlorid.

CHOAK. See CHOKE.

CHOCK, v. i. 1. To fill up a cavity (to choke); as, "the wood-work exactly chocked into the joints."—Fuller. 2. To encounter. See SHOCK.

CHOCK, n. 1. A wedge, or something to confine a cask or other body, by chocking it or stay around it. [Hence the word chock-full, meaning completely filled.—Todd. So chock up means completely up.] 2. An encounter. See SHOCK.

CHOC'O-LATE, n. [Fr. chocolat; Sp., Port. chocolate.] 1. A paste or cake composed of the roasted kernels of the cacao, with other ingredients, usually a little sugar, cinnamon, or vanilla. 2. The liquor made by dissolving chocolate in boiling water.

CHOC'O-LATE-HOUSE, n. A house where company may be served with chocolate.

CHOC'O-LATE-NUT. See CACAO.

CHODE. The old preterit of chide, which see.

CHOICE, n. [Fr. choix.] 1. The act of choosing or selecting from two or more things that which is preferred; election. 2. The power of choosing; option. 3. Care in selecting; as, "they were collected with judgment and choice."—Bacon. 4. The thing chosen; selection. 5. The best part of any thing; that which is preferable; and properly, the object of choice. 6. The act of electing to office by vote; election.—To make choice of, to choose; to select, to separate and take in preference.

CHOICE, a. 1. Worthy of being preferred; very valuable. 2. Holding dear; selecting or using with care; as, choice of one's time, choice as to one's company.—SYN. Select, precious; costly; exquisite; uncommon; rare; sparing, frugal; chary; careful.

CHOICE'-DRAWN, a. Selected with particular care.—Shak.

CHOICE'LESS, a. Having no power of choosing; not free.

CHOICE'LY (chois'ly), adv. 1. With care in choosing; with exact choice. 2. Valuably; excellently; preferably; curiously. 3. With great care, carefully.

CHOICE'NESS (chois'ness), n. Valuableness; particular value or worth.

* CHOIR (kwire), n. [L. chorus.] 1. A collection of singers, especially in divine service, in a church. 2. Any collection of singers. 3. That part of a church appropriated for the singers. 4. That part of a cathedral or collegiate church eastward of the nave, and separated from it usually by a screen of open work, corresponding to the chancel in parish churches.—5. In nunneries, a large hall adjoining to the body of the church, separated by a grate, where the nuns sing the office.

CHOKE, v. t. [Sax. aceocan.] 1. To stop the passage of the breath, by filling the windpipe, or compressing the neck: to suffocate; to strangle. 2. To stop by filling; to obstruct, to block up; as, to choke up a road or harbor. 3. To hinder by obstruction or impediments; to hinder or check growth, expansion, or progress; as, to choke the growth of plants. 4. To smother or suffocate, as fire. 5. To suppress, or stifle; as, to choke the strong conception.—Shak. 6. To offend; to cause to take an exception.

CHOKE, v. i. 1. To have the windpipe stopped. 2. To be offended; to take exceptions.

CHOKE, n. The filamentous or capillary part of the artichoke

CHOKE'-CHER-RY, n. The popular name of a species of wild cherry, remarkable for its astringent qualities.

Thomas Heber Orr's page 170, *chirp* to *choke-cherry*, which includes a definition of *chloroform*.

CHIRP (churp), v. i. [Ger. zirpen.] To make the noise of certain small birds, or of certain insects.

CHIRP, v. t. To make cheerful.—Pope.

CHIRP, n. A particular voice of certain birds or insects.

CHIRP'ER, n. One that chirps, or is cheerful.

CHIRP'ING, ppr. or a. Making the noise of certain small birds.

CHIRP'ING (churp'ing), n. The noise of certain small birds and insects.

CHIRP'ING-LY, adv. In a chirping manner.

CHIRRE, v. i. [Sax. ceorian.] To coo, as a pigeon.

CHIR'RUP, v. t. To cheer up; to incite or animate; to quicken; as, to chirrup one's horse.

CHI-RUR'GEON, n. [Gr. χειρουργος.] A surgeon; one whose profession is to heal diseases by manual operations, instruments, or external applications.

† CHI-RUR'GE-RY, n. [Gr. χειρουργια.] Surgery.

† CHI-RUR'GIC,   }
† CHI-RUR'GIC-AL, } a. Pertaining to surgery; surgical.

CHIS'EL, n. [Fr. ciseau.] An instrument of iron or steel, used either for paring wood or stone.

CHIS'EL, v. t. To cut, gouge, or engrave with a chisel.

CHIS'ELED, pp. or a. Cut or engraved with a chisel.

CHIS'EL-ING, ppr. Cutting with a chisel.

CHIS'LEU, n. [Heb. כסלו.] The ninth month of the Jewish year, answering to a part of November and a part of December, in the modern division of the year.

CHIT, n. [Sax. cith.] 1. A shoot or sprout. 2. A lively child, in familiar language. 3. A freckle, i. e., a push.

CHIT, v. i. To sprout; to shoot, as a seed or plant.

CHIT—CHAT, n. [See CHAT, CHATTER.] Prattle; familiar or trifling talk.

† CHIT'TER, v. i. [Dutch citteren.] To shiver.

CHIT'TER-LING, n. The frill to the breast of a shirt.

CHIT'TER-LINGS, n. pl. [G. kuttel.] The smaller intestines of swine, &c., fried for food.

CHIT'TY, a. 1. Childish; like a babe. 2. Full of chits or sprouts.

* CHIV'AL-RIC (shiv-), a. Partaking of the character of chivalry.

* CHIV'AL-ROUS (shiv'al-rus), a. Pertaining to chivalry, or knight-errantry; warlike; bold; gallant.

* CHIV'AL-ROUS-LY, adv. In a chivalrous spirit.

* CHIV'AL-RY (shiv'al-re), n. [Fr. chevalerie.] 1. Knighthood; a military dignity, founded on the service of soldiers on horseback, called knights: a service formerly deemed more honorable than service in infantry. 2. The qualifications of a knight, as valor and dexterity in arms. 3. The system of knighthood; the privileges, characteristics, or manners of knights; the practice of knight-errantry, or the heroic defense of life and honor. 4. An adventure or exploit, as of a knight. 5. The body or order of knights. —6. In English law, a tenure of lands by knight's service.

CHIVE, n. See CIVE.

CHIVES, n. pl. In botany, slender threads or filaments in the blossoms of plants.

CHLAM'Y-PHORE, } n. [Gr. χλαμυς and φερω.] A small
CHLA-MYPH'O-RUS, } South American quadruped, allied to the armadillo, and covered with a scaly shell like a cloak.—Harlan.

CHLA'MYS, n. [L. and Gr.] A tunic or loose coat worn by the ancients over the vest or doublet.—Elmes.

CHLO-RA-CE'TIC AC'ID, n. An acid formed by the action of chlorine on acetic acid.—Dana.

CHLO'RAL, n. A liquid composed of chlorine, carbon, and oxygen, obtained by the action of chlorine upon alcohol.

CHLO'RATE, n. A compound of chloric acid with a salifiable base.

CHLO'RIC, a. Pertaining to chlorine, or obtained from it. —Chloric acid, that acid of chlorine and oxygen which contains the greatest proportion of oxygen.

CHLO'RID, n. A term applied to combinations of chlorine, corresponding to the oxyds; a non-acid combination of chlorine with another element.

CHLO-RID'IC, a. Pertaining to a chlorid.—Ure.

CHLO'RINE, } n. [Gr. χλωρος.] A greenish yellow gas, ob-
CHLO'RIN, } tained from common salt. It is a powerful agent in disinfecting, and in bleaching.

CHLO-RI'O-DINE, } n. A compound of chlorine and
CHLO-RI-OD'IC AC'ID, } iodine.

CHLO'RIS, n. [Gr. χλωρος.] The greenfinch, a small bird.

CHLO'RITE, n. [Gr. χλωρος.] A soft, olive-green mineral, consisting of minute scales, and somewhat soapy to the touch. It is allied to talc, but contains also silica, magnesia, and alumina.—Dana.

CHLO'RITE, n. A salt formed of chloric acid and a base.

CHLO-RIT'IC, a. Pertaining to or containing chlorite; as, chloritic sand.—Lyell.

CHLO'RO-CAR-BON'IC, } a. Terms applied to a com-
CHLO'RO-CAR'BON-OUS, } pound of chlorine and carbonic oxyd.

CHLO-RO'PAL, n. A greenish, earthy mineral, consisting of silica and oxyd of iron.—Dana.

CHLO-RO-CY-AN'IC, a. Composed of chlorine and cyanogen.

CHLO-ROM'E-TER, n. [Gr. χλωρος and μετρον.] An instrument for testing the decoloring or bleaching powers of chlorid of lime.

CHLO-ROM'E-TRY, n. The process for testing the bleaching power of any combination of chlorine.

CHLO'RO-PHANE, n. [Gr. χλωρος and φαινω.] A variety of fluor spar, from Siberia.

CHLO-RO-PHÆITE, n. [Gr. χλωρος and φαιος.] A rare mineral, found in small nodules.

CHLO'RO-PHYL, n. [Gr. χλωρος and φυλλον.] The green matter of the leaves of vegetables.

CHLO-RO'SIS, n. [Gr. χλωρος.] 1. The green sickness; a disease of females, giving them a pale hue. 2. A disease in plants, giving them a pale hue.

CHLO-ROT'IC, a. 1. Pertaining to chlorosis. 2. Affected by chlorosis.

CHLO'ROUS, a. Chlorous acid is that acid of chlorine and oxygen which contains the smallest proportion of oxygen.

CHLO-ROX-AL'IC, a. Chloroxalic ether, an oxalic ether containing chlorine instead of hydrogen.—Chlorozalic acid, a name formerly used for chloracetic acid.

CHLO'RU-RET, n. The old name of a chlorid.

CHOAK. See CHOKE.

CHO'AN-ITE, n. A zoophyte of the chalk.—Mantell.

CHOCK, v. i. 1. To fill up a cavity (to choke); as, "the wood-work exactly chocked into the joints."—Fuller. 2. To encounter. See SHOCK.

CHOCK, n. 1. A wedge, or something to confine a cask or other body, by chocking into the space around it. [Hence the word chock-full, meaning completely filled.—Todd. So chock up means completely up.] 2. An encounter. See SHOCK.

CHOC'O-LATE, n. [Fr. chocolat; Sp., Port. chocolate.] 1. A paste or cake composed of the roasted kernels of the cacao, with other ingredients, usually a little sugar, cinnamon, or vanilla. 2. The liquor made by dissolving chocolate in boiling water.

CHOC'O-LATE—HOUSE, n. A house where company may be served with chocolate.

CHOC'O-LATE-NUT. See CACAO.

CHODE. The old preterit of chide, which see.

CHOICE, n. [Fr. choix.] 1. The act of choosing or selecting from two or more things that which is preferred; election. 2. The power of choosing; option. 3. Care in selecting; as, "they were collected with judgment and choice."—Bacon. 4. The thing chosen; selection. 5. The best part of any thing; that which is preferable; and properly, the object of choice. 6. The act of electing to office by vote; election.—To make choice of, to choose; to select; to separate and take in preference.

CHOICE, a. 1. Worthy of being preferred; very valuable. 2. Holding dear; selecting or using with care; as, choice of one's time, choice as to one's company.—SYN. Select; precious; costly; exquisite; uncommon; rare; sparing; frugal; chary; careful.

CHOICE'-DRAWN, a. Selected with particular care.—Shak.

CHOICE'LESS, a. Not having the power of choosing; not free.

CHOICE'LY (chois'ly), adv. 1. With care in choosing; with exact choice. 2. Valuably; excellently; preferably; curiously. 3. With great care; carefully.

CHOICE'NESS (chois'ness), n. Valuableness; particular value or worth.

* CHOIR (kwire), n. [L. chorus.] 1. A collection of singers, especially in divine service, in a church. 2. Any collection of singers. 3. That part of a church appropriated for the singers. 4. That part of a cathedral or collegiate church eastward of the nave, and separated from it usually by a screen of open work, corresponding to the chancel in parish churches.—5. In nunneries, a large hall adjoining to the body of the church, separated by a grate, where the nuns sing the office.

CHOIR'-SERV'ICE (kwire-), n. The service of singing performed by a choir.

CHOKE, v. t. [Sax. aceocan.] 1. To stop the passage of the breath, by filling the windpipe, or compressing the neck; to suffocate; to strangle. 2. To stop by filling; to obstruct, to block up; as, to choke up a road or harbor. 3. To hinder by obstruction or impediments; to hinder or check growth, expansion, or progress; as, to choke the growth of plants. 4. To smother or suffocate, as fire. 5. To suppress, or stifle; as, to choke the strong conception.—Shak. 6. To offend; to cause to take an exception.

CHOKE, v. i. 1. To have the windpipe stopped. 2. To be offended; to take exceptions.

CHOKE, n. The filamentous or capillary part of the artichoke.

CHOKE'-CHER-RY, n. The popular name of a species of wild cherry, remarkable for its astringent qualities.

SIXTEENTH THOUSAND.

WALKER AND WEBSTER

COMBINED IN

A DICTIONARY

OF

THE ENGLISH LANGUAGE;

IN WHICH

THE DEFINITIONS OF WEBSTER,
AND THE PRONUNCIATION OF WALKER

ARE UNITED AND BROUGHT INTO CONFORMITY TO THE USAGE OF THE PRESENT TIME;
MANY NEW WORDS ARE INTRODUCED;
AND NUMEROUS SYNONYMOUS TERMS ARE CAREFULLY DISCRIMINATED.

WITH AN APPENDIX,

CONTAINING

WALKER'S KEY TO THE PRONUNCIATION OF SCRIPTURE, GREEK, AND LATIN
PROPER NAMES, AND A VOCABULARY OF MODERN GEOGRAPHICAL NAMES;
TOGETHER WITH THE EXPLANATION OF NUMEROUS CON-
TRACTIONS AND CURRENT PHRASES FROM VARIOUS
LANGUAGES; A CONCISE ACCOUNT OF
HEATHEN GODS AND HEROES;
&c. &c.

BY JOHN LONGMUIR, A.M., LL.D.,
FORMERLY LECTURER IN KING'S COLLEGE AND UNIVERSITY, ABERDEEN.

LONDON: WILLIAM TEGG.

1866.

ABOVE: Walker and Webster Combined, London, 1866. *OPPOSITE:* Page 170 of an authorized Webster octavo, *chirp* to *choke-cherry,* with no definition of *chloroform.*

Index